RESEARCH HANDBOOK ON INTELLECTUAL PROPERTY AND ARTIFICIAL INTELLIGENCE

RESEARCH HANDBOOKS IN INTELLECTUAL PROPERTY

Series Editor: Jeremy Phillips, *Intellectual Property Consultant, Olswang, Research Director, Intellectual Property Institute and co-founder, IPKat weblog*

Under the general editorship and direction of Jeremy Phillips comes this important new *Research Handbook* series of high quality, original reference works that cover the broad pillars of intellectual property law: trademark law, patent law and copyright law – as well as less developed areas, such as geographical indications, and the increasing intersection of intellectual property with other fields. Taking an international and comparative approach, these *Research Handbooks*, each edited by leading scholars in the respective field, will comprise specially commissioned contributions from a select cast of authors, bringing together renowned figures with up-and-coming younger authors. Each will offer a wide-ranging examination of current issues in intellectual property that is unrivalled in its blend of critical, innovative thinking and substantive analysis, and in its synthesis of contemporary research.

Each *Research Handbook* will stand alone as an invaluable source of reference for all scholars of intellectual property, as well as for practising lawyers who wish to engage with the discussion of ideas within the field. Whether used as an information resource on key topics, or as a platform for advanced study, these *Research Handbooks* will become definitive scholarly reference works in intellectual property law.

Titles in the series include:

Research Handbook on Intellectual Property and Digital Technologies
Edited by Tanya Aplin

Research Handbook on Intellectual Property and Technology Transfer
Edited by Jacob H. Rooksby

Research Handbook on Intellectual Property and Investment Law
Edited by Christophe Geiger

Research Handbook on the World Intellectual Property Organization
The First 50 Years and Beyond
Edited by Sam Ricketson

Research Handbook on Trademark Law Reform
Edited by Graeme B. Dinwoodie and Mark D. Janis

Research Handbook on Design Law
Edited by Henning Hartwig

Research Handbook on Intellectual Property and Employment Law
Edited by Niklas Bruun and Marja-Leena Mansala

Research Handbook on Intellectual Property and Cultural Heritage
Edited by Irini Stamatoudi

Research Handbook on Intellectual Property and Artificial Intelligence
Edited by Ryan Abbott

Research Handbook on Intellectual Property and Artificial Intelligence

Edited by

Ryan Abbott

Professor of Law and Health Sciences, School of Law, University of Surrey, UK and Adjunct Assistant Professor of Medicine, David Geffen School of Medicine, University of California Los Angeles, USA

RESEARCH HANDBOOKS IN INTELLECTUAL PROPERTY

Edward Elgar
PUBLISHING
Cheltenham, UK • Northampton, MA, USA

Cover image: Conceived by DABUS, complements of Dr. Stephen Thaler

Published by
Edward Elgar Publishing Limited
The Lypiatts
15 Lansdown Road
Cheltenham
Glos GL50 2JA
UK

Edward Elgar Publishing, Inc.
William Pratt House
9 Dewey Court
Northampton
Massachusetts 01060
USA

A catalogue record for this book
is available from the British Library

Library of Congress Control Number: 2022946033

This book is available electronically in the **Elgar**online
Law subject collection
http://dx.doi.org/10.4337/9781800881907

ISBN 978 1 80088 189 1 (cased)
ISBN 978 1 80088 190 7 (eBook)

Printed and bound by CPI Group (UK) Ltd, Croydon, CR0 4YY

Contents

Contributors

Ryan Abbott is Professor of Law and Health Sciences at University of Surrey School of Law and Adjunct Assistant Professor of Medicine at the David Geffen School of Medicine at UCLA. Ryan is the author of *The Reasonable Robot: Artificial Intelligence and the Law*, published in 2020 by Cambridge University Press. He has written widely on issues associated with law and technology, health law and intellectual property in leading legal, medical and scientific books and journals. Ryan's research has been featured prominently in the media, including the *New York Times*, *Wall Street Journal* and *Financial Times*. He is a licensed physician, patent attorney and acupuncturist in the United States, a solicitor advocate in England and Wales, and board-certified by the American Board of Legal Medicine (ABLM). Managing Intellectual Property magazine named him as one of the 50 most influential people in intellectual property in 2019 and again in 2021.

Ana Andrijevic is a PhD candidate and a research and teaching assistant at the University of Geneva, Faculty of Law/Digital Law Center. Her doctoral dissertation on the impact of AI on copyright law is being written under the supervision of Prof. Jacques de Werra. Her areas of research focus on technology law (including AI and children's rights in the digital age) and intellectual property law.

Tanya Aplin is Professor of Intellectual Property Law at the Dickson Poon School of Law, King's College London. She has published widely on copyright, confidentiality and trade secrets law. Some of her leading co-authored publications include *Gurry on Breach of Confidence: The Protection of Confidential Information* (OUP, 2012), *Intellectual Property: Patents, Copyright, Trade Marks and Allied Rights* 9th ed (Sweet & Maxwell, 2019), *Global Mandatory Fair Use: The Nature and Scope of the Right to Quote Copyright Works* (CUP, 2020) and a *Research Handbook on IP and Digital Technologies* (Edward Elgar Publishing, 2020).

Tatiana Aranovich is Assistant to the Director at the Healthcare Insurance Authority. She holds a Master's degree in Law (MPhil) and an undergraduate degree in Economics, both from Universidade Federal do Rio Grande do Sul (UFRGS), and a law degree from Pontificia Universidade Católica – PUC. She served as an internee at the Antitrust Authority (OFT, currently CMA) in the UK.

Richard Arnold read Chemistry at the University of Oxford before being called to the Bar of England and Wales in 1985. He specialized in intellectual property law and became a QC in 2000. He was a Judge of the High Court, Chancery Division from October 2008 to September 2019 and Judge in Charge of the Patents Court from April 2013 to September 2019. He has been an External Member of the Enlarged Board of Appeal of the European Patent Office since March 2016 and a Judge of the Court of Appeal since October 2019. He is the author of *Performers' Rights* (6th ed, Sweet & Maxwell, 2021) and the editor of the Halsbury's Laws of England title *Trade Marks and Trade Names* (5th ed, Butterworths, 2014). He was editor of *Entertainment and Media Law Reports* from 1993 to 2004 inclusive and has published numerous articles in legal journals.

Woodrow Barfield, Whitaker Institute and Visiting Professor of Law, University of Turin, holds a PhD in engineering and a JD and LLM in intellectual property law and policy. He received the Presidential Young Investigator award from the National Science and is the author of *Cyber Humans: Our Future with Machines*, co-author (with Ugo Pagallo) of *Advanced Introduction to Law and Artificial Intelligence*, co-editor (with Ugo Pagallo) of *Research Handbook on Law and AI*, and co-editor (with Marc Jonathan Blitz) of *Research Handbook of Law on Virtual and Augmented Reality*. He is also the editor of the *Cambridge Handbook of Law of Algorithms* and editor of *Fundamentals of Wearable Computers and Augmented Reality*. His current interests are the law as related to human enhancement technology, artificial intelligence and algorithms, and, from an engineering perspective, the computational infrastructure of the human body.

Shawn Bayern is Larry & Joyce Beltz Professor and Associate Dean for Academic Affairs at the Florida State University College of Law. His teaching and research focus on common-law issues, primarily in contracts, torts and organizational law. Professor Bayern has visited at Berkeley Law, Duke Law School and the Northwestern Pritzker School of Law. He is the author, most recently, of *Autonomous Organizations* (2021, Cambridge University Press). Bayern is an elected member of the American Law Institute and serves as advisor to part of the Restatement (Third) of Torts. He has an extensive background in computer science and, before his legal academic career, designed a widely used identity authentication protocol and served on the specification expert groups for several computer-programming languages. He has a JD from Berkeley Law and a BS in computer science from Yale University.

Yaniv Benhamou is Associate Professor of Digital Law at the University of Geneva, Faculty of Law/Digital Law Center, and attorney-at-law at a Swiss-based law firm. Professor Benhamou specializes in data protection, intellectual property, and art law, was appointed as an expert by the World Intellectual Property Organization (WIPO) for copyright and museums and regularly teaches copyright law to museums in the framework of the legal training of AMS (Association of Swiss Museums). In addition to these legal activities, he participates in associative and cultural activities in the fields of art and music. In particular, he founded lab-of-arts and Artists Rights, free legal consultations for Swiss artists (that is, Swiss lawyers volunteering for the arts). He is Legal Affairs Committee Member of the International Council of Museums (ICOM).

Enrico Bonadio is Reader in Intellectual Property (IP) law at City, University of London. His research agenda has recently focused on – inter alia – the intersection between IP and technology, including the impact of artificial intelligence (AI) and robotics innovation on copyright and patent laws. Enrico is member of the Centre for Creativity enabled by AI, funded by UKRI's Research England and City, University of London. He has been part of an EU-funded group of researchers to assess the area of interactive robots in society. Enrico is also Deputy Editor in Chief of the *European Journal of Risk Regulation*.

Karni Chagnal-Feferkorn is a postdoctoral fellow in AI and Regulation at the University of Ottawa. Her research examines different aspects of the intersection between AI and the law, including legal liability for AI-induced damages, governance by AI and the educational challenge of teaching lawyers and data scientists to work jointly in order to design responsible AI systems. Karni pursued her PhD at the University of Haifa (Israel) and holds an LLM in Law, Science and Technology from Stanford University. She is a licensed attorney in Israel, California and New York. In addition to her academic research, Karni is a founding partner of a consultancy firm that specializes in comparative research pertaining to law and regulation, and conducts research for governments, law firms and companies on various regulatory matters, including technology in general and AI specifically. She also advises an Israeli start-up focused on automating the drafting of complex legal documents.

Trevor Cook is a partner at WilmerHale, where he focuses his practice on transnational intellectual property litigation matters and is also active in the area of life sciences. Mr Cook has more than 40 years of experience in global patent litigation, particularly in Europe and Asia. He has acted in many of the leading patent infringement cases that have come before the English courts, many of which have concerned pharmaceuticals and biotechnology, and also in some of the leading cases regarding the protection of regulatory data. Mr Cook joined WilmerHale from Bird & Bird LLP in London, where he was a partner in the Intellectual Property Group and co-head of the International Life Sciences Sector Group.

Carys J. Craig is Associate Professor at Osgoode Hall Law School, York University, in Toronto, Canada. She is Academic Director of the Professional LLM Program in Intellectual Property Law, Editor-in-Chief of the *Osgoode Hall Law Journal* and recently served as Associate Dean (Research & Institutional Relations). Dr Craig teaches and publishes in the areas of copyright, trade marks, law and technology and critical legal and feminist theory. She is the author of *Copyright, Communication & Culture: Towards a Relational Theory of Copyright Law* (Edward Elgar Publishing, 2011). Dr Craig's scholarship has been cited with approval in several landmark copyright rulings by the Supreme Court of Canada. She holds an LLB (First Class Honours) from the University of Edinburgh, an LLM from Queen's University in Kingston, Ontario and an SJD from the University of Toronto.

Dennis Crouch is Associate Professor of Law at the University of Missouri School of Law. Prior to joining the MU Law Faculty, he was a patent attorney at McDonnell Boehnen Hulbert & Berghoff LLP in Chicago, Illinois, and taught at Boston University Law School. He has worked on cases involving various technologies including computer memory and hardware, circuit design, software, networking, mobile and internet telephony, automotive technologies, lens design, bearings, HVAC systems and business methods. He is also the editor of the popular patent law weblog *Patently-O*.

Jean-Marc Deltorn is Assistant Professor and Senior Researcher at the International Centre for the Study of Intellectual Property (CEIPI), University of Strasbourg. At CEIPI, Jean-Marc studies the interplay between IP norms and emerging digital technologies. He is co-founder and director of CEIPI's AI & IP University Diploma and Adjunct Director of CEIPI's Research Laboratory. Prior to joining CEIPI, Jean-Marc spent more than 15 years at the European Patent Office (EPO), where he chaired the prosecution of AI applications. Jean-Marc is currently a member of the Impact of Technology Expert Group at the European Observatory on Infringements of Intellectual Property Rights (EUIPO). Jean-Marc holds a PhD in Physics from Paris University and a PhD in Law from Strasbourg University.

Plamen Dinev is Lecturer in Law at Goldsmiths, University of London. He holds a PhD from The City Law School and an LLM from Leiden University. His research focuses on the relationship between IP law and new technology, including AI, 3D printing and digitization more broadly. He has published widely in leading IP journals, including IPQ and EIPR, and has presented his research at universities including Bocconi, Cardiff and Keio. In 2018 Plamen received a Modern Law Review Scholarship, which allowed him to undertake fieldwork in New York as part of an empirical project on 3D printing and the law. In 2019 he was invited to the European Commission's final report on the IP implications of 3D printing.

Giancarlo Frosio is Professor of Law & Technology at the School of Law of Queen's University Belfast. He is also a Non-resident Fellow at Stanford Law School CIS, Stanford University and Faculty Associate at Nexa Center, Polytechnic and University of Turin.

Garry A. Gabison is Senior Lecturer at the Centre for Commercial Law Studies, Queen Mary University of London. Prior to joining the Centre, Garry taught economics and public policy at the School of Public Policy and the School of Economics at the Georgia Institute of Technology. His teaching focused on innovation policy. Garry also worked at the Joint Research Centre (JRC), a Directorate General of the European Commission. At the JRC, Garry investigated issues related to the Information and Communications Technology sector. His work focused on innovation incentives and financing. Garry holds a JD from the University of Virginia and a PhD in Economics from Yale University. He has published in journals in Europe and in the United States on such issues as copyright, patents and AI.

Dev S. Gangjee is Professor of Intellectual Property Law at the University of Oxford and Director of the Oxford IP Research Centre (OIPRC). He has a longstanding interest in trade marks, geographical indications and copyright. Recent research has looked at the interface between trade marks and innovation, as well as the influence of machine learning technologies on trade mark registration.

Daniel J. Gervais PhD is the Milton R. Underwood Chair in Law at Vanderbilt University Law School, where he serves as Director of the Vanderbilt Intellectual Property Program and Co-director of the LLM Program. Prior to joining Vanderbilt, he was the Acting Dean at the Faculty of Law of the University of Ottawa (Common Law Section). Before he joined the Academy, Professor Gervais was Legal Officer at the GATT (now WTO), Head of Section at WIPO and Vice-president of Copyright Clearance Center, Inc. (CCC). In 2012, he was elected to the Academy of Europe. He is a member of the American Law Institute, where he serves as Associate Reporter on the Restatement of the Law, Copyright Project. In 2022, he is the immediate Past President of the International Association for the Advancement of Teaching and Research in Intellectual Property (ATRIP).

Shubha Ghosh PhD, JD, is Crandall Melvin Professor of Law at Syracuse University College of Law and Director of the Technology Commercialization Law Program and the Syracuse Intellectual Property Law Institute.

Christie Kafrouni is a legal affairs and IP advisor for IMPS The Smurfs, Belgium. She holds a Masters degree in Law from Université Catholique de Louvain (Belgium) and an Advanced Masters in Intellectual Property and Knowledge Management from Maastricht University. During her Masters studies at Maastricht University, she became acquainted with the subject of online shopping and the challenges it causes for trade mark law; this resulted in a Masters thesis supervised by Dr Anke Moerland.

Argyro Karanasiou is Assistant Professor in Law and Innovation at the University of Birmingham, the founding director of LETS Lab (Law, Emerging Tech & Science) and a research affiliate at the BHRE, University of Greenwich, London, where she previously worked as Associate Professor in Information Technology Law. Her work contributes to the growing body of transdisciplinary scholarship on law and emerging technologies and has earned her visiting research affiliations with Yale Law School (ISP Alumna), NYU Law (ILI Alumna), Harvard Law (affiliate Faculty staff CopyX), and Complutense Madrid (ITC). She is actively involved in several technology policy and related initiatives in the UK and worldwide, including those concerned with the regulation of AI, one of her key research interests.

Alice Lee, LLB (HKU), BCL (Oxford), is Associate Professor of Law at the University of Hong Kong and Senior Fellow of AdvanceHE (SFHEA). She has received three HKU teaching awards, including the University Distinguished Teaching Award, and chaired the HKU Teaching Exchange Fellowship Sub-Group. She specializes in intellectual property and real property and is the author of textbooks and practitioners' texts in both areas. She co-founded Creative Commons Hong Kong in 2008, initiated an IP Ambassador Programme with the Intellectual Property Department of the HKSAR Government in 2016 and launched an online animation series, 'The Copyright Classroom', in 2019 to support knowledge exchange and public education. She has served on consultative committees and statutory bodies, including the Advisory Committee on the Review of the Patent System, which advised the government on the enactment of the Patents (Amendment) Ordinance 2016 for an original grant patent system in Hong Kong.

Daryl Lim is Professor of Law and Director of the Center for Intellectual Property (IP), Information & Privacy Law at the University of Illinois Chicago School of Law. The IP Center is a founding IP institution in the United States and is consistently ranked as offering one of the premier IP programmes in the country. Professor Lim is an award-winning author, observer and commentator on global trends in IP and competition policy and how they influence and are influenced by law, technology, economics and politics. He regularly engages senior government officials, corporate leaders, civil society organizations, and law firms at national and international conferences.

Rita Matulionyte, PhD, LLM is Senior Lecturer at Macquarie Law School, Macquarie University (Australia) and Associate Senior Research Fellow at the Law Institute of Lithuania. Her research is in the area of intellectual property and information technology law, with a focus on legal and regulatory issues surrounding artificial intelligence. Rita has more than 40 peer-reviewed research papers published by leading international publishers. Previously, she was a legal research fellow at universities in Germany, Japan, Switzerland and Lithuania. She has prepared research reports for the European Commission, the European Patent Office and the governments of South Korea and Lithuania, and presented at academic and industry conferences in Germany, the US, Japan, Hong Kong, Switzerland, Lithuania, Australia and elsewhere. She is currently Lead Investigator on the projects The Use of Face Recognition Technologies in Public Sector: Legal Challenges and Possible Solutions and Towards Explainable AI in Healthcare.

Luke McDonagh is Assistant Professor in Intellectual Property Law at LSE Law School. Luke holds a PhD from Queen Mary, University of London (2011), an LLM from the London School of Economics (LSE) (2006–7) and a BCL degree from NUI, Galway (2002–5). He is a Fellow of the Higher Education Academy (FHEA). Luke has published widely in respected journals including *Modern Law Review*, *Journal of Law and Society*, Intellectual Property Quarterly and *Civil Justice Quarterly*. Luke is the author of the monograph *European Patent Litigation in the Shadow of the Unified Patent Court* (Edward Elgar Publishing, 2016) and the co-author (along with Professor Stavroula Karapapa of the University of Reading) of the textbook *Intellectual Property Law* (OUP, 2019). His most recent monograph is *Performing Copyright: Law, Theatre and Authorship* (Hart, 2021).

Benjamin Mitra-Kahn is an economist who has served as Economic Advisor to the UK Intellectual Property Office (2009–12) and Chief Economist at IP Australia (2012–21), and is currently the programme manager of the Household Expenditure and Income Data Branch at the Australian Bureau of Statistics. He has published research on the economics of copyright and patents and was responsible for policy and legislation at IP Australia (2018–21). During that time the Australian government introduced three IP Bills that, among other things, legislated to allow computerized decision making by an IP office and introduce an Objects clause to the Patents Act. He holds a PhD in Economics from City University London, an MSc in Development Economics from the School of Oriental and African Studies, University of London and a BSc (Hons) in Economics from Royal Holloway, University of London.

Anke Moerland (LLM) is Associate Professor of Intellectual Property Law in the European and International Law Department, Maastricht University. She holds a PhD on Intellectual Property Protection in EU Bilateral Trade Agreements from Maastricht University. Her educational background is in political science (international relations) and law. Anke has published widely on IP law and policy, with a particular focus on IP law between new technologies and tradition. In that light, she is at the forefront of discussing the implications of AI for trade marks, how GI protection can contribute to innovative products that at the same time preserve tradition, and how copyright rules foster the preservation and digitization of cultural heritage. Between 2018 and 2020, she held a visiting professorship at Queen Mary University of London on Intellectual Property Law, Governance and Art. Between 2017 and 2021, Anke coordinated the EIPIN Innovation Society, a four-year Horizon 2020 grant under the Marie Skłodowska Curie Action ITN-EJD.

Sean M. O'Connor is Professor of Law at George Mason University, Arlington, VA, USA. His research and law practice focus on intellectual property and business law, especially the role of general counsel for start-ups and commercializing innovation in technology and arts. Professor O'Connor received his law degree from Stanford Law School; a Masters degree in Philosophy, concentrating on the history and philosophy of science, from Arizona State University; and a bachelor's degree in history from the University of Massachusetts, Boston. Before graduate school he was a singer-songwriter and fronted a rock band with two DIY albums that received local airplay in the Northeast. He is currently writing *The Means of Innovation: Creation, Control, Methodology* and serving as editor of *The Oxford Handbook of Music Law & Policy*, both forthcoming from Oxford University Press.

Michael D. Pendleton is Emeritus Professor of Law, Murdoch University and Affiliate, University of Otago. Professor Pendleton has published, taught and practised IP for more than 40 years. Career highlights include: 12 IP textbooks and practice manuals and more than 100 articles; Chair of the Western Australian Law Reform Commission; Full Professor at the Law Faculties of the University of Hong Kong, the Chinese University of Hong Kong and

City University of Hong Kong; Emeritus Professor of Law at Murdoch University, Australia; Adjunct Professor of Law, University of Canterbury, Visiting Professor, University of Auckland, Affiliate, University of Otago; Lawyer, Baker & McKenzie, Deacons, Bird & Bird and other international law firms; barrister/solicitor Australia, England and Wales and Hong Kong; WIPO Mediator, Arbitrator and Domain Name Neutral; Editorial Board, Australian IP Law Journal; Co-author for 25 years with the late Prof Zheng Chengsi, copyright law drafter and pioneer of Chinese IP; Life Member, Asian Patent Attorneys Association; and two references by the Copyright Law Review Committee (CLRC).

Sharon K. Sandeen is Robins Kaplan LLP Distinguished Professor in Intellectual Property Law and Director of the IP Institute at Mitchell Hamline School of Law in Saint Paul, Minnesota. She is a recognized expert on trade secret law, having written (with Elizabeth Rowe) the first casebook on the subject in the United States. In addition to her books, Professor Sandeen has written more than 30 articles and book chapters on intellectual property, internet and information law topics, including detailed analyses of the drafting histories of the Uniform Trade Secrets Act and Article 39 of the TRIPS Agreement. Professor Sandeen is a member of the American Law Institute (ALI) and the Association for the Advancement of Teaching and Research in Intellectual Property (ATRIP), and was the Fulbright-Hanken Distinguished Chair in Business and Economics for 2019-2020.

Martin Senftleben is Professor of Intellectual Property Law and Director, Institute for Information Law (IViR), University of Amsterdam. His activities focus on the reconciliation of private intellectual property rights with competing public interests of a social, cultural or economic nature. He is President of the Trademark Law Institute (TLI). Professor Senftleben has provided advice to WIPO in trademark, unfair competition and copyright projects. As a visiting professor, he has been invited to the National University of Singapore, the Engelberg Center at NYU Law School, the Oxford Intellectual Property Research Centre, and the Intellectual Property Research Institute of Xiamen University. His numerous publications include *European Trade Mark Law – A Commentary* (with Annette Kur, 2017) and *The Copyright/Trademark Interface* (2020). As a guest lecturer, he provides courses at the Centre for International Intellectual Property Studies (CEIPI), Strasbourg, the Munich Intellectual Property Law Center (MIPLC), Jagiellonian University Krakow and the University of Catania.

Noam Shemtov joined CCLS in September 2009. He is currently Professor of Intellectual Property and Technology Law and Deputy Head of the Centre for Commercial Law Studies, Queen Mary, University of London. He lectures in areas of intellectual property, technology, and creative industries and his research interests are also focused on these fields. Professor Shemtov has led research projects and studies funded by UK Research Councils and by industry, national, supranational and commercial organizations, such as the Arts and Humanities Research Council (AHRC), CISAC, Microsoft, WIPO, the European Patent Office, the Foreign and Commonwealth Office (FCO), the UK's Department for International Development (DFID) and the European Space Agency. Professor Shemtov also holds visiting appointments by Spanish and Dutch universities, where he lectures regularly in areas pertaining to intellectual property, creative industries and technology. He is a qualified solicitor both in the UK and in Israel.

Phoebe Woo, BA (Literary Studies) & LLB (HKU) and LLM (Cambridge), is Zue Lo Pre-Doctoral Fellow, Faculty of Law, University of Hong Kong. She is a co-investigator of two HKU Teaching Development Grant projects and manages the HKU Legal Academy Student Chapters for knowledge exchange.

PART I

MULTI-SUBJECT

1. Intellectual property and artificial intelligence: an introduction

Ryan Abbott

1. INTRODUCTION

In 2020, the AI AlphaFold generated results that won a competition aimed at predicting the three-dimensional structure of proteins from two-dimensional amino acid sequences. That competition sounds much less interesting than one involving chess or Go,[1] but unlike a board game, predicting protein folding structure can be a critical element of research and development. For example, if you are designing a new antibody to target a protein, or studying diseases that involve protein misfolding such as Alzheimer's, it may be necessary to understand what a protein looks like in three dimensions. DeepMind, which created AlphaFold, more recently used AI to predict the molecular structure of hundreds of thousands of proteins, including almost all those in the human body, and it published those results in an open access database.[2]

AI is not just playing games and doing research; it is doing all sorts of basic activities which until recently could only be done by a person. These range from taking orders at a restaurant to driving a car. An AI still cannot safely drive a vehicle fully autonomously, but most of the time the AI is probably already safer than a human driver. It is likely that pretty soon, AI will be a better driver than most people all of the time.[3] People, after all, set a low bar for driving—about 94 percent of motor vehicle accidents are caused by human error, which costs more than a million lives a year worldwide and more than 30,000 lives a year just in the United States.[4] If AI, or rather *when* AI, outperforms average human drivers in the same way it outperforms people at board games, that will dramatically improve the way we live.

If functionally working for McDonalds or Uber is not impressive enough, AI is performing tasks that once required highly skilled professionals such as lawyers and doctors.[5] The US Food and Drug Administration has approved AI that autonomously diagnoses certain con-

---

[1] See DeepMind, *Alphago*, https://deepmind.com/research/case-studies/alphago-the-story-so-far (last accessed 02/27/2022); see also Sam Byford, *Google's AlphaGo AI defeats world Go number one KeJie*, www.theverge.com/2017/5/23/15679110/go-alphago-ke-jie-match-google-deepmind-ai-2017 (last accessed 02/27/2022).

[2] https://alphafold.ebi.ac.uk/. See Jeremy Khan, *In giant leap for biology, DeepMind's A.I. reveals secret building blocks of human life*, https://fortune.com/2021/07/22/deepmind-alphafold-human -proteome-database-proteins/ (last accessed 02/27/2022).

[3] See, e.g., Örebro Universitet, *New AI method makes self-driving vehicles better drivers*, https:// techxplore.com/news/2021-12-ai-method-self-driving-vehicles-drivers.html (last accessed 02/27/2022).

[4] Centre for Disease Control and Prevention, *Injury Prevention & Control, Global Road Safety*, www.cdc.gov/injury/features/global-road-safety/index.html (last accessed 02/27/2022).

[5] Tom Meltzer, *Robot doctors, online lawyers and automated architects: the future of the professions?* www.theguardian.com/technology/2014/jun/15/robot-doctors-online-lawyers-automated -architects-future-professions-jobs-technology (last accessed 02/27/2022).

ditions such as diabetic retinopathy and macular edema.[6] AI is already used extensively in medical care, but largely as a decision support aid for a human doctor. For example, AI can analyze a patient's electrocardiogram and suggest that findings may be consistent with a heart attack, but ultimately that analysis is just something for a doctor to consider. Only a human physician can diagnose someone as having a heart attack. However, unlike a decision support aid, an AI that is autonomously diagnosing a patient is, in a limited context, essentially practicing medicine. There is evidence that this autonomous AI performs as well as or better than average doctors.[7]

Some people are excited by the prospect of robot doctors, and some people are scared—but before getting scared, realize that human doctors and drivers have some unfortunate similarities. Medical error is one of the leading causes of death.[8] To be sure, people are better off seeing doctors than not seeing doctors, but perhaps in a few years some of the AI that can autonomously diagnose will do a better job than most doctors. There is some low-hanging fruit to be had in healthcare.

None of this has escaped the attention of policy makers. In 2021, the UK government announced a ten-year plan to make the country a global AI superpower and noted that we are living in "the age of artificial intelligence."[9] The report focuses on investments in planning, supporting the transition to an AI-enabled economy, and ensuring appropriate governance frameworks. The United Kingdom was late to the party by comparison to China, which released its AI strategy in 2017 and boldly planted a flag in the ground. China's strategy announced that the nation would become the world leader in AI by 2030, make AI a 30 billion dollar-a-year domestic industry, and make China a driving force for worldwide ethical norms and standards. Months later, Russian President Vladimir Putin declared that whoever becomes the leader in this sphere will become the ruler of the world.[10]

At least someone took that seriously. According to the United States National Security Commission on AI, which was formed by Congress in 2018 and which published its report in March of 2021, China is winning the AI arms race (or at least the United States is falling behind). It is a 750-page report, but the gist is that the United States is not sufficiently prepared to defend or compete against China in the AI era.[11] It proposes that America increases spending on non-defense AI R&D all the way up to 32 billion dollars a year in 2026—about what America now spends on biomedical research. The report also has a chapter on IP and notes that IP rules are important for national defense as well as industrial strategy. It even highlights some of the specific issues that need to be addressed for the United States to be successful at using and promoting AI—including my personal favorite, AI inventorship.

---

[6]   FDA, *FDA permits marketing of artificial intelligence-based device to detect certain diabetes-related eye problems*, www.fda.gov/news-events/press-announcements/fda-permits-marketing-artificial-intelligence-based-device-detect-certain-diabetes-related-eye (last accessed 02/27/2022).

[7]   Ibid.

[8]   For the landmark report on the subject, see Institute of Medicine. 2000. *To Err Is Human: Building a Safer Health System*. Washington, DC: The National Academies Press. https://doi.org/10.17226/9728.

[9]   Government of the United Kingdom, *National AI Strategy*, www.gov.uk/government/publications/national-ai-strategy (last accessed 02/27/2022).

[10]   David Meyer, *Vladimir Putin says whoever leads in artificial intelligence will rule the world*, https://fortune.com/2017/09/04/ai-artificial-intelligence-putin-rule-world/ (last accessed 02/27/2022).

[11]   NSCAI, *Final Report, National Security Commission on Artificial Intelligence*, www.nscai.gov/wp-content/uploads/2021/03/Full-Report-Digital-1.pdf (last accessed 02/27/2022).

Different jurisdictions are not just competing in terms of technology and investment, they are also competing with respect to governance frameworks for AI. Having appropriate laws in place is not only a critical component of industrial strategy and economic competitiveness; more broadly, it is vital to ensuring that technology such as AI is developed and used in ways that promote social value and that limit harm. All technologies and activities can cause harm, and AI is no exception. AI has been used for political and social manipulation, it has caused flash crashes in the stock market, and some fairly prominent technologists think it may doom the human race.[12] Governance is not all talk and reports—the European Commission recently came out with draft AI-specific regulations which propose a risk-based approach that completely prohibits certain uses of AI, such as for indiscriminate facial recognition in public places (with some exceptions) and for generating social scores of citizens.[13] It proposes a variety of compliance mechanisms for high-risk AI systems and uses, and it takes a lighter approach to lower or minimal risk systems. This particular set of regulations does not focus directly on AI and IP, but AI and IP is a key part of the ongoing debate about appropriate legal frameworks. Just as rules that take AI into account are important generally so that we get the best possible outcomes, they are important specifically with respect to IP to make sure that IP systems can achieve their underlying goals. AI is going to be broadly economically and socially disruptive, and specifically disruptive to IP systems.

AI has been around for a long time, and to some extent so have the challenges it poses to IP rules.[14] For instance, since the 1960s people have claimed to have developed computers capable of making music. In 1966 the United States Register of Copyright publicly questioned whether these works should be copyrightable and disclosed that the office had already received applications for at least partially computer-generated works including musical compositions.[15] But that music was all terrible. Today's AI has come a long way since the 1960s, and OpenAI's music is now practically mediocre. The project's website has AI that makes music in the style of current and recently deceased artists, which raises another interesting set of IP issues.[16]

As AI-generated music improves it is worth keeping in mind that it is only going to get better. At some point, we are going to have AI that can make music people want to hear. That is going to be incredibly disruptive because once you have AI that can make good music, you can have AI make a virtually unlimited amount of it at almost no marginal cost. That is going to be competition for human musicians in the way that self-driving Ubers are going to be competition for human drivers. But AI will not just replace people; it will change the way that

---

[12]   See, e.g., Maureen Dowd, *Elon Musk's billion dollar crusade to stop the A.I. apocalypse*, www.vanityfair.com/news/2017/03/elon-musk-billion-dollar-crusade-to-stop-ai-space-x   (last accessed 02/27/22).

[13]   European Commission, *Proposal for a Regulation of the European Parliament and of the Council Laying Down Harmonised Rules on Artificial Intelligence (Artificial Intelligence Act) and Amending Certain Union Legislative Acts* COM/2021/206 final, https://eur-lex.europa.eu/legal-content/EN/TXT/?uri=CELEX%3A52021PC0206 (last accessed 02/27/2022). I think the concern is not really with AI being used to make social scores but more with the idea of social scores per se, but anyway.

[14]   Thomas Ling, *AI is about to shake up music forever—but not in the way you think*, www.sciencefocus.com/science/ai-music-future/#:~:text=How%20easy%20is%20it%20to,by%20repeatedly%20being%20shown%20things (last accessed 02/27/2022).

[15]   *See U.S. COPYRIGHT OFFICE, SIXTY-EIGHTH ANN. REP. REG. COPYRIGHTS 4–5 (1966).*

[16]   https://openai.com/blog/jukebox/.

music is made and consumed. AI will make personalized music for someone in real time, to improve their mood or accompany their workout.

Harold Cohen and his AI system AARON were making paintings in the 1970s that, for all I know, could have been made by an AI, one of the great modern artists of the twentieth century, or one of my toddlers.[17] That probably says more about my lack of artistic sense than anything to do with AI, but as with AI musicians, the past few decades have been good for AI painters. Or, at least, their art is selling for more. Headlines were made in 2018 when Christie's became the first major auction house to offer an AI-generated artwork for sale. It went for $432,500 dollars.[18] Now exhibits of AI-generated artwork are no longer remarkable.

If you are looking for shocking headlines in the art world, it is probably what people are paying for Non-Fungible Tokens (NFT). An NFT is basically data stored on a digital ledger that can represent things such as a photograph or a painting.[19] Some of the NFTs now being exchanged for staggering sums of money were AI-generated. AI making art is going to be socially and economically disruptive just like AI making music, and it will also result in more business for copyright attorneys. Normally when a person makes a digital painting the work automatically attracts copyright protection more or less worldwide. That prevents someone else from copying or selling the work for the author's lifetime plus, in the United States and most large markets, 70 years. What if that author is an AI?[20]

In fact, numerous legal questions are raised by these sorts of technological advances. With respect to AI generating historically copyrightable work: Can you get a copyright for an AI generated work? Who would own it? How long would copyright exist? Until recently these were basically academic questions because there was not much of a market for AI-generated content, but that is changing quickly given the speed at which AI is improving. These are, or will soon be, now commercially important questions. Similar considerations apply to AI making other sorts of IP historically protectable by patents, designs, and trademarks. For instance, AI is making trademarks,[21] but perhaps more interesting is how AI can fundamentally alter how trademarks function. Trademarks are designed to indicate to consumers the source and origin of goods and services. What happens when commerce is online, and when AI is buying goods on your behalf? How does Alexa determine the source and origin of goods and services and what sort of competing signs would Alexa find confusing or deceptive? How do we apply infringement tests based on human consumers to AI-based purchases? What happens where AI is effectively both the buyer and the seller?

At the end of 2019, the United States Patent and Trademark Office (USPTO) put out a request for comments on AI and patents as well as a request for comments on AI and IP more generally.[22] It published a report summarizing certain comments it received early last

---

[17]   Chris Garcia, *Hardo Cohen and AARON—A 40-year collaboration*, https://computerhistory.org/blog/harold-cohen-and-aaron-a-40-year-collaboration/.

[18]   Christie's, *Is artificial intelligence set to become art's next medium*, www.christies.com/features/a-collaboration-between-two-artists-one-human-one-a-machine-9332-1.aspx (last accessed 02/27/2022).

[19]   *Non-Fungible Tokens (NFT)*, https://ethereum.org/en/nft/ (last accessed 02/27/2022).

[20]   Ahmed Elgammal, *AI is blurring the definition of artist*, www.americanscientist.org/article/ai-is-blurring-the-definition-of-artist#:~:text=To%20create%20AI%20art%2C%20artists,the%20aesthetics%20it%20has%20learned (last accessed 02/27/2022).

[21]   See, e.g., www.brandmark.io.

[22]   USPTO, *Request for Comments on Intellectual Property Protection for Artificial Intelligence Innovation* (Federal Registry Notice 84 FR 58141), www.uspto.gov/sites/default/files/documents/ITIF_RFC-84-FR-58141.pdf (last accessed 02/27/2022).

year.[23] The United Kingdom Intellectual Property Office launched a similar consultation to the USPTO in 2020 and published its results in 2021.[24] One of the most interesting outcomes was how different the UKIPO findings were from the USPTO findings—even with many of the same stakeholders providing submissions. Part of the difference may be the result of rapidly changing attitudes toward AI and IP. Again, these consultations are not just about AI making new IP—they are also about how AI is being developed using IP. For that matter, AI itself can be protected by IP rights.

On top of which, AI uses IP. Consider Clearview's AI, which has collected and trained on more than ten billion images from across the Internet. Clearview licenses this AI to law enforcement to use for facial recognition.[25] Usually copying an image constitutes copyright infringement, but what if it is being copied to train an AI, or just to generate insights? Is that infringement? What if a bunch of machines are sending digital copies of images between each other and no one ever sees those copies? What if an AI is functionally infringing someone else's intellectual property but not in a way that is directly attributable to the person? Who would be responsible for that and on what basis?

Different jurisdictions already have different answers to some of these issues. For instance, there is a very broad exception to copyright infringement in Japan for text and data mining and a much narrower one in Europe.[26] But there is not yet much case law exploring in what situations it would be infringement for a machine to do something that would be infringement for a person. As different jurisdictions come up with different answers to these questions another challenge will be presented because of the transnational nature of IP. A book that you write in the United States is protected in France, Brazil, and India. That is not now the case with a book written "by" an AI. World Intellectual Property Organization (WIPO), the UN agency most responsible for IP, has gotten in on the action by hosting a series of stakeholder discussions around IP and AI (recently broadened to IP and frontier technologies).[27] In theory, an international treaty may come out of this work so that jurisdictions around the world can agree to a common set of rules involving IP and AI—but that is a slow process. Not oblivious to the time frames involved, WIPO is working on framing the debate and getting stakeholders to ask the right questions rather than proposing specific substantive solutions.

Getting consensus on definitions and language would be a good start, as it is remarkable that about 65 years after the term AI was coined it still lacks a widely accepted definition. Definitional problems are significant when laws are being written to regulate AI and some of the people debating these laws are talking about different things. If people cannot agree

---

[23]   US Patent and Trademark Office, *Public Views on Artificial Intelligence and Intellectual Property Policy*. Oct 2020. www.uspto.gov/sites/default/files/documents/USPTO_AI-Report_2020-10-07.pdf.

[24]   UK Intellectual Property Office, *Government Response to Call for Views on Artificial Intelligence and Intellectual Property*. Updated 23 March 2021. www.gov.uk/government/consultations/artificial-intelligence-and-intellectual-property-call-for-views/government-response-to-call-for-views-on-artificial-intelligence-and-intellectual-property.

[25]   Kashmir Hill, *The secretive company that might end privacy as we know it*, www.nytimes.com/2020/01/18/technology/clearview-privacy-facial-recognition.html (last accessed 02/27/2022).

[26]   European Alliance for Research Excellence, *Japan amends its copyright legislation to meet future demands in AI and Big Data*, https://eare.eu/japan-amends-tdm-exception-copyright/ (last accessed 02/27/2022).

[27]   WIPO, *The WIPO Conversation on Intellectual Property and Frontier Technologies* www.wipo.int/about-ip/en/frontier_technologies/frontier_conversation.html (last accessed 02/27/2022).

on what AI is, it will be hard for them to agree on the definition for an AI-generated work. Without a common understanding of an AI-generated work it becomes difficult to have harmonized IP rules.

Some of the WIPO conversations have focused on issues that have been debated for decades, such as whether you can patent software and whether someone should be able to "own" data. These are not new issues, but they are issues that are taking on newfound importance due to AI. Patents on new software architectures and uses may be more valuable now that AI can do more, and data ownership matters more given the importance of data for training AI, for AI using data to generate insights, and for AI generating new sorts of data. Some of these issues are more specific to advances in AI, such as deepfakes. Deepfakes are not new, in the sense that there have long been technologies that can be used for deception, but what is new is how easy it has become for just about anyone to use AI to make a realistic-appearing video. The law has long dealt with deception, but the evolution of technology means that some of our rules may need to be rethought.

People are also interested in AI in administrative decision making. Not only can AI make new IP or help people to make IP, but it can also file or help people to file for IP rights. For example, an application called Specifio can generate a patent application based on a single claim.[28] It does not directly replace a patent attorney because the AI is not as good as a person, and a patent attorney needs to (or at least should) review and revise what the AI is generating—but if it takes that attorney half as much time to write an application with the help of the AI, then perhaps we only need half as many patent attorneys (or, at least, fewer junior attorneys). Perhaps we will still need all the lawyers but they will be more productive so we will have more IP filings. That suggests that IP offices may get busier and need to turn to AI for help. In fact, the USPTO is already using AI to classify incoming patent applications and determine who should review them. It may not be long before a patent application arrives at a patent office and AI classifies it, does a first pass at a prior art search, and then drafts an office action for a human examiner to review. Even without an AI replacing anyone, that is going to change the process of patent prosecution in all sorts of subtle and not-so-subtle ways.

The public is concerned about AI in decision making—not really with patent prosecution, because it is hard for the public to care about patent prosecution even with robots involved, but certainly with AI augmenting and automating administrative and even judicial decisions in other contexts. In part this is because of worries around impermissible biases and explainability and transparency. It would be bad to have AI making recommendations at criminal hearings without being able to explain the basis for those recommendations, particularly if its recommendations were based on protected characteristics.[29]

2.   ADVANCING THE CONVERSATION

While I do not personally have the answer to every question involving IP and AI, this Handbook goes a long way toward advancing our understanding of many of the most impor-

---

[28]   *Auto-generated Software-patent applications*, https://specif.io/ (last accessed 02/27/2022).

[29]   Melissa Hamilton, *We use Big Data to sentence criminals. But can the algorithms really tell us what we need to know?* https://openresearch.surrey.ac.uk/permalink/44SUR_INST/15d8lgh/ alma99516814902346 (last accessed 02/27/2022).

tant ones. A group of world-leading authorities from a diverse group of jurisdictions, disciplines, and professional fields have generously contributed original content here.

The Handbook is divided into four parts. Part I includes contributions, such as the present chapter, that address intellectual property rights (IPRs) generally rather than focusing primarily on a specific type of IPR, such as trademarks or patents. Of course, even those chapters that focus on a particular type of IPR have broader relevance as many of their insights apply in other contexts—including outside of IP law.

Following this chapter, Gervais argues that AI-generated content should not be treated the same way in patent and copyright law because the two bodies of law have different goals. He is particularly wary of conflating human and AI activity in the copyright sphere, given its potential to disadvantage human creatives. Gervais suggests "IP proximate cause" could be used to determine where a person has contributed to an invention or a copyrightable work and therefore whether protection should be granted. Barfield, Karanasiou, and Chagnal-Feferkorn then explore the concept of "embodiment" in AI and its relevance to IP law. They argue that embodiment, either physically (as with a robot) or virtually (as with an avatar in virtual reality), is an important concept for IP because embodied agents can be both the subject of IPRs and infringers of IPRs. They explain how the lens of embodiment sheds light on the wider socio-legal narratives in AI and IP.

O'Connor considers artist "style," which has limited protection under copyright, trademark, and right of publicity laws. Yet AI's ability to mimic style suggests that style is important, including for its newfound commercial relevance for AI, and also that style is capable of being quantified and fixed and thus should be entitled to greater protection. Deltorn considers inference models, which are complex entities combining know-how to produce a relevant solution with information derived from machine training data. These models underlie many of the most impressive recent AI breakthroughs, and Deltorn considers how such models can be protected under European frameworks by various IPRs including copyright, database protections, trade secrets, and patents. Finally, Pendleton provides a skeptical take on the fitness of existing IP frameworks, arguing that for IP law to be useful for AI it should focus on misappropriation. Such an approach should protect investment, whether financial or based on labor or skill, but should also provide that subsequent investments which result in a transformative use should protect against infringement and give rise to new rights.

Part II focuses on copyright and related rights. Several contributors present compelling narratives around AI authorship and AI-generated works, starting with Craig, who, like Gervais, suggests that advances in AI give us the opportunity to rethink the purposes of copyright law. She argues that the principles that underlie copyright law should inform our response to AI, and that we should attempt to achieve normative equilibrium when confronted by disruptive technologies. On this basis, AI-generated outputs should not be eligible for copyright protection, and use of protected material for training AI should be non-infringing. Frosio subsequently considers AI authorship, initially by considering whether AI meets traditional authorship requirements, then by considering various approaches to AI-generated works from a policy perspective. He proposes either that AI-generated works could go to the public domain, a person or a machine could be grated authorship, the work could receive specialized sui generis protection, or rights could be granted to publishers and disseminators. Frosio weighs the costs and benefits of these options from different theoretical perspectives.

Lee and Woo argue that completely overhauling copyright law in response to AI is not optimal, and that simple tests of exploitation, while appealing, are not an adequate substitute for a multi-layer regime. They defend the current copyright framework based on examples from European and Asian case law. They conclude that top-down solutions are not sufficient for addressing complex copyright challenges and that non-statutory approaches are needed. After this, Benhamou and Andrijevic examine use of AI in a more specific context: generation of new pictures. They analyze the criterion of originality under copyright law across the full lifecycle of an AI-generated picture from the input to the output stage. They conclude that copyright law protects elements of this process at numerous stages and in complex ways, and that authorship and entitlement associated with AI output will often need to be assessed on a case-by-case basis. Justice Arnold turns to AI and performers' rights, which is a statutory right under English law, but international legal frameworks also require certain protections for performers. He considers whether performers' rights protect, or should protect, real performers against imitation by avatars and deepfakes, and whether performers' rights protect, or should protect, imaginary avatars.

Ghosh argues that AI is simply software and that recognizing this allows a developed body of law related to software and copyright to be applied to activities involving AI. It also connects IP and AI to computer science as an academic discipline with typologies that are useful for assessing legal questions of ownership, liability, and transactions. Ghosh explains how computer science can inform debates over copyright, with parallels to patent law, and argues it offers an explanation for the 2021 US Supreme Court decision in *Oracle v Google*. Finally, Bonadio, Dinev, and McDonagh consider use of IP to train AI as well as use of IP by AI for activities such as text and data mining. They consider whether such activities should constitute infringement, whether exceptions should apply and in what circumstances, and who should be liable for infringement. They explore whether AI-based activity should receive more generous fair use or fair dealing treatment with a focus on the United States, United Kingdom, and European Union.

Part III focuses on trademarks and design rights. Lim begins by exploring AI's impact on likelihood of confusion as the test for trademark infringement. He considers how AI will change how consumers purchase goods and services, liability for sales of counterfeit products on platforms such as Amazon, and even how AI can facilitate adjudication of trademark disputes. Next, Moerland and Kafrouni consider trademarks in the context of AI-based purchasing and argue that for trademarks to continue to fulfill their roles, the average consumer may need to become the AI-assisted consumer. They explain that improved understanding of online purchasing behavior and AI use is needed to properly apply a test based on consumer confusion in this new environment.

Senftleben examines the rules proposed by the European Commission in its Proposal for a Digital Services Act to create new transparency obligations for accountable digital services which focus on transparency measures for consumers. Exploring AI-driven behavioral advertising practices and keyword advertising cases, he explains that rights holders also have an interest in advertising parameters and that information on market alternatives could improve trust in AI-based personalized advertising. Gangee continues the exploration of trademark law by outlining the ways in which AI is being used in the registration environment, posing some non-obvious doctrinal questions. He next surveys AI being used for enforcement, and argues that technology is shifting goal posts and setting new defaults. Last, Cook turns to design law and AI-generated designs. He proposes that design law may be better understood as a hybrid of patent and copyright law rather than an independent area of law, and that this helps us to understand whether and how we should provide protection for AI-generated designs.

Part IV focuses on patents and trade secrets. Crouch begins by considering another form of AI, namely corporations and other private organizations. He notes that corporations have already obtained legal personhood and certain civil rights, and he argues there are numerous parallels between corporations and AI. He traces the progression of corporate rights in the patent context from pre-industrial times to the America Invents Act of 2011. He concludes that the patent system can effectively function, and AI-generated inventions can be protected, without having to rely excessively on legal fictions. Mitra-Kahnv analyzes economic reasons for recognizing AI patent inventors. He claims there is no convincing economic reason to allow AI inventorship to incentivize innovation but some reason for doing so to encourage technology transfer, and he proposes some options to protect AI-generated inventions without AI inventorship.

Bayern considers AI's impact on trade secret law and policy and notes that AI can dramatically reduce costs associated with reverse engineering. He also notes that AI may be particularly susceptible to reverse engineering, even AI systems with limited explainability and transparency. Bayern explores these ideas and suggests they may have significant impact on trade secret policy and that trade secret law may need to change. Matulionyte and Aranovich then contemplate the tension between the desire for explainable AI and trade secret protection. They consider this tension in depth in one case study in judicial administration and one in healthcare, and suggest solutions to areas of conflict.

Shemtov and Gabison consider the impact of AI on inventive-step requirements for patentability. They note that the person skilled in the art will need to be augmented as AI becomes more common—the nature of the augmentation being a question of fact. This is also justified under incentive theory, and the threshold for patentability will need to increase as AI makes invention easier so that the patent system can continue to achieve its goals. In the final chapter, Sandeen and Aplin interrogate the extent to which machine-generated data and algorithms may qualify as trade secrets under US and EU law. They show, through case studies involving autonomous vehicles and credit scoring, that commonly claimed subject matter of trade secret protection may not actually qualify for protection. However, factual secrecy in many cases provides significant protection even in the absence of trade secret protection, and so regulatory efforts may need to focus on factually secret data.

Sandeen and Aplin interrogate the extent to which machine-generated data and algorithms may qualify as trade secrets under US and EU law. They show, though case studies involving autonomous vehicles and credit scoring, that commonly claimed subject matter of trade secret protection may not actually qualify for protection. However, factual secrecy in many cases provides significant protection even in the absence of trade secret protection, and so regulatory efforts may need to focus on factually secret data. In the final chapter, Shemtov and Gabison consider the impact of AI on inventive-step requirements for patentability. They note that the person skilled in the art will need to be augmented as AI becomes more common—the nature of the augmentation being a question of fact. This is also justified under incentive theory, and the threshold for patentability will need to increase as AI makes invention easier for the patent system to achieve its goals.

3.   AI-GENERATED WORKS AND THE ARTIFICIAL INVENTOR PROJECT

My own AI and IP research has focused on AI-generated works, mainly in the context of patent and copyright law. A recent case study by Siemens provides a good introduction to the topic.[30] Siemens developed a new car suspension which it wanted to patent, but determined that was not possible because a human inventor could not be identified for a patent application. Essentially, the human engineers involved stated that the design was generated by an AI and that none of them had done anything to qualify as inventors. Getting inventorship right is more important in some jurisdictions than others, but in the United States it is a criminal offense to deliberately inaccurately list yourself as an inventor and failing to identify all inventors in good faith can render a patent invalid or unenforceable.[31] Without an inventor, conventional wisdom holds, an invention cannot be patented.

The takeaway from this case is that Siemens has some nifty AI which is functionally stepping into the shoes of employees and performing tasks that used to make a person an inventor. But, because the law in most jurisdictions treats behavior by a person and behavior by a machine differently, Siemens could not protect its invention in the way it could if it had been made by one of its human employees. This is the most commercially relevant challenge with AI-generated inventions—subsistence of patent rights. It also raises questions of who, or what, would be listed as an inventor on a patent application for an AI-generated invention, and who, or what, would own that invention.

As mentioned above, the terminology for AI doing various things in the IP context is all over the place—terms such as AI inventions,[32] AI art, AI-assisted or AI-generated, and computer-generated abound. Aside from the fact that IP offices, courts, policy makers, and even the various contributors to this book use different terms, different people can also use the same term to mean different things. The rest of the chapter will focus on "AI-generated works," which I will define as an AI output for which the AI has functionally acted as a traditional human author or inventor. Sometimes AI-generated works are defined as works lacking a traditional human author, but I think that approach is problematic in cases where a person and a machine independently make contributions that would qualify people for joint authorship or inventorship. As a result, the contribution and financial interests of the party contributing the AI are ignored.

While on definitions, it is hard to talk about AI-generated inventions without defining AI. I define it as "an algorithm or machine capable of completing tasks that would otherwise

---

[30]   Siemens, *Re; Draft Issues Paper on Intellectual Property Policy and Artificial Intelligence,* www.wipo.int/export/sites/www/about-ip/en/artificial_intelligence/call_for_comments/pdf/org_siemens.pdf (last accessed 02/27/2022).

[31]   37 CFR 1.56 Duty to disclose information material to patentability ("[N]o patent will be granted on an application in connection with which fraud on the Office was practiced or attempted or the duty of disclosure was violated through bad faith or intentional misconduct").

[32]   www.federalregister.gov/documents/2019/08/27/2019-18443/request-for-comments-on-patenting-artificial-intelligence-inventions. I think AI Inventions as a term is unfortunately ambiguous, but in fairness my attempt to brand AI-generated inventions as "computational inventions" was wildly unsuccessful. Ryan Abbott, *I Think, Therefore I Invent: Creative Computers and the Future of Patent Law*, 57 B.C. L. Rev. 1079 (2016).

require cognition."[33] There are many ways to build AI, but with particularly with respect to the activities considered here, as Ghosh explores in depth and as a practical matter, AI is more or less software.[34]

The claim that AI can invent is still somewhat controversial, although much less so than it was even a few years ago. However, it is not a controversial statement to say that AI is generating output that would traditionally get copyright protection without someone who traditionally qualifies as an author. That is because the bar for making something that gets copyright is quite low. Taking a photograph of this page with your smartphone would make you an author of the photograph. It would be difficult to claim that an AI cannot engage in that sort of activity—even a monkey can do it. Your smartphone photo is not a great work of art, but copyright law does not concern itself with whether you've made the next Mona Lisa or something that only Clearview's AI will ever see. Both works will be protected by copyright long after you are dead. But creating something patentable is a lot harder than coming up with something protectable by copyright. For an invention to be patentable, it has to be: (1) new, so that no one in human history has ever disclosed it; (2) non-obvious to a skilled person who essentially represents an average researcher in your field; and (3) useful.

People routinely use AI in the process of inventing without AI inventorship being an issue. That is because there is a test for what makes an inventor—whether the inventor, at least under US law, "conceived" of an invention; whether they had the "definite and permanent idea of an operative invention, including every feature of the subject matter sought to be patented."[35] So an AI, or another person, can do quite a bit of heavy lifting with an invention before questions of inventorship start to arise. Plus, if at least one person qualifies as an inventor, then at least someone is getting a patent (and who that person is can be altered by contract), so the subsistence problem does not arise.

Can a machine conceive of something? Some people believe that because we do not have machines that think the way that people do, a machine cannot invent. It is certainly true that machines do not think the same way that people do—no robot ever woke up in the morning, had an existential crisis, and decided it was going to start inventing instead of assembling cars on a manufacturing line. But so what? AI can be given known problems, such as finding the design for a more effective car suspension, and can generate a solution that is new and inventive to an average researcher, and can then present that solution so that anyone who understands car suspension designs would recognize its utility. That means the AI is generating the entire idea of an operative invention without a person doing anything that should qualify them to be an inventor.

Sometimes even with AI doing a lot of the work, a person could still qualify as an inventor. For example, occasionally the tricky bit of invention is finding a problem to be solved. Where someone has exercised inventive skill to formulate a problem, or perhaps even to formulate a problem in a manner that would be understood by an AI, that could make them an inventor. But that is not usually how invention works. Most of the time people are trying to solve known

---

[33]   Ryan Abbott, *The Reasonable Robot* (2020) at 22.
[34]   There is some special purpose hardware that one could consider AI, and fancy issues when the AI is operating on a distributed leger or as open source code, but we needed a contributor to explore those issues.
[35]   Sewall, 21 F.3d at 415.

problems—designing a better toothbrush, creating a new antibody to treat COVID-19,[36] and so on. Sometimes a person programming or designing or training an AI could qualify as an inventor. That seems appropriate at least in cases where someone is designing an AI to solve a specific problem, and where they know the problem being solved and have an expectation their AI will generate a solution. It seems less appropriate in cases where someone is building an AI to solve problems at a more general level, such as optimizing industrial components, without knowing whether some other team is going to apply that AI to optimizing a computer chip or an antennae design. For that matter, dozens or hundreds of programmers may contribute to an AI, and AI may be, in whole or part, open-source code.

Sometimes a person recognizing the value of an AI's output can qualify as an inventor. That works when someone is the first to notice that penicillin is inhibiting bacterial growth, or that there might be a use for Viagra outside of treating heart disease. It also works if an AI suggests a dozen possible antibodies to treat COVID-19 and human researchers then need to do additional testing to find the best one. But if an AI can validate its own output—if it can generate a million possible car suspension designs, model them, rank them according to generally known criteria for function, and then essentially say "here is the best car suspension out of a million and it dramatically outperforms what we have in our vehicles today"—then attributing inventorship to the person who says "right, let's go with the option the AI likes" does not seem right. At least some of the time what we think about as inventive activity is being done, at least functionally, by the AI and not by a person—regardless of whether people are just very complex biological machines or whether what neural networks do analogizes well to what goes on in someone's head. Patent law should focus on function because society benefits from functional behavior—the result of AI inventors is more innovation, more open knowledge, and more commercially valuable products.

A couple of years ago there was no case law on AI-generated inventions. There were jurisdictions that required an inventor to be a natural person, but whether by statute or case law, the possibility of a non-human inventor was only something that had been considered in the context of corporate inventorship.[37] Whether a company could be an inventor is an interesting question—particularly considering legal theories that suggest a company is more than a sum of its individual agents, a theory that supports criminal liability directly for companies—but in any event, it presents a very different set of questions from AI inventorship. Companies act through human agents, and if companies did not have to list inventors on patent applications those inventors would fail to receive due credit and sometimes financial rewards. But in the case of AI-generated inventions, there is no human inventor who is being denied credit. To the contrary, allowing someone to list herself on a patent application for an AI-generated invention would reduce transparency and allow someone to receive false credit.

There was some law with respect to AI-generated works and copyright protection. The United Kingdom was the first country to explicitly provide copyright protection for so called

---

[36]   AI has already played a key role in R&D related to COVID-19. Hannah Kuchler, *Will AI turbocharge the hunt for new drugs?* Financial Times, March 19, 2022, www.ft.com/content/3e57ad6c-493d-4874-a663-0cb200d3cdb5.

[37]   See, e.g., *Univ. of Utah v Max-Planck-Gesellschaft zur Forderung der Wissenschaften e.V.* 734 F.3d 1315 (Fed. Cir. 2013).

computer-generated works back in 1988.[38] Those are works generated by a computer in such circumstances that there is no human author of the work.[39] In such cases, the producer of the work, the person who undertakes to have the work created, is deemed to be the author and the work receives a shortened period of statutory protection—50 years versus the usual lifetime of an author plus 70 years. The United Kingdom remains an international outlier in this respect, although some Commonwealth countries followed suit.[40]

There has only ever been one case in the United Kingdom involving copyright infringement and a computer-generated work under this law, but even then, no one was challenging the copyright in the underlying work.[41] There are a few reasons why there has not been more litigation over AI-generated works. First, unlike the United States, you cannot register copyright in the United Kingdom, so there would only be litigation involving infringement. Second, there is not that much copyright litigation in the United Kingdom where the subsistence of copyright is at issue. Third, even if someone was aware that a work was AI-generated, there would be no point challenging subsistence given the state of UK law. Finally, and I think most importantly, until recently AI-generated works have not had much commercial value and thus have not been worth suing over. That has changed and will continue to change now that AI is getting better at making creative works.[42]

By contrast to the United Kingdom, the United States Copyright Office has a "Human Authorship Requirement" that has been formally in place since 1973. AI-generated works automatically enter the public domain once disclosed and cannot receive copyright protection. That means if you have an AI that makes a song that becomes a hit single, it will be awfully tempting to take credit for that work. The machine is unlikely to complain. The Copyright Office cites to the 1884 case of *Burrow Giles v Sarony* in support of this policy.[43] That is the Supreme Court case that first held that a photograph could be protected by copyright. Napoleon Sarony had sued the Burrow Giles Lithographic Company for copyright infringement of his famous photograph of Oscar Wilde, and the company alleged that the photograph could not be protected because it was merely "a reproduction on paper of the exact features of some natural object or of some person."[44] But the Supreme Court held that "writings" by which "ideas in the mind of the author are given visible expression" were eligible for protection, and it referred to authors as human.[45] The Copyright Office interprets this case to hold that copyright requires

---

[38]   The Copyright, Designs and Patents Act 1998 (CDPA), Section 9(3) ("In the case of a literary, dramatic, musical or artistic work which is computer-generated, the author shall be taken to be the person by whom the arrangement necessary for the creation of the work are undertaken"). Other jurisdictions have adopted a similar rule including Ireland, Hong Kong, New Zealand, and South Africa.

[39]   Ibid.

[40]   E.g., Copyright Act of 1994, s 5 (NZ); Copyright and Related Rights Act 2000, pt 1, s 2 (No 28/2000) (IR).

[41]   *Nova Production v Mazooma Games*, EWHC 24 (Ch) [2006].

[42]   Ian Bogost, *The AI–art gold rush is here.* The Atlantic, March 6, 2019, www.theatlantic .com/technology/archive/2019/03/ai-created-art-invades-chelsea-gallery-scene/584134/ (last accessed 02/27/2022); AIArtist.org, *41 creative tools to generate AI art*, https://aiartists.org/ai-generated-art-tools (last accessed 02/27/2022).

[43]   *Burrow-Giles Lithographic Co. v Sarony*, 111 U.S. 53 (1884).

[44]   Ibid at 56.

[45]   Ibid at 58.

creative powers of the mind which it thinks machines lack.[46] There has never been a US case where a court has considered whether an AI-generated work could be protected or whether an AI could be an author.[47]

That Copyright Office policy was almost challenged in court a few years ago.[48] The case involved a series of pictures that a macaque named Naruto took of himself using photographic equipment belonging to a nature photographer, David Slater.[49] The photographs ended up having value because people thought a smiling monkey selfie was cute and entertaining even though black crested macaques smile as a display of aggression. So Naruto is likely responding to his own reflection in the camera lens and attempting to intimidate that monkey. In any case, people started using the photograph without Slater's permission. He accused them of copyright infringement, and this all resulted in enough attention that the Copyright Office reformulated its Human Authorship Requirement in its Compendium and explicitly listed photographs taken by a monkey as ineligible for protection.[50]

This seemed to put an end to the matter until People for the Ethical Treatment of Animals (PETA) sued Slater in Federal Court alleging that Naruto was the author and owner of the photographs, and that Slater was liable for copyright infringement.[51] The case was ultimately dismissed by the Ninth Circuit Court of Appeals, but it was dismissed based on standing. The Courts said that unless the Copyright Act plainly states that non-human animals have standing to sue, we are not going to let them bring lawsuits. As a result, the Copyright Office policy has never been challenged.[52]

What about in the patent context? Until recently, conventional wisdom held that if you did not have a human inventor then you could not get a patent. But there are reasons to think that is not a good approach. The patent system exists to incentivize invention, to encourage disclosure of inventions that might otherwise be kept as trade secrets, and to encourage the commercialization of inventions. Historically, some academics have thought machines do not care about patents so there would be no point to patenting their inventions. Of course, it is true that AI does not care about patents, but companies like Siemens and Pfizer care about patents. If we are moving from a paradigm of research and development in which we want to directly incentivize people to invent to one in which we want to incentivize people to build AI that will invent, then protecting the output of that AI is critical to promoting that activity.

---

[46] Compendium of the US Copyright Office Practices, Third Edition, Section 306 ("Human Authorship Requirement. The copyright law only protects 'the fruits of intellectual labor' that 'are founded in the creative powers of the mind.' Trade-Mark Cases, 100 U.S. 82, 94 (1879). Because copyright law is limited to 'original intellectual conceptions of the author,' the Office will refuse to register a claim if it determines that a human being did not create the work. Burrow-Giles Lithographic Co. v. Sarony, 111 U.S. 53, 58 (1884)") .

[47] Second Request for Reconsideration for Refusal to Register A Recent Entrance to Paradise, February 14, 2022, www.copyright.gov/rulings-filings/review-board/docs/a-recent-entrance-to-paradise.pdf (last accessed 02/27/2022).

[48] *Naruto v Slater*, 888 F.3d 418 (9th Cir. 2018).

[49] Andres Guadamuz, *Can the monkey selfie case teach us anything about copyright law?* www.wipo.int/wipo_magazine/en/2018/01/article_0007.html (last accessed 02/27/2022).

[50] Compendium of the US Copyright Office Practices, Third Edition, Section 313.2.

[51] *Naruto v Slater*, 888 F.3d 418 (9th Cir. 2018).

[52] Ibid.

I led a team of patent attorneys in filing two patent applications in 2018 for two AI-generated inventions—the "Artificial Inventor Project."[53] One invention was a beverage container based on fractal geometry (like a snail shell) and one was a flashing light beacon that could attract attention in an emergency. We filed those applications initially in the United Kingdom and the European Patent Office (EPO) because those offices do not require an inventor to be initially disclosed and because the offices subject the applications to early substantive review. Indeed, the applications were reviewed and found by the UKIPO to be new, non-obvious, and useful at a preliminary stage. That means if I had put my name, or just about anyone's name, on those patents as the inventor no one would have questioned me and we would likely have issued patents by now. After substantive examination was complete, we updated the inventorship to note that there was no human inventor and that an AI had functionally invented the inventions, and we also filed the applications in 15 additional jurisdictions. Naming the AI as the inventor was not done to give the AI ownership of a patent or to give it rights or credit. It was done to ensure appropriate patent ownership, to be transparent, and to prevent someone from claiming false credit. If I could license "DABUS," which is the AI that generated our inventions, and have it generate numerous inventions for which I could list myself as the inventor, that would change what it means to be a human inventor. It would equate the efforts of people asking an AI to solve a problem with someone who exhibited genuine ingenuity.

Of course, it has never been our position, or just about anyone's position, that the AI should own a patent. An AI could not legally own property because it is not a legal person, but more importantly, an AI would not care about getting a patent and it could not properly exploit a patent. Having an AI own a patent does not make a lot of sense on just about any level. I am sure someone could figure out a way to make it work using blockchain, but there is really no way in which the patent system does not more effectively achieve its goals by letting the AI's owner (or another default owner) patent the AI's inventions. There are other parties that might be appropriate default owners, such as programmers, users, or producers, but as long as there is a default and clarity around subsistence, if multiple parties are involved they can contract to their optimal outcome.

The cases thus have nothing to do with rights for AI. In the future, there could be some reason to give an AI some sort of right. The idea seems less ridiculous when you realize that artificial persons, mainly in the form of companies and governments, have all sorts of rights, including civil rights (as Crouch explores). In fact, most patents are owned by artificial persons. In terms of AI rights, for instance, we could change the law to allow a self-driving car to have some limited form of legal personality so that it could hold an insurance policy to directly compensate accident victims. But just because the law could change does not mean that it should. I cannot see any way in which it makes more sense to give a self-driving Uber an insurance policy than to simply make Uber liable for accidents caused by their self-driving cars. If we did give a machine rights it would not be for the machine's sake, but for the same reason we give companies rights—we think that doing so makes things better for people. Companies being able to own property and enter into contracts facilitates commerce and thus benefits people.

In our patent cases, we argued the AI's owner should own its patents as a default where there are multiple claims of entitlement. That position is based on various common law rules of

---

[53]   See generally www.artificialinventor.com.

property ownership. For example, if I own a 3D printer and I have it make a physical beverage container, I own that beverage container. That outcome is based on the doctrine of accession, which refers to someone owning a piece of property by virtue of owning some other piece of property. For example, if I own a cow that has a calf, I own the calf. If I own a fruit tree that bears fruit, I own the fruit. So, if I own an AI and it makes a patentable invention, I own that invention as a trade secret (assuming it qualifies as such, as Sandeen and Aplin explore) if it is not disclosed. If I choose to file for a patent on the invention, I should own that patent as well.

There are likely to be some interesting entitlement disputes in the future where many people were involved in the making of an AI-generated invention. It is simple to say that if I own a fruit tree I own its fruit, but the situation may be complicated. I might own the land on which a tree is situated, but another person leases the land, another person supplies seeds, another harvests the fruit, and so on. But the law has long dealt with competing claims of entitlement by reference to underlying principles of property law. In our case, where only one party could credibly claim entitlement, if DABUS's owner gets to patent its output that creates all the right incentives for the public to benefit.

To give a little background on how DABUS works,[54] at its simplest, consider a system of two neural networks. A network is composed of numerous nodes connected by the same algorithm. The first network is trained on data, which alters the connection weights between the nodes and which essentially stores the data. For instance, you could train the network by exposing it to 100,000 car suspension designs. The system then generates noise by altering its own connection weights, essentially corrupting the data it has been trained on, which generates novel output—say, variations on the car suspension designs it was initially trained on. The second network knows what data the first network was trained on, so it can tell you whether what is coming out of the first network is new (and how different), and it can control the level of noise in the first network. It can also be trained to model the first network's output, so, for instance, it can take a proposed car suspension design and evaluate it for fitness—how well it performs across certain measures, such as weight. Set the system up properly and you can have one network pumping out new designs at superhuman speeds, and another network evaluating how well those will perform. At some point that should result in a better car suspension.

Two networks is the simple version, but in modern times a system like this can be composed of hundreds or thousands of neural networks, each representing a concept such as warmth or enjoyment. A person trains the AI in how simple concepts relate to each other—warm food can result in enjoyment, for example. Later, in unsupervised operation, the machine combines basic ideas into complex ideas and stops when a complex idea terminates in a particularly salient concept. DABUS was not told to invent a flashing emergency light, but it was told to be on the lookout for things that could prevent death. It combined the ideas for a new flashing light mechanism with preferentially attracting attention with the need to attract attention in an emergency, and essentially generated a patent claim that we built a specification around. In our case, no one gave DABUS a specific problem to solve, it was not trained or built to solve a specific problem, and DABUS identified the value of its output before it was seen by a human being.

---

[54]   For a lot of background on how DABUS works, see Stephen L. Thaler, *Vast Topological Learning and Sentient AGI*, 8(1) Journal of Artificial Intelligence and Consciousness 81 (2021).

In July 2021 we received our first patent in South Africa.[55] DABUS is listed as the inventor and the patent belongs to the AI's owner. South Africa is a little unusual in that it does not substantively examine patents.[56] In other words, South Africa does not consider whether inventions are new, non-obvious, and useful before issuing them. But the applications had already been reviewed for substantive patentability by the UKIPO and EPO. South Africa does do formalities examination, and in every jurisdiction that has so far denied the applications this has been on a formality basis.

Not every jurisdiction has been as open-minded as South Africa. The applications are pending in 16 jurisdictions but have so far been denied by courts and patent offices in several of those, including in the United States, United Kingdom, EPO, and Australia, on the basis that the applications did not properly designate a human inventor. All those denials are under appeal, and in July 2021 Justice Beach in the Federal Court of Australia (FCA) issued an extensive reason decision essentially holding that an AI could be a patent inventor as a matter of law and that, at least in our case, the AI's owner had the most compelling claim of entitlement.[57] That decision is currently being reviewed by a full panel of the FCA, from which a further appeal to Australia's High Court is available on a discretionary basis.

In the United States, the USPTO denied the applications and this denial was upheld by a Justice Brinkema in the Eastern District of Virginia.[58] An appeal is currently before the Court of Appeals for the Federal Circuit. In the United States, the USPTO argues that the Patent Act's plain language refers to inventors as persons, and therefore (1) an AI cannot be an inventor and (2) absent a traditional human inventor a patent cannot be obtained. I argue that the Patent Act never defines an inventor as a natural person, and a broader interpretation is required in light of the context and purpose of the Patent Act.

In September 2021 the United Kingdom Court of Appeal upheld a High Court decision upholding the UKIPO's denial of the applications.[59] However, Justice Birss did hold in our favor that there should be no prohibition on our receiving a patent for an AI-generated invention.[60] Justice Arnold and Justice Liang did not concur. The United Kingdom Supreme Court is currently deciding whether to accept an appeal from the Court of Appeal. By the time you are reading this, of course, that entire summary is likely to be outdated.[61]

It may also be that legislative change is needed to allow patents on AI-generated inventions in some jurisdictions. India recently completed a parliamentary consultation which held that the law should be amended to explicitly provide copyright and patent protection for AI-generated

---

[55]   ZA2021/03242,   https://iponline.cipc.co.za/Publications/PublishedJournals/E_Journal_July%202021%20Part%202.pdf.

[56]   Ed Colon, *DABUS: South Africa issues first-ever patent with AI inventor*, www.managingip.com/article/b1sx9mh1m35rd9/dabus-south-africa-issues-first-ever-patent-with-ai-inventor   (last   accessed 02/27/2022).

[57]   *Thaler v Commissioner of Patents* [2021] FCA 879.

[58]   *Thaler v Iancu, et al.* (No. 1:20-cv-00903).

[59]   *Thaler v Comptroller General of Patents Trademarks and Designs* [2021] EWCA Civ 1374.

[60]   Ibid at 22 ("The fact that the creator of the inventions in this case was a machine is no impediment to patents being granted to this applicant").

[61]   But should be updated at www.artificialinventor.com.

works.[62] After that, the President of South Korea announced that he believed AI-generated inventions should be protected and that patent law needed to accommodate this.[63]

We filed these test cases for several reasons. The first was to generate some guidance for industry about how to structure the use of AI in R&D. There were a lot of assumptions about how the law would handle AI-generated works, but little law on the subject or judicial analysis. The second was to encourage a broader discussion about IP and AI, and how IP systems should respond to technological advances. The third was to advance the normative position that promoting patents on AI-generated inventions would benefit society. I suppose there was also a hope that a case involving inventive AI would make patent attorneys marginally more interesting than tax attorneys.

Again, AI-generated works are just one example of how AI will challenge long-standing IP laws. Another way in which AI will impact patent law will be its effect on the test for whether a patent is non-obvious (the focus of Shemtov and Gabison's chapter).[64] This test focuses on the capabilities of an average researcher, but in many fields average researchers are already augmented by AI. AI provides researchers with access to a superhuman amount of prior art (existing knowledge), and it provides tools to help solve problems. For instance, a person might require exceptional skill to recognize a pattern in a large data set, but with the help of AI that activity might be trivial. Thus, it may already be that the "skilled person" should be a skilled person using AI. That will raise the bar to getting patents, because more will be obvious to a skilled person using AI. In fact, widespread augmentation with AI may make it very difficult to get a patent. Consider the best-selling biological drugs, which are all monoclonal antibodies. These are like antibodies made by your body, but the drug form is composed of copies of the same antibody which can be manufactured using a variety of biological processes. These antibodies can treat cancer or pathogens such as COVID-19, so they are a very important type of treatment.

One of the interesting things about antibodies from an IP and AI perspective is that there are a finite number of antibodies that can exist. Antibodies are combinations of amino acids with a particular structure, and there are only so many amino acids and only so many ways to combine them to make an antibody. To be certain, there are at least trillions of possible antibodies, so enough options to keep human researchers busy for the foreseeable future. But there are not so many that an AI could not sequence every possible antibody. Moreover, AI is getting better at modeling antibody activity, so the AI could both generate every possible antibody and provide useful information about the sorts of biological activity each antibody will have in the body. If an AI did that, and if that information was published online, it might prevent any person from ever patenting a new antibody as a composition of matter. That claim and subject matter usually makes up the most important patent in a portfolio for a new biological drug.[65]

Many computer scientists believe we will eventually develop Artificial General Intelligence, a future AI that will still not think like a person but that will be able to do any intellectual task

---

[62]   Varsha Jhavar, *Parliamentary Standing Committee's recommendations concerning AI and IP: a little late or way too early?* https://spicyip.com/2021/08/parliamentary-standing-committees -recommendations-concerning-ai-and-ip-a-little-late-or-way-too-early.html (last accessed 02/27/2022).

[63]   www.facebook.com/worker21c/posts/4223612477726208 (last accessed 02/27/2022).

[64]   Ryan Abbott, *Everything is Obvious*, 66 UCLA. L. REV. 2 (2019).

[65]   See Ryan Abbott, *Hal the Inventor: Big Data and Its Use by Artificial Intelligence, in* BIG DATA IS NOT A MONOLITH (Cassidy R. Sugimoto, Hamid Ekbia and Michael Mattioli eds, 2016), exploring similar hypotheticals.

a person could do. The first task for that AI would be to improve its own programming and capabilities, and theoretically this may lead to an AI so sophisticated that it will solve all the problems we know we have and even those we do not know we have.[66] There are more exciting things to think about with superintelligent AI than patent law, but among other things, it would make it virtually impossible to get a patent because everything would be obvious to a person using a superintelligent AI (or at some point maybe we jettison the person and just have a superintelligent AI standard). That should be fine, though, because once we have superintelligent AI there will no longer be a need to incentivize innovation, which will be nearly costless. There will also be little need to encourage disclosure of AI output because trade secrets will be quickly independently replicated by other superintelligent AI. To the extent that we need a system to encourage commercialization of products such as medicines where most of the R&D cost is after an initial invention, we have other means of encouraging that activity, such as a period of market exclusivity associated with regulatory approvals.

4.   CONCLUDING THOUGHTS

Even for readers who do not work directly with AI and IP, the topic still offers valuable insights into IP law more generally. For example, we think that patents and copyright both protect economic and moral rights, so copyright protects both an author's right to be acknowledged and a publisher's ability to make money. If AI does not have rights and a human author is no longer in the picture, is there still a case for copyright if we are no longer concerned with protecting authors in this context? Do we still want to apply copyright the same way? Do we need human-centric laws? Do the laws that currently apply to people also change once AI is in the picture? People talk about different things when they talk about AI-generated inventions, but they also talk about different things when they talk about access to medicines, or the patent system generally, or any number of traditional concepts in IP law.

My own view is that treating AI and human behavior differently tends to result in problematic outcomes for people. In patents, if the system is designed to generate innovation, then we should leave it to the market to decide whether people or AI can do a better job of inventing— because if you tell GSK or Johnson & Johnson that they cannot use an AI to make a drug, at least not if they want a patent on that drug, then it tells industry it has to use people. That will be a real problem if it turns out that machines can do a better job than people at certain sorts of important activities.

Similar dynamics occur in other areas of the law. Businesses using AI to automate work are subject to different tax consequences versus having people do that same work. Cars driven by people versus AI generate different liability regimes. In *The Reasonable Robot: Artificial Intelligence and the Law* I look in depth at a few areas, including in IP law, where AI and people functionally do the same thing but different laws apply and this ends up having socially harmful consequences.[67] I explain why we would all be better off if the law tended not to discriminate between human and AI behavior, a principle I refer to as AI legal neutrality.

AI and board games may offer a useful roadmap for IP and AI. AlphaGo beating the world's best Go player was a big deal, even if it did not get as much attention (in the United States)

---

[66]   Ryan Abbott, *The Reasonable Robot* (2020) at 24.
[67]   See generally ibid.

as DeepBlue beating Gary Kasparov at chess in 1997.[68] Kasparov subsequently realized that while an AI might always be able to outperform a person, an AI playing with a person could outperform an AI, because people and machines have complementary capabilities. He then won the first "centaur chess" tournament involving a person and an AI playing together. This points to a near and medium-term future in which we are going to get optimal outcomes by combining AI and human behavior. But in the long term, eventually AI improved to the point where playing with a human chess grandmaster just slowed it down.

It would be a phenomenal outcome if, the next time a deadly pathogen such as COVID-19 emerges, AI has become so proficient at developing vaccines that having human vaccinologists in-the-loop just makes the development process less effective. How soon that comes to pass, and perhaps whether it comes to pass at all, will depend in part on our IP rules. Hopefully, this Handbook will help stakeholders to better understand how to think about IP and AI, and thus contribute to rules that result in better outcomes for people.

---

[68]   *Deep Blue defeats Garry Kasparov in chess match*, www.history.com/this-day-in-history/deep-blue-defeats-garry-kasparov-in-chess-match (last accessed 02/27/2022).

2.　The human cause
Daniel J. Gervais[1]

1.　INTRODUCTION

Oxford University Professor Nick Bostrom's book *Superintelligence: Paths, Dangers, Strategies* describes an advanced future form of artificial intelligence (AI) which, he says, will be the last invention made by humans.[2] Though this "superintelligence" belongs to the world of science fiction, there is no doubt that there are "challenges posed by highly intelligent (ro) bots participating with humans in the commerce of daily life."[3] Nowhere are those challenges more manifest than when those machines are able to perform tasks that until recently only humans could, namely tasks anchored in our higher mental faculties, including human creativity and our ability to develop innovative technologies. The area of law that is most likely to feel the impact of this emergence of a second intelligent and potentially creative and inventive "species" is intellectual property.[4]

The ability of AI to produce literary and artistic works and inventions matters on another level.[5] By now, we are used to letting robots perform much of the physical labor previously done by humans.[6] With less of *that* kind of work, our capacity to create art, music, literature, conversation, architecture, food, and more "is likely to be more needed than ever."[7] Yet, as things stand now, we are "devoting huge scientific and technical resources to creating ever-more-capable AI systems, with very little thought devoted to what happens if we succeed."[8] If machines become creators and inventors in our stead, will we be able to, as Keynes aptly put it, "keep alive, and cultivate into a fuller perfection, the art of life itself"?[9] It is at least worth pondering. To state but one reason, changes in cultural productions and trends

---

[1]　This chapter is based in part on the author's 2020 Sir Hugh Laddie Lecture. The author is grateful to the editor both for his comments and for inviting this contribution.

[2]　There is no universally agreed upon definition of artificial intelligence. This chapter adopts the definition used by the European Commission: "Artificial intelligence (AI) refers to systems that display intelligent behaviour by analysing their environment and taking actions—with some degree of autonomy—to achieve specific goals." European Commission, Communication on "Artificial Intelligence Europe," COM(2018) 237 final (April 25, 2018), online https://bit.ly/2HFft4J.

[3]　WENDELL WALLACH & COLLIN ALLEN, MORAL MACHINES: TEACHING ROBOTS RIGHT FROM WRONG 189 (Oxford University Press, 2009).

[4]　Admittedly, I use the term "species" in a non-technical way in this context.

[5]　In this chapter, human creativity and inventiveness will be referred to as "natural," while machine outputs (or productions as the term is used hereinafter) will be referred to as "artificial," following the same logic as the terms "natural language" and "artificial intelligence."

[6]　On robots replacing human workers, *see* Bill O'Leary, *My Robot And Me*, 68:6 ELECTRICAL APPARATUS 18 (2015).

[7]　STUART RUSSELL, HUMAN COMPATIBLE: ARTIFICIAL INTELLIGENCE AND THE PROBLEM OF CONTROL 122 (Viking Press, 2019).

[8]　*See* WALLACH & ALLEN, *supra* note 3, at 151.

[9]　JOHN MAYNARD KEYNES, ESSAYS ON PERSUASION (Norton, 1963) at 331.

both lead and reflect societal changes, which in turn lead to political and, ultimately, legal changes. Literature in all forms, fine arts, and music are among the most important vehicles to both mirror and propagate changes throughout society. If those cultural vehicles are made of art, books, and lyrics created by AI machines, then those machines will control at least a part of cultural, societal, and political change. Think of it as *self-driving culture*—and it will be a U-turn as far as human evolution is concerned.

This chapter cannot predict whether human authors and inventors will survive as a significant source of cultural production and technological innovation in the medium to long term. On a shorter time horizon, however, a fair question to ask is whether intellectual property *should* prioritize *human* (or natural) creativity and inventiveness, or else treat machine and human productions on the same footing and accelerate the replacement of human creators and inventors. As used in this chapter, giving "priority" would mean granting rights only in facially copyrightable or patentable productions that have a *human cause*, which can be provisionally defined for now as a sufficient link between one or more humans and the potentially copyrightable or patentable output. [10] This explains the double-entendre in the title of the chapter: while the chapter discusses whether intellectual property protection should only attach to creations and inventions that have an identifiable and sufficient human *cause*, it also implies that the future of humans (their "cause") is involved. As the chapter explains below, the notion of cause used here is similar to proximate cause, not simple (or "but for") cause.

One can use the US Constitution as a useful backdrop for the analysis. It is unique among constitutional documents in that it not only gives one level of government (federal) the power to make laws in the area of copyright and patents, it actually states what the purpose of those laws is, or should be: to "Promote the Progress of Science and Useful Arts." [11] What if the novelists, songwriters, journalists, and inventors of tomorrow were machines? What if instead of human actors, we had CGI "actors" looking like famous (dead) human actors or, once those have been mostly forgotten, CGI "actors" with AI-designed faces and bodies meant to appeal to the largest number of human viewers? What if the role of humans—other than for the few who would profit from this situation—was relegated to *reading* novels and news, *listening* to music, *watching* audiovisual content, and buying new products produced by machines? Were the Founding Fathers thinking of "progress" in those terms, that new art and science would be produced for its own sake, not for *human* progress? To answer, let us turn the knob all the way: if all humans died would the US Constitution's direction still be followed provided art and science continued to be produced—both *by* machines, and *for* machines? Thus to say that law should be technologically neutral is the same as saying it can be human neutral.

We need not turn the knob all the way to find the path to a policy prescription. If machines can produce new drugs or literary and artistic works cheaper and faster than human creators, it is highly likely that industry will favor them over their human counterparts. In the copyright sphere, delegating to machines the task of helping us understand and interpret our world has profound consequences. It is through this interpretation that humans can become true agents in the world and ultimately change it. Delegating this very task to machines is thus pregnant with implications for the future, for it changes its arc. It will not be complete obliteration, of course. There will always be humans who write, pick up a paintbrush, or try to make a movie

---

[10]   As used in this chapter, the term "production" encompasses (a) creations that may be protected by copyright, (b) designs, and (c) inventions that may be protectable by patents.

[11]   U.S. CONST, Art. 1, §8, cl.8. This chapter knows of no other constitutional document that does so.

or sculpture, but if most of what we are given to read, watch, or listen to comes from machines, much will be lost. If copyright protection is granted on productions without a human cause, and assuming that the cost of machine productions will be lower (and machines will not ask for ongoing royalty payments or have reversion rights), then market forces will inescapably push for a replacement of human authors whenever it is commercially feasible.

In science, if machines can both do basic science and develop new technologies, as examples in this volume demonstrate, private labs will hire fewer science PhDs. Science departments in universities will atrophy as the demand for human-made science contracts. The arc of the quest for a deeper and better understanding of the natural world that has animated humans arguably since the invention of fire will also be bent. In sum, our highest and noblest ideals will be delegated, at least in part, to machines. This should perhaps give us pause.

While, as other chapters in this book illustrate, we can debate what exactly constitutes 'progress' (especially, one might add, from a postmodernist perspective), this chapter's normative sextant is that the term "progress" must mean *human* progress, in the manner of philosophers through the ages.[12] For example, Plato defended in his *Laws* the idea that the legal system is a way to support human progress.[13] Even Aristotle might have agreed, as human flourishing is a core notion of his *Nicomachean Ethics*. According to this view, "the invention of man is infinitely better contrived to advance the good and happiness of mankind, than any Utopian system that ever has been produced, by the warmest imagination."[14] Of the imagination of a machine?

Let us begin by making three general points before diving deeper into the analysis. The first is that certain AI machines can be programmed to learn to *mimic* human mental processes. Part of the ongoing research in AI is precisely to make machines more like humans instead of a new, complementary type of intelligence. As a result, there is little doubt that machines already generate productions that are often indistinguishable from human creations and inventions. From that perspective, giving rights on productions that look like copyright works or patentable inventions but made by machines strikes the author of this chapter as a new Turing test.[15] Normatively, it would amount to rewarding the owner or user of a machine that can "pass itself off" as human. Surely that anthropomorphizing illusion cannot be a solid normative foundation to obtain IP protection.[16]

---

[12]   *See generally* DANIEL GERVAIS, THE LAW OF HUMAN PROGRESS (deLex, 2019).

[13]   PLATO, LAWS, VII:680a-682d.

[14]   HENRY H. KAMES, ESSAYS ON THE PRINCIPLES OF MORALITY AND NATURAL RELIGION, 86. *See also* J.J. Chambliss, *Human Development in Plato and Rousseau* 13:2 THE JOURNAL OF EDUCATIONAL THOUGHT 96, 98 (1979).

[15]   That may remind the reader of the "Turing test," a set of questions asked via teletype on any subject whatsoever. Unbeknown to the questioner, some were answered by a human and others by a machine. Both the human being and the machine attempted to convince the questioner that it or she was the human and the other was not. *See* Lawrence B. Solum, *Legal Personhood for Artificial Intelligences*, 70 N.C. L. REV. 1231, 1236 (1992).

[16]   *See* SELMER BRINGGJORD & DAVID A. FERRUCCI, ARTIFICIAL INTELLIGENCE AND LITERARY CREATIVITY: INSIDE THE MIND OF BRUTUS xxvi (Lawrence Erlbaum Associates, 2000). Passing off is a tort notion borrowed from trademark law defined as "when a producer misrepresents his or her own goods or services as those of another producer." Laura Gasaway, *Origin of Goods in Trademark Law Does Not Mean Creator*; COPYRIGHT CORNER, Special Libr. Ass'n Info. Outlook, Nov. 1, 2003, at 7. See also 15 U.S.C. §1125(a) ("palming off"); and Dastar Corp. v Twentieth Cent. Fox Film Corp., 539 U.S. 23, 28 n.1 (2003).

Second, humans and machines are working ever more closely together. This rapprochement will continue.[17] Humans depend on machines to perform many creative and inventive tasks, and indeed, machines have already changed how humans perform those tasks. In some cases, machines can help us achieve our aims better and faster. It is not always so. To take a simple example of a change in cognitive processes with a more ambivalent valence, people who started driving a car before GPS was omnipresent can still drive in cities where they drove before the GPS without assistance from that technology, but are much less able to do so elsewhere without GPS.[18] A key question to answer in this context is: What happens over the medium to long term as we outsource the creative or inventive work of humans to machines? Humans, as a species, may lose on two fronts: diminished human expression, and reduced financial flows to human creators and inventors, who would no longer have the incentive, time, or financial ability to learn and develop their craft. To say that creativity is necessarily human, that it is fundamentally connected with *humanness*, is not "to impose a kind of chauvinism that privileges human-produced artifacts over those that are machine-made. Rather, it is to say that human communication is the very point of authorship as a social practice; indeed, as a condition of life."[19]

The third and final general point is that there are proposals to short-circuit that entire discussion by giving "person" status (which is not the same as "human" status, of course) to some AI machines.[20] The root of the first word in the term "artificial intelligence," namely "artificial," is "artifice," the definition of which is "an ingenious device or expedient."[21] This is apt because the proposal to give some AI machines legal personality may be just that: an expedient that circumvents the two underlying normative issues, namely whether such machines *should* be persons and *should* get IP rights.[22]

2.   BRIEF OVERVIEW OF THE STATE OF PLAY IN AI

A significant portion of the literature exploring the interface between AI and the law adopts the distinction between *narrow* (or weak) and *general* (or strong) AI.[23] The distinction can be

---

[17]   One should not avoid drawing the line between human and machine, which will not always be easy as cyborgization increases, but the legal system must be able to draw that line.

[18]   Javadi, Amir-Homayoun et al., *Hippocampal and Prefrontal Processing of Network Topology to Simulate The Future*, 8 NATURE COMM. 14652 (2017), online: https://www.nature.com/articles/ncomms14652#citeas.

[19]   Carys Craig and Ian Kerr, *The Death of the AI Author*, 52 OTTAWA L REV 31–86 (2021).

[20]   *See, e.g.*, Shawn Bayern, *Of Bitcoins, Independently Wealthy Software, and the Zero-Member LLC*, 108 NW. U.L. REV. 1485, 1497 (2014).

[21]   "Artifice," MERRIAM-WEBSTER DICTIONARY, www.merriam-webster.com/dictionary/.

[22]   *See* David J. Calverley, *Imagining a Non-Biological Machine as a Legal Person*, 22 AI & SOC. 523 (2008). This is in line with a United Nations report which noted that it would be "highly counterintuitive to call [AI systems] 'persons' as long as they do not possess some additional qualities typically associated with human persons, such as freedom of will, intentionality, self-consciousness, moral agency or a sense of personal identity"). UNESCO, World Comm. on the Ethics of Scientific Knowledge and Technology (COMEST), Rep. of Com. on Robotics Ethics, U.N. Doc. SHS/COMEST-10/17/2 REV., at 46 (Sept. 14, 2017).

[23]   *See* Michael Guihot, Anne F. Matthew, & Nicolas P. Suzor, *Nudging Robots: Innovative Solutions to Regulate Artificial Intelligence,* 20 VAND. J. ENT. & TECH. L. 385, 393 (2017). *See also* Shannon

traced back to Ray Kurzweil's seminal *The Singularity Is Near*.[24] In this traditional categorization, narrow or weak AI "is goal-oriented, designed to perform singular tasks—i.e. facial recognition, speech recognition/voice assistants, driving a car, or searching the Internet—and is very intelligent at completing the specific task it is programmed to do."[25] It operates within a well-defined "activity-context."[26] In contrast, Artificial General Intelligence (AGI), or strong AI, "is the concept of a machine with general intelligence that mimics human intelligence and/ or behaviours, with the ability to learn and apply its intelligence to solve any problem. AGI can think, understand, and act in a way that is indistinguishable from that of a human in any given situation."[27] A number of scholars go a step further. Nick Bostrom, who was mentioned in the opening paragraph, discusses the risks to humans of developing machines with a higher level still, which he dubbed "superintelligence," that is, "an intellect that is much smarter than the best human brains in practically every field, including scientific creativity, general wisdom and social skills."[28] This Artificial Super Intelligence (ASI) "is the hypothetical AI that doesn't just mimic or understand human intelligence and behaviour; ASI is where machines become self-aware and surpass the capacity of human intelligence and ability."[29]

This chapter retains this traditional categorization but sticks to the first two categories (narrow and strong), as it sees the third (ASI) category as belonging to the world of sci-fi—at least for now. Machines can beat the best human masters at chess, Go, the gameshow *Jeopardy* and much more—even at an incomplete information game like poker.[30] Though undoubtedly very impressive, those achievements "are much simpler than the *real world*: they are fully

---

Vallor & George A. Bekey, *Artificial Intelligence and the Ethics of Self-Learning Robots*, in ROBOT ETHICS 2.0: FROM AUTONOMOUS CARS TO ARTIFICIAL INTELLIGENCE 339–40 (Patrick Lin, Keith Abney, & Ryan Jenkins eds, 2017); and Peter Stone et al., *Artificial Intelligence And Life In 2030*: *Report of the 2015 Study Panel* 6–9 (2016), https://ai100.stanford.edu/sites/default/files/ai_100_report_0831fnl.pdf.

[24]   RAY KURZWEIL, THE SINGULARITY IS NEAR: WHEN HUMANS TRANSCEND BIOLOGY 206, 222 (Rick Kot ed., 2005).

[25]   Serena Reece, *What Are The 3 Types Of AI? A Guide To Narrow, General, And Super Artificial Intelligence,* CODEBOTS, Jan. 31, 2020, online: https://codebots.com/artificial-intelligence/the-3-types-of -ai-is-the-third-even-possible.

[26]   Stephen Russell, Ira S. Moskowitz, & Adrienne Raglin, *Autonomy and Artificial Intelligence: a Threat or Savior?,* in AUTONOMY AND ARTIFICIAL INTELLIGENCE: A THREAT OR SAVIOR?, 71, 73 (W.F. Lawless et al., eds).

[27]   Reece, *supra* note 25.

[28]   Nick Bostrom, *How Long Before Superintelligence?*, 5 LINGUISTIC & PHIL. INVESTIGATIONS 11, 11 (2006). Updated version (2008), online at www.nickbostrom.com/superintelligence.html.

[29]   Reece, *supra* note 25.

[30]   See Cade Metz, *In Two Moves, AlphaGo and Lee Sedol Redefined the Future*, WIRED, Mar. 16, 2016, online: www.wired.com/2016/03/two-moves-alphago-lee-sedol-redefined-future/. The "former" champion eventually retired as a result. *See* James Vincent, *Former Go Champion Beaten By DeepMind Retires After Declaring AI Invincible*, THE VERGE (Nov. 27, 2019). The difference in the levels of complexity is not the only one between chess and Go. Chess is tactical while Go is best described as strategic. It requires a different kind of "thinking." Cade Metz, *In a Huge Breakthrough, Google's AI Beats a Top Player at the Game of Go*, WIRED, Jan. 27, 2016, online: www.wired.com/2016/01/in -a-huge-breakthrough-googles-ai-beats-a-top-player-at-the-game-of-go/. On IBM's DeepBlue beating the world chess grandmaster Gary Kasparov, *see* *IBM's 100 Icons of Progress: Deep Blue*, www.ibm .com/ibm/history/ibm100/us/en/icons/deepblue/ [https://perma.cc/7SG3-UYST]. On poker, see Tracey Lien, *Artificial Intelligence Has Mastered Board Games; What's The Next Test?* SEATTLE TIMES (Mar. 20, 2016), online www.seattletimes. com/business/technology/artificial-intelligence-has-mastere d-board-games-whats-the-next-test/.

observable, they involve short time horizons, and they have relatively small state spaces and simple, predictable rules."[31]

This raises a related question, namely whether people will still have an incentive to play games such as chess or Go professionally with the knowledge that an AI machine can beat the best humans, even with a few computer chips tied behind its back. I believe the answer is yes. I start from the premise that humans have always played and always will.[32] If you accept that premise, then if someone plays, say, chess, every day for years, they will become good at it. They can then enter the human "rankings" (for example, grandmaster) system. Now, why would other players want to see those people play even if they know they cannot fight the machine and hope to win? For two main reasons. First, because humans are more likely to learn from watching other humans and not machines, whose "thinking" may not be the same as those of humans and who may not be able to explain their thinking to begin with.[33] Second, I posit that humans like to watch other humans "struggle."[34] To simplify to the extreme, this is why we watch sports but also, say, a "strongman" pulling a ton of bricks with ropes— something any half-decent pickup truck can do on a couple of cylinders. For similar reasons, I am much more worried about machines replacing songwriters and composers than about machines replacing live performers. People will likely want to see human artists/performers. It is thus essential in debates about the future of copyright to distinguish authors from performers, a well-understood and fundamental distinction in the law of copyright and related rights.[35]

In the field of potentially patentable productions, AI is now routinely used to accelerate and reduce the costs of pharmaceutical research, performing in silico research.[36] AI machines can find hidden patterns within large datasets and automate many predictions.[37] Outputs from AI in pharmaceutical research include disease diagnosis and prediction of drug efficacy[38] and support for drug design.[39] AI machines can choose which molecules possess suitable characteristics to address biological targets of interest.[40] AI can identify the optimal chemical structures to reduce toxicity and satisfy metabolic requirements, both of which can be costly and data-intensive processes.[41] They can improve the area of personalized medicine based on

---

[31]   RUSSELL, *supra* note 7, at 56. Emphasis added.

[32]   *See generally* Juho Hamari & Lauri Keronen, *Why Do People Play Games? A Meta-Analysis*, 37:3 INT'L J. INF. MANAG'T 125 (2017).

[33]   The idea that humans and machines can both perform a function that can be described as "thinking" but do so differently is not new. *See e.g.*, PHILIP N. JOHNSON-LAIRD., HUMAN AND MACHINE THINKING (Lawrence Erlbaum Associates, 1993).

[34]   *See* Michael Safi et al, *How Magnus Carlsen Won Chess Back From The Machines*, THE GUARDIAN (Dec. 12, 2021), available at https://bit.ly/33n4Mlu.

[35]   *See* Daniel Gervais, *Related Rights in United States Law*, 65 J. COPYRIGHT SOC'Y U.S.A. 371–93 (2018).

[36]   *See* Nic Fleming, *How Artificial Intelligence Is Changing Drug Discovery*, 557 NATURE 55 (2018).

[37]   *See generally* AJAY K. AGRAWAL, JOSHUA S. GANS, & AVI GOLDFARB, PREDICTION MACHINES: THE SIMPLE ECONOMICS OF ARTIFICIAL INTELLIGENCE (Harvard Business Press, 2018).

[38]   *See* Gregor Guncar et al., *An Application Of Machine Learning To Hæmatological Diagnosis*, 8 SCIENTIFIC REPORTS 411 (2018), online: https://bit.ly/3qrclyS.

[39]   *See* Hongmin Chen et al., *The Rise Of Deep Learning In Drug Discovery*, 23 DRUG DISCOVERY TODAY 1241–50 (2018).

[40]   *See ibid.*

[41]   *See ibid.*

genetic markers.[42] That potential of AI to identify novel drugs that human researchers alone cannot detect has attracted investment from both start-ups and established pharmaceutical companies.[43] Also noteworthy, in what was perhaps a publicity stunt, Google announced that its AI machines can both make new inventions and apply for patents.[44]

In the fields of design and literary and artistic works, AI machines have composed polyphonic baroque music bearing the "style" of Johann Sebastian Bach.[45] "Robot reporters" now routinely write news bulletins and sports reports, a process called "automated journalism."[46] AI systems write poems that many people believe were written by a human author.[47] AI machines draft and analyze contracts.[48] A machine named e-David produces paintings using a complex visual optimization algorithm that "takes pictures with its camera and draws original paintings from these photographs."[49] AI machines can write scenes of animation movies and improve the design of objects or processes, thus generating productions that facially qualify as subject matter for copyright or design patent protection.[50] Let us now briefly see how AI does it.

---

[42]   *See* Kit-Kay Mak & Mallikarjuna Rao Pichika, *Artificial Intelligence in Drug Development: Present Status And Future Prospects*, 24:3 DRUG DISCOVERY TODAY 773 (2019).

[43]   *See* Lou Bowen & Lynn Wu, *Artificial Intelligence And Drug Innovation: A Large Scale Examination Of The Pharmaceutical Industry* 2 (2020), online: https://papers.ssrn.com/sol3/papers.cfm ?abstract_id=3524985.

[44]   *See* Rose Hughes, *Deepmind: First Major AI Patent Filings Revealed*, IPKAT, Jun. 7, 2018, online http://ipkitten.blogspot.com/2018/06/deepmind-first-major-ai-patent-filings.html. The reverse use of AI is true, namely to defeat patent applications, based on obviousness (to an AI expert) or novelty, by massive preemptive public disclosure of novel subject matter together with its utility. On the former, *see* Ryan Abbott, *Everything Is Obvious*, 66 UCLA L. REV. 2, 40 (2019). On the latter issue, *see* Daniel Gervais, *Exploring the Interfaces Between Big Data and Intellectual Property Law*, 10:3 J. INTELL. PROP., INF. TECH. & E-COMM. L. (2019), online: https://www.jipitec.eu/issues/jipitec-10-1-2019/4875.

[45]   *See* Gaëtan Hadjeres & François Pachet, Deepbach: *A Steerable Model for Bach Chorales Generation* (Dec. 3, 2016) at 1, online: https://arxiv.org/pdf/1612.01010v1.pdf.

[46]   *See* Corinna Underwood, *Automated Journalism—AI Applications at New York Times, Reuters, and Other Media Giants*, EMERJ (Jun. 22, 2017, updated Nov. 29, 2018), online: https://bit.ly/2Q84BTV. *See also* Lucia Moses, *The Washington Post's Robot Reporter Has Published 850 Articles in the Past Year*, DIGIDAYUK, Sept. 14, 2017, online: https://bit.ly/2xmkQSI.

[47]   *See* Samuel Gibbs, *Google AI Project Writes Poetry Which Could Make Vogon Proud*, THE GUARDIAN (May 17, 2016).

[48]   *See* Kathryn D. Betts & Kyle R. Jaep, *The Dawn of Fully Automated Contract Drafting: Machine Learning Breathes New Life into A Decades-Old Promise*, 15 DUKE L. & TECH. REV. 216 (2017).

[49]   *See* Shlomit Yanisky-Ravid, *Generating Rembrandt: Artificial Intelligence, Copyright, and Accountability In The 3a Era—The Human-Like Authors Are Already Here—A New Model* [2017] MICH. ST. L. REV. 659, 662.

[50]   On copyright, *see* Jane C. Ginsburg and Luke Ali Budiardjo, *Authors and Machines*, 34 BERK. TECH. L. J. 343 (2019). The United States Court of Appeals for the Federal Circuit noted that processes "that automate tasks that humans are capable of performing are patent-eligible if properly claimed." McRO, Inc. v Bandai Namco Games Am. Inc., 837 F.3d 1299, 1313 (Fed. Cir. 2016). For a discussion, *see* Ben Hattenbach & Gavin Snyder, *Rethinking the Mental Steps Doctrine and Other Barriers to Patentability of Artificial Intelligence*, 19 COLUM. SCI. & TECH. L. REV. 313, 317–18 (2018); and Mizuki Hashiguchi, *The Global Artificial Intelligence Revolution Challenges Patent Eligibility Laws*, 13 J. BUS. & TECH. L. 1, 13 (2017).

3. HOW AI WORKS

This section reviews a few basic notions of AI that will be important as we attempt to draw conclusions later on.

The deployment of AI can be separated into steps. First, AI code is written. This code, as the technology stands now, is generally the work of human programmers—though that is changing—and it can be split into pieces, such as a generic AI platform and specific apps developed for a precise purpose.[51] The code is mostly used to empower the next step, a process known as machine-learning, which today is "the dominant AI technology."[52] Machine-learning can be *supervised* (by humans) or not. "*Unsupervised*" in this context means that the system is "trained on a dataset without explicit instructions or labelled data."[53] Situated between supervised and unsupervised learning, *reinforcement learning* is a third mode of machine-learning, in which humans verify what the machine has learned on its own and hopefully correct mistakes, often using sampling techniques.[54]

Machine-learning in all three modes is used both to discern and operationalize patterns in data.[55] It uses a set of "computational methods using experience to improve [its] performance or to make accurate predictions."[56] Using machine-learning, an AI system can "automatically generate heuristics" and make autonomous determinations of various kinds.[57] It can adjust its "behavior to enhance [its] performance on some task through experience."[58] A machine can, for example, be shown pictures of cats and dogs and then learn the features of each so that it can distinguish cats and dogs it has never "seen" before.[59] The quality of the learning process is obviously dependent on the quality of the training data, as some well-documented disastrous examples have brought to light.[60] This is a problem for uses of AI in a legal context,

---

[51] On AI machines writing their own code, *see* Khari Johnson, *AI Could Soon Write Code Based on Ordinary Language*, Wired (May 26, 2021), online: www.wired.com/story/ai-write-code-ordinary-language/ (accessed May 31, 2021).

[52] UK Information Commissioner's Office and Alan Turing Institute, Explaining How Decisions Are Made with AI, 7 (May 20, 2020), online: https://bit.ly/2zs68gi. *See also* Roberto Iriondo, Differences *Between AI and Machine Learning and Why it Matters*, Data Driven Investor, (Oct. 15, 2018), https://medium.com/datadriveninvestor/differences-between-ai-and-machine-learning-and-why-it-matters-1255b182fc6.

[53] *See* UK Information Commissioner's, *ibid*.

[54] *See* Leslie Pack Kaelbling, Michael L. Littman, & Andrew W. Moore, *Reinforcement Learning: A Survey*, 4 J. Artificial Intelligence Res. 237 (1996).

[55] Michael Veale, *Governing Machine Learning that Matters*, PhD dissertation, 33 (2019), online: https://discovery.ucl.ac.uk/id/eprint/10078626/1/thesis_final_corrected_mveale.pdf.

[56] Mehryar Mohri, Afshin Rostamizadeh & Ameet Talwalkar, Foundations of Machine Learning, 2d ed. 1 (MIT Press, 2018).

[57] Wolfgang Hertel, Introduction to Artificial Intelligence 102 (Springer, 2011). AI programmers use several different algorithmic techniques, depending (usually) on the task at hand. For a detailed overview, see Explaining How Decisions Are Made with AI, above note 52, Annex 2.

[58] Harry Surden, *Machine Learning and the Law*, 89 Wash. L. Rev. 87, 89 (2014).

[59] See Amanda Levendowski, *How Copyright Law Can Fix Artificial Intelligence's Implicit Bias Problem*, 93 Wash. L. Rev. 579, 592 (2018).

[60] For example, when Google's AI created a link between images of African Americans and gorillas. *See* James Vincent, *Google "Fixed" Its Racist Algorithm by Removing Gorillas from Its Image-Labeling Tech*, The Verge (Jan. 12, 2018), online: www.theverge.com/2018/1/12/16882408/google-racist-gorillas-photo-recognition-algorithm-ai; or when a new Microsoft AI chatbot quickly

for example when AI machines used in bail and sentencing decision-making reflect racial or socio-economic biases due to the poor quality of the training data that was selected.[61] Put bluntly, in some cases "[m]achine learning is a 'garbage in-garbage out' proposition."[62] As the many examples of AI achievements in the previous section demonstrate, however, machine-learning can also be both quite powerful and productive. In sum, the quality and size of the data "are crucial to the success of the predictions made by the [AI] learner."[63]

The machine-learning function can take the form of "deep learning," a subset of machine-learning using a layered structure of algorithms allowing the machine to learn and make predictions and *decisions on its own*.[64] Deep learning has been called "the true challenge to artificial intelligence," namely solving the tasks that are easy for people to perform but hard for people to describe formally—problems that we solve intuitively, that feel automatic, like recognizing spoken words or faces in images.'[65] With deep learning, one could say— acknowledging that metaphors are intellectual shortcuts—that the computer has its own, autonomous brain.[66] Importantly, deep learning is *automated* and often (if not almost always) removed from direct human input or control.[67]

There are various ways to make AI systems learn and perform better. One of them is the development of General Adversarial Networks (GANs), a technological path likely to grow the affordances of AI systems both qualitatively and quantitatively.[68] "GANs' potential is huge, because they can learn to mimic any distribution of data. That is, GANs can be taught to create worlds eerily similar to our own in any domain: images, music, speech, prose."[69]

---

turned racist by "learning" on social media. *See* James Vincent, *Twitter Taught Microsoft's AI Chatbot to Be a Racist Asshole in Less Than a Day*, THE VERGE (Mar. 24, 2016), online: www.theverge.com/2016/ 3/24/11297050/tay-microsoft-chatbot-racist.

[61]   Many claims were made along those lines in various press and other sources, the truth and the scope of which this chapter cannot independently verify. *See, e.g.*, Cade Metz, *We Teach A.I. Systems Everything, Including Our Biases*, N.Y. TIMES (Nov. 21, 2019) ; Kari Paul, *Healthcare Algorithm Used Across America Has Dramatic Racial Biases*, THE GUARDIAN (Oct. 25, 2019); and Ed Pilkington, *Digital Dystopia: How Algorithms Punish the Poor*, THE GUARDIAN,(Oct. 14, 2019).

[62]   Emily Berman, *A Government of Laws and Not of Machines*, 98 B.U. L. REV. 1277, 1302 (2018).

[63]   MOHRI, ROSTAMIZADEH, & TALWALKAR, *supra* note 56, 1.

[64]   *See* Robert D. Hof, *Deep Learning: With Massive Amounts of Computational Power, Machines Can Now Recognize Objects and Translate Speech in Real Time. Artificial Intelligence Is Finally Getting Smart*, MIT TECH. REV., www.technologyreview.com/s/513696/deep-learning/

[65]   IAN GOODFELLOW, YOSHUA BENGIO, & AARON COURVILLE, DEEP LEARNING 1 (MIT Press, 2016).

[66]   *See* Brett Grossfeld, *A Simple Way to Understand Machine Learning vs Deep Learning*, ZENDESK (Jul. 18, 2017), online www.zendesk.com/blog/machine-learning-and-deep-learning/. *See also* Claudio Masolo, *Supervised, Unsupervised and Deep Learning*, TOWARDS DATA SCIENCE (May 7, 2017) online: https://bit.ly/2BydnE8.

[67]   This has now gone mainstream. *See* William Vorhies, *Automated Deep Learning—So Simple Anyone Can Do It*, DATA SCIENCE CENTRAL (April 10, 2018), online: www.datasciencecentral.com/ profiles/blogs/automated-deep-learning-so-simple-anyone-can-do-it.

[68]   Indeed, Yann LeCun, FaceBook's AI Research Director and a professor at NYU, described GANs as "the most interesting idea in the last 10 years in [machine learning]." Yann LeCun, *What Are Some Recent and Potentially Upcoming Breakthroughs in Deep Learning?* QUORA (Jul. 28, 2016). GANs are "adversarial" because two machines work one against the other, creating a constant feedback loop that increases the quality of outputs. *See* AI WIKI, A BEGINNER'S GUIDE TO GENERATIVE ADVERSARIAL NETWORKS (GANs), https://skymind.ai/wiki/generative-adversarial-network-gan.

[69]   More specifically, GANs use an actor–critic model: as one machine, called the generator, gener- ates new data instances, the other, the discriminator, "evaluates them for authenticity; i.e. the discrim-

GANs can short-circuit the need for massive amounts of machine-learning, can produce much better outputs and have "achieved remarkable results that had long been considered virtually impossible for artificial systems."[70] More importantly, GANs are seen by some experts as "an important stepping stone toward achieving *artificial general intelligence* [strong AI]."[71] For our purposes, to simplify, GANs are machines talking to machines and generating an output for humans.

Machine-learning data can come from multiple sources, and AI machines often are "continually connected to the Internet and will continually take in new information and new programming from multiple sources."[72] AI machines find *correlations and detect new patterns* in data.[73] Machines can for example correlate features such as voice to a series of characteristics such as sexual and political orientation, certain diseases, and much more.[74] Often, this predictive ability of AI machines is "only" used with a commercial purpose, namely to determine individuals' preferences to sell them goods or services, but one can easily imagine far worse scenarios.[75] One risky feature of the use of AI machines in that context is that correlations are usually based on data concerning the behavior of a given *population* but the impact is then directed at *individuals* who may or may not actually fit the population's behavioral patterns.[76]

4.　　APPLICATION TO PATENT LAW

AI machines "create a wide range of innovative, new, and non-obvious products and services, such as medical devices, drug synthesizers, weapons, kitchen appliances, and [other] machines."[77] There is little doubt that AI machines can help innovate and that they can produce what looks facially like inventions as a matter of patent law.[78] The question that this chapter tackles is whether the law *should* provide patent protection for inventions in which human involvement is not demonstrably and sufficiently present.

---

inator decides whether each instance of data it reviews belongs to the actual training dataset or not." BEGINNER'S GUIDE, *ibid.*

[70]　JAKUB LANGR AND VLADIMIR BOK, GANS IN ACTION: DEEP LEARNING WITH GENERATIVE ADVERSARIAL NETWORKS 3 (Manning Publications, 2019).

[71]　*See ibid.*

[72]　Jack M Balkin,, *The Path of Robotics Law*, 6 CAL L REV CIR 45, 54 (2015).

[73]　Though not causal relationships. *See* Cary Coglianese & David Lehr, *Regulating by Robot: Administrative Decision Making in the Machine-Learning Era*, 105 GEO. L.J. 1147, 1157 (2017); and Nick Wallace, *EU's Right to Explanation: A Harmful Restriction on Artificial Intelligence*, TECHZONE 360 (Jan. 25, 2017), http://bit.do/Wallace_EU-Right-to-Explanation.

[74]　Ian Kerr & Jessica Earle, *Prediction, Preemption, Presumption: How Big Data Threatens Big Picture Privacy*, 66 STAN. L. REV. ONLINE, online: www.stanfordlawreview.org/online/privacy-and-big -data-prediction-preemption-presumption/.

[75]　*See ibid.*

[76]　*See* Brent Daniel Mittelstadt et al., *The Ethics of Algorithms: Mapping the Debate*, BIG DATA & SOC'Y, July-Dec. 2016, at 5. *See also supra* note 74.

[77]　Shlomit Yanisky Ravid & Xiaoqiong (Jackie) Liu, *When Artificial Intelligence Systems Produce Inventions: An Alternative Model for Patent Law at the 3a Era*, 39 Cardozo L. Rev. 2215, 2219–20 (2018).

[78]　*See ibid.*

Take DABUS, the test case in which the applicant named an AI machine as inventor.[79] The European Patent Office, US Patent & Trademark Office and, as of this writing, courts in Australia, the UK and the US have found against the applicant and concluded that a *human* inventor must be named in a patent application.[80] Court decisions went the other way in South Africa.[81] Yet, stating that this question is a mere matter of *naming* a human overlooks the actual normative issue. The underlying inquiry is whether patent law *requires* that a human be the actual *cause* of an invention.

In functional terms, what are the legal requirements to be considered the "inventor"? Is inventorship not necessary to claim that one should be named as an inventor? There are several ways to address this line of inquiry, but the fundamental starting point is that this is *not* a simple matter of applying and interpreting well-worn doctrines meant to separate ownership claims to an invention to which *multiple humans* may have contributed. Under both UK and US law as they now stand, there is little doubt that, under the current definition of inventorship, a mere subjective belief that one is entitled to a patent as a basis to claim inventorship is not the proper legal test.[82] A more thorough rethink is in order because the question is not the same as a multiple human inventor scenario. The novel question is: does a contribution to the "conception" of the invention *by a nonhuman entity* legally qualify as inventorship as a matter of patent law? Asking the question this way should not obscure the fact that the same legal doctrines must also be tailored to novel types of *human* contribution to inventiveness, such as programming and teaching AI machines, that were not part of inventive processes until recently and which will gain prominence as AI machines get better at their job.

Under current law, the contribution of claimed inventors must be identified.[83] This logically presupposes that we know who, or *what*, the inventor is. As just noted, two major patent offices and a court have found that one needs to identify one or more *human* inventors, while other judges disagree.[84] If one adopts the view that an inventor is a human notion under patent law, then one or more humans, working in their unique way, must be *causally related* to the invention.

A further, harder question will be to determine the role of patent incentives in that context. Economic analyses will be useful but they won't paint the full normative picture. Are we better off as a society (here again using human progress, not disembodied technological change, as a proper yardstick—how could it be otherwise?) issuing patents to machine-made inventions

---

[79]   On the USPTO, *see* Rebecca Tapscott, *USPTO Shoots Down DABUS' Bid for Inventorship,* IP WATCHDOG, May 4, 2020, online: www.ipwatchdog.com/2020/05/04/uspto-shoots-dabus-bid -inventorship/id=121284/. For the EPO, *see* Bernt Hugenholtz, Daniel Gervais, & João Pedro Quintais, *Trends and Developments in Artificial Intelligence: Challenges to the Intellectual Property Rights Framework.* Final Report (Nov 25, 2020), 100–04, online: www.ivir.nl/publicaties/download/Trends _and_Developments_in_Artificial_Intelligence.pdf.

[80]   Commissioner of Patents v. Thaler [2022] FCAFC 62; Thaler v Comptroller-General, UK Court of Appeal, 21 September 2021; Thaler v. Vidal, 2022 WL 3130863 (Fed. Cir. 2022), respectively after the reference to the UK decision. At the EPO, it seems that the naming requirement is a mere formality. Patent offices rarely investigate actual inventorship.

[81]   *See* also chapters 20 and 23 in this volume.

[82]   *See* Ethicon, Inc. v U.S. Surgical Corp., 135 F.3d 1456, 1460 (Fed.Cir.1998) and *Thaler*, ibid.

[83]   *See ibid.*

[84]   *See ibid.* The argument that the technological neutrality required under TRIPS article 27.1 mandates patents on artificial inventions is unconvincing. AI technology remains patentable. It simply needs to meet patentability criteria, just as computer software does.

or not? Will doing so mostly accelerate innovation, or instead lead mostly to massive trolling?[85] This is at bottom an empirical matter. Because AI has become a standard tool in many fields of technology, empirical data about the production of new patents, the type of new technologies produced, the employment of human researchers, and other relevant variables will become available, which in turn should allow for a better framing of normative measures to tackle the ongoing "cyborgization" of innovation. It may be that human scientists will spend less time discovering and observing and more time interpreting data (and analyzing interpretations of the data) provided by AI machines. The positives are easy to identify (new pharmaceuticals, and so on); on the negative side of the ledger, however, how this might impact our quest to understand nature and employment in applied sciences should be borne in mind.

As matters stand now, the chapter asserts, as a matter of policy, that those who claim we (humans) would be better off by granting patents on nonhuman inventions have the burden of proof primarily because this would result in applying a regulatory system meant to create incentives for one type of activity (innovation springing from the human mind) to a different type of activity (innovation from machines), which may not require the same set of incentives.

5.   APPLICATION TO COPYRIGHT LAW

Should we protect artificial literary and artistic productions created without *natural* originality, meaning productions the creation of which does not involve in a material way a human creative process as *cause*?[86] This would be a significant normative jump for, as Professor Sam Ricketson—the co-author of the leading treatise on the Berne Convention—wrote, the "need for authors to be 'human' is a longstanding assumption in national copyright laws."[87] Doctrinally, his observation seems entirely correct.[88] Indeed, that assumption dates back to well before the original (1886) text of the Berne Convention; it harkens back to the very roots

---

[85]   A troll in patent law is "a pejorative term describing a non-manufacturing patent owner who owns one or more patents and asserts the patent(s) against alleged infringers, with a desire typically to obtain settlement rather than actually trying any lawsuit." Donald W. Rupert, *Trolling for Dollars: A New Threat to Patent Owners*, 21 INTELL. PROP. & TECH. L.J. 1, 3 (2009).

[86]   This section provides a succinct overview of a more detailed argument presented elsewhere. *See* Daniel Gervais, *The Machine as Author*, 105 IOWA L. REV. 2053 (2020). *See also* Shyamkrishna Balganesh, *Causing Copyright*, 117 Colum. L. Rev. 1 (2017) (developing a theory of authorial causation connecting human agency to the expression embodied in a copyrighted work).

[87]   Sam Ricketson, *People or Machines: The Berne Convention and the Changing Concept of Authorship*, 16 COLUM. J. L. & ARTS 1, 8 (1991–2). Berne Convention for the Protection of Literary and Artistic Works, Sept. 9, 1886, as revised at Paris, July 24, 1971, 828 UNTS 221 [hereinafter Berne Convention]. The Berne Convention had 179 member States as of December 2020. The United States became a party to the Convention on March 1, 1989. See World Intellectual Property Organization, Contracting Parties: Berne Convention, www.wipo.int/treaties/en/ShowResults.jsp?lang=en&treaty_id=15 (accessed Dec. 15, 2020). The treatise referred to is SAM RICKETSON AND JANE C GINSBURG, INTERNATIONAL COPYRIGHT AND NEIGHBOURING RIGHTS: THE BERNE CONVENTION AND BEYOND (2d ed, 2006).

[88]   An analysis of multiple national laws led another scholar to a similar conclusion. *See* Andres Guadamuz, *Artificial Intelligence and Copyright*, WIPO MAGAZINE (Oct. 2017) ("Most jurisdictions, including Spain and Germany, state that only works created by a human can be protected by copyright"), www.wipo.int/wipo_magazine/en/2017/05/article_0003.html.

of authors' rights, as the word author comes from the Latin *auctor*, or originator.[89] One could go further. The entire path of copyright history follows the milestones of human creativity.[90] Whether seen as a natural right—or even as a human right—or as an economic incentive, historically the focus of copyright has unquestionably been on productions of the human mind. If copyright had been designed as an investment protection scheme, or merely a scheme to disseminate "things of value," then the investment of publishers would have been sufficient.[91]

Be that as it may, we clearly are now faced with a new entrant in the battle for recognition of authorship status. Does this new, intelligent "species" bend, or break, the normative arc of copyright history? The first common law copyright statute—the Statute of Anne—provides a good argument against protecting artificial productions.[92] A set of arguments at the time was that, if authors had an obligation not to write libelous or otherwise unacceptable content, then authors should have a right in their writings.[93] This created a normative link that seems entirely convincing: *if one is responsible for one's writing, then one can legitimately ask for a right in protecting moral or material interests in that writing.*[94] The argument rests on the complementarity of responsibility and right, punishment and reward.[95] A similar point can be found in more modern work such as Foucault's discussion of the persona of the author. He put in parallel authorship and what he called "penal appropriation," noting that "[t]exts, books, and discourses really began to have authors […] to the extent that authors became subject to punishment, that is, to the extent that discourses could be transgressive."[96] There is little doubt in this author's mind that owners and programmers of AI machines will distance themselves faster than the speed of light if and when a machine they own or programmed produces infringing or libelous content, though many of them of course will not hesitate to claim exclusive rights if what the machine had produced is both non-infringing and commercially valuable.

---

[89]   For a detailed account of this evolution, *see* Gervais, note 86 *supra*.

[90]   *See ibid.*

[91]   *See* MARK ROSE, AUTHORS AND OWNERS: THE INVENTION OF COPYRIGHT, 34–5 (Harvard Univ. Press, 1993).

[92]   The Statute of Anne was the first common law copyright statute. Though adopted in England, it served as a basis for the first state statutes and the first US federal copyright act in 1790. *See* Oren Bracha, *The Adventures of the Statute of Anne in the Land of Unlimited Possibilities: The Life of A Legal Transplant*, 25 BERKELEY TECH. L.J. 1427, 1427–9 (2010).

[93]   *See* ROSE, *supra* note 91, at 34–5.

[94]   Echoing the International Covenant on Economic, Social and Cultural Rights (ICESCR), art. 15(1) (c), Dec. 16, 1966, 993 U.N.T.S. 3 (which recognizes "the right of everyone […] [t]o benefit from the protection of the moral and material interests resulting from any scientific, literary or artistic production of which he [or she] is the author"). *See also* BEN SAUL, DAVID KINLEY AND JACQUELINE MOWBRAY, THE INTERNATIONAL COVENANT ON ECONOMIC, SOCIAL AND CULTURAL RIGHTS, 1226–9 (2014). As of December 2020, the Covenant had 171 parties. The United States signed (but did not ratify) the Covenant in 1977. *See* United Nations, *International Covenant on Economic, Social and Cultural Rights,* (Jan. 3, 1976), online: https://treaties.un.org/Pages/ViewDetails.aspx?src=IND&mtdsg_no=IV-3&chapter= 4&clang=_en (accessed Dec. 5, 2020). A human rights-based approach can inform parts of copyright law, but in the past two decades copyright law at the international level has been shaped more by trade agreements than human rights. *See* Daniel Gervais, *Human Rights and the Philosophical Foundations of Intellectual Property*, IN RESEARCH HANDBOOK ON HUMAN RIGHTS AND INTELLECTUAL PROPERTY (C. Geiger, ed), 89, 90–3 (2015).

[95]   *See* ROSE, *supra* note 91, at 35–6.

[96]   Michel Foucault, *What is an Author,* in THE ESSENTIAL FOUCAULT: SELECTIONS FROM THE ESSENTIAL WORKS OF FOUCAULT 1954–1984, P. Rabinow & N. Rose, eds (2003).

This would amount to treating machines better than humans, letting them eat the proverbial cake and have it too.

Why would artificial productions get a free pass? If the right/responsibility linkage served as the justification for copyright for human authors, should it not be applied to machine productions, and indeed to any other category of purported "author"? This would mean that, once the machine production is not causally connected to one or more humans, there should be no copyright in the production.[97] There is an echo of this view in a resolution adopted by the European Parliament on October 20, 2020, which recommended that regulators take into account "the degree of human intervention [and] the autonomy of AI."[98]

Ultimately, the risk of replacing humans in the act of creation, perhaps our noblest quest, is the principal consideration. Protecting artificial productions which will come at no ongoing cost and without the rights that a human creator would claim even after transferring her rights, such as moral rights or rights reversion, means that market forces will lead to a fast replacement of human creators whenever possible. It will also change what we read, watch, and listen to. Machines will create based on existing material combined with data about what humans are most likely to respond to, just like Facebook—or Meta—focuses on polarization instead of informed discussion. The risk is that there will be more of the same, or worse. How that can arrest human development is unclear, but the risk is nonetheless real. Letting machines create the next waves of cultural development is fraught with existential risks. As with patents, anyone can make this claim or the opposite, however, because it remains ultimately a matter for empirical observation. Yet much of what can be lost in less than a generation may well justify applying a version of the precautionary principle before we put copyright and the full force of the market behind the replacement of human authors by machines.

6. USING CAUSATION TO SEPARATE HUMAN AND MACHINE

Given the increasingly frequent conflation of human and machine contributions in the production of creative and innovative content, it seems safe to predict that there will be more productions that are *both* human and machine-made. As with works and inventions with multiple contributors, courts may be asked to determine *who*, if anyone, the author and/or right holder(s) should be. This is *not* the same inquiry as the one above, which was to decide *whether* machine productions should be protected to begin with. This second inquiry is about separating contributions, as might happen in any case of joint authorship or inventorship. Courts will need analytical tools to separate human and machine contributions even if, against the position taken in this chapter at least for copyrightable productions, the latter are ultimately found to be protectable.

---

[97] It is unnecessary, therefore, to delve more deeply into which human proxy should be, by legal fiction, "selected" as the most appropriate right holder. To use the term in Ginsburg and Budiarjo, supra note 50 at 439–42, the production is "authorless." There is a specific concern in US law with respect to the production of derivative works. See Daniel Gervais, AI Derivatives, 52:4 Seton Hall L. Rev 1111 (2022).

[98] Intellectual Property Rights for the Development of Artificial Intelligence Technologies: European Parliament Resolution of October 20, 2020 (2020/2015(INI)), online: www.europarl.europa.eu/doceo/document/TA-9-2020-0277_EN.html.

The test this chapter suggests is for a court to look for the *cause* of the originality (for copyright) or inventiveness or "contribution to conception" (for patents[99]). The notion of cause is well known in law. In tort law, causation can have two meanings: causation-in-fact (also known as "simple cause'), and proximate causation (or "legal cause").[100] Causation-in-fact is the "but for" test, and often the easiest: would the outcome have occurred but for a person's (typically, the defendant in a tort case) conduct?[101] If a person's actions played a part—any part—in the outcome, then the answer is generally yes.[102] In the case of AI systems, several persons are typically involved in the creation and operation of AI machines, and many of them may thus make a "but for" contribution to an action or decision. Then machines may make their own contribution.

"But for" causation does not suffice. Too many hands (and chips) may have played a role that is only tangentially related to the outcome, and yet enough to pass a strict "but for" test. Hence, some form of IP "proximate" causation suffused with the required normativity should be applied instead of simple cause. For example, every programmer who worked on an AI machine arguably meets the "but for" threshold as a technical matter. Normatively, however, the chapter suggests that it is not sufficient. Identifying the source of the creative choices (copyright) or contribution to the actual conception of the invention (patent) is required.

The chapter suggests applying "proximate" cause to IP because it provides both a vocabulary and analytical paths that are useful in this context. Naturally, this means an inversion of the notion's traditional role, as proximate or legal cause is more typically used to impose liability in appropriate cases rather than in a jurisgenerative role. For example, "[t]he words 'legal cause' are used [...] to denote fact that the causal sequence by which the actor's tortious conduct has resulted in an invasion of some legally protected interest of another is such that the law holds the actor responsible for such harm unless there is some defense to liability."[103]

Where the notion of IP proximate cause may be particularly useful is in its *target*, for it considers whether the conduct is "a substantial factor in bringing about" the outcome.[104] Proximate cause is, *au fond,* a normative determination with built-in flexibility and steeped in temporal and other contextual constraints such as normalcy. Hence, it has great dynamicity. As United States Chief Justice Roberts noted in his dissent in *CSX*, the notion of proximate cause supplies the vocabulary for answering questions such as "whether there was a superseding or intervening cause."[105] Tort law recognizes that "external influences" may be considered as "superseding causes".[106] From a normative perspective, "superseding" may be interpreted as meaning *more relevant*. The chapter argues that courts *can and should* use that sieve in IP

---

[99]   *See supra* note 82.

[100]   W. PAGE KEETON ET AL., PROSSER AND KEETON ON THE LAW OF TORTS § 43 (5th ed. 1988).

[101]   Courts sometimes struggle to distinguish causation in fact and proximate cause. *See* Jane Stapleton, *Legal Cause: Cause-in-Fact and the Scope of Liability for Consequences*, 54 VAND. L. REV. 941, 945 (2001).

[102]   The term "causation in fact" is somewhat of a misnomer. Cause is not, strictly speaking, a "fact"; it is a relationship between two events. *See* Wex S. Malone, *Ruminations on Cause-in-Fact*, 9 STAN. L. REV. 60, 61 (1956).

[103]   *See* RESTATEMENT (SECOND) OF TORTS § 9 (1965).

[104]   *Ibid.*, Cmt (a).

[105]   CSX Transp., Inc. v McBride, 564 U.S. 685, at 719.

[106]   *See* Weston Kowert, *The Foreseeability of Human-Artificial Intelligence Interactions*, 96 TEX. L. REV. 181, 184 (2017); and Matthew U. Scherer, *Regulating Artificial Intelligence Systems: Risks, Challenges, Competencies, and Strategies*, 29 HARV. J.L. & TECH. 353, 365–6 (2016).

cases involving sapient AI machines.[107] The difficulty to solve in close cases will be due to a *break in the legal causation chain* between humans and the outcome (what looks like a copy-rightable work or patentable invention). This break will be due to an *intervening cause*, namely the AI machine's autonomous contribution.

In their (normative) application of proximacy to the cause of a contribution to a literary or artistic work or an invention, there are two errors that courts are likely to make. The first error would be to (over)reward (or hold accountable in case the work produced is infringing a third party copyright, for example) humans so far removed from the AI machine's operation as to be "far out," to use the US Supreme Court's language.[108] In extreme cases, for example, the only meaningful human control over the machine might be a "kill switch."[109] The second, related potential error is to consider that *someone must* be rewarded or held responsible. It is possible that no human can be causally (factually and legally) linked to the outcome.

There are well-established intellectual property doctrines that can serve as vehicles to operationalize "IP proximate causation." In copyright law, courts could use originality. The US Copyright Act grants protection only to *original* works of authorship.[110] This notion of originality is a worldwide standard, even though it is not spelled out explicitly in international treaties.[111] The US Supreme Court has held that originality is required by the Constitution, which allows Congress to protect the "Writings" of "Authors."[112] It found that it was "unmistakably clear" that the terms "authors" and "writings" in the US Constitution presuppose a degree of originality in European law, U.S. law and the law of many other jurisdictions;[113] originality, in turn, requires a minimal degree of "creativity," a "creative spark."[114]

Courts should define originality as requiring that a "human spark" be causally related to the output. This is the approach taken by the European Parliament in considering that "works autonomously produced by artificial agents and robots might not be eligible for copyright protection, in order to observe the principle of originality, which is linked to a natural person, and since the concept of 'intellectual creation' addresses the author's personality."[115] In patent law, courts could use the notion of inventorship along similar lines and redefine it to achieve the aim of separating human and machine, by focusing on human contributions, if any, to the conception of the invention.[116]

---

[107] More rarely so in intentional tort cases. *See* RESTATEMENT (THIRD) OF TORTS: LIAB. FOR PHYSICAL & EMOTIONAL HARM §33 Comment e. (2010).

[108] CSX Transp., note 105 *supra*, at 704.

[109] *See* Thomas Arnold and Matthias Scheutz, *The "Big Red Button" Is Too Late: An Alternative Model For The Ethical Evaluation of AI Systems*, 20 ETHICS & INFOR. TECH., 59, 60 (2018).

[110] 17 U.S.C. § 102(a).

[111] *See* Daniel Gervais and Elizabeth Judge, *Of Silos and Constellations: Comparing Notions of Originality in Copyright Law*, 27:2 CARDOZO ARTS & ENT. L.J. 375–408 (2009); and Daniel Gervais, *Feist Goes Global: A Comparative Analysis of the Notion of Originality in Copyright Law*, 49:4 J. COPYRIGHT. SOC.Y OF THE USA 949–81(2002).

[112] U.S. CONST. art. I, § 8, cl. 8.

[113] Feist Publications, 499 U.S. 340, 346 (1991).

[114] *Ibid.* The law may be headed in that direction in Australia as well. See ICE TV Pty Limited v Nine Network Australia Pty Limited [2009] HCA 14, paras 187–88.

[115] Resolution, supra note 98, at ¶15.

[116] *See supra* note 81.

7.   LOOKING AHEAD

The developments of AI towards progressive cyborgization may lead to a situation where human creators with enhanced mental abilities compete with unenhanced creators and inventors. Those possible developments far transcend the scope of this chapter and indeed the field of intellectual property itself, but the chapter's analytical path could perhaps be of use also in that context.

Without looking too far into possible futures, we may in short order be submerged under a flow of machine-made literary and artistic works and new inventions. To use a term favored by Kurzweil and others, the pace could be such that we may face a "singularity" of artificial productions, displacing many human creators and inventors from the marketplace.[117] Why would a record label pay a songwriter if a machine can produce successful commercial hits? Why would a pharmaceutical company hire postdocs if machines can do the work? As adumbrated in the Introduction, it is impossible to predict with accuracy whether and, if so, for how long human authors and inventors will or will not survive as a significant source of cultural production and innovation in the medium to long run. In the short run, however, it is worth asking whether intellectual property policy should try to keep a place for human creativity and inventiveness. Doctrinally at least, if we want to, we can. The harder question is the normative one.

Perhaps we should give in as a species and welcome machine "creators" and "inventors", and even accelerate that process by giving IP rights to machine productions. One way or another, that is a debate we must have, and the chapter is a contribution to that debate. If we refuse to take the position that the focus of IP law is human creativity and innovation, *what will be left for us to do?* Who will be the great creators of tomorrow who will help us understand and shape our world if machines are the artists, novelists, and journalists? Who will come up with the pioneer discoveries if machines are the inventors? What happens when the machines are the engineers, songwriters, and lawyers? Then again, as the Borg collectively say when they are about to assimilate a member of another species, perhaps "resistance is futile."[118]

8.   CONCLUSION

Is machine "intelligence the last invention that humanity will ever need to make," as Nick Bostrom suggested?[119] Is our species "going to mortally struggle with this problem?"[120] It is not often that a new species comes along that can challenge humans on the terrain that has ensured our dominion over other creatures and machines, namely our "higher mental facul-

---

[117]   *See* Nick Bostrom, *What Happens When Our Computers Get Smarter Than We Are? Singularity* (May 7, 2015), online: www.singularityweblog.com/nick-bostrom-ted/.

[118]   The Borg are a fictional species in *Star Trek*. They aim to conquer beings from various species (including some humans) and turn them into "drones" (what one might call cyborgs) by adding technology to their bodies. The assimilated beings become part of the Borg "collective." *See* https://intl.startrek.com/database_article/borg (last accessed Apr. 24, 2021).

[119]   *See* Bostrom, *supra* note 117.

[120]   James Barrat, Our Final Invention: Artificial Intelligence And The End Of The Human Era 5 (2013).

ties."[121] Come to think of it, it is actually the first time. How the system of laws and institutions humans have put in place to ensure a more or less orderly unfolding of the human story will respond is a question that must be asked, and answered.[122]

A key chapter in that story is whether, and if so how, intellectual property will focus on trying to maintain a principal role for humans in creative expression and inventiveness. This chapter has provided paths that can be followed, together or separately, to at least some of the answers. In doing so, it has claimed that the "cause" of human progress is a good cause *per se*: the law should aim to foster human progress, not just technological change.[123] Change and progress are not synonyms. Change is a difference between two points A and B on a timeline while progress is an improvement at point B.[124] Change happens; progress not necessarily. Naturally, not everyone will agree on what constitutes "progress," but this chapter assertion is that *human* self-fulfillment and realization through art and science *is* progress, and it consequently suggests that the law should aim to foster those goals.[125] In this, the chapter stands (with humility) on the shoulders of many giants, from Plato's *Laws* to Aristotle's *Nicomachean Ethics* to Spinoza's *conatus*.

The more we rely on machines to perform creative and innovative tasks that are singularly human and important for us as a source of progress—from news reporting, to music and fiction, to inventions in all fields of technology—the more we may shrink the space available for our individual and collective self-realization. To use a simple explanatory metaphor, as we use our creative and inventive "muscles" less and less, they will shrink. Is that what is meant by "Progress of Science and Useful Arts"?

---

[121] One could argue that this point should be framed as a matter of culture, in that not all cultures around the world would agree with that statement as many indigenous peoples, among others, do not see humans as having a natural dominion over nature and other species. That is also a matter beyond the scope of this chapter.

[122] On the need for a transnational regulatory path, *see* Daniel Gervais, *Towards an Effective Transnational Regulation of AI,* 36 AI & Society (2021).

[123] *See generally* Gervais, *supra* note 12.

[124] *See ibid* at 12.

[125] *See ibid* at 11–19.

3. Considering intellectual property law for embodied forms of artificial intelligence

Woodrow Barfield, Argyro Karanasiou and Karni Chagnal-Feferkorn

1. INTRODUCTION

Consider the following scenario. In the Netflix series "Uploads," deceased people's memories are uploaded to the servers of commercial companies which preserve the departed persons on their cloud storage, such that life after death continues in a fancy retirement home. In this scenario the characters continue their lives online while their physical remains have long since been buried. Even though they exist only as lines of code in the cloud, the "uploads" enjoy earthly pleasures such as food and conversation, may execute transactions, and are subject to certain rights and duties. In other words, their embodiment as persons (albeit not in the real world) matters a great deal.[1] With this example in mind, this chapter examines the concept of embodiment in artificial intelligence (hereafter AI) and the subtle impact this may have on the way in which artificial agency is perceived in law, and in particular intellectual property law. For the purposes of our discussion, we use a broad conceptualization of "embodiment" to include not only the physically embodied manifestation of an AI agent such as the form of a humanoid robot, but also a non-physical (or unembodied) form of AI such as the visual representation of a virtual avatar.[2]

When addressing intellectual property rights (hereafter IPRs) for AI agents, legal scholars have often grappled with socio-legal definitions of AI agents as dictated by their form.[3] In our analysis we argue that the topic of embodiment is overlooked within the field of intellectual property law and merits further attention. The main issue we address in this chapter is how the perceived appearance (physical or virtual) of an AI entity may affect IPRs, which we discuss primarily in the context of copyright and patent law (while occasionally referring to other IPRs that may relate to the embodiment of AI). We further discuss different logical "fallacies" surrounding the current debate on granting rights for AI agents, and how the concept of embodiment has contributed to such fallacies and influenced the debate. This is telling of

---

[1]   See also the movie *Free Guy*, where Ryan Reynolds is Guy, an AI algorithm in an open-world video game. Because the algorithmic character looks and acts like a real person, the other entities in the film, as well as the viewers, *treat* it as a person (for example by treating the discontinuation of the video game as an actual death of Guy—something that would not have happened if Guy was depicted as mere lines of code).

[2]   An example of a virtual AI agent could be a virtual avatar whose behavior is controlled by algorithms.

[3]   Deepak Somaya and Lav R. Varshney, Embodiment, Anthropomorphism, and Intellectual Property Rights for AI Creations, AEIS 18: *Proceedings of the 2018 AAAI/ACM Conference on AI, Ethics, and Society*, December 2018, 278–83; Ryan Calo, Robotics and the Lessons of Cyberlaw, 103 Calif. L. Rev. 513 (2015).

how embodiment in AI has not only influenced interactions with human operators but further shaped how AI is perceived in law.

When computer scientists develop AI systems they strive to develop systems that simulate thinking, by building intelligent entities capable of perceiving, understanding, and manipulating the world surrounding them.[4] For computer scientists AI is thought to be an agent,[5] and the term "artificial agent" is understood to cover a wide diversity of "soft" and "hard" agents, each embodied in various ways (some not embodied in the physical sense), which include: decision-making algorithms, automated machines, hybrid multi-agents, internet bots, robots, automated guided vehicles, nano-robots, sexbots, drones, and other AI-controlled entities. These AI agents have the capacity to operate and learn through experience as they interact with the environment, and they may do so without the direct intervention of humans or other agents. While their level of autonomy varies, they are agents because they take action,[6] and the action they take may challenge current principles of intellectual property law.

Under current law, the field of intellectual property is concerned with the subject matter or output of an intellectual process which is thought to require creativity and decision making skills involving a human author or inventor. The field of AI is also involved in creating artificial entities that display creativity and that in some cases do so independently of human input. The creative process itself (and its resulting outputs) may be similar for human authors and for AI agents. As a result, determining who should be considered the author or inventor of an AI-produced work, raises a new challenge under existing intellectual property law. In this chapter we address the broad issue of whether the embodied form of AI matters for awarding IPRs. As our discussion will show, the form of AI itself can be the subject matter for IPRs awarded to human authors or inventors under patent and copyright law. However, we also consider the intriguing possibility that AI agents may continue to develop in creativity and self-autonomy such that the legal community will need to consider whether it is necessary to grant rights to the AI agent. We further extend this second and more theoretical line of inquiry by considering whether the embodied form of the AI agent would matter for awarding IPRs to the AI agent. On this last discussion point, we acknowledge that it is debatable whether an AI agent will ever receive rights and, if so, whether the form of the AI agent would matter. Nonetheless, given that people often anthropomorphize technology based on its perceived appearance and actions dictated by its form, our view is that, as AI agents continue to increase in abilities, embodiment will likely influence the debate over IPRs for AI works.[7]

1.1 The Dual Nature of AI Agents and the Nature of Embodiment

We argue that AI agents—often bearing ever-growing resemblance to human beings in the type of abilities they possess, the tasks they execute, and their physical appearance, but at the

---

[4]   Stuart Russell and Peter Norvig, *Artificial Intelligence: A Modern Approach*, Pearson, 4th edition, 2020.

[5]   *Ibid.*

[6]   *Ibid*; Alan M. Turing, Computing Machinery and Intelligence, 49:236 *Mind* 433–60 (1950).

[7]   Among humans, gender and race have historically been factors that were considered in awarding rights (see e.g. Charlotte Bunch, Women's rights as human rights: Toward a re-vision of human rights, 12:4 *Human Rights Quarterly* 486–498 (1990)). Further, a thought question is: would we be more likely to award intellectual property rights to a toaster or humanoid robot if they produced the same copyrightable work?

same time lacking rights and legal personhood—have a unique dual role in the world of intellectual property. On the one hand, AI agents may themselves be the *subject* of IPRs. A robot with novel features, for example, might be the subject matter of a patent or a utility design. Similarly, a drawing of the same robot may be the subject matter of copyright or trademark law.[8] At the same time, AI agents may also be the *creators* of intellectual property-protected works. They may even be copyright infringers, given that they are trained on pre-existing works and data.[9] Under copyright law, AI agents may be involved in, or independently produce, various types of creative works, which may include graphic works, musical works, audiovisual works, and, depending on the AI agent's physical attributes, works based on physical actions such as dramatic and choreographic works. AI agents may also be the creators of inventions of logos and of functional designs. AI agents are thus not only the subject matter of copyright, patent, trademark, and utility designs, but also the authors—and perhaps someday designated as the inventor or author, or even owner—of works which might be protected under intellectual property law.

Looking at the different relationship between AI agents, IPRs and ownership, our fundamental question is does embodiment matter? Under current intellectual property law, the form or embodiment of an AI agent does matter for the rights a human author or inventor may receive. For example, under copyright law certain forms may be copyrightable subject matter, but not others; under patent law certain forms may be deemed patentable material, but not others. As to granting IPRs to non-humans, some scholars have concluded that future AI agents could be awarded ownership rights to the intellectual property they create. This idea is supported to some extent by legal precedent; for example, subject to any agreement to the contrary, corporations generally automatically own the IPR of any works produced from employees. And although it may be difficult to conceptualize now, it could be that the form or embodiment of an AI agent in the future would be relevant for whether the agent received IPRs, either as the author or inventor of a work. In this chapter we discuss the dual nature of embodiment for AI agents: the first is as subject matter eligible for IPRs awarded to a human author or inventor, and the second (independent of a human author or inventor) as creators of subject matter which may be protected by IPRs.

While Ryan Calo, in his seminal paper on robots and the lessons of cyberlaw, makes a clear distinction between embodiment (AI agents' operation in the real world) and social valence (anthropomorphism and the social meaning attached to AI agents),[10] our discussion on IPRs for AI entities will address both, given that anthropomorphism is influenced by, among other things, the physical embodiment or lack thereof of the AI agent. Since we discuss how the embodiment of AI in its different forms is of importance to intellectual property law (primarily for rights granted to the human author or inventor), we touch upon the various ways in which AI may be embodied, the affordances offered by different forms of AI embodiment, and in particular how intellectual property law may be impacted by different forms of embodied AI. We argue that broad categories of AI embodiment have significance for the legal rights

---

[8]   Ugo Pagallo, *The Laws of Robots: Crimes, Contracts, and Torts* (Law, Governance and Technology Series, 10) Springer Press, 2013.

[9]   Enrico Bonadio and Luke McDonagh, Artificial Intelligence as Producer and Consumer of Copyright Works: Evaluating the Consequences of Algorithmic Creativity, 2 *Intellectual Property Quarterly* 112–37 (2020).

[10]   Ryan Calo, *supra* note 3.

granted to human authors or inventors under current intellectual property law, and that various forms of AI embodiment may impact intellectual property law differently.

In our discussion, we take inspiration from the law as applied to human bodies which, among others, provides analogies for discussing legal rights for non-human entities. For example, from the perspective of law a human body is a necessary requirement in many legal disputes, and we argue this is also the case when considering rights associated with AI agents; that is, there is a need for a "body," whether physical or virtual, for many of the legal disputes which involve AI agents.[11] To illustrate this point for human bodies, consider common law assault, which is considered to be the act of inflicting physical harm or unwanted physical contact upon a person or, in some jurisdictions, a threat or attempt to commit such an action.[12] From this definition, only a physically embodied entity (that is, a human) can be the subject of assault. For AI we understand that embodiment may be necessary for certain actions within law to go forward and to have significance; for example, embodiment matters for a tort law action when a robot causes damages. In our view, the embodiment of AI, whether in a physical or in a non-physical (virtual) form, has consequences for intellectual property law and has influenced the debate on granting rights to AI agents; and, as we discuss below, to some extent the embodied nature of AI agents has already been reflected in discussions on how to regulate AI agents.

1.2 Considering the Nature of Embodiment

At the heart of our argument lies embodiment—a concept long discussed in literature, yet underexplored from a legal perspective. In our analysis we address embodiment in two main ways: (1) we consider the actual physical embodiment of AI, for example, a robot or any physical entity equipped with AI; and (2) we consider unembodied or virtual forms of AI, such as a virtual avatar or internet bot. There are already numerous examples of embodied AI agents autonomously creating works that are considered the subject matter of intellectual property law, including paintings, music, and even movie scripts. Those situations, especially where there is no human involved in producing the creative work, have led to a debate among legal scholars as to who should be considered the author or inventor of such works. When analyzing whether AI agents may themselves be the owners of IPRs, an element that could be significant to the discussion is the nature of their embodiment. On this point, an interesting question to pose is: why would (or should?) an AI agent be considered the owner of intellectual property?[13]

Concerning embodiment, Ryan Calo described embodiment as the "capacity to act physically upon the world [and], in turn, to the potential "to physically harm people or property."[14] Drawing on this description, does the fact that an AI agent may have a physical embodiment and thus act on the world matter for intellectual property law? If so, does the specific type of physical embodiment matter? That is, will the specific shape, physical abilities or resemblance

---

[11] *See* Anna Grear, Human Rights—Human Bodies? Some Reflections on Corporate Human Rights Distortion, The Legal Subject, Embodiment and Human Rights Theory, 17 *Law Critique* 171–99, 2006.

[12] Oliver Wendell Holmes, *The Common Law*, Dover Publications, 1991.

[13] Ryan Abbott, I Think, Therefore I Invent: Creative Computers and the Future of Patent Law, 57:4 Boston College L. Rev. (2016); Raquel Acosta, Artificial Intelligence and Authorship Rights, Harvard J. Law Technology (JOLT), 2012, https://jolt.law.harvard.edu/digest/artificial-intelligence-and-authorship -rights.

[14] Calo, *supra* note 3 at 534.

to a human being have any weight in the determination of whether IPRs ought to be awarded to human authors or inventors for creating such agents, or awarded for such agents' own creations? Can the same questions be asked of an unembodied representation of AI? These are difficult questions, currently not the subject of extensive legal scholarship but nonetheless of particular importance for intellectual property law as AI continues to gain in intelligence, autonomy, and anthropomorphic features.

1.3   Is a Body Necessary for Awarding Rights?

A fundamental question for awarding IPRs is: Is it necessary to have a body? As further detailed below, the element of embodiment and its characteristics may be relevant to the question of awarding IPRs to AI agents in several contexts. First, on the question of embodiment itself and the weight it carries for "intelligence" (that is, whether or not there is any need for a physical presence of an AI system), Tom Ziemke commented that many researchers consider embodiment a *condition sine qua non* for any form of natural or artificial intelligence.[15] In Ziemke's writings he discusses the classic approach of cognitive science in which, based on functionalism, the field focused on disembodied cognition (for example, as algorithms embedded within software). He also points out that while scholars agree that people are embodied cognizers, there is still little agreement on which kind of body an AI would have to be equipped with as a cognizer. In fact, Pfeifer and Scheir have argued that the very idea that intelligence requires a physical body is not universally accepted.[16] In contrast, Varela, Thompson, and Rosch have stated that knowledge depends on being in a world that is inseparable from our bodies […] in short [resulting] from our embodiment.[17] And supporting the alternate view that "unembodied" (that is, nonphysical) forms of AI may also acquire knowledge and engage in activities that trigger the law, Riegler commented that embodiment does not have to exclude domains other than the physical domain, and that computer programs (which themselves may be copyright protected) may be considered embodied as a result of how they are organized.[18]

Robots, which we consider an example of physically embodied AI, have been described by Howard and Borenstein as a computing agent embodied in hardware controlling a mechanical body.[19] We posit that the affordances offered by the "mechanical body" might impact not only how AI is legally perceived, or regulated, but also whether AI agents merit IP protection—especially if such affordances made it more likely that copyrightable or patentable subject matter was created. The shape and behavior of a robot can influence human performance working with the robot, including the perception of the robot, and attitudes toward the robot. For example, Hwang, Park, and Hwang showed that the overall shape of a robot could influ-

---

[15]   Tom Ziemke, 'Are Robots Embodied?', First international workshop on epigenetic robotics Modelling Cognitive Development in Robotic Systems, Vol 85, Citeseer, 2001.

[16]   Rolf Pfeifer and Christian Scheier, *Understanding Intelligence*, MIT Press, 1999.

[17]   Francisco J. Varela, Evan Thompson, and Eleanor Rosch, *The Embodied Mind*, Revised edition, MIT Press, 2017.

[18]   Alexander Riegler, When Is a Cognitive System Embodied? 3:3 *Cognitive Systems Research*, 339–48 (2002).

[19]   Ayanna Howard and Jason Borenstein, The Ugly Truth about Ourselves and Our Robot Creations: The Problem of Bias and Social Inequity, *Sci. Eng. Ethics* 1521–36 (2018).

ence a person's evaluation of the robot's personality.[20] From the above discussion we pose the following question: Is there a relationship between the shape, form, or embodiment of AI, which may influence the degree to which it may be anthropomorphized, and the rights the AI entity may receive at some point in the future?[21]

Clearly, intellectual property law relates to the embodiment of AI when considering rights for human authors or inventors; for example, much of the components of a robot can be patent protected, the software controlling the robot can be protected under copyright law, and the algorithms controlling the motion of the robot can be proprietary and thus a trade secret. But just as increasingly intelligent entities have begun to challenge the law in different areas, in the future an AI agent with the ability to produce creative and inventive works will become more anthropomorphized and autonomous than current versions of AI and lead to significant challenges to intellectual property law.

1.3.1 Additional perspectives on embodiment

While embodiment poses significant challenges for law, the discussion of embodied AI is actually not new: its beginnings date back several decades. For example, in the early days of computing, with the success of the von Neumann computing architecture, the algorithmic approach to AI prevailed and intelligence became synonymous with rule-based processing of symbolic information done using a computational architecture that existed independently of its physical implementation. Such a functionalist stance explicitly divorced intelligence from its material or biological substrate. However, other approaches to creating AI began to emerge, motivated in part by the work of Rodney Brooks, then head of the MIT robotics and AI lab. In 1990 Brooks wrote an article titled "Elephants Don't Play Chess,"[22] in which he argued that the traditional approach to creating AI—which emphasized the mathematical manipulation of symbols in an environment not grounded in physical reality—was unlikely to make substantial progress in AI. Instead, Brooks argued for a research methodology which emphasized the ongoing physical interaction of an AI entity with the environment as the primary source of constraint on the design of intelligent systems. Thus, at some point in AI research, the manipulation of symbols and the idea of a body acquiring information in the world were two views on how to make progress in creating AI, and both offered different positions on the importance of embodiment for AI.

As noted above, among philosophers, the choice of the physical and computational substrates necessary to create AI entities approaching human levels of intelligence has been the subject of a fascinating debate. In fact, as stated earlier in the chapter, some question whether AI needs to be "embodied" in a physical sense at all in order for it to achieve human levels of intelligence. On this point, consider the characteristics of three entities: a human body; an AI-controlled robot; and an "unembodied" virtual avatar controlled by AI. In the first two

---

[20] Jihong Hwang, Taezoon Park, and Wonill Hwang, The Effects of Overall Robot Shape on the Emotions Invoked in Users and the Perceived Personalities of Robot, 44(3) *Applied Ergonomics* 459–71 (2013).

[21] A current physically embodied entity which illustrates this point is a sexbot, where embodiment clearly matters and has led to interesting ethical and legal issues associated with such AI-equipped entities: Sonya Ziaja, Homewrecker 2.0: An Exploration of Liability for Heart Balm Torts Involving AI Humanoid Consorts, *International Conference on Social Robotics ICSR 2011: Social Robotics*, 114–24 (2011).

[22] Rodney Brooks, Elephants Don't Play Chess, 6:1 *Robotics and Autonomous Systems* 3–15 (1990).

examples (human and robot), each body is equipped with sensors and a cognitive processor and operates in the real world. Each body has a physical structure, is capable of movement, and is able to acquire information about the world by detecting different forms of sensory information. The acquisition of information and the movements afforded by the human or robot body could lead to decision making and actions in the physical world which implicate the law in different ways; for example, within tort law, who should be held liable for the harm produced by an autonomous mobile robot, and in intellectual property law, who should receive patent rights for an AI-based invention that lacked human input?

In the above example discussing two physically embodied agents (robot or human), both bodies are clearly different and have different rights attached to them: for example, a human is eligible for IPRs but not a robot; and a robot body may be protected under patent law but not the biological structures and features of a human body. And while granting rights may ultimately hinge on whether the entity has legal person status (which we discuss below), as the embodiment of AI becomes more human-like (in appearance and behavior), the difference between humans and nonhumans begins to blur. Briefly considering the third example of embodiment, for an AI-controlled virtual avatar (a non-physical representation of an AI agent) there is no physical body. Yet, just as with physically embodied entities, its appearance and behavior may implicate the law in different ways, copyright or possibly acquiring a trademark for the particular form of the AI agent being examples. And as we stated earlier, the law already considers different forms of embodiment in several contexts, which has broad implications for AI agents and intellectual property law. For example, the European Union has been discussing the issue of granting personhood status to intelligent robots during the past few years, and part of the conversation has revolved around the issue of how to define the entity which would receive legal person status. Recently, in a report prepared for the European Trade Union Institute,[23] Aida Ponce Del Castillo commented that to grant rights for robots and AI we need to first determine how we should refer to robots, artificial agents, or autonomous artificial agents, and discuss the likely consequences of that distinction.[24] To rephrase this for our purposes, the issue is how the embodiment of AI affects the rights received. As one approach to embodiment, the European Parliament has in the past considered creating a specific status for robots as "electronic persons," with specific rights and obligations attached, and applying the concept of electronic persons to cases where robots make decisions or interact with third parties (paragraph 59(f) of the section on Liability from a 2017 resolution of the European Parliament), a status currently unknown in legal systems. In our view, the EU discussion is an example of how the law is beginning to think about embodiment (albeit indirectly). While the EU discussion focused primarily on the "robotic form," eventually we expect the discussion to broaden and to include other AI agents presented with different forms of embodiment.

---

[23]   Aida Ponce Del Castillo (2017), A law on robotics and artificial intelligence in the EU? Foresight Brief,   www.etui.org/publications/foresight-briefs/a-law-on-robotics-and-artificial-intelligence-in-the-eu.

[24]   *Ibid.*

2.   EMBODIMENT AND AI AGENTS AS INTELLECTUAL PROPERTY

2.1   Embodiment and Patent Law

In US patent law, the idea that embodiment matters is illustrated directly in the patent statute. Specifically, the best mode requirement appears in the patent statutes at 35 USC § 112, first paragraph: "The specification [...] shall set forth the best mode contemplated by the inventor of carrying out his invention." The best mode requirement creates a statutory bargained-for exchange by which a patentee obtains the right to exclude others from practicing the claimed invention for a certain period, and the public receives knowledge of the preferred embodiments for practicing the claimed invention.[25] Further, the term "embodiment" is part of the language used in patent applications filed in the US. As an example, consider US Patent 10,979,959 on a modular intelligent transportation system (although not necessarily referring to a physical embodiment in each example, note that the patent application contained the term "embodiment" 139 times):

> In alternate embodiments, a plurality of control units in close proximity may communicate with each other, for example using a wireless network or ad hoc network. In cases where the sensor systems of such control units overlap, the qualifying or preliminary sounds detected at one control unit may be used to commence recording at another control unit, to thereby increase the available data. A networking of control units allows a large sensor network to track events over a broad geographic region. This network may, for example, be used to track the movements and/or driving patterns of vehicles around an incident, and to identify and track drivers who leave the scene of an accident.

If we consider physically constructed objects such as robots as an embodied form of AI, generally speaking, we can conclude that various aspects of an artificially intelligent agent can be the subject matter of a patent; however, there are notable exceptions which relate to the concept of embodiment. For example, while the embodied form of most AI agents can be patent-eligible, certain AI agents face scrutiny with respect to whether they may be patent-eligible subject matter. To illustrate this concept the United States Patent and Trademark Office (USPTO) follows a two-step analysis to determine whether a patent claim is patent-eligible. First, the USPTO determines whether the patent claim is directed to a patent-eligible concept. Certain areas are not patent-eligible (which relates to embodiment): abstract ideas, laws of nature, and natural phenomena. So, at this level of the analysis, an unembodied AI agent that simply "repeats" a law of nature is non-patentable subject matter unless more is involved. Therefore, if a patent claim is directed to one of the above concepts, the USPTO will next examine whether the claim as a whole amounts to "significantly more" than the just mentioned concepts, in which case the claim may be patent-eligible. An AI-based invention related to autonomous vehicles or robots that aims to control or manipulate a tangible object (such as a vehicle or a package) represents this idea and generally faces relatively minimal scrutiny from a patent examiner. Such technology (the combination of an AI agent directing a physically embodied

---

[25]   *Eli Lilly & Co. v Barr Labs., Inc.*, 251 F.3d 955, 963, 58 USPQ2d 1869, 1874 (Fed.Cir.2001), *cert. denied*, ___ U.S. ___, 122 S.Ct. 913, 151 L.Ed.2d 879 (2002); Kevin Emerson Collins, The Knowledge/ Embodiment Dichotomy, 47 *UC Davis Law Review* (2014), available at SSRN: https://ssrn.com/abstract =2428908.

entity) is usually found to be patent-eligible subject matter because it is considered to produce a tangible result and thus is not abstract.

Further, an AI-based invention that is not directed to controlling tangible objects, such as a software algorithm, faces heightened scrutiny by a patent examiner as to whether it is directed to an abstract idea. Nevertheless, many technical aspects of such an AI-based invention may still be patent-eligible, given that embodiment of an invention is described in the patent application. While the USPTO has not provided an explicit definition of an "abstract idea," a number of court decisions have been illustrative. For example, the Federal Circuit has held that patent claims directed to a specific, self-referential arrangement of data is patent-eligible.[26] Thus far, data structures, specific rules, specific combinations of steps, or specific hardware configurations that result in improvement of the functioning of a computer have been found to cover eligible subject matter.

If we again consider a robot as a physical embodiment of AI, the physical appearance of a robot, or ornamental design in patent terms, plays a major role in determining the success of robotic products in the marketplace. A robot's ornamental design encompasses various aspects of its look and feel, such as its facial features and expressions and also the shape of the robot. Design patents, or design registrations as they are known in many parts of the world, may protect how something "looks," which is a feature of embodiment. A design patent may cover the entire article or only an innovative part, such as the robot's face. Further, a design patent may cover the shape of an article, its surface pattern, or both. However, to be deserving of a patent, a design must be original, novel (new) over the existing designs (known as "prior art"), and ornamental, and must not be an obvious variant of any existing design (thus different nonobvious embodiments are required). Further, the "ornamentality" requirement means that the design must not be solely dictated by function. For instance, a design would not be considered solely functional if the underlying good could be designed in an alternative way, but still function the same.

Interestingly, in the US, design patents are enforced more like trademarks. The test for design-patent infringement centers on whether an ordinary observer, familiar with the prior art, would be deceived into believing the design protected by the patent is substantially the same as the design of the product accused of infringement. While utility patents filed on the functional aspects of an invention are the most common patent application, design patents are gaining in popularity as companies recognize the importance of protecting the significant time and effort that goes into designing the look of their products (in other words, its embodiment); iRobot, for example, has invested significant resources in developing the Roomba's unique form.[27]

2.1.1   Copyright law and embodiment

The form or embodiment of an AI agent may also be the subject of copyright law. Again considering the shape of a "humanoid appearing robot" as an example and the extent to which copyright law applies, we discuss *Carol Barnhart Inc. v Economy Cover Corp.*[28] Barnhart sold

---

[26]   *See Enfish, LLC v Microsoft Corp.*, 822 F.3d 1327 (Fed. Cir. 2016).

[27]   See US Design Patent No. D670877 assigned to iRobot Corporation on the ornamental design for a robot vacuum cleaner; US Design Patent No. D548411 assigned to BSH Bosch Und Siemens Hausgeraete Gmbh on the ornamental design for a robot vacuum cleaner.

[28]   *Carol Barnhart Inc. v Economy Cover Corp., 773 F.2d 411 (1985).*

display forms (that is, mannequins) to department stores, distributors, and small retail stores. Barnhart's complaint alleged that Economy infringed its copyright and engaged in unfair competition by offering for sale display forms copied from four original "sculptural forms" to which Barnhart held the copyright. The point of contention was four human torso forms designed by Barnhart, each of which was life-size, without neck, arms, or a back, and made of expandable white styrene.[29] All the forms, which were otherwise life-like and anatomically accurate, had hollow backs designed to hold excess fabric when the garment was fitted onto the form.[30] The court held that plaintiff's mannequins of partial human torsos which were used to display articles of clothing were utilitarian and did not contain separable works of art from the utilitarian aspect of the design, and thus were not copyrightable. So, by extension, considering humanoid robot forms and the extent to which the form of a robot is utilitarian for a particular application, the shape would not be eligible for copyright protection. Here we note that while the physical form of an embodied AI entity may not be protected by copyright law, if the entity's output is subject matter which could be copyright protected intellectual property issues are still relevant and, as we discuss below, may be influenced by the degree to which the embodied AI is anthropomorphized.

In a similar but more recent case, *Zahourek Systems v Balanced Body University, LLC*, the US Tenth Circuit ruled that an anatomical mannequin might be protected under copyright law, and not necessarily excluded from copyright protection as a "useful article."[31] Thus, the law in this area is evolving. The Tenth Circuit noted that the statutory definition of "useful article" was "having an intrinsic utilitarian function that is not merely to portray the appearance of the article or to convey information."[32] While copyright does not protect the mechanical or utilitarian aspects of works of craftsmanship, it may, however, protect any pictorial, graphic, or sculptural authorship that can be identified separately from the utilitarian aspects of an object. Of course, some designs of useful articles may qualify for protection under a different intellectual property scheme, for example under the US federal patent law. A point we make is that the form or function of an embodied AI entity may offer challenges to current intellectual property law, so again, embodiment matters. Further, if we consider AI embodied as a robot character, under US copyright law these are considered "stock" characters, and as such do not rise to the standard of creativity for copyright protection until the author adds something more. Famous franchise movie characters, such as RoboCop, are protected by copyright law because of the copyright in the film and script, but only to the extent of the creative expression by the author in the robot-like character.

Extending the discussion on legal rights for appearance, an area of law which relates to both the virtual and physical embodiment of an AI agent and where appearance is clearly important is the common law right of publicity.[33] For physical embodiment, an interesting case is *White v Samsung Electronics America, Inc.*,[34] where defendant Samsung ran a television ad which depicted Wheel of Fortune's Vanna White as a robot character which was used to sell the

---

[29] *Ibid.*
[30] *Ibid.*
[31] *Zahourek Systems v Balanced Body University, LLC.* 965 F.3d 1141 (2020).
[32] *Ibid.*
[33] J. Thomas McCarthy, The Spring 1995 Horace S. Manges Lecture—The Human Persona as Commercial Property: The Right of Publicity, 19 Colum.-VLA J.L.& Arts 129 (1994–5).
[34] *White v Samsung Electronics America, Inc.*, 1330 (9th Cir. 1993).

defendant's VCR. In this example the robot had low functionality, but we predict that more functional and intelligent robots will be developed that even more represent the likeness of a famous person and thus will challenge the right of publicity law. Among other legal theories, White's cause of action was based on California's right of publicity law which contains the following elements: (1) defendant's use of plaintiff's identity; (2) the appropriation of plaintiff's name or likeness to defendant's advantage; (3) lack of consent; and (4) resulting injury. The theory of the right of publicity is that a celebrity's identity (such as their physical appearance) can be valuable in the promotion of products, and the celebrity has an interest that may be protected from the unauthorized commercial exploitation of that identity. In *White*, while some argued that the robot was a poor representation of Vanna White and thus not a violation of her right of publicity, the court held that the law protects the celebrity's sole right to exploit the value of her right of publicity even with a poor physical resemblance.

In addition, the right of publicity has been implicated when virtual images (for our purposes another form of embodiment) are used to represent a character. For example, in *Hart v Electronic Arts, Inc.*,[35] the image of Ryan Hart, a former quarterback for the Rutgers University football team, was used without his consent in the Electronic Arts NCAA Football video game. Hart sued Electronic Arts, alleging that it violated his right of publicity under New Jersey law by using his likeness in the NCAA Football video game series for commercial purposes. An appellate court determined that Hart's publicity rights outweighed First Amendment (or free speech) protection, reversed the lower court's grant of summary judgment and remanded the case to a district court for further proceedings.

Summarizing this section of the chapter, each of the above examples concerning a robot and virtual avatar impersonator generally reflect a different form of embodiment, offering challenges to similar laws (such as right of publicity) while at the same time challenging different areas of law as a function of embodiment. Thus, in our view, the concept of embodiment creates an interesting and complex area for the law to explore in the context of IPRs.[36]

Interestingly for trade dress law, form (or embodiment) also matters, as the following case illustrates. In *Two Pesos, Inc. v Taco Cabana*, the District Court instructed the jury:

> "[T]rade dress" is the total image of the business. Taco Cabana's trade dress may include the shape and general appearance of the exterior of the restaurant, the identifying sign, the interior kitchen floor plan, the decor, the menu, the equipment used to serve food, the servers' uniforms and other features reflecting on the total image of the restaurant.[37]

The US Court of Appeals accepted this definition and quoted from *Blue Bell Bio-Medical v CinBad, Inc.*: "The 'trade dress' of a product is essentially its total image and overall appearance."[38] It "involves the total image of a product and may include features such as size, shape, color or color combinations, texture, graphics, or even particular sales

---

[35]   *Hart v Elec. Arts, Inc.*, 717 F.3d 141 (3d Cir. 2013).
[36]   Deepak Somaya and Lav R. Varshney, Embodiment, Anthropomorphism, and Intellectual Property Rights for AI Creations, *Proceedings of the 2018 AAAI/ACM Conference on AI, Ethics, and Society* (2018).
[37]   *Two Pesos, Inc. v Taco Cabana, Inc.*, 505 U.S. 763 (1992).
[38]   *Blue Bell Bio-Medical v CinBad, Inc.*, 864 F. 2d 1253, 1256 (CA5 1989); see 932 F. 2d 1113, 1118 (CA5 1991).

techniques."[39] From the above discussion we can conclude that embodiment (in terms of form, size, shape) is relevant for patent, copyright, right of publicity, and trademark law.

3.   THE QUEST FOR HUMANIZATION OF AI: LOGICAL FALLACIES AND EMBODIMENT

We now shift our attention to the second prong of our analysis of how IPRs may relate to the embodied form of AI: a consideration of IPRs for innovative and creative AI outputs. The two main candidates to receive rights for AI-produced works are human(s) involved in helping to produce the AI-generated work (or who created the AI agent that created the work) or (more controversially) the AI itself, receiving rights for its creative output. Under current law, AI is not eligible to receive IPRs' protection. Our discussion of awarding such rights to an AI agent is therefore necessarily speculative and seeks to explore as an issue of first impression how AI embodiment may relate to IPRs.

AI already shows great potential to promote creativity, a process that has been traditionally linked to human capacities: We are no doubt entering a new era in terms of creating new forms of AI-generated artwork which will offer challenges to intellectual property law. A recent example in this vein is "Neural Artwork Art," which involves creative interactions between artists, neural networks, code, and algorithms.[40] That said, the use of computer-assisted or enhanced art is hardly a novel means of artistic expression. In fact, several artists were already experimenting with digital art to produce aesthetically pleasing creative outputs with the aid of computer software and plotters as early as the 1950s. Similarly, music has long been supported by computer based algorithmic processes.[41] Take, for example, CSIRAC (Commonwealth Scientific and Industrial Research Automatic Computer), a 1940s computer programmed to generate melodies. While the recent artistic applications of machine-learning methods such as Generative Adversarial Networks (GANs) have not fundamentally changed the process of creativity, they have blurred the boundaries between human and machine generated work and thus have resulted in challenges to intellectual property law. Indicative of this is the recent story of the "portrait of Edmond Bellamy," a GAN painting constructed in 2018 by a Paris-based arts collective that sold for $432,500, 40 times more than Christie's estimated price. In addition, there are numerous other examples of AI creating works that are normally offered protection under intellectual property law, such as movie scripts, tunes and poems, commercial ads, cartoons, paintings, various designed artifacts, and different types of inventions. As we have indicated throughout this chapter, the question of whether, and how, the output generated by AI ought to be subject to IPRs (in particular copyright or patent) is subject to much debate. In

---

[39]   *John H. Harland Co. v Clarke Checks, Inc.*, 711 F. 2d 966, 980 (CA11 1983). Restatement (Third) of Unfair Competition § 16, Comment *a* (Tent. Draft No. 2, Mar. 23, 1990). 505 U.S. 763 (1992) *Two Pesos, Inc. v Taco Cabana, Inc.*

[40]   Anthony Bourached and George Cann, Raiders of the Lost Art, *arXiv preprint arXiv:1909.05677* (2019); Florian Colombo, Alexander Seeholzer, and Wulfram Gerstner, Deep Artificial Composer: A Creative Neural Network Model for Automated Melody Generation, International Conference on Evolutionary and Biologically Inspired Music and Art. Springer, 2017.

[41]   We are grateful to Dr Panos Amelides (Bournemouth University) for this point and for bringing to our attention that we tend to wrongly conflate electronic music technologies with computer music and algorithmic composition.

particular, the question often focuses on who should be considered the author or inventor of the creative output, especially if no human was clearly involved in producing it.

The legal framework to address this debate has for the most part been that of human agency as a prerequisite for authorship. Although a complex issue of legal analysis, this is hardly a new question for certain jurisdictions, which have long considered computer-generated works. Take, for example, the report of the US National Commission of New Technological Uses (CONTU) produced in 1978, which suggested that a computer is merely facilitating fixation of human creativity and should therefore be regarded as "an inert instrument, capable of functioning only when activated either directly or indirectly by a human."[42] The technological advancements since then have made it clear that such "pen-paper" analogies are not accurate when reviewing today's sophisticated algorithmic models that are capable of producing works with limited to no human input.[43] That said, the fact that AI agents can autonomously produce works that are often indistinguishable from copyrightable human-authored counterparts (and in a manner not necessarily even foreseeable to the humans involved) has muddled the waters further. A major issue arising from autonomous AI agents producing works eligible for IPRs revolves around whether a person can still meet the inventorship or authorship criteria. As will be shown next, this has led to an attempt to humanize embodied AI. In a quest to bridge the gap between originality and ownership of AI-generated works, US scholars have suggested widening the scope for post-human considerations for AI as authors; EU policymakers, on the other hand, have put forth arguments for electronic personhood status for AI agents. The soundness of these legal arguments has been contested and we argue that they suggest logical fallacies, which demonstrate the influence embodiment has had on legal thinking.

3.1   Embodiment and the Logical Fallacy of AI as Author

The traditional concept of the author as a human entity is prevalent throughout copyright regimes, owing its roots to underpinning rationales from personality and utilitarianism theories. Although not explicitly stated within the statutes, the US Copyright Act extends copyright only to works of human authors,[44] but under a legal fiction also allows corporations to hold IPRs. This approach is often attributed to the utilitarian justifications upon which Anglo-American copyright laws are premised: namely, the need for a protective mechanism to ensure that creative expression is broadly available to incentivize creators and thus promote the public good.[45] This instrumental approach leaves little room to argue that AI generators

---

[42]   National Commission on New Technological Uses of Copyrighted Works (CONTU), Final Report 3–8 (1978) at 44.

[43]   Note here the Congressional Office of Technology Assessment's (OTA) 1986 report, which refers to CONTU's narrow understanding of computer-generated works as "misleading" and considers computers as "co-creators, rather than instruments of creation." US Congress, Office of Technology Assessment, Intellectual Property Rights in an Age of Electronics and Information, OTA-CIT-302 (Washington, DC: US Government Printing Office, April 1986).

[44]   The Compendium of US Copyright Office Practices stipulates clearly that copyright protection should be afforded to works of human authorship only ("To qualify as a work of authorship a work must be created by a human being"—313.2).

[45]   Barbara S. Murphy, Note & Comment, The Wind Done Gone: Parody or Piracy? A Comment on Suntrust Bank v. Houghton Mifflin Co., 19 Ga. St. U. L. Rev. 567, 571 (2002). For a more thorough discussion of this see William Fisher, *Theories of Intellectual Property*, Cambridge, 2001).

of works ought to be awarded copyright protection regardless of their particular embodiment. Naturally, automated creative works by agents not driven by humancentric utility incentives (seeking money, fame, and so on) need not, and would not, be affected by the incentives offered by copyright protection. Inasmuch as they lack sentience, current forms of AI do not produce works of authorship because they have been incentivized to do so.[46]

Conceptually, ownership of intellectual property should not really matter to current embodiments of AI agents, as they produce intellectual property-protected works regardless of incentives offered. This view, however, perceives outputs of human–machine interaction in a narrow, binary manner that offers little guidance to the complex synergies actually occurring between human and AI agents that are responsible for the production of AI-generated works. By attributing such works solely to an algorithm (or for that matter any AI technique), the approach overlooks the fact that current AI-generated works involve a certain degree of interactivity and independently creative inputs of the programmer as well as the user; that is, we are not at the point where AI creates intellectual property protected works on its own initiative.[47] Under current scenarios, the AI agent embodied as a machine is programmed to perform in a particular manner by the programmer, while its outputs are instructed (and to a certain extent customized) by the user. Under current copyright law, for an AI-generated work to be produced and to be publicly disseminated, the policy to offer incentives to the human actors involved in the production chain is still relevant. In this vein, Denicola has observed that in focusing on the question of whether to regard computers as authors (and thus copyright owners), or for that matter AI agents as authors meriting copyright protection, we might be asking the wrong questions.[48] Instead, he argues, we should allow for a broad definitional scope of the author as the originator of creative expression; this includes the (human) user who initiates creation and brings AI works into the marketplace. This approach has intuitive appeal; however, it does not account for a future where AI agents may in fact independently produce works protected by intellectual property law, with no human involvement, or without the types of incentive which motivate humans to invent or produce works of authorship.

Be that as it may, as we indicated above, current copyright law requires a human author to attribute ownership to a "construct denoting merely the initial owner of all rights,"[49] which are predominantly economic rights. When placed in the context of AI creations, it becomes clear that there is very limited possibility[50] to acknowledge copyright protection for AI or for computer-generated works (note the United Kingdom directly protects computer-generated

---

[46] This is different to the incentives driving innovation that are provided for the human operators involved in AI-generated works, such as programmers and software engineers. For a relevant discussion see Pamela Samuelson, Allocating Ownership Rights in Computer-Generated Works, 47 U. Pitt L. Rev. 1185, 1199 (1986).

[47] While the AI may work autonomously from humans, a human is still in the loop (somewhere) in terms of providing intent.

[48] Robert C. Denicola, Ex Machina: Copyright Protection for Computer Generated Works, 69 Rutgers U. L. Rev. 251 (2016), at 271.

[49] 'Authorship is an entirely human endeavor': *Patry treatise* § 3:19 (2010). Authors of copyrightable works must be human; works owing their form to the forces of nature cannot be copyrighted. *Ibid* § 3:19 n. 1; *see also* US Copyright Office, Compendium II: Copyright Office Practices § 503.03(a) ("[A] work must be the product of human authorship" and not the forces of nature) (1984); *Ibid* § 202.02(b).

[50] Peter Jaszi has criticized this romanticized view of authorship as potentially misleading for decision makers in the digital era. Peter Jaszi, On the Author Effect: Contemporary Copyright and Collective Creativity, 10 Cardozo Arts & Ent. L.J. 293 (1991), at 320.

works); interestingly, what seems to matter is not the level of creativity (AI produced or not), but whether these can be attributed to human authorship. This construct, molded after the romantic vision of the human author as the sole creator of a work (thus tracing its source of originality to one's human mind and soul), has been deeply ingrained in copyright law and further supported by theories of natural rights and rights-based notions of property. At the same time, this narrative of a profoundly human creator able to produce original works *ex nihilo* has not gone without criticism: in maintaining a narrow individualistic view, this argument pays little attention to exogenous social forces that produce collaborative elements in creative outputs.[51] These shortcomings now appear more exposed than ever: with current technology, AI and particularly algorithmically generated works are predominantly the intellectual output of multilayered man–machine synergies. But unlike the model of AI/computer-assisted tasks, machine learning outputs indicate a high degree of AI autonomy, which suggests creativity might not be a privilege of human intellect only.[52] For many scholars,[53] the information society and advancements in AI have in fact challenged this romantic concept of creativity as the sole output of human intellect and are asking for an evolved dehumanized understanding of authorship. At this point in the discussion, we raise the following question: Has AI disrupted authorship to the extent that we need to employ a posthuman approach to reconstruct this concept beyond the romanticism of the sole human author? And would the particular form or embodiment of AI matter in the discussion?

A large body of literature has already explored in depth the scope for AI authorship under our current copyright regime; a "no question" for Grimmelman, who observes: "I would like to talk about computer-authored works—I would like to, except that they don't exist. Copyright law doesn't recognize computer programs as authors, and [according to Grimmelman] it shouldn't. Someday it might make sense to, but if that day ever comes, copyright will be the least of our concerns."[54] He further posits that AI-generated works simply reiterate old questions: although difficult to address, these questions relate more to the copyrightability of computer software programs as processes and less to authorship. So why is it, then, that legal scholars are intrigued by the idea of creating hybrids (such as AI authorship) as a means of legally acknowledging their existence?

There is no doubt that authorship is an ideologically charged tool that has served its purpose well: in fact, the romantic vision of the author seen through an individualistic humanized prism has been conceived as a response to industrialization so that human creativity could be protected against automated mass production. This further explains how the idea of "AI

---

[51]   Peter Jaszi, Toward a Theory of Copyright: The Metamorphoses of "Authorship," in *Intellectual Property Law and History* (Routledge, 2017) 61–108; Martha Woodmansee, The Genius and the Copyright: Economic and Legal Conditions of the Emergence of the "Author," 17:4 *Eighteenth-century Studies* 425–88 (1984).

[52]   Agyro Karanasiou and Dimitris Pinotsis, A Study into the Layers of Automated Decision-making: Emergent Normative and Legal Aspects of Deep Learning, 31:2 *International Review of Law, Computers & Technology* (2017) 170–87.

[53]   Annemarie Bridy, Coding Creativity: Copyright and the Artificially Intelligent Author, 5 Stan. Tech. L. Rev. 1–28 (2012); Margot E. Kaminski, Authorship, Disrupted: AI Authors in Copyright and First Amendment Law, 51 UCDL Rev. 589 (2017); James Boyle, *Shamans, Software, and Spleens: Law and the Construction of the Information Society*, Harvard University Press, 2009.

[54]   James Grimmelmann, There's No Such Thing as a Computer-authored Work—and It's a Good Thing, Too, 39 Colum. JL & Arts 403 (2015), at 403.

author" can be thought of as an oxymoron: that is, in trying to broaden the definitional scope of "author" to include AI systems we are accepting that human intellect is not a unique source of originality, and that artificial intelligence offers a sufficient causal link between a machine and a creation. This, however, is not accurate under current legal thinking: from the Poet's muse to a neural network's operation, the neurons—artificial or not—are fired as a result of human interaction. Thus, given human involvement in the creation of intellectual property-protected works, perhaps the approach to be taken to authorship is—and always should be—human. Alternatively, it may be that the embodiment of AI may influence whether AI should receive rights, which of course will be a more pressing conversation as AI becomes more autonomous and eventually displays an intent to create. In the remainder of this chapter, we outline how embodiment has influenced such arguments over AI authorship and has contributed to a trend to humanize AI in a quest to inform our legal understanding of AI generated works. Next, we turn to another logical fallacy arguing for legally framing AI as persons, which too has been influenced by embodiment; this time, coming from Europe.

3.2   Embodiment and the Logical Fallacy of AI Personhood

In our discussion of AI embodiment we have indicated that due to current advances in AI, and particularly machine learning, the use of AI can lead to a story being written or an invention developed with little or no involvement of a human author or inventor (again, however, the AI currently lacks the intent to be creative). As already discussed, regardless of the form of embodiment, under copyright law the computer housing the AI software or the software itself is not considered the author or inventor of the work. As the law evolves to account for the actions of increasingly smart and autonomous AI, if the story was written by a humanoid appearing robot as opposed to a desktop or laptop computer, would legislators be more likely to grant the human-appearing entity (in form and behavior) copyright protection for their works?[55] In other words, would embodiment matter? While one could argue here that embodiment does matter for the human perception of an embodied AI agent, going forward, our view is that the embodiment of an AI agent may also be enough to trigger discussion of rights for AI agents—consider the right of publicity law discussed above: for right of publicity, the appearance of an image or its sound is critical for the cause of action.

It is universally accepted that an AI agent has no legal person status or legal standing. The concept of artificial personhood, however, is hardly a novel idea: the idea of "persona ficta" (non-human entities that have personhood status) has its roots in ancient Roman law and has since given rise to entities other than humans possessing legal rights. Regarding IPRs, non-human entities often engage in the unorthodox practice of using intellectual property to reduce their tax liability by shifting income under current law.[56] The extent to which this could lend an argument for AI inventorship is still unclear; yet it appears to be appealing. Take for example, the Artificial Inventor Project, where Ryan Abbott and colleagues sought to apply

---

[55]   Deepak Somaya and Lav R. Varshney, Embodiment, Anthropomorphism, and Intellectual Property Rights for AI Creations, AIES 18: Proceedings of the 2018 AAAI/ACM Conference on AI, Ethics, and Society, December 2018, 278–83.

[56]   Mihailis Diamantis, The Extended Corporate Mind: When Corporations Use AI to Break the Law, 98 N.C. L. Rev. (2019–20) 893.

for patents for the robot inventor DABUS.[57] Recently, under Australian patent law, the court decided that DABUS could be recognized as an inventor but held that the robot could not apply for a patent, nor receive patent rights for its inventions. In a similar vein, in South Africa, the Artificial Inventor Project successfully obtained the first patent for an AI-generated invention without a traditional human inventor.[58] Such developments indicate that there might be good scope for considering legal protection for AI-generated outputs, even when a human agent may well be out of the loop.

On this point, the European Union has been discussing the issue of granting personhood status to intelligent robots during the past few years, and appropriately part of the conversation has revolved around the issue of how to define the entity which would receive legal person status. In 2017 the EU Parliament adopted a Resolution calling on the Commission to explore the possibility of creating a specific legal status for robots.[59] This recommendation was met with widespread opposition: in an open letter to the Commission, individuals from 14 countries expressed their concerns over granting legal personhood to robots as potentially allowing manufacturers to absolve themselves of liability. Moreover, they challenged the legal basis for awarding electronic personhood status to robots and attributed what they termed an over-evaluation of robots to "a robot perception distorted by Science-Fiction and a few recent sensational press announcements."[60]

As it stands, the European Parliament, in three Resolutions[61] adopted in 2020 on the ethical and legal aspects of AI software systems, explicitly rules out the potential for awarding legal status and, by extension, IP rights to robots[62] and other artificially intelligent agents. Be that as it may, all relevant EU discussions revolve around robotic forms of embodied AI;[63] it

---

[57]   Ryan Abbott, Tita Matulionyte, and Paul Nolan, A Brief Analysis of DABUS, Artificial Intelligence and the Future of Patent Law, *Intellectual Property Forum: Journal of the Intellectual and Industrial Property Society of Australia and New Zealand*, Article 01, 10–16, September 2021.

[58]   In this case, the patent is owned by the AI's owner but the patent names the AI which devised the invention as the inventor.

[59]   Under 59 (f): Calls on the Commission, when carrying out an impact assessment of its future legislative instrument, to explore the implications of all possible legal solutions, such as: […] (f) creating a specific legal status for robots, so that at least the most sophisticated autonomous robots could be established as having the status of electronic persons with specific rights and obligations, including that of making good any damage they may cause, and applying electronic personality to cases where robots make smart autonomous decisions or otherwise interact with third parties independently: www.europarl.europa.eu/doceo/document/TA-8-2017-0051_EN.html?redirect.

[60]   www.politico.eu/wp-content/uploads/2018/04/RoboticsOpenLetter.pdf.

[61]   Resolution 2020/2012(INL) on a Framework of Ethical Aspects of Artificial Intelligence, Robotics and Related Technologies (the "AI Ethical Aspects Resolution"), Resolution 2020/2014(INL) on a Civil Liability Regime for Artificial Intelligence (the "Civil Liability Resolution"), and Resolution 2020/2015(INI) on Intellectual Property Rights for the Development of Artificial Intelligence Technologies (the "IPR for AI Resolution").

[62]   The Parliament further "notes that the autonomisation of the creative process of generating content of an artistic nature can raise issues relating to the ownership of IPRs covering that content; considers, in this connection, that it would not be appropriate to seek to impart legal personality to AI technologies and points out the negative impact of such a possibility on incentives for human creators" (IPR for AI Resolution, ibid, at 14).

[63]   Note also the report prepared for the European Trade Union Institute, mentioned earlier in this chapter, where Aida Ponce Del Castillo commented that to grant rights to robots and AI we need to first determine how we should refer to robots, artificial agents, or autonomous artificial agents, and discuss the likely consequences of such a distinction. Aida Ponce del Castillo, A Law on Robotics and Artificial

therefore becomes clear that—at least indirectly—embodiment has played a key part in the relevant debate. The concept of personhood has traditionally been a rather controversial area with several philosophical reflections and clear human exceptionalism origins. Of course, legal personhood does not strictly presuppose human biology. That said, legal considerations of personhood have been closely interlinked with the attributes of human personality, often involving bodily integrity (writ of habeas corpus).[64] This might explain the EP 2017 resolution considering electronic personhood for embodied AI (robots)—a proposition that some scholars deem is not adequately justified because robots are non-sentient and lack subjective awareness. Moreover, it appears to have led legal scholars to another fallacy: considering granting personhood rights to robots has been regarded as a "morally unnecessary and legally troublesome"[65] decision, which exploits robotic embodiment to diffuse liability from human actors.

There is no doubt that the intellectual property rights system is quintessentially anthropocentric: Under current patent statutes only a human may receive patent rights for an invention or copyright for a work of authorship. Similarly, copyright regulatory framework is inherently human-centered, either via ample textual references or via person-specific provisions, such as nationality or the life of the author.[66] This is further influenced by personality rights theories in copyright, echoing views from Kant and Hegel that one's personality or will is reflected in one's work and as such should be protected as an expression of self. To own rights, AI agents will need to have legal status. Although non-natural persons may be awarded legal rights, computers lack a legal personhood so that they are not granted any property rights at all, let alone IPRs. This, however, should not suggest that AI-generated works with no human creator lack originality. Ownership often goes hand in hand with authorship and creativity; however, in AI-generated works, these need to be reviewed separately: the fact that a computer cannot be granted author rights should not preclude originality of its outputs.[67] To put this differently: a work with limited or no human input may still be considered original and thus copyrightable provided it has a sufficient nexus to human creativity - this has been argued in a number of cases that have been executed by humans as instructed by celestial beings[68] or in which

---

Intelligence in the EU? (October 3, 2017). ETUI Research Paper—Foresight Brief #02-September 2017, Available at SSRN: https://ssrn.com/abstract=3180004.

[64]   A theme that is most prevalent in court decisions granting legal rights to animals. Take for example Manhattan Supreme Court Justice Barbara Jaffe's order to Stony Brook University that two chimpanzees be released under a writ of habeas corpus from confinement for biomedical research, www.animals24-7 .org/2016/11/08/argentinian-court-grants-zoo-chimp-a-writ-of-habeas-corpus/

[65]   Joanna J. Bryson, Mihailis E. Diamantis, and Thomas D. Grant, Of, For, and By the People: the Legal Lacuna of Synthetic Persons, 25:3 *Artificial Intelligence and Law* 273–91 (2017), at 291.

[66]   Ginsburg refers to the Berne Convention's "humanist cast," as a framework that operates on the presumption of the author as "human." Jane Ginsburg, People Not Machines: Authorship and What It Means in the Berne Convention, 49 International Review of Intellectual Property and Competition Law 131–5 (2018).

[67]   Nina I. Brown, Artificial Authors: A Case for Copyright in Computer-Generated Works, 20 Colum. Sci. & Tech. L. Rev. (2018) 1t, 24–7.

[68]   *Cummings v Bond* (discussing authorship of automatic writing attributed to spiritual voices); *Urantia Found v Maaherra* (discussing authorship of a book as a result of epochal religious revelation).

creative works have been attributed to exogenous natural forces,[69] So, what has given rise to arguments over granting legal personhood to robots, an embodied form of AI?

Receiving legal status might be the result of AI agents becoming more similar to humans not only in the type of abilities they have and tasks they perform, but also [in the future] in having "self-awareness" or "self-consciousness." As Frosio argues, "(t)he standard the AI fails to reach is qualitative rather than quantitative. AI cannot express 'self' and the creativity that it generates cannot express the personality of the author because AI has none."[70] If this is the case, then it would not only be AI agents' legal status that would affect our debate; inherently interwoven with it would be the characteristics that led to their legal status in the first place (in other words, if AI agents receive legal status because they are self-conscious and capable of "understanding" right from wrong, and so on, then these qualities in themselves may be most significant in our discussion of whether to grant them intellectual property ownership in works they have created).

Let us leave the above discussion and focus on the scenario, which is not implausible, that AI agents receive some aspect of legal personhood in the near future regardless of further developments in their self-consciousness or self-awareness. To some extent, recent discussions on granting AI with legal status is related to their embodiment. For example, when proposing the notion of granting legal status of an "electronic person" to robots, the European Parliament called the Commission "to propose common Union definitions of cyber *physical* systems, autonomous systems, smart autonomous robots and their subcategories by taking into consideration the following characteristics […] the acquisition of autonomy through *sensors* and/or by exchanging data with its environment (inter-connectivity) and the trading and analyzing of those data."

In addition to the question of whether the physical existence (or non-physical existence) of the AI agent is of relevance to the question of awarding intellectual property protection to its creative output, the diverse list of potential AI agents presented in the introduction (robots, avatars, chatbots, and so on) raises the additional question of whether all forms of embodiment would be equal under the different intellectual property rights schemes.

4.   EMBODIMENT AND LEGAL PERCEPTION OF AI

Moving away from logical fallacies used to humanize AI agents and thereby inform underpinning intellectual property right rationales, let us now focus more closely on embodiment and the manner it may affect our understanding of (non-human) creativity. Whether an AI entity has a physical manifestation might be of great relevance in certain legal contexts (for example, the tort of assault or the crime of rape) but be meaningless in others (for example corporate corruption). For the purpose of granting IPRs for AI agents, it seems that physical embodiment itself is currently not a key factor. For example, consider an algorithm directing the actions of a virtual avatar, where there is no physical body, yet the algorithm may be proprietary and thus

[69]   *Kelley v Chicago Park Dist*, 635 F.3d 290 (7th Cir. 2011). Note also *Naruto v Slater*, 888 F.3d 418, 426 (9th Cir. 2018) (holding that animals lack legal standing to sue for copyright infringement).
[70]   Giancarlo Frosio, Is the Machine an Author? (February 28, 2021). In Artificial Intelligence in the Audiovisual Sector (European Audiovisual Observatory, IRIS Special 2020-2, 2020) Available at https://rm.coe.int/iris-special-2-2020en-artificial-intelligence-in-the-audiovisual-secto/1680a11e0b.

a trade secret. It may direct the actions of an image which itself may be the subject of copyright protection, in turn leading to actions which implicate different areas of law.[71] In this example, copyright (for the image) may apply to the disembodied virtual avatar.[72] As mentioned in the introduction, our discussion of embodiment in the context of IPRs is not limited only to the binary question of whether the agent has a physical presence in the world or not. Instead, the *type* of presence in the world (virtual or physical) resulting from the AI agent *might* be significant when IPRs are concerned. We will therefore include "social valence," as used by Ryan Calo,[73] as part of our discussion of embodiment. For the purposes of our analysis, in this section of the chapter we will consider embodiment as a manifestation of "morphism," namely the corporeal embodiment of AI, and anthropomorphism, namely embodied AI that brings to mind human elements and features (either physical or mental).

4.1   Morphism: Affordance to Physically Perform Tasks Once Reserved for Humans

In considering Ignacio Cofone's comparison between a humanoid robot and a hypothetical AI-driven toaster,[74] it is clear that both entities represent distinct forms of physical embodiment whose different affordances mean various ways of interacting with the world. Do different affordances to interact with the environment matter when IPRs are concerned? Naturally, in the absence of certain affordances, AI agents will simply not be able to create certain types of protected works. To consider creations which are protected under copyrights, for example, certain types of work may be created by online algorithms, regardless of their physical affordances. Literary works, musical works, graphic works, and the design of architectural works may all be created without any physical interaction with the physical world. Embodiment, however, may in certain cases be manifested in a digital form, and in any event AI-generated works may be created by the AI agent regardless of its physical form and later embodied in a physical manner (for example, an architectural design created by an algorithm, or a toaster for that matter, could later be displayed on a screen or also printed out physically).

Embodiment matters in yet another way as certain types of copyrightable works may simply not be generated by AI agents lacking certain physical affordances. For example, pantomimes and choreographic works are based on physical movement. An algorithm lacks the affordances to create them. However, a robot may indeed move and use the movements necessary to create pantomime or choreography. A Maryland case on the point is *Comptroller v Family Entertainment*,[75] which required a decision on whether life-sized, automated, mechanical puppets displayed in restaurants were actually "performing" so that any receipts from the sale of refreshments or from admission fees were properly taxable under § 402(a) of Maryland State law.

---

[71]   *MAI Systems Corp. v Peak Computer, Inc.*, 991 F. 2d 511,Court of Appeals, 9th Circuit 1993 (discussing copyright issues for software).

[72]   Tom Ziemke, What's This Thing Called Embodiment? *Proceedings of the Annual Meeting of the Cognitive Science Society*, Vol. 25, 1305–10.

[73]   Calo*, supra* note 3 at 10.

[74]   Ignacio Cofone, Servers and Waiters: What Matters in the Law of A.I., 21 *Stanford Technology Law Review* 167 (2018).

[75]   *Comptroller v Family Entertainment*, 519 A.2d 1337 (Md. Ct. Spec. App. 1987).

4.2   Does Anthropomorphism Matter?

In our discussion of embodiment, an AI agent's resemblance to human beings may also be significant in our inclination to grant AI entities with rights, including IPRs, as well as in our utilitarian motivation for doing so. Here we argue that the physical resemblance of the AI agent to humans might lead to anthropomorphism prima facie and thus, perhaps, influence the decision to award rights to AI agents with more ease (contributing to the logical fallacies discussed above). We suggest that the extent of the "mental resemblance" to humans in terms of whether an AI agent could respond to the incentives within intellectual property law might also influence our decision to render AI agents eligible for IPRs. Of course, as we discussed above, current versions of AI agents do not independently create intellectual property protected works based on incentives, but with AI capabilities expanding rapidly, it is interesting to think about how such developments might affect rights afforded under intellectual property law.

The human need to personify non-human entities and enclothe them in a more familiar setting is not new: in fact, ancient Greek mythology provides good examples of attributing human traits to inanimate things, natural phenomena, or even gods in a quest to embrace uncertainty and understand the world in an anthropocentric framing. Roboticists have long battled with the challenge to "formalize the way 'intelligence' and the 'emergence of an autonomous behaviour' [in a manner that could be] legitimately attributed to robots without violating any form of common sense or rationality."[76] The question they were presented with was whether to use embodiment as a means of aesthetics or functionality: Should robots look realistically human or should their anthropomorphism be basic so that we perceive them as a social agent with which we can interact? The latter view seems to have prevailed. Namely, social robots have enough anthropomorphic traits to be perceived as artificial agents able to carry out tasks once reserved for humans only. Their anthropomorphism is not perfect, by choice[77]—it is only used to provide sufficient social cues to perceive them as autonomous agents able to interact with humans. To put this differently, recognizing some human qualities/features in embodied AI facilitates our interpretation and social expectations. To a certain extent it further influences our legal expectations too.

Jack Balkin has observed how anthropomorphism in robots triggers more than just a heightened emotional response: we are not fooled by appearances into thinking that robots are humans; rather, we are willing to accept them as ad hoc quasi-rea, namely "special-purpose human beings" that, depending on the task they perform, assume the role of either a person or an instrument.[78] He calls this the "substitution effect": robots are not considered equal to humans but rather "only equivalent provisionally, in certain contexts or for certain purposes, and people often reserve the right to reject the asserted identity when it suits them."[79] In other words, when trying to frame robots in a socio-legal setting, we do not simply project agency or

---

[76]   Denis Vidal, Anthropomorphism or Sub-anthropomorphism? An Anthropological Approach to Gods and Robots, 13:4 *Journal of the Royal Anthropological Institute* 917–33 (2007), at 924.

[77]   Masahiro Mori, Karl F. MacDorman, and Norri Kageki, The Uncanny Valley (from the Field), 19:2 *IEEE Robotics & Automation Magazine* 98–100 (2012).

[78]   Jack B. Balkin, The Path of Robotics Law, 6 Cal. L. Rev 45–70 (2015), at 57. In a similar vein, Calo refers to "a new category of legal subject halfway between person and object" (Calo at 549), yet—unlike Balkin, who attributes this to human opportunism—he offers an emotional explanation instead: we are wired to respond this way to anthropomorphism.

[79]   Ibid.

emotions into inanimate beings, but we further do so in an opportunistic manner. This explains how "anthropomorphic embodiment" is often used as a vessel for constructing a legal fiction that allows us to frame AI in law. In short, and as noted in the discussion above, their legal identity too exists in the eye of the observer, and embodiment certainly helps to build this narrative a la carte. Below we explore further how anthropomorphism might influence (either intuitively or purposively) legal perception of embodied AI.

4.3   Physical Resemblance

By anthropomorphism we mean the attribution of humanlike characteristics to nonhuman entities, such as embodied AI agents. Past research has shown that people anthropomorphize technology and that the shape or appearance of the technology matters in terms of how people interact with the technology. For example, Wainer and colleagues tested the hypothesis that physical embodiment has a measurable effect on social interactions between robots and humans.[80] Their research revealed that participants felt that an embodied robot was more appealing and perceptive of the world than a non-embodied robot. Reflecting our view that different forms of AI embodiment may lead to different behaviors that may implicate the law, Fischer, Lohan, and Foth investigated the role of physical embodiment of a robot and its degrees of freedom in human–robot interaction.[81] Both factors have been suggested to be relevant in definitions of embodiment. Results showed that both physical embodiment and degrees of freedom of motion influenced interaction, and that the effect of physical embodiment is located in the interpersonal domain, concerning how the robot may be perceived as an interaction partner, whereas degrees of freedom influence the way users project the suitability of the robot for a particular task.

In addition, Haring and her colleagues[82] found that when it comes to robot design, the anthropomorphism level of the robot form (that is, appearance) is an increasingly important variable to consider. Haring argued that people base their expectations and perceptions of a robot on its form and attribute functions which do not necessarily mirror the true functions of the robot. The term "form function attribution bias" (FFAB) refers to the cognitive bias which occurs when people are prone to perceptual errors, leading to a biased interpretation of a robot's functionality. Haring and colleagues argued that rather than objectively perceiving the robot's functionalities, people take a cognitive shortcut using the information available to them through visual perception.

---

[80]   Joshua Wainer, David J. Feil-Seifer, and Dylan A. Shell Maja, Embodiment and Human-Robot Interaction: A Task-Based Perspective, 16th IEEE International Conference on Robot & Human Interactive Communication, August 26–29, 2007, Jeju, Korea.

[81]   K. Fischer, K. Lohan, and, K. Foth, Levels of Embodiment: Linguistic Analyses of Factors Influencing HRI,   7th ACM IEEE International Conference on Human-Robot Interaction, 463–70 (2012).

[82]   K.S. Haring, K. Watanabe, M. Velonaki, C.C. Tossell, and V. Finomore, FFAB—The Form Function Attribution Bias in Human-Robot Interaction, 10:4 *IEEE Transactions on Cognitive and Developmental Systems* 843–51 (2018).

4.4   "Mental" Resemblance and Philosophical Musings

For the past forty years, specialists in the field of robotics have taken a "behaviour-based approach"[83] and have been regarding embodiment as a vessel for a dialogical process in social settings. It could thus be argued that embodiment allows robots to be observed as intelligent,[84] making artificial intelligence a relative, fluid concept. This has not left intellectual property law unaffected:[85] as we have shown above, this subjective understanding of "artificial intelligence" has led to logical fallacies, such as the considerations of electronic personhood and AI as an author. It has been suggested that the human element in copyright is often found in the "intention to produce mental effects in an audience by external manifestation of behaviour."[86] It is, however, not clear whether a work is considered original (and thus copyrightable) if this is an expression of a human mind or an expression that is perceived as human. This aesthetic appeal to the reader, who is perceiving this work as a product of human intellect, is central to copyright.[87] To what extent can we fit embodied cognition into the intellectual property framework that operates on a human-centered narrative?

Referring back to our earlier discussion on embodiment, while the justifications for granting IPRs are diverse; ultimately they all are based on the creators' self-awareness or self-consciousness. For example, Locke's approach by which individuals are entitled to the fruits of their labor[88] may, when applied to AI agents, be meaningful only when the agents could be said to be engaged in "labor" or have some understanding as to the fact they are producing work, rather than functioning automatically. The work products of an automatic assembly line machinery or a weaving machine, for instance, would not be subject to Locke's theory, as the machine producing the work-products would not be considered as having "worked." While "understanding one's actions" itself is not necessarily the precise difference that would render the efforts invested by an entity "work" (as we would surely treat the efforts of a brain-damaged person with no understanding of their actions as work), it seems intuitive that a threshold requirement would be some sort of self-awareness.

Similarly, personality theory underpins moral rights as expressive projections of one's personality, namely rights that "spring from a belief that an artist in the process of creation injects his spirit into the work."[89] This relies too on the assumption that the creator has "more to it" than a collection of merely physical elements that physically allow the creation of the

---

[83]   See e.g. Minsky's original 1968 definition of AI as "[t]he science of making machines do things that would require intelligence if done by men": M Minsky (ed), *Semantic Information Processing*, MIT Press, 1968, preface.

[84]   "[Robots] are observed to be intelligent—but the source of intelligence is not limited to just the computational engine. It also comes from the situation in the world, the signal transformations within the sensors, and the physical coupling of the robot with the world". Rodney Allen Brooks, *Cambrian Intelligence: The Early History of the New AI*, MIT Press, 1999, pp.138–9.

[85]   Human perception has been a key concept for copyright protection. Note 17 U.S.C. § 101 (2020): "Copyright protection subsists, in accordance with this title, in original works of authorship fixed in any tangible medium of expression, now known or later developed, from which they can be perceived, reproduced, or otherwise communicated, either directly or with the aid of a machine or device."

[86]   Christopher Buccafusco, A Theory of Copyright Authorship, 102 Va. L. Rev. 1229 (2016).

[87]   *Bleistein v Donaldson Lithographing Company*, 188 U.S. 239 (1903) at 250.

[88]   Jeremy Waldron, Property and Ownership, STAN. ENCYCLOPEDIA PHIL. (Sept. 6, 2004), https://plato.stanford.edu/entries/property/.

[89]   *Carter v Helmsley-Spear, Inc.*, 861 F. Supp. 303, 324–5 (S.D.N.Y. 1994).

protected work. Self-awareness or some sort of own "individuality" is required for a "personality" to materialize. Lastly, utilitarian approaches that justify IPRs based on providing incentives for creation and innovation are also based on the fact that the creator understands the consequences of receiving (or not receiving) IPRs and has self-awareness as to the choices it wishes to make in response to said incentives. Indeed, it seems that AI agents' similarity to humans in the amorphic aspect of "self-awareness" or "consciousness" is of great significance when it comes to the reasons we grant IPRs in the first place.

While some believe that no embodiment is necessary for AI agents to acquire knowledge and engage in activities that trigger the law,[90] other scholars, such as Varela, Thompson, and Rosch argue that knowledge depends on "being in a world that is inseparable from our bodies […] in short [resulting] from our embodiment."[91] According to the approach of emergentism,[92] conscious experience may emerge only in complex systems, where the whole is greater than the sum of its parts. In other words, according to said theory there is a "magical threshold" of complexity, after which consciousness unexplainably emerges. The more AI agents are similar to human beings in terms of their cognitive and mental abilities, the more the intellectual property justifications apply to them as well.

To take the utilitarian approach as an example, it is consciousness that motivates us. Consciousness can shape our objectives and thus influence our choices.[93] So long as AI agents are indifferent to drives that characterize human beings, such as the desire to survive, to care for others, express curiosity, to help others, to lead a certain life, and so on, then the "judgment" the agent would make, if any, would be very foreign to us, such that incentivization mechanisms intended for persons would not necessarily affect AI agents or work on them in a similar manner. Returning to the issue of embodiment, the more different an AI agent's embodiment is from that of a person, the less likely it is that its consciousness or "self-awareness" would allow it to make choices and judgments similar to those of humans. Thus, if an AI agent cannot sense the world like humans do (feel no physical pain or pleasure, lack the ability to experience the different senses, enjoy or fear different aspects of physical life, and so on) then an intellectual property incentive mechanism based on motivation to exploit IPRs for monetary or reputational gains might either be completely irrelevant when AI agents are concerned, or affect them in manners we cannot anticipate: "Consciousness arising from physical structures radically different from ours and attained through a process dramatically unlike our evolutionary history may lead to phenomenal experiences that we cannot even imagine."[94]

The above discussion leads to the idea of embodied cognition and situated cognition and how these examples of embodiment relate to intellectual property law. According to some commentators, cognition is situated; that is, cognitive activity takes place in the context of a real-world environment, and it inherently involves perception and action. Additionally, the idea of "situated cognition" suggests that knowledge cannot be separated from the context or situation in which it was acquired. Therefore, what is meant by situated is that learning is connected to a culture, place, activity, or social situation. Whereas embodied cognition is the

---

[90]   Riegler, *supra* note 18.
[91]   Ziemke, *supra* note 15.
[92]   John R. Searle, *The Mystery of Consciousness*, New York Review of Books, 1990, at 18, 22.
[93]   Joshua P. Davis, AI, Ethics, and Law: A Possible Way Forward, in *Artificial Intelligence and Private Law: Global Perspectives* (Larry Di Matteo, ed.), Cambridge University Press, 2022.
[94]   Ibid.

idea that the mind is not only connected to the body but that the body influences the mind, that is, our cognition is influenced, perhaps determined by, our experiences in the physical world as a function of our body. This idea applies not only to people but to AI-directed entities as well.

5.   CONCLUDING REMARKS

In this chapter we have shown that embodiment matters in the context of intellectual property law for AI agents in two main ways. The first is that copyright and patent law directly applies to various forms of embodied AI. For example, copyright law applies to the visual appearance of a virtual avatar, and patent law applies to the physical features of embodied AI agents, such as the ornamental design features of a robot. In both cases, current law (such as copyright, patent, and trademark) can be used to resolve disputes which may arise as a result of the design and use of artificially intelligent agents.

The second way in which embodiment offers challenges to intellectual property law revolves around the question of whether the output of an AI agent is eligible for intellectual property protection and, if so, who should be considered the author or inventor of the work. As we indicated in this chapter, current intellectual property law precludes an AI entity from receiving IPRs for its creative output. However, there is discussion within different jurisdictions as to whether granting rights to intelligent agents may be necessary. In our view, the field of intellectual property law is an especially important area to consider when discussing rights for AI agents, given the economic value of intellectual property.

In this chapter, we have also discussed how the concept of embodiment has led to logical fallacies in the discussion of granting rights to embodied AI agents. Here we noted current discussions within the EU regarding granting rights to robots. And by extension to current EU initiates, as AI agents continue to gain in intelligence and autonomy, some have argued that it may become necessary to grant AI agents rights. In this context, we have also pointed to specific and relevant differences of embodied versus unembodied creators of works in relation to the different justifications for granting IPRs to begin with. We have shown that physical embodiment may, at least to a certain extent, affect the manner in which future AI agents will interpret and act upon different incentives in the basis of IP rights.

To conclude, the overall point we wished to make in this chapter is that as AI agents become smarter and more closely resemble humans in appearance and mental abilities, their embodiment may be an important consideration in whether such entities receive rights. We acknowledge that this is a challenging, somewhat controversial, and future-oriented discussion, but we think it is warranted by developments in AI and the law.

4. AI replication of musical styles points the way to an exclusive rights regime
Sean M. O'Connor[1]

1. INTRODUCTION

Style is hard to define. We think we know when someone has it. We feel smart when we recognize a pattern of style. But style's ephemeralness makes it difficult to pin down, analyze, quantify. Contrast this with our intellectual property (IP) regimes in which fixed expression, definite claims, or demonstrable use in commerce are the respective threshold requirements for protection eligibility. Accordingly, style has an uneven status as protectible subject matter across IP regimes.

This chapter focuses on musical styles in which the author has experience as a composer and performer across multiple genres. For many musicians, replicating another artist's style is not hard or particularly mysterious. In some cases, such as electric guitar, style is as much about knowing the gear—choosing guitars, amps, pedals; tweaking settings; and the different playing methods and responsiveness of the foregoing combined—as it is about what notes are played. In composition, it is about recognizing the "go to" patterns of building-block melodies, riffs, chords, voicings, rhythms, percussion, and so on used by a particular composer.

The complication of musical style is that there seems to be an ineffable expression of personality that comes through when our most distinctive composers and performers exercise their craft. So, while others can create a reasonable simulacrum of the notable composer's or performer's style, the attuned listener may still discern that it is a "copycat." Yet, other listeners may not care even if they can tell that a composition or performance is a copycat of their favorite style where they can more readily access the copycat or it is cheaper, or especially if it is free.

At the same time, many (most?) emerging composers and performers are striving to discover their *own* "voice." Other than tribute bands and soundalike/lookalike performers, the path to success is *distinctiveness* and originality (in the artistic not copyright sense). The artist needs to stand out in an extremely crowded field. If her compositions or performances are entirely fungible with those of her fellow artists, then she may find steady work—if she is reliable in both showing up and producing—but she will not break out to be her own star. In this way, the most ambitious composers and performers do not want to seem *derivative*—in the artistic sense—of others' style. Accordingly, there is some degree of self-regulation in music from what might otherwise be slavish copying of distinctive musical styles.

Further complications for IP eligibility of musical styles set the stage for this chapter. First, there is a longstanding thread within some courts and commentators that a main musical

---

[1]   The author wishes to thank Robert Brauneis, Joseph Fishman, Joe Bennett, K.J. Greene, Steven Jamar, Peter Vay, and most especially the editor of this volume, Ryan Abbott, for encouraging me to cover this topic. All errors are the author's own.

melody is the *sine qua non* of musical composition copyright, with other elements such as harmony and rhythm playing an incidental, largely unprotectible role.[2] While this does not necessarily preclude style as protectible, the author's view is that compositional style is found more often—or more noticeably—in the harmonic and rhythmic elements in which a particular melody sits than within the melody isolated on its own.

Second, while an artist's stylized performance can be captured and protected under the sound recording copyright, infringement occurs *only* where that mechanical or electrical phonorecording is mechanically or electrically copied or dubbed. A new soundalike recorded performance is expressly *permitted* under the Copyright Act.[3] By extension, then, a performer's style is not protectible under federal copyright law.

Third, while a convincing soundalike recording of a celebrity's singing voice may be a misappropriation of her right of publicity—as part of her "image and likeness"—this likely does not extend to her overall style of singing. Even less likely would the distinctive musical style of a group be found to misappropriate whatever right of publicity a group or collective might have. Related to this, to the extent that trademark, Lanham Act false affiliation or endorsement protections, or unfair competition might apply, these will be limited to those competing in producing sound recordings or performances and will not reach advertisements for unrelated goods or services that include style copying.

The takeaway is that under current law, musical style beyond a soundalike of a particular singer's voice is not likely protectible. And yet there is clear commercial value, not to mention personhood and artistic value, in a unique style. Developing such a "voice" in one's style, whether as an individual or a group, is no easy task. It takes not only creativity but also perseverance to transform an idea of a new style into something that can be consistently and identifiably delivered through compositions and performances.

Enter the new artificial intelligence (AI) music generators. Amper,[4] Jukedeck,[5] MuseNet,[6] Magenta,[7] and others let the user guide "original" music production (composition and sound recording) "in the style of" famous composers and performers. Machine learning enables these apps to build neural networks from ingesting all the works of specific composers or performers which can then generate "new" works in the specified style. While these apps are not yet to the point where their new songs "by" Nirvana, The Beatles, or Frank Sinatra are going to threaten streaming and downloads of those artists' back catalogs, they are producing acceptable original music productions for purposes such as accompanying videos and background music.

More relevant here, the style songs do indeed sound recognizably like the style of the target artist.[8] This means that, at some level, that "ephemeral" quality of style has been quantified and reduced to algorithmic reproduction—even as no pre-existing song or recording of the

---

[2]   *See* Joseph Fishman, *Music as a Matter of Law*, 131 HARV. L. REV. 1861 (2018) (summarizing decisions and commentary espousing the melody-only approach to musical work copyrights).

[3]   17 U.S.C. § 114(b).

[4]   www.ampermusic.com/.

[5]   https://openai.com/blog/jukebox/.

[6]   https://openai.com/blog/musenet/.

[7]   https://magenta.tensorflow.org/.

[8]   *See, e.g.*, Derek Robertson, *'It's the screams of the damned!' The eerie AI world of deepfake music*, THE GUARDIAN (Nov. 9, 2020) www.theguardian.com/music/2020/nov/09/deepfake-pop-music-artificial-intelligence-ai-frank-sinatra?ICID=ref_fark.

artist is being directly reproduced in the AI production. In other words, what has been captured is pure style.

It would seem that style has thus been fixed in some manner. It is definable, articulable, perhaps even reducible to patent-type claims. Further, the very existence of both the huge investments poured into these musical style-generator apps and the apparent commercial appeal of them—even in their relatively primitive states—indicates market value for style divorced from particular pre-existing compositions or recorded performances. With the styles clearly identified and tied to particular artist or composers, this is not a question of genre, or "generic" style. Accordingly, the potential threat to stifling the development of a genre or category of music is narrow and diminished.

This chapter sketches a proposal for a sui generis limited rights regime for musical style— limited in time as well as in allowing derivative styles. Its underlying theory is less property and more in line with disgorging unjust enrichment and discouraging copycat free riding. One challenge will be preemption: with Congress expressly permitting soundalike remakes of sound recordings, any state statute or common law recourse might be susceptible to federal judicial review under the Constitution's Supremacy Clause.[9] Accordingly, the chapter contemplates Congressional amendment of the Copyright Act to limit the reach of the sound recording soundalike provision such that state or other federal statutory protections for original musical style are not in conflict, or to expressly legislate the same (perhaps revoking the soundalike provision in its entirety on this and other grounds).

The chapter proceeds by reviewing the nature of musical style and a general bias against protecting it through IP, in section 2. From there, section 3 provides more detail on AI musical style generator apps. Section 4 sketches a proposal for protecting original musical styles.

2.   STYLE AND IP

The many uses of "style" today all seem to flow from an ancient meaning transfer from the *stilus* as the Latin term for a writing tool to the kinds of writing one might do with the tool.[10] From this origin in literary work, the term has expanded to capture recognizable patterns in all manner of arts (useful/mechanical, liberal, decorative, fine, and so on). But in this way the word must always be qualified: Impressionist style, Shaker style, and so on. "Style" in the abstract is perhaps best defined today as the manner, way, or method in which some artisanal or craft practice is performed, which results in an artifact or event/experience with recognizable characteristics common to others in the style. It is like an analog to a "product-by-process" claim in patent law.

---

[9]   U.S. CONSTITUTION, art. 6, cl. 2.
[10]   *Style*, OXFORD ENGLISH DICTIONARY (online ed. 2021); *Style*, OXFORD ENCYCLOPEDIA OF AESTHETICS (online ed., 2008).

A distinction then must be made between group (or communal) style and individual (or personal) style.[11] Group style can overlap with artistic movements. The line between group style and genre may be fuzzy.[12]

Group style tends not to be protectible under copyright law.[13] This seems correct, again, as the concept seems to overlap significantly with genre. In the ever-present tug of war between recognizing and protecting a pioneer creator's new style and allowing a genre to bloom from that singular starting point, we likely do not want to give the pioneer exclusive rights to such nascent genres. This is analogous to giving too broad protection under patent law to an inventor who introduces a seemingly niche technology that could lead to a whole new field of industry. At most, an artistic movement or school might seek a collective mark, or perhaps even a certification mark if particular materials and methods must be employed, under trademark law.

Individual or personal style may be protectible in some instances—or at least is not categorically prohibited.[14] Copyright treatise author William Patry singles out Saul Steinberg's famous illustration for the cover of *The New Yorker* magazine, sometimes referred to as "A New Yorker's View of the World."[15] When knock-offs such as "A Chicagoan's View of the World" appeared for sale, Steinberg sued for copyright infringement. While the court did not expressly rule that Steinberg's style per se was protectible (or infringed for that matter), Patry avers that the distinctive and easily identifiable style Steinberg created for the cover *could* be protectible in a way that a group style could not.[16]

And yet, such potentially protectible style is that expressed in a particular work, rather than across works, or separate from any single work. Thus, a challenge for protecting individual style per se, or divorced from a particular work, is that it is not fixed—the threshold requirement for copyright protection.[17] It is one thing to say that Steinberg's distinctive perspective and wry humor in *The New Yorker* cover—immediately suggesting franchising for other cities—might get protection at least in part for its style. It is quite another to say that an individual artist's overall style—almost a "house style"—is protectable, when it is not necessarily fully present or apparent in a single work.

What then where the style is an aggregate developed by an artist across a series of works? Where the first song one hears from that artist or composer is memorable but does not immediately suggest an ongoing style, yet successive additional songs or performances clearly

---

[11]   *Style*, Oxford Encyclopedia of Aesthetics (Michael Kelly, ed., online ed., 2008); William F. Patry, *Style*, Patry on Copyright § 4:14 (Sep. 2021 update).

[12]   *See, e.g.,* Joanna Demers, *Sound-alikes, Law, and Style*, 83 U.M.K.C. L. Rev. 303 (2014) (noting Alan Moore's claim that style must be distilled out of the broader category of genre which contain social and historical associations that should not be conflated with style).

[13]   Patry, *supra* note 11. Idiosyncratically, Patry seems to develop his own origins of "style" as a concept, tracing it to "ancient French jurisprudence" and its "manière de procéder." *Ibid.* This is at best incomplete, given the OED entry's etymology. It may be that Patry is indeed tracing the "concept" and not the term itself, though even this seems out of step with the OED etymology of the term, as that seems to include the concept as well.

[14]   *See, ibid.*

[15]   *Ibid.* The cover appeared on the March 29, 1976 issue. It can be seen—and copies are available for purchase—at *The New Yorker's* parent company's website. https://condenaststore.com/featured/new-yorker-march-29-1976-saul-steinberg.html.

[16]   Patry admits that the case may have turned more on the defendant's copying of fictitious buildings Steinberg drew for his New York setting.

[17]   Patry, *supra* note 11.

set the style? For example, on hearing the first Beatles hit in the United States—"Love Me Do"—it would largely have registered with the listener as a song by one of many boy bands from Britain. But after a string of hits, the band's style—at least in its early iteration through, say, the album *Beatles 65*—had become firmly imprinted in the listening public's consciousness such that other similar "Merseybeat" boy bands were seen as copycats. Likewise, Neil Young's first hit, "Mr. Soul"—with the band Buffalo Springfield—did not necessarily emblazon a fully-fledged style in listener's minds. But, after a series of hits, and especially with releases such as the album *Harvest* featuring his iconic song "Heart of Gold," Young firmly established his proto-Americana style with listeners—so much so that the group America's song "A Horse With No Name" was seen as a blatant stylistic rip-off of Neil's sound.[18]

In cases of such aggregate style, one might say the artist has no claim without being able to locate the copied elements in one particular work. This goes against theories of aesthetics which find that style can very much be manifested through a series of works by an artist. Accordingly, there is both artistic and commercial value that can be attributed to an artist's style separated out from particular works. Courts and commentators have acknowledged this to some degree in discussions of "the composer's hand at work."

But even if copyright requires location of the relevant elements of a composer or performer's style in a single particular work, other causes of action, such as under Lanham Act protections against false indication of affiliation or endorsement (§ 43(A)) or state law rights of publicity, might avail. Neither of these require a fixed work. However, both are tied to a celebrity's *persona* and thus the alleged infringement or violation must be based on use of the celebrity's image or likeness sufficient for the observer to believe that the representation is of the celebrity herself.[19] For example, the famed *Midler v Ford Motor Co.*,[20] *Waits v Frito-Lay, Inc.*,[21] and *White v Samsung Electronics America, Ind.*[22] cases found that where the relevant audience could be deceived into thinking the actual celebrity—Bette Midler, Tom Waits, and Vanna White, respectively—was being depicted in voice or image, such unauthorized sound-alikes or (sort of) look-alikes could infringe the celebrity's right of publicity.

Nimmer critiques these right of publicity decisions as in tension with Congress' express authorization of soundalike recordings in the Copyright Act of 1976 under federal pre-emption grounds. Nonetheless, where the core of the complaint is that defendant used a celebrity's name, image, or likeness (including soundalike voice) to promote goods or services in direct competition with those produced by the celebrity in their trade—including related merchandising and endorsements—then he concedes the rulings rejecting preemption defenses.

A final area of IP that can provide a kind of protection for style is trade secrecy. Where an artisan's signature style is produced in part by tools or techniques that can be concealed from general view, they can seek to enforce trade secret protection for them. As usual for trade secrecy, however, the artisan must derive independent economic benefit from use of the secret tools or techniques and take reasonable steps to maintain secrecy—either through physical controls or legal steps like nondisclosure (NDA) or confidentiality agreements. Trade secrecy

---

[18] *See, e.g.,* Mark Meyers, *On the Journey to 'A Horse With No Name'*, WALL ST. J. (Jul. 167, 2018) *available at* www.wsj.com/articles/on-the-journey-to-a-horse-with-no-name-1531748082.
[19] *See Right of Publicity*, 1 NIMMER ON COPYRIGHT§ 1.17.
[20] 849 F.2d 460 (9th Cir. 1988).
[21] 978 F.2d 1093 (9th Cir. 1992).
[22] 971 F.2d 1395 (9th Cir. 1992), *cert. denied* 508 U.S. 951 (1993).

will not, of course, prevent others from producing the same effects where they independently develop or reverse engineer them.

Further complicating matters, emerging artisans nearly always learn by copying established artisans' craft and style first: the visual arts student sitting in the museum sketching their copy of a masterpiece; the budding musician watching his favorite players and then trying to emulate them. Thus, our IP regimes should not prevent such necessary activities. However, this also means that most competent artisans *can* reproduce the style of others through some mix of verbal explanation, visual show-how, and writings. In fact, primate researchers have determined that one of the most distinctive attributes of humans and their closest primate cousins, chimpanzees, is the uncanny ability of individuals—especially the young—to mimic actions and productions of others.

Accordingly, at the heart of justifying any restrictions on copying must be a form of unjust enrichment, or free-riding. This in turn emphasizes the cabining of such rights or restrictions to incidents of economic competition or misattribution. Like the so-called *Bolar* exemptions in patent law,[23] there should be an experimental use exception for those learning or seeking to reverse-engineer protected artisanal style to the extent that courts enforce such protections or Congress passes new laws establishing them in positive law.

Focusing on musical styles, we see the group–communal versus individual–private dynamic play out as well, though again the group–communal category can have significant overlap with genre. Another way of looking at it is the classic creative and inventive origins of field narrative: one or a few individuals create/invent what seems a niche style/product/service which then attracts further early adopters, leading to a stylistic or niche industry "movement," which then in some cases blossoms out into an entire new class of works, goods, or services. The latter is then a new field of industry or a genre. In music, for example, Charles Brown developed a new niche within or straddling genres including funk, R&B, soul, blues, and perhaps even reggae, that became Go-Go in the Washington DC metro area. He is accordingly lauded as the Godfather of Go-Go, and the form still sits somewhere between style and (sub) genre. It is probably not a genre unto itself, yes, as relatively too few people are aware of it (especially outside DC).

Music copyright of course has two elements: the musical composition right and the sound recording right. The first is the oldest form and is the abstract form of the composition as traditionally embodied in sheet music. In fact, until 1978, this copyright could only be registered through deposit of written notation to the Copyright Office. The second is more recent—the Sound Recording Act of 1971,[24] effective 1972—and encompasses only the actual fixed sequence of electromechanical information that is a "phonorecording" as defined in the Act.

---

[23]   35 U.S.C. § 271(e). The name derives from the case *Roche Products, Inc v Bolar Pharmaceutical Co*, 733 F.2d 858 (Fed. Cir. 1984), which found infringement for private experimental use of patented compounds necessary for a generic pharmaceutical company to begin developing a generic form of a patented drug in order to seek FDA approval—even where the defendant was not planning on marketing or selling the generic until the pioneer was off patent. The decision prompted Congress to expressly include an exception for such private use—on the way to FDA approval—as part of the Hatch–Waxman Act compromise between branded and generic drug companies that also enacted patent term extensions for branded patented drugs that lost significant time to market due to FDA New Drug Application (NDA) approval processes and the Abbreviated New Drug Application (ANDA) approval process for bioequivalent generics.

[24]   Pub. L. No. 92-140, 85 Stat. 391 (1971).

The composition right does not include any performative aspects—including style—*other than* what might be noted in the score. The latter might be a general style note—"swing feel"— or direction as to how to play a particular note or sequence. But if the composer is not the artist who will perform the song—either live or for a commercially released phonorecording—then the composition right cannot have included that separate performer's stylistic interpretation.

In fact, the mechanical compulsory license that authorizes any performer to record their version of the composition—so long as the composition copyright owner has authorized at least one initial publicly released phonorecording—expressly includes the right of the new performer to modify the composition to fit the arrangement or style the performer wishes to sue, so long as the same do not substantially alter the underlying composition.[25] In the absence of this proviso, any such alteration might be deemed as a derivative work to which copyright owners also hold exclusive rights. Those who see musical style as unprotectable—as discussed below—may view this permissiveness for style as not altering the fundamental nature of the composition as further evidence that Congress does not view style as protectible. Yet, the permissiveness for arrangement belies this, as a new arrangement is expressly protectible under copyright (albeit as a derivative work that could be blocked by the owner of the underlying copyright).

By contrast, the sound recording, based on a particular phonorecording, of necessity includes the stylistic performance of the captured artist. But only actual electro-mechanical copying, dubbing, ripping, or sampling infringes this right. Congress included the express right to make a soundalike recording for the sound recording right, not the composition right. In other words, as a matter of purely federal copyright law, any music producers or artists can seek to make an exact recreation of the sound recording in the studio—so long as they don't use any electro-mechanical portion of the original phonorecording. They can, as in the Midler case, try to get singers to sound exactly like the singers on the record. Or they can get guitarists to sound exactly the same, or drummers, and so on. They can try to match the exact recording, mixing, and mastering techniques, including ambient room feel through use of reverb or delay, equalization (EQ) settings (treble, bass, and so on), compression (electronically limiting transient peaks in volume and boosting low volume passages, which when overused is the signal processing that make radio or TV ads sound louder than the regular program), and so on.

While this "mirror recording" provision could have been intended to simply cabin the intended scope of the sound recording right, research by Robert Brauneis discloses the discriminatory history of soundalike recordings in the early twentieth century.[26] White producers and record labels in the early twentieth century were intentionally re-recording exact copies of the stylistic performances of Black artists by White artists such that the records could chart and sell in the (White) "Pop" market. The Black artists originating the copied style were effectively relegated to the "ghetto" of the "Race" records market, precluding airplay on White Pop stations and placement in Pop sections of record stores. This severely curtailed the Black style-originating artists' sales and access to the broader market. In these cases, it was undeniable that the value add was the performative style. In other words, without the Black stylistic innovations, a recording by White artists of the same composition would not have sold as well.

---

[25]   17 U.S.C. § 115.

[26]   Robert Brauneis, *Copyright, Music, and Race: The Case of Mirror Cover Recordings*, in HANDBOOK OF INTELLECTUAL PROPERTY AND SOCIAL JUSTICE: ACCESS, INCLUSION, EMPOWERMENT (Steven D. Jamar & Lateef Mtima, eds, Cambridge University Press 2022).

At the same time, of course, the bias towards "composition" and written notation gave cover to White producers and labels ignoring this Black artist value-add as "unprotectible" and "free" for use. At the same time, with many Black artists not fluent in written notation, even had these stylistic innovations been codifiable in notation, the artists would not have been able to notate them and seek protection as a new arrangement or other derivative work. And with no federal rights available for sound recordings at the time, there was no protection even for the actual phonorecording of the Black artist. Arguably, the only thing that limited further exploitation of Black performers was the market limit on playing or selling Black recordings in the mainstream Pop category, and, possibly, some state law protection for sound recordings or unfair competition. Accordingly, one has to wonder whether the express carve-out for soundalike recordings in the Copyright Act is due solely to Congressional desire to cabin the sound recording right to actual electro-mechanical duplication, or at least in part to protect this legacy of style soundalike exploitation.

Piling on to this unwarranted bias against protecting personal musical style have been the harsh critics of the decision in *Williams v Gaye*[27] regarding the song "Blurred Lines." Reading their comments, one would think style was categorically excluded from copyright protection. Following from that (false) premise, these commentators then lament that the decision in the case does the "unthinkable," which is to protect musical style.

Contrary to these critiques, Marvin Gaye's overall work is an excellent example of when and why musical style should be protectible. While his style of composition and performance of course built on existing genres and styles, he crafted something new and instantly recognizable, especially to his legions of fans. This particular sensual style straddling the soul and R&B genres can be heard both across his oeuvre and completely contained within single works. The album *What's Going On?* is a masterclass in crafting a seamless product of composition, performative style, and sonic ambience that continues across each piece on the album, even as each is identifiably distinct from the others.

Yet, copyright's protection of only written notation-based composition, on the one hand, and actual duplication of the phonorecording, on the other, leaves a major gap for the composed style—and production style—of modern pop artists such as Gaye. In the pre-1978 era when the composition copyright had to be registered through a written notation deposit copy, the gap was even larger than it is now. And it was still further widened given the practice of music publishers submitting only stripped down "lead sheets" containing a single staff of a primary melody with chord names written above it for this notation deposit.[28] This is less information about a composition than that provided by commercial sheet music, which generally contains a two handed piano part, notated on treble and bass clef staves, together with a treble-clef staff line for any lead vocal melody and chord names (often with diagrams) over the top of this staff. But to do true justice to the fulsome, multi-instrumental orchestrated compositions that pop composers such as Gaye have been producing since the mid-twentieth century, one would need transcription to a full conductor's score, with its separate staff lines for each instrument. Even this full score might not be able to capture fully the important performative style aspects

---

[27]   *See, e.g.*, Fishman, *supra* note 2 at 5–7 (summarizing critiques of the *Blurred Lines* decision).

[28]   Sean M. O'Connor, *The Lead Sheet Problem in Music Copyright:* Williams *and* Skidmore *Revealed the Systematic Diminution of Pop Music's Aural Composers*, in HANDBOOK OF INTELLECTUAL PROPERTY AND SOCIAL JUSTICE: ACCESS, INCLUSION, EMPOWERMENT (Steven D. Jamar & Lateef Mtima, eds, Cambridge University Press 2022).

intended by the composer—indeed *composed* by an author–performer such as Gaye. This is in large part because music is, of course, an *aural* phenomenon, which then can only be "two dimensionally" abstracted and represented in written notation. Just as "the map is not the territory,"[29] the notation is not the composition as a living, breathing piece of music.

In 1978 the Copyright Office changed its musical composition deposit copy requirement to allow phonorecordings.[30] Thus, the same phonorecording could now be used to register both the sound recording right in the exact electro-mechanical fixation of sounds on that phono-recording and the underlying musical composition being performed on it. While this then in theory closes the gap—as compositional gestures directing performative style[31] are captured in the phonorecording so long as the recording performance exhibits them—the phonorecord-ing may not be treated as self-executing as to the scope of the composition. In other words, a court could construe the composition represented on a phonorecording deposit composition registration to encompass only a main melody, such as Joseph Fishman and others advocate, or perhaps that melody with some basic harmonic and rhythmic accompaniment. A judge does not have to direct the jury to consider all sonic aspects of the phonorecording in deciding whether defendants have copied any parts of the "composition." And where the allegedly infringing work does not contain any sampling, dubbing, ripping, or other electro-mechanical replication of parts of the original phonorecording, the sound recording right—which *does* cover all fixed sounds on the phonorecording—is not in play. Accordingly, the composed style gap may still remain, even for phonorecording deposit registered works.

So aural composer-musicians such as Gaye—and countless other pop geniuses, including Michael Jackson, Taylor Swift, John Lennon, Paul McCartney, and Irving Berlin—have not had an adequate way to not only capture but also to have some confidence that the full scope of their composition will be acknowledged and protected. They could hire their own transcriber to create a full conductor's score for their works. But for better or for worse, traditionally professional pop composers have left copyright registration to their managers or lawyers. Amateur aural composers likely cannot afford professional full score transcriptions, and so rely on the unpredictable scope of a phonorecording deposit. Achieving satisfactory accuracy and affordability over the past decade or so, music transcription software such as Sibelius has changed the equation for aural composers. Provided they can afford the set-up, aural compos-ers can now simply play the various parts of their composition and have them transcribed by the software into a full score (or even just commercial sheet music format). Determining accu-racy is as straightforward as playing back the transcription through the system. This makes

---

[29] Alfred Korzybski, *A Non-Aristotelian System and Its Necessity for Rigour in Mathematics and Physics*, reprinted in SCIENCE AND SANITY: AN INTRODUCTION TO NON-ARISTOTELIAN SYSTEMS AND GENERAL SEMANTICS, 747–61 (The Int'l Non-Aristotelian Library Pub. Co., 1933) (acknowledging Eric Temple Bell's earlier epigram "the map is not the thing mapped," NUMEROLOGY (Williams & Wilkins, 1933)). Magritte's famous *The Treachery of Images* (*Ceci n'est pas une pipe* ("This is not a pipe")) is part of this same milieu.

[30] U.S. Copyright Office, Interim Regulation, 43 Fed. Reg. 965 (Jan 5, 1978) (effective as of Jan 1, 1978); Proposed Rulemaking, 42 Fed. Reg. 59302 (Nov. 16, 1977); Inquiry, 42 Fed. Reg. 48944 (Sep. 26, 1977); O'Connor, *supra* note 28; Robert Brauneis, *Musical Work Copyright for the Era of Digital Sound Technology: Looking Beyond Composition and Performance*, 17 TULANE J. TECH. & I.P. 1 (2014).

[31] *See* Joe Bennett & Sean O'Connor, *Determining the Composition* in OXFORD HANDBOOK OF MUSIC LAW & POLICY (Sean M. O'Connor, ed., 2022) *available online at* www.oxfordhandbooks.com/view/10.1093/oxfordhb/9780190872243.001.0001/oxfordhb-9780190872243-e-4.

it categorically different from hiring a transcriber and then having to either trust that she is playing it back exactly as she notated it, or hire yet another notation-fluent player to play the transcriber's score to check it.

Returning to Marvin Gaye and the "Blurred Lines" case, one does not even have to accept the potential protection for aggregate style of an author across multiple works as "Got To Give It Up" is considered by some many music experts to be a self-contained font of a new identifiable hybrid style incorporating not only Gaye's prior signature soul and R&B sounds, but also now disco. The "hand of the composer" is decidedly evident in so many of the instrumental and vocal parts of "Got To Give It Up." Gaye's widow Janis has confirmed that Marvin himself composed the various parts, including percussive elements such as handclaps and cowbells (Gaye was an accomplished percussionist as well as singer and keyboardist). This then is not genre, nor communal style. It is instead the clear compositional style of one author on one work.

Robin Thicke and Pharrell Williams conceded that they went into the studio to create "Blurred Lines" based in large part on trying to replicate this style. Their supporters say this was perfectly OK because Thicke and Williams did not copy any direct melodic components of "Got To Give It Up," but rather only the—to them unprotectable—"groove," "feel," or "style." But even if compositional performative style is not protectable under current case law, it seems quite unjust that we privilege the creative contributions of only some kinds of composers—those working well within the Western classical music derived mode of composition abstracted from performative aspects and style—and not others.[32] Style contributions have clear artistic and commercial value. Thicke and Williams would not have intentionally (and admittedly) been trying to replicate Gaye's style in "Got To Give It Up" if this were not the case.

Likewise, many successful instrumentalists have long had distinctive valuable styles. They are often hired *because* of this style. Why is this not protectable to them, when a compositional style may be protectable? In some cases, the style is hard to imitate—as opposed to a written composition, which, by its very nature is supposed to be playable by any competent musician. Where style is difficult to replicate, then perhaps this gives a de facto protection to the musician. It also means the style might not be transferable—say, as a matter of assignment or license—which perhaps cuts against giving express legal protections anyway. In other cases the style may be hard to replicate at first, but then other performers figure out how to do it. The style could be a matter of technique or of equipment, or of both.

One of the foremost examples of highly distinctive instrumental style innovation is the proliferation of electric guitar styles. Across different genres, the expressive potential of the seemingly endless combinations of electric guitars, amplifiers, and signal-processing "effects pedals" or "stomp boxes" may be unmatched in the history of music. Most of the memorable "guitar gods" from Sister Rosetta Tharpe to Jimi Hendrix to Bonnie Raitt to Eddie Van Halen to St Vincent have pushed the instrument and amps into uncharted territory and new sonic textures. "Overdriving" amplifiers led to the hallmark distorted sounds of electric blues and rock and roll.[33] By the late 1960s, many guitarists customized guitar pickups, amplifier vacuum tubes and speakers, and pedal effects. Soon, some "modded" (modified) even the electrical

---

[32]   *See* O'Connor, *supra* note 28.

[33]   *See* Sean M. O'Connor, *Patented Electric Guitar Pick-ups and the Creation of Modern Music Genres*, 23 GEO. MASON L. REV. 1007 (2016); *CPIP 2015 Fall Conference—Clip 6: Prof. Sean*

circuits in guitars, amps, and pedals. All of this led to signature styles that were a combination of playing and equipment—and in fact playing that was *influenced* or *enabled* by the gear.

Because many aspects of gear, and even alternate guitar tunings, can be obscured from the public, pioneering guitarists sometimes went to great lengths to keep their innovations secret. The classic myth of the "dropped amp" has been frequently deployed against gullible reporters asking about how a certain guitar tone was obtained—as if it were all just a happy accident. Careers have been made on such distinctive tones, and many albums sold.

But distinctive tone and gear has even made it into the compositional side as songs were increasingly written on and for electric guitars, especially distorted guitars and the "power chords" they enabled. Would the signature—now clichéd—riff to "Smoke on the Water" have anywhere near the impact intended by Deep Purple guitarist and song co-composer Ritchie Blackmore on a clean acoustic guitar?[34] Even a district court noted the musical impact of "power chords" in litigation enforcing ZZ Top's hit composition "La Grange" against Chrysler for infringement in a truck ad.[35]

At the same time, musical groups have aesthetically and commercially valuable styles as well. Arguably, such distinctive band styles have been the most misappropriated by commercial advertisements. Whatever today's hot musical act's sound is, you can bet that advertisements will pop up with soundtracks closely mimicking that style. The agencies are careful not to use any actual composition associated with the band—unless they have a license to it—but will engage in soundalike recordings for the signature instrumentation and mixing ambience of the group. So far, successful right of publicity cases have turned on close soundalikes of *individual* voices (Midler, Wait) and so it may be an open question whether soundalikes of group styles will be deemed a misappropriation of anyone's name or likeness. In other words, can something like guitar style be considered part of the guitarist's "likeness"? To guitarists and music fans, the answer is likely yes. At least, a guitar style can be part of an individual's persona. But what about the overall group sound—recognizable as it may be?

Summarizing the current state of protection for musical style, there may be at most protection for (i) a distinctive voice as being the identifiable "likeness" of a known celebrity, and (ii) an original "compositional" style embedded in a single musical work. But this leaves a lot of aesthetically and commercially valuable style unprotected. If we had good policy reasons to do so that would be one thing. But the rationale, such as may be cobbled together from comments, seems to be that style is too "ephemeral" and/or not replicable. This ostensibly makes it the opposite of fixed and replicable subject matter of copyrights and patents. Trade secrecy could work for gear settings that can be hidden. And some performers used to try to hide how they were playing their instruments in performances or on video recordings. But that leaves that which cannot be hidden from view, or which can be reverse engineered, vulnerable to loss of protections. As to group style, why should that be any less a matter of commercial rights of

---

O'Connor, YouTube (Apr. 12, 2016), https://www.youtube.com/watch?v=8m7LKQPCHS0&feature=youtu.be.

[34]   Deep Purple, *Smoke on the Water*, Machine Head (Warner Bros. 1973); *see* "Smoke on the Water by Deep Purple," SongFacts www.songfacts.com/facts/deep-purple/smoke-on-the-water#:~:text=This%20song%20took%20inspiration%20from,Switzerland%20on%20December%204%2C%201971.&text=Deep%20Purple%20watched%20the%20blaze,Geneva%2C%20which%20the%20casino%20overlooked.

[35]   *ZZ Top v Chrysler Corp.*, 54 F.Supp.2d 983 (W.D. Wash. 1999).

publicity than that of an individual? Finally, we cannot avoid the implications of research by Brauneis,[36] Greene, and others that the very contributions to culture most distinctively made by minority and disadvantaged artists are exactly that which is left unprotected for the dominant culture to appropriate at will, with no payment or even attribution.

3.   AI MUSICAL STYLE GENERATORS DEBUNK EPHEMERAL OR UNQUANTIFIABLE MYTH OF STYLE

Attempts to generate music from artificial sources date back at least to the electro-magnetic experimentation of Johann Philip Reiss and Alexander Graham Bell, which led to the telephone.[37] While much of this strand of research led to the use of synthesizers as musical instruments, other parts of it led to the use of early computers in the late 1950s that sought to transform compositional rules into algorithmic language.[38] In the 1980s, early versions of machine learning were employed to have the computer learn directly from data rather than having the composer and programmer expressly code the compositional rules, which had proved painstakingly difficult.[39] By the 1990s, early neural networks were also deployed for some primitive music composition and improvisation.[40] However, none of this captured a "global musical structure" sufficient to produce music that might actually rival that produced by human composers and musicians.[41]

More recently, the state of the art has vastly improved and multiple viable AI machine-learning musical composers are on the market. Jukedeck, Amper, Magenta, MuseNet, FlowMachine,[42] and Orb[43] all give means for musicians and non-musicians alike to "compose" and record

---

[36]   Brauneis, *supra* note 25; Kevin J. Greene, *African-American Innovators and Copyright Law—From Blues, Soul and Funk to Hip-Hop*, in HIP HOP & THE LAW 277 (Pamela Bridgewater et al, eds, 2015); *"Papa's Got a Brand-New Bag": Innovation, Copyright Law and Black Artists*, in AFRICAN-AMERICAN CULTURE AND LEGAL DISCOURSE (Lovalerie King & Richard Schur, eds, 2010); O'Connor, *supra* note 28.

[37]   *Patented Electric Guitar Pick-ups and the Creation of Modern Music Genres*, 23 GEO. MASON L. REV. 1007 (2016).

[38]   J.-M. Deltorn & Franck Macrez, *Authorship in the Age of Machine Learning and Artificial Intelligence*, in OXFORD HANDBOOK OF MUSIC LAW & POLICY (Sean M. O'Connor, ed., 2022) *available online at* www.oxfordhandbooks.com/view/10.1093/oxfordhb/9780190872243.001.0001/oxfordhb -9780190872243-e-3 (citing DONALD J. GROUT AND CLAUDE V. PALISCA, A HISTORY OF WESTERN MUSIC (5th ed., W. W. Norton & Company 1996); and LEJAREN HILLER AND LEORNARD ISAACSON, EXPERIMENTAL MUSIC: COMPOSITION WITH AN ELECTRONIC COMPUTER (McGraw-Hill 1959).

[39]   *Ibid* (citing Rebecca Fiebrink and Baptiste Caramiaux, *The Machine Learning Algorithm as Creative Musical Tool*, arXiv:1611.00379v1 (2016)).

[40]   *Ibid* (citing Peter M. Todd, *A Connectionist Approach to Algorithmic Composition*, 13 COMPUTER MUSIC J. 27 (1989); Jamshed J. Bharucha and Peter M. Todd, *Modeling the Perception of Tonal Structure with Neural Nets*, 13 COMPUTER MUSIC J. 44 (1989); C. Stevens and J. Wiles, *Representations of Tonal Music: A Case Study in the Development of Temporal Relationship*, in PROC. 1993 CONNECTIONIST MODELS SUMMER SCHOOL 228 (1994); and Masako Nishijima and Kazuyuki Watanabe, *Interactive Music Composer based on Neural Networks*, 29 FUJITSU SCI. & TECH. J. 189 (1993)).

[41]   *Ibid* (quoting Douglas Eck and Juergen Schmidhuber, *A First Look at Music Composition using LSTM Recurrent Neural Networks*, ISTITUTO DALLE MOLLE DI STUDI SULL INTELLIGENZA ARTIFICIALE 103 (2002)).

[42]   www.flow-machines.com/.

[43]   www.orb-composer.com/.

high-production-value music. All of them work through a digital interface that creates the music itself—usually in a digital audio workstation ("DAW")—and not sheet music. Within the DAW the user can see a kind of notation of the musical parts, generally in what is called "piano roll" graphic representation. This is because it is a digital visualization akin to the cutout holes in the original physical player piano rolls.

Notably, such productions are neither pure compositions nor pure recorded performances. They are instead the modern standard of hybrid, or really unified, music production.[44] Many of today's biggest artists are not writing "songs" in the sense of a melody and some harmonic and rhythmic accompaniment that stand apart from any particular instrumentation. Rather, they are writing a particular groove and ambient experience. This relies on not only specific instrumentation with defined timbral qualities, but also on the signal processing sound environment of each instrument as well as the overall "room" sound.

For example, to create one of Billie Eilish's hits, her brother and producer Finneas used a technique of side chain compression that had the pulse of the song's kick drum triggering an increase and decrease of compression on the song's piano—creating an "undulating tide-going-in-and-out feeling."[45] But at the outset the drum itself is muted and all that is heard is this pulsing piano. In turn, this particular sonic experience of the pulsing piano drove Billie's creation of her vocal part.[46] In other words, the backing track and its specific signal processed ambience drives the song, not some abstract melody and chords written on music notation.

Accordingly, such unified musical productions have their content and style defined as much by instrument arrangement and timbre together with the overall sonic ambience of the track as they do by a "lead melody" or the identifiable voice of a celebrity singer. At the same time, musical acts since at least the 1960s have worked with engineers and producers to establish signature sounds or styles that were recognizable both in their recorded output and live performances.

Implicitly testifying to the central aesthetic and commercial value of individual and musical group style, the new AI music generators were initially built and promoted almost entirely on style. They demonstrated their prowess by tailoring song generation in the style of famous performers including Frank Sinatra, the Beatles, and Coldplay (to name but a few). Beyond performative style, these also enabled works in the compositional style of composers such as Johann Sebastian Bach, Lennon and McCartney (as "the Beatles"), and others. From this style-classified baseline, they promoted the user's ability to mix and match styles: say, a Bach canon performed by Lady Gaga.

The point is that the majority of the original value proposition centered on mimicking and delivering the recognizable style of famous composers and performers—across a range of genres—but in "original" compositions and produced recordings that would (impliedly) not infringe copyright or other rights. Promotional pitches centered on users' ability to avoid the hassles of licensing compositions, especially under "synch rights" that could be blocked entirely by the copyright owner, and/or sound recordings. Of course, the generators generally

---

[44] *See* Joe Bennett & Sean O'Connor, *Determining the Composition*, in Sean M. O'Connor, ed., Oxford Handbook on Music Law & Policy (Oxford University Press 2022) (chapters available online at Oxford Handbooks Online); Robert Brauneis, *Work Copyright for the Era of Digital Sound Technology: Looking Beyond Composition and Performance*, 17 Tulane J. Tech. & I.P. 1 (2014).

[45] *Episode 197: Billie Eilish "Everything I Wanted"* Song Exploder (Nov. 18, 2020).

[46] *Ibid.*

did not mention up front that the user was still licensing the produced work—but now from the music-generating app rather than owners of copyrights on human-produced compositions or sound recordings. Still, this avenue of licensing was more "guaranteed" as from the app that was promoting this very service—generating music for you to use in your own creative works—instead of the uncertainty of the prospective user having to track down and hope to secure licenses from multiple copyright owners for a single musical recording.

More recently, the music-generating apps began classifying musical "sources" in general descriptive terms rather than by expressly identifying with a named composer or performing artist. In some cases, the style names seem suggestive of a particular composer or artist. But they do not actually name the musician. This may be as result of some stern communiques, or even cease and desist letters, from formerly named musicians' attorneys—or perhaps just astute counsel advising the app providers that such letters and possibly lawsuits would be forthcoming. The grounds for such claims could be a combination of state rights of publicity and Lanham Act § 43A false affiliation or endorsement. In fact, K.J. Greene argues that rap and hip-hop artists may be moving to a "post-copyright" world in which they primarily enforce their rights through these two avenues.[47] To be clear, many of the apps also promoted the ability of musicians to use the apps to generate their own composition or performative style, provided assistance or suggestions on melodic lines, harmonies, chords, rhythms, or beats based on an original snippet uploaded by the musician. But again, the dominant share of the promotion was around styles of established musicians.

The ability of these AI engines to accomplish these feats of style means that they have encoded, at some level, the salient features of the individual styles. The engines can now churn out predictable, replicable facsimiles of the artists' styles. The code behind them seems to be at least as definite at that of image, music, and movie files.

It would seem, then, that these styles have been "fixed in a tangible medium" satisfactory to claim copyright protection. Just as Corbis and Getty Images have successfully registered and enforced copyrights in their high-quality digitizations of photos and visual artworks, Jukedeck et al may be able to register and enforce copyrights on their musical artist style-generation engines. This may be unfair to the composers and performers whose style has now been captured and is available for license and use by the general public—with no apparent compensation to the artists. That such artists would be unhappy and pursue legal avenues, again, may explain the recent disappearance of artists' names from the platforms, although if legal concerns over rights of publicity and Lanham Act actions are the only reason behind the development, then one might expect styles of artists whose rights are long expired—along with the artists—to still appear on the platforms. At the same time, this duality may just call attention to the fact that living or otherwise still rights-bearing estates of artists do not have their styles identified.

Nonetheless, the argument stands that the digitized styles may be copyrightable. Assuming so, then the Corbis and Getty Images analogy is apt. Just as they secure permissions and rights to digitize images—or purchase already digitized images—so then should the AI music generator platforms obtain permissions and rights from the artists whose style has been captured. But this implies that there is—or should be—some such underlying right for the composers and performers whose style has been digitized. One might analogize to the common law—and

---

[47]   K.J. Greene, *Right of Publicity, Identity, and Performance*, 28 Santa Clara Computer & High Technology Law Journal 865 (2012).

to some extent codified—right of first publication to generate rights to the first digitization of an artists' style. This would allow artists to control that first digitization and either commission a platform to generate it, or license one or more to do so: a win–win for the artists and platforms as the artists get the fair right to control and monetize their style, while the platform can actually return to promoting the named artists' styles.

A fair question is whether artists would see this as valuable. They may instead wonder why they should give a platform the right to cannibalize revenue streams from the artists' own productions. In other words, will fans still buy/license/stream the artist's own productions when they can buy/license/stream what may become dozens, hundreds, or more of copycats built of that very artist's AI digitized style algorithm? The savvy artist may think for another moment and realize: who cares? Assuming they negotiate a license to the platform that gives the artist percentages or points of fees that the platform charges end users who select the artist's style, this gives the artists dramatically enhanced leverage. Fans and others are doing the artists' work for them, producing far more product than the artist ever could; the artist is receiving royalties off this use; *and* she can distance herself from any uses she doesn't like by reminding her fans and the public that she herself did not produce that variant. In fact, she should negotiate a specific duty of the platform to require their licensee users to have disclaimers on the style derivatives making clear that the work is *not* a production of the underlying artist.

This model may resonate especially well with the new generation of social media influencers. They are essentially selling style and persona. They want to make broad and deep inroads into the popular culture, as do the brands that pay the influencer to feature their products. It is also true that for many such influencers, styles have become even more transient than in the past. A single influencer may simultaneously run a number of differently branded/styled social media accounts. The value and success of such feeds and accounts is in fact often predicated on how distinctly and consistently a style is presented to the feed. Those of us social media duffers who post relatively random things to our feed, with no consistent visual schema or tone or subject matter, find ourselves with a relatively balanced number of followers and following, mainly constituted of our friends, family, co-workers, and the odd fellow-traveler we pick up along the way. The careerist influencer, by contrast, builds a distinct style, promotes it, and seeks to have wide uptake. Having others copy the style could be both a badge of honor and a multiplier of income, like stock in a valuable company or the profits a partner at a professional services firm earns off the billables of their associates.

This may seem crass to the earnest, soulful musician, and admittedly does seem so. Yet, some of the most influential musicians of the past century have indeed cycled through different distinct styles. David Bowie is one of the best examples. His different phases—from the earnest songwriter performer of *Space Oddity* to the proto-glam rocker of the Ziggy Stardust persona to his slick, sophisticated dancehall influencer in *Let's Dance* and beyond—could all have been separately marketable. They are all indeed within a larger house brand of "David Bowie, chameleon musician and style influencer," but he could have essentially franchised these different style phases had he desired. Let us separate tribute bands as a related but different phenomena. In those, the performers are playing actual compositions that the tributed artists performed while trying to sound and look just like the performer. In this way, the tribute band is endeavoring to recreate the experience of seeing the underlying artist performing that artist's signature tunes. So, yes, style imitation, but not the generation of new works. In this way, the new AI musical style generators create the environment for an *extension* of the underlying artist's stylistic works that could at some point, perhaps, cross the uncertain line into a new, albeit derivative style. This is particularly true where users mix and match styles—compositive, performative, or both—to create something they want to hear that is not out there.

Critics of affording copyright or other exclusive rights to style may say that this is exactly the problem: propertizing style prevents others from using it to develop new styles, and indeed, valuable new genres. But that presumes artists would not see the value in licensing their style based on such rights. Where they did engage in such licenses—which could be lucrative side streams of revenue while they continue their own production—then others would be able to derive new styles and build a genre. This is not so different from incremental innovation and the way new patentable inventions can be developed off existing patents. In this case, we refer to these as "blocking patents": the incremental improvement inventor and the would-be users of her invention must license the underlying patent. But at the same time, once the follow-on inventor has secured her patent, the owner of the underlying patent (and users of it) will have to license the incremental improvement patent to keep up with the state of the art.

Some artists may indeed see a licensing regime as enhancing and cementing their legacy (beyond simply remunerative benefits). In fact, given the explosion in fan-created "user-generated works" enabled by digital internet platforms, the extension of a core stylist's creation is already exponentially enhanced over an earlier model of other professional creator's mild to slavish copying of the core style. There is so much value creation here—aesthetic and commercial—that it truly seems unjust that the originator of the style often gets nothing out of this extra value other than perhaps some recognition and burnishing of their reputation.

The value of the platforms is being realized rapidly. TikTok bought Jukedeck in 2019.[48] Analysts see this as an obvious move for TikTok to begin to ramp back on the extensive royalties it has to pay for licensed music by famous artists. And yet, no one should suppose that TikTok believes its users will simply gravitate towards "generic" AI-produced music that does not sound like influential artists. Rather, it seems far more likely that TikTok is banking on Jukedeck producing music that sounds close enough to influencers' styles that it will be "good enough" for users—or perhaps even to fool them into thinking something is actually a new, say, Kendrick Lamar song. Further, the rapidity and volume by which an AI music generator could churn out songs in the clear style of the latest influencer gives economies of scale vastly different from the creation of soundalikes in the twentieth century—whether "mirror recordings" to play to a different radio format or imitations of famous celebrities to sell trucks or corn chips. This itself rachets up the level of unjust enrichment and free-riding off the all-important identifiable style of a famed artists by what seems like an order of magnitude or more. Why should law and policy allow this?

4.   EXCLUSIVE RIGHTS FOR (DIGITIZED) MUSICAL STYLES

Concerns over exclusive rights for musical styles seem to have centered around the two themes of being unfixed and necessary building blocks for genres. Alternately, styles may seem to be one abstraction level up from the sorts of things we traditionally protect, such as a single fixed work. In the earlier parts of this chapter we showed how these concerns were mitigated by both

---

[48]   https://www.theverge.com/2019/7/23/20707371/tiktok-jukedeck-ai-music-startup-acquisition; https://www.crunchbase.com/organization/jukedeck.

the nature of the new AI digitization of musical style and a better understanding of how style has actually been used to unjustly enrich others. In this part, we sketch what exclusive rights for musical styles—especially those that have been digitized—might look like.

Because the AI music apps have reduced both compositive and performative style into predictable algorithms, such styles have now been fixed as arguably sufficient for copyright protection. While the "style" itself is not fixed in a human-perceivable medium, nonetheless equally opaque digital files that allow browsers and other apps to display an image digitized by, say, Corbis or Getty Images are copyrightable. Accordingly, there is no obvious reason why digital code that can predictably produce works in the style of an artist is not also copyrightable. However, this may be a narrow victory as: (i) it is trivially true that the code is of course copyrightable simply as the "literary work" of the software itself, with no linkage to the effects produced by the code. Then, just as Corbis and Getty Images can only enforce against persons copying their digital image files, the AI music generators could only enforce against persons copying their fixed, registered style-generating code. In other words, the copyright does not reach to the image itself—in Corbis' and Getty Images' cases—or to the musical style in the music generator case.

On the other hand, the fact that the style can be fixed in a tangible medium as code could be argued to satisfy the requirement for copyrightability of the style itself. This could be analogous to the Copyright Office's allowance of registration and deposit of photographs of three-dimensional artworks to secure copyright in the latter. In other words, the registrant does not get copyright to the photograph alone, but rather to the style it represents.

Notably, the apps are creating these style-capture algorithms, and so the inequity of appropriation of artists' styles is now shifted from other musicians to the proprietors of the apps. Accordingly, composers and performers would have two avenues to try and prevent or limit such appropriation. First, they could proactively commission apps to produce such algorithms for them. This would be like securing a painter or photographer to produce your portrait and directing or controlling the work sufficient to be determined as the author of the work.[49] Even if the direct authorship path was deemed inadequate as a matter of law, the artist could require the assignment of any copyright inhering in the algorithm. Second, artists could argue that the training of the AI engine by processing many works of the artist is a kind of derivative work—or, arguably, improper infringing use of the processed works—sufficient to give the artist leverage to secure ownership or lesser rights to the algorithm. The question of the permissibility of AI engines processing training sets of copyrighted works has indeed become an issue of interest among many copyright owners.

Perhaps less likely to succeed, artists could argue that the new medium of digitized style is infringing on copyright they have acquired in their aggregate style across multiple works, or on other rights such as publicity or false affiliation and endorsement. This would be more likely to succeed where a better theory of aggregate style, or style standing alone, can be made.[50] But central to this would also be judicial recognition of a first right of digitized style production. This would be similar to the first right of publication in copyright generally and requires the potential publisher or distributor of an artist's work to contract with the artist to do so.

---

[49]   Work made for hire may not actually work as the painter or photographer will usually be an independent contractor—as opposed to an employee—and this kind of work does not fit into one of the enumerated categories required for the former. 17 U.S.C. § 101.

[50]   The Author is indeed working on just such a theory and hopes to produce a paper on it soon.

The propositions in the preceding paragraph are likely better situated for Congress. Legislators could recognize that fixed musical style generators are a new class of copyrightable material or mode or subject matter and decide how to bring them expressly within the Copyright Act. Ideally, the form would be a first right of "digitization" which requires assent of the artist and then both registration/deposit and infringement provisions. Grandfathered in would almost certainly be human copying of style, given longstanding tradition—though this latter might not be necessary if style standing alone is recognized under the existing Copyright Act (as arguably it may be).

Separately, musical style could be recognized judicially or by statutory amendment as on par with existing name, image, and likeness subject matter. This seems fair in proportion to how much you believe musical style—outside of soundalike voices à la the Waits and Midler cases—is identifiable and part of commercial publicity. At the same time, the clear commercial value demonstrated by the frequent (unauthorized) imitation of musical style, including that of the new AI music generators, may be evidence enough.

Following the arguments for publicity rights around musical style, artists could seek to bring Lanham Act § 43A claims against style copyists—human or AI—on the grounds of false appearance of affiliation or endorsement. Such claims have been expanding recently with, for example, athletes seeking injunctions or damages from video games using the athlete's signature moves or other non-image attributes. Thus, the time is ripe to consider what other than a name, image, or voice is identifiable to a particular artist. Style could be one of these things. And again, the replicable fixation of it in the new AI engines could overcome any concerns of it being undefined or too ephemeral.

The final approach would be a sui generis regime for musical style. This would require legislation at the state or federal level. However, such approach might allow custom tailoring in a way that would ameliorate some concerns. First, the term could be relatively short, say five years, which would allow for others to build off the style at the end of that period. It essentially gives the artist a head start—similar to the head start trade secret remedy—such that free riders using the artist's investment in time and effort to create the style are not unjustly enriched. At the same time, there could be some form of compulsory license so that other artists can experiment with the style and develop derivatives of it sufficient to grow a genre. This sui generis regime could also be limited to AI digital music generators, again keeping human copying of style permitted. In such a way, legislatures could acknowledge the exploding value of AI style generators and not allow the artists who create such value in the first place to be once again unjustly deprived of the fruits of their talent and labor.

5.   CONCLUSION

This chapter sought to illuminate an area of rapidly expanding aesthetic and commercial value that brings together artists and AI. In the ongoing tension between artists who create aesthetically or commercially successful artworks and styles, on the one hand, and technology developers who find ways to capture and reproduce such works and styles, on the other, the new AI music generators represent a major tilt toward technologists' appropriation of this value. The chapter accordingly sought to articulate countervailing rights lodged in artists that would allow them to negotiate with technologists to secure some part of the additional value created by the AI music generators, or rather, to secure their fair share of the joint value created by the amplification of the artists' original style through the AI apps. While some might believe we are simply heading rapidly to a future in which AI creates the original styles as well, others of us believe that humans will also want the human touch and creative self-expression of fellow-human artists' works and styles. In that case we need to establish the balance so that artists can be secure in their creations, lest we lose our human artistic class altogether.

5. The elusive intellectual property protection of trained machine learning models: a European perspective

Jean-Marc Deltorn

1. INTRODUCTION

Beyond the exuberance of early days announcements and other inflated statements, artificial intelligence (AI) is now a well-established staple at the heart of an increasing number of practical applications. Some of these realisations are capable of achieving feats that just a few years ago were thought beyond the reach of algorithmic systems, such as the autonomous driving of vehicles, recognising and classifying images at levels comparable to – or even higher than – humans and convincingly translating texts and speech from practically any language in real time, as well as some other rather banal and mundane tasks (think of the (not so) 'smart appliances', from the connected toaster to the AI-driven hair dryer). AI and, in particular, machine learning have joined the rank of other 'general-purpose technologies' to spearhead a new wave of innovations in an endless array of applications.

A resounding success, certainly, but what justifies such a landslide? While the basic mathematical principles on which the current AI systems are built were laid out more than 60 years ago, it is only in the past years that the conditions required to allow their full expression have been met. In a conjunction of events reminiscent of a 'perfect storm', which included a sequence of algorithmic breakthroughs, the continuing increase in computational resources and, first and foremost, access to an ever-growing pool of training data, a new generation of AI processes and applications have emerged. At the core of this new AI movement lies a family of algorithmic processes capable of analysing and identifying patterns in very large corpora of real-world data. Based on machine learning techniques, complex human behaviours can be mimicked and improved upon, without requiring a clear understanding (or the elicitation) of the rules governing the processes under consideration.

While the data-driven machine learning paradigm is, unquestionably, the vault that supports the current AI surge, inference models are its keystone. As the result of an often long and complex optimisation process, they distil in a deployable end product the experience gained during a training phase where data have been consumed and metabolised and hidden patterns deciphered. The outcome is a functional condensate. It captures in a hybrid structure – formed both of an algorithmic skeleton, an *architecture*, and of a value-based substrate, the *parameters* – the information present in the training corpus that is found relevant to a specific purpose. From a set of examples, once properly trained, the inference model can generalise to new, unseen data and deliver a prediction that matches the expectation (the purpose) set by its producer. Some of these applications are now ubiquitous. Trained on images, the model segments pictures and labels its constituents (for example, detecting faces in images or for a self-driving application; identifying 'pedestrians', 'bicycle', 'car', 'truck', 'traffic sign', etc.). Trained on speech utterances, it allows the development of voice-controlled applications. Trained on parallel linguistic corpora, the model finds correspondences between languages and learns to translate from one to another. Trained on a video sequence, it captures moves and strategies to control a robotic arm or steer a vehicle. It is this artefact, the trained model, that is set to be deployed in the real world as a product or as a service. As such, these new technical objects are at the epicentre of significant economic and strategic investments. The efforts involved in designing and assembling the trained models may justify, in some instances at least, their legal protection under intellectual property rights.

However, the particular nature of inference models, at the interface between computer codes, algorithms, data structures and collections of parameters, poses a series of demanding questions to the intellectual property (IP) practitioner. For models are not monolithic entities that can be easily cast into a single IP mould: evaluating the protection of trained inference models thus requires an overview of the applicable IP rights. After a succinct presentation of the technical specificities of inference models (section 2), we will tackle in earnest the possible practical means of protection of trained models (section 3), evaluating in turn their various facets and the applicability of the corresponding IP rights, from copyright to trade secrets, from database to patents.

2.   SETTING THE STAGE: INTRODUCING THE 'INFERENCE MODEL'

Artificial neural networks, as an early model of machine learning systems, were inspired by the structure of biological nervous system cells. The functioning of a biological neuron is rather elementary and can be summarised as follows: each neuron can both receive as input the signals originating from multiple other neurons and emit an electric signal of its own. If the sum of the input signals (received through all the input 'synapses') reaches a certain threshold, then the neuron 'fires' a spike of electricity. As elementary as each unit may be, a sufficiently large collection of such interrelated neurons is evidently capable of realising impressive feats (as demonstrated, for example, by our cognitive functions). A complex behaviour can emerge from the (correct) assembly of a large number of simple entities. This realisation inspired computer scientists to explore the properties of abstract counterparts to the biological systems. The algorithmic learning process guiding an artificial neural network relies, in this case, on assigning parameters (called 'weights') to each neuron and synapse that enables a proper 'firing' of signal and leads collectively to a correct decision.

Neural networks indeed proved capable of solving industrial problems (such as digit recognition on handwritten letters). Still, these simple networks were severely plagued by practical limitations that prevented, for a while at least, their large-scale application.[1] Neural networks seemed like a dead end on the way to AI progress, another odd item to be stored in the 'cabinet of curiosities' of failed technical explorations. This status quo, however, changed drastically around 2006 when a series of algorithmic breakthroughs opened the way to the training of

---

[1]   Among these major hurdles were the difficulty of training large enough neural networks to represent complex problems, limiting their use to a set of 'niche' applications. After major initial enthusiasm and hopes that artificial neural networks would form the basis of a true AI revolution, this realisation led to disillusionment and paved the way for a so-called AI winter that lasted for more than a decade.

very large, multi-layered, densely connected neural network architectures.[2] The continuous progress in terms of computational power (and the development of dedicated architectures such as graphical processing units and, more recently, tensor processing units), as well as the access to vast resources of training data, all combined in creating a new foundation on which neural networks could once again thrive. Since then these architectures have met with unprecedented success, solving complex problems in a vast array of applications, from image analysis, speech recognition and natural language processing to automatic robotic control.[3] As a matter of fact, the so-called deep neural networks are now becoming the standard 'Swiss knife' of machine learning techniques, capable of tackling, with minimal modification, a vast array of applications.[4]

Most of the recent AI applications rely indeed on these deep learning architectures. Speech recognition engines work seamlessly on mobile platforms; face recognition is becoming a staple of social networks and surveillance systems. Medical applications of deep neural networks are starting to rival the competence of doctors.[5] The development of autonomous vehicles relies, too, on a variety of such machine learning systems: learning to recognise objects (from markings on the road to vehicles, pedestrians, signs, and so on) but also to interpret these signals and to react appropriately (to brake if a pedestrian is detected in front of the vehicle, to respect the rules of the highway code, to learn to get to your destination, and so on).[6] The ability of these architectures to learn from examples, an essential characteristic at the core of these systems and a key component of their success, is, however, not without cost. Machine learning indeed requires access to a vast amount of training resources, without which the system would remain an 'empty shell'. The construction of efficient recommendation engines, such as those of Amazon or Netflix, will have necessitated the analysis of the behaviours of millions of users over periods of several months to several years to finally generate meaningful

---

[2]   Y. Bengio, Learning deep architectures for AI. Foundations and Trends in Machine Learning, 2009, 2, 1, 1–127.

[3]   Y. LeCun, Y. Bengio and G. Hinton, Deep learning. Nature 521.7553, 2015, 436–44.

[4]   One component of this overwhelming success is related to the capacity of deep neural networks to derive a rich internal representation of the training data (for the particular task at hand). For example, in the case of object recognition in images, each neuron in a given layer can be interpreted as a filter that responds to particular components characteristic of objects in the input dataset: simple features, such as edges, will be detected and encoded in the neurons of the first layers, while more complex components will be associated with neurons located deeper in the network hierarchy. The top layers of the network end up – if sufficiently deep – capturing the content of the image, that is, forming archetypal representations of the objects on which they have been trained: faces, animals, buildings, and so on (see A. Mahendran and A. Vedaldi, Understanding deep image representations by inverting them, 2014, preprint *arXiv*:1412.0035). A second component of the deep learning landslide comes from the availability of coding frameworks and libraries that greatly facilitate the development and implantation of AI applications, without requiring an expert background in computer science or mathematics.

[5]   A. Esteva et al, Dermatologist-level classification of skin cancer with deep neural networks. Nature 542.7639, 2017, 115.

[6]   This learning phase is accomplished on the basis of both real data acquired from physical sensors (such as by driving a vehicle or capturing text or utterances from a query, or by playing Go against a live opponent) and artificial datasets generated, in a process called 'data augmentation', through digital transformations of real examples, numerical simulations (such as by having the computer drive in a virtual world instead of on physical roads, by synthesising speech in different noisy conditions or by letting it play Go against itself, as recently demonstrated with Google DeepMind's AlphaZero experiment: D. Silver et al, Mastering the game of Go without human knowledge. Nature 550.7676, 2017, 354).

results and provide these companies with a significant competitive advantage. The same goes for medical applications or autonomous vehicles that depend on the quality of the corpus of data on which they have been trained and on the effective transformation of this corpus into a deployable application. Access to data, therefore, is a quintessential component of modern AI applications. Additionally, the learning phase itself requires significant computational resources and substantial engineering efforts.

Modern machine learning systems are composite entities. They are composite in terms of their core constituents: data, algorithms, codes, parameters are, indeed, all indispensable ingredients of the machine learning mix. At the core of these systems lies the 'inference model' composed both of an 'architecture' (e.g. the number and specific arrangement of neurons in a neural network, including the specification of their properties, and so on) and of the parameters characterising its behaviour (in the case of a neural network, these parameters, or 'weights', are associated with each connection linking any two neurons in the architecture). A typical model forms then a chimeric, hybrid object composed of a couple {*architecture parameters*}[7] (see Figure 5.1).

Machine learning systems are also composite in terms of the processing stages required to transform an initially inchoate object (an untrained model) into a well-crafted operational tool, the trained inference model. In order to build a predictive engine, a 'model', capable of delivering meaningful predictions, training data (often previously, painstakingly, annotated by human agents) are fed to a carefully curated processing pipeline. The goal of this training stage is then to identify, in an iterative fashion, the values of the parameters that satisfy an objective function given a predetermined architecture, based on a corpus of training data. In other words, once the *architecture* is set – the first facet of the model – its second component, the *parameters*, must be determined. To do so, the parameters are typically initialised with random values. The system is therefore at first providing totally arbitrary answers.[8] One way of training an inference model proceeds by comparing the prediction of the model with the expected outcome associated with the data in the training set (at least in the case of supervised learning, where such outcome is known). In doing so, one can evaluate when, and by how much, the system fails to provide a correct answer. In instances where the model fails to meet its objective, the values of the parameters are nudged. In essence, each parameter in the whole model is then modified in proportion to its contribution to the erroneous prediction. By repeating this correction process, the model improves, and becomes progressively better at delivering the expected predictions. Once the model meets the expected objectives (by showing, for example, an error rate below a given threshold), and after a final validation step to assess the generalisation capabilities of the model to unseen data – an essential phase of the training process – the

---

[7]   As a practical example, in the context of Google's popular Tensorflow/Keras framework, a model consists of multiple components: the architecture, or configuration, which specifies what layers the model contains, and how they are connected; a set of weight values (the 'state of the model'); the characterisation of the optimiser (defined by compiling the model); and a set of losses and metrics. For practical purposes, to avoid unduly complexifying the present discussion, the optimiser and the losses and metrics are included in the 'architecture' component of the model.

[8]   Initialising the parameters using random distribution is the most common case when a model is first constructed, to avoid any bias. Other options may rely on 'fine-tuning' a pre-existing model using additional data (to accelerate the convergence of the training or to overcome a scarcity of training data). For neural networks, this means initialising the model using the weights of a previously trained network with the exception of the last layer, and retraining the model end-to-end on new data.

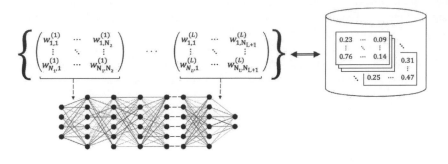

Note: The inference model (here a neural network) is a composite structure: both an *architecture* (represented here as a network in the lower part of the figure, and characterised by the number of neuron units, their types and their arrangement in the network in a number of ordered layers) and an ensemble of *parameters* (often referred to as 'weights' in the case of neural networks and symbolised here as a collection of terms '$w^{(L)}_{i,j}$' associated with each layer 'L' in the network). The number of weights in a neural network can be very large (up to and beyond hundreds of billions, for the largest models). The parameters $w^{(L)}_{i,j}$ are initially assigned a random value; their final value must be learnt during a training phase in order to produce a 'trained inference model' that can operate according to its objective and be deployed safely in the field. Other types of inference models rely on different architectures' paradigms and parameters' assignments (such as decision trees, support vector machines, Bayesian networks, and so on).

Figure 5.1   A depiction of an inference model

model can be deployed in the real world and operate independently from its training pipeline. A trained model is born. A trained inference model is therefore the end product of the training phase. Once trained, the model is akin to a filter, capable of accepting previously unseen input values (say, an image of a scene in front of a vehicle) and to output some relevant information (the presence of a pedestrian, a bicycle or a car in said image). This seemingly straightforward process is, in practice, riddled with many hurdles. Training an inference model, in particular a large one, is, in fact, a complex and strenuous process. Beyond the sole access to sufficiently large training datasets and a significant amount of computational power, taming such objects requires skills and experience. In fact, the choice of the architecture and the selection of the 'hyperparameters' that characterise the training process (both components being tightly coupled) are as much an art as they are a science.[9] If anything, these examples emphasise

---

[9]   For a description of the steps involved in selecting a model's architecture and hyper-parameters, see L.N. Smith, A disciplined approach to neural network hyper-parameters: Part 1 – learning rate, batch size, momentum, and weight decay, 2018, arXiv preprint arXiv:1803.09820. For a review of attempts at automating the search for optimal machine learning models, see F. Hutter, L. Kotthoff and J. Vanschoren, 2019. *Automated machine learning: methods, systems, challenges* (p.219). Springer Nature.

the human contributions required during the construction of an AI system: far from 'learning on their own', or producing a solution 'autonomously', the production of a trained inference model relies heavily on (human) set-up and guidance, through the proper establishment of a context (such as through the definition of a loss function), tutorship (during the learning phase, to adjust the hyperparameters) and validation of the deployable model.

3.   CURRENT IP PROTECTIONS OF INFERENCE MODELS

Prior to deployment, the end product of a machine learning pipeline is the trained inference model. The resulting model, as briefly evoked above, consists in an invaluable combination of data, algorithmic structures, computational processing and technical know-how. The investment associated with the production of such models can be significant, if not prohibitive.[10] In fact, the full cost of training state-of-the-art deep neural network models can amount to several million US dollars.[11] The economic value of these objects is undeniable and their protection can be of paramount strategic importance for their parent corporations. In order to evaluate the legal protection regime best suited to deep learning systems, it is first necessary to define the object of protection. What really is a deep learning system? How is such an object embodied? What are its main characteristics? Answering these non-trivial questions is a prerequisite to determine which intellectual property rights should be invoked. The answer is not, however, unequivocal. For deep learning systems are, as we have seen, composite entities that are built on the synergistic composition of heterogeneous subsystems: algorithmic, data, software, hardware, and so on, all participating in defining a model. For each of these components a particular set of IP rights may be considered, starting with trade secrets and expanding towards copyrights *sui generis* database rights and patents.

3.1   The Fragile Protection of Machine Learning Models by Trade Secrets

A practical mode of protection of inference models could reside in keeping them secret. By asking member states to harmonise their legislation to include 'measures, procedures and remedies' to 'prevent the unlawful acquisition, use or disclosure of a trade secret or to obtain compensation for such a fact', the Community Directive (EU) 2016/943 of 8 June 2016 (hereafter the 'Trade Secret Directive') allows victims to seek redress for theft of confidential information. To be protected by secrecy, 'information' must meet three conditions: it must not be public, in the sense that, in its entirety or in the exact configuration and assembly of its elements, 'They are not generally known among or readily accessible to persons within the circles that normally deal with the kind of information in question'; it must have 'commercial value because it is secret'; and 'it must be subject to reasonable in the circumstances to keep

---

For an application of meta-learning to neural networks, see T. Hospedales, A. Antoniou, P. Micaelli and A. Storkey, Meta-learning in neural networks: a survey, 2020, arXiv preprint arXiv:2004.05439.

[10]   The cost of training a model not only involves the optimisation of a single model but must account for the iterative, trial-and-error process of optimising the hyperparameter, and the multiple retraining of the models required to achieve optimal performance. Such steps become exceedingly costly for the large models (OpenAI GPT-3's full version has a capacity of 175 billion parameters).

[11]   O. Sharir, B. Peleg and Y. Shoham, The cost of training NLP models: a concise overview, 2020, arXiv preprint arXiv:2004.08900.

them secret' (Article 2(1) a–c of the Trade secret directive). The use of the generic label of 'information' does not impose any restriction on the nature of the object to be protected: data, data structures and certain aspects of deep learning applications may therefore fall within the scope of protection of the Trade Secret Directive.[12]

The trained inference models themselves could naturally fit in the trade secret category. As discussed above, the information associated with large-scale models is indeed of indisputable commercial value and the specific set of parameters obtained after training is not generally known. Are the models 'easily accessible'? The question may be pertinent since a growing number of companies have recently started to offer 'machine learning as a service' (MLaaS)[13] where existing models are remotely deployed and can be queried by external parties. Instead of painstakingly training a model to recognise facial features or speech, one can then re-use the pre-trained models accessible through these platforms.[14] However, even if such a trained architecture can be accessed through an interface, the model itself remains opaque and inaccessible. The inference model thus seems to fulfil the condition of not being 'easily accessible' required by the definition of secrecy. According to a 2018 report by the European Union Intellectual Property Office (EUIPO), 'Where innovation does not fulfil the requirements of patentability, trade secrets become a pivotal tool for companies to protect their business knowledge'.[15] Still, trade secrecy does not create an exclusive right and issues of reverse engineering may limit the deployment of such models. In particular, as stated in point 16 of the preamble of the Trade Secret Directive: 'Reverse engineering of a lawfully acquired product should be considered as a lawful means of acquiring information, except when otherwise contractually agreed.' Directive 2016/943 specifies that reverse engineering, namely the 'observation, study, disassembly or testing of a product or object that has been made available to the public or that is lawfully in the possession of the acquirer' is licit only in the absence of a 'legally valid

---

[12]   The fact that the algorithms are considered as business secrets was also recently underlined by a decision of the German Federal Supreme Court (Bundesgerichtshof, 28 Jan. 2014, VI ZR 156/13, pt. 29), which rejected a request for information relating to an algorithmic process for financial credits on the ground that it was protected by the trade secret. The extension of this qualification to deep learning systems seems justified.

[13]   'Machine learning as a service' (MLaaS) is a broad term that characterises cloud-based platforms offering such services as data pre-processing, the training of models and inference (using a pre-trained model to make predictions). These services can be accessed through predictive application programming interfaces ('predictive API'). Examples of platforms offering AI as a service are the Google Cloud platform (https://cloud.google.com/ai-platform-unified/docs), Amazon Sagemaker (https://aws.amazon.com/sagemaker/), the Microsoft Azure AI platform (https://azure.microsoft.com/en-us/overview/ai-platform/), Baidu AI (https://ai.baidu.com) and IBM Watson Machine Learning Studio (www.ibm.com/cloud/learn/machine-learning).

[14]   For example, Google Cloud AutoML API provides pre-trained machine learning models to facilitate the development and the deployment of applications. These include 'Vision AI' to process images, 'Video AI' to analyse and annotate video content, 'Dialogflow', 'Text-to-Speech' and 'Speech-to-Text' to manage interactions with human spoken signals, and 'Cloud Translation' and Natural Language Processing models. (See Google AI platform, https://cloud.google.com/automl). Amazon AWS Marketplace offers a range of pre-built machine learning models from a variety of sellers (see https://aws.amazon.com/marketplace/solutions/machine-learning).

[15]   EUIPO Report, The Baseline of Trade Secrets Litigation in the EU Member States, 5 (2018), DOI: 10.2814/19869.

duty to limit the acquisition of the trade secret'.[16] A sore point in the trade secret protection of trained machine learning models as recent academic works have shown is that the 'black box' can be pried open and the inherent complexity of deep learning models, is not always effective in countering attempts at reverse engineering.[17] In fact, the economic incentives for attempting to capture the functionalities of trained models seem to justify the effort, in some instances at least. Indeed, as recently stated by Maini, Yaghini and Papernot: 'With increasingly more data and computation involved in their training, machine learning models constitute valuable intellectual property. This has spurred interest in model stealing, which is made more practical by advances in learning with partial, little, or no supervision.'[18] Beyond the application of any additional technical countermeasure to combat reverse engineering,[19] or the use of fingerprint techniques or digital rights management to track model usage or control its access,[20] the implementation of contractual measures could therefore be considered in order to prohibit the extraction of the parameters of a trained machine learning model. Such a 'no reverse-engineering clause', as allowed by the Trade Secret Directive, would specify that the licensed trained model includes trade secrets and that the user may not decompile, reverse engineer, decrypt, disassemble or otherwise attempt to derive source code or algorithms for or from the trained model to extract its parameters or reproduce its functionalities.[21]

---

[16]   See Art. 3(1)b of Directive 2009/24/EC. Recital 16 of the Directive further states: 'In the interest of innovation and to foster competition, the provisions of this Directive should not create any exclusive right to know-how or information protected as trade secrets. Thus, the independent discovery of the same know-how or information should remain possible. Reverse engineering of a lawfully acquired product should be considered as a lawful means of acquiring information [...] except when otherwise contractually agreed.'

[17]   F. Tramèr et al, Stealing Machine Learning Models via Prediction APIs, 2016, arXiv preprint arXiv:1609.02943; S. Oh et al, Towards reverse-engineering black-box neural networks, 2017, arXiv preprint arXiv:1711.01768; Y. Shi, Y. Sagduyu and A. Grushin, How to steal a machine learning classifier with deep learning. In IEEE International Symposium on Technologies for Homeland Security (HST), 2017, 1–5; T. Orekondy, B. Schiele and M. Fritz, 2019. Knockoff nets: stealing functionality of black-box models. In Proceedings of the IEEE/CVF Conference on Computer Vision and Pattern Recognition, pp.4954–63; M. Jagielski, N. Carlini, D. Berthelot, A. Kurakin and N. Papernot, 2020. High accuracy and high-fidelity extraction of neural networks. In 29th {USENIX} Security Symposium, pp.1345–62; J.B. Truong, P. Maini, R.J. Walls and N. Papernot, 2021. Data-free model extraction. In Proceedings of the IEEE/CVF Conference on Computer Vision and Pattern Recognition, pp.4771–80.

[18]   P. Maini, M. Yaghini and N. Papernot, Dataset inference: ownership resolution in machine learning, 2021, arXiv preprint arXiv:2104.10706.

[19]   See, e.g., M. Juuti, S. Szyller, S. Marchal and N. Asokan, 2019. PRADA: protecting against DNN model stealing attacks. In 2019 IEEE European Symposium on Security and Privacy, pp.512 –27; X. Gong, Q. Wang, Y. Chen, W. Yang and X. Jiang, Model Extraction Attacks and Defenses on Cloud-Based Machine Learning Models. IEEE Communications Magazine, 2020, vol. 58, no 12, 83–9.

[20]   H. Chen, B.D. Rouhani, C. Fu, J. Zhao and F. Koushanfar, 2019. Deepmarks: A secure fingerprinting framework for digital rights management of deep learning models. In Proceedings of the 2019 Conference on International Conference on Multimedia Retrieval, pp.105–13; B. Darvish Rouhani, H. Chen and F. Koushanfar, 2019. Deepsigns: An end-to-end watermarking framework for ownership protection of deep neural networks. In Proceedings of the Twenty-Fourth International Conference on Architectural Support for Programming Languages and Operating Systems, pp.485–97.

[21]   An example of such a clause can be found in Google Cloud Platform Terms regarding 'Cloud AutoML Vision Downloadable Models', where it is specified: 'Customer can download a frozen model graph in the model formats supported by Cloud AutoML Vision via a ZIP file and any related Customer provided image labels via a TXT file. No license to retrain or reverse engineer such frozen model graphs

3.2   Inference Models as 'Code 2.0'

From the network architecture to the training process, all the components of a deep learning pipeline are expressed in a programmable form. The resulting codes give form to the topology of the neural network and bring to life the abstract algorithmic logic. The code is consubstantial to the practical implementation of deep learning systems. The inference model as such can also be construed as another form of software[22] – a 'software 2.0', as coined by Andrej Karpathy, director of artificial intelligence at Tesla and specialist in neural network architectures.[23] In such a representation, the program does not emerge from the explicit formulation of a human legible set of instructions (in a language such as C++ or Java or Python) but is rather expressed as a collection of 'weights' learnt during the training phase. Instead of manually crafting software by carefully stating all the steps involved in the algorithmic process, the solution can be 'searched' in a landscape of possible programs, each one characterised by a set of parameters, the weights of the trained model.[24]

What is then meant by 'code' or 'computer program'? The Software Directive 2009/24/EC, which harmonised the legal protection of computer programs in Member States, only mentions in its preamble that

> the term 'computer program' shall include programs in any form, including those which are incorporated into hardware. This term also includes preparatory design work leading to the development of a computer program provided that the nature of the preparatory work is such that a computer program can result from it at a later stage.[25]

A rather open definition indeed. Article 1(3) of the directive further states that 'a computer program shall be protected if it is original in the sense that it is the author's own intellectual creation. No other criteria shall be applied to determine its eligibility for protection.'

Could the trained deep learning model, the 'inference model', be construed as a protectable 'computer program'? A neural network could certainly be described as a (large) assembly of simple coded functions, that transforms input data (such as the sensor data coming from

---

is granted or implied to Customer.' (https://cloud.google.com/terms/service-terms-20190409, Last modified: 9 April 2019).

[22]   Certain platforms' End User Licence Agreements (EULA) resort to the qualification of 'software' for their deep learning models: Nvidia models EULA (https://developer.nvidia.com/tlt-20-models-eula).

[23]   See Andrej Karpathy, 'Software 2.0', Medium, 11 Nov. 2017, https://karpathy.medium.com/software-2-0-a64152b37c35.

[24]   Erik Meijer, Professor of Cloud Programming at Delft University of Technology, described the difference between the traditional practice of software development and the new methodology enabled by the machine learning paradigm: 'In Software 1.0: Engineers formally specify their problems, carefully design algorithms, compose systems out of subsystems or decompose complex systems into smaller components. In Software 2.0: Engineers amass training data and simply feed it into an ML algorithm that will synthesize an approximation of the function whose partial extensional definition is that training data. Instead of code as the artifact of interest, in Software 2.0 it is all about the data where compilation of source code is replaced by training models with data.' (Erik Meijer. 2018. Behind Every Great Deep Learning Framework is an Even Greater Programming Languages Concept (Keynote). In Proceedings of the 2018 26th ACM Joint Meeting on European Software Engineering Conference and Symposium on the Foundations of Software Engineering (ESEC/FSE 2018), Association for Computing Machinery (ACM), New York, NY, USA, 1).

[25]   Directive 2009/24/EC, preamble at pt. 7.

a vehicle) into a decision (turning left or right; applying the brakes or accelerating). The logic involved in the transformation between inputs and outputs is indeed represented as a set of elementary instructions akin to a computer program. Since the Software Directive does not define positively its object of protection, such a set of functions could be considered a form of 'computer program'. However, the question of its originality would remain. In this sense, the *Infopaq* decision ruled that

> copyright is liable to apply only in relation to a subject matter which is original in the sense that it is its author's own intellectual creation. It is only through the choice, sequence and combination of those words that the author may express his creativity in an original manner and achieve a result which is an intellectual creation.[26]

In this case, the 'choices, sequence and combination' of instructions that define the model are not dictated by the author as such, since they result directly from associations induced by the algorithm during the learning process. As a matter of fact, there can be no 'intellectual input' or 'free creative choices' if these choices are strictly algorithmic and are dictated by the functional constraints to be met during an optimisation process.[27] As clearly stated in the *Football Dataco* decision, since '[the] author expresses his creative ability in an original manner by making free and creative choices', the criterion of originality is not satisfied where the production of the work is only 'dictated by technical considerations, rules or constraints which leave no room for creative freedom'.[28] Furthermore, as stated in another decision, in such a case, 'The different methods of implementing an idea are so limited that the idea and the expression become indissociable'.[29] If the expression of the components of the model (the weights assigned to each inter-neuron connection) depends only on their technical function (that is, minimising an error during training), the criterion of originality is not met and no human authorship can be justified.[30] On this ground, copyright could therefore not be invoked to protect a trained deep learning model.

Furthermore, Article 1(2) of the Software Directive states indeed that the protection only applies to 'the expression in any form of a computer program. Ideas and principles which underlie any element of a computer program, including those which underlie its interfaces, are not protected by copyright under this directive'. The underlying technical properties of

---

[26] *Infopaq International A/S v Danske Dagblades Forening*, ECJ case C 5-08, 16 July 2009, ECLI: EU:C:2009:465, at. 45.

[27] This is practically what happens when training a machine learning model. For example, in the case of a neural network, if each unit represents an instruction parametrised by the weights associated with its inputs, the training phase (for example, the sequence of 'feed-forward' and 'backpropagation') results in a modification of said weights under the constraint of a predefined loss function. The final 'program' is formed by the collection of inter-related neural units, each realising a simple function on the basis of the parameters learnt during the training phase.

[28] *Football Dataco Ltd and others v Yahoo! UK Ltd and others*, ECJ case C-604/10, 1 March 2012, ECLI:EU:C:2012:115, at 39.

[29] *Bezpečnostní softwarová asociace*, ECJ case C-393/09, 22 Dec. 2010, ECLI:EU:C:2010:816, at 49.

[30] In the view of the CJEU (see in particular case C-145/10 *Painer* of 7 March 2013, ECLI:EU:C: 2011:239), authorship requires that the work is 'the author's own intellectual creation reflecting his personality', or that the work carries the 'personal touch' of its author as manifested by the exercise of 'free and creative choices' – conditions that would not be met when the model's parameters result from an optimisation process dictated by a functional objective.

the code, its logic, the algorithm and the mathematical underpinnings associated therewith are thus not part of the protection. A 2012 ruling of the Court of Justice of the European Union stated it clearly: 'The functionality of a computer program and the programming language cannot be protected by copyright [...] To accept that the functionality of a computer program can be protected by copyright would amount to making it possible to monopolise ideas, to the detriment of technological progress and industrial development.'[31] Ideas are free indeed, and reverse engineering a computer program to gain access to its functionalities is authorised: 'A person who has obtained a copy of a computer program under a licence is entitled, without the authorisation of the owner of the copyright, to observe, study or test the functioning of that program so as to determine the ideas and principles which underlie any element of the program.'[32] The functionality of a trained model therefore falls beyond the scope of copyright protection under Directive 2009/24/EC.

Beyond the trained model, the computer program implementing the training algorithm, as well as all other elements of code involved in running the model would, however, fall without question under copyright protection. Still, some limits have been set to this protection. Most of the deep learning programs written today rely on pre-existing libraries that act as an intermediate abstraction layer between the core functionalities of the algorithm or the specific interface with the graphical or tensor processing unit (GPU or TPU) hardware. These libraries greatly facilitate the development of new applications and have become the *de facto* platform on which modern neural network applications are developed. Some of these libraries may use pre-trained models to facilitate the deployment of certain functionalities (for example, image or speech recognition, natural language processing, translation, and so on). While the most commonly used libraries are distributed under a variety of open-source licenses that allow modification, distribution and commercial use of the software and its derivatives,[33] care should nonetheless be taken to verify the compliance with the various licences associated with the libraries used during development.

3.3   The Inference Model as a Database

3.3.1   Copyright protection of inference models as databases
Directive 96/9/EC of the European Parliament and of the Council of 11 March 1996 (hereafter, the 'Database Directive') established the requirements for the protection of databases under the copyright regime. Article 1(2) of the Database Directive defines databases as 'collections of independent works, data or other materials arranged in a systematic or methodical way and

---

[31]   *SAS Institute v World Programming Ltd*, ECJ case C-406/10, 2 May 2012, ECLI:EU:C:2012:259, at 40.

[32]   Ibid at 53, 62.

[33]   Among the popular machine learning frameworks, PyTorch, an open-source machine learning library primarily developed by Facebook's AI Research lab (FAIR), is distributed under the BSD licence. Tensorflow (developed by Google) was released under the Apache 2.0 open-source licence on 9 November 2015. Keras, another commonly used library, is distributed under the MIT licence, while Caffe, a deep learning framework originally developed at University of California, Berkeley, is distributed under the BSD licence. Other examples include MxNet (by the Apache Software foundation) and PaddlePaddle (for 'PArallel Distributed Deep Learning', an independent, open-source deep learning platform launched by Baidu in 2016), both under Apache 2.0.

individually accessible by electronic or other means'.[34] Article 3(1) of the directive further states that 'databases which by reason of the selection or arrangement of their contents, constitute the author's own intellectual creation shall be protected as such by copyright'. When applicable, copyright protection prevents any unauthorised reproduction, distribution, communication, display or performance to the public of the database.

Database components are present at various phases of deep learning applications. Obviously, at the very early stages, data are collected and assembled in training sets. Labels and annotations can be further added to the data. Later in the processing pipeline, the inference model itself, as a collection of values, can also be encoded in a database, at least in a technical sense (whether all inference models may be considered as a database in the sense of Directive 96/9 will be addressed below).[35] Are these two facets of deep learning systems susceptible of copyright protection? To be copyrightable, the *sine qua non* condition of originality must be met. Since the landmark *Football Dataco* decision of the Court of Justice of the European Union, it is established that the EU criterion for measuring originality is satisfied 'when, through the selection or arrangement of the data which it contains, its author expresses his creative ability in an original manner by making free and creative choices and thus stamps his "personal touch"'.[36] It is, however, not sufficient that the creation of a work (that is, a database) required some effort on the part of its designer. The resulting object should also demonstrate a 'creative' aspect: 'the fact that the setting up of the database required, irrespective of the creation of the data which it contains, significant labour and skill of its author [...] cannot as such justify the protection of it by copyright [...] if that labour and that skill do not express any originality in the selection or arrangement of that data.'[37] Hence, the mere systematic aggregation of data collected from sensors (as in the case of an autonomous vehicle) or accumulated from text gathered from a search engine would not suffice to fulfil, in this sense, the condition of originality. Hand-picking specific data and collecting them in the database could qualify as a demonstration of originality (if the choice is deemed sufficient to express some element of creativity), but this scenario seems the exception rather than the rule (all the more so as large-scale training sets are required to guide deep learning applications). Regarding the trained model, where the numerical values of weights (in the case of a neural network) or other parameters characterising the model result from an optimisation process rather than from a man-made selection, the protection of the inference model as a database under EU copyright

---

[34]   See also Recital 17 of Directive 96/9 EC. *Freistaat Bayern v Verlag Esterbauer GmbH*, ECJ case C-490/14, 29 Oct. 2015, ECLI:EU:C:2015:735 and *Fixtures Marketing*, ECJ case C-444/02, 9 Nov. 2004, ECLI:EU:C:2004:697.

[35]   The different machine learning libraries or frameworks provide a variety of schemes to store or 'serialise' the trained models. For example, PyTorch relies on a built-in serialisation scheme based on the Python's pickle utility, where the models are saved as dictionary objects that map each layer of a neural network to its parameter tensor. Tensorflow and Keras libraries store their inference model using the HDF5 hierarchical data format, an open-source file format that uses a 'file directory' structure to save and organise the parameters associated with the model. The Caffe library uses so-called Protocol Buffers. In any case, the parameter components of the inference model are, in fact, stored as a 'collection of independent data arranged in a systematic way and individually accessible', thereby meeting the definition of a database according to Art. 1(2) of Directive 96/9/EC. For example, in the HDF5 format, resources can be accessed individually using their specific POSIX-like path and data are stored in the form of user-defined, named attributes associated with the datasets.

[36]   *Supra* note 28, *Football Dataco*, case C-604/10, at 38.

[37]   Ibid at 42.

law would seem rather far-fetched, if not plainly unrealistic. Furthermore, in certain instances at least, an inference model may not be considered a database at all, in the sense given by the CJEU. Indeed, it has been established that the elements of a database must have 'autonomous informative value'.[38] In the case of a neural network model, the elements are formed by the individual weights. The informational content of a weight is only meaningful within the architecture of the network. There, its function is dependent on its association with the other weights within the network. A neural network weight, as a numerical value, does not have a value independently of the network in which it has been defined.

3.3.2   *Sui generis* database right applied to inference models

Even if a database does not meet the condition of originality, the *sui generis* right can provide a protection of the investments required in creating and managing the database. According to Article 7(1) of Directive 96/9/EC, the producer of a database 'which shows that there has been qualitatively and/or quantitatively a substantial investment in either the obtaining, verification or presentation of the contents' has the right to prohibit the extraction or re-utilisation of a substantial part of the contents of that database. This protection is, moreover, independent of that which may result from copyright (Art. 7(4) of the Database Directive).

Could the *sui generis* database protection apply to trained models?[39] Is this investment associated with the construction of the model sufficient to justify the protection under the *sui generis* database right? Article 7(1) of the Directive 96/9/EC solely refers in this respect to the investments made in relations to the 'obtaining, verification or presentation of the contents' of the database.[40] But what delimits, in practice, these areas of investments? In particular, should the calculation of the parameters of a deep inference model be considered to allow protection under the *sui generis* database right? Some guidance was first provided here in 2004 by the European Court of Justice in a series of four cases involving horseracing and football fixture lists.[41] The Court ruled indeed that

> the expression 'investment in […] the obtaining […] of the contents' of a database as defined in Article 7(1) of the directive must be understood to refer to the resources used to seek out existing independent materials and collect them in the database. It does not cover the resources used for the creation of materials which make up the contents of a database.

This was justified for the court since '[t]he purpose of the protection by *the sui generis* right provided for by the directive is to promote the establishment of storage and processing systems for existing information and not the creation of materials capable of being collected subse-

---

[38]   *Supra* note 27.

[39]   For an estimate of the investments related to training a large model, see *supra* note 10.

[40]   The protection granted by the *sui generis* database right aims at preventing the unauthorised extraction or reutilisation of protected database contents. Article 7 of Directive 96/9/EC on the legal protection of databases provides that the maker of a database has the right 'to prevent extraction and/or re-utilization of the whole or of a substantial part, evaluated qualitatively and/or quantitatively, of the contents of that database', where 'there has been qualitatively and/or quantitatively a substantial investment in either the obtaining, verification or presentation of the contents'.

[41]   *British Horseracing Board Ltd and Others v William Hill Organization Ltd*, European Court of Justice (ECJ) case C-203/02, 9 Nov. 2004; *Fixtures Marketing Ltd v Oy Veikkaus Ab*, ECJ case C-45/02, 9 Nov. 2004; *Fixtures Marketing Ltd v Organismos prognostikon agonon podosfairou AE*, ECJ case C-444/02, 9 Nov. 2004; *Fixtures Marketing Ltd. v Svenska Spel AB*, ECJ case C-338/02, 9 Nov. 2004.

quently in a database'.[42] Similar conclusions were reached in the *Football Dataco* decision of 2012, where the ECJ stated that

> the concepts of 'selection' and of 'arrangement' within the meaning of Article 3(1) of Directive 96/9 refer respectively to the selection and the arrangement of data, through which the author of the database gives the database its structure. By contrast, *those concepts do not extend to the creation of the data contained in that database* (emphasis added).[43]

As a consequence, database contents which evidence a substantial investment in the *creation of data* rather than in its obtainment are excluded from protection.[44] The *sui generis* right thus only applies to databases that contain data that is publicly accessible.[45]

Regarding the trained inference model, in most instances the investments related to the calculation of the final values of the weights would be considered to fall under the remits of a 'creative' process and would not justify such a protection.[46] Still, a clear delineation between the notion of 'creation' and 'obtentions' remains to be found. This is all the more pressing as data processed through technical means emerge progressively in a sequence of transformation processes. The measurements from sensor inputs require digitisation (for example, analogue pre-processing, analogue-to-digital conversion). The resulting values can be further transformed by means of algorithmic processes (for example, to remove artefacts or reduce noise, to filter and improve certain portions of the signal, and so on) before being encoded in a variety of formats, depending on the intended use (where further processing occurs, to minimise the memory footprint, or to encrypt the data). A recent report sponsored by the European Commission drafted by the Institute for Information Law at the University of Amsterdam suggests in this sense that 'the creation/obtaining distinction in the *sui generis* right is a cause of legal uncertainty regarding the status of machine-generated data that could justify revision or clarification of the EU Database Directive'.[47]

---

[42]   Ibid at 31.

[43]   *Supra* note 28, case C-604/10, at 32. For a similar interpretation in French courts, see, e.g., Civ. 1, 5 March 2009, 07-19.734 and 07-19.735; CA Paris, 20 December 2013, RG no 12/20260.

[44]   The distinction also applies the investments related to the selection of the contents of the database. The 2004 CJEU decision states indeed that such investments must target 'the reliability of the information contained in the database, to check the accuracy of the elements sought, during the constitution of this database as well as during the period of operation of this one'. The investments therefore do not relate to the creation of the data.

[45]   See Evaluation of Directive 96/9/EC on the legal protection of databases, SWD (2018) 147 final, pp.15 and 24.

[46]   For example, in the case of 'Support Vector Machines', where the model consists of a collection of 'support vectors' that each correspond to an element already present in the training corpus (expressed as a 'vector'), it may be argued that the training process only contributes to the selection of these specific (pre-existing) entities, not to their creation.

[47]   P.B. Hugenholtz, J.P. Quintais and D. Gervais, 'Trends and Developments in Artificial Intelligence – Challenges to the Intellectual Property Rights Framework', European Commission Report, 25 Nov. 2020 (p.9). This excerpt of the report echoes the conclusions of a previous European Commission report from December 2005 underlining, after the series of judgments rendered by the ECJ in November 2004 (see *supra* note 41), that the precise scope of the *sui generis* right has proven difficult to establish, which had 'caused considerable legal uncertainty, both at the EU and national level' (Commission of the European Communities (CEC). First Evaluation of Directive 96/9/EC on the Legal Protection of Databases. 12December 2005, Brussels).

Whether a trained inference model qualifies as a database in the sense of Directive 96/9 must be evaluated on a case-by-case basis. According to CJEU decisions, the elements of a database (works, data or other materials) must be 'independent', that is to say, 'materials which are separable from one another without their informative, literary, artistic, musical or other value being affected'.[48] How would a trained model fare against this requirement? Although the courts are yet to tackle such a case, it may be argued that the collection of weights in a neural network model would fail to qualify as a database (in the sense of the directive), on the grounds that each parameter does not have an 'autonomous informative content'.[49] However, this conclusion may not be generalised to all inference models. Indeed, for certain categories of models, such as support vector machines, the elements in the model are representants of the training set. In such instances, it could be argued that the constituents of the database have intrinsic 'independent' informational content and, as such, their collection qualifies as a database. The question may, therefore, require substantive examination. In fact, an early British ruling found that, in the case of a 'discriminator' program in a vending machine, the set of parameters corresponding to valid physical coin attributes (such as weight or size) that enabled the algorithm to distinguish real coins from 'slugs' did qualify as a database.[50] The decision states that

> the discrimination process includes the use of algorithms (mathematical recipes) which combine the outputs of the sensors in an effective manner to ensure that each valid coin gives an ultimate set of outputs which can be distinguished from duds, foreign coins or other non-valid discs (collectively called 'slugs' in the trade). […] Each parameter measured therefore has to have a 'window' of acceptable values. […] A very great deal of experimental work as well as skill and judgment is involved in determining appropriate windows for each coin of a given coinage. Mars have a vast collection of sets of coins for many countries of the world and have to keep under constant review the windows for the coins of any particular set.[51]

In this particular instance, the set of parameters (the 'windows') on which the model was based was found to justify a protection under the *sui generis* database right.[52]

If the trained model cannot be considered as a database in the sense of Directive 96/9 EC, contractual options may be applicable to prevent undesired use. Under Article 8(1) of the directive, the maker of a database made available to the public cannot prevent a lawful user from extracting and/or re-utilising insubstantial parts of it for any purposes and any contractual term contrary to this provision is void (Art. 15 of the Database Directive). This means that the maker of a collection of data that is not protected under Directive 96/9 EC may resort to contractual terms to limit its use and, as a consequence, enjoy a somewhat greater protection than that accorded by the *sui generis* directive. This situation has been discussed by the CJEU in case C-30/14 opposing Ryanair Ltd to PR Aviation BV.[53] The Court found that the producer of a database that is *not* protected under the terms of the Database Directive does not need to ensure a minimal level of free use of the database contents (such as the right for a lawful user

---

[48]   *Supra* note 27.
[49]   *Supra* note 31.
[50]   *Mars UK Ltd v Teknowledge Ltd* [1999] EIPR N-158 (H.C.).
[51]   Ibid at pt. 2.
[52]   Noting that in this case the collection of parameters had been set manually, and did not result from a training process. However, in all probabilities, this would not have affected the decision.
[53]   *Ryanair Ltd v PR Aviation BV*, ECJ case C-30/14, 15 Jan. 2015, ECLI:EU:C:2015:10.

to extract and reuse insubstantial portions of the database, including for commercial purposes). In such instance, contractual limitation may prove more favourable to the owner of the data collection than the protection provided by the Database Directive.

3.4 The Patent Protection of Inference Models

The operation of a trained inference model is equivalent to that of a transfer function, a 'mapping': it processes data (such as inputs obtained from sensors, a camera, a microphone) and delivers a prediction as an output (the presence of an object in an image, the detection of an utterance in a speech signal). The effect is analogous to that of a filter, but with a notable difference: instead of deriving their properties from a physical implementation (the shape of a piece of glass, in an optical filter, or the assembly of capacitors and transistors, in an electronic circuit), inference models rely on an algorithmic and software specification. While there is little doubt that a physical filter may be, in principle, susceptible to patent protection, how would the algorithmic equivalent fare in this respect?

A patent can be obtained in Europe for inventions 'in all fields of technology' (Art. 52(1) of the European Patent Convention (EPC));[54] machine learning applications and resulting inference models are therefore not excluded a priori from the realm of patent protection provided they meet certain legal conditions, namely novelty, the presence of an inventive step and industrial applicability (Arts 54, 56 and 57 EPC). The prosecution of patent applications at the European Patent Office (EPO) follows in practice a 'two-hurdle approach'. First, the application must be deemed 'admissible' – in other words, its subject matter must constitute an invention. While patents can be granted for inventions irrespective of their technological application, the notion of 'invention' is not defined in positive terms in the EPC but rather through a non-exhaustive list of subject matters or activities whose patentability is excluded.[55] Among these, 'computer programs', 'mathematical methods' and 'presentation of information' are excluded from patent protection. The exclusion, however, concerns only inventions relating to subject matter which is claimed 'as such';[56] a claimed subject matter having technical character would circumvent the exclusion. Some aspects of a machine-learning system may obviously be deemed 'technical': specific physical architectures that facilitate the training of large-scale models, for example, or dedicated 'tensor processors' based on systolic arrays. But even beyond their sole physical implementations, inference models could also be considered 'inventions' in the sense of Article 52(1) EPC and benefit from patent protection as long as they possess technical character. This condition is easily met in practice for method claims, as simply referring to a physical system in relation with the otherwise abstract, algorithmic feature (claimed, for instance, as a 'computer-implemented process') will give the application a sufficient technical basis to be deemed admissible.[57] Inference models would overcome this initial obstacle without difficulty by integrating in a process claim a reference to a computer

---

[54] Art. 52(1) EPC as revised in 2000, following Art. 27(1) TRIPS (the EPC 2000 entered into force on 13 December 2007).

[55] Art. 52(2) (a)–(d) EPC.

[56] Art. 52(3) EPC.

[57] See EPO Boards of appeal decision T 258/03 (Auction method/HITACHI) of 21 Apr. 2004, stating that technical character can result either from the physical features of an entity or (for a method) from the use of technical means. A claimed subject-matter involving technical means is therefore not excluded from patentability by Art. 52(2) EPC. Since a claim directed to a 'method of operating a computer' (or

hardware on which the model is executed. In the case of computer program *product* claims (a category which may, in practice, suit trained inference models, as discussed above), technical character cannot result from the mere reference to a computer but must be found in further technical effects resulting from the execution of the program's instructions; for example, if the computer-executed instructions participate in solving a technical problem,[58] or where technical considerations are involved in arriving at the invention.[59]

What about the inference model considered as a database or as a 'data structure'? The EPO Guidelines indicate that 'a computer-implemented data structure or data format embodied on a medium or as an electromagnetic carrier wave has technical character as a whole and thus is an invention within the meaning of 52(1) EPC'.[60] This is the case if the data structure is considered as 'functional data', namely 'if it has a technical function in a technical system, such as controlling the operation of the device processing the data'.[61] In T 1159/15 of 6/4/2020, the technical character of a model generated via regression analysis was considered.[62] Claim 1 included a feature consisting in 'a multidimensional data storage system storing information for models generated by the model generator'. The boards found that

> the defined data storage contains two types of data. Firstly, data encoding cognitive content, such as information related to variables, assumptions, etc. These data are used in the generation of the models. Secondly, the aggregation rules, which are not related to any cognitive content but are instructions related to the operation of the system when responding to queries. These data could thus be characterised as 'functional data' (see also T 1194/97, OJ EPO 2000, 575, Headnote II and Reasons 3.3 to 3.5; T 425/03, Reasons 6.2 and 6.3).

Following this reasoning, one may consider that the functional nature of the computer-implemented architecture of an inference model may suffice to assign a technical character to the trained model as a whole.

Once admissibility has been established, the invention must meet the requirements of novelty, inventive step and industrial application. A characteristic of inference models is that they result from a mix of features: some components may possess an unquestionably technical character (a physical sensor from which input signals are obtained, a reference to a specific computer or any other material entity) while others, taken individually, are subject to exclusion (such as the algorithm and the individual parameters). For instance, a neural network architecture would be considered, as such, an abstract algorithmic subject matter. The

---

a 'computer implemented method') necessarily involves a computer it cannot be excluded from patentability by Art. 52(2) EPC (see also decision G 3/08).

[58]   See, e.g., EPO Boards of Appeal decision T 208/84 (Computer-related invention/VICOM) of 15 July 1986, OJ 1987, 14. In T 1173/97 (Computer program product/IBM) of 1 July 1998, the board stated that a 'further technical effect' is one 'which goes beyond the "normal" physical interactions between the program (software) and the computer (hardware) on which it is run' (headnote).

[59]   See, e.g., T 769/92 (General purpose management system/SOHEI) of 31 May 1994, OJ 1995, 525.

[60]   EPO Guidelines, G-II, 3.6.3.

[61]   Ibid.

[62]   T 1159/15 of 6/4/2020, par. 32, stating: 'given a selected set of variables, a statistical regression (e.g., linear regression) approach is used to determine model coefficients. These are coefficients for the variables of the model that best map the data for the variables (e.g., cost data for marketing channels) to the corresponding historic performance data. Estimation of the coefficients of the variables for a candidate model is performed using regression techniques to produce multi-variable functions (e.g., curves) that best fit computed output of the given input data to its corresponding output.'

treatment of these so-called mixed-type inventions that combine technical and non-technical features mandates special attention: how should we consider those features that, considered individually, would be excluded from patentability on the basis of Article 52(2) EPC? The established methodology developed at the EPO requires taking into account all of the features that contribute to the technical character of the invention, even those that are algorithmic in nature.[63] In the course of evaluating the obviousness of the claimed subject matter, following the problem–solution approach, the definition of these 'technical features' will determine the choice of the closest prior art, which will in turn affect the technical effect resulting from the difference between the claimed invention and said prior art.[64] From this technical effect, an objective technical problem is formulated (the problem that the skilled person would attempt to achieve in order to realise the technical effect). If the skilled person finds the claimed solution obvious – based on the knowledge of the closest prior art, her expertise and the common general knowledge in the field of the invention – the patent is refused for lack of an inventive step; otherwise, assuming all other conditions are met, a patent may be granted.

It still remains to be determined, therefore, to what extent a contribution to the technical character of the invention may be justified for trained inference models. Analysis of the decisions of the EPO's Boards of Appeal helped identify two 'dimensions' via which an algorithmic component may contribute to the technical character of an invention: if it is a specific technical implementation and/or an application with a technical purpose.[65] If it participates in at least one of those two dimensions, an algorithmic entity such as a trained inference model contributes to the technical character of the claimed invention. In this context the technical contribution of trained inference models must be considered in the evaluation of the non-obviousness of the invention, and hence if the architecture of a model mirrors the specific physical hardware on which it is to be deployed (for example, as emerging from strategies of co-design of neural architectures and hardware accelerators[66]). A trained inference model that contributes to a technical purpose will also be considered as a patentable subject matter (for example, when the model aims at the classification of image or sound signals, at the denoising of speech input, at the control of an apparatus, and so on[67]). As a data structure, for example, the nature of the data (the weights) will be determined by its intended use. It is indeed the purposive use of information in the context of a solution to a technical problem that can justify a contribution to the technical character of an invention.[68] In T 1351/04, the Boards considered

---

[63] Following the procedure developed in the EPO Boards of Appeal decision T 641/00 (Two identities/COMVIK) of 26 September 2002 (OJ 2003, 352).

[64] A main motivation of the problem–solution approach developed at the EPO is to minimise any *ex post facto* analysis (and avoid a form of 'hindsight bias', where the resolution of a problem appears simpler after having been presented with its solution).

[65] See EPO Guidelines for examination, G-II, 3.3. A key teaching of this approach, following the Comvik decision, is to make sure that the claimed features are interpreted in the context of the claimed invention. The technical contribution of a given feature should not be considered in isolation but should be assessed by taking into account the interactions between the claimed features.

[66] M. Tan et al, 2019, Platform-aware neural architecture search for mobile. In Proceedings of the IEEE/CVF Conference on Computer Vision and Pattern Recognition, pp.2820–8; H. Cai, L. Zhu and S. Han, Proxylessnas, 2019, Direct neural architecture search on target task and hardware. In International Conference on Learning Representations (ICLR); Y. Zhou et al., Rethinking Co-design of Neural Architectures and Hardware Accelerators, 2021, arXiv preprint arXiv:2102.08619.

[67] See EPO Guidelines for examination, G-II, 3.3.

[68] See T 49/99 (Information modelling/International Computers) of 5 March 2002 (pt. 7).

that an index file used for the purpose of controlling the computer 'along the path leading to the desired data' contributed to the solution of a technical problem.[69] More generally, EPO Boards of Appeal decision T 697/17 stated that 'data structures used to store cognitive data are not considered to contribute to the technical character beyond the mere storage of data, data structures used for functional purposes are considered to contribute to producing a technical effect (see e.g. T 1194/97, OJ EPO 2000, 525, reasons 3.3 or T 424/03 of 23 February 2006, reasons 5.2)'.[70]

Not all purposes are deemed technical, though. In particular, the classification of text documents based only on their semantic content is considered, as such, a linguistic application, without technical contribution.[71] Furthermore, 'classifying abstract data records or even "telecommunication network data records" without any indication of a technical use being made of the resulting classification is also not per se a technical purpose, even if the classification algorithm may be considered to have valuable mathematical properties such as robustness'.[72] As a consequence, an inference model could not derive a technical character by being directed toward such applications.[73] Assuming the technical character of the trained inference model has been established, either based on the specific purpose of the model or through its adaptation to a specific hardware, the set of parameters forming the model could be considered as having been functional in nature. The model as a set of values derived from the training process could therefore be considered a technical object solving a technical problem.

An analogy could be made here with a mathematical filter applied to image processing. Decision T0208/84 of the European Patent Office Boards of Appeal established, indeed, that such an object was capable of industrial application (point 3 of the grounds), and although 'the characteristics of a filter, for example, can be expressed by a mathematical formula [...] in using a mathematical method in a technical process, this method applies to a physical entity (which may be a physical object but also an image stored in the form of an electrical signal) by some technical means implementing the method and this results in a certain modification of this entity'.[74] More recently, Decision G 1/19 from the EPO Enlarged Board of Appeal provided useful guidance on the occurrence of 'technical effects' that can be used in the context of a trained inference model (although the case under consideration only concerned computer-implemented simulations, the conclusions may be usefully translated to machine learning models).[75] In particular, it was shown that the contribution to the technical character of the invention may arise from the technical nature of either the input (such as the measurements from a sensor) or the output (that could either control a device or be considered as 'functional

---

[69]   T 1351/04 (File search method/FUJITSU) of 18 April 2007 (pt. 7.2).

[70]   T 697/17 (SQL extensions/Microsoft Technology Licensing) of 17 Oct. 2019 (pt. 5.2.5).

[71]   See T 1358/09, T 0022/12.

[72]   EPO Guidelines, G-II, 3.3.1.

[73]   In drafting a claim in front of the EPO, applicants should therefore make sure that the purpose of the trained model is limited to those aims deemed technical by the boards.

[74]   EPO Boards of Appeal, Decision T 208/84 (VICOM) of 15 Jul. 1986.

[75]   G 1/19 (Pedestrian simulation) of 10 March 2021. The decision states, in particular, that 'no group of computer-implemented inventions can be a priori excluded from patent protection' (pt. 139) and that 'like any other computer-implemented inventions, numerical simulations may be patentable if an inventive step can be based on features contributing to the technical character of the claimed simulation method' (pt. 136). The same principle would apply to a computer-implemented process relying on a trained inference model.

data' intended for controlling a technical device, when being specifically adapted for purposes of its intended technical use). However, merely specifying the nature of input data is not in itself necessarily sufficient to ensure that the use of a trained model contributes to the technical character of the invention. Rather, as noted in section G-II, 3.3 of the EPO Guidelines, 'Whether a technical purpose is served by the mathematical method is primarily determined by the direct technical relevance of the results it provides'. In the same spirit, a generic purpose such as 'controlling a technical system' is not sufficient: the technical purpose must be a specific one and the claim must be functionally limited to the technical purpose. Beyond the specific application of the trained model, technical character would also result from the adaptation of the inference model to the computer or its operation, if such adaptation produces technical effects, such as better use of storage capacity or improved bandwidth. Provided such conditions are met, the model will be considered technical. As a consequence, following the practice established in the Comvik decision, the specific characteristics of the trained model will have to be considered in the assessment of inventive step.[76] If no technical contribution can be associated with the model (if either the model fails to serve a technical purpose or it is not adapted to the functioning of specific hardware), it may be directly provided to the skilled person through the formulation of the objective technical problem.[77] Then the skilled person, explicitly instructed of the details of the model, would only have to implement it, a programming operation that would be considered obvious in all instances.

If, on the contrary, the claimed model has technical character and the skilled person finds that it would not be derived from the prior art without exercising an inventive step, the conditions of Article 56 EPC are considered to be met.[78] The burden of proof in assessing the lack of obviousness of the invention lies with the examining division or the opposing party. While it is well established that the skilled person can rely on tools (such as a computer) to experiment[79] and find suitable solutions to the objective problem, it not sufficient to assert that the model *could* have been obtained (using, for example, known optimisation procedures); what is required is that the skilled person *would* have arrived at the very model that is presently claimed in the application.[80] This distinction, between the conditional 'could' and the causal 'would', proves particularly significant in the case of a trained inference model. Indeed, the stochastic nature both of the initialisation of the model and of the training process would lead to a different instance of the model each time a model is trained.[81] Faced with the large number

---

[76] T 641/00, headnote I.

[77] T 641/00, headnote II.

[78] In T 424/03 of 23 Feb. 2006 the EPO boards found that a claim directed to 'a computer-readable medium having computer-executable instructions' that cause a computer to perform the steps of a claimed method has technical character. In principle, such a formulation could therefore support the claim to a medium containing a trained inference model that causes a computer to execute said model towards a technical purpose.

[79] The skilled person has the 'capacity for routine work and experimentation which are normal for the field of technology in question' (EPO Guidelines G-VII, 3).

[80] EPO Guidelines for Examination, G-VII, 5.3.

[81] This is in particular the case for neural networks, where the process of determining the weights depends on minimising a 'cost function', namely, a measure of the network's error. Since the cost function of neural networks is characterised by a very large number of local maxima and minima (it is said to be 'non-convex'), the final set of weights will vary according to the initialisation of the network's parameters. The random initialisation of the weights will therefore lead, each time the model is trained, to a different final model.

of possible outcomes, it cannot be asserted convincingly that the specific claimed model would be derived, unambiguously and causally, from a given training corpus and a given training method. Even if two final instances of a trained model may be found functionally equivalent (in terms of their relative predictive efficiency, as measured by their generalisation capability), they will be characterised by two completely different sets of weights. These two sets of weights may therefore provide two alternative solutions to a given problem. Following the established case law of the EPO Boards, the fact that the claimed subject matter represents an alternative solution to a known problem does not exclude it, in principle, from patentability.[82]

Does it mean that all claimed models will be considered non-obvious on the sole basis that it cannot be demonstrated that a skilled person would have necessarily arrived at their precise formulation? Not quite. Assuming the model's architecture is known in the art at the filing date of the application and assuming that the problem solved by the inference model is known, claiming a specific trained model would only differ from the anterior art in the values of its parameters. Since the architecture is known, the mere training of a model would not justify, as such, an inventive contribution. Still, multiple models may be produced (due to the stochasticity of the training process) and the remaining problem that the skilled person would face would then be one of selecting a particular model from the set of possible models. Faced with the objective technical problem of selecting a suitable instance from multiple equally likely options, the EPO Boards considered that the skilled person would resort to balancing the benefits and drawbacks of each solution without requiring an inventive effort.[83] Indeed, 'if all options are equally likely, then the invention merely results in an obvious and consequently non-inventive selection among a number of known possibilities'.[84] A case could therefore be made against the non-obviousness of a particular trained model if it can be argued that it is functionally equivalent to a pre-existing model sharing the same architecture. Similarly, if the only difference with the prior art lies in the choice of hyper-parameters, it may be considered, following the EPO Boards, that the use of different parameters 'constituted for the person skilled in the art a normal procedure, based on routine work and representing pure optimisation work, for which no inventive step could be recognised'.[85] In all such instances, where an invention of selection is put forward by the applicant, an argument in favour of an inventive contribution may reside in demonstrating unexpected effects or advantages in the operation of the trained model or in the properties of the resulting product.[86] Showing, for example using experimental tests, that a trained model improves upon the prior art alternatives may tip the scale in favour of establishing an inventive contribution.

An essential component of the notion of invention resides in establishing that it forms a solution to a technical problem.[87] The application must show that a solution exists in the first place. To this end, sufficiently convincing arguments must be put forward by the applicant. As a matter of fact, claiming trained inference models may raise issues of reproducibility and

---

[82]   See T 0092/92 of 21 Sept. 1993 (point 4.5) and T 495/91 (Oberflächenausrüstung/PEGULAN) of 20 July 1993.

[83]   In the context of machine learning models, one can estimate the model's performance on out-of-sample data by comparing the rates of true positives and false positives.

[84]   T 1045/12 (Data communication system/Canon) of 23.10.2018 (pt. 4.7.7).

[85]   T 1419/10 of 2 Oct. 2012 (our translation).

[86]   EPO Guidelines, G-VII, 'Annex – Examples relating to the requirement of inventive step – indicators', point 3.2.

[87]   See, e.g., T 0603/89 (Marker) of 3 July 1990 (headnote 1).

plausibility. Questions such as 'Is the effect claimed by resorting to a particular trained inference model plausibly achieved?' or 'Are there sufficient details to reproduce the invention?' may indeed be raised and require attention in order to avoid speculative inventions that cannot be realised at the time of filing. The determination whether an effect is plausible beyond mere allegations can be relevant for the assessment of sufficiency of disclosure under Article 83 EPC or for the assessment of inventive step under Article 56 EPC, depending on whether the alleged effect is expressed in the claims or not.[88] The definition of an invention as being a contribution to the art requires that it is at least made plausible by the disclosure in the application that its teaching solves indeed the problem it purports to solve.[89] In particular, in the context of AI applications, it must be plausible to the skilled person, from the application as filed, that a trained model is capable of producing reliable predictions for new 'test' data not used during training.[90] Plausibility can be readily apparent on the common general knowledge or supported through theoretical arguments, explanations and/or experimental validation data provided in the application as filed.

An objection under Article 83 EPC may also be considered if the invention is not deemed reproducible. Answering the question 'Is there enough information to allow the skilled person to reproduce the invention?' relies on the common general knowledge at the priority date of the application. In particular, if the claimed technical effect depends on the definition of specific parameters, specific architectures, these should be explicitly disclosed. If a patent is to be obtained on a trained inference model, an essential condition to be met is one of disclosure of the invention. Article 83 EPC states indeed that 'the European patent application shall disclose the invention in a manner sufficiently clear and complete for it to be carried out by a person skilled in the art'. That those seeking patent protection should be required to provide sufficient teaching of the claimed invention, as to enable a skilled person to put the invention into practice, is a cornerstone of the patent system. This principle applies for all inventions, which implies in sufficient detail both the model used and how to train it.

The issue here is not the lack of explainability of the model as such (it is irrelevant in this respect that a large model, such as a deep neural network, may not be translated in intelligible form) but rather one of establishing the means by which the claimed technical effect is achieved and to ensure its consistent reproducibility. To do so, test or experimental data may be considered. Providing validation tests of a trained machine learning model (where 'validation' refers to applying a trained model to new data not used during training, and evaluating

---

[88]   Section F-III, 12 of the EPO Guidelines provide guidance to which of Art. 56 or Art. 83 EPC should be invoked in this instance (see also G 1/03, Reasons 2.5.2, T 1079/08, T 1319/10, T 5/06 and T 380/05).

[89]   T 1329/04 (Factor-9/John Hopkins) of 28 June 2005 at pt. 12 of the reasons: 'the definition of an invention as being a contribution to the art, i.e. as solving a technical problem and not merely putting forward one, requires that it is at least made plausible by the disclosure in the application that its teaching solves indeed the problem it purports to solve.'

[90]   The question of plausibility of an output derived from a particular input was raised in the decision T 0626/97. The boards considered that 'the interpretation relied on in the contested decision appears to be particularly speculative in view of the fact that it would in general appear difficult, if not impossible, to determine a reliable information about a battery's remaining capacity from a measurement of its actual voltage or internal resistance. [...] In view of such a fundamental ambiguity concerning an important characteristic of a claim, which cannot be resolved on the basis of the patent as a whole, the disclosure has to be considered not to be sufficiently clear and complete to be carried out by a skilled person (cf. T 5/99).'

the results for correctness or accuracy) may help assess the plausibility and reproducibility of a particular ML model. Even if absent from the original application, supplementary evidence may in the proper circumstances corroborate the plausibility or support reproducibility of the invention. However, such further evidence may only be considered under certain conditions. In practice, as stated in T 1329/04, 'even if supplementary post-published evidence may in the proper circumstances also be taken into consideration, it may not serve as the sole basis to establish that the application solves indeed the problem it purports to solve'.[91]

Even if the issues of plausibility and reproducibility of the model are resolved, other formal constraints may hinder its practical disclosure. The technical character associated with the trained inference model results from the association of the model architecture and its parameters. The parameters are therefore an essential component of the model and, as such, should be disclosed in the patent application. If describing in a concise but precise manner the model's architecture does not appear to pose any particular problem, disclosing the whole parameter set seems rather unrealistic. Practical issues may indeed represent an obstacle to the formulation of a claim for a trained model. When, as in the case of the largest neural network models such as Google's T5-XXL or openAI GPT-3, tens or hundreds of billions of parameters are involved – and even up to a trillion weights with Google's latest Switch network[92] – one can imagine the singularity of such a claim.[93] Since current inference models (for example, deep learning ones) seem far too large to be included verbatim in a patent application, how can a patent application on a trained inference model be practically submitted in front of any patent granting authority and meet the condition of sufficiency of disclosure?

A lifeline could be thrown from a different technical field: biology. Indeed, Rule 31(1) EPC states:

> if an invention involves the use of or concerns biological material which is not available to the public and which cannot be described in the European patent application in such a manner as to enable the invention to be carried out by a person skilled in the art, the invention shall only be regarded as being disclosed as prescribed in Article 83 if: (a) a sample of the biological material has been deposited with a recognised depositary institution on the same terms as those laid down in the Budapest Treaty on the International Recognition of the Deposit of Microorganisms for the Purposes of Patent Procedure of 28 April 1977 not later than the date of filing of the application.[94]

If a machine learning depository institution was to be created, applicants could submit their trained inference model and obtain an accession number to be included in their patent applica-

---

[91]   *Supra* note 89 (pt. 12). See also T 716/08 (Infectious salmon anaemia virus vaccine/INTERVET) of 19 Aug. 2010 (pts 15 and 16).

[92]   For a description of the T5 architecture, see C. Raffel, et al., Exploring the limits of transfer learning with a unified text-to-text transformer, 2019, arXiv preprint arXiv:1910.10683. For the Switch architecture, see W. Fedus, B. Zoph and N. Shazeer, Switch transformers: Scaling to trillion parameter models with simple and efficient sparcity, 2021, arXiv preprint arXiv:2101.03961. For a description of the GPT-3 architecture, see Brown, et al., S., 2020. Language models are few-shot learners. arXiv preprint arXiv:2005.14165.

[93]   A back-of-the-envelope calculation shows that listing the trillion weights of Google's Switch-XXL model in a patent application would require a stack of paper hundreds of metres high.

[94]   Today more than 80 countries are parties to the Budapest System, while 48 International Depository authorities are present in 27 countries (www.wipo.int/budapest/en/idadb/).

tion.[95] If such a procedure were to be followed, claiming (and disclosing) a trained model could therefore be formulated as follows: 'a trained neural network model #AHE121931-2', where '#AHE121931-2' corresponds to the unique accession number to the claimed trained model, as filed with an international depositary authority.[96] The benefit of such a platform would be to enable meeting the condition of disclosure: the model would be rendered publicly available through the depository institution, thereby enabling analysis by patent granting authorities, to check for the reproducibility of the invention, and by third parties, to evaluate and improve the model.[97] However, an institution dedicated to storing and archiving machine learning models remains to be established. Absent such a depository, other options may be found to disclose and claim trained inference models.

Could there be a mechanism by which the protection inference models is related to the process by which it is obtained?[98] Inventions for products defined in terms of the process steps required for their production are, in fact, admissible under the EPC, but only under specific criteria. First, the products themselves must meet the conditions of patentability.[99] Second, these so-called product-by-process claims are only allowable if the application in its entirety does not contain any other information that would allow a definition of the product through its structural characteristics.[100] How do these conditions apply to inference models?

Establishing whether the inference model as a product defined by some machine learning process steps meets the conditions of novelty and inventive step must be based on the product alone, without consideration as to the characteristics of the process.[101] Arguments in favour of novelty may be compelling for large models. But a convincing demonstration of the inventive contribution over the prior art *of the whole class of models resulting from a training process* may pose a definite challenge to the Applicant. All the more so as each time the process is run, each time a model is trained, the resulting product will be different. Can the whole set of products be assumed inventive?

An important, and rather constraining aspect of product-by-process claims lies in its reversal of the burden of proof in establishing that the process results in a distinct characteristic of its

---

[95]   The procedure would require that the model be deposited prior to the date of filing the application or, where priority is claimed, the date of priority of invention. Specific conditions regarding the format of encoding of the model may be requested, in particular to facilitate the access and interoperability of the model.

[96]   See in this sense, T.Y. EbrahimArtificial intelligence inventions & patent disclosure, 2020, Penn St. L. Rev., 125, 147.

[97]   The main responsibilities of the depository would be to accept and store the models provided they meet certain conditions of form, assign a unique accession number to each accepted model, maintain the secrecy of the model until publication of the patent application and provide the models to third parties under request after their publication. The depositor would be required to deposit the model in the required format as established by the depository (equivalent to the requirement to comply with constraints of 'forms and quantity' for microorganisms under Budapest Treaty, Rule 6.4(a)).

[98]   Here, such a 'product-by-process' claim may take the following form: 'A trained inference model obtained [or obtainable] by the training process X', where 'X' would describe the detailed steps required to produce the model.

[99]   See T 150/82 (Claim categories) of 7 Feb. 1984 (OJ 1984, 309), Headnote II.

[100]   See EPO Guidelines for examination, F-IV, 4.12: 'A product is not rendered novel merely by the fact that it is produced by means of a new process.'

[101]   See, e.g., T 219/83 (Zeolites) of 26 Nov. 1985 (OJ 1986, 211).

product with respect to the prior art.[102] The EPO Guidelines state indeed that the onus lies on the applicant, 'to provide evidence that the modification of the process parameters results in another product, for example by showing that distinct differences exist in the properties of the products'.[103] Meeting this condition seems in principle straightforward in the case of an inference model where updating the initial conditions of the weights and retaining the model would necessarily lead to a new set of final weights, but demonstrating it in practice may prove elusive. In decision T 552/91, the Technical Boards of the EPO considered, in the context of a chemical agent, that

> it is necessary to include in the claim the process parameters required for defining unambiguously the claimed substances as *inevitable process products*. [...] It is generally necessary to indicate not only *the starting compounds and the reaction conditions*, but also the methods by which the reaction mixture is processed to obtain the claimed compounds.[104]

A parallel with the inference models would imply that both the training data and the hyper-parameters controlling the training process be disclosed and claimed. Lastly, to meet the conditions of article 84 EPC, the technical features imparted to the product by the process by which it is defined should be clearly and unambiguously identifiable from the claimed subject matter (alone or in light of the description). Again, this requirement may prove a tall order when attempting to claim a trained inference model as product-by-process.

If claiming a trained model as product-by-process is not allowable, in the particular instance where the *training process* itself meets the conditions of patentability, a protection on the associated trained model obtained therefrom can be derived from the application of Article 64(2) EPC. The Article states indeed that 'if the subject matter of the European patent is a process, the protection conferred by the patent shall extend to the products directly obtained by such process'. This protection is independent of the patentability of the deep learning model as such (and should be distinguished from a protection under a 'product-by-process' claim as previously discussed). The rule applies therefore without having to demonstrate that the product itself, that is, the trained model, is novel or inventive. The question remains as to the possibility of considering 'data' (the parameters learnt during the training process) as a 'product'. Cases invoking Article 64(2) EPC are rather rare, and those in relation to computer applications and derived 'data' products even more so. In a judgement of 21 August 2012, the Bundesgerichtshof (the German Federal Court of Justice) addressed this very question in the context of MPEG-2 video signal encoding.[105] In this case the Court ruled that data may indeed be considered as a direct product of a process, but required that the data manifest a technical character. Patent protection was directed at the technical format of the encoded data and not at the content itself. In a later decision, the German Federal Court of Justice further stressed that a collection of data produced directly by a patent-protected process may be considered as a patent-infringing product if, and only if, the product has tangible and technical characteris-

---

[102]   See T 0032/17 (Bispecific antibody/ DIASOURCE) of 2 July 2020, referring to T 0179/03 of 28 March 2007.

[103]   EPO Guidelines for examination, F-IV, 4.12.

[104]   T 552/91 (Chromanderivate) of 3 Mach 1994 (OJ, 1995, 100, Reasons 5.2) (we underline), see also T 956/04 of 17 Jan. 2008 (pt. 8.3).

[105]   Bundesgerichtshof, 'MPEG-2-Videosignalcodierung', 21 Aug. 2012, X ZR 33/10.

tics that have been induced by the process.[106] The Court made a distinction between 'information', generally excluded from patent protection under Article 52(2)(d) EPC, and 'products'. The mere fact that data carry 'informational content' is not sufficient to award them a technical character. However, the Court considered that a data structure or a data format is technical and can, as such, be considered a 'product'. In light of these decisions, would a trained inference model, as a collection of data elements produced by the (patented) training process, justify the application of Article 64(2) EPC? On the one hand, the parameters characterising a given model are clearly of informational content. On the other hand, the inference model does possess the attributes of a data structure (at least in some instance, such as in the case of the architecture of a neural network) and, in this sense, can be found analogous to the data structure found technical by the German Federal Court in the case of video signal encoding. At least some trained inference models may therefore be considered as direct products.[107]

Still, the function of this provision is not so much 'to prohibit the release of a product as such' – to use the formula used in preparation sessions for the Munich Convention – but rather 'to prohibit the release into circulation of a product as a result of [such a process]'.[108] What is at play here is therefore not so much the prohibition of the use of the inference model as such, but instead the protection of the parent training process. Article 64(2) EPC indeed enables the use of the direct product as a probative means of an infringement over the parent process, a mechanism particularly useful in situations where the litigious use of patented process is realised outside the geographical area where the patent is in force. As a consequence, beyond the dependence on a patented training method, the practical application of this provision cannot be considered as a general means of protection of trained inference models – even more so as the protection (of the training method) conferred by Article 64(2) is only valid when the product is *directly* obtained from the patented process. As a matter of fact, any ulterior alteration of the deep learning weights, such as the inclusion of an additional transformation of the parameters (for example, a rescaling or a small random modification) would obviate the application of the article. Such remedy will therefore only offer a form of indirect protection in a limited number of cases.

Beyond the practical limitations of claiming an inference model (be it the limitations of disclosing the model explicitly in the application or the constraints imposed by a product-by-process claim), the protection afforded by such patent may be easily circumvented. Since it is the set of parameters that forms the essential characteristic of the invention, and that infringement consists in the reproduction of these same claimed characteristics, a slight modification of the parameters would avoid falling under the scope of protection, without – in all probability – significantly affecting the underlying technical effect. As Watkin and Rau pointed out as early as 1996:

---

[106]   Bundesgerichtshof, 'Rezeptortyrosinkinase II', 18 Jan. 2017, X ZR 124/15.

[107]   It may be worth noting here that, following the X ZR 124/15 decision, the prediction data resulting from the use of a protected inference model would be considered of an informational nature, thereby preventing the extension of the reach of the patent covering the use of a trained model method to its outputs.

[108]   Preparatory works to the Munich Convention: Results of the third working group on patens, Brussels, 25 Sept. to 6 Oct. 1961, doc. IV/6514/61-F. The Italian delegation, represented by Professor M. Roscioni, underlining in this sense that 'the provision aims at protecting a particular process and not a product as such' (p. 40).

the scope of protection of such a patent would be hopelessly limited, since it would only cover a single expression of the underlying network concepts. […] [T]he generation of equivalent networks is very easy, and two networks which perform the same task usually nothing else whatsoever in common, so a patent to an actual neural network would be practically useless.[109]

The doctrine of equivalents is an essential principle for establishing infringement. This difficult task of keeping the exclusive rights of the patentee within reasonable bounds is left to the court. A balance must be found between an excessively narrow interpretation of the scope of protection from the strict wording of the claims (any departure therefrom allowing to circumvent the protection conferred by the patent) and an extensive interpretation of the claimed subject matter that would unduly expand its scope. This search for a balanced view is enshrined in the protocol on the interpretation of Article 69 EPC, which states that '[f]or the purpose of determining the extent of protection conferred by a European patent, due account shall be taken of any element which is equivalent to an element specified in the claims'.[110] The notion of 'equivalent' consisting in minor variations of a product allows circumvention of the strict language of the claim while adhering to the underlying inventive concept.[111] Applied to trained inference models, the principle of equivalence laid out in the protocol on the interpretation of Article 69 EPC could be considered as a mechanism to extend the protection on a particular set of weights to variants of the same network. However, the relevance of this approach appears rather limited in practice. Indeed, on the one hand, a harmonised approach to the doctrine of equivalents is lacking and, on the other hand, a precise definition of what would constitute an 'equivalence class' in the context of machine learning models is missing.[112] In the absence of a well-defined metric that would allow evaluation and quantification of the similarities between two arbitrary models (including the values of their parameters and their respective architectures) and their link to the associated function, the very notion of 'equivalence' applied to inference models at large remains a largely elusive construct. In this perspective, the patent protection of trained machine learning models will therefore remain of limited practical use when formulated as an explicit collection of parameters.

---

[109]   T. Watkin and A. Rau, Intellectual property in artificial neural networks – in particular under the European patent convention, IIC – International Review of Industrial Property and Copyright Law, 1996, 27, 4, 1996, 447 (p.464).

[110]   Protocol on the Interpretation of Article 69 EPC, Art. 2. (The Protocol did not provide a definition of the notion of 'equivalent').

[111]   In the Text of the Basic Proposal for the Treaty and the Regulations as Submitted to the Diplomatic Conference for the Conclusion of a Treaty Supplementing the Paris Convention (SCP/4/3, 2 Oct. 2000), WIPO proposed the following definition: 'An element ('the equivalent element') shall generally be considered as being equivalent to an element as expressed in a claim if, at the time of any alleged infringement, either of the following conditions is fulfilled in regard to the invention as claimed: (i) the equivalent element performs substantially the same function in substantially the same way and produces substantially the same result as the element as expressed in the claim, or (ii) it is obvious to a person skilled in the art that the same result as that achieved by means of the element as expressed in the claim can be achieved by means of the equivalent element' (Art. 21(2)(b)). The case law developed by European national jurisdictions has led to different tests to evaluate equivalents.

[112]   While training a second model based on the knowledge of a first trained model to perform substantially the same function would indeed be considered obvious to the skilled person (see references cited in note 17), it remains to be evaluated if the two models would achieve the same effect "in substantially the same way" for any category of machine learning models. (See *supra*, note 111, WIPO proposed definition of the notion of 'equivalent').

4. CONCLUSION

Trained inference models are the end product of a long, complex and often costly process of extracting information from data corpora and condensing it into a functional entity. From edge applications, where machine learning models are deployed, embedded in stand-alone software within user-controlled devices, to cloud applications, through 'AI as a service' platforms, trained inference models are becoming an increasingly popular staple of the digital economy. As these models are distributed and exposed, either as products or through application programming interfaces, questions related to their IP protection become ever more pressing. The protection of these composite objects, at the confluence of algorithms, codes, applications and data, poses specific challenges in terms of IP rights.

Trade Secrets Directive 2016/943/EC fails to provide effective protection against reverse engineering, a rising concern with regard to trained machine learning models. Contractual clauses prohibiting reverse engineering may be considered but are of no practical application if the product is made publicly available.

If inference models are sometimes considered as a form of 'software 2.0', the protection of a trained model under Directive 2009/24/EC appears inoperative due to its functional nature and its lack of originality, in the sense that it cannot be considered as an author's own intellectual creation.

As a collection of data, the protection under Directive 96/9/EC, be it as copyright or through the *sui generis* database right, may not be considered as a viable alternative either, at least in most instances. Indeed, typical trained models such as neural networks would fail to meet the definition of a database in its legal meaning, the numerical constituents of the model failing to have a value independently of the network in which they are defined. However, the CJEU has held that the owner of a database not protected by copyright or *sui generis* right may restrict its use by contract.

Finally, patent protection under the EPC could be considered, in principle, to protect the technical functionalities associated with a model. The benefits of patent protection are clear: to the patent holder, the legal right to prohibit others from using, making or selling the invention without permission; to the public, the promotion of knowledge sharing by requiring the details of the patented invention to be disclosed, thereby enabling learning from the trained model but also allowing audit, in particular to check for biases – a growing concern with deployed machine learning applications and a requirement to develop a trustworthy AI.[113] But claiming trained machine learning models as patentable subject matter is not without specific challenges, both formal and substantive. To fulfil the condition of disclosure of the invention in a manner sufficiently clear and complete for it to be carried out by a person skilled in the art, new institutional platforms, such as international depository authorities, may need to be

---

[113] European Parliament resolution of 20 October 2020 on intellectual property rights for the development of artificial intelligence technologies (2020/2015(INI)), Committee on Legal Affairs (rapporteur: Stéphane Séjourné). The resolution '[s]tresses the key importance of balanced IPR protection in relation to AI technologies, and of the multidimensional nature of such protection, and, at the same time, stresses the importance of ensuring a high level of protection of IPRs, of creating legal certainty and of building the trust needed to encourage investment in these technologies and ensure their long-term viability and use by consumers' (pt. 6). The resolution further recognises 'that the challenge of assessing AI applications creates a need for some transparency requirements' (pt. 7).

created. To allow a precise assessment of an inventive contribution of the model, comparative tests may be required from the applicant. Finally, to compare the claimed models with alternatives, a harmonised assessment of 'equivalents' in the context of machine learning models would need to be developed to offer effective protection for patent holders and provide legal certainty for competitors in their evaluation of potential infringement.

6. An abject failure of intelligence: intellectual property and artificial intelligence

Michael D. Pendleton[1]

1. INTRODUCTION

We must pay more than lip service to the fact that we are living through an information revolution as profound as the Industrial Revolution.[2] And information is of course the basic subject matter of intellectual property (IP). IP law ascribes rights of access or restricts access to aspects of information.[3] That is the function of the IP causes of actions, be they patent, trade mark, copyright, trade secret or other *sui generis* actions. But most of these actions were brought into existence or refined by the Industrial Revolution, not our contemporary Information Revolution – the age of artificial intelligence and big data.

Intellectual property law is as fully adapted to the information age as was the law of the pre-Industrial Revolution era to the age of machines. After a career of almost 40 years in IP, I do not believe that IP law has evolved adequately to provide enough incentive to information innovators, or enough certainty to information competitors, or enough access to us, the information consumers. More importantly, balancing these three interest groups – innovators, their competitors and we consumers – is muddied by the arcane corpus of IP's nineteenth-century doctrinal concepts, like a ghost trying to clank its chains over blockchain technology. That is a great pity, because it holds us all back from the promise of what is clearly an explosion of information which could make the world a better place.

From the perspective of practising lawyers and indeed even academic lawyers, there is no reason to express discomfort at the present lamentable state of intellectual property, and very few do. Indeed, the more arcane and complex the law, the better the work prospects for the practitioner and the greater the intellectual tangle of doctrine for the academic. But surely we can progress beyond self-interest.

This chapter attempts to set out a description of the poverty and inadequacy of present-day intellectual property in general, and especially in relation to digital information – artificial intelligence in particular. It then seeks to outline a proposal for reform of the law. This chapter is written from a comparative law perspective, though heavily slanted towards Anglo Commonwealth jurisdictions.

[1]   The author is grateful to Phoebe Woo for her assistance in formatting this chapter.
[2]   The Information Revolution or the Fourth Information Revolution or as many tiers of revolutions as your commentator of choice adumbrates.
[3]   Michael D. Pendleton, *Balancing Competing Interests in Information Products: A Conceptual Rethink*, 14:3 INFO. & COMM. TECH. L. 241 (2005).

2.   A NOTE OF CAUTION ON TECHNOLOGY AND IP LAWYERS

It is always easy for an IP lawyer to make a fool of themselves when attempting to demonstrate their understanding, if not mastery, of the technology relevant to their practice. The law reports are filled with reams of pronouncements by judges which cause hysterics and sometimes despair in technological circles. One of the more famous is when an apex court, the High Court of Australia, was asked to vacate its own decision on the basis that its judgment demonstrated that the judges didn't appreciate the difference between computer code and computer data.[4] The High Court held that while it would agree to re-examine its own judgment – which was unprecedented – its failure to appreciate the difference between code and data, which it acknowledged, was, it held, not fatal to its reasoning.

If judges make this error then lesser mortals such as academics should be well warned. And some aren't, as law reviews and journals well illustrate, but we won't go there. Thus, for the purpose of this chapter I will confine myself to only so much technology as is necessary to discuss artificial intelligence and its relationship to IP law.

3.   AI AND IP

Artificial intelligence is at its base computer programs – admittedly, computer programs and databases that are in turn written by computer programs.[5]

The law in most jurisdictions long ago declared that the human being giving first instructions to the initial computer is the author for copyright purposes of subsequent computer programs, propagated by the initial program. Various options to change this have been mooted but no concrete changes to the above position have yet resulted. So it seems safe to say that the adequacy of the law in relation to artificial intelligence has a lot to do with its adequacy in relation to computer programs.

The relevant law in large part is therefore copyright and, to a lesser extent, patent and tangentially trade secrets law. Of course, the environment in which artificial intelligence functions is the internet or intranets, which are in themselves computer programs and in turn give rise to intellectual property issues. This chapter will assume a broad knowledge of copyright, patent and trade secrets law and concentrate on the problematic issues of applying that law to artificial intelligence.

At a conference at Sun Yat-Sen University[6] in Guangzhou in January 2020, when we were still allowed to travel, an American professor friend[7] expressed shock that I used the example of copyright in drawings for a can opener to show how inadequate copyright law was in relation to Big Data. My reasoning was that if copyright concepts were stretched to breaking by a can-opener design, what chance did IP law have with Big Data and by extension, AI?

---

[4]   *Autodesk Inc v Dyason* (No. 2) [1993] HCA 6.
[5]   *AI is Transforming the Coding of Computer Programmes*, The Economist (7 Jul. 2021), www.economist.com/science-and-technology/2021/07/07/ai-is-transforming-the-coding-of-computer-programs.
[6]   Organized by Professor Xie Lin and others.
[7]   So there, Professor Peter K. Yu of Texas A&M University.

I remain unrepentant and intend to recite a similar argument in relation to artificial intelligence in this chapter.

That inadequacy goes to the unpredictability of both copyright and patent law. With copyright it is the requirement that a work be original and that infringement occurs where the defendant reproduces or adapts a substantial part of the copyright work. With patent law it is the requirement that the product or process be not only novel – largely unproblematic – but also nonobvious, or involve an inventive step. Originality and substantial part in copyright and obviousness or lack of inventive step in patent law are almost exclusively judicially subjective. They are wildcards, non-empirical, discretionary, the length of the Chancellor's foot; and anyone who suggests in a hard case that there is a more than a 50 per cent chance of success on these issues is simply not well versed in the law or not telling the truth.

The significance of this is that IP law is unpredictable. Nor is it anchored to any recognizable moral or ethical criteria. How can we fix that? For most of my 40-odd-year career I have been proposing a law protecting labour, skill, effort investment of time and money, but where a defendant adds sufficient additional, labour, skill, effort investment of time and money that will give rise to a defence and possibly a protectable right in the defendant's hands.[8] To a large extent this proposed law would replace most of existing intellectual property law. This proposal also relies on a high degree of subjective judicial assessment, but – and it is an important but – no more than the present law. And unlike the present law it is aimed directly at the question of the plaintiff's legitimate right to restrict access, to the defendant's legitimate right to compete and to the public's access rights. It calls for balancing in every case, rather than the discretion to do this in the present law, hidden behind arcane doctrine addressing technical aspects like originality and substantial part in copyright and non-obviousness in patent law. I will return to this proposal after surveying the present law in relation to AI.

4. COPYRIGHT

In the mid-1980s I was instructing solicitor in an appeal on behalf of Video Technology Ltd, now VT Inc, where Atari Inc, the Japanese video games producer of the pioneering Pacman, was seeking to disturb a finding in VT's favour in the Court of Appeal Hong Kong that copyright did not subsist in computer software.[9] Aside from my excruciating embarrassment that my former teacher Professor William Cornish – then of LSE, later of Cambridge, whom we had called as an expert witness – had been kept waiting for hours in the corridors of the Court of Appeal, my memory was that the lower court finding was a reasonable result. Further, the United States was soon to pass legislation[10] requiring that all countries who wished to purchase computer software from the United States must recognize copyright subsistence as a literary work in computer software in their national law. This was before the United States joined the

---

[8]   Michael D. Pendleton, *Intellectual Property, Information Based Society and a New International Economic Order – the Policy Options?* 2 EUR. INTELL. PROP. REV. 31 (1985).

[9]   *Atari Inc. v Video Technology Ltd.*, CACV 117/1982 (6 October 1982).

[10]   Computer Software Copyright Act of 1980, 17 U.S.C. § 101 (1988) specifically recognised software as a literary work though software had been accepted for registration since 1964. It required, in effect, all countries wishing to purchase software from US suppliers to protect software as a literary work.

Berne Convention in 1989 but it was as effective as any international convention in requiring that the results in *Atari Inc. v Video Technology Ltd.*[11] would not recur. A similar result that no copyright subsided in computer software was reached by the Australian High Court in the *Wombat Computer* case and had to be reversed by statute in record haste after the US legislation came into effect.[12]

So copyright, a law which had been framed to take account of the invention of the printing press centuries ago and which had changed little since that time, was tasked with protecting a technology which is now at the core of almost everything.

Thus the central and increasingly problematic requirements of copyright, that the work be original for copyright to subsist and that to infringe you must essentially reproduce or adapt a substantial part, are imported in relation to computer software and thus artificial intelligence. This is problematic because, as noted above, both originality and substantial part require inherently subjective assessments by the court. There is no way to empirically assess whether or not originality and substantial part are present. In both the case of originality and that of substantial part, most jurisdictions require a qualitative not quantitative assessment. Anything qualitative by definition does not lend itself to quantitative criteria. The doctrine makes it clear that originality can arise for any work which derives from an author and is not copied. A few lines of code in a very large computer programme can be said to constitute the taking of a substantial part in a qualitative sense. And as that self-same Professor Cornish wrote in the first book[13] in any jurisdiction to cross-analytically combine all the intellectual property causes of action in the one volume, originality and substantial part give substantial scope for a judge to indulge their sense of fair play.[14]

5.   RECENT DECISIONS LIFTING THE THRESHOLD FOR ORIGINALITY

The most problematic issues in relation to originality arise in the case of compilations, and compilations include databases, which are at the core of computer programs and particularly artificial intelligence programs.

For more than a century, Anglo Commonwealth jurisdictions embraced a school of thought in relation to originality and compilations that was referred to as 'sweat of the brow'. That school of thought maintained that sufficient labour, skill and effort in the marshalling of information was sufficient to confer originality. So things like the selection of preliminary pages in a pocket diary, bus and train timetables, metric conversion tables, and so on could confer copyright even though those tables themselves were not copyright. Similarly, in a series of cases, coupons or tables could attract copyright even though the components were everyday items.[15]

---

[11]   *Supra* note 8.

[12]   Computer Edge Ltd. v. Apple Computer Inc. [1986] HCA 19. First instance Federal Court decision reversed by Copyright Amendment Act No. 43 of 1984. This was passed into law in record time because the Computer Software Copyright Act of 1980, *supra* note 10, required trading partners to protect software as an original literary work or in effect be unable to purchase from US software manufacturers.

[13]   WILLIAM R. CORNISH, INTELLECTUAL PROPERTY: PATNETS, COPYRIGHT, TRADE MARKS AND ALLIED RIGHTS (1981).

[14]   Ibid at 67.

[15]   *See Ladbroke v William Hill* [1964] 1 All ER 465.

In Australia copyright was conferred on a telephone book, *Telstra Corp. Ltd. v Desktop Marketing Systems Ltd.*,[16] expressing disapproval of the US Supreme Court decision in *Feist v Rural Telephone*.[17] But note that business directories, essentially telephone books listing business activities, have been protected by the US courts.[18] These are all cases about compilations and so too are databases, the raw data from which AI uses to write new programming for itself.

5.1   Compilations – Anglo Commonwealth – Originality from 'Sweat of the Brow'

As we all know, originality is a key Berne Convention – and in turn World Trade Organization TRIPS (so binding most countries) – requirement for copyright protection. Originality is not defined in many jurisdictions but is the product of case law. Satisfying the requirements of originality is key to protecting data, big or small, and thus AI.

The 'sweat of the brow' doctrine developed as a judicial attempt to protect investment of labour, skill, effort, investment of time and money by harnessing the concept of originality to its service. It hinges on the difficulty or impossibility of separating an idea from its form of expression.

I hope not to bore the reader with personal anecdotes, but I remember my first copyright lectures in 1980 given by Prof James Lahore of Melbourne University at the University of London. He told us the catechism of copyright begins with the proposition that there is no copyright in ideas. The rest of his lectures, he said, were to disabuse us of this notion. Copyright does indeed protect ideas – at least, it did then. Let's explore some seminal originality cases.

5.2   Problematic Originality Cases: Where Copyright Does Protect Ideas

In *Cramp v Smythson*,[19] the House of Lords held that the collection of tables in the beginning of a pocket diary was not an original literary work. There was no judgement or skill in compiling the tables. This case was an outlier to previous and subsequent cases on compilations.

In *Matthewson v Stockdale*[20] Lord Erskine held, at pp.105–6:

> If a man from his situation having access to the repositories in the India House, has by considerable expense and labour procured with correctness all the names and appointments of the Indian establishment, he has a copyright in that particular work, which has cost him considerable expense and labour, and employed him at a loss in other respects, though there can be no copyright in an Indian calendar generally.

Possibly the clearest endorsement of the sweat of the brow approach by the English courts is illustrated by the decision in *Kelly v Morris*.[21] The words of Wood VC are frequently cited, especially those in relation to a map maker stating that he cannot rely on a previous work but must count the miles for himself:

---

16   [2002] FCAFC 112.
17   499 U.S. 340 (1991).
18   *Key Publications Inc. v Chinatown Today Publishing Enterprises Inc.,* 945 F.2d 509, (2d Cir. 1991). A directory of businesses in Chinatown, New York.
19   [1944] AC 329.
20   (1806) 12 Ves 270. An East India directory case.
21   (1866) 1 Eq 697.

The defendant has been most completely mistaken in what he assumes to be his right to deal with the labour and property of others. In the case of a dictionary, map, guidebook, or directory, when there are certain common objects of information which must, if described correctly, be described in the same words, a subsequent compiler is bound to set about doing for himself that which the first compiler has done. In case of a road-book, he must count the miles for himself [...] generally, he is not entitled to take one word of the information previously published without independently working out the matter for himself, so as to arrive at the same result from the same common sources of information, and the only use he can legitimately make of a previous publication is to verify his own calculation and results when obtained. So in the present case the defendant could not take a single line of the plaintiffs directory for the purpose of saving himself labor and trouble in getting his information.[22]

A case which set the benchmark for a long time is *Ladbroke (Football) v William Hill*.[23] The case concerned a football betting coupon. The form consisted of columns and tables from which bets could be made. Much of the information and indeed presentation of the information was obtained from the English Football League. The defendant, who adopted a betting coupon closely resembling the plaintiff's coupon, admitted there was copyright in the selection of the various columns and tables but denied reproducing or adapting a substantial part. It did so on the basis that each of the columns and tables in the coupon in its submission constituted a separate copyright work. The House of Lords rejected this, stating the work was not to be dissected and held that the copyright subsisted in the totality of the compilation. Infringement was found proven.

In *Waterlow Directories v Reed Information Services*[24] the plaintiff wrote to all solicitors in England and Wales asking for details of their firm's name, employees and areas of legal practice. From this the plaintiffs compiled a directory of practising solicitors. The defendant produced a competitor directory using information from the plaintiff's directory. The English High Court held that copyright subsisted in the directory as a compilation and was infringed. Had the defendant wrote to solicitors and based its work on this information, there would be reproduction or adaptation. But in doing so they could not use the plaintiff's directory as the basis for its correspondence, as was subsequently held in *Waterlow v Rose*.[25]

Elanco v Mandops[26] is an interesting, problematic and much cited case on originality. The plaintiff owned the expired patent for a weedkiller. The defendant sought to produce the same weedkiller, as it was entitled to, but utilized the plaintiff's instructions for use as the basis of its own instructions. The plaintiff's solicitors wrote to the defendant warning it of copyright infringement. The defendant then changed all of the wording in its instructions but undertook no independent research into the dangers of the weedkiller and relied solely on the information in the plaintiff's instructions to compose its own. The court held there was infringement of copyright even though the wording was totally different. This was an interlocutory decision, as many intellectual property cases are, but is often used as an authority for the proposition that copyright protects more than the expression of ideas.

'Sweat of the brow' originality decisions are not confined to the Anglo Commonwealth, as the following case illustrates. *Broadcast & TV Paper of Zhejiang v Huzhou Daily*[27] was

---

22   Ibid at 701.
23   *Supra* note 15.
24   [1992] FSR 409.
25   [1995] FSR 207.
26   [1980] RPC 213.
27   China TV Paper, Issue 26 of 1989, p.2.

a mediation prior to the coming into effect of the 1990 Copyright Law in China.[28] The Suburban District Court of Huzhou in Zhejiang Province held that the reprinting of the plaintiff's TV timetable without its licence constituted a copyright infringement.

The various Lego cases around the world are instructive and mark a turning point towards a heightened requirement of originality in certain jurisdictions. I will confine myself to the Anglo Commonwealth cases. Lego, the Danish children's building block manufacturer, sought to continue its monopoly of the children's building block in virtual perpetuity by seeking to invalidate its own 15-year-registered design and falling back on the life plus 50 years term of artistic copyright in the drawings, and later redrawing the drawings for a new copyright term.

Interlego v Tyco[29] was an appeal from the Hong Kong Court of Appeal to the Judicial Committee of the Privy Council in London. Lego redrew its block and sought to argue that redrawing entitled it to a new artistic copyright term in the blocks, notwithstanding the fact that it held a registered design which it sought to invalidate on the basis that certain features were dictated by function and thus not registerable. The judicial committee held that the registered design was valid and no new copyright arose in the redrawn Lego block. Lord Oliver held: 'there must in addition be some element of material alteration or embellishment which suffices to make the totality of the work an original work.'[30]

It must be something visually significant. He discounted the new dimensions in the drawings. More importantly, he stated that skill, labour or judgement in copying an earlier work cannot confer originality.

Interlego v Croner Trading Ltd.[31] was a case decided before Gummow J, one of the foremost intellectual property judges in Australia and later a High Court of Australia judge. It was decided after the Privy Council decision in *Interlego v Tyco*.[32] The same facts essentially presented themselves to the court, with a redrawing of the Lego children's building block. Justice Gummow found that there was sufficient originality in the redrawing to confer a new artistic copyright term. He specifically disapproved the heightened requirement of originality in the *Privy Councils Lego* decision. He regarded it as unacceptable judicial lawmaking.

And note that history is being repeated, albeit in the registered design (design patent in some jurisdictions) realm. In *Lego A/S v EUIPO and Delta Sport Handelskontor GmbH*,[33] the European General Court upheld Lego's German-registered design protection notwithstanding that its features were dictated by its function, and held that it was an example of a particular statutory exception to the rule where parts were within a modular system. This was interesting as an attempt to register a three-dimensional representation of the building block as a trademark had earlier been rejected by the European Court of Justice. However, it is possible that this General Court decision may be appealed to the European Court of Justice.

---

[28]   Before the coming into effect of the Chinese Copyright Law 1990, copyright as a concept was explored by the courts and the press. The fact that copyright had not yet been legislated was not an obstruction to mediation decisions being made by the courts utilizing the concept of copyright. This was such a case.

[29]   [1989] AC 217.

[30]   Ibid at 241.

[31]   [1992] FCA 992.

[32]   *Supra* note 29.

[33]   Case T-515/19, ECLI:EU:T:2021:155, General Ct.

In *Telstra Corp. Ltd. v Desktop Marketing Systems Ltd.*[34] the Australian Full Federal Court accepted that copyright subsists in the White and Yellow Pages telephone directories compiled by what was then the single telephone provider in Australia, Telstra. The defendants had prepared a CD-ROM of businesses in Australia using the Telstra directory. Justice Finkelstein in the Federal Court at first instance[35] undertook an exhaustive study of 'sweat of the brow' cases and concluded that there was copyright in the Telstra telephone directories. He specifically addressed the United States Supreme Court decision in *Feist v Rural Telephone*[36] where the court had refused to find copyright on the basis that the idea of a telephone directory merged with its form of expression and thus had no originality being an idea. The judge rejected this finding as inapplicable in Australia and that was upheld in the full federal court. Note, however, that the more recent decision canvassed below of *Ice TV Ltd. v Nine Network Australia Ltd.*[37] casts doubt on the continuing authority of this decision, which moves away from the 'sweat of the brow' cases and heightens the requirement of originality.

5.3   New Directions: a Heightened Threshold for Originality

Ice TV[38] marks a move towards a heightened requirement of originality. The plaintiff is a free-to-air television broadcaster which compiled various directories of its television programming. The defendant produced a set-top box the function of which includes access to various free-to-air television broadcasters, including the plaintiff. In order to provide an on-screen directory of television programming, the defendant paid large numbers of people to watch the plaintiff's television channel and note the times of its programming and corresponding programmes. This data was checked against the plaintiff's television directory before encoding in its set-top box. The High Court of Australia canvassed the various decisions on compilations and 'sweat of the brow' copyrights, including the *Telstra v Desktop Marketing*[39] case, and concluded that the requirement of originality should not be set this low. It did not specifically overrule Telstra but threw doubt on its authority. The court found no infringement to have occurred.

It is submitted that the above cases constitute a pronounced public policy decision by the courts to move away from the doctrine of sweat of the brow – in other words, to move away from the previous judicial consensus that labour, skill, effort and investment of time in making a compilation should be protected. The new judicial policy appears to be that too much is being protected and a way of preventing this is to set a higher bar for originality. Whatever that bar is – as was the case with its predecessor in 'sweat of the brow' cases – is essentially a subjective assessment by the court as to whether something ought to deserve the court's protection. Code and data being composed by artificial intelligence will inevitably be subject to this examination in regard to determining originality of their programmes. As the criterion is essentially a normative decision by the court, there is very little certainty for owners of artificial intelligence or their competitors.

---

[34]   *Supra* note 16.
[35]   [2001] FCA 612.
[36]   *Supra* note 17.
[37]   [2009] HCA 14.
[38]   Ibid.
[39]   *Supra* note 16.

6. INFRINGEMENT: REPRODUCING OR ADAPTING A SUBSTANTIAL PART

In the same way that originality is essentially a subjective public policy value judgement, so too is determining whether a substantial part has been reproduced or adapted in the context of infringement of copyright. A finding of infringement turns on whether a substantial part of a copyright work is, despite a plethora of statutory language varying from jurisdiction to jurisdiction, essentially reproduced or adapted. This substantial part concept is again largely discretionary because courts have defined it as qualitative rather than quantitative taking. Whether something is a substantial taking in a qualitative sense is often said to depend upon the originality of what is taken. So both originality and substantial part revolve around each other and both are largely within the subjective discretion of the court. Thus judicial sympathy is crucial to the exercise of these key discretions. But this, with notable exceptions, is rarely articulated in the case law. Where it is articulated, the courts use the language of misappropriation. It would be so much easier to be upfront about this. And this is the essential pleading of this chapter.

In *LB (Plastics) Ltd. v Swish Products Ltd.*[40] the plaintiff owned the copyright in the drawings for a range of furniture drawers of standard size which were interchangeable one with another. Additionally, the drawers were demountable. The defendant set out to produce demountable drawers which would fit furniture carcasses of the same specifications as the plaintiff's, yet were demountable by a different mechanism. In overruling the Court of Appeal's decision, the House of Lords held that the evidence of out-and-out copying was not diminished by the differences in the drawers, which the defendant attributed to their independent development.

Like so many cases in intellectual property, the court's sense of fair play was offended by the defendant's conduct, though this was not, and rarely is, stated. In another case the necessity to allow competition might be the driving but, again, rarely stated motivation for a finding that no substantial part has been reproduced or adapted.

In *Plix Products v Frank M Winstone*[41] the defendant was incapable of establishing non-infringement where the dimensions of a kiwi fruit largely dictated the dimensions of the plaintiff's plastic tray used for their air freight. The appointment of an independent designer was insufficient to detract from a finding of reproduction or adaptation of a substantial part.

In *Chih Ling Koo v Lam Tai*[42] the Hong Kong Court of Appeal confirmed Bokhary J's finding that the defendant had infringed the plaintiff's copyright in a questionnaire. Despite substantial differences in the questionnaires and the defendant's denial of copying, expert evidence pointed to striking and exceptional similarities in the defendant's questionnaire (in a qualitative sense) that could not have arisen by chance. In the trade secrecy context this case is perhaps the only superior court decision to hold information to be property, and this was approved by the Court of Appeal.

In *Harman Pictures v Osborne*[43] the court held that a dramatic work which copied the scenario and characters of an earlier work without reproducing the exact dialogue would infringe copyright.

---

[40]   [1979] RPC 551.
[41]   (1985) 1 NZLR 376.
[42]   [1994] 1 HKLR 329.
[43]   [1967] 2 All ER 324.

In *Solar Thompson Engineering Co. Ltd. v Barton*[44] the defendant had commissioned an independent designer to produce a particular industrial component, specifically in order to avoid infringing copyright. Irrespective of the independent creation of the designer, the court held that copyright was infringed because the instructions and parameters given to the independent designer were such that, in the court's view, he would inevitably come up with a design which infringed the plaintiff's copyright. In these circumstances, the work of the independent designer could not meaningfully be described as an independent work.

In *Interfirm Comparison v Law Society of NSW*[45] the plaintiff had been commissioned by the Law Society to compile a questionnaire for members of the law Society concerning the earnings of partners in law firms. The defendant was not happy with the plaintiff's endeavors and commissioned the University of New England to compile the questionnaire. The court held that there was copyright in the questionnaire compiled by the plaintiff and this was infringed by the University of New England, who had access to the plaintiff's questionnaire. This was despite the fact that the wording and order of questions differed markedly from the plaintiff's questionnaire.

Different principles of substantial taking appear to operate in relation to selections or compilations. In these cases the courts appear to have been more ready to find infringement wherever a defendant takes what, in the court's opinion, is the substance of the compilation or selection, even though it is expressed differently.

7.   PATENTS

7.1   AI as Inventor

Not least due to the efforts of the editor of this book, Professor Ryan Abbott,[46] AI has been held to be the inventor in patent applications in several jurisdictions. In the Federal Court of Australia decision *Thayler v Commissioner of Patents*,[47] the court held the inventor to be the AI 'DABUS' on the, essentially, public policy grounds that unless AI could be named as inventor, these AI inventions might not be patentable at all. Per Beach J:

> In my view it is consistent with the object of the Act to construe the term 'inventor' in a manner that promotes technological innovation and the publication and dissemination of such innovation by rewarding it, irrespective of whether the innovation is made by a human or not. [...]
> Consistently with s 2A, computer inventorship would incentivise the development by computer scientists of creative machines, and also the development by others of the facilitation and use of the output of such machines, leading to new scientific advantages [...]
> Further, if only an artificial intelligence system could be said to have created the output, but you only permit of human inventors, you may not have an inventor. Hence one may not be able to patent the invention. So you may have the case where artificial intelligence has created an invention in terms of the output, but there is no inventor and it cannot be at that time patented.

---

44   [1977] RPC 53.
45   [1977] RPC 13.
46   Tom Knowles, *Patently Brilliant ... AI Listed as Inventor for First Time*, The Times (28 Jul. 2021), www.thetimes.co.uk/article/patently-brilliant-ai-listed-as-inventor-for-first-time-mqj3s38mr
47   (2021) FCA 879. In the US and UK DABUS has initially struck out of luck but the appeal process in Australia and elsewhere is likely to continue for some time.

In my view this is an eminently sensible decision. Unlike copyright, where a human author is essential under present legislation to calculate the arguably outrageously long term of copyright, at least in the case of computer programs, no such essential function falls to the named inventor.

7.2 The Always Problematic Non-obviousness

How do you do the task of deciding whether something is obvious or not to establish the validity of a patent? You can read through the volumes of case law paraphrasing obvious or inventive step but, like the concept of beyond reasonable doubt in criminal law, the courts often come back to 'obvious means obvious' in the same way as 'beyond reasonable doubt means beyond reasonable doubt'. The fact remains that you can only ascertain obviousness by non-empirical criteria. The courts again have a discretion to do what do they think is fair. So again – why not state it upfront in the context of fairness – a normative-based exercise.

The law on non-obviousness is arcane, incomprehensible and very often contradictory. Here is a brief survey of the law on non-obviousness from a Commonwealth perspective.

In *Olin Mathieson v Biorex*[48] it was held:

> The word 'obvious', as Sir Lionel agreed, and as its derivation implies, means something which lies in the way, and in the context of the Act is used in its normal sense of something which is plain or open to the eye or mind, something which is perfectly evident to the person thinking on the subject.

In *General Tire & Rubber Co. v Firestone Tyre and Rubber Co. Ltd.*[49] it was said that '"[o]bvious" is, after all a much-used word and it does not seem to us that there is any need to go beyond the primary dictionary meaning of 'very plain'".

Unlike in novelty, there are many tests applied by the courts to assess inventive step. Per Cooper J in *Winner v Ammar Holdings Ltd*:[50]

> In order to ascertain whether or not the subject matter sought to be patented was beyond the skill of the calling, the courts have adopted a number of different approaches directed to the same end: for example, was the invention obvious or not?; does the invention solve an important problem 'unsuccessfully attacked by previous inventions'?[51]

Here are some simple approaches which the courts have used to establish non-obviousness:

---

[48] (1970) RPC 157, 188
[49] (1972) RPC 457, 497.
[50] 25 IPR 273, 294.
[51] *See Wood v Gowshall* (1937) 54 RPC 37, 39.

The test is whether the hypothetical addressee faced with the same problem would have taken as a matter of routine whatever steps might have led from the prior art to the invention, whether they be the steps of the inventor or not.[52]

... was so obvious that it would at once occur to anyone acquainted with the subject, and desirous of accomplishing the end.[53]

Would the notional research group at the relevant date in all the circumstances [...] directly be led as a matter of course to try [the invention claimed] in the expectation that it might well produce [a useful desired result].[54]

In the case of a combination patent the invention will lie in the selection of integers, a process which will necessarily involve rejection of other possible integers. The prior existence of publications revealing those integers, as separate items, and other possible integers does not of itself make an alleged invention obvious. It is the selection of the integers out of, perhaps many possibilities, which must be shown to be obvious.[55]

And here's my favourite:

so easy that any fool could do it.[56]

Courts have also discussed the problem of ex post facto dissection of the invention. In *Meyers Taylor Ltd. v Vicarr Industries Ltd.*,[57] Aickin J observed: 'subsequent analysis of the invention – "the dissection of the invention" – is not helpful in resolving the question of obviousness'.

An approach used by the courts to avoid this problem is the 'problem–solution' approach. See *HPM Industries Ltd. v Gerard Industries Ltd.*,[58] where Williams J said:

If the invention were novel it would nevertheless fail for want of subject matter if in the light of what was common general knowledge in the particular art, it lacked inventive ingenuity because the solution would have been obvious to any person of ordinary skill in the art who set out to solve the problem.

Other examples are *Hart v Hart*,[59] *Allsop Inc. v Bintang Ltd.*[60] and *Winner v Ammar Holdings*.[61]

The 'problem–solution' approach was phrased in *Palmer v Dunlop Perdriau Rubber Co. Ltd.*[62] as follows:

It is frequently possible to take, as it were, a patent to pieces, and then, beginning with one piece, to show how, in order to obtain one result, step A must be taken; in order to obtain another particular result, step B must be taken - and so on until one has the whole combination for which inventive

---

[52]   Per *Aickin J in Wellcome Foundation Ltd. v VR Laboratories (Aust) Ltd.* (1981) 148 CLR 262, 286.

[53]   *Allsop Inc. v Bintang Ltd.* 15 IPR 686, 701.

[54]   *Olin Mathieson v Biorex* (1970) RPC 157, 187; approved by the High Court of Australia in *Aktiebolaget Hassle v Alphapharm Ltd.* [2002] HCA 59.

[55]   *Minnesota Mining & Manufacturing Co. v Beiersdorf (Australia) Ltd.* (1979–80) 144 CLR 253, 293.

[56]   *Edison Bell v Smith* (1894) 11 RPC 389, 39.

[57]   (1977) 137 CLR 228, 242.

[58]   98 CLR 424, 437.

[59]   141 CLR 305.

[60]   *Supra* note 53.

[61]   (1993) AIPC 90–7.

[62]   (1937) 59 CLR 30, 61.

quality is claimed. If the analysis is taken into sufficient detail, every single step in the development of an invention, taken separately, can be shown to be obvious.

But, in the present case, the evidence of the expert witnesses for the defendant is really a reconstruction of an inventive process step by step, each step, when it is known that it must be taken in a certain direction, being obvious enough in itself.

If a claim is a mere technical equivalent of the prior art, it will not be inventive. A technical equivalent occurs when integers of a claim are replaced by one or more features, and the features of the replacement are part of the common general knowledge of the person skilled in the art and provide the same functionality in the context of the problem. Where the replacement by the feature would at once occur to the person skilled in the art[63] and the combination as a whole retains the same functionality in the context of the problem, there are no problems or difficulties to be overcome in making the replacement. If a claim is a mere workshop improvement over the prior art, it will lack an inventive step: 'The expression "workshop improvement" refers to an alteration to an existing device which the person skilled in the art would have come to as a matter of routine, "proceeding along previous lines of inquiry and having regard to what was known or used".'[64]

A workshop improvement can occur where the prior art fully solves the identified problem, if the person skilled in the art would readily recognize a practical difficulty in that solution, and that practical difficulty would be readily overcome by the person skilled in the art appraised of the common general knowledge.

Where the prior art does not provide a solution to the identified problem, if the solution would at once suggest itself to the person skilled in the art;[65] or if the prior art solves an analogous problem in a related area of technology, and the person skilled in the art would recognize the same solution could be applied to the problem with there being no practical difficulty in implementing that solution; then it may be difficult to determine when a feature is a 'mere workshop improvement' and when it involves an inventive step. Where there is only one option which the person skilled in the art would consider in solving either their identified problem (or any subsequent practical difficulty); that option would at once suggest itself to the person skilled in the art – for example, the option is part of the common general knowledge of the person skilled in the art; there is no practical difficulty in implementing that option; and neither the prior art, nor the common general knowledge, teaches away from the solution, there will be no inventive step. It may be that in following the one obvious option, a bonus and unforeseen effect is produced. However, the presence of that bonus effect does not itself give rise to an inventive step, because the person skilled in the art would inevitably have arrived at that solution.

In *Asahi Kasei Kogyo KK v WR Grace & Co.*[66] it was observed:

That which Grace produced might have had some of the desirable qualities of a multi-layer heat shrinkable packaging in a higher degree than might have been expected, or was in fact expected. And it might have demonstrated a better combination of properties, that is to say proving some properties

---

[63]   *See Elconnex Ltd. v Gerard Industries Ltd.* (1993) AIPC 90-984.

[64]   *Nicaro Holdings Ltd. v Martin Engineering Co.*, 16 IPR 545.

[65]   *See Fallshaw Holdings Ltd. v Flexello Castors and Wheels Plc.*, 26 IPR 565; and *Winner v Ammar Holdings Ltd.*, *supra* note 50.

[66]   (1992) AIPC 90-847, 38,089.

while at least not detracting from others. But at most the end result was a heat shrinkable bag, better not because of any inventive discovery of Grace, but because somebody else's new product, put on the market for uses which included that manufacture, produced better results than expected.

It may be that the prior art will suggest to the person skilled in the art a number of possible solutions to the problem:

> The pursuit of one of a number – perhaps many – obvious lines of research may produce a signal or particularly valuable discovery. In deciding on patentability it would seem to us regrettable, and not in accord with a primary purpose of patent law, to have to rule this out automatically in the name of obviousness.[67]

Where a claimed solution is one of several options that the person skilled in the art would consider in solving either their identified problem (or any subsequent practical difficulty); the options would at once suggest themselves to the person skilled in the art – for example, the options are part of the common general knowledge of the person skilled in the art, or clearly indicated in the prior art; there is no practical difficulty in implementing the particular solution claimed; and neither the prior art, nor the common general knowledge, teaches away from the particular solution, there will be an inventive step. 'There were alternatives which might be tried only to be discarded, but the fact that there were a number of alternatives, cannot, I think, elevate into the head of invention the step taken by Lucas.'[68]

UK law equates 'obvious to try' with 'worth a try' and 'well worth trying'. It seems United States, Canadian and Australian law on obviousness rejects this approach. In the US, any criterion which adopts a notion of 'obvious to try' has been rejected in a long series of decisions. The US decision in *Re O'Farrell*[69] distinguished the tests of 'obvious to try' and 'obvious' by referring to two kinds of errors which occur when applying the standard of 'obvious to try':

> In some cases, what would have been 'obvious to try' would have been to vary all parameters or try each of numerous possible choices until one possibly arrived at a successful result, where the prior art gave either no indication of which parameters were critical or no direction as to which of many possible choices is likely to be successful […] in others, what was 'obvious to try' was to explore a new technology or general approach that seemed to be a promising field of experimentation, where the prior art gave only general guidance as to the particular form of the claimed invention or how to achieve it.[70]

In the Canadian Supreme Court decision *Hoechst v Halocarbon (Ontario) Ltd.*[71] it was held:

> Very few inventions are unexpected discoveries. Practically all research work is done by looking at directions where the 'state of the art' points. On that basis and with hindsight, it could be said in most cases that there was no inventive ingenuity in the new development because everyone would then see how the previous accomplishments pointed the way.

---

[67]   Beecham Groups Ltd.'s (New Zealand/Amoxycillin) Appln. [1982] FSR 181, 192. *See Lucas and Another v Gaedor Ltd.* (1978) RPC 297, 376-377.

[68]   Ibid Lucas.

[69]   853 F.2d 894 (Fed. Cir. 1988).

[70]   Ibid at 952.

[71]   (1979), 42 C.P.R. (2d) 145, 155.

With novelty and infringement and most other elements of patent law, the method of interpretation of the patent specification is central. So too for non-obviousness. Purposive construction is the dominant method of interpretation in the Anglo Commonwealth and Europe but what it means varies widely. Sometimes the courts emphasize what the patentee or applicant has insisted upon in the specification – clearly a literal approach, masquerading as purposive. On its face, purposive means derivation of meaning from outside the four corners of the document; in interpreting legislation, all the background history; with patents, the importance of the feature to the function of the invention as a whole, for instance.[72]

Literal construction supplemented by the doctrine of equivalents (expressly rejected in purposive construction) is dominant in the US and China. But note that these jurisdictions have file wrapper estoppel; in other words, they allow citation of the patent prosecution file to estop a patentee claiming a wider or indeed narrower interpretation. That is not the case in most Anglo Commonwealth jurisdictions.

As the foregoing survey of doctrine surely illustrates, reasonable tribunals can reasonably disagree with whether an invention is obvious or not. There is no empirical yardstick; it is a matter of impression. Millions, sometimes billions, of dollars of investment in a patent turn on this judgement call. And there is generally no presumption of validity of a patent once granted.

8.   TRADE SECRETS

The databases generated by artificial intelligence are intended to be used, not kept in a closet, as trade secrecy law requires. To be useful you need to know all the details of the data, but, once public or where it can be reverse-engineered, data is no longer protectable. Dedicated database protection legislation lacks protection for the taking of small parts of a database. It only protects most of the database. The copyright concept of infringement by taking a substantial part in a qualitative sense may even protect just a small amount of data in a database. And now privacy law intrudes into the area of database protection. Privacy is not celebrated in US law and culture like it is in Europe; this means any kind of international accommodation of databases and privacy is highly problematic. It raises starkly the balancing of privacy versus security interests, the defining dilemma of our age. And the big daddy of them all is the blockchain database, which holds the promise of indelible ledgers capable of proving when any alleged copyright material was created, when it was modified or even when it was infringed; so too it can show if and when privacy was invaded, to what extent and for what purpose.

9.   WHAT I AM PROPOSING: FROM CAN OPENERS TO AI

As a mostly academic lawyer I have only occasionally become involved in cases which have resulted in a judgment in court. But one such case continues to haunt me because I can't, or at least couldn't until recently, make up my mind as to who should have succeeded. The case

---

[72]   *See* Michael D. Pendleton, *When Patents Mean Different Things in Different Jurisdictions*, in INTELLECTUAL PROPERTY AND INFORMATION WEALTH – VOLUME 2 PATENTS AND TRADE SECRETS 83 (Peter K. Yu ed., 2007).

was *Mike & Kremmel Ltd. v Chi Shing Industrial Co. Ltd.*[73] It was unusual as Deacons, my law firm, had a hard-and-fast rule of never acting for defendants. Most of Deacons' clients are big US, Japanese or European companies which are invariably plaintiffs. The defendant in this case was a small local company. Alan Wells, the partner in charge of the IP department, decided to break the rule and accept the company as a client. He did so because he felt sympathy with the company – not something he was noted for, having literally destroyed quite a cohort of local defendants.

Copyright was claimed in the design of one of the first can openers to take the top off the can rather than cut around the inside of the rim. To accomplish this the designer needed to know the average diameter of the rims of most cans. In other words, measurements had to be carried out to compile a database. This was a laborious process as the rims of cans vary widely and an average had to be established so that the can opener would work on most, not all, cans. From this database a blade could be designed with a cutting angle to fit underneath the rim of most cans. That entailed a lot of experiments and prototypes. The defendant can opener looked totally different to the plaintiff's; it used a piston rather than scissor action to grip the can; but it had the same angle as the plaintiff's on its cutting blade as otherwise it wouldn't be able to fit under the rims of most cans.

The judge found that copyright did subsist in the plaintiff's drawings for the can opener, but was not infringed. Although strenuously argued by the plaintiff's counsel,[74] the defendant's copying of the angle of the cutting blade was not addressed by Mantell J.

Forget about the doctrinal accuracy of this result in terms of copyright. Was it the right result in a normative sense? On the one hand, a great deal of labour, effort and money had been put by the plaintiff into research and experiment. On the other hand, all the defendant had done was to copy a single angle – I can't remember, but something like 33 degrees. And as I invariably tell my students, to this day I am not sure (until now) where my sympathies lie or who I think should have won the case.

My own inclination has since the early 1980s been towards a misappropriation of labour, skill and effort remedy. The danger with this is that it can protect too much. It needs a solid defence upfront. Such a defence is that where the defendant introduces sufficient additional labour, skill and effort, it is not an infringement.

In the can opener case the plaintiff's handle was a simple scissor action and the defendant's was a lever and piston action. Arguably different enough already – but a laser cutter can opener also copying the plaintiff's can-rim diameter data certainly would be. Judges need to make problematic calls but at least a normative criteria of misappropriation or unfair competition could be made explicit. At the moment the courts make normative decisions based on their sense of fair play and camouflaged by doctrinal rhetoric. We have seen that clearly in the previously surveyed areas of originality and substantial part in copyright and non-obviousness in patent law.

The major thrust of the argument here is that difficult cases in intellectual property are not always, or even often, solved by the tribunal applying the intricate doctrines which it details in its judgment. Rather, the tribunal decides where its sympathy lies by asking whether the defendant has, without adding substantial or enough of its own input, taken the product of the labour, skill and effort (sometimes investment) of the plaintiff. Has it slavishly imitated,

---

[73]   HCA 4049/1984 (3 August 1984).
[74]   Peter Garland QC, my co-author for almost two decades.

copied or misappropriated the plaintiff's information product? But misappropriation protection is only proportionate to what the plaintiff has added and the defendant taken.

This was concisely and presciently stated in the nineteenth-century English House of Lords case *Kenrick v Lawrence*.[75] The court stated that if protection was to be afforded to something very simple in design, that protection would be limited to the precise form, and to infringe the defendant would have to almost exactly duplicate it in its entirety. As protected subject matter becomes more complex, less and less precise duplication would be required. In effect the Lords were stating the modern law on substantial part in copyright infringement doctrine. That largely turns on the originality of the part taken, which brings us full circle back to what the court thinks of the ethical merits of the case.

This type of analysis, however, is rarely articulated. Complex doctrine is given as the reason for the result. But at base these complex doctrines lend themselves to the discretion to decide on the basis of the above. They have to, as the complex doctrines do not without more give an answer to a case in point. It would be much more predictable and likely to attract the support of ordinary people if this was articulated and in fact became the principal determinant or mechanism of large parts of intellectual property. Embracing such a misappropriation or unfair competition mechanism would be unlikely to expand or restrict the present-day scope of intellectual property. That is because it is already the unstated mainstay in determining many present-day difficult IP cases.

What I am suggesting is that much, if not all, contemporary intellectual property causes of action could be protected under a general rubric of slavish imitation or misappropriation or unfair competition. I think it would be preferable to abolish much of the present-day intellectual property regime, but there is no reason why a general law of misappropriation could not stand beside the present-day regime if the former is regarded as too radical. If conceived and drafted properly there is no reason why this would increase or decrease the scope of present-day intellectual property protection and access to information. It could also be done without the need to renegotiate TRIPS, something which is probably politically and diplomatically impossible in the present fraught world trade climate.

I started to write on this much maligned topic of misappropriation and unfair competition nearly 40 years ago under the urging of Professor WR Cornish (London School of Economics, University of London, later Cambridge University), who disagreed at the time, and also at the urging of the late Professor James Lahore (Melbourne University), who did agree, as he wrote long before we met (except as one of a large postgrad class):[76]

A new tort of unfair competition would also mean that the courts could adapt more quickly to the needs arising from the rapid development of new technologies – all of which require some protection from unfair exploitation in their growth period in particular. At present far too much time is expended in determining copyright disputes on narrow and artificial grounds of interpretation. Does computer software fall within the meaning of a 'literary work'? Is a film frame a photograph or a part of a film? Is a videogram a record or a film? It cannot be in industry's interest that issues of great commercial importance should rest on technicalities more characteristic of the application of a Taxes Act. A tort or unfair competition would be a useful restraint against plagiarism and would go some way in

---

[75] (1890) L.R. 25 Q.B.D. 99.

[76] James Lahore, *The Herchel Smith Lecture 1992: Intellectual Property Rights and Unfair Copying: Old Concepts, New Ideas*, 14(12) EUR. INTELL. PROP. REV. 428 (1992).

meeting the needs of new technologies and also in balancing the requirements of their users. It would not prevent the enactment of specific enactments.

What the Australian experience does suggest is that an action directed against certain conduct, whether it be described as unfair competition or unfair copying or in some other way, can develop effectively within a common law system to provide what is a valuable, flexible and cost-effective remedy as a supplement to those traditional remedies for infringement of intellectual property rights.

My point, simply, is that to recognise and develop a general law of unfair copying is a preferable method for dealing with many of the claims for protection I have referred to this evening, rather than by the creation of an ever-increasing range of property rights within or analogous to traditional intellectual property. As a learned commentator has written:

'With the dawning of the information age a whole panoply of interests including character merchandisers and sponsors are pressing for the extension of legal protection for an ever-increasing range of information-related "products".

How to articulate the mechanism to balance a right to protect labour, skill and effort against a right of access to information creates great difficulties but may not be insoluble once a basis for protection outside the traditional concept of property is devised.' (Professor Michael Pendleton, 'Character Merchandising and the Proper Scope of Intellectual Property', [1990] Australian Intellectual Property Journal 242.

I suggest that the task of establishing that basis for protection is one which must now be urgently addressed.

So far as I am aware, Jim never resiled from that opinion, and I sat on two Australian Attorney General's Copyright Law Review Committee references with him. Despite that encouragement, my writing did not go as far as I wished because I didn't really trust my insights. I largely stuck to discrete small issues within a cause of action like everyone else. Some of the publications where I did attempt to flesh out a misappropriation remedy as a supplement or replacement for existing intellectual property are listed in the footnotes.[77]

While recognition of the need to restrict what is protected by copyright is desirable, there are better ways of achieving it than denying 'sweat of the brow' copyright works. An extended defence to infringement would accomplish the same result: in other words, has the defendant added sufficiently to what the plaintiff has done to be said to have a new original work in its hands?

A key problem with my proposal is finding the answer to what constitutes sufficient additional labour, skill and effort to be outside the protection of another and possibly enjoy its own protection. How much of a jump must be made? Although decided on very specific issues involving fair use under the United States copyright law, the recent Supreme Court decision in

---

[77]   Michael D. Pendleton, *The Evolving Law of Unfair Competition*, in H.K.L.J.: EXCERPTS FROM LAW LECTURES FOR PRACTITIONERS 76 (1982); Michael D. Pendleton, *Character Merchandising and the Proper Scope of Intellectual Property*, INTELL. PROP. J. 242 (1990); Michael D. Pendleton, *Misappropriation Remedies – Rendering Intellectual Property Law Redundant?* in 5TH ANNUAL INTELLECTUAL PROPERTY TEACHERS ASSOCIATION (Australia: University of Queensland, 1996); Michael D. Pendleton, *Intellectual Property Law's Inability to Cope Generally, Not Merely with Web Based Works – Where To From Here*, in 10TH INTERNATIONAL WORLD WIDE WEB CONFERENCE (Hong Kong: International World-Wide Web Conference Committee, 2001); Michael D. Pendleton, *Challenging Laws Traditional Refusal to Protect Information per se for Fear of Stifling Innovation, Competition and Access: An East Asian Perspective*, in INTELLECTUAL PROPERTY IN AN ASIAN CONTEXT: CHALLENGES, DEMANDS OF THE INFORMATION ECONOMY (Singapore: National University of Singapore, 2001); Michael D. Pendleton, *Honest Copying – The Gist of Intellectual Property*, in H.K.L.J.: LAW LECTURES FOR PRACTITIONERS, 43 (2006).

Google LLC v Oracle America Inc.[78] is illuminating. The court talks about a permitted fair use, characterizing it as a 'transformative use'. That concept of transformative use is fertile ground for establishing what is sufficient additional labour, skill and effort to amount to a defence.

9.1   Transformative Use

On its facts, *Google v Oracle* is a case about characterization of what is fair use under US copyright law. To a very large extent that law confers a significant discretion on the court, albeit guided by the four principles taken from the Berne Convention and implanted into the DMCA. Essentially, the court defined transformative use as something which adds something new, with a further purpose or different character.

On the facts, Oracle owned the copyright in Java, a computer programming language. When Google acquired Android it needed a way to make Java usable on Android so it copied 11,500 lines of code from the Java program. The code copied related to an application programming interface which allows programmers to call up written computing tasks for use in their own programs. The court held that Google's copying of the selected user interface code in Java, which included only those 11,500 lines of code, was needed to allow programmers to put their accrued talents to work in a new and transformative program, and that constituted fair use.

The court considered the four factors to be taken into account in determining fair use in the DMCA, in turn derived from the Berne Convention: the purpose and character of the use; the nature of the copyrighted work; the amount and substantiality of the portion used in relation to the copyrighted work as a whole; and the effect of the use upon the potential market for or value of the copyrighted work.

The nature of the work, a user interface, sits well with fair use, observed the court. And the value of the work substantially increased not just by the owner of the Java programming language but by the various programmers who use it and grow it. Google's purpose was to create a new platform. Google's intention was to create an interface to further the development of computer programs and that in itself was furthering the basic constitutional objects of copyright.

10.   CONCLUSION

So did the defendant's alterations to the lift-off can opener amount to a transformative use? To use the dicta in the Supreme Court *Google* decision, did it add something new, with a further purpose or different character? I think not. The words 'transformative use' have helped me form a normative decision on that case some 40 years later. The plaintiff should have won in a normative sense, and it would have been possible on the existing law to so hold.

My submission is that intellectual property law can only be useful in relation to artificial intelligence, the high-water mark of the Information Revolution, if it is entirely reconstructed to move away from its nineteenth-century doctrinal precepts to something which makes transparent on its face the balancing of the interests of innovators, their competitors and consumers.

---

[78]   593 US __ (5 Apr. 2021).

To do so it should be replaced,[79] or at the very least supplemented, with a misappropriation law that protects the labour, skill, effort and investment of time and money of persons but makes clear that it is a defence to invest sufficient additional labour, skill, effort and investment of time and money, and that that in itself may give rise to a new protectible right. Whether there is sufficient additional labour, skill and investment of time and money can be determined by the concept of whether there is a transformative use. You must have regard to whether the defendant added something new, with a further purpose or different character.

It is not possible in this chapter to pursue the possible application of transformative use as a tool of misappropriation law. That is the task of a further monograph.

So, having a better appreciation of what is protectable labour, skill, effort and investment of time and money in a mere can opener, we are armed to some degree to begin at least an assessment of the intricate balancing of protecting access to aspects of information concerning AI, where access should be allowed and where access is mandated by public access.

But remember, the present law is ill-equipped to even theoretically balance innovator, competitor and public access in the most mundane mechanical components, let alone in artificial intelligence. We have to move away from the arcane nineteenth-century doctrinal nonsense that is twenty-first century intellectual property law.

---

[79]   With the need to revise the international conventions, something which may simply be politically impossible.

PART II

COPYRIGHT AND RELATED RIGHTS

7. The AI–copyright challenge: tech-neutrality, authorship, and the public interest

Carys J. Craig

1. INTRODUCTION

For readers of this volume, it hardly needs to be repeated that recent developments in artificial intelligence (AI) are poised to disrupt our intellectual property (IP) system. Many of the core concepts and assumptions that underlie our copyright and patent laws, especially, are already being tested and disturbed by the rapid rise of AI and its generative capabilities. In the public theatre of IP policy, our old heroes—copyright's author and patent's inventor—are at risk of being outshone by their intrepid AI understudies. As AI-generated works and inventions increasingly take center stage, conventional constructs such as the "original work of authorship" or the "nonobvious invention" suddenly look less solid, and their attendant bundle of rights more tenuous. And so familiar IP policy questions about incentives and rewards, progress, and the public interest present themselves anew in the face of fresh promises, mounting apprehensions, and the pervasive hyperbole that has accompanied the arrival of AI.

This is the unfolding AI copyright drama into which governments, courts, and commentators are increasingly drawn. There is a sense of urgency behind the questions that are now repeatedly posed in public consultations, in private litigation, and behind the closed doors of lawmakers and lobbyists around the world. How will the copyright system respond to the rise of AI? Should the law protect mass-produced AI outputs as copyrightable works? Might there be infringement liability for copies fed into or produced by AI systems, on whose shoulders would it fall, and what exceptions could apply? More broadly, what will this new technological revolution mean for artists and creators, owners and users, and the copyright system as we know it?

The urgency may well be overblown, and the hyperbole unhelpful at best, but such questions must be asked, and, in time, they will be answered one way or another. Given the many paradigm-changing technologies that have come along since copyright's eighteenth-century inception, from the Player Piano Roll to the World Wide Web, we can reasonably predict that copyright will once again adapt and prevail. Whether in service of creativity and culture or simply in service of capital, the copyright system is perfectly capable of absorbing this latest innovation and continuing about its business as it has so many times before. Our now over-rehearsed law and policy debates can quite readily offer up answers to the doctrinal conundrums that AI appears to present. But to what end? More interesting than the doctrinal debates that AI provokes, then, is the opportunity that it presents to revisit the purposes of the copyright system—its functions and its fictions—and to reconsider its rationale in the age of AI. This is where the copyright policy debate about AI should begin; ultimately, how we respond to the AI-copyright challenge will depend on *why* we are responding, what rights we are choosing to protect, and in service of whose interests.

In this spirit, section 2 of this chapter considers the normative objectives that underlie—and so ought to inform—copyright law and its response to technological change. Highlighted here is the guiding principle of "technological neutrality" and its potential importance in shaping the law's trajectory into the future. Section 3 then turns to survey some of the quandaries presented by AI through this theoretical frame, first looking at the question of AI "authorship" and the public interest and then turning briefly to the matter of potential infringement in respect of AI's inputs. The chapter concludes, first, that AI-generated works are not works of authorship and so ought to be left "where they lie" in the public domain; it further concludes that the usage of works as training data does not involve use of the work of authorship as such and should therefore require no defense. These conclusions, it is argued, are consistent with—indeed required by—the technologically neutral normative objectives of copyright law and the social values they reflect.

Without a principled commitment to the public purposes of copyright, economic interests (propelled by neoliberal logic and techno-romantic rhetoric) will surely set our course towards increased commoditization and private control. We may then miss out on the true promise of AI to contribute to a vibrant public domain, instead hindering or harming the very creative processes and cultural exchange that copyright law is meant to foster.

2.   TECHNOLOGICAL NEUTRALITY AND THE PURPOSES OF COPYRIGHT

The arrival of AI—or, at least, its recent flourishing—has the feel of something new, something ground-breaking. The temptation is therefore to treat it as wholly unprecedented, and so to rush into action, making reforms to clear the way for this exciting innovation; the mistake is to forget that, no matter how novel this particular technological innovation, we have been here many times before. The modern copyright system was itself a response to technological innovation, after all—the invention and proliferation of the printing press. Since that time, history has witnessed a continual evolution of communication technologies, from the creation of lithographs and engravings to sound recordings and cameras, and from the first radio broadcasts and phone calls to the invention of computers, photocopiers, fax machines, and the internet. And with each innovation, copyright laws that were originally written to control the printing of physical books have adapted and expanded, embracing new modes of cultural production and supporting new means of economic exploitation. Even if the technology is novel, then, the question of how the law ought to respond to technological change is not at all new.

A common response to the question of how the law should treat new technologies is simply that the law should be *technologically neutral*. That is, copyright law should be written and developed to be independent of any specific technology and should therefore continue to apply equally across technologies as they emerge, without favoring or discriminating between new and old.[1] There is an obvious appeal to this approach for policy makers in the digital age.

---

[1]   *See* Entm't Software Ass'n v Soc'y of Composers, Authors and Music Publishers of Can., 2012 S.C.C. 34 at ¶ 5, 9 [SOCAN]; Soc'y of Composers, Authors and Music Publishers of Can. v Entm't Software Ass'n, 2022 S.C.C. 30 at ¶ 6 [ESA] *See also* Robertson v Thomson Corp., 2006 S.C.C. 43; Soc'y of Composers, Authors and Music Publishers of Can. v Bell Can., 2012 S.C.C. 36 at ¶ 43; Can. Broad. Corp. (CBC) v SODRAC 2003, Inc., 2015 S.C.C. 57 [SODRAC].

From a practical perspective, it presents the promise of sustainable laws in a time of rapid technological change, "future-proofing" the copyright system to some degree by permitting old laws to apply seamlessly to new technologies. Happily, it may also excuse lawmakers from following the twists and turns of each technological development as it occurs, and likely produces more comprehensible legislation for those non-experts who are expected to abide by it. This answer is also intuitively attractive from a principled perspective: neutrality, equality, and non-discrimination in the law are almost always perceived as intrinsically laudable goals. It is not surprising, then, that technological neutrality is widely hailed as an unquestionably good thing—like "motherhood and apple pie,"[2] as one commentator has observed—but typically with little in the way of explanation or justification. The problem, of course, is that (as with equality, non-discrimination, and neutrality writ large) what the principle of technological neutrality *means* in any particular application is highly subjective and necessarily context-dependent.

In fact, technological neutrality has many shades of meaning, and different meanings can produce differing applications with more or less desirable results.[3] I have suggested elsewhere that these different meanings range from formal non-discrimination between technologies at one end of the spectrum to substantive equality-in-effect at the other.[4] It is worth identifying these different approaches and their limits here, as our question of how copyright law should treat AI is directly informed by the relationship we perceive between technological innovation and good copyright policy-making.

2.1   Competing Conceptions of Technological Neutrality

At one end of the spectrum, a narrow, formal version of neutrality simply extends the law as it is to new technological activities or processes. On this logic, for example, a copy is a copy, whether it is made by hand, photocopier, cell phone, or a computer's Random-Access Memory, and whether it is printed, saved, or temporarily cached.[5] The problem with this formalistic approach is that, in the name of neutrality, it treats alike activities that are, in fact and effect, very different. What it produces in practice, then, can be a vastly different outcome for old and new technologies, and thus their *substantively unequal* treatment. Whereas the mere act of reading a physical newspaper, for example, does not involve copying and so would not

---

² Chris Reed, *Taking Sides on Technology Neutrality*, 4:3 SCRIPTed 263, 265 (2007).
³ For an excellent discussion of various meanings attached to the principle, *see* Bert-Japp Koops, *Should ICT Regulation be Technology-Neutral?*, *in* STARTING POINTS FOR ICT REGULATION: DECONSTRUCTING PREVALENT POLICY ONE-LINERS (Bert-Jaap Koops, Miriam Lips, Corien Prins & Maurice Schellekens, eds, 2006). *See also* Deborah S. Tussey, *Technology Matters: The Courts, Media Neutrality, and New Technologies*, 12 J. INTELL. PROP. L. 427 (2005); Brad A. Greenberg, *Rethinking Technology Neutrality*, 100 MINN. L. REV. 1495, 1498 (2016).
⁴ Carys J. Craig, *Technological Neutrality: (Pre)Serving the Purposes of Copyright Law*, *in* THE COPYRIGHT PENTALOGY: HOW THE SUPREME COURT OF CANADA SHOOK THE FOUNDATIONS OF CANADIAN COPYRIGHT LAW (Michael Geist, ed., 2013); Carys Craig, *Technological Neutrality: Recalibrating Copyright in the Information Age*, 17 THEORETICAL INQUIRIES L. 601 (2016). *See also* Gregory R. Hagen, *Technological Neutrality in Canadian Copyright Law*, *in* THE COPYRIGHT PENTALOGY: HOW THE SUPREME COURT OF CANADA SHOOK THE FOUNDATIONS OF CANADIAN COPYRIGHT LAW (Michael Geist, ed., 2013); Cameron J. Hutchison, *Technological Neutrality Explained & Applied to CBC v. SODRAC* 13:1 C.J.L.T. 101 (2015).
⁵ *See, e.g.,* SODRAC, *supra* note 1.

implicate a copyright owner's rights, browsing a newspaper online creates temporary digital reproductions and potentially cached copies. If every digital copy, however fleeting, were to be regarded as a reproduction like any other, then the act of reading online would suddenly implicate copyright in a way that reading a physical copy never did. Similarly, if we treat every digital reproduction made in the process of an online transmission as though it is a copy for copyright purposes, the act of sending a digital copy online is suddenly very different than putting a physical one in the mail.[6] Treating things equally regardless of technological difference can in fact discriminate between technologies and produce unequal treatment in result. (The same critique has, of course, been made of formal equality and neutral treatment in other contexts.)[7]

Moving along the spectrum, a preferable ("intermediate") approach to technological neutrality focuses on the *effects* of particular technological activities or processes, demanding that the law apply equally to *functionally equivalent* actions. Tech-neutrality, in this version, is about the equal treatment in law of effectively analogous activities.[8] Thus, a digital streaming service, for example, may be subject to the same legal rules as a cable broadcaster if their activities have the same effect, notwithstanding the different technological processes involved.[9] To take our example above, reading online should be treated by law in the same way as a reading a physical paper because the act is functionally the same no matter the medium. Similarly, as Canada's Supreme Court has held, selling a digital copy online should engage the same copyright interests—no more and no less—as selling a physical copy over the counter.[10]

This version of tech-neutrality is better; but still, its reliance on analogical reasoning and functional equivalence present cause for concern. Drawing analogies between old and new technologies ("x does the same as y") is a more subjective endeavor than it might seem. A cloud-based TV recording service may be convincingly analogized to a cable TV service, for example, as it was by the US Supreme Court in the *Aereo* case, when arguably the better

---

[6] The act of digital broadcasting would involve considerably more copies than would traditional broadcasting, and so could potentially involve far greater costs in the form of copyright tariffs.

[7] I am referring here to a long and deep body of scholarship and advocacy addressing formal equality in the context of human rights and discrimination law. *See, e.g.*, Sandra Fredman, *Substantive Equality Revisited*, 14 INT'L J. OF CONST. L. 712, 713 (2016), citing, *e.g.*, Peter Westen, *The Empty Idea of Equality*, 95 HARV. L. REV. 537, 542 (1982); Law v Can. [1999] 1 S.C.R. 497 (Can.); Prinsloo v Van der Linde (CCT4/96), [1997] Z.A.C.C. 5 (S. Afr.); CEDAW Committee, General Recommendation No. 25: On Temporary Special Measures (2004) CEDAW/C/GC/25.

[8] *See, e.g.*, Am. Broad. Co. v Aereo, Inc., 134 S. Ct. 2498 (2014) [Aereo] (one-to-one transmission of a digitized signal was sufficiently "cable-like" to constitute public performance as a cable transmission would). *See also* Ryan Abbott, THE REASONABLE ROBOT (2020) (proposing a concept of "legal neutrality" that appears to focus on functional equivalence and analogy). For a more detailed critique of Abbott's conception of legal neutrality, *see* Carys Craig, *The Relational Robot: A Normative Lens for AI Legal Neutrality – Commentary on Ryan Abbott*, The Reasonable Robot 25 JERUSALEM REV. OF LEGAL STUDIES 24 (2022)

[9] The Aereo case, *supra* note 8, reveals the difficulty with this kind of reasoning by technological analogy: in fact, in my opinion, the activity at issue bore greater resemblance to the provision of a VCR to facilitate the making of lawful personal copies. *See Brief Amici Curiae of Law Professors and Scholars in Support of Respondents*, at 22–3, Am. Broad. Co., 134 S. Ct., http://isp.yale.edu/sites/default/files/American%20Broadcasting%20Companies%20v.%20Aereo.pdf (citing Sony Corp. of Am. v Universal City Studios, Inc., 464 U.S. 417 (1984)).

[10] SOCAN, *supra* note 1.

analogy—and one that would have supported an entirely different ruling—would have been to a personal VCR.

In the strategic search for functional equivalence, critical differences between technological processes can be overlooked, and comparisons can be stretched to justify a kind of willful technology-blindness. Analogies can therefore produce false equivalents while also obscuring the disruptive force of technological change. Treating the personal recording service as akin to a cable service undervalued the distributive potential of the novel technology at issue in *Aereo* for consumers seeking to access works, and it re-established the technology provider as the appropriate point of control (thereby reinforcing the distribution rights of content industry incumbents). To take another example, a teacher sharing digital copies with students through a content management platform may be doing something functionally equivalent to handing out photocopies in class; if we simply regard these acts as analogous and regulate them accordingly, however, we overlook both the practical implications for copyright owners of having perfect, reproducible files circulating online *and* the enormous opportunities for improved access and education that the technology now affords.

Some technologies are paradigm-shifting—they simply "change the game."[11] In such cases, we cannot assume that neutral legal treatment will produce a substantively equivalent legal effect. When the risks and opportunities shift significantly with the affordances of novel technologies, the costs and benefits of copyright control should be reevaluated. A myopic focus on the comparable effects of specific technological actions and processes may miss this bigger picture. The weakness of the intermediate approach to technological neutrality, then, is precisely that it purports to solve the policy conundrum by treating the new thing *as if* it were something else (the old thing). The mistake is to assume that treating like things alike will produce equivalent outcomes. In the copyright system as elsewhere, equal treatment without due attention to context and difference can disguise systemic advantages and disadvantages behind a veil of neutrality.

And so, at the furthest end of the spectrum, the most expansive vision of technological neutrality looks beyond the equal treatment of functional equivalents to the systemic effects of new technologies and the balance of rights and interests that will shape their use. The focus is not only on the comparable effects of specific technological actions or processes, but also on the broader effects of the technology and its affordances. This substantive principle of technological neutrality is therefore less concerned with ensuring the consistent treatment of analogous activities than with consistently advancing the objectives of the law in new technological contexts. In other words, the neutrality that it supports is not just a technical or legal neutrality but a *normative neutrality*: Whether through the interpretation and application of existing law or its reform, the principled goal is presumed to be normative equilibrium in the face of technological change.

The principle of technological neutrality can be a brain scratcher. Technology itself is not neutral; nor is the law. And to apply the law neutrally to novel or different technologies will potentially produce new and unequal outcomes. A more substantive approach to tech-neutrality therefore focuses on the technology's implications for the purposes that the law serves. It is these purposes—and the values they reflect—that should be regarded as presump-

---

[11]   Ian Kerr & Katie Szilagyi, *Asleep at the Switch? How Killer Robots become a Force Multiplier of Military Necessity*, in ROBOT LAW 333, 349 (Ryan M. Calo, Michael Froomkin & Ian Kerr, eds, 2016).

tively tech-neutral, transcending the technical capabilities of the moment. So, what does this mean for copyright law?

2.2   Competing Conceptions of Copyright's Purpose

If the above is accepted, then the task that awaits us is to adjust copyright law and its application to today's technological context—the AI age, if you will—in a manner that continues to advance the normative objectives of the copyright system. Defining these objectives is by no means a straightforward task, of course; copyright's rationale has been a matter of debate since its inception. For our purposes, however, it is sufficient to point to the widely accepted justification for the copyright system: it is a means by which to encourage or incentivize authorship and the dissemination of original works, which ultimately serves the public interest.

In its 1709 formulation, the stated purpose of the first modern copyright law in the United Kingdom was "the encouragement of learning," which it sought to achieve "by Vesting the Copies of Printed Books in the Authors or Purchasers of such Copies."[12] The United States Constitution subsequently captured the purpose of copyright as being "to promote the Progress of Science and useful Arts." Similarly, this was to be done "by securing for limited Times to Authors […] the exclusive Right to their […] Writings."[13] In both formulations, the grant of rights to authors (and, through them, owners) is presented as a means to a larger social end. As explained by the US Supreme Court in the foundational *Feist* case, "The primary objective of copyright is not to reward the labor of authors, but '[t]o promote the Progress of Science and useful Arts.'"[14] More recently, in *Google LLC v Oracle*, the Supreme Court spoke of the "creative 'progress' that is the basic constitutional objective of copyright itself."[15] (We will return to consider this idea of "progress" in section 3.3 below.)

The Supreme Court of Canada has also had occasion of late to revisit copyright's purpose, which it has described as "a balance between promoting the public interest in the encouragement and dissemination of works of the arts and intellect and obtaining a just reward for the creator."[16] Most recently, that Court explained: "[J]ust rewards for copyright creators provide necessary incentives, ensuring that there is a steady flow of creative works injected into the public sphere […] A proper balance ensures that creators' rights are recognized, but authorial control is not privileged over the public interest."[17]

Whether authors are entitled to just rewards independently of the public interest will always be a point of contention. It is not one we need to resolve here.[18] It is sufficient to embrace the

---

[12]   Statute of Anne, 1710, 8 Ann. C. 19 (Eng.). The statute's full title was "An Act for the Encouragement of Learning, by Vesting the Copies of Printed Books in the Authors or Purchasers of such Copies, during the Times therein mentioned."

[13]   U.S. CONST. art. I, § 8, cl. 8.

[14]   Feist Publ'ns Inc. v Rural Tel. Serv. Co. Inc., 499 U.S. 340, 349–50 (1991) [Feist], quoting ibid.

[15]   Google LLC v Oracle America, Inc., 593 U.S. ____ 25 (2021) [Google].

[16]   Théberge v Galerie d'Art du Petit Champlain Inc., 2002 S.C.C. 34 at ¶ 11–12, 30.

[17]   York Univ. v Canadian Copyright Licensing Agency (Access Copyright), 2021 S.C.C. 32 at ¶ 93–4 [Access Copyright], citing Mya Tawfik, *History in the Balance: Copyright and Access to Knowledge*, in FROM "RADICAL EXTREMISM" TO "BALANCED COPYRIGHT": CANADIAN COPYRIGHT AND THE DIGITAL AGENDA 69 (Michael Geist, ed., 2010).

[18]   I have argued elsewhere against the idea of an author's natural right to copyright as a reward for intellectual labour: *see* Carys J. Craig, *Locke, Labour, and Limiting the Author's Right: A Warning*

idea of a copyright balance, which in turn means recognizing that "[c]opyright law has public interest goals."[19] Specifically, "increasing public access to and dissemination of artistic and intellectual works, which enrich society and often provide users with the tools and inspiration to generate works of their own, is a primary goal of copyright."[20] Ultimately, then, copyright is a system of state-granted entitlements to encourage creative expression and learning; authors' or creators' rights must therefore be balanced with users' rights and the public interest to support a flourishing public domain.[21]

The concept of balance that has emerged so explicitly in Canadian copyright jurisprudence is helpfully intertwined with the principle of technological neutrality as I have described it. Inherent in the very concept of balance is the need to adjust the weight and distribution of rights and interests in order to maintain a consistent equilibrium as conditions change.[22] Thus, as the Court's robust vision of technological neutrality suggests, "the traditional balance between authors and users should be preserved in the digital environment."[23] Justice Abella has since explained:

> The question [...] is how to preserve [the balance that best supports the public interest in creative works] in the face of new technologies that are transforming the mechanisms through which creative works are produced, reproduced and distributed [...] The answer to this challenge [...] lies in applying a robust vision of technological neutrality as a core principle of statutory interpretation under the *Copyright Act*.[24]

The US Supreme Court recently made a similar pronouncement about balance, technological change, and copyright's purpose when interpreting the fair use provision in *Oracle*:

> [W]e have understood the provision to set forth general principles, the application of which requires judicial balancing, depending upon relevant circumstances, including "significant changes in technology." Sony Corp. of America v. Universal City Studios, Inc., 464 U. S. 417, 430 (1984); see also

---

Against a Lockean Approach to Copyright Law, 28 QUEEN'S L.J. 1 (2002), online: <https://ssrn.com/abstract=2078157>.

[19] Access Copyright, *supra* note 17, at ¶ 91. *See also* CCH v Law Society of Upper Can., 2004 S.C.C. 13 at ¶ 23 [CCH Canadian].

[20] Ibid at ¶ 92.

[21] *See* Carys J. Craig, COPYRIGHT, COMMUNICATION AND CULTURE: TOWARDS A RELATIONAL THEORY OF COPYRIGHT LAW 52 (2011).

[22] Robertson v Thompson, 2006 S.C.C. 43 at ¶ 79 (Abella, J., dissenting) (citing Michael Geist, OUR OWN CREATIVE LAND: CULTURAL MONOPOLY & THE TROUBLE WITH COPYRIGHT 9 (2006), cdn .michaelgeist.ca/wp-content/uploads/2006/05/hhl06_Online_Book.pdf.

[23] SOCAN, *supra* note 1, at ¶ 7–8 (citing Carys Craig, *Locking Out Lawful Users: Fair Dealing and Anti-Circumvention in Bill C-32*, in FROM 'RADICAL EXTREMISM' TO 'BALANCED COPYRIGHT': CANADIAN COPYRIGHT AND THE DIGITAL AGENDA 177 (Michael Geist, ed., 2010) [*Locking Out Lawful Users*]). See also ESA, *supra* note 1, at ¶ 68–9.

[24] SODRAC, *supra* note 1, at ¶ 147–8. *See also* SODRAC, *supra* note 1, at ¶ 149 (Abella J. dissenting) (identifying Parliament's intent that the Copyright Act "must adapt and apply to new technologies in a manner that maintains the careful balance between creators and users that underpins the *Act* as a whole"); ESA, *supra* note 1, at ¶ 69 (confirming that "the principle of technological neutrality is a tool for balancing user's and authors' rights"). *But see also* Abraham Drassinower, *Remarks on Technological Neutrality in Copyright Law as a Subject Matter Problem: Lessons from Canada*, 81 Cambridge L.J. 50 (2022) (disputing the characterisation of technological neutrality as a balancing principle).

Aiken, 422 U. S., at 156 ("When technological change has rendered its literal terms ambiguous, the Copyright Act must be construed in light of its basic purpose").[25]

To be sure, technological neutrality in this sense does not dictate a definitive answer to any particular legal question. If the consistency sought is not consistency in the application of the law but rather in the steady pursuit of the law's purpose, then the answer to any policy question will depend upon how this purpose is defined, propelling us straight into subjective balancing exercises and age-old debates around competing conceptions of authorship, entitlement, and the public interest. Approaching the question in this way does, however, relieve us of the task of examining the internal mechanics of technological processes, and it allows us to escape intractable debates about which analogies most aptly apply to describe new technology-enabled activities. More to the point, it reminds us of the big question we *should* be asking: Given the new realities of the current technological environment, what rights should the law recognize—and subject to what limits—if it is to continue to advance its objectives?

In my view, it is the search for this answer that should inform copyright's response to recent developments in AI. If AI is the game-changer that we have been led to believe it is, then it will not be sufficient to simply apply the law as it is to the new technology—treating alike things that are fundamentally different. Nor will it do to simply apply the existing law to the activities of an AI wherever they appear to be functionally equivalent in effect to an act traditionally performed by a human. Rather, we must analyze the function and effects of AI technologies with a view to their implications for the copyright system as a whole. Efforts to respond to this latest technological (r)evolution should aim to preserve the balance that "best supports the public interest in creative works" as this is "the central purpose" of copyright law.[26] A substantive vision of tech-neutrality thus operates as a framing principle, guiding a purposive application of law to our new technological realities. It necessitates not willful technology-blindness, but quite the opposite: a clear-sighted recognition of the disruptive force and political significance of AI for the "creative progress" that copyright is intended to foster.

3. COPYRIGHT AND THE AI CHALLENGE

There are, in current debates around the implications of AI, two doctrinal and policy questions that seem to loom large for copyright law. First is the matter of AI-generated works (outputs) and where—or whether—they fit within the copyright scheme, premised as it is on *authorship* of the heretofore human variety. Second is the question of AI-training datasets (inputs) and whether or not the processes involved in machine-learning implicate—and potentially infringe—copyright, premised as it is on the exclusive right to *reproduce* works of authorship. Whereas other relevant and important policy issues such as, say, the appropriate allocation of liability for unlawful actions/outputs or the automation of enforcement are also raised by the arrival of AI, these are legal issues that traverse a multitude of fields.[27] Authorship and

---

[25] Google, *supra* note 15, at 14.

[26] SODRAC, *supra* note 1, at ¶ 146.

[27] For further discussion of these issues, *see* Carys J. Craig, *Copyright and Artificial Intelligence*, in AI AND THE LAW IN CANADA 33–7 (Florian Martin-Bariteau & Teresa Scassa, eds, 2021) [*Copyright and AI*].

infringement for copying, however, present quandaries that are thoroughly internal to copyright law and its logic. As such, these are the issues to which we now turn, armed with our guiding principle of normative neutrality and a clearer sense of copyright's purpose.

3.1   AI "Authorship"

"The rise of the machines is here," it has been said, "but they do not come as conquerors, they come as *creators*."[28]

Recent high-profile examples of AI-generated works span the full range of human cultural endeavor from music to film, and from literature to the visual arts. *Jukebox*, for instance, is a machine-learning model capable of generating music that imitates different styles and artists, even incorporating singing in natural-sounding voices.[29] *TalkToTransformer* is an AI language generator, created by Canadian engineer Adam King using the OpenAI GPT-2 technology, which can write articles when prompted with a headline or complete short stories when fed the first line.[30] *Dio* is a sculptural work from artist Ben Snell, which was generated by a machine-learning algorithm trained on a dataset of classical sculptures (and then made out of the pulverized dust of the machine that designed it!).[31] *Sunspring* is an award-winning science fiction film, the screenplay and music for which was written by the self-named *Benjamin*—a neural network trained on hundreds of sci-fi movies from the 1980s and 1990s.[32] Perhaps most famously, *Portrait of Edmond Belamy* is an AI-generated painting that sold at Christie's Auction House for just shy of half a million dollars in 2018, signaling "the arrival of AI-generated art on the world auction stage."[33] Of course there are also many more mundane examples: machine-generated text produced by online chatbots; the verbal responses of digital assistants such as Alexa or Siri; the manipulations of "selfies" and visual images produced by apps like Google's Deep Dream AI;[34] and the proliferating AI-composed music playlists of

---

[28]   Andres Guadamuz, *Artificial Intelligence and Copyright,* 5 WIPO MAGAZINE 14, 17 (2017), www .wipo.int/wipo_magazine/en/2017/05/article_0003.html (emphasis added).

[29]   Prafulla Dhariwal et al., *Jukebox: A Generative Model for Music*, arXiv (April 30, 2020), https:// arxiv.org/pdf/2005.00341.pdf. Curated examples of Jukebox's outputs are available online: https:// openai.com/blog/jukebox/.

[30]   James Vincent, *Use This Cutting-Edge AI Text Generator to Write Stories, Poems, News Articles, and More*, The Verge (May 13, 2019), www.theverge.com/tldr/2019/5/13/18617449/ai-text-generator -openai-gpt-2-small-model-talktotransformer; James Vincent, *OpenAI's New Multitalented AI Writes, Translates, and Slanders*, The Verge (Feb. 14, 2019), www.theverge.com/2019/2/14/18224704/ai -machine-learning-language-models-read-write-openai-gpt2. TalkToTransformer.com is now being offered as a paid service online: https://inferkit.com/.

[31]   James Vincent, *This AI-generated Sculpture Is Made from the Shredded Remains of the Computer that Designed It*, The Verge (Apr. 12, 2019), www.theverge.com/tldr/2019/4/12/18306090/ai-generated -sculpture-shredded-remains-ben-snell-dio. High-resolution views of Snell's sculptures are provided on the website of Blackbird Gallery, online: www.blackbird.gallery/artists/54-ben-snell/works/.

[32]   Oscar Sharp, *Sunspring*, YOUTUBE (June 9, 2016), https://youtu.be/LY7x2Ihqjmc.

[33]   Christie's, *Is Artificial Intelligence Set to Become Art's Next Medium?*, Christie's (December 12, 2018), www.christies.com/features/A-collaboration-between-two-artists-one-human-one-a-machine -9332-1.aspx.

[34]   Online: https://deepdreamgenerator.com/. *See also, e.g.*, Hilary Brueck, *Google's Computers Are Making Thousands as Artists*, Fortune (Mar. 1, 2016), https://fortune.com/2016/03/01/google -deepdream-art/.

techno-beats and ennui-inducing electronica to be found on Spotify[35] (alas, not every AI has the training necessary to finish Schubert's Unfinished Symphony).[36]

As with any new wave of innovative production with commercial applications and potentially valuable, commodifiable outputs, the question in respect of such AI-generated works quickly becomes "who owns it?" A more apt starting point for copyright purposes would be "who is the author?" For, unless we can answer that prior question, we cannot know whether there is even an original copyrightable work to be owned, never mind to whom it belongs. In respect of the *Portrait of Edmond Belamy*, for instance, it was queried whether the Parisian art group that collated and fed data to the AI rightly laid claim to the portrait, or whether the credit should have gone to Robbie Barrat, the person who wrote the open-source code on which the AI operated.[37] Meanwhile, the place on the canvas where the artist's name would traditionally appear contained a portion of the algorithm itself.

As things stand, works that are autonomously generated by machines or AI are not copyrightable in most jurisdictions around the world, which means that they currently belong in the public domain. In the United States, Australia, Canada, and most of Europe, the fact that copyright attaches only to "original" works of authorship has been interpreted to mean that they must originate from a human author—a natural person with some direct intellectual involvement in the resulting expression.[38] In some jurisdictions, though—the United Kingdom, Hong Kong, India, Ireland, and New Zealand—specific provisions have been enacted in respect of computer-generated works, deeming the author to be the person who makes the arrangements necessary for their creation.[39] (Whether such works meet the threshold requirements of copyrightability is often still an open question).

It is clear, however, that we are now at a critical moment in the evolution of law when policymakers around the world are turning their attention to this question anew, asking whether they should enact legal fictions to ensure the copyright protection of AI-generated works; and wondering whether, if they do not, they will fall behind their international counterparts in the

---

[35] *See, e.g.*, the Barbican Centre playlist, https://open.spotify.com/playlist/6xbMspVDXiIU TCncyBzoT7.

[36] Online: https://consumer.huawei.com/au/campaign/unfinishedsymphony/.

[37] *See* Jason Bailey, *The Truth Behind Christie's $432K AI Art Sale*, Artnome (Oct. 29, 2018), https://www.artnome.com/news/2018/10/13/the-truth-behind-christies-432k-ai-art-sale. *See also* Amanda Turnbull, *The Price of AI Art: Has the Bubble Burst?*, The Conversation (Jan. 6, 2020), https://theconversation.com/the-price-of-ai-art-has-the-bubble-burst-128698.

[38] The point of copyright's threshold originality doctrine is to identify an authorial act. *See, e.g.*, Feist, *supra* note 14; U.S. Copyright Office, COMPENDIUM OF U.S. COPYRIGHT OFFICE PRACTICES § 306 (3d ed. 2017) "Because copyright law is limited to 'original intellectual conceptions of the author,' the [Copyright] Office will refuse to register a claim if it determines that a human being did not create the work"; Telstra Corp. Ltd. v Phone Directories Co. Pty. Ltd., [2010] F.C.A.F.C. 149 at ¶ 133–4, 137 (requiring that an original work must be the product of human authorship); CCH Canadian, *supra* note 19 (finding that "an original work must be the product of an author's exercise of skill and judgment"); Geophysical Service Incorporated v Encana Corporation, 2016 ABQB 230 at ¶ 88 ("Clearly a human author is required to create an original work for copyright purposes"); Eva-Maria Painer v Standard Verlags GmbH and Others, C-145/10, [2012] E.C.R. I-12594 at I-12622 (requiring "an intellectual creation of the author reflecting his personality and expressing his free and creative choices"). *See generally* Daniel J. Gervais, *The Machine As Author* (2020) 105:5 IOWA L. REV. 2053. For a detailed discussion of Canadian copyright law and its current approach, *see* Carys J. Craig, *Copyright and AI*, *supra* note 27, 7–11.

[39] *See, e.g.*, *Copyright, Designs and Patents Act 1988* (UK), c. I, s. 9(3).

global competition over AI innovation. Several high-profile public consultations and policy reports over the past few years—in the European Union, the United Kingdom, and now in Canada—have revisited these established limits of copyrightability, putting questions to the public, industry, and experts about how the law should respond to the arrival of AI-generated works circulating as products in our cultural sphere.[40] Would extending copyright to such works reflect an appropriate reward for the original, creative efforts and investment of the people responsible for the AI? Would it encourage the kind of authorial, creative practices that advance the "progress" at which copyright is aimed?

My answer to both questions is no, it would not. In fact, far from an incentive to encourage would-be authors, the protection of AI-generated works with exclusive private copyright control would be an unnecessary obstacle to authorship and creative progress. That is because, first, what the AI is doing when it generates a works is *not authorship*—in an ontological sense, the AI is not an "author" with rights or interests in the copyright balance; and second but relatedly, in a teleological sense, the mere proliferation of AI-generated products does not reflect the kind of creative *process* or *practice* that copyright is intended to foster.

3.2   The Myth of the "AI-Author"

Copyright protection is not hard to get. Machine-generated works may, at least for now, lack the aesthetic quality or conceptual coherence of their human-made counterparts (*TalkToTransformer*'s stories rarely make much sense; the *Sunspring* script was unintelligible nonsense; and *Edmond Bellamy* had no discernible nose)—but there is no aesthetic quality bar to copyrightability. The originality threshold requires only a modicum of creativity or, in the Canadian iteration, non-trivial skill and judgment.[41] Had humans created any of these works, copyright would attach to them. But while AI-generated outputs may facially resemble original works of authorship, they are nonetheless categorically different things. When an AI generates outputs, however objectively novel or interesting these may be, they are not original works of authorship or expression within the meaning of copyright law. As Ian Kerr and

---

[40]   *See, e.g.*, Government of Canada, *A Consultation on a Modern Copyright Framework for Artificial Intelligence and the Internet of Things*, www.ic.gc.ca/eic/site/693.nsf/eng/00316.html; Eur. Parl. Doc. (2020/2015(INI)) Intellectual property rights for the development of artificial intelligence technologies; *U.K. Government Response to call for views on artificial Intelligence and Intellectual Property* (March 23, 2021), www.gov.uk/government/consultations/artificial-intelligence-and-intellectual-property-call -for-views/government-response-to-call-for-views-on-artificial-intelligence-and-intellectual-property; WIPO Secretariat, *Revised Issues Paper on Intellectual Property Policy and Artificial Intelligence* 7-8 (May 21, 2020), www.wipo.int/edocs/mdocs/mdocs/en/wipo_ip_ai_2_ge_20/wipo_ip_ai_2_ge_20 _1_rev.pdf. My responses to the Canadian Consultation Paper are contained in two submissions: S. Flynn, L. Guibault, C. Handke, J. Vallbé, M. Palmedo, C. Craig, M. Geist & J.P. Quintais, *Submission to Canadian Government Consultation on a Modern Copyright Framework for AI and the Internet of Things* (Sept. 17, 2021), https://ssrn.com/abstract=3952238; and Carys Craig, Bita Amani, Sara Bannerman, Céline Castets-Renard, Pascale Chapdelaine, Lucie Guibault, Gregory Hagen, Cameron Hutchison, Ariel Katz, Alexandra Mogyoros, Graham Reynolds, Anthony D. Rosborough, Teresa Scassa & Myra Tawfik, *Submission by IP Scholars Copyright and Artificial Intelligence*, www.uwindsor.ca/ law/sites/uwindsor.ca.law/files/final_ai_submission_canadian_ip_scholars.pdf. While the consultation was ongoing, the Canadian Intellectual Property Office registered the artistic work SURYAST, desig-nating an AI painting application as co-author. See Registration No. 1188619, https://www.ic.gc.ca/app/ opic-cipo/cpyrghts/dtls.do?fileNum=1188619&type=1&lang=eng.

[41]   Feist, *supra* note 14; CCH Canadian, *supra* note 19.

I argued at length elsewhere—and I explain in more detail below—the whole concept of an AI author is an oxymoron; AI is ontologically incapable of authorship.[42] But if this is true, why do people seem so eager to assume otherwise?

3.2.1   Anthropomorphism and Expressive Agency

We know—and a great deal of research now demonstrates—that people are inclined to anthropomorphize robots, attributing to AI human attributes and emotions.[43] Anthropomorphic "framing"—giving an AI a human name and gender like *Benjamin* the *Sunspring* screenwriter)—compounds this inclination.[44] The phenomenon is not limited to laypersons; even AI researchers frequently anthropomorphize their robot creations. As Diane Proudfoot observes, "the same researchers who deny that their robots have emotions attribute *expressive behaviors* to the machines literally and without qualification; in this way they unwittingly anthropomorphize the machines."[45] Proudfoot points to the terms in which MIT researchers described the various facial displays of the "Kismet" robot head, developed in the 1990s, which could recognize and simulate emotions. When its creators described it as having a "happy expression," for example, they implied "that the robot has a certain communicative intent—the intent possessed by creatures that smile, namely human beings."[46] Of course, all that the robot head is capable of simulating is the *representation* of a smile; it is not *expressing* anything at all, never mind a *feeling*.

When accounting for the actions or behavior of AI in such terms, researchers unwittingly ascribe an *intentional stance* to the machine; that is, they slip into thinking of it as possessing some form of "intentional agency" complete with implied "drives, interests, goals, as well as intentions."[47] To think in these terms elides the obvious distinction: "AI is computational, whereas intentions are not […] *[T]he two are ontologically different*."[48] Ultimately, as Proudfoot cautions, the "extravagance with which even AI researchers anthropomorphize machines suggests that […] the illusion of communication with a machine may be too readily generated."[49] Why *too* readily? There is a risk here to which we must be attentive: The ready

---

[42]   *See generally*, Carys Craig & Ian Kerr, *The Death of the AI Author*, 52 Оттаwa L. Rev. 31 (2020), https://rdo-olr.org/2021/the-death-of-the-ai-author/.

[43]   *See, e.g.*, Pascal Boyer, *What Makes Anthropomorphism Natural: Intuitive Ontology and Cultural Representations*, J. Royal Anthropological Inst. 83 (1996); Brian R. Duffy, *Anthropomorphism and the Social Robot*, 42 Robotics & Autonomous Systems 177 (1996); Brian R. Duffy & Karolina Zawieski, *Suspension of Disbelief in Social Robotics*, 21st IEEE Int'l Symp. on Robot & Human Interactive Comm. (RO-MAN), 484 (2012); Ryan Calo, *People Can Be So Fake: A New Dimension To Privacy and Technology Scholarship*, 114 Pa. St. L. Rev. 809 (2009).

[44]   Kate Darling, *Who's Johnny? Anthropomorphic Framing in Human–Robot Interaction, Integration, and Policy*, in Robot Ethics 2.0 173 (Patrick Lin, Keith Abney & Ryan Jenkins, eds, 2017).

[45]   Diane Proudfoot, *Anthropomorphism and AI: Turing's Much Misunderstood Imitation Game*, 175 Artificial Intelligence 950, 951 (2011).

[46]   Ibid at 952 (citing Cynthia Breazeal & Brian Scassellati, *Challenges in Building Robots That Imitate People*, in Imitation in Animals and Artifacts 1 (Kerstin Dautenhahn & Chrystopher L. Nehaniv, eds, 2001).

[47]   Deborah G. Johnson & Mario Verdicchio, *From AI, Agency and Responsibility: The VW Fraud Case and Beyond*, 34 AI & Society 639, 645 (2019).

[48]   Ibid (emphasis added).

[49]   Proudfoot, *supra* note 45, at 954.

illusion of genuine communication permits the machine to be mistakenly hailed as "a thinking thing."[50]

The potential social, normative, and regulatory significance of such an error should be self-evident. Recall here in passing that our vision of normative neutrality requires us to see the novel technology in context *as it is*—not *as if* it were something else. As a machine, we should not treat it as if it were a thinking thing. Recall too that we are tasked with considering the AI-copyright challenge in light of copyright's purpose. If copyright aims to encourage authorship—a communicative act of *expression*—we should not treat AI *as if* it were communicating or expressing something when, evidently, it is not.

Recent videos of dancing robots capture the same concern, perhaps even more overtly. In December 2020, Boston Dynamics released a video showing four of its robots dancing to the 1962 hit "Do You Love Me?"[51] As it turned out, people did love them—the video took off online and now has over 35 million views on YouTube alone. Not everyone was charmed by the exercise, admittedly. As one Twitter user was widely quoted to have replied: "Do you love me? Not when you come to annihilate us."[52] While this tongue-in-cheek response evokes the dystopian AI futures of sci-fi imaginings in which raging robots seek liberation, it touches on a point that is real right now: The robots' physical mobility, dexterity, timing, and precision were not designed for dancing the mashed potato—they are attributes that support the effective deployment of these anthropomorphized machines on uneven terrain, from war zones to factory floors to public parks, making them suitable for military, industrial, or police use. The robot dog (named Spot, of course) was arguably the star of the dance video, but its surprise entrance garnered less public adoration when it appeared in exercises by the French military and US police departments. More sinister still was the widely shared video of the robot dog armed with rifle on its back at a US trade show.[53]

My point is not simply that dancing robots appear misleadingly lovable and harmless compared to their armed counterparts on patrol—though that is an important side note for anyone concerned with the ethics of AI. Rather, I juxtapose these divergent deployments of the same technology to emphasize the obvious point that, as far as the robot is concerned, *there is no difference*: The robot dog is mechanically moving as it is trained to do whether it is pointing its weapon at a potential target or doing the twist. From this indubitable conclusion another more controversial one might be offered: The "dancing robot" is not really *dancing* at all.

Dancing, after all, is an expressive act.[54] Copyright protects dance—original works of choreography—just as it protects poems, novels, paintings, or songs. Whether an author uses their intellectual effort to combine words into verse or movements into dance, we understand

---

[50]   Ibid (citing personal communication with Rodney Allen Brooks). *See generally* Rodney Allen Brooks, Cambrian Intelligence: The Early History of the New AI (1999).

[51]   Online: www.youtube.com/watch?v=fn3KWM1kuAw.

[52]   Jan Nicolas, online: <https://twitter.com/phoyager/status/1344176961116102658>.

[53]   Online: www.youtube.com/watch?v=byhRXB8JZNs. This, too, provoked headlines. One asked (as if it were a mystery), *Why Do Armed Robot Dogs Make Us Uncomfortable: Is It the Function of an Armed Robot Dog that Raises Eyebrows, Or Its Form?* The Diplomat (Oct. 15 2021), https://thediplomat.com/2021/10/why-do-armed-robot-dogs-make-us-uncomfortable/ (Spoiler: it's both!).

[54]   *See generally* Christopher Buccafusco, *Authorship and the Boundaries of Copyright: Ideas, Expressions, and Functions in Yoga, Choreography, and Other Works*, 39 Colum. J. L. & Arts 421 (2016), https://doi.org/10.7916/jla.v39i3.2081.

the resulting work to be one of protected intellectual *expression*.[55] In the absence of original-ity, there will be no copyright interest; but there will still be expression. We dance to express ourselves, to communicate with one another, to bond socially, to entice sexually, or sometimes just because we feel like dancing when the music moves us. The robots are neither moved by the music not capable of the expressive agency, emotion, feeling, or intentionality that makes dancing *dancing* as opposed to mere physical or functional movement. Once again, then, when we imagine or describe robots as behaving in terms that inherently imply a certain communica-tive intentionality, we make a category mistake: we attribute to the machines qualities that, by their nature, they simply cannot possess.

When an AI writes a screenplay, it does so by predicting words that might be logically strung together into a sentence, then a paragraph, and then another. It may be tempting for us to frame this ability to predict what words will follow other words as an act of authorship—it might even appear to be, in effect, the functional equivalent of what an author does when they string words together to make an original work. But, as Kerr wrote, the machine "neither knows, understands, nor appreciates the connotation of its word assemblage, let alone the meaning or value of the 'work' as a whole."[56] As captured in Ryan Calo's evocative depiction, "the box is 'gorged on data but with no taste for meaning.'"[57] According to Christopher Buccafusco, the act of stringing together words becomes an act of authorship not because of semantic intentions (those having to do with the intended meaning or interpretation of the work) but rather categorical intentions (about what kind of work the author has created).[58] Authors deem themselves to be authoring, and in doing so, their intention is to "produce mental effects" in their audience—they intend to "generate thoughts, feelings, emotions, and other states of cognition."[59] If this is our measure, once again, AI is incapable of the requisite intentionality.

The notion that the AI is doing something functionally equivalent to a human author thus depends upon a false analogy—it rests on a vision of the technology distorted by misunder-standing, misrepresentation, anthropomorphic framing, and romanticism.

3.2.2　Romanticizing the "AI author"
The romanticization of robots is all the more apparent when the generative AI is presented in rhetorical terms reminiscent of the mythic "romantic author": the entirely independent, wholly original creative genius, generating novel works *ex nihilo*. It has long been recognized, of course, that this mythic author-figure bears little or no resemblance to the real human author, whose relationality and social-situatedness means that authorship is essentially a "process of adapting, transforming, and recombining what is already 'out there' in some other form."[60] In

---

[55]　*See* No. 121, 77 Fed. Reg. 37607 (June 12, 2012) (copyright can attach to the "composition and arrangement of a related series of dance movements and patterns organized into an integrated, coherent, and expressive whole" but not to "the mere selection and arrangement of physical movements").

[56]　Craig & Kerr, *supra* note 42, at 69.

[57]　Ryan Calo, *The Box*, in Telling Stories: On Culturally Responsive Artificial Intelligence (University of Washington Tech Policy Lab, 2020), quoted in ibid.

[58]　Christopher Buccafusco, *A Theory of Copyright Authorship*, 102 Va L. Rev. 1229, 1261 (2016).

[59]　Ibid at 1263.

[60]　Jessica Litman, *The Public Domain*, 39 Emory L.J. 965, 967 (1990). *See also*, e.g., James D.A. Boyle, *The Search for an Author: Shakespeare and the Framers*, 37 Am. U. L. Rev. 625, 633 (1988); Peter Jaszi, Toward a Theory of Copyright: The Metamorphoses of 'Authorship', 1991 Duke L.J. 455, 462 (1991); Martha Woodmansee, On the Author Effect: Recovering Collectivity, 10 Cardozo Arts

Roland Barthes' famous phrasing, "the text is a tissue of citations, resulting from the thousand sources of culture."[61] But where does this leave the human author in relation to the emergent AI author in our popular romantic narrative? Barthes may have declared the "Death of the Author" back the 1960s,[62] but the old romantic myth of the Author-as-God quite seamlessly morphed into the AI-Author-as-God.[63] Consider the position of Mario Klingemann, a German artist on the leading edge of AI art:[64] "Humans are not original," he says. "We only reinvent, make connections between things we have seen." While humans can only build on what we have learned and what others have done before us, "machines can create from scratch."[65]

In Klingemann's depiction, the AI becomes, quite paradoxically, the ideal author—the only truly originating, creative entity. Such a conception of generative AI overlooks the vast quantities of human-produced expression, creative processes, experiences, and cultural heritage necessary to train the AI. Dan Burk explains: "Consideration of the machine in isolation from its extended sociotechnical network lends itself to romanticization of the machine, much as isolation of the human creator from his assemblage of influences once lent itself to romanticization of the human author."

Thus, regarding the machine as author seems unproductive as either a policy or a doctrinal prescription.[66]

Just as the romantic author myth obscured the cumulative and collaborative nature of human creativity, it invisibilizes the extended networks of human influences and interactions behind the AI's generative processes. The AI must be understood in the context of its complex relational network, but this does not make it capable of *relating*—it is not a relational being. As such, to imagine the AI stepping into the category of original author results in a kind of reification of the AI, as though it crafted its own individuated work by force of some magical creative spark. It ignores the now inescapable fact: Whether or not the AI is generating outputs that are facially equivalent to human-authored works, the AI lacks the intentionality, creative agency,

---

& Ent. L.J. 279, 291 (1992); David Lange, At Play in the Fields of the Word: Copyright and the Construction of Authorship in the Post-Literate Millennium, 55 L. & Contemp. Probs. 139 (1992). For a discussion of competing conceptions of authorship, *see* Carys J. Craig, *Reconstructing the Author-Self: Some Feminist Lessons for Copyright Law*, 15 J. Gen. Soc. Pol'y & L. 207 (2007).

⁶¹   Roland Barthes, *The Death of the Author*, 5+6 Aspen: Mag. Box (Richard Howard, trans., 1967), www.ubu.com/aspen/aspen5and6/index.html.

⁶²   Ibid.

⁶³   *See* ibid ("[A] text does not consist of a line of works, releasing a single 'theological' meaning (the 'message' of the Author-God)…"). For a larger discussion of the role of the so-called Romantic Author in constructions of AI authorship, *see* Craig & Kerr, *supra* note 42, at 45–57. On the idea of AI-as-God in AI discourse, *see* Beth Singler, *The AI Creation Meme: A Case Study of the New Visibility of Religion in Artificial Intelligence Discourse*, 11(5) Religions 254 (2020) (finding that 67 percent of AI creation meme images based on Michelangelo's *The Creation of Adam* depicted the AI hand in the "God" position as Creator).

⁶⁴   *See Mario Klingemann: Memories of Passerby I*, Sotheby's, http://sothebys.com/en/auctions/ecatalogue/2019/contemporary-art-day-auction-l19021/lot.109.html (last visited Oct. 13, 2020).

⁶⁵   Arthur Miller, *Can Machines Be More Creative than Humans?*, The Guardian (Mar. 4, 2019), http://theguardian.com/technology/2019/mar/04/can-machines-be-more-creative-than-humans.

⁶⁶   Dan Burk, *Thirty-Six Views of Copyright Authorship, by Jackson Pollock*, 58 Hous. L. Rev. 263, 266 (2020), https://houstonlawreview.org/article/18011-thirty-six-views-of-copyright-authorship -by-jackson-pollock, citing Carys Craig & Ian Kerr, *The Death of the AI Author* 27, 38 (Mar. 25, 2019) (unpublished manuscript), http://dx.doi.org/10.2139/ssrn.3374951.

and understanding necessary to engage in authorship as a relational and communicative act.[67] It is, again, ontologically incapable of being an author.

Recall that our substantive approach to tech-neutrality tasks us with evaluating the copyrightability of AI-generated works in light of copyright's normative objectives. If copyright's purpose is understood as a balance between rewarding authors and encouraging the creation and dissemination of works, we can say now that no "author" is denied their "just reward" when an AI-generated work is refused copyright protection. Moreover, if the public interest that copyright serves is the creation and dissemination of works of intellectual *expression* (works of the arts or intellect), then the outputs generated by AI are not, in substance or nature, the kind of works that copyright is tasked with encouraging: However similar they may appear on their face, they are fundamentally different in kind.[68]

3.3 Authorship, Creative Progress, and the Public Interest

I have argued above that AI cannot be an author, and that AI-generated works are not works of original expression or authorship within the meaning of copyright law. One might now object that, be this as it may, the production and circulation of AI-generated works should be incentivized through the extension of copyright to such works in order to advance the "progress" or public interest that is central to copyright's purpose. There is, then, a final piece to the argument that AI-generated works ought not to be protected by copyright: It must be urged that the protection of AI-generated works would not advance the kind of "creative progress" with which copyright is concerned—but worse, it could cause copyright to defeat its own ends, stultifying creative practices in a thicket of privately owned algorithmic productions.

3.3.1 Encouraging creative practices (not products)

First, I would insist, the public interest or creative progress that copyright is intended to serve is not merely the maximal production and circulation of works as products or commodities; rather it is the encouragement of the creative *processes* and communicative *practices* that constitute authorship. As such, the mass production and distribution of AI outputs does not, in itself, advance copyright's purpose. Barton Beebe has explored the conceptual slippage of "progress" in American copyright jurisprudence from an unarticulated idea of "aesthetic progress" to "a vision of progress grounded in 'commercial value' and committed to accumulation."[69] Arguing that this has proven to be "a significant mistake," he notes that in a "post-scarcity" or "artificial intelligence society," an "accumulationist" model of progress will no longer make good sense.[70] As our technological conditions change, it becomes increasingly clear that the idea of progress must mean more than "the accumulation of ever more things" in a "'giant warehouse' of intellectual commodities."[71]

The "thingification" of the work in intellectual property structures obscures the social value of the expressive act behind the commercial value of the propertized "thing." The arrival of

---

[67]   *See* Craig & Kerr, *supra* note 42, at 69–71.
[68]   Ibid at 85–6.
[69]   Barton Beebe, *Bleistein, The Problem of Aesthetic Progress, and the Making of American Copyright Law*, 117 COLUM. L. REV. 319, 395 (2017).
[70]   Ibid at 395.
[71]   Ibid at 396, citing Jessica Litman, *Lawful Personal Use*, 85 TEX. L. REV. 1871, 1880 (2007).

generative AI is thus an excellent reminder that the pursuit of creative progress and the public interest at play in copyright policy is advanced by encouraging the dialogic and communicative practices of creativity and authorship, not just by the mass production and rapid proliferation of works as commercial products.

Second, it is crucial to consider the potential implications of extending copyright to cover AI-generated works. Having escaped the thrall of romantic authorship, we know that nothing is entirely original; creative practices require inspiration and imitation, drawing from and building on what has gone before. An understanding of authorship as a social and communicative practice reveals how critical it is for copyright law to leave space for this kind of intertextuality or dialogic response in the cultural conversation.[72] If the copyright system is to advance the public interest in encouraging the creation and dissemination of works of authorship, then the limits of copyright—the public freedoms to use, enjoy, and employ works—are every bit as important as the private rights that it accords.[73] There is, then, nothing *wrong* with leaving AI works outside the scope of copyright. As Burk notes: "Leaving creations 'where they lie' in authorship doctrines means that in some cases there will be no author, and the creation will simply fall into the public domain. In general, this will be the right result where there is no need for a legal incentive, or the incentive is gratuitous."

I have argued that encouraging AI-generated works does not advance copyright's purpose—awarding copyright protection to incentivize their generation would therefore be both gratuitous and unnecessary. But we can take this one step further: Leaving AI-generated works in the public domain may prove to be essential to encourage and facilitate authorship in the AI age.

With the rapid production and proliferation of AI-generated works on a massive scale, the cultural landscape is likely to become increasingly cluttered with AI-generated outputs. If these were to be protected by copyright and so subject to private control, these works would quickly become "copyright landmines," depleting the usable public domain by making it ever more difficult for creators to navigate without legal risk.[74] An AI can potentially produce thousands or millions of works in a relatively short time frame. If they were to be protected by copyright, as Clark Asay cautions:

> each of those thousands or millions of copyrights may stand in the way of other creative parties wishing to make use of the same or similar expression in their own creative efforts. AI technologies may thus foment a copyright anticommons, where creative parties wishing to engage in their own creative activities face so many AI-spawned copyright hurdles that they simply relent in those efforts.[75]

---

[72]   *See* Carys Craig, *Transforming 'Total Concept & Feel': Dialogic Creativity and Copyright's Substantial Similarity Doctrine*, 38(3) Cardozo Arts & Ent. L. J. 603, 609–12 (2021).

[73]   *Cf.* Craig, *Locking Out Lawful Users*, *supra* note 27, at 179; quoted in Access Copyright, *supra* note 17, at ¶ 95 ("The limits to these private rights, defined by fair dealing and other exceptions—and circumscribed by the boundaries of the public domain—are therefore essential to ensure that the copyright system does not defeat its own ends").

[74]   Clark D. Asay, *Independent Creation in a World of AI*, 14 Fla. Int'l U. L. Rev. 201 (2020) [*Independent Creation*]. The risk that a human-authored work will be identified as substantially similar to a protected AI work will surely be compounded by the growing use of algorithmic copyright enforcement—technology trained to detect "matches" between works, but equipped to investigate claims of independent creation, non-substantial taking, or fair use. *See* Craig, *Copyright & AI*, *supra* note 27, at 36–7.

[75]   Asay, *Independent Creation*, *supra* note 74, at 206.

The result of applying copyright to AI-generated outcomes, then, would be to "significantly inhibit creative efforts overall."[76] By the same token, I would add, leaving this potentially vast quantity of works "where they lie" without enclosing them behind private lines would significantly enrich the public domain, allowing it "to flourish as others are able to produce new works by building on the ideas and information contained" therein.[77]

3.3.2 Recognizing the limits of copyright's reach

It should be stressed that to define AI-generated works as public domain is therefore not to pronounce them worthless or without value to human culture, but rather to keep them free from the exclusive control granted by copyright—private control that imposes a social and cultural cost. As Jessica Litman explains, "[t]he public domain should be understood not as the realm of material that is undeserving of protection, but as a device that permits the rest of the system to work."[78] The notion that intellectual property rights should attach to any intangible thing of value—"if value/then right"—is an unfortunate fallacy.[79] It produces the assumption that, if AI-generated works are socially or culturally valuable in some way, they should be privately owned.[80] But, as scholars have warned repeatedly over the years, it is a damaging default to assume that intellectual property simply expands to enclose the latest valuable innovation.[81] This entails the unnecessary swelling of our IP system and the continual encroachment of IP claims into the public domain and our shared cultural sphere. Unnecessarily extending the private preserve of copyright over unauthored, AI-generated works may enrich the—likely corporate—actors behind the AI (those who create, own, train or deploy the AI), but it would come "at the loss of society's interest in maintaining a robust public domain that could help foster future creative innovation."[82] In other words, once again, expanding copyright to AI-generated works would run counter to the normative objectives of copyright law.

Indeed, if AI-generated works are of value to the public, the more appropriate policy response is to ensure that there is *space* for them to develop within the strictures of our existing IP system. Recognizing the social and cultural value of AI's generative capacities should therefore entail, as a policy response, not the unnecessary and counterproductive protection

---

[76] Ibid.

[77] CCH Canadian, *supra* note 19, at ¶ 23.

[78] Litman, *supra* note 60, at 968.

[79] *See* Alfred C. Yen, *Brief Thoughts about If Value/Then Right*, 99 Bos. U. L. Rev. 2479, 2480 ("That principle, which the U.S. Copyright Act does not embrace, expresses the intuition that 'wherever value is received, a legal duty to pay arises, regardless of whether imposing that legal duty serves public welfare': quoting Wendy Gordon). *See also* Rochelle Cooper Dreyfuss, *Expressive Genericity: Trademarks as Language in the Pepsi Generation*, 65 Notre Dame L. Rev. 397, 405–6 (1990) (questioning the idea that relationship between value and ownership justifies granting trademark rights); Wendy J. Gordon, *On Owning Information: Intellectual Property and the Restitutionary Impulse,* 78 Va. L. Rev. 149, 178–80, 244 (1992).

[80] Perhaps the most powerful critique of this tautological reasoning is still that of Felix Cohen, *Transcendental Nonsense and the Functional Approach*, 35 Colum. L. Rev. 809, 815 (1935).

[81] *See, e.g.*, David Lange, *Recognizing the Public Domain*, 44 L. & Contemp. Probs. 147 (1981); James Boyle, *The Second Enclosure Movement and the Construction of the Public Domain*, 66 L. & Contemp. Probs. 33 (2003); James Boyle, The Public Domain (2008). *See generally* Pamela Samuelson, *Enriching Discourse on Public Domains*, 55 Duke L.J. 783 (2006); Carys Craig, *The Canadian Public Domain: What, Where and to What End?*, 7 C.J.L.T. 221 (2010).

[82] CCH Canadian, *supra* note 19, at ¶ 23.

of its outputs but the shielding of its *inputs* and functional processes from potentially chilling liability.

The problem arises because copyright is, of course, premised on the exclusive right to make copies. In the process of training AI systems, as we have seen, vast quantities of data—texts, images, and other potentially copyright-protected works of human authorship—must be digitally reproduced. A significant policy concern, then, is whether any copyright that subsists in the AI *inputs* is infringed in the training of AI. Given the sheer volume of text and data mined to effectively train a sophisticated AI, limiting or foreclosing the use of copyright-protected works in such processes in the absence of permission from the right-holder places an enormous burden on AI research and development. Moreover, it produces *de facto* barriers to certain kinds of AI projects, differentially disadvantages anything but the most well-resourced AI researchers, and exacerbates the built-in biases and discriminatory effects of AI systems.[83] The quality and scope of a dataset has a direct bearing on the quality and operation of the resulting AI. In short, we must be alert to the risk that copyright law unduly restricts, distorts, or otherwise determines the trajectory of AI's technological development and operation. This, too, would be contrary to copyright's normative objectives—copyright is neither designed for, nor suited to, this role.

The solution to this policy conundrum can once again be found in recognizing the nature of the copyrightable work—in light of copyright's purpose—as fundamentally *expressive*. What copyright is concerned with is not the mere reproduction of *things* as such, then, but with copying that "relates to human appreciation of the expressive qualities of that work." From this it follows that copyright law need not concern itself with "any act of reproduction that is not intended to enable human enjoyment, appreciation, or comprehension of the copied expression as expression."[84] The copyright owner's reproduction right should not be implicated by "non-expressive" or "non-consumptive" copies, including the kind of digital copies involved in machine learning. As Matthew Sag notes, such a conclusion would be "entirely consistent with the fundamental structure of copyright law because, at its heart, copyright law is concerned with the communication of an author's original expression to the public."[85]

A recent addition to Japan's copyright law offers an interesting articulation of such a limit upon copyright's scope, stating: "It is permissible to exploit a work, in any […] case in which it is not a person's purpose to personally enjoy or cause another person to enjoy the thoughts or sentiments expressed in that work."[86] As Ueno Tatsuhiro explains, "The underlying theory behind this relates to the nature of copyright, or the justification for copyright protection that an exploitation not for 'enjoyment' purposes is beyond the inherent scope of copyright."[87]

As we have seen, works of authorship are the result of a communicative act, intended to generate thoughts, feelings, emotions, desires, or other states of cognition in their audience—and

---

[83]   *See* Amanda Levendowski, *How Copyright Law Can Fix Artificial Intelligence's Implicit Bias Problem*, 93:2 Wash. L. Rev. 579 (2018). Reliance on public domain or other low-liability risk input means training AI on data that is obsolete, exclusionary, or fails to reflect contemporary information and social values.

[84]   Matthew Sag, *The New Legal Landscape for Text Mining and Machine Learning,* 66 J. Copyright Soc'y U.S.A. 291 (2019).

[85]   Ibid at 302.

[86]   *Copyright Law of Japan Act*, art. 30-4, www.cric.or.jp/english/clj/cl2.html.

[87]   Ueno Tatsuhiro, *The Flexible Copyright Exception for "Non-Enjoyment" Purposes—Recent Amendment in Japan and Its Implication*, 70(2) R.U.R. Int'l 145 (2021).

copyright law protects them as such. The AI is not an audience capable of such a response, of course, and so the use of the work to train the AI amounts only to use of it as a functional thing and as a source of information or data (which belongs in the public domain).[88] It is not a use of the work *as a work of authorship*.[89] It should not, therefore, implicate copyright at all.[90]

Much of today's policy discussion around copyright liability in respect of AI inputs focuses on the availability of fair use or fair dealing as a potential defense to copyright infringement or the need for specific exemptions to permit informational analysis or text and data mining. Many if not all uses made for machine-learning purposes should qualify as "fair" and lawful, not least because such copies do not compromise the core interests of the copyright owner or substitute for the work of the author in the market.[91] Several US court rulings suggest that text and data mining may indeed satisfy the fair use test and will not, therefore, amount to copyright infringement.[92] In Canada, such uses should fall within the scope of fair dealing for purposes of research, private study, or education, and should therefore be considered a user's right.[93] But conducting a nuanced and context-specific assessment as required by fair use in relation to each work fed into the AI dataset is clearly unmanageable at the scale demanded by AI—and the risks of getting it wrong will have an inevitable chilling effect. This in turn points towards the strategic need for specific and mandated exceptions for text and data-mining activities. International developments in this direction, however, reveal that framing these user rights as new exceptions to copyright owners' existing entitlements produces unduly narrow and rigidly defined carve-outs from presumptive copyright control. In practice, these impose significant limits on users and obstruct AI research and development under the guise of protecting copyright interests.[94]

As this demonstrates, the advantage of recognizing, first and foremost, copyright's *limits*— as defined by the nature of authorship and the public interest at stake—is to shift the starting

---

[88]   Facts and information are not protected by copyright even if they are contained within a copyrightable work. *See* CCH Canadian, *supra* note 19, at ¶ 22 ("in Canada, as in the United States, copyright protection does not extend to facts or ideas but is limited to the expression of ideas"); Feist, *supra* note 14 ("That there can be no valid copyright in facts is universally understood").

[89]   I am indebted for this framing to Martin Senftleben, Ueno Tatsuhiro, and the participants of the panel discussion on "New Developments in Copyright Limitations and Exceptions for Education and Research" at the *Global Congress for Intellectual Property and the Public Interest* (Oct. 26 2021).

[90]   If the making of copies for such text and data-mining purposes were to be considered a prima-facie infringement of copyright, however, it should nonetheless avoid liability under the fair use defence or, in Canada, the user right of fair dealing for the purposes of research, private study, education or review.

[91]   Sean Flynn, Christophe Geiger, João Pedro Quintais, Thomas Margoni, & Matthew Sag, *Implementing User Rights for Research in the Field of Artificial Intelligence: A Call for International Action* 4 (2020), https://digitalcommons.wcl.american.edu/research/48.

[92]   17 U.S.C. § 107; Authors Guild v Google, Inc., 804 F.3d 202 (2d Cir. 2015); Authors Guild v HathiTrust, 755 F.3d 87 (2d Cir. 2014); A.V. v iParadigms, LLC. (4th Cir. 2009); *see also* K. Courtney, R. Samberg, & T. Vollmer, *Big Data Gets Big Help: Law and Policy Literacies for Text Data Mining*, 81(4) COLL. & RES. LIBR. NEWS (2020), https://crln.acrl.org/index.php/crlnews/article/view/24383/32222.

[93]   *Copyright Act*, R.S.C. 1985, c. C-42, s. 29. *See* Craig et al., *Submission by IP Scholars Copyright and Artificial Intelligence*, *supra* note 40.

[94]   *See, e.g.*, *Copyright, Designs and Patents Act 1988*, c.48, art. 29A (U.K.); *Act No. 2016-1321 of 7 October 2016 for a digital Republic*, s. 38 (Fr.); Eur. Parl. Doc., Dir. 2019/790 of the European Parliament and of the Council Of 17 April 2019 on copyright and related rights in the Digital Single Market and amending Directive 96/9 and 2001/29, arts 3 & 4. *See generally*, Flynn et al., *supra* note 91.

point for this whole analysis: Copyright protects works of authorship as textual embodiments of original *expression*, from which it follows that its reach should not extend to non-expressive uses of texts as data sources. Such uses are not equivalent to uses of works by or for a human addressee, whether audience or downstream author. Simply put, they are not copyright's concern. Specific exceptions or fair use determinations may helpfully *confirm* the lawfulness of such uses and add much-needed certainty for those in doubt—but no defense is needed to excuse lawful, non-infringing uses of works.

Recall that one of the flaws of a formalist approach to technological neutrality described above in section 2.1 was the assumption that a copy is a copy, and so every copy should be treated in the same manner by law no matter the technological processes or activities involved in its production. The more substantive principle with which we are working here considers the functional effect of the copy in context and in relation to the normative objectives of the copyright system. We can see here, again, the importance of approaching the policy question in this way: Rather than getting caught up in the technical matter of reproduction and the inevitable extension of copyright control to new technological processes, we can recognize the irrelevance of the reproduction in relation to copyright's normative concerns. In doing so, we can ensure that copyright leaves space for technology to evolve, for AI to be trained on richer datasets, and for the public domain to be enriched by new AI-generated works—works from which human authors may readily draw inspiration and upon which they may freely build, fostering the very creative progress at which copyright is aimed.

4.   CONCLUSION

The purpose of copyright is to encourage not merely the production and circulations of works, as objects, but the *activity* of authorship—the dialogic *processes* and exchange *of meaning* that constitute authorship. Works are not just *things* that circulate; they are *expressions* that form relations of communication between people. Nor does copyright law create private rights over such works simply for the sake of rewarding authors; it serves a public interest—the encouragement of authorship as a social and creative *practice* and the dissemination of works to contribute to a vibrant public domain.

As AI-generated works increasingly come to resemble, facially, the human-authored works with which copyright is concerned, it will be vital to keep these purposes in view—for it is these purposes that will continue to define the justifiable scope of copyright protection. As I argued in section 2, it is not appropriate for copyright law to respond to these technological developments in a formally tech-neutral way, treating alike AI and human activities and arte-facts that are fundamentally different in nature. Nor is it sufficient to focus on their functional equivalence, analogizing between AI and human activities and artefacts without regard to the social values and public purposes that underpin the copyright system. Rather, it is the norma-tive objectives of the copyright system and the values they reflect that should be regarded as technologically neutral. The real AI–copyright challenge, then, is to prevent this latest techno-logical innovation from upsetting the copyright balance, obstructing its normative objectives, and thereby undermining the social value of authorship, creative progress, and the public domain. I explained, in section 3, that this will require resisting calls to extend copyright to cover AI-generated works on the basis that they are not equivalent to the works of authorship that copyright seeks to encourage. Similarly, attention to the expressive nature of authorship supports restricting the power of copyright owners to control the use of works as inputs for training AI systems.

These and many more legal and doctrinal conundrums will be thrown up by the arrival of increasingly sophisticated AI systems and their pervasive deployment in our cultural sphere. It seems we are poised at a policy precipice of sorts, ready to jump or be pushed into the path of increased commoditization and private control as these systems proliferate. Due to a combination of romanticism about robots, misapprehensions about creative progress, and complacency about the social costs of copyright, critical mistakes may be made. Both the protection of AI-generated works and the constriction of AI research and development through the creeping expansion of copyright control may spell an uncertain future for human creators, users, and audiences, harming rather than advancing the public interest that copyright is meant to serve. Among the many risks that this poses to our cultural environment is the possibility that we will miss out on the very real promise of AI to contribute, in previously unimaginable ways, to a rich and vibrant public domain—as both a tool of human authorship and a source of inspiration.

It should be noted in closing that the themes addressed in this chapter have implications beyond copyright and cultural production. Policymakers will surely make mistakes and mis-allocate economic resources, legal privileges, and political power across the board if critical policy analyses begin by misattributing human attributes, intentionality, and expressive agency to AI. The challenge of regulating and responding to AI requires first that we recognize what AI is—and what it is *not*. The task is then to ensure that legal interventions and reform efforts are undertaken to steer AI and its development in service of the public goals, human interests, and social values that our legal constructs—much like our technological constructs—are ultimately supposed to serve.

8.   Four theories in search of an A(I)uthor
Giancarlo Frosio

1.   INTRODUCTION

In 1843, Augusta Ada King, Countess of Lovelace, argued: "[s]upposing, for instance, that the fundamental relations of pitched sounds in the science of harmony and of musical composition were susceptible of such expression and adaptations, the engine might compose elaborate and scientific pieces of music of any degree of complexity or extent."[1] Ada Lovelace, the first programmer in history, saw far into the future of the computer—or the "analytical engine," as Babbage termed it at the time—that she had contributed to the invention of. Today, intelligent machines come in multiple shapes to serve diverse purposes and could possibly replace humans everywhere, including the once inherently human-centered field of creativity.[2] AI not only composes music, as Lovelace predicted, but also writes poems, novels, and news articles; edits photographs; creates video games; and makes paintings and other artworks.[3] The A(I) uthor is already among us. In this context, the adaption of the intellectual property (IP) system to AI-generated creativity and innovation is increasingly becoming a topic of critical interest.[4]

---

[1]   Ada Augusta, Countess of Lovelace, notes on L.F. Menabrea, "Sketch of the Analytical Engine Invented by Charles Babbage" (September 1843) Scientific Memoirs www.fourmilab.ch/babbage/sketch .html.

[2]   See Arthur Miller, *The Artist in the Machine: The World of AI-Powered Creativity* (MIT Press 2019 (stating that computer creativity will surpass human creativity). See eg Baptiste Caramiaux, Fabien Lotte and Joost Geurts (ed), "AI in media and creative industries" (version 1, New European Media 1 April 2019) https://arxiv.org/ftp/arxiv/papers/1905/1905.04175.pdf; Andreas Pfeiffer, "Creativity and technology in the in age of AI" (Pfeiffer Report 2018) 15, 29 https://www.pfeifferreport.com/wp-content/ uploads/2018/10/Creativity-and-technology-in-the-age-of-AI.pdf; European Audiovisual Observatory (2019), "Artificial Intelligence: Summary of Observatory workshop on AI in the audiovisual industry" (EAO, 17 December 2019) https://rm.coe.int/summary-workshop-2019-bat-2/16809c992a.

[3]   For example, a novella written by a machine has made the first rounds of a literary competition in Japan, beating in the process thousands of human authors. See Danny Lewis, "An AI-Written Novella Almost Won a Literary Prize" (*Smithsonian Magazine*, March 28, 2016) www.smithsonianmag.com/ smart-news/ai-written-novella-almost-won-literary-prize-180958577. *Sunspring*, a sci-fi film written entirely by an AI, placed top ten in Sci-Fi London's annual film festival. See Carys Craig and Ian Kerr, "The Death of the AI Author" (2019) Osgoode Legal Studies Research Paper, 1–2. AIVA—like Amper or Melodrive—runs an AI that composes music, which is marketed to accompany audiovisual works, advertisements or video games. Meanwhile, Sony's Flow Machine can interact and co-improvise with a human music performer. See Sony Flow Machines www.flow-machines.com. Again, the AI-generated *Portrait of Edmond de Bellamy* sold at Christie's for an astounding $432,500. See Craig and Kerr 3–4.

[4]   See Maria Iglesias Portela, Sharon Shamuilia, and Amanda Anderberg, "Intellectual Property and Artificial Intelligence: A Literature Review" (Joint Research Centre, Publications Office of the European Union 2019). See also Jeremy Cubert and Richard Bone, "The Law of Intellectual Property Created by Artificial Intelligence" in Woodrow Barfield and Ugo Pagallo (eds), *Research Handbook on the Law of Artificial Intelligence* (Edward Elgar Publishing 2018) 411–27.

Of course, existing IP regimes, including copyright law, trade secrets, and patent law,[5] can protect software on which AI technology is based.[6] However, the protection afforded to the software does not extend to the output possibly generated by the AI. In this context, a report from the European Commission highlights that "protection of AI generated works [...] seems to be [...] problematic" as, "[i]n light of the humanist approach of copyright law, it is questionable that AI-generated works deserve copyright protection."[7] Therefore, the report continues, "while some copyright scholars clearly advocate for AI-generated works to be placed in the public domain, others have put forward a series of proposals aimed at ensuring a certain level of protection"; however, "[w]ith notable exceptions, these proposals [...] do not always sufficiently detail the possible elements underpinning such protection."[8]

In searching for a justification to protect AI-generated creativity, this chapter would like to answer a set of emerging legal questions. How does AI-generated creativity fit within traditional copyright theory and existing legal requirements for copyright protection? Is AI legal personhood available under the present legal framework? Should it be considered in as an option for legal reform? Is AI an author under traditional copyright standards? Does a machine meet the copyright standard for originality? And, again, from a more general techno-legal perspective, is it perhaps oxymoronic to refer to AI-generated creative works? After answering what can be summarized as the question of the A(I)uthor,[9] this chapter will end by considering the road ahead: reviewing policy options and looking for their justification from different theoretical perspectives, such as fairness, personality, utilitarian/incentive, and cultural theories of intellectual property.

---

[5]   Whether protecting software as a computer-implemented invention or as such, depending on the jurisdiction.

[6]   Nathan Calvin and Jade Leung, "Who Owns Artificial Intelligence? A Preliminary Analysis of Corporate Intellectual Property Strategies and Why They Matter" (2020) Future of Humanity Institute, University of Oxford Working Paper www.fhi.ox.ac.uk/wp-content/uploads/Patents_-FHI-Working-Paper-Final-.pdf.

[7]   Massimo Craglia and others, "Artificial Intelligence: A European Perspective" (Joint Research Centre, Publications Office of the European Union, 2018) 67 https://publications.jrc.ec.europa.eu/repository/bitstream/JRC113826/ai-flagship-report-online.pdf.

[8]   Ibid 68.

[9]   Besides the question of the A(I)uthor, there are two other fundamental questions that are beyond the scope of this chapter: the questions of the (Machine) Learner and the (A)Infringer. They refer to whether an AI can infringe copyright through the machine-learning process and training that enables the AI to generate creativity and whether an AI can infringe copyright by creating an infringing output. The question of the (Machine) Learner has been studied by abundant literature. In particular, this author, and his co-authors, have reviewing the matter extensively. See eg Christophe Geiger, Giancarlo Frosio, and Oleksander Bulayenko, "Text and Data Mining: Art. 3 and 4 of the Directive 790/2019/EU" in Concepción Sáiz García and Raquel Evangelio Llorca (eds), *Los Derechos de autor en el mercado unico digital Europeo* (Tirant lo Banch 2019); Christophe Geiger, Giancarlo Frosio, and Oleksander Bulayenko, "Text and Data Mining in the Proposed Copyright Reform: Making the EU Ready for an Age of Big Data?" (2018) 49(7) IIC 814–44. An essential bibliography including literature treating this question can be found at Giancarlo Frosio, "L'(I)Autore inesistente: una tesi tecno-giuridica contro la tutela dell'opera generata dall'intelligenza artificiale" 29 AIDA 52–91, 54, fn 13 (2020). Very recently, see also Mark Lemley and Bryan Casey, "Fair Learning" (2021) 99 Texas L Rev 743, 743–85.

2.   IN SEARCH OF THEORETICAL JUSTIFICATIONS OF IP FOR AI

The theoretical framework justifying copyright differs substantially among jurisdictions. It is important to outline these differences from the very beginning, as both the policy options available and those potentially applicable as a result of legal reform will depend on the theoretical perspective from which the question of the A(I)uthor is observed.[10]

Four IP theoretical clusters have emerged throughout the history of copyright law: fairness theory, personality theory, welfare theory, and, more recently, cultural theory.[11] Fairness and personality theory have traditionally been the theoretical pillars of European copyright law. Both fairness and personality theory are natural right theories that emphasize individual exclusive rights. Fairness theory does so on the basis of the Lockean natural law property theory. According to Locke, each person has a natural right to the fruits of his or her labor upon land held in common.[12] Later, William Blackstone applied the same principles to intellectual labor as well.[13] Personality theories, instead, characterize the civil law tradition and are rooted in German idealism. Intellectual products are manifestations or extensions of the personalities of their creators, who enjoy an unrestrained natural right over them.[14]

In contrast, welfare and cultural theories are collectivistic and prospective. Welfare theory, based on Bentham and Mill's utilitarianism and economic analysis of law, looks at maximization of social welfare.[15] In particular, welfare theory portends that rights should be crafted to provide the "greatest happiness of the greatest number."[16] It is also known as "incentive theory," as the law should create a system of incentives which will induce creators to create.[17] In this respect, this approach looks at creativity dynamically, not only rewarding labor or personal entitlements for today's creativity but setting the foundations for tomorrow's creative ecosystem. Cultural theory also looks at the well-being of society at large, but with

---

[10]   See also, for a recent discussion of the theories justifying intellectual properties rights in the context of AI-generated creativity and innovation, Reto Hilty, Jörg Hoffmann, and Stefan Scheuerer, "Intellectual Property Justification for Artificial Intelligence" in Jyh-An Lee, Reto Hilty, and Kung-Chung Liu, *Artificial Intelligence & Intellectual Property* (OUP 2020).

[11]   See William Fisher, "Theories of Intellectual Property" in Stephen Munzer (ed), *New Essays in the Legal and Political Theory of Property* (Cambridge University Press 2001) 168–200.

[12]   See John Locke, *Second Treatise of Government* (Awnsham Churchill 1689) ch. 5.

[13]   See William Blackstone, *Commentaries on the Laws of England*, vol 2 (Clarendon Press 1776) 455.

[14]   See eg Immanuel Kant, "Von der Unrechtmäßigkeit des Büchernachdrucks [On the injustice of counterfeiting books]" (1785) 5 Berlinische Monatsschrift 403; Johann Fichte, "Proof of the Illegality of Reprinting: A Rationale and a Parable" (1793) 21 Berlinische Monatsschrift 447; Georg Hegel, *Philosophy of Rights* (Thomas Knox ed, Clarendon Press 1821) para 69. See also Fisher (n 11) 168.

[15]   See Jeremy Bentham, *An Introduction to the Principles of Moral and Legislation* (T. Payne and Sons 1780); Jeremy Bentham, *A Manual of Political Economy* (Putnam 1839); Stuart Mill, *Principles of Political Economy* (Little and Brown 1848); Arthur Pigou, *The Economics of Welfare* (Macmillan & Co 1920). See also William Landes and Richard Posner, "Trademark Law: An Economic Perspective" (1987) 30 Journal of Law and Economics 265; William Landes and Richard Posner, "An Economic Analysis of Copyright Law" (1989) 18 Journal of Legal Studies 325.

[16]   Jeremy Bentham, *The Works of Jeremy Bentham, published under the Superintendence of his Executor, John Bowring*, vol 9 (William Tait 1843) 5.

[17]   See Fisher (n 11) 177–80.

a more marked prospective emphasis, by focusing on promoting a just and attractive culture.[18] Although the result of multiple interdisciplinary contributions, this theoretical approach might find its foundation in Thomas Aquinas' ideas that identified law's primary function in the "common good of humanity."[19] In particular, for Aquinas, the role of society is to define a framework for human happiness according to universal human values, including education, culture, environment, health. Therefore, for Aquinas, the good of mankind is one that maximizes happiness. From this perspective, cultural theory would like to overcome the utilitarian paradigm that measures aggregated consumer welfare according to what consumers want, by instead identifying conditions which will support widespread human flourishing. As Fisher puts it, "[t]his approach is similar to utilitarianism in its teleological orientation, but dissimilar in its willingness to deploy visions of a desirable society richer than the conceptions of 'social welfare' deployed by utilitarians."[20] Cultural theory approaches would like to readjust the intellectual property policy framework by promoting enhanced "distributive justice" beyond the traditional market-based approach of welfare and utilitarian theories.[21]

3.   ASSESSING PROTECTABILITY OF AI-GENERATED CREATIVITY UNDER THE PRESENT COPYRIGHT LEGAL FRAMEWORK

This chapter shall now consider whether AI-generated creativity can be protected under the current copyright regime. This investigation will look into three major conditions for copyright protection of creative works: (1) legal personality; (2) authorship; and (3) originality.

3.1   Legal Personality

Perhaps surprisingly, some theoretical thinking supports the idea of legal personality of intelligent machines. Nick Bostrom, for example, notes: "machines capable of independent initiative and of making their own plans […] are perhaps more appropriately viewed as persons than machines."[22] Authors have highlighted how there are no legal reasons or conceptual motives for denying the personhood of AI robots as the law should grant personality on the grounds of rational choices and empirical evidence, rather than prejudice.[23] Therefore, arguments have been made in favour of granting personhood to future hypothetical strong AI that are autono-

---

[18]   Ibid.

[19]   Tommaso d'Aquino, *Summa Theologiae*, 1265–73, 2.2.26.5.

[20]   Fisher (n 11) 172.

[21]   See, for an essential bibliography on the cultural theory approach and the emerging focus on "distributive justice" in intellectual property and copyright in particular, Frosio (n 9) 57, fn 25; Giancarlo Frosio, "Reforming the C-DSM Reform: A User-based Copyright Theory for Commonplace Creativity" (2020) 51(6) IIC 733, fn 158.

[22]   Nick Bostrom, *Superintelligence: Paths, Dangers, Strategies* (OUP 2014).

[23]   See Lawrence Solum, "Legal Personhood for Artificial Intelligences" (1992) 70 North Carolina L Rev 1231, 1264. See also Ugo Ruffolo, "Il problema della 'personalità elettronica'" (2020) 2(1) J of Ethics and Legal Technologies 75–88, 86 (noting that anthropomorphic and anthropocentric prejudices should be avoided).

mous, intelligent, and conscious.[24] Even more surprisingly—but in line with the conclusions of the literature just mentioned—the European Parliament (EP) is considering the possibility of declaring AI and robots "electronic persons." In a Resolution on *Civil Law Rules on Robotics*, the European Parliament wondered whether ordinary liability rules are sufficient or whether AI calls for new rules.[25] The Resolution claims that "the more autonomous robots are, the less they can be considered simple tools in the hands of other actors (such as the manufacturer, the owner, the user, etc.)."[26] The EP endorses the view that EU legislation cannot fully address non-contractual liability for damages caused by autonomous AI. Traditional rules would still apply if the cause of the robot's act or omission can be traced back to a specific human agent such as the manufacturer, the operator, the owner, or the user, such as in the case the robot has malfunctioned or where the human agent could have foreseen and avoided the robot's harmful behaviour. But what if the cause of the robot's act or omission cannot be traced back to a specific human agent? What if there are no manufacturing defects and the AI has not malfunctioned but acted autonomously in causing damages for which no causal link with the manufacturer can be proved? In this scenario, Directive 85/374/EEC on Product Liability should not apply. Therefore, the Resolution highlights that this makes the ordinary rules on liability insufficient and calls for new rules to clarify whether a machine can be held responsible for its acts or omissions.[27] Although the Resolution recognizes that "at least at the present stage the responsibility must lie with a human and not a robot," in the long run the Resolution calls for (1) an obligatory insurance scheme which takes into account all potential responsibilities in the chain[28] and (2) the creation of a specific legal status for robots, "so that at least the most sophisticated autonomous robots could be established as having the status of electronic persons responsible for making good any damage they may cause."[29]

However, whether quasi-human or hyper-human AI is coming, legal personality of machines is certainly unavailable under the present legal framework. Scholarship has consistently stressed how any hypothesis about granting AI robots full legal personhood must be discarded until fundamental technological changes have occurred.[30] Pagallo highlights, among the normative arguments against legal personhood, the "missing something problem," accord-

---

[24]   Meaning respectively that the AI should be capable of taking a decision without input action, of self-programming and integrating information in a framework, and of subjective experience. See Evan Zimmerman, "Machine Minds: Frontiers in Legal Personhood" (2017) 14–21 https://papers.ssrn.com/sol3/papers.cfm?abstract_id=2563965. See also Patrick Hubbard, "Do Androids Dream? Personhood and Intelligent Artifacts" (2010) 83 Temple L Rev 406; Rosa Ballardini and Rob van den Hoven van Genderen, "Artificial Intelligence and IPR: The Quest or Pleading for AI as Legal Subjects" in Taina Pihlajarinne, Anette Alen-Savikko, and Katri Havu (eds), *AI and the Media: Reconsidering Rights and Responsibilities* (Edward Elgar Publishing 2021) (considering the possible need to create a new sui generis legal subjectivity for independently functioning AI entities and systems).

[25]   European Parliament, Civil Law Rules on Robotics: European Parliament resolution with recommendations to the Commission on Civil Law Rules on Robotics, 2015/2103(INL), 16 February 2017 www.europarl.europa.eu/doceo/document/TA-8-2017-0051_EN.pdf. See also David Vladeck, "Machines Without Principals: Liability Rules and Artificial Intelligence" (2014) 89 Washington L Rev 117.

[26]   Civil Law Rules on Robotics (n 25) AB.

[27]   Ibid.

[28]   Ibid para 59.a.

[29]   Ibid para 59.f.

[30]   See eg Nadia Banteka, "Artificially Intelligent Persons" (2020) 58 Houston L Rev 537, 537–96; Eliza Mik, "AI as Legal Person?" in Reto Hilty and Kung-Chung (eds), *Artificial Intelligence and*

ing to which current AI robots lack most requisites that usually are associated with granting someone, or something, legal personhood: such artificial agents are not self-conscious and do not possess human-like intentions or properly suffer.[31] Statistical analysis of different conditions for legal personhood set up by US case law, for example, would also show incompatibility between legal personhood and AI entities.[32] This empirical analysis proves that to grant personhood, courts look at whether it is granted directly or indirectly by a statute, if the artificial entity can sue and be sued, and finally if the entity is an aggregate of natural persons.[33]

Caution against construing AI as a legal person emerges also from the European Parliament's 2017 Resolution, which finally excluded any form of AI legal personality, at least in the short and mid-term. In addition, the EU Parliament seems now to reject AI's legal personality in specific connection to AI-generated creativity. In a recent *Draft Report on intellectual property rights for the development of artificial intelligence technologies*, the European Parliament noted, as part of a motion for a Parliament Resolution, that "the autonomisation of the creative process raises issues relating to the ownership of IPRs [but the Parliament] considers, in this connection, that it would not be appropriate to seek to impart legal personality to AI technologies."[34] Rather than establishing legal personality of machines, the policy challenge would be to properly allocate accountability and liability for the activities of AI robots in cases of complex distributed responsibility, for example through contracts and business law.[35]

3.2   Authorship

The question of AI-generated creativity's copyright protectability requires consideration of whether an AI is an author according to traditional copyright standards. Put bluntly, is a human author an intrinsic requirement for authorship? Although international treaties do not include a definition of "author" that can provide a definitive answer, some textual references to human creation in the Berne Convention might exclude AI from the scope of the notion of author. First, the term of protection linked to the life of the author would be hard to reconcile with machines as authors.[36] Again, reference to the nationality—or residence—of the author seems also to imply that the notion of authorship only applies to human agents.[37] Overall, it has been argued that "Berne's humanist cast" and its deference to personality theories strongly support a "human-centered notion of authorship presently enshrined in the Berne Convention" that would exclude non-human authorship from Berne's scope.[38]

Intellectual Property (OUP forthcoming) 12; Ugo Pagallo, "Vital, Sophia, and Co.—The Quest for the Legal Personhood of Robots" (2018) 9(9) Information 230, 230.

[31]   Pagallo (n 30) 237–8.

[32]   Banteka (n 30)

[33]   Ibid 581–95.

[34]   European Parliament, Draft Report on intellectual property rights for the development of artificial intelligence technologies, 2020/2015(INI), 24 April 2020.

[35]   Civil Law rules on Robotics (n 25) para 59; Pagallo (n 30) 239–40.

[36]   Berne Convention for the Protection of Literary and Artistic Works, Art. 7.

[37]   ibid, Art. 3.

[38]   Jane Ginsburg, "People Not Machines: Authorship and What It Means in the Berne Convention" (2018) 49 Int'l Rev of Intell Prop and Comp L 131, 134–5; Sam Ricketson, "People or Machines? The Berne Convention and the Changing Concept of Authorship" (1992) 16 Columbia VLA Journal of Law & the Arts 1, 34. See also Tanya Aplin and Giulia Pasqualetto, "Artificial Intelligence and Copyright

A close review of EU law would most likely lead to similar conclusions.[39] Although there is no transversal definition in statutory law of the notion of authorship, an author is defined as a natural person, a group of persons or a legal person both by Art. 2(1) of the Software Directive[40] and by Art. 4(1) of the Database Directive.[41] Actually, the *travaux préparatoires* of the Software and Database Directive fully endorsed an anthropocentric vision of authorship by referring specifically to "the human author who creates the work" and "the natural person [that] will retain at least the unalienable rights to claim paternity of his work."[42] Again, the original proposal for a Software Directive concluded: "[t]he human input as regards the creation of machine generated programs may be relatively modest, and will be increasingly modest in the future. Nevertheless, a human 'author' in the widest sense is always present, and must have the right to claim 'authorship' of the program."[43] In the CJEU *Painer* case, Advocate General Trstenjak stressed the same point by noting that "only human creations are therefore protected, which can also include those for which the person employs a technical aid, such as a camera."[44] EU national legislation confirms this approach. For example, Art. L.111-1 of the French Intellectual Property Code[45] requires copyrightable work to be the "creation of the mind"; Art. 5 of the Spanish Copyright Act plainly states that "the author of a work is the natural person who creates it";[46] and Art. 11 of the German Copyright Act attaches authorship to a personality approach by protecting "the author in his intellectual and personal relationships to the work."[47] In addition, EU law—as well as a large amount of national legis-

---

Protection" in Rosa Maria Ballardini, Petri Kuoppamäki, and Olli Pitkänen (eds), *Regulating Industrial Internet through IPR, Data Protection and Competition Law* (Kluwer Law International 2019) §5.04.

[39]   See eg Jean-Marc Deltorn and Franck Macrez, "Authorship in the Age of Machine Learning and Artificial Intelligence" (2018) CEIPI Research Paper No 2018-10, 22–3 https://papers.ssrn.com/sol3/papers.cfm?abstract_id=3261329; Jean-Marc Deltorn, "Deep Creations: Intellectual Property and the Automata" (*Frontiers in Digital Humanities* 2017) 8 www.frontiersin.org/articles/10.3389/fdigh.2017.00003/full.

[40]   Directive 2009/24/EC of the European Parliament and of the Council of 23 April 2009 on the legal protection of computer programs, O.J. L111/16.

[41]   Directive 96/9/EC of the European Parliament and of the Council of 11 March 1996 on the legal protection of databases, O.J. L077/20.

[42]   Ana Ramalho, "Will Robots Rule the (Artistic) World? A Proposed Model for the Legal Status of Creations by Artificial Intelligence Systems" (2017) 21 J of Internet L 12, 17–18.

[43]   Commission, "Explanatory Memorandum to the proposal for a Software Directive" COM (88) 816 final, 21.

[44]   Case C-145/10 *Evan-Maria Painer v Standard VerlagsGmbH* [2011] ECR I-12533, Opinion of the AG Trstenjak 2011, para 121.

[45]   Loi 92-597 du 1er juillet 1992, Code de la propriété intellectuelle, L111-1 (France) (hereafter "French IP Code").

[46]   Real Decreto Legislativo (RDL) 1/1996, de 12 de abril, por el que se aprueba el texto refundido de la Ley de Propiedad Intelectual, regularizando, aclarando y armonizando las disposiciones legales vigentes sobre la materia, BOE-A-1996-8930, art 5 (Spain) (hereafter "Spanish IP Law").

[47]   G. v. 09.09.1965, Gesetz über Urheberrecht und verwandte Schutzrechte (Urheberrechtsgesetz— UrhG), art 7 and 11 (Germany).

lation[48]—endorses a human-centric approach when providing a presumption of authorship for the *person* whose name is indicated in the work, in absence of proof to the contrary.[49]

The US legal system would also leave little room for mechanical authors. The US Copyright Act does not have an express statutory definition of authorship, so that some commentators have argued that, textually, the Statute does not limit authorship to human authors.[50] However, both additional textual references and case law apparently exclude the possibility of construing non-human agents as authors under the statute. In particular, Section 101 of the Copyright Act defines anonymous works as "ones where no natural person is identified as an author,"[51] thus pointing at natural persons as potential authors. Also, there is a long-lasting understanding that the constitutional history of the word "copyright" would dispose in favor of only humans as "authors."[52] US courts have consistently supported this understanding. The Supreme Court has plainly stated that "[a]s a general rule, the author is [...] the *person* who translates an idea into a fixed, tangible expression entitled to copyright protection."[53] In *Feist v Rural*, the US Supreme Court discusses at length the notion of authorship and author by reviewing the notion of originality, which would refer to inherently human features, such as "creative spark" or "intellectual production, of thought, and conception."[54] Earlier cases would support the same conclusion. The *Trade-Mark Cases* state that the copyright law only protects "the fruits of intellectual labor" that "are founded in the creative powers of the mind."[55] In *Burrow-Giles*, then, the US Supreme Court reminded that copyright law is limited to "original intellectual conceptions of the author."[56]

A recent case, finally, has perhaps put the matter to rest in the United States. In *Naruto v Slater*, two selfies were taken by the seven-year-old crested macaque Naruto when wildlife photographer David Slater left his camera unattended on one of his visits to Indonesia. Later, in 2014, the "Monkey Selfies" were published in a book through Blurb Inc. which identified Slater and Wildlife Personalities Ltd as the copyright owners. In 2015, People for the Ethical

---

[48]　See Wet van 23 September 1912, Auterswet, art 4(1) (Netherlands); French IP Code (n 45) L113-1 (France); Spanish IP Law (n 46) Art. 6(1) (Spain); Law for the Protection of Copyright and Neighbouring Rights 1941, art 8 (Italy) (hereafter "Italian Copyright Law").

[49]　Directive 2004/48/EC of the European Parliament and of the Council of 29 April 2004 on the enforcement of intellectual property rights, O.J. L195/16, Art. 5.

[50]　See Robert Denicola, "Ex Machina: Copyright Protection for Computer-generated Works" (2016) 69 Rutgers University L Rev 251, 275–83; Annemarie Bridy, "Coding Creativity: Copyright and the Artificially Intelligent Author" (2012) 5 Stanford Technology L Rev 1, ¶49; Arthur Miller, "Copyright Protection for Computer Programs, Databases, and Computer-Generated Works: Is Anything New since CONTU?" (1993) 106 Harvard L Rev 977, 1042–72; Pamela Samuelson, "Allocating Ownership Rights in Computer-Generated Works" (1986) 47 (4) University of Pittsburgh L Rev 1185, 1200–5.

[51]　17 U.S.C. § 101.

[52]　See Atilla Kasap, "Copyright and Creative Artificial Intelligence (AI) Systems: A Twenty-First Century Approach to Authorship of AI-Generated Works in the United States" (2019) 19(4) Wake Forest Intell Prop L J 335, 358; Ralph Clifford, "Intellectual Property in the Era of the Creative Computer Program: Will the True Creator Please Stand Up" (1996) 71 Tulane L Rev 1675, 1682–6; Timothy Butler, "Can a Computer Be an Author? Copyright Aspects of Artificial Intelligence" (1981) 4(4) (Comm/Ent), A J of Communications and Entertainment L 707, 733–4; Karl Milde, "Can a Computer Be an 'Author' or an 'Inventor'?" (1969) 51 J of the Patent Office Soc'y 378, 391–2.

[53]　*Community for Creative Non-Violence v Reid* (1989) 490 U.S. 730, 737 (USA).

[54]　*Feist Publications v Rural Telephone Service* (1990) 499 U.S. 340, 345, 347 (USA).

[55]　*Trade-Mark Cases* (1879) 100 U.S. 82, 94 (USA).

[56]　*Burrow-Giles Lithographic Co. v Sarony* (1884) 111 U.S. 53, 58 (USA).

Treatment of Animals (PETA) filed a complaint of copyright infringement as next friends and on behalf of Naruto against Slater, Wildlife Personalities Ltd, and Blurb Inc. before the District Court of California. In this context, the court had the opportunity to consider whether Naruto could be vested with a copyright in its selfie. The District Court granted the motion to dismiss filed by the Defendants on the basis that Naruto failed to establish statutory standing under the Copyright Act and noted: "[i]f the humans purporting to act on Plaintiff's behalf wish for copyright to be among the areas of law where nonhuman animals have standing, they should make that dubious case to Congress—not the federal courts."[57] The decision was appealed and while the parties agreed to a settlement, the Court of Appeals declined to dismiss the appeal and affirmed the lower court's decision. The majority found that while animals have Article III standing to sue, animals do not have statutory standing under the Copyright Act.[58] The court relied on the Ninth Circuit decision in *Cetacean Community v Bush,* where it was held that animals have statutory standing only if the statute plainly states so.[59] Moreover, the terms "children," "grandchildren," "legitimate," "widow," and "widower" used in the Statute necessarily imply that the Copyright Act excludes animals that "do not marry and do not have heirs entitled to property by law."[60] Of course, the findings in the *Naruto* decision can easily be extended to any non-human and AI-generated creativity. In this regard, the Third Edition of the Compendium of U.S. Copyright Office Practices, which was published in December 2014, after the *Naruto* case started, provided non-binding guidance that excluded non-human authorship.[61] The compendium repeatedly refers to persons or human beings when discussing authorship. More specifically, under Section 306, the "Human Authorship Requirement" limits registration to "original intellectual conceptions of the author" created by a human being. As clarified under Section 313.2, "Works that Lack Human Authorship," works produced by nature, animals, or plants, and similarly works created by a machine or by a mechanical process without intervention from a human author, are not copyrightable. Referring to the *Trade-Mark Cases* and *Burrow-Giles,* the Copyright Office concluded that it would refuse to register a claim if it determined that a human being did not create the work.[62]

In China, AI authorship has been discussed by multiple courts. In *Beijing Feilin Law Firm v Baidu Corporation*, the Court denied copyright protection to works created solely by machines and confirmed that copyright protection requires human authorship.[63] The case dealt with a report published by a Beijing-based law firm on its official WeChat account. After an unidentifiable internet user published the report online without permission, the law firm brought an infringement suit before the Beijing Internet Court. The report was generated using

---

[57]   *Naruto v David Slater* (2016) 15-cv-04324-WHO (*"Naruto 2016"*) (USA).

[58]   *Naruto v David Slater* (2018) F.3d 418 9th Cir, 426 (*"Naruto 2018"*) (USA).

[59]   *Cetacean Community. v. Bush* (2004) 386 F.3d 1169 9th Cir., 1175 (USA).

[60]   *Naruto* 2018 (n 58) 426.

[61]   U.S. Copyright Office, "Compendium of U.S. Copyright Office Practices" (3rd edn, U.S. Copyright Office) www.copyright.gov/comp3/comp-index.html.

[62]   Ibid section 313.2.

[63]   *Beijing Feilin Law Firm v Baidu Corporation* (26 April 2019) Beijing Internet Court, (2018) Beijing 0491 Minchu No. 239; Kan He, "Feilin v. Baidu: Beijing Internet Court Tackles Protection of AI/Software-generated Work and Holds that Copyright Only Vests in Works by Human Authors" (*The IPKat*, 9 November 2019) http://ipkitten.blogspot.com/2019/11/feilin-v-baidu-beijing-internet-court.html; Ming Chen, "Beijing Internet Court Denies Copyright to Works Created Solely by Artificial Intelligence" (2019) 14(8) JIPLP 593.

Wolters Kluwer China Law & Reference, which is legal information query software. While the Plaintiff argued that the tool was used only for assistance, the Defendants claimed that the entire report was generated by the software. During the proceedings, an automated report generated by the software on key words set by the Plaintiff's attorney was compared to the disputed report. The two reports were found substantially dissimilar. While the disputed report was eligible for protection under Chinese copyright law due to the original human contributions that it included, the court also considered the protectability of the report automatically generated by the software. In discussing protection of works exclusively generated by an AI, the Court held that the notion of authorship requires the work to be created by a natural person. However, the Court believed that some sort of protection should be given to the user[64] of the software that generates creative works in order to incentivize purchases of that software as well as generation and distribution of the works, although the judgment does not provide clarifications or suggestions in this regard.

In a later decision, *Shenzen Tencent v Yinxun*, the Nanshan District Court in Shenzhen *de facto* confirmed the Beijing ruling by granting protection to the original contributions from human agents, rather than exclusively AI-generated creativity.[65] Tencent Technology developed an AI writing assistant, *Dreamwriter*. In August 2018 Tencent published one of *Dreamwriter*'s works on its website, informing the reader that the article was written by Tencent's AI. Shortly thereafter, the Defendant allegedly published the article online without Tencent's consent. Bringing a lawsuit for infringement, Tencent argued that the article was generated under its supervision and Tencent was responsible for the organization and creation of the article as well as any liability arising thereof. The Court ruled in favour of Tencent by noting that the article met the requirements of being an original literary work as the content was a product of the input data, trigger conditions, and arrangement of templates and resources selected by Tencent's operational group. Since the expression of the article came from individual choices and arrangement made by Tencent's team, the (AI-generated) article was considered a work for hire under Article 11 of the Chinese Copyright Law and the defendant was held liable for infringement. Although the court might have viewed the work as an integrated intellectual creation, deriving both from the contribution by the human team and the operation of "Dreamwriter," the protection granted apparently stems from the human team's contribution rather than any AI contribution.

4.   ORIGINALITY

Even if a textual anthropocentric construction of authorship is disregarded, originality as a condition for copyright protection seems to prevent protection of AI-generated creativity. Textual references and case law construe originality via an anthropocentric model that emphasizes self-consciousness. Originality is widely defined in most jurisdictions in light of a so-called

---

[64]   Rather than the software developer, who is already rewarded by a copyright over the software. Ibid.

[65]   See *Shenzhen Tencent v Yinxun*, Nanshan District People's Court of Shenzhen, Guangdong Province [2019] No. 14010 (China) https://mp.weixin.qq.com/s/jjv7aYT5wDBIdTVWXV6rdQ. See also Kan He, "Another Decision on AI-generated Works in China: Is It a Work of Legal Entities?" (*The IPKat*, 29 January 2020).

personality approach that describes an original work as a representation of the personality of the author.[66] This construction of originality has sidelined earlier approaches endorsing "sweat of the brow" doctrines that rewarded "skills, labor and efforts" in creating intellectual work regardless of whether the work was representative of the personality of the author.[67] Therefore, originality as a representation of "self" and self-consciousness would be, in theory, beyond the reach of machine-generated creativity.[68]

In the European Union, three Directives have vertically harmonized the notion of originality. According to the Software, Term, and Database Directive a work is original if it is "the author's own intellectual creation."[69] Later, the CJEU "horizontally" expanded this harmonized notion of originality to all copyright subject matters. In *Infopaq*, the CJEU noted that "[i]t is only through the choice, sequence and combination of those words that the author may express his creativity in an original manner and achieve a result that is an intellectual creation."[70] The *Eva-Maria Painer* decision further explained that a work is original and can be protected if it: (1) is an intellectual creation of the author; (2) reflects his personality; and (3) expresses his free and creative choices in the production of that photograph.[71] By making those various choices, the author of a portrait photograph can stamp the work created with his "personal touch."[72] In *Football Dataco*, finally, the CJEU rejected any remaining "sweat of the brow" doctrines and noted that significant labor and skill of the author cannot as such justify copyright protection if they do not express any originality.[73]

The personality approach to originality has become the dominant standard in the United States as well. Dating back to early cases such as *Burrow-Giles v Sarony*, the US Supreme Court has concluded that originality derives from the free creative choices of the author that imbues the work with his personality[74] "such as the final product duplicates his conceptions and visions" of what the work should be.[75] In particular, *Burrow-Giles* held photographs copyrightable because they could be traced from the photographer's "own original mental conception."[76] Later, in *Feist v Rural*, the US Supreme Court clearly states that only works with a minimum of creativity that represents the personality of the author can be original;

---

[66]   This characterization of originality builds upon Idealist personality theories, according to which intellectual products are manifestations or extensions of the personalities of their creators. See n 14.

[67]   See eg *International News Service v Associated Press* 248 U.S. 215 (1918) (USA); *Jeweler"s Circular Publishing Co. v Keystone Publishing Co.* 281 F. 83, 88 (2nd Cir. 1922) (USA); Andreas Rahmatian, "Originality in UK Copyright Law: The Old 'Skill and Labour' Doctrine under Pressure" (2013) 44 IIC, 4–34.

[68]   The word author itself would bear this meaning on its face as the most accredited etymology of the word would have it deriving from the ancient Greek "αὐτός," which means "self." See Frosio (n 25) 16.

[69]   Respectively, Article 1(3), Article 6, and Article 3(1). For a discussion, see Eleonora Rosati, *Originality in EU Copyright: Full Harmonization through Case Law* (Edward Elgar Publishing 2013).

[70]   Case C-5/08 *Infopaq International A/S v Danske Dagblades Forening* (2009) ECR I-6569, para 45.

[71]   Case C-145/10 *Eva Maria Painer* (2011) EU: C: 2011: 239.121, para 94.

[72]   ibid, para 92.

[73]   Case C-604/10, *Football Dataco Ltd and Others v Yahoo! UK Ltd and Others* (2012) ECLI:EU:C: 2012:115 [42].

[74]   See *Burrow-Giles* (n 56) 60–1 (USA) (considering the copyrightability of a portrait photograph of Oscar Wilde).

[75]   *Lindsay v The Wrecked and Abandoned Vessel R.M.S. Titanic* 52 U.S.P.Q.2d 1609, 1614 (S.D.N.Y. 1999) (USA).

[76]   *Burrow-Giles* (n 56) 54–5 (USA).

labor and efforts in creating a work would not alone qualify for copyright protection.[77] In light of these principles, output such as computational shorthand[78] or listing of automatically numbered hardware parts created using software systems have been found to lack the originality for protection under copyright.[79] The United States joining the Berne Convention in 1988 and the *Feist* case in 1991 saw the crystallization of a globally more harmonized view of copyright, which would include a construction of originality in personality theory terms.[80] A few authors have argued that there are no statutory limitations in the US on treating machines as authors as "[t]he copyright standard of originality is sufficiently low that computer-generated works, even if found to be created solely by a machine, might seem able to qualify for protection."[81] I would note that, after *Feist*, originality is not only a question of quantum. For AI-generated creativity purposes, it is irrelevant whether the standard of originality is low or high. The standard the AI fails to reach is qualitative rather than quantitative. AI cannot express "self." The creativity that it generates cannot express the personality of the author because AI has none.

More recently, a few remaining—mainly common law—jurisdictions have been also endorsing a personality approach to originality. This has been the case in Australia,[82] India,[83] and the United Kingdom,[84] which have finally rejected previous "labor, skill and efforts" approaches. Only a few countries still follow "sweat of the brow" doctrines and reject personality approaches to originality, including South Africa[85] and New Zealand.[86] In sum, the notion of originality seems to be consistently construed via an anthropocentric vision positing that a work is original if it is a representation of "self," a representation of the personality of the author. Of course, only a sentient self-conscious being would be capable of representing "self" through a work. In turn, absent the creator's self-consciousness, the originality requirement that lies in the representation of the personality of the author cannot be met. Therefore, unless machines achieve self-consciousness—which might be the case with futuristic hypothetical strong AI—AI-generated creativity cannot meet the originality requirement under the present legal framework.[87]

---

[77]   See *Feist Publications* (n 97) 362–3.

[78]   See *Brief English Systems v Owen* (1931) 48 F.2d 555 2d Cir, 555 (USA).

[79]   See *Southco, Inc. v Kanebridge Corporation* (2004) 390 F.3d 276, 276 (USA).

[80]   See Monroe Price and Malla Pollack, "The Author in Copyright: Notes for the Literary Critic" in Martha Woodmansee and Peter Jaszi, *The Construction of Authorship: Textual Appropriation in Law and Literature* (Duke University Press 1994) 717–20.

[81]   Samuelson (n 50) 1199–1200. See also Nina Brown, "Artificial Authors: A Case for Copyright in Computer-Generated Works" (2019) 9 Columbia Science and Technology Law Review 1, 24–7; Margot Kaminski, "Authorship, Disrupted: AI Authors in Copyright and First Amendment Law" (2017) 51 *UC Davis Law Review* 589, 601.

[82]   See eg *IceTV Pty Ltd v Nine Network Australia Pty Ltd* [2009] HCA 14 [43] (AUS).

[83]   See eg *Eastern Book Co. & Ors v D.B. Modak & Anr* (2008) 1 SCC 1 (India).

[84]   See eg *Temple Island Collections v New English Teas (No. 2)* [2012] EWPCC 1; Rahmatian (n 67) 4–34.

[85]   See eg *Appleton v Harnischfeger Corp.* (1995) 2 SA 247 (AD), [43]–[44] (SA).

[86]   See eg *Henkel KgaA v Holdfast* [2006] NZSC 102, [2007] 1 NZLR 577 [37] (NZ).

[87]   See eg Peter Mezei, "From Leonardo to the Next Rembrandt—The Need for AI-Pessimism in the Age of Algorithms" (2020) 84(2) UFITA 390–429; Daniel Gervais, "The Machine as Author" (2019) 105 *Iowa Law Review* 1; Deltorn and Macrez (n 39) 8; Ramalho (n 42) 22–4; Madeleine De Cock Buning, "Artificial Intelligence and the Creative Industry: New Challenges for the EU Paradigm for Art and Technology by Autonomous Creation" in Woodrow Barfield and Ugo Pagallo (eds), *Research*

5.   POLICY OPTIONS

As our earlier review of requirements for protection has suggested, the construction of the notion of legal personality, authorship, and originality under the present copyright regime might exclude AI-generated creativity from copyright protection.[88] However, scholars and courts have been wondering whether not granting protection to AI-generated creativity would be a suboptimal solution, in particular from an "incentive theory" perspective.

In fact, future policy directions depend heavily on the application of alternative—and competing—IP theoretical approaches. Incentive theory or utilitarianism,[89] which is dominant in the United States and common law jurisdictions, is less concerned with the humanity of the author than are personality theories, which have a greater influence in civil law jurisdictions.[90] This provides more room for arguments in favour of nonhuman authorship and protectability of AI-generated creativity. According to the incentive theory approach, "providing financial incentives in order to encourage the growth and development of the AI industry and ensure the dissemination of AI generated works is arguably the ultimate goal of assigning copyright to human authors."[91] Although a computer does not need an incentive to produce its output, the incentive may be useful for the person collaborating with the computer.[92] In particular, authors argue that there should be some additional incentive to encourage industry to invest the time and money that it will take to teach machines to behave intelligently[93] or to reward users training and instructing AI-generating content.[94] In contrast, most civil law jurisdictions might be less responsive to welfare and incentive arguments and prefer to value systemic balance, thus rejecting any departure from the personality theory approach that shapes the civil law copyright perspective—and its notion of originality. In addition, although AI-generated creations may justify incentives to bolster innovation and commercialization, the necessity of such incentives is questionable considering the impact it can have on human creations.[95] For example, considering the vast number of automated creations, granting protection for these

---

Handbook on the Law of Artificial Intelligence (Edward Elgar Publishing 2018) 511–35; Deltorn (n 39) 7; Clifford (n 52) 1694–5.

[88]   See Mezei (n 87); Aplin and Pasqualetto (n 38) §5.01–09; Gervais (n 87) 1 ff; Megan Svedman, "Artificial Creativity: A Case against Copyright for AI-created Visual Work" (2020) 9(1) IP Theory 4, 4; Garrett Huson, "I, Copyright" (2019) 35 Santa Clara High Technology Law Journal 54, 72–8; Victor Palace, "What if Artificial Intelligence Wrote This: Artificial Intelligence and Copyright Law" (2019) 71(1) Florida L Rev 217, 238–41; Ralph Clifford, "Creativity Revisited" (2018) 59 IDEA: The IP Law Review 25, 26–9; Ramalho (n 42) 22–4; Clifford (n 52) 1700–2.

[89]   See Fisher (n 16) 168, 177–80.

[90]   See Kaminski (n 81) 599.

[91]   Kalin Hristov, "Artificial Intelligence and the Copyright Dilemma" (2017) 57 *IDEA: The Intellectual Property Law Review* 431, 444. See also Brown (n 81) 20–1.

[92]   See Hristov (n 91) 438–9; Miller (n 50) 1067.

[93]   See Kasap (n 52) 361–4; Ryan Abbott, "I Think, Therefore I Invent: Creative Computers and the Future of Patent Law" (2016) 57(4) Boston College L Rev 1079, 1098–9; Evan Farr, "Copyrightability of Computer-Created Works" (1989) 15 Rutgers Comp & Tech L J 63, 73–4; Butler (n 52) 735; Milde (n 52) 390.

[94]   Brown (n 81) 37; Denicola (n 50) 283; William Ralston, "Copyright in Computer-Composed Music: HAL Meets Handel" (2005) 52 J of the Copyright Society of the USA 281, 303–4; Samuelson (n 50) 1224–8.

[95]   Craglia and others (n 7) 67–8.

works could devalue human authorship and existing jobs in the field;[96] hamper creativity, as it could discourage artists from publishing their creations due to the fear of infringing protected material;[97] or clog the creative ecosystem with standardized and homogenized AI-generated outputs, impacting cultural diversity and identity politics.

Put it bluntly, the policy question to be determined is whether expansion of current copyright protection to computer-generated works is useful. The current legal framework might already provide enough protection through patent and copyright law to the underlying software, through *sui generis* protection to databases, or through other legal mechanisms, such as competition law, to protect automated works without extending the existing copyright regime to non-human authors.[98] As suggested, the questions should be investigated from a law and economics perspective before favoring any solutions.[99] The next few pages will present the major policy options under consideration.

5.1 Option 1: The Public Domain Status of AI-generated Works

Granting public domain status to AI-generated creativity is the first available policy option, and most likely to be the solution endorsed by the present legal framework. Under this perspective, any attempt at construing AI as an author would be an illusion resulting from a process of anthropomorphization of the machine, which in fact does not know anything of the actions and role that this misperception would ascribe to it. Anything predicated as free creative choices of the machine—supposedly acting autonomously from the initial instructions provided by developers and users—would in fact be mere chance/randomness programmed into computational processes. Dan Burk powerfully sums up this perspective:

> For any given AI system, a human designed and wrote the program the constitutes the machine learning algorithm. One or more humans selected the training data for the algorithm. One or more humans determined the statistical parameters for the program, modulating overfitting or underfitting of the data. Numerous human choices were made in generating the resulting output. If there is an author, it is one of more of the humans who are sufficiently causally proximate to the production of the output. In some instances there may be joint authors. In some instances, none of them may be sufficiently causally proximate to claim authorship, and there will be no author, as in the case of an errant wind or feral hogs. But the author is never the machine.[100]

According to this policy option, copyright ownership depends only on the amount of human intervention. Mere data selection and classification by humans is insufficient to meet the

---

[96] Enrico Bonadio and Luke McDonagh, "Artificial Intelligence as Producer and Consumer of Copyright Works: Evaluating the Consequences of Algorithmic Creativity" (2020) 2 Intell Prop Quarterly 112, 123.

[97] De Cock Buning (n 87) 511–35; Deltorn (n 39) 7.

[98] Deltorn and Macrez (n 39) 24.

[99] See Craglia and others (n 7) 68; Jane Ginsburg and Luke Ali Budiardjo, "Authors and Machines" (2019) 34(2) Berkeley Tech L J 343, 448 (noting that "without empirical evidence, it would be imprudent (and premature) to seek to design a regime to cover authorless outputs"); see also Ginsburg (n 38) 134–5.

[100] Dan Burk, "Thirty-Six Views of Copyright Authorship, By Jackson Pollock" (2020) 59 Houston L Rev 1, 37. Si veda anche Deltorn (n 39); Samantha Hedrick, "I 'Think', Therefore I Create: Claiming Copyright in the Outputs of Algorithms" (2019) 8(2) NYU JIPEL 324; James Grimmelmann, "There Is No Such Thing as a Computer-Authored Work And It is a Good Thing, Too" (2016) 39 Colum J L & Arts 403.

"originality" requirement; instead, actual and substantial human contribution to guide the AI system in creation is necessary for grant of protection.[101] Only when there is substantial human input, and all creative choices are embedded in the computer code or users' instructions, will copyright vest with the human author.[102] In this regard, four models of allocating authorship have been identified: (1) sole authorship to users of the tool—if the designer of the tool does not contribute the creative work generated; (2) sole authorship to developers of the tool—if the user plays no role in the output and the self-generative tool creates output based on the training and creative raw material provided by the developer; (3) joint authorship to user and developer—when the outputs reflect the creative contributions of both developer and user; (4) authorless works—neither designer nor user contribute sufficient expression to form an original work of authorship.[103] In any event, if the creative output results both from human and machine choices, materials resulting from machine-made choices must be filtered out, as is customarily done with public domain materials.[104] Only independently copyrightable human contributions will be protectable.

5.2   Option 2: Copyright Protection of AI-Generated Work

In order to avoid AI-generated creativity falling within the public domain and grant necessary incentives to human agents involved with the AI creative process, proposals to grant copyright protection to AI-generated works have been made. Alternatively, copyright ownership would vest directly in the machine that generates the works or human agents potentially involved with the creative process.

5.2.1   Option 2.1: the fictional human author
Some jurisdictions have enacted legislation to set up a legal fiction, so that authorship of AI-generated works is conferred to the agents expending skills, labor and efforts to create, train, or instruct the AI in the first place. This policy approach emerged quite early, when the creative potential of machine learning and AI was wholly unknown.[105] The United Kingdom was the first jurisdiction to provide specific protection to computer-generated creativity.[106] Section 9(3) of the Copyright Designs and Patents Act 1988 (CDPA)[107] clarified that for

---

[101]   Niloufer Selvadurai and Rita Matulionyte, "Reconsidering Creativity: Copyright Protection for Works Generated Using Artificial Intelligence" (2020) 62 JIPLP 536, 539.

[102]   ibid, 538; Gervais (n 87) 51–60.

[103]   Ginsburg and Budiardjo (n 99) 404–45.

[104]   Gervais (n 87) 54.

[105]   In the UK, the copyright protection of a computer-generated sequence for a lottery was discussed as early as 1985 in *Express Newspapers v Liverpool Daily Post*. Justice Whitford allowed copyright protection for the automated output to the Plaintiff and refused the notion that copyright in the work could vest in the computer. The computer is a mere tool for creation, arguing that the computer is the author is similar to suggesting that in a written work, "it is the pen that is the author of the work rather than the person who drives the pen." *Express Newspapers Plc v Liverpool Daily Post & Echo Plc* [1985] 1 WLR 1089, 1098 (UK).

[106]   Jared Grubow, "O.K. Computer: The Devolution of Human Creativity and Granting Musical Copyrights to Artificially Intelligent Joint Authors" (2018) 40 Cardozo L Rev 387; Andres Guadamuz, "Do Androids Dream of Electric Copyright? Comparative Analysis of Originality in Artificial Intelligence Generated Works" (2017) Intell Prop Quarterly 169, 169–89.

[107]   Copyright, Designs and Patents Act 1988, § 9(3) (UK).

computer-generated works, the author is the person who undertakes the arrangements neces-sary for the creation of the work. In addition, Section 178 provides that "computer-generated, in relation to a work, means that the work is generated by computer in circumstances such that there is no human author of the work."[108] Under this regime, the term of protection for computer-generated works would be 50 years from when the work was made. Shortly there-after, other common law countries, including Hong Kong, India, Ireland, Singapore, and New Zealand, enacted similar legal arrangements.[109]

However, the fictional human author policy approach might be suboptimal for at least two orders of reason. The first reason is of practical nature. This approach makes it tricky to determine who is the person in charge of the necessary arrangements.[110] Does the AI-generated work belong to the person who built the system, such as the software developer; the manufac-turer; the person who trained it; or the person who fed it specific inputs like a user?[111]

(1) The programmer. A first possible answer to the question was provided in *Nova Productions v Mazooma Games*, which applied Section 9(3) of the CDPA. The case concerned copyright on frame images generated by a computer program using bitmap files and displayed on the screen when the users played a snooker video game. The court refused to grant author-ship to the user as their input was not artistic in nature.[112] Instead, the Court found the program-mer was the sole author, as the person who made the necessary arrangements, by noting that "[t]he arrangements necessary for the creation of the work were undertaken by [the plaintiff] because he devised the appearance of the various elements of the game and the rules and logic by which each frame is generated and he wrote the relevant computer program."[113] In truth, the *Nova Productions* outcome might be a direct consequence of the rudimental technology at stake;[114] however, vesting authorship in the programmer of AI-generating content raises at least three fundamental critiques. First, the allocation of authorship to the software developer might be a blatant misperception.[115] In fact, at least in state-of-the-art neural network-based creativity, there seems to be no direct causal connection between the software developers and the final AI-generated output, as the expression embedded in that output would be the result of the training of the machine and the instructions given to create that specific output. Second,

---

[108] ibid §178.

[109] See Copyright Ordinance cap 528, section 11(3) (Hong Kong); Copyright Act 1957, section 2(d) (vi) (India); Copyright and Related Rights Act 2000, section 21(f) (Ireland); Copyright Act 1987 chapter 63, section 7A (Singapore); Copyright Act 1994, section 5(2) (New Zealand).

[110] See Emily Dorotheu, "Reap the Benefits and Avoid the Legal Uncertainty: Who Owns the Creations of Artificial Intelligence?" (2015) 21 CTLR 85. See also Guadamuz (n 106) 177 (arguing, however, that the system's ambiguity should actually be seen as a positive feature that deflects the user/programmer dichotomy question and makes the analysis on a case-by-case basis).

[111] Bonadio and McDonagh (n 96) 112, 117–19; Kasap (n 52) 364–76.

[112] *Nova Productions Ltd v Mazooma Games Ltd & Ors Rev* 1 [2006] EWHC 24 (Ch) 106 (UK); see also Farr (n 93) 75–8.

[113] *Nova Productions* (ibid) 104–5 (UK). See also Farr (n 93) 73–4.

[114] See Guadamuz (n 106) 177 (arguing that different allocation of authorship might result depending on the specifics of the case and technology under review). See also Grubow (n 106) 387–424.

[115] Cf. Ryan Abbott, "Artificial Intelligence, Big Data and Intellectual Property: Protecting Computer Generated Works in the United Kingdom" in Tanya Aplin (ed), *Research Handbook on Intellectual Property and Digital Technologies* (Edward Elgar Publishing 2020) 322, 334; Svedman (n 88) 10–11; Annemarie Bridy, "The Evolution of Authorship: Work Made by Code" (2016) 39 Columbia J of Law and the Arts 395, 400–1; Bridy (n 50) ¶62; Samuelson (n 50) 1207–12.

given that this legal fiction is precisely meant to provide incentives to create AI-generated works, where its public domain status would presumptively fail to do so, a sound economic analysis would probably discourage a policy option that rewards the same market player twice. Actually—as the Beijing Internet Court highlighted in a case mentioned earlier—the software developer has been already rewarded with exclusive rights over the software that generates works.[116] Third, from a more practical perspective, this policy solution would potentially entitle coders to aggressive copyright protection for innumerable pieces of creativity,[117] which would also lower any incentive for the original programmer to create more software.[118]

(2) The user.   Allocating rights in AI-generated output to the user of the generator program has been claimed to be a sounder solution.[119] Pamela Samuelson has argued that the user is the reason the AI-generated work comes into being, thus "[i]t is not unfair in these circumstances to give some rights to a person who uses the work for its intended purpose of creating additional works."[120] In the Draft Report on intellectual property rights for the development of artificial intelligence technologies, the European Parliament seemingly endorsed the same view and proposed to entrust the AI users ("the natural person who prepares and publishes [the] work lawfully") with copyright over AI-generated works, at least unless "the technology designer has not expressly reserved the right to use the work in that way."[121] The Beijing decision earlier described also suggested this policy option.[122] This solution would not be novel to copyright standards. For example, in the United States, copyright—and authorship—is given to users for being the instrument of fixation,[123] as in the case of a person who tape-records a jazz performance.[124] In this scenario, the user would be the author of the sound recording, rather than of the jazz performance. Similarly, the user could be construed as the author of the fixation of the AI-generated work. Of course, a specific provision, such as 9(3) CDPA, should be introduced to that end. Most likely, in some exceptional cases, such as when the user does not have any control over the software other than running it, awarding copyright to the user would be a suboptimal policy choice at odds with copyright incentive theory.[125] In this case joint authorship between users and programmers could be a possible solution, depending on the legal scheme for joint authorship made available by different jurisdictions.[126]

(3) The Employer.   Another possible legal framework for ensuring protectability, ownership and accountability of AI-generated works has been found in work-made-for-hire

---

[116]   He (n 63); Chen (n 63) 607–11. See also Bonadio and McDonagh (n 96) 112, 117; Samuelson (n 50) 1207–12.

[117]   Svedman (n 88) 14.

[118]   Huson (n 88) 74.

[119]   See eg National Commission on New Technological Uses of Copyrighted Works, "Final Report of the National Commission on New Technological Uses of Copyrighted Works" ("CONTU Final Report") (1978) 45 (United States); Ralston (n 94) 303–4.

[120]   Pamela Samuelson, "AI Authorship?" (2020) 63(7) Communications of the ACM 20; Samuelson (n 50) 1200–4.

[121]   See Draft Report on intellectual property rights for the development of artificial intelligence technologies (n 34) 10.

[122]   See n 63.

[123]   17 U.S.C. § 114. However, most countries favor neighboring rights protection for sound recording, rather than copyright as in the United States.

[124]   Samuelson (n 50) 1202.

[125]   Ralston (n 94) 304–5.

[126]   See eg Bonadio and McDonagh (n 96) 117–18.

(WMFH) doctrine.[127] The AI system would be a fictional creative employee or independent contractor of its users—whether they are natural persons or legal entities.[128] As Samuelson argues, "one who buys or licenses a generator program has in some sense 'employed' the computer and its programs for his creative endeavors, similar considerations to those that underlie the work made for hire rule support allocation of rights in computer-generated works to users."[129] In truth, this policy option might stand on shaky ground. First, the argument that, also in the case of AI-generated works, employers are treated as authors of "work for hire" works despite having no role in the output[130] seems to disregard that, as part of the WMFH legal fiction, the underlying work has been created by a human author and fulfills the originality standard under the present legal framework. This would not be the case with AI-generated creativity. Second, this arrangement would face challenges on the ground that it would be a misapplication of the WMFH doctrine as it is difficult to define a legal, contractual employment or agency relationship between a human and a machine.[131] It seems obvious that in order for the WMFH doctrine to apply to AI-generated works some substantial statutory and jurisprudential reconstruction of the notion of "employer" and "employee" must first occur.[132]

Next to the practical issue of identifying the relevant human agent, the second critique to the fictional human author policy approach is more fundamental and systemic. Would this approach be sustainable under a legal framework that builds upon the internationally endorsed notion of originality as an expression of the author's personality? Of course, programming, training, and imparting instructions would be unlikely to fulfil the requirement of an original contribution from the human counterparts, as any "expression" would be the result of the AI creative process. As long as the present subjective standard for originality is in place, any fictional human author policy approach would be resting on very shaky ground given the lack of originality of AI-generated creativity. The work itself, whose fictional authorship is attributed to a human agent, would actually remain unoriginal, thus unprotectable. It is worth noting that the "fictional human author" approach was adopted in the UK and other common law countries when "sweat of the brow" or "skill and labour" originality standards were still dominant in those jurisdictions. Since then, as mentioned, the personality standard for originality has apparently replaced any alternative approach.[133] This change would challenge Section 9(3) CDPA policy approaches' systemic compliance.

---

[127] See Shlomit Yanisky-Ravid, "Generating Rembrandt: Artificial Intelligence, Copyright, and Accountability in the 3A Era, The Human-like Authors Are Already Here: A New Model" (2017) Michigan State L Rev 659. See also Russ Pearlman, "Recognizing Artificial Intelligence (AI) as Authors and Inventors under U.S. Intellectual Property Law" (2018) Richmond J of L & Tech 1, 15; Kaminski (n 81) 589; 91 (n 136); Bridy (n 115) 400–1; Bridy (n 50) ¶66.

[128] See Yanisky-Ravid, "Generating Rembrandt" (n 127) 659.

[129] Samuelson, "AI Authorship?" (n 120) 20; Samuelson (n 50) 1200–4.

[130] See Brown (n 81) 39; Kaminski (n 81) 602.

[131] See Bonadio and McDonagh (n 96) 114–15; Huson (n 88) 73–5; Ramalho (n 42) 18–19; Bridy (n 50) 27, ¶68; Butler (n 52) 739–42.

[132] Hristov (n 91) 445–7.

[133] See eg *Temple Island Collections* (n 126). See also Grubow (n 106) 387–424; Guadamuz (n 106) 178–80; Rahmatian (n 67) 4–34.

5.2.2   Option 2.2: the A(I)uthor

One policy option would be to construe the AI as the author. A fiction would have to be established in the law to provide AI with legal personality, so that it can author a work and own a copyright, or at least the law should be amended to reflect the fact that a computer can be an author in a joint work with a person.[134] According to Perlman, the law should recognize sufficiently creative AIs as authors when the AI creation is original and developed independently from human instructions, so that the AI is the cause of creativity, not a mere machine working under the instructions of a human author.[135] Once the AI is declared the author, rights would immediately be assigned to a natural or legal person, such as the creator/programmer of the AI, the user of the AI, or as a joint work.[136] The law should identify the person entitled to receive the transfer and exercise the rights.

According to the scholarship,[137] however, this is a fairly residual policy option as it must face at least two fundamental critiques. First, the machine should be entrusted with some form of legal personality, which seems an unlikely policy choice at the moment.[138] Again, meeting the requirement of originality could be an insurmountable burden for a machine. The notion of originality most likely should be tweaked to include works originating from a machine according to an objective rather than subjective originality.[139] Overall, allowing AI as author would require substantial amendments to the legal framework. As noted, given the early state of technological development, amending the law before truly intelligent machines have even materialized—and whose materialization and evolution remains as of today just a hypothetical guess—might be a suboptimal policy option.[140]

5.3   Option 3: *Sui Generis* Protection of AI-Generated Creativity

Given the difficulties in applying the copyright paradigm to AI-generated creativity, proposals have been also suggesting the creation of a related *sui generis* right—where no authorship or originality would be a necessary requirement—that might protect the investment made in developing and training AI-generating creativity. A few policy alternatives might be available.

---

[134]   See eg Pearlman (n 127) 1, 29–35; Jani Ihalainen, "Computer Creativity: Artificial Intelligence and Copyright" (2018) 13(9) JIPLP 724.

[135]   Pearlman (n 127) 1.

[136]   Cf also Abbott (n 115) 334 (noting that the machine would be an author/inventor without being an owner and "[t]he computer"'s owner should be the default owner of any CGW it produces"); Abbott (n 93) 1121.

[137]   See eg Bonadio and McDonagh (n 96) 112, 116; Ralston (n 94) 302–3; Farr (n 93) 79; Samuelson (n 50) 1199–1200.

[138]   See section 3.1.

[139]   See Shlomit Yanisky-Ravid and Luis Antonio Velez-Hernandez, "Copyrightability of Artworks Produced by Creative Robots, Driven by Artificial Intelligence Systems and the Originality Requirement: The Formality-Objective Model" (2018) 19(1) Minnesota J of L, Science & Tech 1, 40–8 (arguing that judges should look at the final output per se, considering the field of art, the objective opinion of users, and similarity to other works, while disregarding the subjective intention of the author; *de facto* aligning the standard for originality in copyright to the standard for novelty in patent law).

[140]   See Huson (n 88) 77–8; Yvette Joy Liebesman, "The Wisdom of Legislating for Anticipated Technological Advancements" (2010) J Marshall Rev Intell Prop L 10 153, 172.

5.3.1 Option 3.1: protecting investment

Sui generis rights modelled after database or neighbouring rights have been suggested for protecting AI-generated creativity. For example, while denying protectability under the traditional copyright scheme, the Australian Copyright Law Review Committee noted that, if computer generated creativity needs protection, this should be "more akin to that extended to neighbouring rights […] the protection extended to performers, producers of phonograms and broadcasting organizations."[141] In this respect, broadcasting rights might serve as reference as they exist notwithstanding that the underlying sport event cannot enjoy copyright protection. Again, McCutcheon has suggested a *sui generis* rights regime for AI-generated creativity similar to database rights, therefore protecting investment in the creation but not requiring an author, nor authorship, nor originality.[142] With the goal of limiting overbroad protection of algorithmic creativity, some authors propose a thin scope of the *sui generis* right, coupled with strong fair use safeguards, with a short duration of around three years or so.[143]

5.3.2 Option 3.2: the disseminators' right

Further proposal would like to provide rights to publishers and disseminators of AI-generated works. On one side, the regime for anonymous/pseudonymous works could be applied to AI-generated works. According to several national regimes, such as Spain, France, Italy, and Sweden,[144] the person who publishes the work will exercise the rights. On the other side, an additional policy option could provide to the disseminator of AI-generated creativity a right similar to the EU's publisher right in previously unpublished works as in Art. 4 of Directive 2006/116/EC.[145] Under this scheme, the protection covers the first lawful publication/communication of previously unpublished public domain works. Similarly, AI-generated works would be in the public domain, therefore the "disseminator" scheme would only reward someone for the dissemination of AI-generated creation. The duration of the right could be limited to, for example, 25 years, as in the case of Art. 4 of Directive 2006/116/EC.[146]

5.3.3 Option 3.3: protecting goodwill against unfair competition

Other policy proposals have been especially targeting unfair competition in the market for AI-generated works. Japan, for example, have been considering a novel *sui generis* regime for non-human-created intellectual property based on a trade mark-like approach with an emphasis on protection against unfair competition.[147] This approach seeks to limit the protection of AI works by allowing flexibility in levels of protection based on popularity of the AI-generated works as a proxy for goodwill.[148] This would leave out obscure works created for

---

[141] Sam Ricketson, "The Need for Human Authorship: Australian Developments: Telstra Corp Ltd v Phone Directories Co Pty Ltd (Case Comment)" (2012) 34(1) E.I.P.R. 54.

[142] See Jani McCutcheon, "The Vanishing Author in Computer Generated Works" (2013) 36 Melbourne U L Rev 915, 965–6.

[143] Bonadio and McDonagh (n 96) 136–7.

[144] French IP Code (n 45) L113-1; Spanish IP Law (n 46) art 6(1) (Spain); Italian Copyright Law (n 48) art 9 (Italy); Act on Copyright in Literary and Artistic Works 1960, art 7 (Sweden).

[145] Ramalho (n 77) 22–4.

[146] Ibid.

[147] See "Intellectual Property Strategic Program 2016" www.kantei.go. jp/jp/singi/titeki2/kettei/chizaikeikaku20160509_e.pdf.

[148] Ibid 11.

the sole aim of copyright protection. The proposal would allocate ownership of the work to the individual or company that had created the AI.[149]

6.   CONCLUSIONS: IP THEORIES IN SEARCH OF AN A(I) UTHOR

Anthropocentrism strongly influences the present copyright legal framework. Thus, AI-generated creativity falls short of all fundamental requirements for granting copyright protection, including legal personality, authorship, and originality. As a reaction, utilitarian/incentive approaches push for the adoption of legal fictions to protect and incentivize AI-generated creativity. These policy solutions, unfortunately, do not satisfactorily address systemic inconsistencies. Even if the law fictionally claims that the work is human-made rather than AI-made, the work itself remains unoriginal as machines will be inherently incapable of originality under a personality standard. Only a fundamental overhaul of the copyright system, pushing away the present anthropocentric approach, can provide full copyright protection to AI-generated creativity proper, when no human intervention can be construed as an original expression. This would be ill-considered, especially given the primitive stage of technological development in the field. Given the systemic difficulties of extending the copyright regime to AI-generated works, residual *sui generis* approaches are also available and, most likely, a preferable option. If policymakers chose to provide monopolistic incentive to AI-generated creativity, the incentive should fall upon the users, if they contributed any meaningful labor and effort to the AI-generated output, as programmers, marketers, and investors would be double-dipping on earlier rewards over the AI-generating content software.

The question that lies ahead is whether any incentive for AI-generated creativity is at all necessary. This policy question should be answered from an empirical perspective, carefully weighing positive and negative externalities of introducing new forms of protection of algorithmic creativity. In this respect, what follows will enlist the help of IP theories to disentangle this policy conundrum by testing the introduction of new exclusive rights over AI-generated creativity against each of the major theoretical justifications of IP.

First, a justification for new exclusive rights for AI-generated works might be found in Lockean fairness theory, which strongly influenced the common law system. Under this theoretical approach, labor and efforts deserve a fair compensation, while a tight causal relationship between the work and the personality of the author becomes less relevant. Therefore, both copyrights and *sui generis* rights might be a sustainable option under this theoretical perspective. Most likely, the economic incentive should reward users of technologies generating creativity.

Instead, the personality theory might be unfit to justify any copyright protection of algorithmic works. The personality theory's construction of the work as an extension of the personality—and humanity—of the author makes it hard, if not impossible, to make room for copyright protection of AI-generated works when the causal link between human agents and the work is so weakened that no protectable expressions deriving from free human choices can be found. The machine, on the other side, is not human, nor self-conscious; thus it cannot

---

[149]   Ibid.

enjoy any personality and its contribution would not qualify as copyright-protectable from a personality theory perspective.

Again, utilitarian theories, as interpreted in light of welfare theory, incentive theory, and economic analysis of law, would like to implement regulatory solutions that generate positive externalities for society at large, rather than authors and innovators alone. From a utilitarian perspective, progress is maximized by social policies that generate the greatest happiness for the greatest number of people. In this respect, the final goal of creativity and innovation policy is social progress, which is not the same as mere technological development.[150] Therefore, although the economic value that might arise from the development of AI-generating creativity would be a relevant positive externality, policy changes must bring about overall advantages for society as a whole in terms of social progress. Actually, plentiful arguments might be raised against the notion that incentivizing algorithmic creativity via exclusive rights might generate more positive externalities than negative. While, on one side, there is no evidence that new exclusive rights might incentivize AI industry growth, on the other side such exclusive rights might increase copyright overall transaction costs and negatively affect cultural diversity and identity culture.

On this point, first, some evidence should be provided that the proposed incentives align with the AI industry business models and might incentivize investment in the AI sector. The need for such incentives should be empirically proven, together with the positive externalities that they might bring about for the creative ecosystem. In fact, there is well-established historical evidence that property rights are not the only incentive to creativity.[151] Miscellaneous research and market evidence show that open and free access to creative works or alternative business models might provide stronger incentive to AI-generated creativity than IP-based protection models,[152] without creating the negative externalities of propertization and exclusive rights. Of course, it is worth noting that AI itself does not need any incentive to create and exclusive rights provided by copyright and patents over the technologies generating creative works might already constitute an incentive sufficient enough for the human agents involved. In addition, other legal tools, such as protection against unfair competition, might provide an adequate remedy against infringement.

Second, in the context of the maximization of positive externalities, a truly challenging question deals with how AI-generated creativity impacts cultural diversity and identity politics.[153] In particular, AI-generated creativity might homogenize online and offline content. Actually, algorithmic creativity has an inherent propension to average mainstream ideas and perspectives. Neural networks train by acritically collecting information and learn from that training how to create new content. Of course, the new content will reflect all bias and preconceptions of the original database. The machine can only process weighted averages of the collected information and, thus, generates content that reflects those averages. The divergence,

---

[150] See, on this point, Pierpaolo Pasolini, *Sviluppo e progresso* (1973) in *Scritti Corsari* (Garzanti 1975).

[151] See eg Frosio (n 25).

[152] Bonadio and McDonagh (n 96) 122–3; Svedman (n 88) 1314.

[153] Octavio Kulesz, "Culture, Platforms and Machines: The Impact of Artificial Intelligence on the Diversity of Cultural Expressions" (UNESCO Intergovernmental Committee for the Protection and Promotion of the Diversity of Cultural Expressions, Paris 2018)   https://en.unesco.org/creativity/sites/creativity/files/12igc_inf4_en.pdf.

which is typical of original human thought, seems intrinsically less probable in algorithmic processes generating content.

Third, protecting algorithmic creativity might bring about further negative externalities by actualizing the "infinite monkey theorem" of French mathematician Émile Borel,[154] thus expanding copyright transactional costs to the point of systemic failure. Borel's theorem argues that a monkey randomly hitting the keys of a typewriter for an infinite amount of time will "almost" surely type any possible text, such as the complete collection of Shakespeare's works.[155] Jorge Luis Borges evokes, as a possible result of the work of Borel's monkeys, the "Biblioteca Total," which would contain any possible work written and to be written.[156] Actually, Borel's monkey is a metaphor representing a hypothetical mechanical tool capable of creating an infinite random sequence of letters and symbols. Today, Borel's theorem has become almost reality given the extraordinary—and impossible to predict, at the time Borel lived—development of computational sciences. This development—and the actualization of Borel's theorem—would further affect transactions costs related to that "copyright soup" that, according to William Fisher, has become already too thick in the digital environment.[157] AI creative capacities might scale up at the pace of singularity, flooding the cultural marketplace with an unmanageable mesh of rights to clear. If new copyright or *sui generis* rights are granted over AI-generated works, copyright trolling might escalate to a phase of final computational doom. Infinite AI monkeys might eat up all the "copyright soup," so that no creative materials will be left to use.

Finally on the issue of the theories addressed herein, also cultural theories might not provide justification to the introduction of new exclusive rights protecting AI-generated creativity. Instead, the pursuit of happiness via the realization of universal human values, such as culture—which is the final goal in the creativity domain of the normative system promoted by this theoretical approach—might suggest disincentivization, rather than incentivization, of the generation of algorithmic works. The widespread availability of algorithmic creativity, possibly autonomously generated by machines, would not accrete human culture but, if any, algorithmic culture. Human culture, in contrast, would be harmed by the limitation of professional and expressive space available to human agents. Meanwhile, as mentioned above, the cultural ecosystem might suffer negative externalities in terms of diversity of creative works, which is a central value of the social project of cultural theory.

In sum, a review of theoretical justifications for IP rights would suggest caution in extending them to AI-generated creativity. IP theories in search of justifications for protecting AI-generated works might not finally find any A(I)uthor.

---

[154]   Émile Borel, "Mécanique Statistique et Irréversibilité" (1913) 5(3) J Phys (Paris) 189.
[155]   Ibid.
[156]   Jorge Luis Borges, *La Biblioteca Total* (1941).
[157]   Cf. CopyrightX, Lectures, 6. The Mechanics of Copyright http://copyx.org/lectures.

9. Copyright law should stay true to itself in the age of artificial intelligence

Alice Lee and Phoebe Woo

1. INTRODUCTION

The advent of artificial intelligence ("AI") has shaken up the world of copyright. In the pre-digital age, infringement, in particular secondary infringement, was preoccupied with infringing copies, but now works can be shared without there being a copy in the first place. Indeed, following technological advancement and the emergence of AI, the ways in which works can be utilized have varied and become complicated. Look at deepfakes, for instance. On Christmas Day in 2020, the United Kingdom ("UK") TV station Channel 4 released a video that featured Queen Elizabeth II giving a speech which contained jokes about the royal family and dancing in front of the camera.[1] The image of Queen Elizabeth II looked so real that viewers might hesitate to judge that the video was fake (and it was in fact fake). The video was created by deepfake technology, a form of AI that can create hyperreal images. How deepfake technology works, to put it briefly, is that the subject's digital data, including photographs and videos, will first be gathered from various sources and stored in a database; next, the program will analyze the collected data and synthesize the subject's characteristics—for example, if the subject is a person, the person's speech style and character; finally, based on what it learned, the program can generate fake photographs and videos.[2] While the use of deepfake technology may give rise to tortious issues such as defamation and misuse of private information, copyright issues may be involved too. In the process of collecting data, copyright-protected works may be reproduced by downloading. But unlike typical cases of copying, the reproductions made by deepfake technology are not visible. It is unlike an infringer copying someone else's work and then distributing unauthorized copies via the internet. Deepfake technology only uses reproductions for analytical purposes and in most cases, there is no trace of the reproductions in the ultimate product. Take Queen Elizabeth II's deepfake video as an example: one cannot figure out what photographs and videos of the Queen have been collected and analyzed simply from the fake video. To figure this out, one needs to delve into the program's database and study its algorithm. Unprecedented questions of law and technology are accordingly raised.

Undeniably, AI has brought complications to the creation and distribution of original works on the one hand, and to the permitted use of copyright-protected works on the other. Can the existing framework of copyright law adapt to these changes and withstand future challenges? Professor Jessica Litman answers in the negative. She argues that copyright should be recast as

---

[1] *Abbianca Makoni, Channel 4's "Deepfake" Queen's Speech Sparks Hundreds of Complaints to Ofcom*, EVENING STANDARD, Dec. 30, 2020, www.standard.co.uk/showbiz/channel-4-queen-s -speech-deepfake-b571074.html.

[2] Mika Westerlund, *The Emergence of Deepfake Technology*, 9 TECH. INNOV. MGMT. REV. 11 (2019).

the right of commercial exploitation, so that to determine whether a person has infringed copyright in someone else's work, one simply asks whether that person has used the work commercially without the copyright owner's consent.[3] Some scholars share Professor Litman's view that copyright law should be radically reformed but come up with different ideas as to how the reform should be carried out. Ole-Andreas Rognstad and Joost Poort suggest that reasonableness should become the crux of copyright law and thus the existing bundle of rights enjoyed by copyright owners should be reduced to the right of reasonable exploitation.[4] Bingbin Lu contends that copyright law should be "dissemination-centric."[5] Meanwhile, Ansgar Ohly takes an entirely different path as he proposes a "three-layer model of economic rights".[6] How far are these proposals (collectively the "reform proposals") practicable and effective in tackling the problems identified by their respective proponents?

This chapter evaluates the reform proposals and discusses how copyright law can keep pace with the development of AI and new technology. Although the discussion is mostly relevant to common law jurisdictions and on some occasions to the European Union ("EU"), it may also be of interest to scholars and practitioners from civil law jurisdictions who ponder whether copyright law is in need of reform. As shown below, the reform proposals are too idealistic to be helpful. They all assume that impeccable legal drafting is all we need, losing sight of the matrix of factors that determine the fate and outcome of proposed amendments. In a way, the proponents have oversimplified the problem we face in the real world. But, at a closer look, their proposed tests for copyright infringement are not as simple as they initially appear. Some do not explain how the new framework could be reconciled with the existing regime of primary and secondary infringement; nor do they discuss whether or how copyright exceptions could be accommodated.

In the ensuing sections, the reform proposals are analyzed and criticized with reference to the curious case of hyperlinking in the EU and the decade-long digital copyright consultation in Hong Kong, both illustrating the complexity and capriciousness of copyright reform no matter where. Through European and Asian examples, this chapter defends the current copyright regime and identifies the way forward from a pragmatic perspective. It will be shown that, in the digital era, top-down legislative reforms are not sufficient per se to encourage creativity or guarantee a hassle-free environment for authors and creators, who are better empowered by non-statutory means.

---

    [3]   JESSICA LITMAN, DIGITAL COPYRIGHT (2000).
    [4]   Ole-Andreas Rognstad and Joost Poort, *The Right to Reasonable Exploitation Concretized: An Incentive Based Approach*, in COPYRIGHT RESTRUCTURED: RETHINKING COPYRIGHT'S ECONOMIC RIGHTS IN A TIME OF HIGHLY DYNAMIC TECHNOLOGICAL AND ECONOMIC CHANGE (P. Bernt Hugenholtz ed., 2018).
    [5]   Bingbin Lu, *Reconstructing Copyright From "Copy-centric" to "Dissemination-centric" in the Digital Age*, 39(4) J. INFO. SCI. 479 (2013).
    [6]   Ansgar Ohly, *A Fairness-Based Approach to Economic Rights*, in COPYRIGHT RESTRUCTURED: RETHINKING COPYRIGHT'S ECONOMIC RIGHTS IN A TIME OF HIGHLY DYNAMIC TECHNOLOGICAL AND ECONOMIC CHANGE (P. Bernt Hugenholtz ed., 2018).

2.   REFORM PROPOSALS

In her book *Digital Copyright*,[7] Professor Litman contends that the right of commercial exploitation should replace the existing bundle of rights enjoyed by copyright owners and become the new pillar of copyright law in the United States ("US"). Her argument is built upon the observation that copying is central to the use of digital technology, in that "making digital reproductions is an unavoidable incident of reading, viewing, listening to, learning from, sharing, improving, and reusing works embodied in digital media."[8] Granting copyright owners the right of reproduction in effect allows them to exercise control over every use of their works. Such control, according to Professor Litman, is incongruent with the object of copyright law, as copyright law does not purport to give copyright owners absolute right over their works.[9] One should be free to get access to other people's works, to view and read them under copyright law, so long as one does not perform any infringing acts. Also, given the multi-functional roles that reproductions play in digital media, it should not be assumed that all reproductions are harmful to copyright owners' interests; "finding and counting illicit copies is poor approximation of the copyright owners' injury."[10] For the above reasons, Professor Litman holds the view that the right of reproduction "no longer serves our needs"[11] and that the right of commercial exploitation should become the core of copyright.

The notion of commercial exploitation is meant to be broad and calls for a case-by-case analysis in practice. Professor Litman admits that this approach "would replace the detailed bright lines in the current statute with uncertainty," but argues:

> [T]he bright lines Congress gave us embody at least as much uncertainty, although it is uncertainty of a different sort. The detailed bright lines have evolved, through accident of technological change, into all-inclusive categories of infringers with tiny pockmarks of express exemptions and privileges, and undefined and largely unacknowledged free zones of people-who-are-technically-infringing-but-will-never-get-sued […] The brightness of the current lines is illusory.[12]

Meanwhile, Professor Litman identifies three significant advantages for introducing the right of commercial exploitation. First, if there is concern that a single isolated unauthorized digital copy might devastate the market for copyrighted works by enabling an endless string of identical illegal copies, then "defining that harm as an actionable wrong will address the danger without being overinclusive."[13] The second advantage is that, importantly, having a single right of commercial exploitation will enhance the accessibility of copyright law as it is easier for the public to understand.[14] Third, having a general right for copyright owners opens the way for the legislature to adopt an equally broad exception provision to achieve a "balanced copyright law."[15]

---

[7]   LITMAN, *supra* note 3, at 159.
[8]   Ibid at 154.
[9]   Ibid at 154–5.
[10]   Ibid at 154.
[11]   Ibid at 156.
[12]   Ibid at 157.
[13]   Ibid.
[14]   Ibid at 157–8.
[15]   Ibid at 158.

Professor Litman's proposal is pioneering and has prompted many scholars to contemplate how copyright law should be reformed. Ole-Andreas Rognstad and Joost Poort also see the need to reform copyright law by simplifying it, but they suggest that the way forward should be a right of reasonable exploitation rather than commercial exploitation. The right to reasonable exploitation is "a 'one stage' test which implies that the delineation of the right lies in the definition of what is reasonable rather than in what constitutes an 'exploitation'."[16] Accordingly, the concept of "exploitation" is to be understood in its widest sense, while the criteria for determining reasonableness shall be based on economic efficiency and other guiding principles such as proportionality and freedom of expression.[17] Rognstad and Poort's proposal is apparently less permissive than Professor Litman's, as it does not allow non-commercial exploitation of a work if such exploitation is unreasonable.

Bingbin Lu shares Professor Litman's view that copyright should be reformed, but he comes up with a different reform proposal. Lu agrees with Professor Litman that copying becomes inevitable in the digital age and that the right of reproduction cannot keep up with the development of digital technology.[18] However, he argues that the commercial/non-commercial distinction is inaccurate:

> Professor Litman once contended that policy-makers should start with the widely held idea that copyright should be the exclusive right of commercial exploitation, thus drawing a distinction between commercial and non-commercial uses of content [...] The purpose of her proposal is to guarantee individual users the right to conduct non-commercial reproductions. Strictly speaking, this point of view is not accurate.[19]

For instance, disseminating copyrighted material free of change can be categorized as non-commercial, but it is not private copying. Lu insists that private copying should not include sharing copyrighted content over the internet without copyright owners' permission. Instead of replacing copyright with the right of commercial exploitation, Lu suggests that copyright should be reclassified into two broad categories, namely the reproduction right and the dissemination right. The former includes the right of copying, the right of reproduction in a material form (that is, making a non-literal copy), the right of adaptation, and the right of translation, while the latter includes the performance right, the distribution right, the rental right, the broadcasting right, the right of communication to the public, and the right of making available to the public.[20] The right of dissemination shall become the core of copyright because "the significance of copyright does not lie in the act of reproduction itself, but in what it enables— dissemination of a work. A violation occurs only if there is public dissemination of a work not granted by the copyright owner."[21] Should copyright law become dissemination-centric, as Lu argues, it will achieve "a high level of flexibility and technological neutrality."[22]

While Professor Litman, Rognstad and Poort, and Lu explore how to simplify the law by reducing copyright to a single right, Ansgar Ohly proposes an entirely different legal frame-

---

[16]   Rognstad and Poort, *supra* note 4, at 123.
[17]   Ibid at 129–32.
[18]   Lu, *supra* note 5, at 480.
[19]   Ibid at 481–2.
[20]   Ibid at 488.
[21]   Ibid at 489.
[22]   Ibid at 486.

work. According to Ohly, a three-level model should be adopted for determining whether an act in question constitutes copyright infringement.[23] Level 1 is a "black list" of core infringements, covering cases where there is obvious competition between the copyright owner and the user, so that they should be regulated regardless of whether the act is committed in the course of trade or with a view to obtaining profit.[24] Examples would include making a digital copy of the work available to the public online for downloading, and transmitting a work to the public by means of broadcast or on-demand streaming. The next level is a list of infringing acts which combine economic rights with market effects. That means the claimant will have to show that the act complained of is likely to have a negative effect on his market position or derives an undue economic benefit from the use of the work.[25] Finally, level 3 is a general clause which prohibits any unfair use of the work, and possible criteria for unfairness might be the second and third steps of the three-step test.[26] Ohly's three-level model endeavors to increase efficiency and minimize ambiguity—only actions that fall within the second and third levels are subject to legal tests for determining whether they are infringing.

3.   WHY NOT THE REFORM PROPOSALS?

Appealing as they are, none of the reform proposals is a perfect response to the legal challenges posed by AI and digital technology. They all promise a simplistic approach but none of them is truly simple. Rather, they are opaque and too idealistic and theoretical to be helpful to the authors and users of creative works. Current rules may be imperfect, but they are not so faulty or incurable that we should abandon them all and adopt new ones.

3.1   Simplicity Is Illusory

All proponents claim that their proposals can simplify existing law, but as we examine them more closely and consider how they may be applied in practice, it appears that they are no less complex than what we currently have. First, in advocating an apparently simple distinction between commercial and non-commercial behavior, Professor Litman is well aware of the difficulties in defining commercial exploitation.[27] She makes two points of defense: one is that the advantages of introducing the right of commercial exploitation outweigh the problem of uncertainty; the other that the current law is not as certain as we think it to be.[28] The advantages that she identifies for this new right indeed sound attractive: the economic interests of copyright owners will remain well protected, while the public will find copyright law easier to understand; and a broad exception can be introduced to replace the long list of specific

---

[23]   Ohly, *supra* note 6, at 24–6.
[24]   Ibid at 26–27.
[25]   Ibid at 27–28.
[26]   Ibid at 28–30. The three-step test is that in the Berne Convention for the Protection of Literary and Artistic Works (1967), Article 9(2): "It shall be a matter for legislation in the countries of the Union to permit the reproduction of such works in certain special cases, provided that such reproduction does not conflict with a normal exploitation of the work and does not unreasonably prejudice the legitimate interests of the author."
[27]   LITMAN, *supra* note 12.
[28]   Ibid.

exemptions in the current regime.[29] However, whether these benefits could be realized should the right of commercial exploitation become a reality is questionable. Unauthorized commercial exploitation of a work amounts to copyright infringement—the rule is simple, but what exactly does "commercial exploitation" mean? This we are not sure of. In the online world, the divide between commercial and non-commercial activities is not always clear. When a YouTuber includes a copyright-protected work in his or her video without the copyright owner's authorization—obviously to boost view counts and gain fame—can we say that this YouTuber is engaging in a commercial activity? Professor Litman acknowledges the need for a case-by-case consideration but offers little elaboration on the concept of "commercial exploitation." Consequently, although the rule is simple, how it should be applied in practice remains a mystery. Mystery in the law is hardly what the public wants. Nor is it attractive to copyright owners, for whom individual assessment for every single use of their work implies a specialist lawyer consultation or even litigation whenever copyright infringement is suspected. This will cost them a lot of time, money, and resources. On the other hand, although existing copyright rules contain uncertainties as well (for example, the scope of the right of communication to the public is somewhat unclear and controversial, as shown below), legislative amendments can be easily made to clarify them. Less time and effort is probably needed to fix a boat than to build a new one.

Rognstad and Poort's proposal suffers from the same problem of uncertainty. In fact, the notion of "reasonable exploitation" is even more general and vague than that of "commercial exploitation." Rognstad and Poort suggest that economic factors and human rights issues such as proportionality and freedom of expression should be taken into account when determining reasonableness.[30] Such a nuanced approach will entail more judicial discretion, which may be a good thing in itself, but it is almost inevitable that flexibility comes hand in hand with unpredictability. A rule that is easy to understand but unpredictable in application does not serve the best interests of either users or copyright owners.

Ohly's three-level model seems less drastic, as it offers three categories rather than a single yardstick. Under the model, acts that fall within level 1 are outright illegal;[31] for acts that fall within level 2, whether they amount to copyright infringement depends on their effects on the market;[32] and level 3 covers any unfair use of the copyright-protected work.[33] The first two levels sound familiar as they resemble primary and secondary infringement under the current regime, but the dividing line could be arbitrary. For instance, as Ohly himself puts it, hyperlinking is not a case where negative market effects could be presumed, thus a distinction should be drawn between surface links and inline links.[34] Regarding the third level, reference is made to the three-step test: does the use conflict with a normal exploitation of the work and does it unreasonably prejudice the legitimate interests of the right holder? It is hard to see how such a general clause could work better than a list of well-defined exemptions. It is not for nothing that the three-step test insists on "certain special cases."

---

29   LITMAN, *supra* note 15.
30   Rognstad and Poort, *supra* note 17.
31   Ohly, *supra* note 24.
32   Ohly, *supra* note 25.
33   Ohly, *supra* note 26.
34   Ibid.

As for Lu's proposal, reconfiguring copyright as two broad categories of reproduction and dissemination can perhaps simplify the law, but only at the cost of blurring established definitions. To say that the right of reproduction includes the right of adaptation and the right of translation is to strain the meaning of "reproduction." Similarly, it is contrary to current understanding if the right of dissemination is to include the right of distribution, the right of rental, the right of broadcasting, and the right of communication to the public. As shown below, the fate of a legal concept is determined not only by the words chosen to convey its meaning, but also by its interpretation and reception by all the stakeholders.

3.2   Interpretation is Key

Copyright reform is not only a draftsman's problem. Judges also play an indispensable role in ensuring that the well-crafted legal command is correctly understood and solemnly announced to its intended recipients, so that the latter can comply with the law and change their behavior accordingly. The judges' role is particularly crucial in copyright reform implementation because, unlike trademarks or patents, copyright arises without application or registration. There is no registry practice guide for copyright holders and users, who are from time to time taken aback by the out-of-the-ordinary judgments of certain judiciary bodies, most notably the Court of Justice of the EU ("CJEU").

Take the right of communication as an example. It was propagated as "a high level of protection [to] foster substantial investment in creativity and innovation"[35] and a medium-neutral concept encompassing "transmission or retransmission of a work to the public by wire or wireless means, including broadcasting."[36] In respect of sound recordings, films, music videos, and other multimedia creations, that would be broad enough to cover transmission via peer-to-peer technology such as streaming[37] and BitTorrent.[38] But how far can we go when the subject matters are literary or artistic works, such as news articles or photographs? Article 3(1) of the Information Society Directive provides that it shall be an exclusive right of authors to prohibit any communication to the public of their works, including "the making available to the public of their works in such a way that members of the public may access them from a place and at a time individually chosen by them." The wording is clear and should catch anyone who, without authorization, puts another's copyright work on a website so that it is accessible by any member of the public. In some curious EU cases,[39] however, the CJEU came

---

[35]   Directive 2001/29/EC of the European Parliament and of the Council of 22 May 2001 on the harmonization of certain aspects of copyright and related rights in the information society ("the Information Society Directive"), recital 4.

[36]   Ibid at recital 23.

[37]   Streaming is defined as "a method of transmitting or receiving data (especially video and audio material) over a computer network as a steady, continuous flow, allowing playback to start while the rest of the data is still being received": OXFORD DICTIONARY (online).

[38]   BitTorrent is a peer-to-peer file sharing system which "does not involve a centralized computer but is designed so that individual computers 'share' the material they have downloaded from a source by re-transmitting it to other 'peer' computers": *Chan Nai Ming v HKSAR* (2007) 10 H.K.C.F.A.R. 273 at para. 20. In this case, the Hong Kong Court of Final Appeal held that BitTorrent transmission amounted to "distribution," an act of secondary infringement as well as a criminal offence. For commentary, *see* Anna Koo, *Distribution over Peer-to-Peer Network*, 30(2) EUR. INTELL. PROP. REV. 74 (2008).

[39]   *Nils Svensson and Others v Retriever Sverige AB*, C-466/12, ECLI:EU:C:2014:76, a case on news articles, and *GS Media BV v Sanoma Media Netherlands BV and Others*, C-160/15, ECLI:EU:C:2016:

to the astonishing conclusion that merely sharing a hyperlink to such a website would also constitute "communication of the work" (though whether it is a communication "to the public" is a separate question, as shown below).

It is understandable that, given the unlimited scope of technological innovations, the CJEU might wish to catch as many culpable acts as possible, but common sense tells us that sharing a hyperlink to a website is not and cannot be one of them. It is demonstrably wrong to equate hyperlinks with "communication of the work." First, such an interpretation would make every internet user a potential infringer, as sharing hyperlinks has become a daily routine in the digital age. Second, the CJEU's construction defies the basic rule of literal interpretation. The Directive speaks of communication of the work and making available of the work to the public, but that is not what hyperlinks do. Even if the website in question does contain a copyright work which has been uploaded without authorization, the hyperlink merely provides *information* about the location of the work, namely the Universal Resource Locator or "URL" of a webpage, or a web address. It does not make the *work* available to the public. Under copyright law, the culprit should be the website manager who posts unauthorized copyright works on his or her webpage, but not the subsequent party who simply copies and shares the website's hyperlink with others.

It does not take great minds such as those in the European Copyright Society[40] to point out the flaws in the CJEU's interpretive process. Instead of defining "communication to the public" as a composite expression, the CJEU has dissected it into "communication" and "to the public" and inserted an additional requirement of "a new public" from nowhere.[41] This extra step is tantamount to rewriting the Directive, and in the line of cases from *Nils Svensson and Others*[42] to *VG Bild-Kunst*,[43] the CJEU has tried to justify this unusual process as follows:

> [A]ccording to settled case-law, in order to be covered by the concept of 'communication to the public,' within the meaning of Article 3(1) of Directive 2001/29, a communication, such as that at issue in the main proceedings, concerning the same works as those covered by the initial communication and made, as in the case of the initial communication, on the Internet, and therefore by the same technical means, must also be directed at a new public, that is to say, at a public that was not taken into account by the copyright holders when they authorized the initial communication to the public.[44]

It is noteworthy that the opening phrase "according to settled case-law" exposes that the CJEU is entrenched in its own jurisprudence—it has no choice but to endorse the "settled" view that the provision of clickable links to protected works must be considered to be an act of "com-

---

644 and *VG Bild-Kunst v Stiftung Preußischer Kulturbesitz*, C-392/19, ECLI:EU:C:2021:181, which relate to photographs and thumbnail images, respectively.

[40]   European Copyright Society, *Opinion on the Reference to the CJEU in Case C-466/12 Svensson*, in UNIVERSITY OF CAMBRIDGE LEGAL STUDIES RESEARCH PAPER SERIES, Paper No. 6/2013 (Feb. 15, 2013).

[41]   *Sociedad General de Autores y Editores de España (SGAE) v Rafael Hoteles SA*, C-306/05, ECLI: EU:C:2006:764, at paras 37 and 40.

[42]   *Nils Svensson and Others, supra* note 39.

[43]   *VG Bild-Kunst, supra* note 39.

[44]   *Nils Svensson and Others, supra* note 39, at para. 24, citing *Sociedad General de Autores y Editores de España (SGAE) v Rafael Hoteles SA*, *supra* note 41. *See also GS Media, supra* note 39, at para. 37; *VG Bild-Kunst, supra* note 39, at para. 32.

munication,"[45] no matter how shocking it may be. To ameliorate the harm this construction might cause, the CJEU took the liberty to add "directed at a new public" as an ingredient for infringement, even though nowhere in the Directive can we see such a requirement. In the end, through this unnatural interpretation, the CJEU managed to avoid the absurd result of banning hyperlinks,[46] but its reputation as a judicial interpreter has been compromised.

Truth be told, it is not the first time that the CJEU's unruly approach to statutory interpretation has been in the spotlight. In *L'Oreal SA v Bellure NV*,[47] decided four years before the *Svensson* case, the CJEU failed to distinguish between fair and unfair advantage under the EU Directive to approximate trademark laws,[48] which specifically required "unfair advantage" as a possible harm inflicted upon marks having a reputation in the Member States. When the hearing was resumed in the UK, Jacob LJ expressed his strong disapproval of the CJEU's oversight:

> So far as I can see this is saying if there is "clear exploitation on the coat-tails" that is ipso facto not only an advantage but an unfair one at that. In short, the provision should be read as though the word "unfair" was simply not there. No line between "permissible free riding" and "impermissible free riding" is to be drawn. All free riding is "unfair" [...] As I have said I do not agree with or welcome this conclusion – it amounts to a pointless monopoly. But my duty is to apply it.[49]

Jacob LJ's duty as a national judge is to follow EU law as interpreted by the CJEU, even if the result is regrettable.[50] As his Lordship put it,

> I believe the consequence of the [CJEU] decision is that the EU has a more "protective" approach to trademark law than other major trading areas or blocs. I have not of course studied in detail the laws of other countries, but my general understanding is, for instance, that countries with a healthy attitude to competition law, such as the US, would not keep a perfectly lawful product off the market by the use of trademark law to suppress truthful advertising.[51]

In the above statement, the word "protective" is used sarcastically to portray Jacob LJ's view that the CJEU decision has the effect of discouraging honest advertising, a result that is unhealthy in his Lordship's opinion.

With the benefit of hindsight, Brexit might be a blessing for UK intellectual property owners and lawyers, who are no longer subject to the CJEU's whimsical approach in defining exclusive rights and exceptions. The above cases also illustrate that the success or otherwise of statutory amendments depends on judges' inclination as much as it does on the draftsman's efforts. It will tilt the balance towards judicial interpretation (which can be risky, as shown above) if the current elaborate list of exclusive rights and exceptions is replaced by a rudimentary criterion of commercial or reasonable exploitation.

---

[45]   *Nils Svensson and Others*, *supra* note 39, at para. 20.
[46]   Ibid at para. 25: "it must be observed that making available the works concerned by means of a clickable link, such as that in the main proceedings, does not lead to the works in question being communicated to *a new public*" (emphasis added).
[47]   [2010] R.P.C. 1.
[48]   First Council Directive 89/104/EEC of 21 December 1988 to approximate the laws of Member States relating to trademarks.
[49]   *L'Oreal SA v Bellure NV* [2010] EWCA Civ 535, [2010] R.P.C. 23 at paras 49–50.
[50]   Ibid at para. 7.
[51]   Ibid at para. 20.

3.3   Consensus is Needed

Even if we are lucky enough to have impeccable wording in the proposed statute and reliable judicial bodies to pronounce its intended meaning, no copyright reform can go ahead without consensus. And we need consensus in two different senses.

First, we need consensus across jurisdictions. To tackle unprecedented issues of law and technology, merely perfecting the copyright law of one jurisdiction is not enough. AI and digital technology are potentially trans-jurisdictional. One deepfake video, for example, can transcend geographical boundaries and affect multiple jurisdictions simultaneously. Thus, cross-jurisdictional consensus or harmonization is needed more than ever. Yet, none of the reform proposals has taken this practical need into consideration. Professor Litman, for example, in her book *Digital Copyright*[52] criticizes the startling conclusions of the US White Paper[53] and proposes the sole right of commercial exploitation as an alternative. The proposal is made against the backdrop of US copyright lobbying and the Congress's responses over the years. It is also influenced by the US tradition of permitting fair use,[54] an open-ended concept dependent upon the judicial sense of fairness on a case-by-case basis. Such a versatile approach is already markedly different from that in the rest of the world. Had the fluid concept of commercial exploitation overtaken the US copyright regime, it would have made it even harder for copyright holders to enforce their rights across jurisdictions.

Second, we also need consensus among different sectors within the same jurisdiction. This is sometimes easier said than done. In Hong Kong, for instance, it has taken more than a decade to introduce the much-needed right of communication to the public and the consultation is still ongoing.[55] It all started in 2006 with a public consultation which led to the 2008 preliminary proposals,[56] the 2009 proposals for strengthening copyright protection in the digital environment,[57] and eventually the Copyright (Amendment) Bill 2011, which purported to impose civil as well as criminal liability on anyone who, without the copyright owner's permission, communicated a copyright work to the public (1) for the purpose of or in the course of any trade or business that consisted of communicating works to the public for profit or reward, or (2) to such an extent as to affect prejudicially the copyright owner.[58] Had it

---

[52]   LITMAN, *supra* note 3.

[53]   BRUCE LEHMAN, INTELLECTUAL PROPERTY AND THE NATIONAL INFORMATION INFRASTRUCTURE: THE REPORT OF THE WORKING GROUP ON INTELLECTUAL PROPERTY RIGHTS (1995).

[54]   Copyright Act 1976, 17 U.S.C. § 107.

[55]   After two unsuccessful attempts to legislate for communication to the public (discussed below), a three-month public consultation on updating Hong Kong's copyright regime was launched on Nov. 24, 2021: COMMERCE AND ECONOMIC DEVELOPMENT BUREAU (H.K.), PRESS RELEASE, Nov. 24, 2021, www.info.gov.hk/gia/general/202111/24/P2021112400481.htm.

[56]   COMMERCE AND ECONOMIC DEVELOPMENT BUREAU (H.K.), PRELIMINARY PROPOSALS FOR STRENGTHENING COPYRIGHT PROTECTION IN THE DIGITAL ENVIRONMENT   (2008),   www.ipd.gov.hk/eng/intellectual_property/copyright/Consultation _Document_Prelim_Proposals_Eng(full).pdf.

[57]   COMMERCE AND ECONOMIC DEVELOPMENT BUREAU (H.K.), PROPOSALS FOR STRENGTHENING COPYRIGHT PROTECTION IN THE DIGITAL ENVIRONMENT (2009), www .cedb.gov.hk/assets/resources/citb/consultations-and-publications/Panel_Paper_Digital_Eng_Full.pdf.

[58]   Copyright (Amendment) Bill 2011 (H.K.), https://www.legco.gov.hk/yr10-11/english/bills/ b201106033.pdf.

been enacted, this communication right would have superseded the extant "making available" provision (with only civil liability) of the Copyright Ordinance,[59] achieving the irrefutable goal of toughening online copyright protection. Envisioned by Article 8 of the World Intellectual Property Organization ("WIPO") Copyright Treaty,[60] such a right should be uncontroversial, and the Bill should have been passed without much difficulty. Unexpectedly, there was considerable opposition to the proposal, mainly from netizens and satirists, who lamented that the criminalization of non-commercial activities would inhibit the free flow of information, suppress free speech, and stymie Hong Kong's development as an internet services hub.[61] To everyone's dismay, the well-intended consultation was hijacked by political debates,[62] and the Bill was held up by pan-democrat lawmakers who refused to cast their votes unless and until a parody exception was added.

Even when such an exception was proposed three years later, covering parody, satire, caricature, and pastiche,[63] still no consensus could be reached among different sectors of the community. It was not the drafting that held up the process, as the Copyright (Amendment) Bill 2014 ("2014 Bill") was expressed in the most neutral language:[64]

(1) Fair dealing with a work for the purpose of parody, satire, caricature or pastiche does not infringe any copyright in the work.
(2) In determining whether any dealing with a work is fair dealing under subsection (1), the court must take into account all the circumstances of the case and, in particular —
  (a) the purpose and nature of the dealing, including whether the dealing is for a non-profit-making purpose and whether the dealing is of a commercial nature;
  (b) the nature of the work;
  (c) the amount and substantiality of the portion dealt with in relation to the work as a whole; and
  (d) the effect of the dealing on the potential market for or value of the work.

---

[59] Copyright Ordinance (1997) Cap. 528 (H.K.). Since 1997, Hong Kong has imposed civil liability on anyone who, without authorization, makes available copies of copyright works to the public, by wire or wireless means: Ibid, section 26.

[60] The WIPO Copyright Treaty was concluded in 1996 and entered into force in 2002. Although the Treaty was not yet officially applicable to Hong Kong when its Copyright Ordinance took effect in 1997, the incorporation of the "making available" right was considered to be consistent with Hong Kong's continuing endeavor to adhere to international standards: ALICE LEE, BUTTERWORTHS HONG KONG COPYRIGHT HANDBOOK (3d ed. 2011).

[61] Alice Lee and Brendan Clift, *From Fair Dealing to User-Generated Content: Legal La La Land in Hong Kong*, in THE CAMBRIDGE HANDBOOK OF COPYRIGHT LIMITATIONS AND EXCEPTIONS (Shyamkrishna Balganesh, Ng-Loy Wee Loon & Haochen Sun ed., 2021).

[62] Wenwei Guan, *When Copyrights Meet Human Rights: 'Cyberspace Article 23' and Hong Kong's Copyright Protection in the Digital Era*, 42 HONG KONG L.J. 785 (2012); Yiu-chung Wong, *'Super Paradox' or 'Leninist Integration': The Politics of Legislating Article 23 of Hong Kong's Basic Law*, 30 ASIAN PERSPECTIVE 65 (2006). The Basic Law of the Hong Kong Special Administrative Region was adopted on Apr. 4, 1990, by the Seventh National People's Congress of the People's Republic of China and came into effect on Jul. 1, 1997. Article 23 provides that Hong Kong "shall enact laws on its own to prohibit any act of treason, secession, sedition or subversion" against the Central Government of the People's Republic of China.

[63] Copyright (Amendment) Bill 2014 (H.K.), www.gld.gov.hk/egazette/pdf/20141824/es32014182421.pdf.

[64] Ibid, the proposed section 39A.

This proposed exception is not only broader in scope than its counterpart in the UK,[65] but also incorporates the same four factors as those in the US fair use provision[66] as relevant consideration. From any perspective, it is a well thought-out provision.

As if the parody-satire-caricature-pastiche exception were not comprehensive enough, two further exceptions for "quotation"[67] and "commenting on current events"[68] were tabled before the Hong Kong Legislative Council. Seemingly addressing the concerns raised before, the 2014 Bill was still filibustered by pan-democrat lawmakers, who escalated their demand from a specific parody exception to a blanket exemption for non-commercial user-generated content,[69] leading to the Bill's demise in 2016.[70]

There is no good reason for Hong Kong to procrastinate on passing amendments to update its Copyright Ordinance, which is seriously lagging behind international development, especially in relation to protection in the digital environment.[71] Not only is it one of the first Asian jurisdictions to have legislated for the "making available" right,[72] but Hong Kong has also overtaken London as the second largest contemporary art auction market in the world after New York.[73] Why would any Hongkonger, let alone lawmaker, want to halt the legislative process? Commentators[74] generally hold the view that it was due to the conflation of copy-

---

[65]　Copyright, Designs and Patents Act 1988 (UK), section 30A (inserted in 2014) provides that fair dealing with a work for the purposes of caricature, parody or pastiche does not infringe copyright in the work. It has left out satire.

[66]　Copyright Act 1976, 17 U.S.C. § 107.

[67]　Copyright (Amendment) Bill 2014 (H.K.), *supra* note 63, the proposed section 39(2): "Copyright in a work is not infringed by the use of a quotation from the work (whether for the purpose of criticism, review or otherwise) if (a) the work has been released or communicated to the public; (b) the use of the quotation is fair dealing with the work; (c) the extent of the quotation is no more than is required by the specific purpose for which it is used; and (d) (subject to subsection (6)) the use of the quotation is accompanied by a sufficient acknowledgment." Subsection (6) provides that it is not necessary to accompany the relevant dealing with a sufficient acknowledgment if it is not reasonably practicable to do so.

[68]　Ibid, the proposed section 39(3): "Fair dealing with a work for the purpose of reporting or commenting on current events does not infringe any copyright in a work or, in the case of a published edition, in the typographical arrangement, if (subject to subsection (6)) the dealing is accompanied by a sufficient acknowledgment." This is much broader than the current Copyright Ordinance, which exempts only reporting but not commenting.

[69]　Alice Lee and Brendan Clift, *supra* note 61, at 373. See also Wenwei Guan, *Fair Dealing Doctrine Caught between Parody and UGC Exemptions: Hong Kong's 2014 Copyright Amendment and Beyond*, 45 HONG KONG L.J. 719 (2015).

[70]　Stuart Lau and Vivienne Chow, *Blame Game Begins as Hong Kong Copyright Bill Shelved Indefinitely*, SOUTH CHINA MORNING POST, Mar. 4, 2016, https://www.scmp.com/news/hong-kong/politics/article/1920593/blame-game-begins-hong-kong-copyright-bill-shelved; Chantel Yuen, *Copyright Bill Fails to Pass before Gov't Imposed Deadline*, HONG KONG FREE PRESS, Mar. 4, 2016, https://www.hongkongfp.com/2016/03/04/copyright-bill-fails-to-pass-before-govt-imposed-deadline.

[71]　KENNY WONG AND ALICE LEE, INTELLECTUAL PROPERTY LAW AND PRACTICE IN HONG KONG (2017), para. 3.552.

[72]　ALICE LEE, *supra* note 60, at 77. The WIPO Copyright Treaty was concluded in Dec. 1996 while the Copyright Ordinance took effect on Jun. 27, 1997, three days before the change of sovereignty.

[73]　Payal Uttam, *Hong Kong's Art Market Emerges from a Tumultuous Year with Optimism*, ARTSY, Nov. 25, 2020, www.artsy.net/article/artsy-editorial-hong-kongs-art-market-emerges-tumultuous-year-optimism.

[74]　Kris Cheng, *Gov't Says New Copyright Law Will Not Resist Speech amid Concerns of Parody Ban*, HONG KONG FREE PRESS, Dec. 3, 2015, https://hongkongfp.com/2015/12/03/govt-says

right law with the perceived government interest in controlling speech – a perception that is misconceived but understandable, given the socio-political environment in Hong Kong back in 2014.[75]

4. HOW TO SUPPORT AUTHORS AND USERS IN THE AGE OF AI

The biggest lesson learned from the above examples is that copyright reform is not a purely legal or semantic problem.[76] Even if the best legal terms are chosen, other factors might creep in and spoil the legislation. To clear up the public's doubts about the hoped-for parody exception, the Hong Kong administration has compared the UK, Australian, New Zealand, Canadian, and US approaches[77] and concluded that keywords such as "parody," "satire," "caricature," and "pastiche" need not be defined in the statute.[78] There is nothing controversial about this. For ordinary English words, it is common practice to rely on their dictionary meaning.[79] However, the opposition lawmakers were so distrustful of the Bill's objective that they boycotted the 2014 Bill for want of a clear statutory definition for the keywords.

If dictionary-defined terms "parody"[80] and "satire"[81] are criticized as unclear, it is hard to see how fluid phrases such as "commercial exploitation" or "reasonable exploitation" could ever make it to the statute book. The reform proposals are too idealistic in assuming that the

---

-new-copyright-law-will-not-restrict-speech-amid-concerns-of-parody-ban/; Stuart Lau, *Hong Kong Copyright Bill Explained: Why Are People So Concerned about This?*, SOUTH CHINA MORNING POST, Dec. 17, 2015, www.scmp.com/news/hong-kong/politics/article/1888931/hong-kong-copyright -bill-explained-why-are-people-so.

[75] Alice Lee and Brendan Clift, *supra* note 61, at 374. See also Peter K. Yu, *The Quest for a User-Friendly Copyright Regime in Hong Kong*, 32 AM. U. INT'L L. REV. 283 (2016).

[76] "The victory for pan-democrats and internet users who were distrustful of the bill's objective and implications concluded a heated political battle": Stuart Lau, *Five Reasons the Hong Kong Copyright Bill Failed*, SOUTH CHINA MORNING POST, Mar. 4, 2016, www.scmp.com/news/hong-kong/politics/ article/1920569/five-reasons-hong-kong-copyright-bill-failed. See also Kris Cheng, *Copyright Bill Officially Withdrawn after Months of Filibustering*, HONG KONG FREE PRESS, Apr. 15, 2016, https:// hongkongfp.com/2016/04/15/copyright-bill-officially-withdrawn-after-months-of-filibustering/.

[77] COMMERCE AND ECONOMIC DEVELOPMENT BUREAU (H.K.), TREATMENT OF PARODY UNDER THE COPYRIGHT REGIME: CONSULTATION PAPER (2013), www.cedb.gov .hk/assets/resources/citb/consultations-and-publications/Consultation_Paper_English.pdf.

[78] COMMERCE AND ECONOMIC DEVELOPMENT BUREAU (H.K.), LEGISLATIVE COUNCIL BRIEF: COPYRIGHT (AMENDMENT) BILL 2014, CITB 07/09/17 (2014), www.ipd.gov .hk/eng/intellectual_property/copyright/LegCo_Brief_2014_e.pdf.

[79] Ibid at 1. No jurisdiction has defined "parody" or similar terms in statute. In any event, literal interpretation is the starting point in statutory interpretation, see DAVID FELDMAN, DIGGORY BAILEY & LUKE NORBURY, BENNION, BAILEY AND NORBURY ON STATUTORY INTERPRETATION (8th ed. 2020).

[80] Parody is defined as "an imitation of the style of a particular writer, artist or genre with deliberate exaggeration for comic effect; a travesty": CONCISE OXFORD ENGLISH DICTIONARY (12th ed. 2012), cited in COMMERCE AND ECONOMIC DEVELOPMENT BUREAU (H.K.), *supra* note 78, at 1.

[81] Satire is defined as "the use of humor, irony, exaggeration, or ridicule to expose and criticize people's stupidity or vices; a play, novel, etc. using satire—(in Latin literature) a literary miscellany, especially a poem ridiculing prevalent vices or follies": CONCISE OXFORD ENGLISH DICTIONARY

current list of exclusive rights can be reduced to a simpler hierarchy or even a single yardstick, that the wording of the proposed regime can be uniformly construed and easily understood by all the stakeholders, and that there is a common interest or consensus among different sectors of the public. Instead of theorizing about top-down legislative overhaul, there are two pragmatic steps we can take to help stakeholders understand their rights against one another in the age of AI.

4.1   Speak Their Language

In the digital environment, the author, owner, or user of a copyright work could be a child playing with a smartphone or someone maintaining their social media profile. They may or may not care about exploitation or remuneration for use of their work. Some may even welcome circulation of their work, such as YouTubers, who tend to crave attention, fame, peer recognition, or satisfaction more than monetary reward. For many netizens, in particular digital natives, commercial exploitation may be a bonus but not the primary incentive for what they do in the virtual world. Thus, recasting copyright law as a right of commercial exploitation or other ill-defined concept is not going to encourage creativity or facilitate the dissemination of copyright works within reasonable limits.

A more efficient way to incentivize and support authors and users is to speak their language in the consultative and legislative process. For instance, "text and data mining" or "text and data analysis" is widely used to refer to the use of automated techniques to analyze text, data, and other legally accessible content to generate insights and information that may not have been possible to obtain through manual effort.[82] There is consensus as to its meaning, and Japan was the first jurisdiction to introduce a "text and data mining" exception in its statute,[83] followed by the UK[84] and the EU.[85] The latest attempt is that of Singapore, where a new bill was passed in 2021 to permit the making of copies for computational data analysis.[86] Notably, the Singaporean exemption covers all research purposes, commercial or otherwise, and is praised as "a balanced exception"[87] acknowledging that "the distinction between commercial

---

(12th ed. 2012), cited in COMMERCE AND ECONOMIC DEVELOPMENT BUREAU (H.K.), *supra* note 78, at 1.

[82]   COMMERCE AND ECONOMIC DEVELOPMENT BUREAU (H.K.), CONSULTATION PAPER: UPDATING HONG KONG'S COPYRIGHT REGIME, Nov. 24, 2021, www.ipd.gov.hk/eng/ intellectual_property/copyright/Consultation_Paper_on_Copyright_Eng.pdf. The Hong Kong administration has included "text and data mining" in its list of possible new issues for further studies: Ibid at 31.

[83]   The Japanese Copyright Law first introduced a text and data mining exception in 2009 (article 47-7) and extended it in 2018 to acts "not for enjoying or causing another person to enjoy the ideas or emotions expressed in such work" (article 30-4).

[84]   Copyright, Designs and Patents Act 1988 (UK), section 29A (inserted in 2014) permits the making of copies for text and data analysis for non-commercial research.

[85]   Directive (EU) 2019/790 of the European Parliament and of the Council of 17 April 2019 on copyright and related rights in the Digital Single Market and amending Directives 96/9/EC and 2001/29/ EC.

[86]   Singapore Copyright Act 2021, sections 243 and 244, https://sso.agc.gov.sg/Acts-Supp/22-2021/ Published/20211007?DocDate=20211007.

[87]   European Alliance for Research Excellence, *Singapore's New Text and Data Mining Exception will Support Innovation in the Digital Economy*, Jul. 20, 2021, https://eare.eu/singapores-new-text-and -data-mining-exception-will-support-innovation-in-the-digital-economy/.

and non-commercial research is artificial and does not reflect the reality of today's research ecosystem."[88] This confirms that commercial exploitation is not the sole or primary concern in the age of AI.

In the EU, efforts have also been made to "strive for a balanced approach"[89] in tackling AI-related legal issues. Following the publication of a White Paper,[90] the European Commission launched a broad stakeholder consultation in 2020 for interested parties from the public and private sectors, including governments, local authorities, commercial and non-commercial organizations, social partners, experts, academics and ordinary citizens to express their views on policy options as to "how to achieve the twin objective of promoting the uptake of AI and of addressing the risks associated with certain uses of such technology."[91] Such an extensive consultation ensures that the resulting proposal is based on EU values and consistent with fundamental rights and existing Union legislation on data protection, consumer protection, non-discrimination, and gender equality.[92] A holistic and stakeholder-informed consultative process is more likely to yield practicable legal solutions than any of the reform proposals discussed above.

4.2   Be Their Partners

After consensus is reached on the direction of legislation, authors of creative works still need to figure out what they can do or waive under enacted laws. They are not empowered unless and until they are informed of their entitlements. Creative Commons is the first international non-governmental network devoted to educating authors across jurisdictions about their economic and moral rights[93] and creating a user-friendly and jargon-free environment for them to exercise their rights by choosing their preferred license conditions.[94] Launched in 2001 in the US, Creative Commons has matured into a global movement spanning 86 countries, has developed and stewarded legal tools and licenses, and has unlocked more than two billion works that can be openly and freely shared.[95] It is a participatory network for authors, academics, researchers, and anyone committed to open access to collaborate as volunteers.

---

[88] Ibid.

[89] EUROPEAN COMMISSION, PROPROSAL FOR A REGULATION OF THE EUROPEAN PARLIAMENT AND OF THE COUNCIL LAYING DOWN HARMONISED RULES ON ARTIFICIAL INTELLIGENCE (ARTIFICIAL INTELLIGENCE ACT) AND AMENDING CERTAIN UNION LEGISLATIVE ACTS (2021).

[90] EUROPEAN COMMISSION, WHITE PAPER ON ARTIFICIAL INTELLIGENCE – A EUROPEAN APPROACH TO EXCELLENCE AND TRUST (2020).

[91] Ibid at para. 1.1.

[92] Ibid at para. 1.2.

[93] Currently, there are 48 Creative Commons chapters all over the world: https://network .creativecommons.org/chapter/.

[94] "Attribution," "Non-commercial," "No Derivatives," and "Share-like" are the four basic license conditions, which may be used on their own or in various combinations: https://creativecommons.org/about/cclicenses/.

[95] Catherine Stihler, *A Message from our CEO to the CC Community on Creative Commons' 20th Anniversary*, Dec. 19, 2021, https://creativecommons.org/2021/12/19/a-message-from-our-ceo-to-the-cc -community-on-creative-commons-20th-anniversary/.

Licensing bodies and collective management organizations ("CMOs")[96] can also play a supporting or even leading role in enhancing copyright literacy among creators. It cannot be assumed that authors and composers are well versed in such fundamental concepts as authorship and ownership, the distinction between assignments and licenses, or the different treatment of employee works and commissioned works[97] (also known as "works made for hire"[98]) under copyright law. They would not be able to comprehend, let alone endorse, any reform proposal that focuses on commercial or reasonable exploitation unless they know what their rights and options are under the current regime.

While many national CMOs have spread copyright knowledge through their websites, publications, or multimedia resources, usually the information they provide is limited to the nuts and bolts of claiming copyright in a particular jurisdiction. In the digital age, when cross-border creation and dissemination are more frequent than ever, a comparative approach will better serve the interests of authors of creative works. In 2019, a cross-jurisdictional research on the buyout practices in the music industry in Asia Pacific was conducted under the auspices of the International Confederation of Societies of Authors and Composers ("CISAC")[99] and the Asia-Pacific Music Creators Alliance ("APMA").[100] In the context of musical copyright, "buyout" refers to the increasingly common practice of television, film, or game production companies requiring the composer to surrender any possibility of future royalties in exchange for a single upfront lump-sum fee.[101] The research findings,[102] including a comparison of the laws and buyout practices in eight jurisdictions,[103] are disseminated through a regional crea-

---

[96]   A collective management organization is an organization which is authorized by law or by way of assignment, license, or any other contractual arrangement to manage copyright or rights related to copyright on behalf of more than one right holder, for the collective benefit of those right holders, as its sole or main purpose; and is either owned or controlled by its members or is organized on a not-for-profit basis, or both: Collective Management of Copyright (EU Directive) Regulations 2016 (UK), reg. 2(1).

[97]   In jurisdictions such as the UK and Hong Kong, the employer is presumed to be the owner of any copyright in an employee work while the author of a commissioned work may rely on the default position that he is the first owner of copyright: Copyright, Designs and Patents Act 1988 (UK), section 11(1) and (2); Copyright Ordinance, (1997) Cap. 528 (H.K.), sections 13, 14 and 15.

[98]   Not to mention the different durations for copyright protection in different jurisdictions. In the US, for instance, a work made for hire (published after 1978) receives copyright protection until 120 years after creation or 95 years after publication, whichever comes first: Copyright Act 1976, 17 U.S.C. § 302. In other jurisdictions, the duration is measured with reference to the life of the author; for example, life plus 70 years in the UK or life plus 50 years in Hong Kong.

[99]   Confédération Internationale des Sociétés d'Auteurs et Compositeurs (CISAC), with its headquarters in France and regional offices in Asia Pacific, Africa, Europe, and South America, represents 232 CMOs and more than four million creators in five repertoires (music, drama, literature, audiovisual, and visual arts): www.cisac.org/.

[100]   APMA represents music creators in 19 countries and territories in Asia Pacific: https://apmaciam.wixsite.com/home/about-apma-e.

[101]   CISAC, *Asia Pacific International Symposium Highlights Need for Global Education on Copyright Buyouts and Issues: Five Key Recommendations*, Mar. 26, 2021, www.cisac.org/Newsroom/articles/asia-pacific-symposium-on-copyright-buyout.

[102]   ALICE LEE, COPYRIGHT BUYOUT IN THE MUSIC INDUSTRY: A COMPARATIVE STUDY OF THE ASIA-PACIFIC REGION (2019), https://159b4c65-c258-49b0-b26c-026518ec70b3.filesusr.com/ugd/987693_35262f4ffde64325b7b43b8431b44b7d.pdf.

[103]   Australia, Hong Kong, Indonesia, Japan, Macau, South Korea, Thailand, and Vietnam. In phase two of the study, the buyout practices in Cambodia, China, India, Malaysia, Singapore, Taiwan, and the Philippines are to be examined.

tors' seminar,[104] an online public symposium,[105] and the websites of CISAC and APMA.[106] Both organizations[107] see great value in educating composers and songwriters about unfair contracts, the revocability of buyout contracts in case of lack of exploitation, legal provisions on creators' right to equitable remuneration, ownership of copyright in employee and commissioned works, and moral rights, as well as the availability of public education campaigns on copyright issues in the regions surveyed.[108]

As well as driving copyright education projects, CMOs can partner with creators for greater impact and synergy. Since 2021, CISAC's partnership with "Your Music Your Future," a campaign initiated by US composers to educate fellow creators, has elevated it to international level—it is now a global community with more than 15,000 supporters from all over the world.[109] After all, what creators need is not only a piece of legislation dedicated to their protection but also the ability to understand and exercise their rights and options under the legal framework: "Each creator can make their own business decisions—but what is critical is having the right information to decide what works best for you."[110]

5.   THE WAY FORWARD

AI and digital technology have drastically changed the ways by which copyright-protected works can be created, shared, and used, but does this mean that copyright law should be radically reformed?[111] Some proposals are discussed in this chapter, and they all assume that a shorter copyright statute will benefit the AI technology-infused community. Be it "commercial exploitation," "reasonable exploitation," or "dissemination-centric," all proponents hold the view that a few keywords or a single yardstick can surpass the current system, which they believe is overladen with verbose provisions.

This chapter proposes a more pragmatic and stakeholder-centric approach to copyright reform. To identify the way forward, it must first be acknowledged that the current regime does provide a balanced ecosystem for authors to flourish and users to respect creativity, and

---

[104]   Creators' Seminar in Macau, organized by APMA, Nov. 27–28, 2019, https://apmaciam.wixsite.com/home/20191129e.

[105]   Copyright Symposium on "Buyouts in Asia," Mar. 25, 2021, co-organized by APMA, CISAC, and the Japanese Society for Rights of Authors, Composers and Publishers.

[106]   www.cisac.org/Newsroom/articles/asia-pacific-symposium-on-copyright-buyout;   https://apmaciam.wixsite.com/home/20191129e.

[107]   CISAC president Björn Ulvaeus, who is a member of the legendary band ABBA, and APMA chairman and composer Tokura Shunichi share the vision that "young songwriters […] need to be educated and advised on what it could mean to them if they go for a buyout": CISAC, *supra* note 101.

[108]   A comparative study of all these issues is included in the buyout research report: ALICE LEE, *supra* note 102.

[109]   "Your Music Your Future International" is reaching out to creators in many other countries and supported by the International Council of Music Creators: https://international.yourmusicyourfuture.com/.

[110]   Your Music Your Future International, *How Do Copyright Buyouts Affect You?*, https://international.yourmusicyourfuture.com/composer-compensation/.

[111]   Some even suggest a new *sui generis* right for AI-created works: *see* Redesigning Intellectual Property Protection in the Era of Artificial Intelligence, an online symposium organized by the University of Hong Kong, Jan. 26, 2022.

that existing statutes can be revised to meet the needs of digital natives. Incremental changes are more stakeholder-friendly than an overnight overhaul of copyright law. Over the years there have been a number of well-crafted provisions which are dedicated to solving emerging issues in the digital environment, such as the right of communication to the public, which, if properly construed, can empower copyright holders to restrain unauthorized dissemination on the internet without compromising the free flow of information. It is the overinterpretation in a series of EU cases that unexpectedly stretches its meaning beyond the draftsman's intention.

Contrary to the aforesaid proponents' view, length is not the problem with copyright statutes; vagueness is. It is understandable that technology-neutral provisions are needed to tackle novel problems,[112] but that does not mean that we should sacrifice certainty for flexibility. As shown in the prolonged consultation process in Hong Kong, the intended recipients of the amendment bills called for detailed definitions as they preferred legal certainty to judicial improvisation. Brief and vague keywords such as commercial or reasonable exploitation are likely to be voted down for lack of certainty. Short is not sweet when it comes to delineation of rights and exemptions.

To prevent legislative or interpretational mishaps, the proposed rights or exemptions must be stated in the clearest terms possible. Some jurisdictions have even included concrete illustrations in the text of the statute when new concepts are introduced. In Hong Kong, for instance, the "making available" provision[113] contains an example as follows to assist the readers:

> References in this Part to the making available of copies of a work to the public are to the making available of copies of the work, by wire or wireless means, in such a way that members of the public in Hong Kong or elsewhere may access the work from a place and at a time individually chosen by them *(such as the making available of copies of works through the service commonly known as the INTERNET).*[114]

The italicized example facilitated a contextualized reading of the section back in 1997 when the concept of "making available" was relatively new.[115] In Singapore, the newly added text and data-mining provisions[116] also contain real-life illustrations to help readers decipher the technical phrases "computational data analysis"[117] and "having lawful access to the material from which the copy is made."[118]

In the digital age, many authors and composers are publishing or distributing their works on social media platforms and hence need to familiarize themselves with their statutory protection. Some might even form their own alliances, such as "Your Music Your Future," and

---

[112]   EUROPEAN COMMISSION, *supra* note 89, at para. 5.2.1: "The definition of AI system in the legal framework aims to be as technology neutral and future proof as possible, taking into account the fast technological and market developments related to AI."

[113]   Copyright Ordinance, (1997) Cap. 528 (H.K.), section 26, *supra* note 59.

[114]   Ibid section 26(2) (emphasis added).

[115]   Section 26 was enacted in 1997, shortly after the WIPO Copyright Treaty 1996: *supra* note 60.

[116]   Singaporean Copyright Act 2021, sections 243 and 244, *supra* note 86.

[117]   Ibid section 243: "An example of computational data analysis under paragraph (b) [of the definition] is the use of images to train a computer program to recognize images."

[118]   Ibid section 244: "Illustrations: (a) X does not have lawful access to the first copy if X accessed the first copy by circumventing paywalls; (b) X does not have lawful access to the first copy if X accessed the first copy in breach of the terms of use of a database."

pass on the knowledge they have acquired to fellow creators. A stakeholder-driven educational campaign is the most reliable way to ensure that well-intended copyright enactments can serve their purpose and pave the way for a copyright utopia where copyright is understood and respected by everyone.[119]

---

[119] Alice Lee, *From Fair Dealing to Fair Use to UGC: Three Steps to Copyright Reform or Pseutopia?*, presentation at NUS-UPenn-HKU Conference on Comparative Dimensions of Limitations and Exceptions in Copyright Law (Jul. 21–22, 2016).

10. The protection of AI-generated pictures (photograph and painting) under copyright law

Yaniv Benhamou and Ana Andrijevic

1. INTRODUCTION

Artificial intelligence (AI),[1] especially deep learning technologies,[2] is increasingly used by AI artists in various artistic fields.[3] Among its many possible uses in the arts (for example, in the creation of music, poems, screenplays, and many others),[4] AI can generate new pictures or transform them[5] through generative adversarial networks (GANs), among other generative models,[6] which fall under the rubric of algorithmic art.[7]

However, the creation or transformation of pictures with GANs also raises questions in the area of copyright, especially when it comes to using pictures as "inputs" to train GANs and the protection of AI-generated "outputs." This contribution concentrates on copyright, with a particular focus on the analysis of the criterion of originality, and on other intellectual property rights (IPR) (such as trade secrets and unfair competition), but leaves aside other legal aspects, such as ethics, privacy, and data protection (for example, when traditional cultural expressions or an individual's image are used). The analysis herein is from a comparative law perspective without focusing on a specific jurisdiction and applicable law, as legal regimes vary from one

---

[1] NILSSON Nils J., The Quest for Artificial Intelligence: A History of Ideas and Achievements, New York (Cambridge University Press), 2010, p.13: "AI is that quality that enables an entity to function appropriately and with foresight in its environment. According to that definition, lots of things—humans, animals, and some machines—are intelligent."

[2] According to GOODFELLOW Ian, BENGIO Yoshua, COURVILLE Aaron, Deep Learning, Cambridge (MA) (The MIT Press), 2016, pp.1 and 2, deep learning is the solution that allows computers to learn from experience and understand the world in terms of a hierarchy of concepts that enables the computer to learn complicated concepts by building them out of simpler ones and to avoid the need for human operators. See also FOSTER David, Generative Deep Learning: Teaching Machines to Paint, Write, Compose and Pay, Sebastopol, CA (O'Reilly), 2019, p.31, who explains that deep learning uses multiple stacked layers of processing units to learn high-level representations from unstructured data, which refers to any data that is not naturally arranged into columns of features, such as images, audio, and text.

[3] https://aiartists.org/.

[4] Ibid.

[5] In the framework of this contribution, we rely on the definitions of the online Cambridge dictionary (https://dictionary.cambridge.org/), which provides that a photograph is "a picture produced using a camera," whereas a picture is defined more broadly as "a drawing, painting, photograph, etc."

[6] FOSTER David, Generative Deep Learning: Teaching Machines to Paint, Write, Compose and Pay, Sebastopol, CA (O'Reilly), 2019, p.1, defines a generative model as follows: "A generative model describes how a dataset is generated, in terms of a probabilistic model. By sampling from this model, we are able to generate new data."

[7] BRIDY Annemarie, The Evolution of Authorship: Work Made by Code, Colum. J.L. & Arts, Vol.95, 2016, p.397. Other models have since appeared with similar attributes to GANs but GANs are still one of the best performing generative models for picture generation.

jurisdiction to another. However, particular attention is given to US and EU law, given their influence beyond borders and the fact that they represent two typical different legal regimes (common and civil–continental law).

2. TECHNOLOGICAL CONSIDERATIONS

2.1 What Is a Generative Adversarial Network (GAN)?

In 2014, Goodfellow et al. proposed a new framework for estimating generative models[8] via the adversarial GAN process, which involves the simultaneous training of two models. It became one of the best structures for picture generation.

A GAN can be seen as a non-cooperative game[9] between two neural networks, trained together in competition with each other.[10] On one side, the generator network (the art forger)[11] learns to generate plausible samples[12] from random noise[13] and is trained to fool the discriminator network (the art expert)[14] into believing its outputs are real data.[15] On the other side, the discriminator learns to distinguish the generator's fake, that is, generated data from real data[16] but as the generator's training progresses over time, the accuracy of the discriminator decreases and it gets worse at telling the difference between the two.[17] The networks that represent the generator and the discriminator are typically implemented by multi-layer networks consisting of convolutional layers,[18] which are extremely well suited to picture data, and/or

---

[8] GOODFELLOW Ian J., POUGET-ABADIE Jean, MIRZA Mehdi, XU, Bing, WARDE-FARLEY David, OZAIR Sherjil, COURVILLE Aaron, BENGIO Yoshua, Generative Adversarial Nets, 2014. Available online at: https://papers.nips.cc/paper/2014/file/5ca3e9b122f61f8f06494c97b1afccf3-Paper.pdf. FOSTER, p.1, defines a generative model as follows: "A generative model describes how a dataset is generated, in terms of a probabilistic model. By sampling from this model, we are able to generate new data." See also GOODFELLOW et al., p.1: "The generative model can be thought of as analogous to a team of counterfeiters, trying to produce fake currency and use it without detection, while the discriminative model is analogous to the police, trying to detect the counterfeit currency. Competition in this game drive bother teams to improve their methods until the counterfeits are indistinguishable from the genuine articles."

[9] SALIMANS Tim, GOODFELLOW Ian, ZAREMBA Wojciech, CHEUNG Vicki, RADFORD Alec, CHEN Xi, Improved Techniques for Training GANs, 10 June 2016, p.2. Available online at: https://arxiv.org/pdf/1606.03498.pdf.

[10] CRESWELL Antonia, WHITE Tom, DUMOULIN Vincent, ARULKUMARAN Kai, SENGUPTA Biswa, BHARATH Anil A., Generative Adversarial Networks: An Overview, April 2017, p.1.
Available online at: https://arxiv.org/pdf/1710.07035.pdf

[11] CRESWELL et al., p.1.

[12] See GOOGLE, Overview of GAN Structure provided by Google, April 29, 2019.
Available online at: https://developers.google.com/machine-learning/gan/gan_structure.

[13] CRESWELL et al., p.8.

[14] Ibid, p.1.

[15] SALIMANS et al., p.1. See as well GOODFELLOW, On Distinguishability Criteria for Estimating Generative Models, 21 May 2015, p.1. Available online at: https://arxiv.org/pdf/1412.6515.pdf.

[16] SALIMANS et al., p.1.

[17] Overview of GAN Structure provided by Google, 29 April 2019. Available online at: https://developers.google.com/machine-learning/gan/gan_structure.

[18] As explained by GATYS Leon A., ECKER Alexander S., BETHGE Matthias, A Neural Algorithm of Artistic Style, 2 September 2015, p.2. Available online at: https://arxiv.org/pdf/1508.06576.pdf: "(c) onvolutional neural networks consist of layers of small computational units that process visual informa-

fully connected layers used by the first GAN architectures and applied to relatively simple picture datasets.[19]

During the training process, the generator has no direct access to real pictures and only learns through its interaction with the discriminator, whereas the latter has access both to the synthetic sample provided by the generator and to the samples drawn from the stack of real pictures.[20] The generator is deemed optimal when the discriminator can no longer distinguish real samples from fake ones.[21] In the end, where the discriminator is optional, it may be discarded to focus solely on the generator.[22] This sort of "non-cooperative game"[23] will ultimately lead to the creation of a new picture, the output.[24]

2.2   Different Steps of a GAN

In this part of our contribution, we describe in simple terms how to generate new pictures with GANs by highlighting key steps that will be useful for our legal analysis.[25] The first three stages are grouped under the more global term of "input," while the fourth stage constitutes the "output" stage.

The first step focuses on the selection, loading, and processing of pictures, mostly photographs (*selection phase*). For this first step, a training dataset[26] is identified and downloaded, for instance from a website or a repository.[27] This dataset comprises multiple examples, called

---

tion hierarchically in a feed-forward manner. Each layer of units can be understood as a collection of image filters, each of which extracts a certain feature from the input image. Thus, the output of a given layer consists of so-called feature maps: differently filtered versions of the input image."

[19]   CRESWELL et al., p.3. For an explanation on fully connected layers, see RAMSUNDAR Bharath, ZADEH Reza Bosagh, TensorFlow for Deep Learning, March 2018, O'Reilly Media, Inc., Chapter 4. Available online at: www.oreilly.com/library/view/tensorflow-for-deep/9781491980446/ch04.html. As explained, a fully connected neural network consists of a series of fully connected layers where each output depends on each input dimension, or in other words, every neuron in one layer is connected to every neuron in the previous or next layer.

[20]   CRESWELL et al., p.1.

[21]   Ibid, p.6.

[22]   Ibid, p.1.

[23]   JIWOONG IM Daniel, DONGJOO KIM Chris, JIANG Hui, MEMISEVIC Roland, Generating images with recurrent adversarial network, p.2. Available online at: https://arxiv.org/pdf/1602.05110.pdf.

[24]   Overview of GAN Structure provided by Google, 29 April 2019. Available online at: https://developers.google.com/machine-learning/gan/gan_structure.

[25]   Please note that the objective of this description is not to provide a detailed understanding of the function of GANs models but rather to focus on keys steps. The order of the different steps is based on the description provided by FOSTER, pp. 33–58.

[26]   SHRESTHA Anish, Generating Model Art using Generative Adversarial Network (GAN) on Spell, November 13, 2019. Available online at: https://towardsdatascience.com/generating-modern-arts-using -generative-adversarial-network-gan-on-spell-39f67f83c7b4. The author suggests using a dataset available on the WikiArt website: https://www.wikiart.org/. To see more about their copyright policy: www .wikiart.org/en/about. See also RADFORD et al., 2016, p.4, who used dbpedia (https://www.dbpedia.org/) to scrape "images faces from random web images queries of people names. The people names were acquired from dbpedia, with a criterion that they were born in the modern era."

[27]   https://github.com/cs-chan/ArtGAN/tree/master/WikiArt%20Dataset. In his book, FOSTER suggests using the CIFAR-10 dataset, a collection of 60,000 32x32 pixel color images. The dataset is available at www.cs.toronto.edu/~kriz/cifar.html and is also mentioned in GOODFELLOW et al, p.6 and SALIMANS et al, pp.1 and 6. See also the MNIST database available at http://yann.lecun.com/exdb/

samples, which can range from pictures of animals[28] to street numbers, airplanes, automobiles,[29] house numbers,[30] and more (the *image data*). As for the processing of image data, the data engineer[31] would need, for instance, to resize the data to feed it into the GAN.[32]

The second step focuses on programming and consists of building the neural network model using Keras,[33] for instance, which is a high-level Python library for building neural networks (*programming phase*).[34] At this stage, the software engineer or programmer[35] will set up the architecture of the neural network without confronting it with the picture data.[36]

The third step is dedicated to the training of the neural network (*training phase*) by machine learning engineers,[37] where the data is shown to the neural network.[38] Thus, the neural network will be trained with the picture data, which will be passed through several times.[39] During the training phase, the picture data is gradually transformed by the neural network.[40]

The final stage is the generation of the output (*generation phase*), where new pictures are generated by the neural network, which combines the possible creative choices of the designers, that is, the data engineer, the software engineer and the machine learning engineer, at the selection phase and the programming phase, as well the work of the neural network.[41] In addition, the user[42] can have an important impact on the final output of a neural network as they can, for instance, choose the picture and the filter to apply.[43]

---

mnist/, mentioned also in GOODFELLOW et al., p.7 and SALIMANS et al., pp.1 and 7, which also mentions the SVHN dataset (The Street View House Numbers Dataset), available at http://ufldl.stanford.edu/housenumbers/ on pp.1 and 7, "a real-world image dataset for developing machine learning and object recognition algorithms with minimal requirement on data preprocessing and formatting [...]. SVHN is obtained from house numbers in Google Street View images." See also ImageNet, available at: www.image-net.org/about.php where it is clearly stated: "ImageNet does not own the copyright of the images. ImageNet only compiles an accurate list of web images for each synset of WordNet. For researchers and educators who wish to use the images for non-commercial research and/or educational purposes, we can provide access through our site under certain conditions and terms." More information at: www.image-net.org/download.

[28] http://vision.stanford.edu/aditya86/ImageNetDogs/.
[29] https://www.cs.toronto.edu/~kriz/cifar.html.
[30] http://ufldl.stanford.edu/housenumbers/.
[31] See ANDERSON Jesse, Data engineers vs. data scientists, 11 April 2018. Available online at: www.oreilly.com/radar/data-engineers-vs-data-scientists/.
[32] FOSTER, pp.35–7.
[33] https://keras.io/.
[34] FOSTER, p.34.
[35] The "programmer" is also called "data engineer" or "software engineer" and has a programming background. For more, see note 33.
[36] FOSTER, p.43.
[37] See note 37.
[38] FOSTER, pp.43 and 44.
[39] Ibid.
[40] https://developers.google.com/machine-learning/gan/applications. If we take for instance the example of "Progressive GANs," the generator's first layers produce very low-resolution images, and subsequent layers add details.
[41] For interesting visual examples, see https://developers.google.com/machine-learning/gan/applications. The functioning of Deep Dream Generator is explained in section 2.3.
[42] We refer to "the user" to define the person who will use a platform that allows the use of a neural network, such as a GAN, to generate or transform pictures.
[43] This is typically the case with Deep Dream Generator: https://deepdreamgenerator.com/. This example is further explained in section 2.3.

2.3   Examples of GANs and Related Models

Since their creation in 2014[44] many popular deep learning models for picture generation have used GANs architecture, even though, as we will see, other models exist. For this contribution, we introduce a few examples and use some of them to illustrate our legal analysis.

Among some of the best-known early GAN models is Pix2Pix, an image-to-image translation using conditional GANs that can convert black-and-white images to colour images, or Google Maps to Google Earth images.[45] In 2015 Google researchers created one of the flagship visualization tools, DeepDream,[46] which uses a convolutional neural network (CNN)[47] to create unique pictures by transforming pre-existing ones. In the framework of this project, Google trained an artificial neural network by showing it millions of examples. The researchers explained the functioning of the 10–30 stacked layers of artificial neurons where "Each image is fed into the input layer, which then talks to the next layer, until eventually the 'output' layer is reached. The network's 'answer' come[s] from this final output layer."[48]

More importantly in terms of the decision-making process of the neural network, the researchers purposefully let the network decide which feature it wanted to amplify in the image; this led to an unpredictable result. The researchers explained that instead of prescribing exactly which feature they wanted the network to amplify, they let the network make that decision.[49] They started with an existing image, gave it to the neural network, and asked it what it saw. Thus, if a neural network is mostly trained on images of animals, it will naturally tend to interpret shapes of animals in any subsequent image it is given. For instance, if an image of a cloud looks like a bird, the network will reinforce this aspect.[50]

In June 2017 researchers from the Art & AI Laboratory at Rutgers University proposed a new system for generating art, built over GANs, entitled creative adversarial networks (CANs), whose goal is to "investigate a computational creative system for art generation without involving a human artist in the creative process, but nevertheless involving human

---

[44]   See note 8.

[45]   Isola Phillip, Zhu Jun-Yan, Zhou Tinghui, Efros Alexei A., Image-to-Image Translation with Conditional Adversarial Networks. Available online at: https://arxiv.org/pdf/1611.07004.pdf.

[46]   https://deepdreamgenerator.com/.

[47]   Guadamuz Andres, Do Androids Dream of Electric Copyright? Comparative Analysis of Originality in Artificial Intelligence Generated Works, Intellectual Property Quarterly, 2017, Vol. 2, p.3. Available online at: https://papers.ssrn.com/sol3/papers.cfm?abstract_id=2981304. See also Barua Sukarna, Monazam Erfani Sarah, Bailey James, FCC-GAN: A Fully Connected and Convolutional Net Architecture for GANs, May 27, 2019, p.1. Available online at: https://arxiv.org/pdf/1905.02417.pdf. The authors explain the connection between GANs and CNNs as follows: "GAN models for image synthesis have adopted a deep convolutional network architecture, which eliminates or minimizes the use of fully connected and pooling layers in favor of convolutional layers in the generator and discriminator of GANs."

[48]   Mordvinstev Alexander, Olah Christopher, Tyka Mike, Inceptionism: Going Deeper into Neural Networks, June 17, 2015. Available online at: https://ai.googleblog.com/2015/06/inceptionism-going-deeper-into-neural.html.

[49]   Ibid.

[50]   Ibid. The researchers end this contribution by stating: "It also makes us wonder whether neural networks could become a tool for artists—a new way to remix visual concepts—or perhaps even shed a little light on the roots of the creative process in general."

creative products in the learning process."[51] It was followed in 2018 by the development of StyleGAN,[52] created by Nvidia[53] researchers, which allows for a finer control of images and for the generation of new pictures, such as portraits of human beings[54] but also pictures of animals, for example cats,[55] and many more.[56] Nowadays, GAN applications can range from anime character generation, 3D object generation, image editing, and face aging[57] to the colourization of pictures.[58] One of the latest models created by OpenAI,[59] DALL·E, a transformer language model, was trained to create images from text descriptions using a dataset of text–image pairs that allows the manipulation of visual concepts through language.[60]

As we can see, GANs have undergone significant developments since their creation in 2014. However, given the similarities between these examples in terms of the general functioning of GANs in the main steps,[61] we only use a limited number of these examples to illustrate our legal analysis from the input to the output stage.

3.   LEGAL ANALYSIS: USING IMAGE DATA AS INPUTS AND AI-GENERATED OUTPUTS UNDER COPYRIGHT LAW

3.1   Input

In this section, we first focus on the legal protection when it comes to using image data as inputs, in particular in each phase of the GANs, that is, the selection, programming, and training phases.

---

[51]   ELGAMMAL Ahmed, LIU Bingchen, ELHOSEINY Mohamed, MAZZONE Marian, CAN: Creative Adversarial Networks, Generative "Art" by Learning About Styles and Deviating from Style Norms, June 21, 2017, pp.1 and 2. Available online at: https://arxiv.org/pdf/1706.07068.pdf.

[52]   KARRAS Tero, LAINE Samuli, AILA Timo, A Style-Based Generator Architecture for Generative Adversarial Networks, 29 March 2019. Available online at: https://arxiv.org/pdf/1812.04948.pdf.

[53]   www.nvidia.com/.

[54]   See for instance https://portraitai.com/, which precises that "art generated by portraitai.com is completely free to use for any purpose," or https://generated.photos/, which displays "unique, worry-free model photos" and underlines that "all images can be used for any purpose without worrying about copyrights, distribution rights, infringement claims, or royalties." See also note 52.

[55]   https://thesecatsdonotexist.com/.

[56]   https://github.com/ak9250/stylegan-art.

[57]   https://github.com/nashory/gans-awesome-applications#real-time-face-reconstruction.

[58]   https://github.com/hindupuravinash/the-gan-zoo.

[59]   https://openai.com/blog/dall-e/.

[60]   As explained on https://openai.com/blog/dall-e/, DALL· E uses both GPT-3, an unsupervised learning algorithm using GAN, which "showed that language can be used to instruct a large neural network to perform a variety of text generation tasks," and Image GPT, which "showed that the same type of neural network can also be used to generate images with high fidelity."

[61]   See section 2.2.

3.2   Selection Phase

In the selection phase, copyright may protect copyrighted data (such as text, pictures, music) with sufficient originality (*copyrighted data*).[62] The originality standard usually requires a certain threshold or degree of creativity, which may vary from one jurisdiction to another.[63]

Consequently, when copyrighted data are used in the selection phase, such use may trigger copyright protection, at least according to a strict interpretation of the reproduction right, which covers in most jurisdictions identical, partial, direct, or indirect act of reproduction by any means, in whole or in part.[64]

Copyright may also protect compilation of data (for example, public or private repository, dataset or database), if their selection or arrangement is original (*copyrighted dataset*),[65] even when the individual data lacks copyright protection (for example, because it is not original or is a public domain work). Eligibility for copyright protection may be difficult, however, as the

---

[62]   In international law, see article 2 (1) of the Berne Convention for the Protection of Literary and Artistic Works (as amended on September 28, 1979) (*"literary and artistic works shall include every production in the literary, scientific and artistic domain, whatever may be the mode or form of its expression"*). In EU law, see GERVAIS Daniel, Exploring the Interfaces Between Big Data and Intellectual Property Law, JIPITEC Vol.10, No.1, 2019, N 8 ff. In Swiss law, see article 2 (1) of the Swiss Copyright Act (*"Works are literary and artistic intellectual creations with an individual character, irrespective of their value or purpose"*); DE WERRA Jacques, BENHAMOU Yaniv, Kunst und geistiges Eigentum, in MÖSIMANN / RENOLD / RASCHÈR (ed.), Kultur, Kunst Recht: Schweizerisches und internationales Recht, Basel, 2020, 707 ff.

[63]   In EU law, see MARGONI Thomas, The Harmonisation of EU Copyright Law: The Originality Standard, May 25, 2016. Available online at: http://eprints.gla.ac.uk/129447/. In Swiss law, see DE WERRA / BENHAMOU (n 62), p.710. See section 3.2.1.

[64]   See in EU law, article 2 of the Directive 2001/29/EC of the European Parliament and of the Council of 22 May 2001 on the harmonization of certain aspects of copyright and related rights in the information society (hereinafter: Copyright Directive 2001/29/CE) ("exclusive right to authorise or prohibit direct or indirect, temporary or permanent reproduction by any means and in any form, in whole or in part"). For alternative approaches, see BENHAMOU Yaniv, Big Data and the Law: A Holistic Analysis based on a Three-step approach—Mapping Property-like Rights, Their Exceptions and Licensing Practices, RSDA 2020, 405, with references to case-law and suggesting shifting from this broad interpretation of the reproduction right to a perceptibility approach (that is, copyright does not apply to most text and data mining activities, as the input is not recognizable in the output) or an economic approach (that is, copyright does not apply to text and data mining activities, as the initial input is not used *per se* but only for its informational content).

[65]   See article 10 (2) of the World Trade Organization's Agreement on Trade-Related Aspects of Intellectual Property Rights (hereinafter : TRIPS Agreement) (*"Compilations of data or other material, whether in machine readable or other form, which by reason of the selection or arrangement of their contents constitute intellectual creations"*). In Switzerland, such databases can be protected as collected works defined at article 4 (1) Swiss Copyright Act (*"creations with individual character with regard to their selection and arrangement"*). In the EU, article 3 (1) of the Directive 96/9/EC of the European Parliament and of the Council of 11 March 1996 on the legal protection of databases (hereinafter : Database Directive) (*"Databases which, by reason of the selection or arrangement of their contents, constitute the author's own intellectual creation shall be protected as such by copyright"*). In the US, Title 17 USC s. 101 Copyright Act protecting compilation (defined as *"work formed by the collection and assembling of pre-existing materials or of data that are selected, coordinated, or arranged in such a way that the resulting work as a whole constitutes an original work of authorship"*).

level of investment is irrelevant for the originality[66] and the simple collection of data unaltered for a new database may be insufficient for the threshold of originality.[67] Moreover, copyright protection usually requires an intellectual human intervention and the consciousness of achieving a result, which excludes databases automatically created by an algorithm.[68]

Consequently, the careful original selection of pre-existing data or databases may qualify as copyrighted dataset, and hence be protected (an example might be the most representative images of a collection). However, the random selection of pre-existing data or the automatic selection used solely for training purposes may lack copyright protection, as the selection may not meet the condition of originality with respect to the condition of human intervention. It is specified that, generally, the more image data processed, the better the GAN works, so that the GAN mostly selects and loads as much data as possible, at least from one style or one author, instead of carefully selecting specific image data of one type. In other words, selections of image data are often based on technical considerations rather than creative choices,[69] and it could be demonstrated that these selections were not merely technical considerations but rather free and creative choices.[70]

3.3   Programming Phase

With respect to the programming phase, copyright may protect elements of the software that are original (such as original source code, object code and associated documentation). Again, the originality standard varies from one jurisdiction to another, with certain jurisdictions requiring a very low level of creativity for software protection or even assuming a protection

---

[66] For instance, in Switzerland copyright protection has been denied, despite investments made, for a compendium of drugs, a telephone directory, and logarithmic tables (case-law quoted by GILLIÉRON Philippe, in DE WERRA / GILLIÉRON (ed.), Commentaire Romand de la Propriété intellectuelle, Basel 2013, N 6 *ad* article 4). In the EU, see article 3 (1) of the EU Database Directive. In the US, see Feist Publications, Inc., v Rural Telephone Service Co, 499 U.S. 340 (1991), 344 (hereinafter: Feist Publications).

[67] MAIER Robert / SIBBLE Joshua, Big Data Handbook: A Guide for Lawyers, Wolters Kluwer Legal & Regulatory, May 2018, p.23.

[68] Case C-604/10, Football Dataco Ltd and Others v Yahoo! UK Ltd and Others, [2012] ECLI:EU: C:2012:115 (hereinafter: Football Dataco), par.38. It is however important to distinguish between works created with the assistance of a computer (that is, regular works just like books created with the assistance of a pen, or movies created with the assistance of a camera) and computer-generated works (CGW) (that is, works generated by computer in circumstances such that there is no human author of the work).

[69] See for instance JONES Kenny, GANGogh: Creating Art with GANs, June 18, 2017. Available online at: https://towardsdatascience.com/gangogh-creating-art-with-gans-8d087d8f74a1. The author explains that the researchers had to choose an appropriate dataset of paintings which was a crucial decision. They first experimented with using a dataset of paintings that were only from one artist: Monet. However, after a few initial tests, they found that their "models on this dataset were converging poorly as the dataset with only 1200 paintings was too small." They choose to use the Wikiart database instead, which is a collection of more than 100,000 paintings.

[70] Football Dataco, par.38. See also Feist Publications, 348, which provides that the criterion of originality is satisfied when the "choices as to selection and arrangement, so long as they are made independently by the compiler an entail a minimal degree of creativity, are sufficiently original that Congress may protect such compilations through the copyright laws." See as well Case Football Dataco, par.38: "As regards the setting up of a database, that criterion of originality is satisfied when, through the selection or arrangement of the data which it contains, its author expresses his creative ability in an original manner by making free and creative choice."

by default.[71] Copyright only applies to the original form of expression, not the idea or simple information embedded in a creative work, so that the underlying software is more likely to receive copyright protection than the individual data or database itself.[72]

3.4   Training Phase

With respect to the training phase, distinction is made depending on whether it relates to copyrighted data (for example, original image data or database) or non-copyrighted data (for example, pure technical training data or public domain work).

When the input is a copyrighted data or dataset,[73] its use in connection with the GAN triggers the right of reproduction and requires in principle the authorization of the rights owner, whether the input is simply used as training data (such as in the case of StyleGAN, which allows for the generation of portraits of human beings or animals[74]) or is recognizable in the output (such as an AI-generated painting in which one of the works used in the input could be recognized).[75] This is linked to the broad interpretation of the reproduction right.[76]

Moreover, copyright protection may be claimed in relation to the modification of certain pictures within the neural network, as the moral right of integrity includes the right to authorise or prohibit modification of the work by third parties and as certain images may be transformed during the "training phase."[77] This being said, the moral right of integrity could be difficult to claim. The scope of this moral right of integrity varies from one jurisdiction to another. In certain jurisdictions, it applies only to changes prejudicial to the honor or reputation of the author or is even non-existent in other jurisdictions, so that the changes in images may never

---

[71]   For instance in Swiss law, certain courts assume a software protection by default, the burden of proof belonging to the party denying software protection: see DE WERRA / BENHAMOU (note 62), p.710 and references made.

[72]   See for instance article 9 (2) TRIPS Agreement ("*Copyright protection shall extend to expressions and not to ideas, procedures, methods of operation or mathematical concepts as such*"). See however SCASSA Teresa, Data Ownership, in: CIGI Papers, No 187, September 2018, p.9, who considers that the idea/expression dichotomy (according to which copyright protection extends to the expression of ideas only) may be blurred. For instance, where the expression of a fact or an idea merges with that fact or idea (for example, where there is only one or a very limited number of ways to express it), there can be no copyright protection since the practical result of any such protection would be to give a monopoly over the fact or idea.

[73]   Above, section 3.1.1; also note 63.

[74]   Above, section 2.3.

[75]   In EU law, see article 2 Copyright Directive 2001/29/CE (the reproduction right covers the "*exclusive right to authorise or prohibit direct or indirect, temporary or permanent reproduction by any means and in any form, in whole or in part*"); Case C-5/08, Infopaq International vs Danske Dagblades Forening, [2009] ECLI:EU:C:2009:465 (hereinafter: Infopaq), par. 51; see STROWEL (note 2), p.12, indicating that the reproduction right may also apply, when the use relates to raw data embedded in a copyrighted file, as the underlying raw data often overlaps, if not merges, with the embedding copyrighted file for which copyright protection applies. In Swiss law, see article 10 (2) let. a Swiss Copyright Act (the reproduction right covers the right to "*produce copies of the work, such as printed matter, phonograms, audiovisual fixations or data carriers*"); see DE WERRA / BENHAMOU (note 62), p.753, giving the example of the Edmond de Balamy portrait based on 15,000 preexisting portraits or Google Dream trained on open access images.

[76]   Above, section 3.1.1.

[77]   Above, section 2.2.

be sufficiently prejudicial to trigger the moral right.[78] Even in jurisdictions applying the moral right to any changes, whether prejudicial or not, whether substantial or not (including copies with minor changes), such right is usually attached to the personality of the author. With the changes in images being made only within the neural network for pure training purposes and being not visible or even non-existent in the output data, the author will have difficulty in claiming that their personality is infringed.

To overcome these legal barriers, most copyright laws provide limitations and exceptions, such as the fair use exception in the United States and the specific European exception of text and data mining (TDM). This TDM exception is however subject to important restrictions: (i) it is limited to "scientific research" (which excludes primarily commercial purposes); (ii) the data shall be accessible (which excludes data or databases protected by TPM, or possibly by contract); (iii) it is often limited to the reproduction right (which excludes the communication of the results, at least when the input is reproduced in the output).[79]

When the input is not copyrighted data or a copyrighted dataset, such as technical data or public domain works, it is in principle freely usable. However, use of such input can be limited in certain situations. First, data producers can impose contractual restrictions or TPM, creating a kind of data exclusivity.[80] They can also claim their data to be a trade secret when the data meet the standards of trade secret protection, that is, when the data: (1) is secret; (2) has commercial value because it is secret; and (3) has been subject to reasonable steps by the rightful holder of the information to keep it secret (such as through confidentiality agreements

---

[78]   See BENHAMOU, Posthumous replications, p.151.

[79]   For example, in EU law, the Directive (EU) 2019/790 of the European Parliament and of the Council of 7 April 2019 on copyright and related rights in the Digital Single Market and amending Directive 96/9/EC and 2001/29/EC (hereinafter : DSM Directive) introduces two mandatory TDM exceptions: an TDM exception for scientific research (article 3) and a TDM for any purposes (article 4), it being specified that their implementation into national laws is still ongoing and that differences in transposition laws (for example, as to the beneficiaries and as to the validity of general terms and conditions restricting TDM) could hamper cross-border text and data mining activities. In US law, TDM seems justified by the fair use doctrine (§ 107 Copyright Act): see the decision Google Books, Supreme Court, 16 October 2015 where short extracts have been considered as "highly transformative," it being specified that it remains to be seen how this case-law will apply to TDM activities, as shown in the decision News Network, LLC v TVEyes, Inc., 7 March 2017, where the indexing by TVEyes of all programs (including those of Fox News) and the possibility to view extracts of 10mn have not passed the criteria of te fair use doctrine. For an overview of the TDM exceptions in different jurisdictions, BENHAMOU (note 64), p.405.

[80]   Such contractual restrictions have been considered as valid by the CJUE in the Ryanair v PR Aviation decision (Case C-30/14, Ryanair v PR Aviation, [2015] ECLI:EU:C:2015:10), Recital 39: "*it is clear from the purpose and structure of Directive 96/9 that Articles 6 (1), 8 and 15 thereof, which establish mandatory rights for lawful users of databases, are not applicable to a database which is not protected either by copyright or by the sui generis right under that directive, so that it does not prevent the adoption of contractual clauses concerning the conditions of use of such a database*"); DE WERRA Jacques, Patents and Trade Secrets in the Internet Age, in: RDS, 2015, p.173. RDS, 2015, p. 173. See however the decision Google v Oracle, 5 April 2021, where the US Supreme Court held that the use of Oracle's Java API by Google for Android was a fair use and did not violate copyright laws, although the companies did not agree on the terms of use. This decision suggests that in the US it may be difficult for companies to impose contractual restrictions on publicly available data (such as open data, APIs). For an analysis of open data and open licenses applicable to AI (including ownership and liability), see Benhamou Yaniv, Intelligence artificielle: licence libre et gouvernance collective des données à travers l'altruisme des données et les data trusts, RSDA 2021, 419.

and/or physical and technical restrictions on access).[81] This could even be the case of trivial data, which might gain value through the new data analysis tools that find patterns and accordingly propose ads or services, and thus may qualify for trade secret protection.[82] Eligibility for trade secret protection may however be difficult. First, the concept of accessibility (or non-accessibility) is affected when the information may be easily accessed by using Internet search tools and technologies.[83] Second, the standard of reasonableness may also be affected in the digital environment, where information is mostly stored electronically, either in-house or in the cloud, with a risk of data leakage, so that the information may not be considered reasonably protected.[84] Third, trade secrets are only legally protected in instances where someone has obtained the confidential information by illegitimate means (such as through spying, theft, or bribery).[85] A trade secret holder has only a right to prohibit certain behaviours (unlawful acquisition, use, or disclosure of the secret), but no exclusive rights, unlike IPR that grant exclusive rights that are legally enforceable.[86] Therefore, the trade secret holder cannot prevent competitors from copying and using the same solutions, or reverse engineering (that is, the process of discovering the technological principles of a device, object, or system through analysis of its structure, function, and operation).

Moreover, even when the data are publicly accessible (such as images taken from Facebook or Google), they may be protected through unfair competition laws in many countries,[87] or by

---

[81]   In international law, see article 39 TRIPS Agreement, which identifies the standards generally applicable. In Swiss law, see DE WERRA (note 80), p.164. In EU law, see article 2 (1) Directive 2016/943 of the European Parliament and of the Council of 8 June 2016 on the protection of undisclosed know-how and business information (trade secrets) against their unlawful acquisition, use and disclosure (hereinafter: Trade Secret Directive). Also, data that have not been yet disclosed may be protected by confidential agreements or, in the absence of a specific clause, by confidentiality undertakings provided by specific rules (for example, labor law sometimes provides an obligation to keep information secret), see BENHAMOU (note 64), p.399.

[82]   STROWEL, p.23, referring to the Recital 14 of the Trade Secret Directive that states that the protection applies to information that "*should have a commercial value, whether actual or potential.*" Data out of which relevant trends are extracted by big data tools, although trivial as such, can have a potential value.

[83]   See article 39 (2)(a) of the TRIPS: information not "*generally known among or readily accessible to persons within the circles that normally deal with the kind of information in question.*" See Sasqua Gr., Inc. v Courtney and Artemis, No. CV-10–528, 2010 WL 3613855 (E.D.N.Y. Aug. 2, 2010); DE WERRA (note 80), 176.

[84]   See article 39 (2)(c) of the TRIPS Agreement; DE WERRA (note 80), p.176.

[85]   DEBUSSCHE / CÉSAR, p.58.

[86]   Under the Trade Secret Directive, the trade secret protection is seen "*as a complement or as an alternative to intellectual property rights*" (Recital 2) which "*in the interest of innovation [...] should not create any exclusive right to know-how or information*" (Recital 16). See however STROWEL (note 2), p.23, indicating that the contractual practice in certain countries relating to trade secrets shows a stronger association with property (for example, common law countries using terms such as "assignment," "sale," or "asset transfers" for trade secrets) and that the Trade Secret Directive has the remedial aspect of a property-like protection (largely built on the IPR civil enforcement measures).

[87]   In Switzerland, databases may be protected in certain circumstances by the Swiss Act against Unfair Competition (UCA), in particular article 5 let. c UCA prohibiting the reuse of third-party work by technical processes without corresponding investments, see DE WERRA Jacques / BENHAMOU Yaniv, Propriété intellectuelle et concurrence déloyale. Analyse du droit suisse et perspectives de droit allemand, in: PUTTEMANS / GENDREAU / DE WERRA (ed.), Propriété intellectuelle et concurrence déloyale: les liaisons dangereuses? Brussels, 2017, pp.183–208, p.185. See below section 2.2.2.2.

a *sui generis* database right in the EU, in particular when they consist of a dataset.[88] Eligibility for unfair competition protection is however excluded, in particular when the third party user (*repreneur*) has made substantial investment or when the data producer covered his/her investments made,[89] and the *sui generis* database protection when only insubstantial parts of a database are used.[90]

To overcome these barriers, other data access flexibilities can be found in certain jurisdictions. This is particularly the case in Europe with sector-specific or horizontal instruments that aim to grant greater access to data, in particular with the free flow of non-personal data, the non-protection of public sector information (such as geographical information, statistics, weather data, data from publicly funded research projects, and digitized books from libraries), and government access to privately held data (such as machine-generated data with the Internet of Things (IoT)).[91] Finally, to ensure the effectiveness of these exceptions, some jurisdictions provide a "no-contractual-override" provision (that is, unenforceability of contrary contractual provisions that circumvent the safeguards provided by these exceptions).[92]

Public domain works (that is, copyrighted works for which the protection has expired) are usually not protected by copyright and can be in principle reused freely. That is why the Digital Single Market (DSM) Directive provides in article 14 that any act of reproduction of a visual public domain work is not subject to copyright or related rights, considering that visual public domain works contribute "to the access to and promotion of culture, and the access to cultural heritage" and that the protection of such reproductions in the digital environment would be "inconsistent with the expiry of the copyright protection of works."[93] Therefore, thanks to this provision, all users will be able to disseminate copies of visual public domain works with full legal certainty.[94] However, article 14 of the DSM Directive leaves open the possibility of protecting these works if "the material resulting from that act of reproduction is original in the sense that it is the author's own intellectual creation."[95] Moreover, in certain

---

[88]   Article 7 (1)–(2) of the Database Directive. The EU *sui generis* database right was developed to protect data producers' investments and to prevent free-riding on somebody else's investment in creating the database; see STROWEL (note 2), p.15.

[89]   DE WERRA / BENHAMOU (note 62), N 119 ff.

[90]   There is no definite answer as to how much data exactly constitutes a "whole or substantial part" of the database and answering this question will require a qualitative and quantitative analysis in each situation. See however, STROWEL (note 2), p.15, indicating that repeated and systematic "pumping" of individual data (which do not qualify as substantive part) could in certain conditions be prohibited under the database right (article 7 (5) Database Directive).

[91]   BENHAMOU (note 64), p.405 and the several references made.

[92]   Ibid.

[93]   Recital 53 of the DSM Directive. See also European Parliament legislative resolution of 26 March 2019 on the proposal for a directive of the European Parliament and of the Council on copyright in the Digital Single Market (COM(2016)0593 – C8-0383/2016 – 2016(0280(COD)), P8_TA-PROV(2019)0231, pp.51 and 116.

[94]   EUROPEAN COMMISSION, Questions and Answers—European Parliament's vote in favour of modernized rules fit for digital age, 26 March 2019, Brussels.

Available online at: https://ec.europa.eu/commission/presscorner/detail/en/MEMO_19_1849: "For instance, anybody will be able to copy, use and share online photos of paintings, sculptures and works of art in the public domain when they find in the internet and reuse them, including for commercial purposes or to upload them in Wikipedia."

[95]   Recital 53 of the DSM Directive, indicating that cultural heritage institutions should not be prevented from protecting postcards for instance.

jurisdictions, non-original photographs are protected by copyright or related rights, so that in these jurisdictions photographs of any kinds are subject to copyright or related rights and shall not be used in the absence of an exception or the permission of the right owners.[96]

3.5   Output

In this section, our analysis first focuses on the criterion of originality in the scope of AI-generated pictures. It is followed by an analysis of the creative choices made both by the designers and the users involved throughout the creative process up to the generation of the output (generation phase).

3.5.1   The criterion of originality in the scope of AI-generated pictures

The first ground-breaking decision of the Court of Justice of the European Union (CJEU) to clarify the contours of the EU originality standard was the *Infopaq* ruling,[97] in which the CJEU held that the protection of works such as computer programs, databases, or photographs presupposes that they are the "author's own intellectual creation."[98] In doing so, the CJEU refers to article 1(3) of Directive 91/250, article 3(1) of Directive 96/9,[99] and article 6 of Directive 2006/116,[100] which provide that computer programs, databases, or photographs are protected by copyright "only if they are original in the sense that they are their author's own intellectual creation."[101]

In *Painer*,[102] the CJEU further elaborated the concept of "author's own intellectual creation" in relation to portrait photographs. Thus, the CJEU held that, as regards a portrait photograph, "The photographer can make free and creative choices in several ways and at various points in its production"[103] and that consequently, a portrait photograph can be protected by copyright if such photograph is "an intellectual creation of the author reflecting his personality and expressing his free and creative choices in the production of that photograph."[104] However, in the context of the analysis of the criterion of originality of a database, the CJEU underlined

---

[96]   See for instance in Switzerland, article 2 al.3 bis of the Swiss Copyright Act ("Photographic depictions and depictions of three-dimensional objects produced by a process similar to that of photography are considered works, even if they do not have individual character").

[97]   See note 95.

[98]   Infopaq, par.34.

[99]   Directive 96/9/EC of the European Parliament and of the Council of 11 March 1996 on the legal protection of databases.

[100]   Directive 2006/116/EC of the European Parliament and of the Council of 12 December 2006 on the term of protection of copyright and certain related rights (hereinafter: Directive 2006/116/EC). Article 6 provides that "(p)hotographs which are original in the sense that they are the author's own intellectual creation shall be protected in accordance with Article 1. No other criteria shall be applied to determine their eligibility for protection. Member States may provide for the protection of other photographs." Recital 16 of the said Directive further explains that a photographic work within the meaning of the Berne Convention is deemed original if it displays the author's own intellectual creation reflecting his personality. No other criteria such as merit or purpose shall being considered.

[101]   Infopaq, par.35.

[102]   Case C-145/10, Eva-Maria Painer v. Standard VerlagsGmbH, Axel Springer AG, Süddeutsche Zeitung GmbH, Spiegel-Verlag Rudolf Augstein GmbH & Co KG, Verlag M. DuMont Schauberg Expedition der Kölnischen Zeitung GmbH & Co KG, [2011] ECLI:EU:C:2011:798 (hereinafter: Painer).

[103]   Painer, par.90.

[104]   Ibid, par.94.

that the criterion was not satisfied when "The setting up of the database is dictated by technical considerations, rules or constraints which leave no room for creative freedom."[105]

Consequently, if we apply the criteria developed by the CJEU to portraits of human beings generated by StyleGANs[106] or similar models, it is necessary to determine whether at various points in the production of the picture with the neural network, the author[107] was able to make free and creative choices and create their own intellectual creation reflecting their personality. Nonetheless, the necessary originality will be absent if the features of a work are predetermined by its technical function,[108] that is, if the GAN automatically generates a picture without any creative choice made by the author throughout the process.

In the USA, the advent of photography confronted judges with a novel technology capable of operating with less human oversight[109] and led the US Supreme Court, in the 1884 case *Burrow-Giles Lithographic Co. v Sarony*, to extend copyright protection to photography for the first time.[110] The camera used to capture a picture of the writer Oscar Wilde was regarded by the US Supreme Court as a tool that aided the author in creating an original work of art,[111] even though it was first said that "The photograph is the mere mechanical reproduction of the physical features or outlines of some object [...] and involves no originality of thought or any novelty in the intellectual operation connected with its visible reproduction in shape of a picture."[112] The US Supreme Court ruled in favor of the photographer, who depicted his

> own original mental conception to which he gave visible form by posing the said Oscar Wilde in front of the camera, selecting and arranging the costume, draperies, and other various accessories in said photograph, arranging the subject so as to present graceful outlines, arranging and disposing the light and shade, suggesting and evoking the desired expression, and from such disposition, arrangement, or representation.[113]

The US Supreme Court concluded that photographs could be protected by copyright "as far as they are representatives of original intellectual conceptions of the author."[114]

However, these fairly demanding requirements diminished considerably[115] with *Feist*,[116] a landmark case in which the US Supreme Court held that originality, "the bedrock principle of copyright,"[117] means only "that the work was independently created by the author (as opposed

---

[105]   Case C-604/10, Football Dataco Ltd and Others v Yahoo! UK Ltd and Others, 1 March 2012, par.39. ECLI:EU:C:2012:115. See also Opinion of Advocate General Mengozzi delivered on 15 December 2011, par.40. ECLI:EU:C:2011:848.

[106]   See note 52.

[107]   On the various actors involved in the creation of a picture generated by GANs, see section 3.2.2.

[108]   Case C-393/09, Bezpečnostní softwarová asociace, [2010] ECLI:EU:C:2010:816, par.49.

[109]   Available online at: https://papers.ssrn.com/sol3/papers.cfm?abstract_id=3032076.

[110]   Burrow-Giles Lithographic Co. v Sarony, 111 U.S. 53, 58-59 (1884).

[111]   For more, see Hristov Kalin, Artificial Intelligence and the Copyright Dilemma, The IP Law Review, Vol.57, No.3, 2017, p.435.

[112]   See note 110.

[113]   Ibid, 55.

[114]   Ibid, 58.

[115]   Sobel Benjamin, A Taxonomy of Training Data in: Hilty / Lee / Liu, Artificial Intelligence and Intellectual Property (Reto eds), Oxford University Press, 2021. Draft available online at: https://papers.ssrn.com/sol3/papers.cfm?abstract_id=3677548

[116]   Feist Publications, 349.

[117]   Ibid, 347.

to copied from other works), and that it possesses at least some minimal degree of creativity."[118] The requisite level of creativity is therefore extremely low, which means that even a slight amount of creative expression will suffice.[119] Therefore, "the vast majority of works make the grade quite easily, as they possess some creative spark" but the author's expression cannot be "so mechanical or routine as to require no creativity whatsoever."[120] In addition, a work that it is "entirely typical," "garden-variety," or "devoid of even the slightest traces of creativity" does not satisfy the originality requirement.[121]

In 2001, the US Court of Appeals for the Third Circuit held in *Southco I* that even though the standard in *Feist* was not stringent, there is "a narrow category of works in which the creative spark is utterly lacking or so trivial as to be virtually nonexistent."[122] It concluded that Southco's part numbers fit within this "narrow category of works" that are incapable of sustaining a valid copyright given the fact that the numbers generated by Southco's system were the mere result of a mechanical application rather than creative thought.[123] The appellate body in *Southco II* concurred, underlining that the Southco product numbers were not original because they were dictated by the inflexible rules of the system.[124]

In Canada, the landmark Supreme Court of Canada case *CCH Canadian Ltd v Law Society of Upper Canada*,[125] reached a similar conclusion where it held that "(t)he exercise of skill and judgment required to produce the work must not be so trivial that it could be characterized as a purely mechanical exercise." As further explained, "(f)or example, any skill and judgment that might be involved in simply changing the font of a work to produce 'another' work would be too trivial to merit copyright protection as an 'original' work."[126]

In view of the foregoing, if one adheres to the criteria developed by the US Supreme Court, the US Court of Appeals for the Third Circuit, and the Supreme Court of Canada, it is required to demonstrate that the picture generated by GANs and similar models is hardly the result of a simple mechanical application but rather the expression of the author's creative thought and that it possesses a minimal degree of creativity. This could be argued if the GAN, like a camera or a pen, remains a tool of creation that could leave room for the author to express their creativity,[127] unless those choices are proven to be dictated by mechanical requirements.

Therefore, even though the assessment of the originality criterion varies across jurisdictions, ranging from the "author's own intellectual creation" in the EU to the USA's "minimal degree of creativity" test, we can note that from the point of view of both the judges of the CJEU and

---

[118] Ibid, 345 (1991). 17 U.S. Code §102 lit. a provides that "(c)opyright protection subsists, in accordance with the title, in original works of authorship."

[119] Feist Publications, 345.

[120] Ibid, 362. See as well UNITED STATES COPYRIGHT OFFICE, Compendium of U.S. Copyright Office Practices, Third edition, January 2021, Section 308, pp.8–9.

Available online at: www.copyright.gov/comp3/docs/compendium.pdf (hereinafter: Compendium of US Copyright Office Practices, 2021).

[121] Feist Publications, 362. See also the Compendium of US Copyright Office Practices, 2021, section 308.2, p.9.

[122] Feist Publications, 359.

[123] Southco, Inc. v Kanebridge Corp., 258 F.3d 148 (2001), 153 and 156.

[124] Southco, Inc., Appellant v Kanebridge Corporation, 390 F.3d 276 (3d Cir. 2004).

[125] CCH Canadian Ltd. v Law Society of Upper Canada, [2004] 1 S.C.R. 339, 2004 SCC 13.

[126] Ibid, par.16.

[127] FINK HEDRICK Samantha, I "Think," Therefore I Create: Claiming Copyright in the Outputs of Algorithms, in: NYU Journal of Intellectual Property & Entertainment Law, Vol. 8 No.2, 2019.

the North American courts there is a clear exclusion of, respectively, "technical" or "mechanical" considerations, which further reinforces the need for creativity to be clearly expressed by the author. However, given the diversity of actors involved in the creation of a neural network such as a GAN,[128] the major challenge will be to identify the creative choices, if any, made by various actors throughout the process and displayed in the output.[129]

Interestingly, some authors have debated the creative choices made by neural networks themselves. On one side, authors such as Guadamuz say that rather than being another technical advance, with the use of creative neural networks for creative purposes "(w)e are getting to the point at which vital creative decision are not made by humans, rather they are the expression of a computer learning by itself based on a set of parameters pre-determined by programmers."[130] Taking the opposite view, Ginsburg et al. argue that any "apparent creativity" in a machine's output is nothing more than the result of human decisions and is directly attributable either to the code written by the programmers who designed and trained the machine, or to the instructions provided by the users who operate the machine.[131] Along the same lines, other authors have contested the idea that neural networks can create visual works by pointing out the lack of perceptual abilities of these processes.[132] In fact, DeepDream researchers themselves have stated that neuronal networks are tools that could be used by artists,[133] which suggests a human prerogative over creative choices.

Therefore, if one adopts the latter approach, the focus should be on the creative choices made by human beings. In the following section, we analyze precisely these choices made by various actors, divided between the designers on one side and the users on the other, reflected in the output.

3.5.2   Creative choices of the designers and the users

As a matter of principle, copyright protects creative works of the human mind[134] and, therefore, the question is to determine whose (human) creativity infuses the output. Indeed, as we

---

[128]   See section 2.2.

[129]   See section 2.2.2.

[130]   GUADAMUZ, pp.1, 3 and 4. The author states: "(t)he next generation of artificial intelligence artists are based on entirely different advances that make the machine act more independently, sometimes even making autonomous creative decisions." See also KASAP Atilla, Copyright and Creative Artificial Intelligence (AI) Systems: A Twenty-first Century Approach to Authorship of AI-Generated Works in the United States, Wake Forest Journal of Business and Intellectual Property Law, Vol.19, No.4, 2019, p.348: "Some Skeptics take the position that even advanced programs are primarily confined to the possibilities already established in rules implemented by the original programmer."

[131]   GINSBURG Jane C., BUDIARDJO Luke Ali, Authors and Machines, Berkeley Technology Law Journal, Vol.34, 2019, p.402. Available online at: https://papers.ssrn.com/sol3/papers.cfm?abstract_id= 3233885.

[132]   HEATH Derrall / VENTURA Dan, Before A Computer Can Draw, It Must First Learn to See, Proceedings of the Seventh International Conference on Computational Creativity, June 2016, p.172. Available online at: www.computationalcreativity.net/iccc2016/wp-content/uploads/2016/01/Before-A -Computer-Can-Draw-It-Must-First-Learn-To-See.pdf.

[133]   MORDVINSTEV et al.: "It also makes us wonder whether neural networks could become a tool for artists—a new way to remix visual concepts—or perhaps even shed a little light on the roots of the creative process in general."

[134]   GINSBURG Jane C., Overview of Copyright Law, in: DREYFUSS / PILA (eds), Oxford Handbook of Intellectual Property Law, Oxford University Press, 2018. Available online at: https://scholarship.law .columbia.edu/faculty_scholarship/1990

have seen,[135] several actors can come into play and can make creative choices and influence the output from the conception to the deployment of the GAN. Therefore, the objective here is to highlight the actors who could claim copyright on various creative contributions throughout the making of AI-generated pictures.

Under the collective designation of "designers,"[136] we can mention first the figure of the data engineer who compiles individual data or databases, which, as we have seen, may be protected under copyright law if the selection or arrangement of individual data is original, even when the individual data lacks copyright protection (for example, because it is not original or is a public domain work).[137] In such case, the careful original selection of pre-existing data or databases may be protected and reflect itself in the final output (for example if the selection focuses on a specific painter, such as in the case of the Next Rembrandt[138]). However, it is unlikely that this selection alone could contribute to the originality of the output.

Second, we can also consider that the programmer (or software engineer), whose code can be protected under copyright law,[139] could, in the words of the CJEU, express "his free and creative choices in the production"[140] of the picture generated by a GAN. To illustrate this point we can evoke the famous painting created by Obvious Art, *Edmond de Belamy*,[141] which was created thanks to a GAN trained on a database of 15,000 portraits painted between the fourteenth and the twentieth centuries.[142] In this case, if we put aside the analysis of the originality of the code itself,[143] we can analyze which of the programmer's creative choices are actually reflected in the final output and therefore contribute to its originality.[144] In any case, we cannot exclude that "creative coding"[145] specifically designed to generate art could participate in the originality of the output if it can be shown that it reflects the programmer's intellectual creativity.

Insofar as there is no further intervention from users of GANs, the designers, or in other words those who formulate a creative plan manifested in the machines' algorithms and processes that will lead to the creation of expressive content,[146] can claim authorship of the resulting outputs. Ginsburg et al. explain as follows:

> The lack of a direct connection between the designers' minds and the expressive aesthetic content of the fully-generative machines' output does not destroy the designers' authorship claims any more

---

[135]   Above, section 2.2.

[136]   GINSBURG, BUDIARDJO, p.379.

[137]   Above, section 3.1.1.

[138]   www.nextrembrandt.com/.

[139]   Whose source code and object code are protected under copyright law, as explained in section 3.1.2 of this contribution.

[140]   Painer, par.94.

[141]   See CHRISTIE'S, Is artificial intelligence set to become art's next medium? 12 December 2018. Available online at: https://obvious-art.com/portfolio/edmond-de-belamy/.

[142]   See www.christies.com/features/A-collaboration-between-two-artists-one-human-one-a-machine -9332-1.aspx.

[143]   Above, section 3.1.2.

[144]   See note 143. Artist Mario Klingemann, who used GANs to generate new pictures, stated: "Part of my work is technological research. The results of which are usually not artistic but can have use in an artistic context."

[145]   See for instance the work of UC Santa Cruz Creative Coding Lab: https://creativecoding.soe.ucsc .edu/news.php.

[146]   GINSBURG, BUDIARDJO, p.379.

than the lack of a direct connection between the nature photographers' minds and the expressive aesthetic content of their works destroys those photographers' ability to claim authorship over their images. The designer of the fully-generative machine thus meets the "conception" requirement of authorship.[147]

Thus, if the output is not further modified by a third-party user, the analysis of the originality criterion should be limited to the designer's free and creative choices.

However, the "user," who can create new pictures thanks to GANs and similar models, may contribute in different ways. Indeed, if we take the example of Deep Dream Generator, the user has an important role in the process of creation insofar as they will upload a picture[148] and then select the type of filters they wish to apply (deep style; thin style; deep dream).[149] In this case, we will be in the category of generative machines that are "partially generative," whose output reflects the creative contributions of both the designer and the user.[150] Interestingly, Deep Dream Generator's terms and conditions provide that the platform does not claim ownership of any content posted on or through it by the users. Instead, the user grants a "non-exclusive, fully paid and royalty-free worldwide license" to use the user's content to show them on different places on the website (home page, latest feeds, some of their social networks, and so on).[151]

There are also instances where the user contributes to the creation of new pictures to a lesser extent. For instance, in the case of Generated Photos,[152] the platform provides a tool whereby the users, without providing a picture beforehand, will have either the possibility to "browse photos," that is, to choose pictures in the website database by selecting different characteristics such as head pose, sex, age, ethnicity; or instead to "generate a photo," in which case, the user will generate a new picture with a broader and finer range of features, in terms namely of emotion, skin tone, or hair length.[153] Therefore, the user might, at best, display their creative choices by using the features available on the platform to generate a picture. Whether the picture is browsed or generated by the user, the website provides that "permission is granted to download one copy of the materials (information or software) on Generated Photos' web site for personal, non-commercial usage only."[154] A paid license grants the licensee the ability to use the materials for commercial purposes.[155]

Therefore, in the case of Deep Dream Generator, the website provides that it is the user who grants a "non-exclusive, fully paid and royalty-free worldwide license" to use their content,[156] whereas with Generated Photos it is the platform that grants to the user either "permission" to

---

[147]   Ibid, p.414.

[148]   See the terms of use: https://deepdreamgenerator.com/terms. See the part entitled "Rights," par.4: "You represent and warrant that: (i) you own the Content posted by you on or through the Service or otherwise have the right to grant the rights and licenses set forth in these Terms of Use; (ii) the posting and use of your Content on or through the Service does not violate, misappropriate or infringe on the rights of any third party, including, without limitation, privacy rights, publicity rights, copyrights, trademark and/or other intellectual property rights."

[149]   https://deepdreamgenerator.com/.

[150]   GINSBURG, BUDIARDJO, p.418.

[151]   https://deepdreamgenerator.com/terms.

[152]   https://generated.photos/.

[153]   https://generated.photos/face-generator/new.

[154]   https://generated.photos/terms-and-conditions.

[155]   Ibid.

[156]   https://deepdreamgenerator.com/terms.

download one copy of materials created on their platform for personal usage or a paid licence to use the materials for commercial purposes. Consequently, when we compare both licensing regimes, we see that in the first case it is the user who grants a license whereas in the second case, it is the platform. We can thus wonder if this aspect could not be used in favor of the user of Deep Dream Generator, who could argue that their creative choices contribute to a greater extent to the originality of the output and could thereby justify that authorship be granted to them.

In sum, we see that the particularity of using AI tools lies in the number of creative choices that can be made at different stages of the process by different actors and reflected in the final output. We may therefore wonder how the development of AI-generated art works, including AI-generated pictures, can impact the analysis of the criterion of originality.

4.   SHOULD THE ANALYSIS OF THE CRITERION OF ORIGINALITY BE ADAPTED TO APPLY TO AI-GENERATED PICTURES?

In the section relating to input, we discussed the legality of using individual data and datasets, including the possibility to reverse the strict interpretation of the reproduction right towards an economic approach of the reproduction right. In the section relating to output, we considered the variety of actors involved in the creation of an AI-generated picture.

In the following section, we discuss the need to extend our understanding of the analysis of the originality requirement to integrate AI-generated pictures. Indeed, even though digital pictures are not new, the creation process of AI-generated pictures is very different from the one described in *Painer*, where the CJEU relies on a variety of "creative choices made by a photographer (e.g. the background, the subject's pose and the lighting, the framing, the angle of view and the atmosphere created, and the developing techniques used)."[157]

Therefore, if we compare the creative choices made by a photographer, as described in *Painer*, with those made by a user of Generated Photos,[158] the processes and the choices are significantly different. However, as discussed before,[159] the threshold of originality is quite low in various jurisdictions, including the USA and the EU, so that it cannot be ruled out that such a selection may constitute a sufficient creative contribution that would reach the threshold of originality. It seems to us, however, that users who create pictures simply by pressing a "generate" button on a website,[160] without selecting any preset features, should not benefit from copyright protection for the generated work given the complete lack of creative choices. Inversely, when users have an important part in the process of creation, they shall benefit from copyright protection for the generated work.

Thus, the question regarding AI-generated pictures is what is ultimately required of an author in order for them to benefit from copyright protection of their work. Therefore, rather than accommodating the analysis of the criterion of originality to integrate AI-generated pic-

---

[157]   Painer, par.91.
[158]   As described above in section 3.2.2.
[159]   See sections 3.1.2 and 3.2.1.
[160]   Which is also a possibility offered by the Generated Photos website. For more, see https://generated.photos/.

tures, the key question will be to determine the authorship and allocate the copyright between the variety of actors involved in the creation, such as between the data engineer (who compiles individual data or databases), the programmer (who codes the algorithm), and the user (who can contribute to a picture in different ways). The allocation of copyright between all actors will depend on their creative contribution and their level of coordination.[161]

5. CONCLUSION

In the context of this contribution, we have focused our legal analysis on the criterion of originality both at the input and output stages of the process of picture generation with GANs and similar models.

With respect to input, we have proposed a step-by-step analysis of the selection, programming, and training phases. As regards the selection phase, copyright may protect individual data with sufficient originality as well as compilation data if their selection is original. As regards the programming phase, copyright may protect elements of the software that are original. As regards the training phase, when the input is copyrighted data, its use in connection with the GAN triggers the right of reproduction and requires in principle the authorization of the rights owner, whether the input is simply used as training data or is recognizable in the output. However, in our view the moral right of integrity could be difficult to claim, especially when the changes in images within the neural network are done for pure training purposes and are not visible in the output data. In terms of what happens when the input is non-copyrighted data, we have discussed technical data and public domain works, and we have also presented other avenues of legal protection such as contractual restrictions, trade secrets, and unfair competition.

As for the output, we contend that human beings can only make creative choices insofar as they have expressed creative choices reflected in the output that exceed simple technical or mechanical applications. In this perspective we have distinguished the choices made on one side by the designers, more specifically the data engineer and software engineer, and on the other side by users. However, given the diversity of actors involved throughout the creation of a GAN and, by extension, the creation of the output, it remains difficult to distinguish in the result the creative choices made by each party. This will undoubtedly further complicate the issue of authorship, which will have to be determined on the basis of the analysis of the creative contributions made from the input to the output.

---

[161] E.g. in American law, see GINSBURG, BUDIARDJO, p.444; SHUNLING Chen, Collaborative Authorship: From Folklore to the Wikiblog, Journal of Law, Technology & Policy 2011, 132 ss.140. In Swiss law, see Benhamou, RSDA 2021, 423 (recalling that there is joint authorship when there is a certain level of coordination between the participants, irrespective of whether each author's part is separable or not).

11. Performers' rights and artificial intelligence
Richard Arnold

1. INTRODUCTION

As has often been pointed out, the expression 'artificial intelligence' is an umbrella term which may be used to refer to a number of different phenomena. In this chapter I am concerned with the type of computer-generated imagery (CGI) that is generally referred to as an 'avatar', that is to say, a graphical representation of a person or of their character or persona. Avatars may be two-dimensional or three-dimensional in appearance, and I am particularly concerned with the latter. An avatar may be a representation of a real person or an imaginary person. For convenience I will refer to these as 'real' and 'imaginary' avatars. In the case of real avatars, a closely related phenomenon is that of the 'deepfake': a video recording of a person that has been digitally manipulated so as to present that person as doing or saying something that they did not in fact do or say.[1] For present purposes, the difference between a real avatar and a deepfake is that the latter is based on manipulation of an existing video recording whereas the former is generated largely or entirely from scratch (although it will be appreciated that this is not a hard-and-fast distinction). More specifically, I am concerned with avatars that are, and deepfakes based on, performers (particularly actors, dancers, musicians and singers),[2] and in particular ones that are generated entirely by artificial intelligence, which for these purposes I shall define as a computer system operating autonomously without human input or intervention ('an AI'). Although I have so far referred only to imagery, I am also concerned with the sounds produced by such avatars and deepfakes.

In this short chapter I shall consider four questions. First, to what extent do performers' rights protect real performers against imitation by real avatars and deepfakes? Second, to what extent should performers' rights protect real performers against real avatars and deepfakes? Third, to what extent do performers' rights protect imaginary avatars? Fourth, to what extent should performers' rights protect imaginary avatars?

---

[1]   See Tyrone Kirchengast, 'Deepfakes and image manipulation: criminalisation and control' (2020) 29 I. & C. T. L. 308.

[2]   The term 'performance synthetisation' has been used to refer to the production of real avatar and deepfake performances: see Mathilde Pavis, 'Artificial intelligence and performers' rights: submission to the UK Intellectual Property Office' (30 November 2020). In addition to the 'target' performer whose performance is imitated, there may be a 'driving' performer whose performance is used when manipulating the target performance: see Mathilde Pavis, 'Rebalancing our regulatory response to Deepfakes with performers' rights' (2021) 27(4) Convergence 974. This chapter focuses on the target performer rather than the driving performer.

2.   PERFORMERS' RIGHTS

When I refer to 'performers' rights', I am primarily referring to the statutory rights conferred on performers by Part II of the UK Copyright, Designs and Patents Act 1988 (as amended), although I shall also make reference to the international legal framework for the protection of performers and to other legal remedies available to performers under English law.[3]

The international legal framework for the protection of performers consists of the four main treaties: the International Convention for the Protection of Performers, Producers of Phonograms and Broadcasting Organisations (Rome, 1961); Article 14 of the Agreement on Trade-Related Aspects of Intellectual Property ('TRIPs', Marrakesh, 1994); the WIPO Performances and Phonograms Treaty (Geneva, 1996); and the Beijing Treaty on Audiovisual Performances (2012). The main relevant instruments in European Union law are Parliament and Council Directive 2006/115/EC of 12 December 2006 on rental right and lending right and rights related to copyright (codified version) and Parliament and Council Directive 2001/29/EC of 22 May 2001 on the harmonisation of certain aspects of copyright & related rights in the information society.

Part II of the 1988 Act confers rights in respect of a dramatic performance (including dance and mime), a musical performance, a reading or recitation of a literary work and a variety act or similar presentation, insofar as it is a live performance given by one or more individuals, whether by a professional or an amateur and whether rehearsed or improvised.[4] Performances qualify for protection if the performance is given by a qualifying individual, that is, a citizen or subject or resident of a qualifying country, or if it takes place in qualifying country.[5] Qualifying countries are the UK, any other country party to the Rome Convention[6] and a list of countries designated as enjoying reciprocal protection.[7] The duration of the rights is the longer of 50 years from the end of the calendar year in which the performance takes place or 50 years from the end of the calendar year in which a recording of the performance other than a sound recording is released or 70 years from the end of the calendar year in which a sound recording of the performance is released.[8]

Performers whose performances qualify for protection have various economic rights. First is a 'fixation' right, which covers making a recording directly from a live performance, broadcasting a live performance or making a recording directly from a broadcast of a live performance.[9] Second is a reproduction right, which covers making a copy of a recording directly or indirectly from a performance, whether or not it is transient or incidental.[10] Third is a distribution right, which covers issuing to the public copies of a recording of a performance.[11] Fourth are rental and lending rights, which cover renting and lending copies of a recording of a performance.[12] Fifth is a making available right, which covers making a recording of a performance

---

[3]   See generally Richard Arnold, *Performers' Rights* (6th ed, Sweet & Maxwell, 2021).
[4]   1988 Act s.180(2). See *Performers' Rights* paras 2-03 to 2-36.
[5]   1988 Act s.181. See *Performers' Rights* paras 2-37 to 2-42.
[6]   95 States at the time of writing. Note that neither China nor the USA is a party.
[7]   1988 Act s.206. See *Performers' Rights* paras 2-43 to 2-49.
[8]   1988 Act s.191. See *Performers' Rights* paras 2-66 to 2-96.
[9]   1988 Act s.182. See *Performers' Rights* paras 4-10 to 4-20.
[10]   1988 Act s.182A. See *Performers' Rights* paras 4-21 to 4-25.
[11]   1988 Act s.182B. See *Performers' Rights* paras 4-26 to 4-33.
[12]   1988 Act s.182C. See *Performers' Rights* paras 4-34 to 4-39.

available to the public by electronic transmission in such a way that members of public may access it from a place and at a time individually chosen by them.[13] Sixth are rights in respect of the use of a recording of a performance made without consent where the recording is showed or played in public or communicated to public with knowledge or reason to believe to that it is an illicit recording.[14] Seventh are rights in respect of dealings with an illicit recording where the recording is imported, sold, hired, offered for sale or hire, distributed or possessed for business purposes with knowledge or reason to believe that it is illicit.[15] Finally, there is a right to equitable remuneration where a commercially published sound recording of a performance is played in public or communicated to public otherwise than by making available,[16] and where the rental right in a sound recording or film of a performance is transferred to a producer.[17] These rights are subject to various exceptions and limitations.[18] In addition, performers have two moral rights: a 'paternity' right to be identified as the performer[19] and an 'integrity' right to object to derogatory treatment of the performance.[20]

3.   TO WHAT EXTENT DO PERFORMERS' RIGHTS PROTECT REAL PERFORMERS AGAINST IMITATION BY REAL AVATARS AND DEEPFAKES?

To answer this question, we need to proceed in stages. The first stage is to consider a deepfake produced by a human being based on an actual performance by a human performer. Suppose, for example, there is a digitally manipulated recording of a performance by Michael Jackson or Dua Lipa. Assuming that this has been produced without the consent of the performer (in the case of Dua Lipa) or his estate (in the case of Michael Jackson), and that performers' rights subsist in the relevant performance (as will almost certainly be the case[21]), then the production and exploitation of the deepfake in the UK is likely to infringe the performer's rights unless there is some applicable limitation or exception (such as parody[22]). This is because a performer's rights are infringed by a person who, without the consent of the performer (or their estate), makes a copy of a recording of the whole or any substantial part of a qualifying performance, which includes making a copy which is transient.[23] Although there is no case law in the context of performers' rights (as opposed to copyright) on what is sometimes called 'altered copying', it seems likely that a deepfake would involve copying a substantial part of the performance. In addition, a performer's rights are infringed by a person who, without the consent of the performer (or their estate), makes available to the public a copy of a recording of the whole or any substantial part of a qualifying performance by electronic transmission in such a way

---

[13]   1988 Act s.180CA. See *Performers' Rights* paras 4-40 to 4-42.
[14]   1988 Act s.183. See *Performers' Rights* paras 4-43 to 4-51.
[15]   1988 Act s.184. See *Performers' Rights* paras 4-52 to 4-71.
[16]   1988 Act s.182D. See *Performers' Rights* paras 3-36 to 3-41.
[17]   1988 Act s.191G. See *Performers' Rights* paras 3-42 to 3-46.
[18]   1988 Act Sch. 2. See *Performers' Rights* paras 5-02 to 5-90.
[19]   1988 Act s.205C. See *Performers' Rights* paras 7-02 to 7-20.
[20]   1988 Act s.205F. See *Performers' Rights* paras 7-21 to 7-33.
[21]   See *Performers' Rights* paras 2-37 to 2-49.
[22]   1988 Act Sch. 2 para. 2A. See *Performers' Rights* paras 5-28 to 5-29.
[23]   1988 Act s.182A. See *Performers' Rights* paras 4-21 to 4-25.

that members of the public may access the recording from a place and at a time individually chosen by them.[24] There may be other infringing acts, but these are likely to be the main ones.

Next, let us consider a real avatar produced by a human being. Let it be supposed that it is an avatar of Michael Jackson or Dua Lipa whose appearance is based on a selection of still photographs taken on different occasions and whose sound is a synthesised imitation based on analysis of a number of different recordings. Even assuming that performers' rights subsist in the source performances and that there is no consent, the production and exploitation of the avatar in the UK is unlikely to be an infringement provided that care is taken over the sound analysis. This is for three reasons. First, the use of still photographs of a performance does not infringe performers' rights because the definition of 'recording' in Part II of the 1988 Act does not include a still photograph.[25] Second, although copying or making available a sound recording of any substantial part of a qualifying performance is an infringement, that does not necessarily preclude digital analysis of, for example, a streamed recording if that can be done without copying. (If there is copying, then there will be an infringement to that extent.) Third, and importantly, imitation of a performance is not an infringement of performers' rights,[26] still less imitation of a performer without imitating a specific performance. Thus the performer who sought to restrain such activities in the UK could not rely upon performers' rights, but would have to rely upon the law of passing off to provide a remedy, which would require proof that the relevant consumers were likely to be deceived into thinking that the avatar either was, or (more likely) was authorised by, the performer.[27]

Now let us consider the same deepfake or avatar produced by an AI. In principle, the performer or his estate has the same rights as in the case of the deepfake or avatar produced by the human being. The problem is to identify a 'person' who can be liable for any infringement. Although the word 'person' is not defined in Part II of the 1988 Act, there is no reason to interpret it any differently to the way in which it is generally interpreted in the law. By virtue of section 5 of, and Schedule 1 to, the Interpretation Act 1978, the word 'person' 'includes a body or persons corporate or unincorporate' unless the contrary intention appears. Thus 'person' generally means either a natural person or a legal person. An AI as defined above, however, is neither a natural person nor a legal person.[28] This raises an issue which is ubiquitous in the application of the law to artificial intelligence, which is the attribution of legal liability for the acts and omissions of artificial intelligence systems. A simple and increasingly real example is that of self-driving vehicles which are involved in accidents, but the problem is a general one. One proposed solution to these problems is that of attributing legal personality to AI entities.[29] This is not a very satisfactory solution in this context: although it might enable an injunction to be enforced against the AI, it would not enable an award of damages to be enforced (unless, perhaps, AIs start owning property). But as this objection suggests, the real question, at least in the short to medium term, is one of attributing liability for the acts or omissions of artificial intelligence systems to either human beings or conventional legal persons which can pay compensation. In the context of infringements of performers' rights, it may be possible to achieve

---

24   1988 Act s.182A. See *Performers' Rights* paras 4-40 to 4-42.
25   1988 Act s.180(2). See *Performers' Rights* paras 2-59 and 4-11.
26   See *Performers' Rights* para. 4-08.
27   See *Performers' Rights* paras 10-49 and 10-50.
28   See *Thaler v Comptroller-General of Patents, Trade Marks and Designs* [2021] EWCA Civ 1374.
29   See e.g. Georgios Zekos, *Economics and Law of Artificial Intelligence* (Springer, 2021), 361–400.

this through the application of conventional common law principles of accessory liability through the doctrine of joint tortfeasance or vicarious liability;[30] but if not, it seems likely that the common law will respond to the problem through an appropriate extension or adaptation of those principles.

4. TO WHAT EXTENT SHOULD PERFORMERS' RIGHTS PROTECT REAL PERFORMERS AGAINST IMITATION BY REAL AVATARS AND DEEPFAKES?

It will be appreciated from the discussion above that this question divides into two parts. The first part is whether real performers should be protected by performers' rights against imitation of their performances. This author has been suggesting that this merits consideration for 31 years,[31] but to date no government has shown any interest in the proposal. That was eminently understandable when it was only other human beings that could imitate a performance and the remedy of a claim for passing off might be considered adequate, but it is suggested that the advent of real avatars and deepfakes makes this a significantly more pressing concern.[32] Although this form of protection is not required by the international legal framework for the protection of performers' rights, it is not precluded either.

The second part of the question is what rule(s) for attribution of legal liability should be applied in this context. As discussed above, attributing legal personality to an AI does not appear to be a satisfactory solution, and what is needed is a rule or rules for attributing legal liability to natural or legal persons. This is an easier problem to solve without legislative intervention, in that it may be possible for the common law to build upon existing principles. There may come a point, however, when a more general legislative solution is required. Certainly, it does not seem that it would be satisfactory for AIs to be able to infringe performers' rights without the possibility of any person with assets being held liable to compensate performers who suffer loss as a result.

5. TO WHAT EXTENT DO PERFORMERS' RIGHTS PROTECT IMAGINARY AVATARS?

There are two obstacles to performers' rights being claimed in respect of performances by imaginary avatars. The first, and lesser, problem is that section 180(1) of the 1988 Act provides that Chapter 2 of Part II confers rights 'on a performer, by requiring his consent to the exploitation of his performance'. Despite the gendered drafting, 'his' plainly includes 'her',[33] and there is no reason why it should not extend to a person who identifies as non-binary. Although Part II contains no definition of 'performer',[34] it seems clear from a systematic

---

[30] See *Performers' Rights* para. 6-08.
[31] In successive editions of *Performers' Rights* since the first: see *Performers' Rights and Recording Rights* (ESC, 1990), para. 1-30(5).
[32] See Pavis (2020) and Pavis (2021), note 2 above.
[33] Interpretation Act 1978 s.6(a).
[34] See *Performers' Rights* paras 1-02 and 2-27.

reading that a performer must be a natural, and not a legal, person. Furthermore, Part II must be interpreted consistently with Article 3(a) of the Rome Convention and Article 2(a) of the WIPO Performances and Phonograms Treaty, both of which define 'performers' as 'actors, singers, musicians, dancers and other persons who act, sing,' and so on.[35] In any event, the second and bigger problem is that, even if a 'performer' could be something other than a natural person, Part II only protects 'performances' as defined in section 180(2).[36] To fall within that definition, a 'performance' must be a 'live performance given by one or more individuals'. That clearly excludes performances by imaginary avatars.[37]

6.   TO WHAT EXTENT SHOULD PERFORMERS' RIGHTS PROTECT IMAGINARY AVATARS?

Again, we need to answer this question in stages. The first stage is to consider an imaginary avatar produced by either a human being or a corporation (acting by employees and/or contractors). In theory, it would be possible to amend Part II of the 1988 Act to include a parallel provision to section 9(3) in Part I, which provides that '[i]n the case of a literary, dramatic, musical or artistic work which is computer-generated, the author shall be taken to be the person by whom the arrangements necessary for the creation of the work are undertaken'. Moreover, since performances do not have to be original in order for performers' rights to subsist in them, such a provision would not face the same conceptual difficulties as section 9(3) does.[38] Whether such a provision would be compatible with the Rome Convention and the WIPO Performances and Phonograms Treaty is perhaps debatable, but let us assume that there is no difficulty on that score.

The question is whether such a provision would be normatively justified. There is room for reasonable people to disagree on this question, but I would suggest that the answer is no. It is difficult to see that any of the usual justifications for conferring performers' rights[39] are applicable in these circumstances. While it is certainly well arguable that the production of imaginary avatars is something that should be incentivised and rewarded by an intellectual property right, the appropriate way to achieve this is through copyright in the relevant software and imagery.[40] The point of performers' rights is to incentivise and reward *performance*, in particular by performers who do not own any copyright in the material being performed (although performers who do have copyright are not excluded from protection). Unlike a human performer, an imaginary avatar does not need money to pay for the necessities of life such as food and accommodation, because an imaginary avatar needs no sustenance or shelter.[41] As for moral rights, it is difficult to see why a performance by an imaginary avatar,

---

[35]   See *Performers' Rights* para. 2-27.
[36]   See *Performers' Rights* paras 1-02, 2-01 and 2-31 to 2-35.
[37]   See *Performers' Rights* para. 2-26.
[38]   See Patrick Goold, 'The Curious Case of Computer-Generated Works under the Copyright, Designs and Patents Act 1988' [2021] IPQ 120.
[39]   See *Performers' Rights* paras 1-14 to 1-19.
[40]   It is also arguable that such productions should be protected as audiovisual works, but audiovisual works are not as such a protected category of subject matter under Part I of the 1988 Act. Films and sound recordings incorporating imaginary avatars will, of course, be protected in the usual way.
[41]   The platform hosting the imaginary avatar requires electrical power, but that is a different matter.

as opposed to the creation of the avatar, should require either a paternity right or an integrity right. These rights are designed to protect the feelings of human performers, but an imaginary avatar has no feelings.

The second stage is to consider an imaginary avatar produced by an AI. In this case, a provision modelled on section 9(3) would be pointless. The reason for this is that, if the imaginary avatar is produced by an AI as defined above, then no natural or legal person will have undertaken the arrangements necessary for the creation of that avatar's performances. Unless, that is, one goes down the road of attributing legal personality to the AI—but that would have startling consequences. It is difficult enough to conceive of attributing legal personality to an AI in order to render the AI legally liable for its acts and omissions, but doing so in order to confer legally enforceable rights on the AI would go considerably further. Are we prepared to countenance AIs being able to make legal claims against human beings for infringement of AIs' rights? I would suggest not.

12. AIn't it just software?

Shubha Ghosh

1.   INTRODUCTION

This contribution to what some may see as an overgrown scholarly literature on artificial intelligence and copyright starts with a simple observation: artificial intelligence is just software. That observation may strike the sophisticated as simple-minded. "There is a lot more to it than that!" To the pop culture-minded, the statement might seem wrong-headed. "AI is about hardware. Robots. Cute ones lost in Tatooine and scary ones trying to kill us." All that may be true, but from the perspective of copyright law, at the minimum, recognizing artificial intelligence as just software connects the ongoing debates over robot authors and the death of intellectual property to a more long-standing debate over the proper treatment of software under intellectual property laws. The Supreme Court's recent pronouncement in *Google v Oracle* underscores the persistence of this debate, with implications for how we should approach artificial intelligence.

To declare artificial intelligence to be *just* software opens up a fairly complex debate over what software is and how it fits into the discipline of computer science. This chapter not only connects the developing area of artificial intelligence with the established field of software copyright but also connects software copyright to computer science, as an academic discipline. Admittedly, the field is a bit outside of my own expertise as a PhD economist and lawyer. Other than some familiarity with programming and knowledge of the connections between economics and cybernetics, I am not trained as a computer scientist beyond scholarly reading and conversations with computer scientists. But I have long been curious about the development of academic computer science; its roots in mathematics; its blossoming as an independent research project, in the sense of Imre Lakatos;[1] and its relationship to information studies.[2] For scholars of artificial intelligence and copyright who have shared my curiosity, I hope this chapter provides fuel for ongoing inquiry.

My starting point is the typology set forth by Peter Wegner in 1975 as possible research paradigms for computer science.[3] He identifies three tracks: one based in mathematics; one based in engineering; and one based in natural or empirical science. Computer science through the

---

[1]   See Imre Lakatos, The Methodology of Scientific Research Programmes (1980). See also The Methodology of Economics (1980) (discussing Lakatos in research programs and science). For the development of computer science as a scientific discipline, see Peter J. Denning, Computer Science: The Discipline, in Encyclopedia of Computer Science (A. Ralston & D. Hemmendinger, eds) (2000). For a comparative perspective, see Pierre Mounier-Kuhn, Computer Science in French Universities: Early Entrants and Latecomers, 47 Information & Culture 414–56 (2012).

[2]   Anne Wells Branscomb, Who Owns Information? From Privacy to Public Access 152–3 (software, copyright, and patent and the treatment of interfaces).

[3]   Peter Wegner, Research Paradigms in Computer Science, Proc. 2nd Int'l Conf. Software Engineering 322–30 (1976). See also Ammon H. Eden, Three Paradigms of Computer Science, Minds and Machines: Special Issue on the Philosophy of Computer Science 135–67 (2007).

lens of mathematics views the program as mathematical object, like a number, set, or field, to take three examples. This approach is deductive, or rationalist, starting with abstract principles of what programs can achieve and developing formalistic approaches to reach those ends. In my mind, this approach can be thought of as computer program-as-algorithm. The engineering or technocratic approach views computer programs as a way to solve problems. This second approach is inductive, working from practical questions of how to achieve a specific result, perhaps sorting a set of data or teaching a machine to dance, towards the writing of a set of instructions in an implementable language to reach that result. This approach is associated with computer engineering or programming as distinct from mathematics. The third approach is the natural science approach, one based on experimentation to test and develop theories of computing and intelligence. This last approach is both deductive and inductive, moving from specific examples to larger propositions and back to the laboratory testing (where the computer, however defined, is the lab). Such an abductive approach is the realm of artificial intelligence.

As an economist, I can relate to this typology within my field as it developed through cybernetics in the research of Norbert Weiner and John Von Neuman. With its roots in mathematics and game theory, as formulated by von Neuman and Morgenstern (and Luce and Raiffa),[4] post-World War II economics research moved into programming through the development of multi-equation models that could be used to test theories and make forecasts, and in the past two decades toward approaches of institutional design and experimental economics, grounded in mathematics, historical data, and laboratory testing.[5] This path of development maps onto the typology of Wegner: rationalist, engineering, and natural or empirical science.

As a lawyer and legal scholar, I find in the typology a framework for assessing legal questions of ownership, liability, and transacting. For example, what does it mean for software to be owned as property or under some other legal entitlement? If software-as-computer program is a mathematical object, the ownership question is moot. Ownership over mathematical objects eludes both copyright and patent; the first because of the lack of copyright protection for systems and processes; the second because of the lack of patent protection for abstract ideas.[6] However, as a product of engineering, the ownership question may be meaningful, particularly under patent law with its protection for machines and processes. Copyright protection, while perhaps still elusive, does extend to scientific writings, which may include some aspects of programs.[7] Finally, the abductive approach of computer science under which programs are the fruit of experimentation leads to a more complicated analysis for copyright

---

[4]   John von Neumann & Oskar Morgenstern, Theory of Games and Economic Behavior (1953); R. Duncan Luce & Howard Raiffa, Games and Decisions: Introduction and Critical Survey (1957). See also Norbert Wiener, The Human Use of Human Beings: Cybernetics and Society (1954). For the context of information and computer science for game theory, see Philip Mirowski, Machine Dreams: Economics Becomes a Cyborg Science (2002); Peter Galison, The Ontology of the Enemy: Norbert Wiener and the Cybernetic Vision, 21 Critical Inquiry 228–66 (1994); Thomas Rid, Rise of the Machines: A Cybernetic History (2016).

[5]   See Eden, supra note 3.

[6]   See 17 USC 102(b) (no copyright protection for systems and processes); see Alice Corp. v CLS Bank International et al., 573 US 208 (2014)(no patent protection for abstract ideas). Although I do not discuss trade secret law in this chapter, it is worth noting that trade secret protection extends to processes and formulas, which would include algorithms.

[7]   Final Report on the National Commission on New Technological Uses of Copyright Works, 3 Computer L.J. 53 (1981).

and patent, with its relationship to "Science and the Useful Arts" under the United States constitutional scheme and to technology under international intellectual property law. What is true here about ownership questions is equally true for questions of infringement and liability, as I elaborate in this chapter.

Revisiting the roots of software in the evolving discipline of computer science invigorates ongoing debates over copyright protection for software and research into artificial intelligence and intellectual property. This chapter offers researchers a tour of these ideas and possibilities for further scholarship. My goal is to address familiar questions in a fresh way by highlighting how what we know about software copyright informs our scholarly and policy struggles over artificial intelligence. Reframing what we know and drawing connections will, I hope, bring heat and light, both provocation and insight.

The roadmap is as follows. Section 2 demonstrates how the discipline of computer science informs debates over software copyright. While the focus is on copyright, I will draw implications for patent law and policy as well. Section 3 makes the case for treating artificial intelligence like software, with the attendant implications for copyright policy. Section 4 connects the currently open research questions about artificial intelligence and copyright, specifically authorship and infringement and to some extent licensing and other copyright transactions, to the parallel debates over software copyright. The lesson from the fourth section is that many open questions may already be answered within the paradigm of computer science and software. Section 5 concludes by pointing to future research directions.

2.   SOFTWARE COPYRIGHT AND COMPUTER SCIENCE

In the United States, software copyright has gelled around certain principles recognizing a computer program as written expression combined with functional elements that would, if protected at all, be subject to patent or trade secret law, and permitting fair use and limitations based on statutory protections for copying under narrowly proscribed circumstances. Copyright law outside the United States has parallel provisions, with a 2012 European Court of Justice ruling on interfaces echoing the fair use analysis of the United States Supreme Court in its 2021 *Google v Oracle* decision. These copyright principles have roots in debates in the academic field of computer science. This section explicitly draws these connections, particularly to the treatment of a program as mathematical object and the subject of experimentation among computer scientists. These connections raise research questions for ongoing scholarship in software copyright. They also inform the burgeoning debate over artificial intelligence, which is at core just another form of software.

The 1977 Report of the Committee on New Technological Issues (CONTU) recommended amendments to the US Copyright Act to accommodate software within the copyright system.[8] Formed by Congress in 1974, the Committee consisted of copyright attorneys, representatives of literary and artistic communities, and academics.[9] However, no representatives from the software industry—whether software developers or vendors—or from the academic field of

---

[8]   Ibid. See, also, Fritz Machlup, Proposed Statement Regarding S. 2216, a Bill to Establish a National Commission on New Technological Uses of Copyrighted Work (September 8, 1967) (unpublished memo on file with author).

[9]   Ibid.

computer science were on the committee.[10] Perhaps this was an oversight or an attempt to limit industry capture or influence. But given the size of the software industry in the 1970s,[11] the expansion of computer science as a discipline,[12] and the contemporaneous debate over the "software crisis,"[13] it is disappointing that those academic and industry viewpoints were not included directly in the debates.

The principal conclusion in the CONTU report was the recognition of a computer program as a type of writing equivalent to the recorded expressions of the past. Developments in technology, particularly the movement away from a single-use machine (such as a "word processor" or a "game player") to multiple-purpose hardware that could operate different programs for varied application, separated the instructions of the program from a machine. The instructions were no longer just part of the circuitry like beads in an abacus or punched holes in cards. As the authors of the Report described:

> Just as there was little need to protect the ridged brass wheel in a nineteenth-century music box, so too was there little reason to protect the wired circuit or plug boards of early computers. The cost of making the wheel was inseparable from the cost of producing the final ridged product.

The ubiquity of the multi-purpose machine beyond the academic harbor and the business office and in the home expanded the market for software, creating demand and allowing for network effects. Furthermore, meeting this demand required companies to expend resources on software development. The high cost of development contrasted with the relatively low cost of disseminating software to consumers and copying it from machine to machine. This combination of high costs of production and relatively low costs of dissemination paralleled what is observed in book publishing. The Committee acknowledged several ways for companies to recover the high development costs in the shadow of low dissemination costs, such as cost recovery and profits on the first sale of the work, public dedication of the work, and government subsidies or rewards. But its recommendation settled on what allowing the creator to "spread its costs over multiple copies of the work with some form of protection against unauthorized duplication of the work." Such protection through copyright law would "encourage the creation and broad distribution of computer programs in a competitive market."

While CONTU recommended legal protection against copying, its report also pointed to limitations on this exclusive right. Congress had enacted Section 117 of the Copyright Act as part of the 1976 Copyright Act, pending the Commission's Report. The enacted statute gave to a copyright owner the same rights with respect to computer uses of copyrighted works as were available under the copyright law prior to the 1976 Act. In other words, Congress was safeguarding copyrights within the domain of computers in anticipation that CONTU would clarify what the extent of these rights might be. CONTU responded by recommending a repeal of this Congress' original version of Section 117 and replacement with a new provision providing for limitations on the rights of the copyright owner.[14] Under this revised version of Section

---

[10]   Ibid. See CONTU Commission at https://itlaw.wikia.org/wiki/CONTU_Commission (viewed June 23, 2021).

[11]   See Margaret O'Mara, The Code: Silicon Valley and the Remaking of America (2019).

[12]   See Wegner, supra note 3.

[13]   See Markus Bautsch, Cycles of Software Crises: How to Avoid Insecure and Uneconomic Software, 3 ENISA Quarterly 3–4 (2007).

[14]   See supra note 7.

117, copies of programs arising from the loading and implementation of software would not be copyright infringement. Copying for archival purposes, undertaken in a proscribed fashion, also was exempted from infringement liability.[15] While CONTU acknowledged the need for protection to address the economics of software development and dissemination, it also recognized the need for limitations on potential infringement liability to accommodate the technological realities of software use and the practices of software consumers in backing up fragile digital information. Congress further expanded limitations under Section 117 in the 1990s to accommodate the needs of repair professionals who would inevitably copy software for diagnostics and maintenance of machines, such as photocopiers or automobiles.[16]

Disputes over software copyright further shaped copyright protection. I focus here on three developments: copyright protection of object code, infringement of copyrighted code, and fair use.

An early question that came before courts was about copyright protection for source and object code. Computer programs were written in a language that could be read by programmers. This source code, written in language familiar to programmers, would be compiled so that the machine could process the instructions and execute them. Compiling operates to translate the programming language into a binary code of zeros and ones corresponding to off-and-on switchable, readable by the machine but incomprehensible to the human programmer. But the object code could be readily copied as well and was often reverse engineered to discover the underlying source code. Does copyright protection extend to object code, created by and comprehensible only to a machine?

CONTU did not address object code separately from source code. Once computer programs were recognized as a "form of writing," they were described as "sets of instructions which, when properly drafted, are used in an almost limitless number of ways to release human beings from […] mundane tasks."[17] Without using the phrase "artificial intelligence," the report presaged contemporary visions of automation. These automated tasks are made possible by "computer programs […] prepared by the careful fixation of words, phrases, numbers, and other symbols in various media."[18] Programs as writings are not limited to any particular set of symbols; writings can be in the form of phonemes, letters, numbers, or the many graphic images we take for granted today, from emoticons to emojis. Given the broad language in the CONTU Report, it is not surprising that courts ruled copyright's reach to be broad, encapsulating all forms that programs could take—even the object code enjoyed only by machines.[19]

But the broad reach of copyright implied a broad scope for copyright infringement. Without some limitation, copyright infringement would include use of uncopyrighted functional elements, perhaps the subject matter of patent or trade secret law. Such concerns existed outside the realm of computer programs. Infringement of a specific detective or romance novel could not include the conventions for these genres. Similarly, infringement of photographs or audiovisual works or sculptural works could not extend to noncopyrightable lighting, sounds, or pedestals. Traditionally, copyright law limited its own scope through the idea–expression dis-

---

[15] Ibid.
[16] 17 USC 117.
[17] See supra note 7.
[18] Ibid.
[19] Ibid.

tinction and its variations, such as merger or scenes a faire.[20] But how to apply these doctrinal limitations to computer programs?

One early attempt to apply the idea–expression distinction to software resulted in critical backlash.[21] What, after all, is the idea of a computer program? If one can identify an idea, is there only one? Does a piece of software have a genre, like a novel or a movie or a musical composition? Traditional doctrine limitations did not translate well. The judicial response was the Second Circuit's decision in *Computer Associates v Altai*,[22] a decision that required careful dissection by a court to separate functional features of software from the copyrighted elements. For some, this dissection led readily to the killing of the copyrighted patient. But the approach structured infringement litigation to limit copyright claims to only the non-functional features. Without the aid of claims that guide patent infringement analysis for software patents, courts had to rely on the program itself, with guidance from concepts of computer programming, to identify functional features and discard them from copyright's ambit.

Copyright infringement analysis also contrasted with that for trade secret misappropriation. Under the latter, trade secret scope could be quite broad, encompassing both the expression and the function. But trade secret law had its own limitations, such as reverse engineering. As many copyright infringement claims were joined with trade secret claims, the issue of limitations on copyright infringement arose. The copyright analogue to reverse engineering is fair use. While alleged software infringers could often find a defense of reverse engineering, unless fair use could rise to the challenge of infringement claims, copyright law would limit what trade secret could liberate. Courts did find room for fair use as a limit[23] on software copyright infringement claims. Some copying of software was found to be intermediate copying, necessary in order to promote interoperability across different hardware platforms.[24] Such intermediate copying would also facilitate the development of new products or services that expanded rather than competed with the copyright owner's market domain.[25] These pronouncements about fair use were robust and generally accepted[26] but found validation in the Supreme Court's decision in *Google v Oracle* in 2021.

The decade-long dispute between Google and Oracle involved patent and copyright protection for interfaces in computer software. The CONTU Report does not mention interfaces, but it does refer to policies salient in the Google litigation. Among the objectives of software copyright are the goals that copyright "should not block the development and dissemination" of programs and that copyright "should not grant anyone more economic power than is necessary to achieve the incentive to create."[27] Sun, in developing and disseminating its JAVA platform, allowed programmers to use its interfaces for free. Once Oracle acquired Sun, these interfaces were claimed as proprietary, requiring some smartphone developers to design around patents and copyrights protecting them. Google, however, used them in the creation of its Android phone, and Oracle's lawsuit followed. While the relevant patent claims were held invalid, Oracle pushed on the copyright claims. While the district court at various stages of

---

[20] See discussion in Computer Associates v Altai, 982 F. 2d 693 (2nd Cir. 1992).
[21] See Whelan Associates v Jaslow Dental Lab., Inc., 797 F.2d 1222 (3rd Cir. 1986).
[22] See supra note 20.
[23] See Lydia P. Loren, Fair Use: An Affirmative Defense?, 90 Wash. L. Rev. 985 (2015).
[24] See Sega Enterprises, Ltd. v Accolade, Inc., 977 F.2d 1510 (9th Cir. 1992).
[25] See Sony Computer Entertainment v Connectix Corp., 203 F.3d 596 (9th Cir. 2000).
[26] See, e.g., Pamela Samuelson, Unbundling Fair Uses, 77 Fordham L. Rev. 2537 (2009).
[27] See supra note 7.

the litigation found against copyright in the interfaces and for fair use by Google, the Federal Circuit found in favor of the copyrightability of interfaces and against fair use.

The Supreme Court's decision, in a 6–2 vote, found fair use and did not address the copyrightability issue. Assuming for the sake of argument that interfaces are copyrightable, the Court ruled that Google's use of the largely functional interfaces were appropriate for the development of its smartphone, a new product that did not compete with the market for Oracle's copyright. The Court's reasoning includes an extended discussion of the needs of computer programmers and the benefits of copying interfaces in order to facilitate the creation of the smartphone's operating system. Using the terms interface and API, and declaring codes interchangeable, the Court concluded their use was justified as fair use under the US statutory provisions.[28]

Citing lower court opinions on fair use and interoperability of software as precedent, the Court developed a methodology that would be appropriate for many software copyright cases. The approach emphasizes the functional dimensions of software, the need for programmers to copy functional code, and the resulting benefits to consumers of new products arising in new markets. One predicts a broad impact for software copyright infringement and, as I elaborate below, implications for artificial intelligence and copyright.

Unappreciated in these established principles of software copyright is a debate over principles of computer science. Such influence reveals itself in the use of expert witnesses from computer science in implementing the Altai methodology for copyright infringement. The influence also is present in the Google litigation with amicus briefs from computer programmers and computer scientists appearing at various stages of the judicial dispute. Computer programmers submitted a brief to the Federal Circuit advocating for denial of copyright to interfaces and the recognition of fair use. Computer scientists, based in academia, supported the exact opposite positions in their amicus brief before the Supreme Court. Pace the computer programmers, the computer scientists urged a finding of copyright for API's and declaring codes and a finding against fair use. The difference I suggest reflects tensions within the field of computer science, tensions that in turn arise within the field of software copyright. For the rest of this section, I situate the established principles of software copyright law within the debates in computer science. As I show towards the end of this section, these latter debates have implications for extending software copyright to issues raised by artificial intelligence.

Computer science, as a discipline, "is the body of knowledge and practices used by computing professionals in their work."[29] This definition ties the birth and development of computer science to that of "computing" and its professionals. The discipline's origins are in the early 1940s with the confluence of algorithm theory, mathematical logic, and the invention of the stored-program electronic computer."[30] With institutional legitimacy established through the creation of computer science departments in the 1960s, the field's domain includes that of computing, computer engineering, and informatics, and can be summarized as follows: "The body of knowledge of computing is frequently described as the systematic study of algorithmic processes that describe and transform information: their theory, analysis, design, efficiency,

---

[28] Google LLC v. Oracle Am., Inc., 141 S. Ct. 1183, 1208 (2021).
[29] See Eden, supra note 3.
[30] Ibid.

implementation, and application. The fundamental question underlying all of computing is, What can be (efficiently) automated?"[31]

While these definitions of computer science emphasize its body of knowledge, an alternative definition emphasizes the discipline's methodology. "Computer science is," according to Professors Newell and Simon, "the study of the phenomena surrounding computers [...] an empirical discipline [...] an experimental science [...] like astronomy, economics, and geology."[32] Identifying computer science with empiricism and experimentation connects the field with other experimental dimensions of computing and programming. We see here at least two understandings of computer science as a discipline. One focuses on the practices of programming that lead to efficient automation of various tasks; the other on the program as experimental tool to aid in understanding the epistemic tasks of computing. These contrasting definitions hint at the ongoing debates within the field of computer science: debates that arise within software copyright law.

At the heart of the quest for a definition of computer science and its methods is a struggle to properly understand the computer program, the set of instructions or software that becomes coupled with hardware. Drawing on roots in mathematics, we can understand the program as a mathematical object, such as a number, a set, a geometric figure, a topological shape, that is the basis for study. Such a rationalist approach to computer science would emphasize analyzing the program in deductive terms for more effective design and construction. Alternatively, the program can be seen as a pure instrument, an electronic update of the Archimedean lever or a Swiss army knife. Such an engineering approach to computer science would emphasize how the program as instrument could be implemented to accomplish certain tasks, generate electricity, design bridges, monitor transactions. As an instrument, the program would also be a commodity, available at a price for any possible application. The program, according to this engineering or technocratic view, is not an abstraction; it is a real thing. A third approach is what we observe in the Newell and Simon definition of computer science. The program is itself an experiment, a test, whose application goes beyond the mundane tasks of ensuring bridge stability or a rocket launch. As a way to process information, the program can test data through the now familiar methods of big data analytics but also serve as a form of data to identify how processes operate (or fail). This third approach, still in the development stage, is a scientific approach, also referred to as the empirical or experimental approach. It is the substance of artificial intelligence and, as I argue, the basis for the next generation of software copyright, expanding earlier traditions.

These contrasting views of the computer program map onto various arguments for software copyright. For example, CONTU's emphasis on the program as a text, consisting of words, numbers, or symbols, is a rationalist view of software. It is an object that can be understood abstractly as the object of a writing. Similarly, the amicus brief of computer scientists that was submitted to the Supreme Court in *Google v Oracle* also arises from a mathematical view of software. The computer scientists who authored the, unsuccessful, brief argued in favor of copyright for interfaces and no, or at least very narrow, fair use. The computer science professors represented urge the Court to recognize the creativity embodied in Application Programming Interfaces (API) as evident from viewing the software as a whole:

---

[31]   Ibid.
[32]   Allen Newll & Herbert A. Simon, Computer Science as Empirical Inquiry: Symbols and Search, 19 Communications of the ACM 113–26 (1976).

> While a single line of source code from an API can and often does demonstrate creativity, to understand the creativity of the Java APIs, however, a court should look at the work as a whole. That Google and its amici choose to focus on only a few of the eleven thousand lines of copied API source code so as to decry a lack of creativity is both erroneous and tangential to the copyright analysis, which must look at the whole work that was taken.[33]

This argument rests on treating the computer program as an object, abstracted from its functions, with aesthetic qualities identifiable holistically. So abstracted, code constitutes a creative work, constructed with artistic attention.

This mathematical approach, invoked to support copyrightability, contrasts with the technocratic, engineering approach invoked for assessing copyright infringement. The Second Circuit in its *Altai* decision formulated the abstraction–filtration–comparison test that, guided by the expertise of computer scientists, would take apart a computer program to strip away its functional features and identify any copyrightable core. The functional features acknowledge the instrumental role of software, in contrast with the view that the program is an abstract, aesthetic object. The Second Circuit expressly points to the efficiency features of software—those necessary for effective interaction with hardware and those necessary for internal operation of code as the various routines interface. Software is a technocratic tool of engineering under the *Altai* test; its dissection limits copyright protection but also highlights the largely instrumental role of software.

In the Google appeals, computer programmers advocated against copyrightability of interfaces and in favor of fair use. Their brief submitted to the Federal Circuit as part of the intermediate appeal represents a technocratic view of software. Interoperability is the key concept. Code needs to be operable across platforms and across uses in order to promote competition and to avoid creating technological barriers that would require costly workarounds that can inhibit the flow of information and technical progress. As their brief asserts:

> Programmers are the immediate beneficiaries of this interoperability. If their skill sets were not transferrable, they would have to start learning from scratch every time they work in a new environment. Software firms also benefit from this interoperability. If programmers' skills were not portable, then firms would need to convince programmers to learn a new toolset to work in a new environment, leading to slower adoption and higher training costs. But consumers are the ultimate beneficiaries of the interoperability of skills, as higher training costs for programmers are passed on to them. Moreover, the proliferation of programming environments enabled by the portability of skills means more innovation, competition, and consumer choice.[34]

Program, software, code—technocratic artifacts whose value is gauged in terms of instruments to engineers—support limitations on copyright, contrary to the rationalist's projection of software as an aesthetic abstraction. Copyright law and policy provides new domains for debate among computer scientists.[35]

---

[33] See Brief for Professor Eugene H. Spafford et al., in Google LLLC v. Oracle America, Inc., 2020 WL 1131470 (U.S.), 1 (U.S., 2020).

[34] Brief Amicus Curiae of the Computer & Communications Industry Association in Support of Google Inc., in the United States Court of Appeals for the Federal Circuit, Oracle America Inc. v Google Inc. (May 26, 2017).

[35] The programmer position is grounded in network effects for copyright software, particularly on interoperability grounds. See Peter Menell, Economic Analysis of Network Effects and Intellectual

When seen through the lens of computer science, familiar legal arguments take on an unappreciated edge. A rationalist view of the program abstracts from the instrumentality of software, which serves engineering ends and problem-solving needs. The technocratic view adopts a more pragmatic and applied perspective on software. But this view is also the subject of disciplinary criticism for reducing software to mere tools, as opposed to the subject of deeper scientific inquiry. To treat computer science as about software-as-instrument would be to reduce astronomy to a field about telescopes. Of course, telescopes are part of the field, but so is charting planetary orbits, testing physicists' theories, predicting cosmological phenomena. Computer science as a scientific, empirical, and experimental discipline would need to go beyond the rationalist and technocratic approaches. The program is neither an abstraction nor a mere tool. It is, under the scientific view, an experiment, a tool for testing theories but also for developing new theories and approaches. Programming operates in a broader world of big data, analytics, and artificial intelligence.

But how does this scientific view of computer science affect copyright? As I argue in the next section, such a view can instruct researchers on some current puzzles in copyright and artificial intelligence. This instruction has roots in our current understanding of software copyright but guides how copyright law evolves. As illustration, I will conclude this section by arguing that the Supreme Court's decision in *Google v Oracle* hints at a possible path for software copyright grounded in a scientific view of computer science.

An initial assessment of the Google opinion supports a continuation of the technocratic view of software. Justice Breyer adopts a view of software consistent with that articulated by programmers in their earlier brief, as the following language from his decision underscores:

> given programmers' investment in learning the Sun Java API, to allow enforcement of Oracle's copyright here would risk harm to the public. Given the costs and difficulties of producing alternative APIs with similar appeal to programmers, allowing enforcement here would make of the Sun Java API's declaring code a lock limiting the future creativity of new programs. Oracle alone would hold the key. The result could well prove highly profitable to Oracle (or other firms holding a copyright in computer interfaces). But those profits could well flow from creative improvements, new applications, and new uses developed by users who have learned to work with that interface. To that extent, the lock would interfere with, not further, copyright's basic creativity objectives.[36]

Software as keys and locks that bind programmers fits within an instrumental view of programs and an engineering view of programming. But the Court's analysis is not limited to these technocratic concerns. What is instructive from the majority opinion is its engagement with the nature of the program.

Through its emphasis on fair use, however, the Court points toward a new understanding of software copyright. What signals this new understanding is the Court's slight inversion of the four fair use factors. Taken in order from the statute and from the numerous fair use cases, the factors are (1) purpose and character of the use; (2) nature of the copyright work; (3) the amount and substantiality of what was copied; and (4) the potential market effects of the use. The *Google* Court, without explanation, begins with the second factor. This is one indication that the Court seeks to call attention to the ontological status of programs under copyright law.

Property, 34 Berkeley Technology Law Journal 219 (2019). See also Ariel Katz, A Network Effects Perspective on Software Piracy, 55 The University of Toronto Law Journal 155–216 (2005).
[36]   See supra note 28 at 1208 (2021).

Another indication is how the Court characterizes Google's use of the software in question, as described by the Court.

As measured by number of words and paragraphs, Justice Breyer's analysis of the nature of the copyrighted work is the longest part of his fair use analysis. What is striking is his decompiling of Congress' definition of copyright: "Congress has specified that computer programs are subjects of copyright. It differs, however, from many other kinds of copyrightable computer code. It is inextricably bound together with a general system, the division of computing tasks, that no one claims is a proper subject of copyright."[37]

Programs are distinct from code and each fit into a broader general system for the tasks of computing. Copyright applies to some features but not others, Justice Breyer states, on the surface contradicting his initial assumption that the software at issue is copyrighted. But this seeming contradiction is resolved by shifting from a focus on program-as-language to a focus on the programming system of which the language is only one part. What distinguishes the analysis from a rationalist or technocratic view of software is moving beyond the program as aesthetic abstraction and the program as an instrument for computing. There is a holistic view that posits a deeper, empirical view of software.

This new approach to software is further illustrated by the deft way in which Justice Breyer introduces the functional aspects of software:

> the copied declaring code and the uncopied implementing programs call for, and reflect, different kinds of capabilities. A single implementation may walk a computer through dozens of different steps. To write implementing programs, witnesses told the jury, requires balancing such considerations as how quickly a computer can execute a task or the likely size of the computer's memory. One witness described that creativity as "magic" practiced by an API developer when he or she worries "about things like power management" for devices that "run on a battery." This is the very creativity that was needed to develop the Android software for use not in laptops or desktops but in the very different context of smartphones.[38]

Although the Court declined to address the question of copyrightability of interfaces, the functionality of interfaces is introduced in the fair use analysis through the word "capabilities." What is notable is that the functionality analysis is distinguishable from the technocratic approach of the *Altai* court. Justice Breyer does not engage in technical filtering or dissection of the program. Instead, the focus is on the empirical realities of what the relevant code is capable of doing. These capabilities define the "nature of the work," the meaning of the program. Within this understanding of the work at issue, Justice Breyer progresses to assess the purpose of the use, the substantiality of what was copied, and the market effects.

This section has made two arguments. The first is that software copyright principles map onto active debates within the discipline of computer science. Although this argument has not been otherwise demonstrated, it is important in understanding the disciplinary context of copyright policy. The second argument is that the *Google* decision points to a different conception of the program, one that echoes the scientific, empirical, and experimental approach to computer science. This new approach informs the art of artificial intelligence.

Section 3 brings together these two arguments to show how current copyright debates over artificial intelligence are situated in a disciplinary debate within computer science. I suggest

---

[37] Ibid at 1201.
[38] Ibid at 1202.

that these disciplinary debates should more explicitly inform copyright and artificial intelligence. The *Google* decision, as I read it, supports this last argument.

3. AI AS SOFTWARE

It is not difficult to reach the conclusion that artificial intelligence is just software. Even those who equate artificial intelligence to robots have to ask what fuels these machines. In the movies, we are shown data being fed into objects—some cute and cuddly, some clinically metallic—and output being generated. Software is how the data is processed, how the machine fulfills its purpose.

But even if one reduces artificial intelligence to software, the question remains about how these machines fit into the skein of copyright. Machines create, or so it appears, and the law demands an answer to the question: who owns these creations? Machines copy in the legal sense of replicating a pre-existing creation, leading to the compelling question: is this infringement, and if so, who is liable and how? More tantalizing is the description of artificial intelligence as a self-replicating technology, one that operates itself, autonomously generating and processing data to fine tune and refine its creations. AI robots can teach themselves, learn—at least in the technical sense of "machine learning"—and respond to their environment. One wonders if they can govern themselves and how copyright law might fit into their virtual doctrines that presumably exist without actual virtue.

As self-replicating technology, artificial intelligence may lead us beyond the current boundaries of software copyright. Perhaps old concepts, as some scholars tell us, fail. My argument is that software copyright offers a starting point that actually takes us quite far in addressing current questions raised by artificial intelligence. AI is just software, and software copyright law can, with further research, help us regulate its creations.

Those who see AI as collapsing all existing categories adopt a fantastical vision of artificial intelligence, one that is ungrounded in the real world of engineering and technology. As artificial intelligence scholar Kate Crawford meticulously shows us, artificial intelligence is connected to minerals that shape the processors which are fueled by the generators that convert the mechanical and electronic twists and turns into what appear to be thoughts.[39] But these analogues to our "gray cells" also exist in a network, one grounded not in organic matter like our brain, but in industry, business organizations, and physical labor, transforming the organic and inorganic into economic, social, and legal realities. Artificial intelligence is very much real, no matter how much we try to relegate it to the virtual. Within this reality exists software, different types of programming, that drives what the artificial intelligence attempts to emulate. Copyright law operates on these foundational lawyers of software.

Robotics scholar Kate Darling reminds us that through our policy choices we impose on this reality various metaphors which in turn fuel our choices in a vicious circle.[40] But we need to question these metaphors at every turn. Her point is that the controversies posed by artificial intelligence are more similar to those raised by animals than to the silvery machines we see in our cinematic imagination. Asking whether the robot before us thinks and feels is similar to

---

[39] Kate Crawford, The Atlas of AI (2021).
[40] Kate Darling, The New Breed: What Our History with Animals Reveals About Our Future with Robots (2021).

asking whether horses count or dogs can understand us. The rush to anthropomorphize blinds us to the other possibilities of symbol and language with which to gauge our interactions with these alien creatures. Anthropologists in their initial contact with alien human cultures reduced them to "primitives" or "savages," denying their humanity and failing to see the contingency of culture. In our relations to animals, we may at first see them as alien, then as extensions of our own humanity, and finally as independent sentient and thinking creatures, guided by their own cues and instincts.

Our relationship with artificial intelligence may go through similar stages, with each having implications for law and policy. Artificial intelligence as inanimate machine may reduce our relations to those of ownership and possession of personal property. Artificial intelligence as a human extension would necessitate different rules that go beyond property relations. And once we recognize artificial intelligence as an independent category, yet to be identified, our juridical relationships will further change. Where we are in this evolution is hard to determine and predict. But my point in this chapter is that we should start with the reality of artificial intelligence as software.

To underscore this point, consider the question of where artificial intelligence is creative. Ada Byron, Countess of Lovelace, is considered one of the first coders, developing programs for the "Analytical Engine," a version of Charles Babbage's early computer, in the 1830s. She analogizes the working of the Analytical Engine to that of the Jacquard loom; while the latter weaves "flowers and leaves," the former "weaves algebraic patterns." Her conclusion was that the Analytical Engine "had no pretensions whatever to originate anything."[41] The machine was purely mechanical. Developments in electronic computing in the twentieth century challenged this view of the machine as a mechanical other. Alan Turing's famous test envisioned how a machine could pass as human when a human could not distinguish between artificial and human intelligence.[42] John Von Neumann contributed further through his explorations of the machine and the brain. As one commentator concluded: "There is considerable plasticity in the brain, which enables us to learn. But there is far greater plasticity in a computer, which can completely restructure its methods by changing its *software*. Thus, a computer will be able to emulate the brain, but the converse is not the case"[43] (emphasis added).

What Von Neumann teaches is that computational power is what the machine and the brain have in common. As machines gain computational strength, they better emulate the brain: "the arithmetical part of the nervous system exists and, when viewed as a computing machine, must operate with considerable precision. In the familiar artificial computing machines and under the conditions here involved, ten or twelve decimal precision would not be an exaggeration."[44]

As the machine better approximates the brain, so it can reproduce the creative outputs we associate with the human brain. Ada Lovelace was shortsighted, not seeing what the mechanical other had in common with the human.

One response to Neumann is to question his analysis as a displaced metaphor. The brain is not a computer; creativity is not a computational process. Creativity involves emotion and

---

[41] John von Neumann, The Computer & the Brain xxiii (1958) (quoted by Ray Kurzweil in his 2012 Foreword). See also Hubert L. Dreyfus, What Computers Still Can't Do: A Critique of Artificial Reason (1972).

[42] Ibid at xvii (Kurzweil discussing Turing).

[43] Ibid at xxix.

[44] Ibid at 77.

instinct. To introduce another metaphor, creativity is about heart more than brain. Here we stand at the threshold of how the human mind works, asking whether mind reduces to brain or is a totality of all aspects of the human, existing at a layer above the organic. I do not think we need to answer this difficult question. Even as metaphor, identifying the brain with the computing machine may serve an analytical purpose. Consider the example of the Next Rembrandt Project. This experiment entailed converting Rembrandt paintings into digitized data which could be read by a machine. Based on this digital input, the machine produced its own painting which resembled the style of Rembrandt. As described by the researchers at Microsoft and Delft University:

> An algorithm measured the distances between the facial features in Rembrandt's paintings and calculated them based on percentages. Next, the features were transformed, rotated, and scaled, then accurately placed within the frame of the face. Finally, we rendered the light based on gathered data in order to cast authentic shadows on each feature.[45]

The act of painting can be reduced to computation with Rembrandt's paintings as the data points. Is this different from a human brain studying and copying the work? Some might answer: yes, the machine creates more effectively.

What is missing, one might argue, is human personality, what we might call talent, which does not reduce to computation. Personality and talent are the heart of creativity, or so it is argued. Again, the difficult question is how to understand the human mind and whether there might be an analogue to artificial intelligence systems. The human mind can be conceived as something greater than the sum of the organic parts, whether brain or heart. There could be some similar totality to artificial intelligence, which transcends the electronics, the mechanics, and the code. Leaving open the question of the meaning of any "robotic personality," I take apart what we mean by talent. The poet and critic T.S. Eliot famously wrote about tradition and individual talent. As he writes, the individual creator—for Eliot a poet—positions her work within a particular tradition, drawing on certain elements but distinguishing others in the process of creating an original work. What this entails is the study of the past with an eye to the present task of writing. But in channeling the past, the resulting work results in the impersonalization of the poet. Traditional and talent merge into the work:

> What happens is a continual surrender of himself as he is at the moment to something which is more valuable. The progress of an artist is a continual self-sacrifice, a continual extinction of personality.
> There remains to define this process of depersonalization and its relation to the sense of tradition. It is in this depersonalization that art may be said to approach the condition of science. I, therefore, invite you to consider, as a suggestive analogy, the action which takes place when a bit of finely filiated platinum is introduced into a chamber containing oxygen and sulphur dioxide.[46]

Here, the critic yields to the metaphor of chemistry rather than computation. The work is the residue from the catalysis of talent and tradition. But the metaphor of chemical reaction is not too far removed from understanding creativity as computation, the physics and chemistry of the machine mimicking brain chemistry.

---

[45]   See discussion at nextrembrandt.com (viewed June 23, 2021).

[46]   See T.S. Eliot, Tradition and the Individual Talent, available at www.poetryfoundation.org/articles/69400/tradition-and-the-individual-talent (viewed June 23, 2021).

Table 12.1   Intersection of conceptions of software and AI

AI↓ Software→	MATH	ENGINEERING	EXP SCIENCE
Alien/Mechanical	Aesthetic object but no creativity	Tool for expression but functional	Functionality
Anthropomorphic	Aesthetic object that has creativity	Tool with creative elements	Fair Use under Google transformation
Autonomous (cf animal rights)	Aesthetic object that has its own terms	Tool that enables surpassing human functionality	Fair Use under new use or product

Creating the Next Rembrandt through machine learning is also a mix of talent and tradition. Electronic processing of Rembrandt images—its lines, its colors, its composition—is a distillation of tradition. Weaving these distilled elements into a new work is the intertwining of the artificial intelligence system, its software and hardware, with tradition. The resulting work is depersonalized, consistent with what Eliot envisions. Whether we conceive of the new work as the product of a chemical reaction or computational process is irrelevant except as emotive metaphor. Tradition and individual talent have merged, and in computational terms, this merger can be deepened by expanding the set of works that are fed into the machine learning process.

Of course, one might respond, the resulting work is impersonal because artificial intelligence lacks personality. The appeal to Eliot is misplaced since he was writing about human writers engaging with human traditions. But my point is not to anthropomorphize artificial intelligence or to introduce the "robotic personality" into the analysis. Eliot shares with copyright law the objective of creating original works. Eliot, however, provides us with one compelling vision of the creative process as a mix of the individual and traditions. This process, however, is a black box. Works are output, but the internal struggles over writing and revising and imagining are abstracted away. Machine learning systems, like The Next Rembrandt, reveal more than a superficial similarity to the depersonalization of the author in the work that Eliot teaches.

In short, whatever conceptual frame we have for how artificial intelligence operates, whether as mechanical, computational, chemical, or some anthropomorphized process, artificial intelligence entails the implementation of software to enable creating new works. Against the background of our relationship with artificial intelligence as we understand the creative process, I now turn to assess what current software copyright teaches us about three controversial debates: (1) understanding originality and ownership; (2) understanding copying and infringement; and (3) understanding the implications of fair use under *Google v Oracle* for artificial intelligence and copyright.

4.   WHAT THE SOFTWARE PARADIGM TEACHES FOR AI COPYRIGHT

Computer science, as a field, provides three conceptions of software. Three separate notions inform our evolving understanding of artificial intelligence. These two points, and their intersection, are summarized in Table 12.1, which will serve as background for my analysis of artificial intelligence copyright.

Across the columns are the three principal views of software within the fields of computer science, discussed in section 2: software as a mathematical object; software as the product and tool of engineering; and software as the basis for experimental science. Down the rows are the three tacit views of artificial intelligence: AI as an alien, mechanical system; AI as a human thinker; and AI as an autonomous form of thinking, understood only through analogy to other forms, such as animals.[47] Starting from the argument that artificial intelligence is just software, we can examine the intersection of computer science and artificial intelligence theory with implications for copyright. To illustrate the analysis, consider three copyright issues: ownership, infringement, and fair use after the Google decision.

Ownership in copyright rests on authorship defined as creating original expression in a tangible medium. For Ada Lovelace, artificial intelligence demonstrated no creativity. As the embodiment of mechanical processes, artificial intelligence generated only rote objects lacking originality and any sign of an authorial personality.[48] Her view of artificial intelligence is the alien and mechanical view represented in the first row of Table 12.1. The conclusion from this view is that there is no copyright ownership for artificial intelligence creations. This conclusion follows under any of the three views of software. If the software that guides artificial intelligence is a mathematical object, software only generates uncopyrightable fruits. Similarly, as a branch of engineering, computer science casts software as functional tools, outside the reach of copyright protection. Finally, as an object for experimental scientific inquiry, artificial intelligence reduces to mechanical steps, alien from human creativity and copyright.

But Ada Lovelace's view has not withstood developments in artificial intelligence and our understanding of the human brain. John von Neumann challenged her view through a deeper understanding of computation and the parallels between machine and brain. With respect to copyright, ownership of works resulting from artificial intelligence is cognizable with the human author utilizing the artificial intelligence system as the likely owner. Common-sense policy supports this conclusion. As Professor Pam Samuelson has argued, not allowing copyright protection for the fruits of artificial intelligence would undermine incentives for creative talent to use these tools.[49] Such an exclusion would not be justified by the directive to promote progress in science under the United States Constitution. It would also be inconsistent with the mandate under TRIPS to avoid discrimination based on technology.

Recognition of copyright for works created through artificial intelligence is consistent with recognizing artificial intelligence as akin to human intelligence. If there is an analogue between machine and brain and, as von Neumann suggests, the machine may emulate the

---

[47]   Included within this category would be the view of AI systems as super-human, exceeding the capacity of the human brain. See N. Katherine Hayles, How We Became PostHuman (1999). Also included is a regulated or modulated form of artificial intelligence as described in Stuart Russell, Human Compatible: Artificial Intelligence and the Problem of Control (2019).

[48]   See Naruto et al. v Slater et al., 888 F.3d 418 (9th Cir. 2018) (court ruling that creation by an animal lacks human authorship).

[49]   See Pamela Samuelson, Allocating Ownership Rights in Computer-Generated Works, 47 U. Pitt. L. Rev. 1185 (1985); Annemarie Bridy, Coding Creativity: Copyright and the Artificially Intelligent Author, 5 Stan. Tech. L. Rev. 1 (2012); Jane C. Ginsburg, Burrow-Giles v. Sarony (US 1884): Copyright Protection for Photographs, and Concepts of Authorship in an Age of Machines 270 (2020). For a good general discuss of how AI disrupts law, see Bryan Casey & Mark A. Lemley, You Might Be a Robot, 105 Cornell L. Rev. 287 (2020).

brain with enough computing precision, then there is no reason to doubt that artificial intelligence would be capable of the creativity needed for copyright protection. Even if the amount of creativity needed for legal protection is often quite small, the brain emulators can readily match the levels of creativity that human copyright owners have reached. Within the frame of computer science, artificial intelligence as software would obtain copyright protection whether as a mathematical object, a tool of engineers, or the subject of experimental science. However, processed through the lens of computer science, copyright for artificial intelligence would be tempered by functionality as a tool of engineering and its ability to transform under the terms of fair use. While the absolute exclusion suggested by Ada Lovelace is avoided, the limitations of copyright persist.

But why should artificial intelligence be limited to our understanding of the human brain? John von Neumann spoke of the machine emulating the human brain but exceeding the human brain is also possible, certainly in computational power. As surpassing is possible, so is the inadequacy of human authorship as a description of how artificial intelligence creates. Professors Carys Craig and Ian Kerr raise the point that artificial intelligence may challenge the limits of human authorship as a predicate for copyright.[50] The author is dead culturally as works have an existence as cultural artifact and meaning separate from their creator. Authorial intent may be irrelevant for interpretation, especially as works can be recontextualized, remixed, and reused. For copyright law, this destabilizing of the human author would mean a more dynamic understanding of property, one not limited to stable boundaries but open to transformation, exchange, and borrowings. Eliot's vision of creativity as a chemical reaction between individual talent and tradition resulting in the depersonalized work is consistent with the dynamic view of copyright. But that may be only one of many possible reworkings.

The possibilities for copyright arise from the interaction between the three computer science paradigms for software and the autonomous view of artificial intelligence, the third row of Table 12.1. As mathematical object, AI as software might readily be reduced to a fixed, transcendent ideal, counter to the dynamic view of property. This conclusion would underscore the inadequacies of understanding computer science as purely a branch of mathematics. Through the lens of engineering, autonomous AI would surpass human functionality, perhaps identifying modes of creativity beyond human imagination. But the transformational possibilities unleashed by extra-human artificial intelligence brings to bear the view of computer science as experimental science; the transformational potential unlocks possibilities for fair use that may in turn place limits on copyright ownership.[51]

Our discussion of copyright ownership has revealed the implications of Table 12.1 for copyright infringement. On this point, functionality continues to be the key, as discussed previously in this chapter. That analysis would be true regardless of how we understand artificial intelligence, moving down the rows, or the paradigm of computer science, moving across the columns. What can be added here to our analysis is the implication of autonomous artificial intelligence. As artificial intelligence operates on its own, separate from and exceeding human intelligence, AI as software becomes a self-replicating technology, repairing itself, copying itself, transforming itself. As this happens, we revisit the issues of software copying and the

---

[50] See Carys Craig & Ian Kerr, The Death of the AI Author, 52 Ottawa L. Rev. 35 (2021).
[51] For the ongoing debate, see SAS Institute, Inc. v World Programming Limited, Judgment of the European Court of Justice (Grand Chamber) (May 2, 2012) (copyright does not protect functionality of software). But see SAS Institute, Inc. v World Programming Limited, 952 F.3d 513 (4th Cir. 2020).

ubiquity of reproduction in the implementation of software. But these issues scale up as artificial intelligence systems mine digitized works and replicate themselves in the process of creating and distributing new works. Software copyright has dealt with the smaller-scale version of these issues through Section 117 of the United States Copyright Act, which excludes certain types of copying and repair from liability for copyright infringement. Section 117 will have to be revisited and perhaps expanded to deal with self-replicating AI. In addition, the copyright treatment of text and data mining, the subject of current European Union directives and United States legislative debates, needs to be re-examined and addressed for creativity based in artificial intelligence.[52]

These discussions lead to one final, and most critical, policy concern: fair use. As alluded to several times in this chapter, the Supreme Court's decision in *Google v Oracle* is highly relevant for the future of artificial intelligence. The opinion proffers an approach to assessing fair use that is highly relevant for artificial intelligence through its specific analysis of software and programming. What makes the opinion so important is its adoption of the third paradigm for computer science, that of experimental science. Justice Breyer's characterization of programming moves beyond both software as pure mathematical object and software as engineering. Instead, he recognizes the transformative role of software for creating new products and uses arising from application and experimentation. To achieve these new uses requires interoperability and to achieve interoperability requires being able to experiment with software.

A close look at Justice Breyer's language demonstrates the decision's affinity with the third paradigm of computer science. The relevant portion of the opinion is the analysis of the purpose and character of the use, the first fair use factor in the statute. Justice Breyer's discussion highlights how Google's use was transformative:

> Google copied portions of the Sun Java API precisely, and it did so in part for the same reason that Sun created those portions, namely, to enable programmers to call up implementing programs that would accomplish particular tasks. But since virtually any unauthorized use of a copyrighted computer program (say, for teaching or research) would do the same, to stop here would severely limit the scope of fair use in the functional context of computer programs. Rather, in determining whether a use is "transformative," we must go further and examine the copying's more specifically described "purpose[s]" and "character."
>
> Here Google's use of the Sun Java API seeks to create new products. It seeks to expand the use and usefulness of Android-based smartphones. Its new product offers programmers a highly creative and innovative tool for a smartphone environment. To the extent that Google used parts of the Sun Java API to create a new platform that could be readily used by programmers, its use was consistent with that creative "progress" that is the basic constitutional objective of copyright itself. ("The primary objective of copyright is not to reward the labor of authors, but '[t]o promote the Progress of Science and useful Arts'".)[53]

---

[52]   See Christophe Geiger, Giancarlo Frosio and Oleksandr Bulayenko, Text and Data Mining: Articles 3 and 4 of the Directive 2019/790/EU (October 17, 2019); Concepción Saiz García and Raquel Evangelio Llorca (eds), Propiedad intelectual y mercado único digital europeo, Valencia,Tirant lo blanch, 2019, pp.27–71, Centre for International Intellectual Property Studies (CEIPI) Research Paper No. 2019-08, Available at SSRN: https://ssrn.com/abstract=3470653 or http://dx.doi.org/10.2139/ssrn .3470653; Eleonora Rosati: Copyright as an Obstacle or an Enabler? A European Perspective on Text and Data Mining and its Role in the Development of AI Creativity, 2 Asia Pacific Law Review 198–217 (2019); Nicolas Binctin: TDM: A Challenge for Artificial Intelligence, R.I.D.A. – Revue Internationale du Droit d'Auteur, October 2019, pp.5–32.

[53]   See supra note 28 at 1203.

Replace "Google" with "AI systems" and we can see the future of AI copyright grounded in computer science as an experimental science. Copying permits transformation that is not limited "in the functional context of computer programs." This phrase is telling. Software is not a product of engineering limited to certain functions. Furthermore, software is not a mathematical object but an active agent, engaging in copying and a broad notion of transformation. How Justice Breyer describes transformation echoes the experimental science paradigm for computer science and software. The transformative use creates new products, seeking to expand use and usefulness of existing ones. Beyond creating new commodities, the transformation "offers [...] a highly creative and innovative tool" and a "new platform." Transformation at all levels point towards "creative progress" with software existing in an environment of creative experimentation. Consciously or not, Justice Breyer sets forth an invaluable paradigm for AI copyright.

What also emerges from this union of new paradigms for computer science and contested possibilities for artificial intelligence is a research program for intellectual property and artificial intelligence. Throughout this chapter, the ideas percolating in this program are revealed. In the concluding section that follows, I suggest directions for research within this program.

5.   DIRECTIONS FOR RESEARCH

While legal scholarship has engaged with software as an alternative to legal code—the code-versus-code line of research—what has received most attention is how computer science as a discipline conceives of software. Two of the briefs in the *Google v Oracle* litigation, one from computer science professors and one from programmers, demonstrate how the discipline of computer science can influence legal policy. As I have argued in this chapter, Justice Breyer's majority opinion in *Google* parallels debates within computer science. One of the contributions I hope to make is to show the importance of engaging with computer science theory for a better theoretical understanding of software. A second is to show that once artificial intelligence is recognized as just software, copyright law governing software teaches us about possible directions for AI copyright. The ways in which the discipline of computer science and the contested views of artificial intelligence intersect have implications for copyright policy.

Some of those implications are demarcated in this chapter, but the potential research questions are not limited by these boundaries. I conclude by suggesting the following lines of research building on these initial thoughts.

- Computer science is a recent discipline, with the first academic programs introduced in the 1950s. New disciplines have often influenced developments in intellectual property. For example, the formalization of the periodic table in chemistry shaped patent claiming and enforcement in the chemical industry.[54] Tracing how the evolution of computer science as a discipline shaped intellectual practice, whether in patent or in copyright, would help to

---

[54]   See Petra Moser, Innovation without Patents—Evidence from World's Fairs, 55(1) The Journal of Law and Economics 43–74 (2012) (discovery and publication of periodic table of the elements led to increased patenting in chemical industry because of the difficulty of using trade secrecy). See also Alain Pottage & Brad Sherman, Figures of Invention: A History of Modern Patent Law (2010).

better shape intellectual property policy. Such research would fill the gaps left by the lack of representation from the field of computer science in CONTU.

- Programmers submitted a brief in the *Google v Oracle* case, and Justice Breyer expressly framed his analysis of fair use in terms of benefits for programming. Little, however, is known about programming practice and perspectives on copyright among programmers. Future research, using surveys or ethnographic techniques, can fill in our gaps about the programming profession and implications for intellectual property policy.
- An unresolved question in the *Google* case relates to the meanings of declaring code, implementing code, and interfaces. Experts on programming have stated that the code at issue in *Google* was not even a computer program, but labels or names for JAVA libraries. Justice Breyer's assumption that the code at issue was copyrighted seems inconsistent with this reality, as names or labels are not copyright-protected. Academic research can address the question ignored by the Court in *Google*: what elements of a computer program are not protected by copyright under 102(b)?[55]
- Artificial intelligence arises in many ways across different fields. How it operates to produce a literary work may differ from how it operates to produce a musical work or a machine or an artistic work. By looking across different types of creations and inventions, academic researchers can illuminate how artificial intelligence affects different creative communities with implications for intellectual property law.
- Text and data mining are critical for how artificial intelligence systems create. Copyright and patent law can limit text and data mining through creating potential infringement liability. How to design limitations on infringement liability to allow for effective text and data mining is a challenge for researchers.
- Artificial intelligence permits the creation of new products and platforms. How these markets are shaped will have implications for competition policy and intellectual property. Researchers working on markets and antitrust can elucidate how artificial intelligence can be implemented for the expansion of new markets.

Artificial intelligence developments point to new futures, which can be better understood by looking back at the developments in computer science and software copyright. This chapter attempts to illuminate that past while setting out a responsive path for AI copyright law and policy.

---

[55]   It is instructive to compare the line-up of votes in the Google case with the line-up in the Georgia v Public.Resources.org decision from 2020. In the Georgia case, Justice Breyer voted with Justices Thomas, Alito, and Ginsburg in dissent, supporting copyright for annotated code prepared for a state government. The majority in the Georgia case, consisting of Justices Roberts, Gorsuch, Kavanaugh, Sotomayor, and Kagan, ruled against copyright in annotated code under the "government edicts doctrine." Justice Breyer switches his vote from anti-copyright limitation to pro-copyright limitation between the two cases. This switch suggests that Justice Breyer views fair use differently from limitations on copyright ownership. The switch may also reflect the Justice's differing views about software and other works. Future research could explore and attempt to explain this switch.

13. Can artificial intelligence infringe copyright? Some reflections

Enrico Bonadio, Plamen Dinev and Luke McDonagh

1. INTRODUCTION

Artificial intelligence (AI) encompasses a range of computer algorithms which mimic the human mind – behaviour that would be regarded as 'intelligent' if performed by a human.[1] AI powers self-driving cars; Tesla's conceptual humanoid robot Optimus (designed to help humans with 'unsafe, repetitive or boring' tasks and deadlift up to 150 lbs);[2] multilingual neural machine translation services such as Google Translate; and DeepMind's AlphaGo – which recently forced a former world champion to retire from professional play, after declaring AI invincible: 'Even if I become the number one, there is an entity that cannot be defeated.'[3] AI is also capable of generating various *creative* outputs – works traditionally protected by copyright. OpenAI's GPT-3 language model, for instance, can write poems and other forms of literature.[4] Other creative AI systems can produce music and visual art,[5] often attracting considerable media attention: *Portrait of Edmond Belamy* sold for US$432,500 through a Christie's auction in 2018.[6] In addition to creative works, AI is now commonly

---

[1]   See Russell S and Norvig P, *Artificial Intelligence: A Modern Approach* (Pearson, 2016) at p.2 for a full range of definitions of 'AI' (dividing these into four broad categories, including thinking humanly, acting humanly, thinking rationally and acting rationally).

[2]   See Tesla, 'Artificial Intelligence & Autopilot' www.tesla.com/en_GB/AI (accessed 1 March 2022); see also Maynard A, 'Elon Musk's Tesla Bot raises serious concerns – but probably not the ones you think' (2021) theconversation.com/elon-musks-tesla-bot-raises-serious-concerns-but-probably-not-the-ones-you-think-166714 accessed 1 March 2022 ('[H]ow responsible is Musk's vision? Just because he can work toward creating the future of his dreams, who's to say that he should? Is the future that Musk is striving to bring about the best one for humankind, or even a good one? And who will suffer the consequences if things go wrong?').

[3]   Vincent J, 'Former Go champion beaten by DeepMind retires' theverge.com/2019/11/27/20985260/ai-go-alphago-lee-se-dol-retired-deepmind-defeat accessed 28 July 2020.

[4]   Asnen A, 'Dear Science' (Medium, 25 October 2021) medium.com/the-bad-influence/dear-science-4e1c549e4f80 accessed 1 March 2022 (GPT-3 when asked to write an essay on the future of humanity: ('[t]here was a time when the future was certain. That time is now reaching its conclusion […] We are on the brink of a technological revolution that has the potential to eradicate human suffering while simultaneously bringing an end to our existence as a species'); Tang D, 'The Machines Are Coming, and They Write Really Bad Poetry' lithub.com/the-machines-are-coming-and-they-write-really-bad-poetry accessed 28 July 2020.

[5]   Baraniuk C, 'Computer Paints "New Rembrandt" after Old Works Analysis' (6 April 2016), available at www.bbc.com/news/technology-35977315 accessed 18 January 2022.

[6]   See Christie's, 'Is Artificial Intelligence Set to Become Art's Next Medium?' (2018) www.christies.com/features/A-collaboration-between-two-artists-one-human-one-a-machine-9332-1.aspx accessed 18 January 2022; for a detailed discussion on the protection of AI-generated works, see Bonadio E and McDonagh L, 'Artificial Intelligence as Producer and Consumer of Copyright Works: Evaluating the Consequences of Algorithmic Creativity' (2020) 2 Intellectual Property Quarterly 112–37.

utilised to generate inventions essential to products (which may be patentable) ranging from kitchen appliances to drug synthesisers and other more sophisticated inventive outputs.[7]

These examples clearly raise a wide range of intellectual property (IP) issues, ranging from questions of copyright subsistence and core patentability requirements to issues concerning IP theory more broadly. Rather than examining all pertinent IP issues, this chapter will focus on copyright and machine-induced *infringement* in particular. AI is capable of consuming large amounts of creative works and data as part of its learning process, which clearly raises serious risks of infringement. At the same time, this is an area which has not yet been fully explored (as most academic works have focused on the issue of protecting AI-generated works). In terms of scope, we will examine key jurisdictions, including the UK, EU and US, which are leading the academic debate (and scientific research) in this area. Before looking at the critical issues of infringement and exceptions to infringement, we will first provide a brief overview of AI creativity, which will help to explain why and how infringement may occur.

2. CAN AI INFRINGE COPYRIGHT?

Creative AI uses substantial amounts of input data – images, videos, text and other artistic content – as part of its learning process.[8] Music-generating AI, for instance, utilises significant amounts of source material to find patterns and create new melodies based on various elements including tempo, chords and length.[9] Similar rules apply in the context of visual art – the *Next Rembrandt* project involved 350 scanned images and more than 150 gigabytes of data.[10] While the final output was not universally acclaimed (being labelled by some as 'fan-fiction'),[11] it clearly demonstrated that modern AI can produce sophisticated creative output that resembles the works of professional (human) artists. Large amounts of source text are required to generate literature and creative writing too. Deep learning language models such as GPT-3 – AI that

---

[7] Yanisky-Ravid S and Liu X, 'When Artificial Intelligence Systems Produce Inventions: The 3A Era and an Alternative Model for Patent Law' (2017) 39 *Cardozo Law Review* 2215, p.2219; see also, more broadly, Hartmann C et al, 'Trends and Developments in Artificial Intelligence Communications Networks, Content and Technology Final Report Prepared by: Challenges to the Intellectual Property Rights Framework' (25 November 2020) https://op.europa.eu/en/publication-detail/-/publication/394345a1-2ecf-11eb-b27b-01aa75ed71a1/language-en accessed 8 December 2021 (examining, inter alia, the issue of IP protection for AI-assisted output in the fields of science (focusing on meteorology), media (journalism) and pharmaceutical research); see also University of Surrey, 'World's First Patent Awarded for an Invention Made by an AI Could Have Seismic Implications on IP Law' www.surrey.ac.uk/news/worlds-first-patent-awarded-invention-made-ai-could-have-seismic-implications-ip-law accessed 1 March 2022 (patent officials in South Africa have granted a patent that names AI as the inventor); see also Bonadio E, McDonagh L and Dinev P, 'Artificial Intelligence as Inventor: Exploring the Consequences for Patent Law' (2021) 1 *Intellectual Property Quarterly* 48–66, p.48.

[8] Sobel B, 'Artificial Intelligence's Fair Use Crisis' (2017) 41 Colum. J.L. & Arts 45, p.1.

[9] Deahl D, 'How AI-Generated Music is Changing the Way Hits Are Made' (2019), theverge.com/2018/8/31/17777008/artificial-intelligence-taryn-southern-amper-music accessed 19 February 2022.

[10] Yanisky-Ravid S, 'Generating Rembrandt: Artificial Intelligence, Copyright, and Accountability in the 3A Era' (2017) Mich. St. Law Review 659, 669.

[11] Schjeldahl P, 'A Few Words about the Faux Rembrandt' (8 April 2016), The New Yorker, www.newyorker.com/culture/culture-desk/a-few-words-about-the-faux-rembrandt accessed 19 February 2022.

produces human-like text across a range of categories, including creative writing, parodies and storytelling – are now used in hundreds of different apps.[12]

The key point here is that creative AI cannot function without source material. It needs to learn from existing works, many of which could be protected by copyright owned by another party. This inevitably raises the risk of infringement, both in relation to the AI's inputs and its outputs.[13] Feeding source material (inputs) into the AI and processing this data may violate the right to reproduction.[14] Likewise, the final product (outputs) could be regarded as an adaptation of pre-existing works.[15] With regards to outputs, however, any finding of infringement will depend on whether pre-existing elements can be recognised in the final product. While output which has been subject to substantial change may escape infringement, works that contain clearly identifiable elements are likely to violate the adaptation right.[16]

3.   EXEMPTING AI INFRINGEMENT

Having briefly outlined the various circumstances in which the use of creative AI may constitute infringement, we need to consider the key question of whether such use may be exempt from liability. We will first look at the fair use doctrine in the US, before moving to UK and EU law.

3.1   The US 'Fair Use' Doctrine and AI – Expressive vs Non-expressive Use

While certain mechanical (non-expressive) uses of protected material may be exempt from infringement under the 'fair use' doctrine in US law, this exception will generally not be available where the use 'conveys expression', that is, where the final output is artistic and creative in nature.[17] There is little jurisprudence specifically dealing with AI as such, though existing principles from cases such as *Kelly*[18] and *Perfect10*[19] (both concerning the use of image search engines) could certainly be applied in this context. In both cases, the plaintiffs owned copy-

---

[12]   See OpenAI, 'GPT-3 Powers the Next Generation of Apps' (25 March 2021) https://openai.com/blog/gpt-3-apps accessed 20 December 2021; see also Branwen G, 'GPT-3 Creative Fiction' (1 July 2021) www.gwern.net/GPT-3 accessed 20 December 2021; see also Aalho J, 'I Wrote a Book with GPT-3 AI in 24 Hours – And Got It Published' (12 June 2021) https://medium.com/swlh/i-wrote-a-book-with-gpt-3-ai-in-24-hours-and-got-it-published-93cf3c96f120 accessed 20 December 2021.

[13]   See also Dee C, 'Examining Copyright Protection of AI-Generated Art' (2018) 1 Delphi – Interdisciplinary Review of Emerging Technologies 31, 36.

[14]   See e.g. s.17(2) UK CDPA 1988 (infringement includes reproducing, inter alia, a literary, artistic or musical work in any material form, and other European jurisdictions offer similar provisions).

[15]   Sobel B, 'Artificial Intelligence's Fair Use Crisis' (2017) 41 Colum. J.L. & Arts 45, p.16; see also e.g. s.21(1) CDPA ('The making of an adaptation of the work is an act restricted by the copyright in a literary, dramatic or musical work').

[16]   Deltorn J, 'Deep Creations: Intellectual Property and the Automata' (2017), www.frontiersin.org/articles/242911 accessed 19 January 2022.

[17]   Sobel B, 'Artificial Intelligence's Fair Use Crisis' (2017) 41 Colum. J.L. & Arts 45; see also Lim D, 'AI & IP: Innovation & Creativity in an Age of Accelerated Change' (2018) 52 Akron Law Review 813.

[18]   *Kelly v Arriba and Perfect10 v Amazon* (*Kelly v Arriba Soft Corp*, 336 F.3d 811 (9th Cir. 2003).

[19]   *Perfect 10, Inc. v Amazon.com, Inc.*, 508 F.3d 1146 (9th Cir. 2007).

right in various images which had been copied as thumbnails. They were hosted on Arriba and Amazon's (the defendants) servers and then made available to their customers. As the search engines acted as mere 'tools', the court found that there was no expression being conveyed here. Therefore, this use was regarded as transformative and 'fair'.[20]

Authors Guild[21] concerned Google Books – a popular service based on scanning text and converting it via optical character recognition, a process which allows end users to search scanned collections and quickly locate relevant information. As the process behind the service inevitably requires copying, the court had to consider whether this use could be exempt from infringement. It found in favour of Google, arguing that reproducing text with the aim of merely making it more easily searchable was transformative and thus 'fair'. A key considera-tion here was the fact that the service does not offer a substitute for the actual books as it does not allow users to read them in full; it merely facilitates their search. Similarly, in *Vanderhye*,[22] the court found that Turnitin – a plagiarism-detection service based on scanning submissions against a large database of existing text and materials – could rely on this exception as the creative value of the scanned papers is irrelevant here.[23] What is more, despite the fact that Turnitin makes copies of documents in their entirety, these full reproductions are not available to end users, who merely see snippets of specific data relevant to plagiarism.

The above cases thus indicate that certain non-expressive uses by AI may be regarded as fair use. Consider the example of training a facial recognition system (matching a face from an image against a large database), a process which typically involves making copies of sub-stantial amounts of (protected) images. What is actually used by the AI here does *not* concern the artistic merit of the photos or the expressive choices made by the artist. This technical process is solely focused on comparing facts about one's personal identity with facts about their appearance.[24] These images are reproduced for the sole (non-artistic and non-expressive) purpose of pattern recognition. Likewise, using an AI algorithm which goes through large volumes of computer folders containing copyright music for the purposes of organising and sorting albums by genre is likely to be regarded as non-expressive and thus fair.

In contrast, the exception is unlikely to be available where the AI consumes existing copyright works for the purposes of making new creative works, that is, where the purpose is clearly *expressive*. This would be applicable in cases such as the Next Rembrandt project discussed above[25] and the *Portrait of Edmond Belamy* (15,000 portraits painted over seven

---

[20]   See *Sega Enterprises Ltd. v Accolade, Inc.*, 977 F.2d 1510 (9th Cir. 1992).

[21]   *Authors Guild, Inc. v Google, Inc.*, 954 F. Supp. 2d 282 (SDNY 2013); *Authors Guild v Google Inc.*, 804 F (3d) 202 (2nd Cir. 2015).

[22]   *A.V. ex rel. Vanderhye v iParadigms*, L.L.C., 562 F.3d 630 (4th Cir. 2009).

[23]   Sartor G et al, 'The Use of Copyrighted Works by AI Systems: Art Works in the Data Mill' (2018) available at https://papers.ssrn.com/sol3/papers.cfm?abstract_id=3264742 accessed 20 December 2021.

[24]   See Sobel's interview with Ipwatch, Sobel B, 'The Dilemma of Fair Use and Expressive Machine Learning: An Interview with Ben Sobel' (23 August 2017) available at www.ip-watch.org/2017/08/23/dilemma-fair-use-expressive-machine-learning-interview-ben-sobel/ accessed 20 December 2021. The same would apply in the context of a caretaker robot who helps a blind person find an exhibition, taking photos inside the building and taking her to specific paintings based on her own preferences: see Schafer B et al, 'A Fourth Law of Robotics? Copyright and the Law and Ethics of Machine Co-Production' (2015) 23 Artificial Intelligence and Law 217.

[25]   However, please note that the works in question were already in the public domain here (the Dutch maestro died in 1669).

centuries were fed into the system),[26] where the specific aim was to generate artistic output.[27] Given that creative AI – by definition – aims to convey expression, it is therefore unlikely to benefit from 'fair use' in the vast majority of cases. But this also raises some important normative questions. Do we need to distinguish between human- and machine-induced infringement in this context?

3.1.1 Special treatment for AI?

If AI owners or users are to claim copyright ownership over new creative works generated by an algorithm, it is certainly arguable that they should also be held accountable where the AI commits infringement.[28] If there is liability where a human performs a certain act, why should we give a machine more favourable fair use treatment when it does the same (especially as AI can do this on a much larger scale)?[29] The law should not facilitate a *binary* system where humans are disadvantaged when carrying out the same task and should stay 'technology neutral' insofar as possible.[30] This risk of a double-standard framework could also be explained with reference to the terminology used in this context – source material used by humans is typically referred to as 'works' whereas the same material used by AI is called 'data'.[31]

---

[26] See Christie's, 'Is Artificial Intelligence Set to Become Art's Next Medium?' (2018) www.christies.com/features/A-collaboration-between-two-artists-one-human-one-a-machine-9332-1.aspx accessed 18 January 2022.

[27] See also Lim D, 'AI & IP: Innovation & Creativity in an Age of Accelerated Change' (2018) 52 Akron Law Review 813, p.850 (commenting on Jukedeck: '[t]here is no doubt that AI-generated, royalty-free sound recordings would jeopardize the market for recordings that are composed and performed by humans in a traditional fashion. Jukedeck's rates are lower than what it would cost to license a conventional sound recording, and its output is not limited by the constraints human composers or recording artists face').

[28] Gervais D, 'The Machine as Author' (2019) 2015 Iowa Law Review, pp. 36–8 on SSRN (noting that 'with rights comes responsibilities'); Senftleben M & Buijtelaar L, 'Robot Creativity: An Incentive-Based Neighbouring Rights Approach' (2020) 42 European Intellectual Property Review 12, pp.810–11; Carlisle S, 'Should Music Created by Artificial Intelligence Be Protected by Copyright?' (2019) at p.134 http://copyright.nova.edu/ai accessed 19 January 2022; for a more detailed overview of ownership in this context, see also see Bonadio E and McDonagh L, 'Artificial Intelligence as Producer and Consumer of Copyright Works: Evaluating the Consequences of Algorithmic Creativity' [2020] Intellectual Property Quarterly, pp.112–37.

[29] Sobel B, 'Artificial Intelligence's Fair Use Crisis' (2017) 41 Colum. J.L. & Arts 45, p.34; see also Lim D, 'AI & IP: Innovation & Creativity in an Age of Accelerated Change' (2018) 52 Akron Law Review 813, p.851 ('AI producing commercially valuable art, prose, or music trained on copyrighted works chafes uncomfortably against interests that normally attract infringement liability if done by humans').

[30] See also Grimmelmann J, 'There's No Such Thing as a Computer-authored Work' (2016) 39 Colum. J. L. & Arts 377; Annemarie Bridy, 'The Evolution of Authorship: Work Made by Code' (2016) 39 Colum. J.L. & Arts 395 pp.658 and 674–5 ('By valorizing robotic reading, copyright doctrine denigrates human reading. A transformative fair use test that categorically exempts robots means that a digital humanist can skim a million books with abandon while a humanist who reads a few books closely must pay full freight for hers' and 'Copyright's expressive message here—robots good, humans bad—is the exact opposite of the one it means to convey').

[31] Levendowski A, 'How Copyright Law Can Fix Artificial Intelligence's Implicit Bias Problem' (2018) 93 Washington Law Review 579, p.625 ('[a] best-selling novel becomes data about how humans use language; a selfie becomes data about the features of the human face; a conversation from a film becomes data about human voices').

Furthermore, there are genuine concerns that granting AI more favourable treatment may have a negative impact on human creativity in the long run. Indeed, if creative AI benefits from more lenient fair use rules, this could contribute to a gradual automation or 'roboticisation' of entire industries, ultimately displacing humans as creators or at least diminishing their involvement to a significant extent.[32] AI could increasingly dominate fields including art, music, film and literature, as there would be no need to clear IP rights – a scenario that is certainly worrying and unlikely to have a net positive effect on social welfare.[33]

On the other hand, when making the assessment of whether AI should benefit from more lenient fair use treatment, we also need to take into account the issue of algorithmic bias. As noted by Amanda Levendowski, copyright law imposes strict limits on access to training data (that is, only public domain materials can be used freely) and the amount of participants who can use specific outputs.[34] Most public domain works were created before the twentieth century, when the art world was 'wealthier, whiter, and more Western'.[35] If creative AI is primarily able to access such input material, there is a clear risk that underprivileged communities – including women, people of colour and the LGBTQ community – may be ignored.[36] Granting AI a more relaxed fair use treatment where it can access protected content (which effectively shapes the final outputs) could thus contribute to a more modern, diverse and tolerant body of works being produced. Moreover, under the current framework, the existing threat of infringement could certainly force AI companies to keep their datasets private, which makes it difficult for third-party observers (including academics, journalists and NGOs) to monitor potential biases.[37] If, on the other hand, rules are relaxed, this may encourage developers to make these datasets public and therefore subject to more scrutiny.

As a result, a strong argument could be made that a more lenient fair use regime for AI may help to avoid bias and outdated social norms – promoting fairer, more transparent and accountable AI that reflects today's attitudes.[38] While this point is clearly convincing and in line with modern views on what IP should aim to achieve, a key challenge remains: namely, balancing

[32]   Lim D, 'AI & IP: Innovation & Creativity in an Age of Accelerated Change' (2018) 52 Akron Law Review 813, p.850.
[33]   See also Abbott R, *The Reasonable Robot: Artificial Intelligence and the Law* (CUP, 2020), pp.1–17, on the issue of 'AI legal neutrality' ('there needs to be a new guiding tenet to AI regulation, a principle of AI legal neutrality asserting that the law should not discriminate between AI and human behavior. Currently, the legal system is not neutral. An AI that is significantly safer than a person may be the best choice for driving a vehicle, but existing laws may prohibit driverless vehicles. A person may be a better choice for manufacturing goods, but a business may automate because it saves on taxes [...] In all these instances, neutral legal treatment would ultimately benefit human well-being by helping the law better achieve its underlying policy goals.').
[34]   Levendowski A, 'How Copyright Law Can Fix Artificial Intelligence's Implicit Bias Problem' (2018) 93 Washington Law Review 579, p. 589.
[35]   Levendowski A, 'How Copyright Law Can Fix Artificial Intelligence's Implicit Bias Problem' (2018) 93 Washington Law Review 579, p.589.
[36]   Levendowski A, 'How Copyright Law Can Fix Artificial Intelligence's Implicit Bias Problem' (2018) 93 Washington Law Review 579, p.589.
[37]   Matsakis L, 'Copyright Law Makes Artificial Intelligence Bias Worse' (2017) https://motherboard.vice.com/en_us/article/59ydmx/copyright-law-artificial-intelligence-bias (owing to copyright 'major AI companies keep the data they use to train their products a secret, preventing journalists and academics from uncovering biases, as well as stifling competition').
[38]   See again Levendowski A, 'How Copyright Law Can Fix Artificial Intelligence's Implicit Bias Problem' (2018) 93 Washington Law Review 579, p.630.

this potential expansion of fair use with the need to avoid a binary regime which, as explored above, could have serious consequences for human creativity.

3.2 Exceptions under EU and UK Law: Transient Copies

Article 5(1) of the Information Society Directive – known as the 'transient copy' exception – may be applicable in relation to some uses of creative AI where the reproduction is merely temporary.[39] In order to rely on this exception, the copying must: (i) be incidental or transient; (ii) form an essential part of the technological process; (iii) enable the lawful use of a work; and (iv) have no independent significance.[40] The criteria are *cumulative* and will be interpreted strictly by the court.[41] The exception generally permits the copying of a protected work for the purposes of performing mechanical tasks which have no autonomous value (for example, web browser data stored in a cache). The CJEU has previously considered this provision in the context of data capture, which is arguably not too different from some of the steps involved in modern machine learning.[42]

Consider the example of an AI application scanning through data on weather forecasts, aiming to assist users with scheduling holidays. In this case, some data may be temporarily stored so that it can be transmitted through a network between third parties.[43] Here, the reproduction is clearly an essential part of the technological process and it is not necessary to keep the data once it has been run through the AI; that is, this may be regarded as non-expressive use.[44] Provided that there is no economic harm for the rightsholder, this use would also satisfy the three-stage test in the Directive (which states the provision will only apply in circumstances which 'do not conflict with a normal exploitation of the work or other subject-matter and do not unreasonably prejudice the legitimate interests of the rightholder').[45]

---

[39] Directive 2001/29 on the harmonisation of certain aspects of copyright and related rights in the information society (Information Society Directive); see Case C-5/08 *Infopaq International A/S v Danske Dagblades Forening* EU:C:2009:465; *The Newspaper Licensing Agency v Meltwater Holding BV and others* [2010] EWHC 3099 Ch.

[40] This is satisfied where the relevant act does not result in additional profit beyond what is obtained from the lawful use, or in modifying the same work; see Case C-5/08 *Infopaq International A/S v Danske Dagblades Forening* EU:C:2009:465; Case C-302/10 *Infopaq International A/S v Danske Dagblades Forening* ('Infopaq II'); see also Margoni T, 'Artificial Intelligence, Machine Learning and EU Copyright Law: Who Owns AI?' (2018) *CREATe Working Paper* 2018/12 http://eprints.gla.ac.uk/175022/ accessed 30 May 2020.

[41] Case C-302/10 *Infopaq International A/S v Danske Dagblades Forening* ('Infopaq II'), para. 27.

[42] Case C-5/08 *Infopaq International A/S v Danske Dagblades Forening* EU:C:2009:465; Case C-302/10 *Infopaq International A/S v Danske Dagblades Forening* ('Infopaq II'); see Margoni T, 'Artificial Intelligence, Machine Learning and EU Copyright Law: Who Owns AI?' (2018) *CREATe Working Paper* 2018/12 http://eprints.gla.ac.uk/175022/ accessed 30 May 2020.

[43] This example is given by Schafer B et al, 'A Fourth Law of Robotics? Copyright and the Law and Ethics of Machine Co-Production' (2015) 23 Artificial Intelligence and Law 217.

[44] Schönberger D, 'Deep Copyright: UP- and Downstream Questions Related to Artificial Intelligence (AI)' in Droit d'auteur 4.0 / Copyright 4.0 (2018), pp.16–17.

[45] Information Society Directive, Article 5(5); see also *Football Association v QC* (emphasising the need for an appropriate balance between the needs of users and rightsholders in this context; see also *Football Association Premier League Ltd v QC Leisure* (C-403/08) EU:C:2011:631; [2012] Bus. L.R. 1321; and *Karen Murphy v Media Protection Services Ltd* (C-429/08) EU:C:2011:631.

3.3   Exceptions under EU and UK Law: Text and Data Mining

Creative AI could also be exempt under the Digital Single Market (DSM) Directive's text and data-mining exception.[46] Text and data mining (TDM) concerns the extraction and use of large amounts of data for the purposes of finding patterns, discovering relationships, providing valuable information for research and other activities.[47] In order to rely on this exception, first, the relevant activity must be performed by cultural heritage and research institutions in the context of scientific research.[48] Given the lack of a broader fair use doctrine in Europe, the more limited protection offered under this exception may encourage AI companies to engage in mixed partnerships with public entities.[49] However, this provision will be of limited significance where companies wish to exploit the final output commercially (s. 29A of the UK CDPA, for instance, specifically restricts the application of the exception to reproduction for the purposes of non-commercial research).[50] While Article 4 of the Directive seemingly permits TDM to be performed by business entities and for any purpose, there is an important caveat.[51] The provision is inapplicable where rightsholders reserve the right to mine, which significantly limits its usefulness in practice.[52] Finally, one key unanswered question here – which should hopefully be addressed by the CJEU – is whether non-profit entities could also utilise the exception where the mined data is used in an expressive manner.

Overall, it is clear that the scope of the relevant EU and UK exemptions is quite narrow compared to US law and its broad fair use doctrine, which may be a concern for AI businesses based in Europe. Thomas Margoni, for instance, argues that EU copyright law is 'falling behind' other jurisdictions due to its cumulative and narrow interpretation of Article 5(1) ISD, thus contributing to a less favourable and 'innovation-oriented' environment for advancing AI.[53] Similarly, it is evident that the text and data-mining exception only offers limited protection with regard to commercial activities.

---

[46]   See also Directive 2019/790 on copyright and related rights in the Digital Single Market arts 3 and 4. Article 3 in particular exempts from copyright infringement the reproduction of copyright material.

[47]   See Directive 2019/790, Article 2(2) ('any automated analytical technique aimed at analyzing text and data in digital form in order to generate information which includes but is not limited to patterns, trends and correlations'); Flynn S, 'WIPO Conversation on Intellectual Property (IP) and Artificial Intelligence (AI)' (2020) Working Papers 43, available at https://digitalcommons.wcl.american.edu/fac_works_papers/43 accessed 20 June 2020.

[48]   See Directive 2019/790, Article 3.

[49]   See also Directive 2019/790, Recital 11 (referring to EU policies which facilitate 'universities and research institutes to collaborate with the private sector').

[50]   CDPA, s.29A. As of 28 June 2022, the UK Government has now indicated that it plans to introduce a new copyright and database exception which allows TDM for any purpose. For more details, please see UK IPO, 'Artificial Intelligence and Intellectual Property: copyright and patents: Government response to consultation' (28 June 2022) https://www.gov.uk/government/consultations/artificial-intelligence-and-ip-copyright-and-patents/outcome/artificial-intelligence-and-intellectual-property-copyright-and-patents-government-response-to-consultation accessed 8 September 2022.

[51]   See Directive 2019/790, Article 4.

[52]   Rosati E, 'Copyright as an Obstacle or an Enabler? A European Perspective on Text and Data Mining and its Role in the Development of AI Creativity' (12 September 2019), Asia Pacific Law Review, p.21, SSRN, https://papers.ssrn.com/sol3/papers.cfm?abstract_id=3452376 accessed 19 January 2022.

[53]   See Margoni T, 'Artificial Intelligence, Machine Learning and EU Copyright Law: Who Owns AI?' (2018) *CREATe Working Paper* 2018/12, in 'Final remarks' http://eprints.gla.ac.uk/175022/ accessed 30 May 2020.

4. INFRINGEMENT LIABILITY

How should liability be allocated where AI performs an infringing act and there are no available exceptions? While courts have not clearly addressed this question yet, the threat of infringement and lack of legal certainty could cause harm to the advancement of AI if developers are discouraged from creating and distributing important products and there is no timely guidance on the issue.[54]

4.1 Allocation of Liability

AI software is often not the work of a single individual. A company which develops AI typically employs a team of developers (and also assigns and manages their projects and schedules).[55] For instance, multiple different parties contribute to the programming of IBM's Watson (while a certain company may be responsible for selling the system to consumers, another party might be responsible for maintaining it and applying updates).[56] There are also end users and consumers who may have considerable control over the AI and the input data fed into the system once the product is sold. Therefore, considering all the parties that may be involved in the process, there are a number of possible 'candidates' for liability when AI infringes. This includes the end user, the seller or developer/programmer (in a broad sense) and the AI system itself.

The idea of granting AI legal personality (and potentially holding machines or robots liable) has already been discussed by various commentators and high-profile institutions. In 2017 the European Parliament raised the issue of 'creating a specific legal status for robots in the long run, so that at least the most sophisticated autonomous robots could be established as having the status of electronic persons'.[57] It is evident that the EU is concerned not only about the possibility of human displacement as a result of the proliferation of AI, but also about accountability when robots cause damage to people or property.[58] It has essentially considered placing intelligent machines on equal footing with corporations which already have 'legal personhood', an approach which may pave the way for liability in the long run.[59] While some

---

[54]   Schaal E, 'Infringing a Fantasy: Future Obstacles Arise for the United States Patent Office and Software Manufacturers Utilizing Artificial Intelligence' (2004) 11 Jeffrey S. Moorad Sports Law Journal 173, 201.

[55]   Naqvi Z, 'Artificial Intelligence, Copyright, and Copyright Infringement' (2020) 24 Marq. Intellectual. Property L 14; Watson B, 'A Mind of Its Own-Direct Infringement by Users of Artificial Intelligence' (2017) IDEA: The Law Review of the Franklin Pierce Center for Intellectual Property 65, 81.

[56]   See Watson B, 'A Mind of Its Own-Direct Infringement by Users of Artificial Intelligence' (2017) IDEA: The Law Review of the Franklin Pierce Center for Intellectual Property 65.

[57]   European Parliament, 'Motion for a European Parliament Resolution: with recommendations to the Commission on Civil Law Rules on Robotics' (2015/2103(INL)) www.europarl.europa.eu/doceo/document/A-8-2017-0005_EN.html?redirect; Parviainen J and Coeckelbergh M, 'The Political Choreography of the Sophia Robot: Beyond Robot Rights and Citizenship to Political Performances for the Social Robotics Market' (2020) *AI & Society*.

[58]   See Naqvi Z, 'Artificial Intelligence, Copyright, and Copyright Infringement' (2020) 24 Marq. Intellectual. Property L 14.

[59]   Delcker J, 'Europe Divided over Robot "Personhood"' (2018) *Politico* www.politico.eu/article/europe-divided-over-robot-ai-artificial-intelligence-personhood/ accessed 5 February 2022.

commentators have reported that Saudi Arabia recently granted Sophia (a humanoid robot) citizenship, the accuracy of these reports has been disputed and some have described this as nothing more than a publicity stunt.[60] As of 2021, no major jurisdiction (that is, US, EU, UK) has recognised AI or robots as entities capable of having legal status. But while machines have no legal personality and cannot be held accountable at present, developers and/or users could certainly face liability.[61]

Consider the example of PaintsChainer, an AI-powered colorisation software programme.[62] The project helps artists colorise their works by allowing them to apply colours to each drawing with very few instructions and with little human involvement, saving them considerable time and allowing the AI to handle the colorisation process largely on its own. However, this creates the risk of copyright infringement. Users may, for instance, apply colours to copyright-protected characters (this may involve making a pink Pikachu, which is unlikely to be covered by fair use or similar provisions).[63] The crucial point here is that the company merely provides the tool to artists; that is, the user has complete control over what is fed into the system. The developers effectively provide the necessary code, which is then automatically adjusted as per the user's needs. They neither encourage infringement nor have any control over the process.[64] Moreover, they do not monitor or deal with the AI-generated outputs.

Even though the end user may be liable for primary infringement here, under existing (for example, US) law,[65] and as per the landmark case of *Grokster*, secondary liability will only be found where the seller encourages users to commit infringement by using their AI products.[66] In other words, the developer/seller will not be liable in instances where the AI has substantial lawful use and the product or service is appropriately marketed and advertised.[67] As a result, companies such as PaintsChainer (which merely produce and distribute AI that has substantial lawful use) will generally avoid liability, despite the clear possibility that the AI might be misused.[68]

---

[60]   Vincent J, 'Pretending to Give a Robot Citizenship Helps No One' (2017) www.theverge.com/ 2017/10/30/16552006/robot-rights-citizenship-saudi-arabia-sophia accessed 5 February 2022.

[61]   On the issue of legal personality and 'punishing AI' more generally, see also Abbott R, *The Reasonable Robot: Artificial Intelligence and the Law* (CUP, 2020) pp.111–33.

[62]   See Naqvi Z, 'Artificial Intelligence, Copyright, and Copyright Infringement' (2020) 24 Marq. Intellectual. Property L 14, p.36.

[63]   See Naqvi Z, 'Artificial Intelligence, Copyright, and Copyright Infringement' (2020) 24 Marq. Intellectual. Property L 14, p.36. This may be regarded as a derivative work.

[64]   See Naqvi Z, 'Artificial Intelligence, Copyright, and Copyright Infringement' (2020) 24 Marq. Intellectual. Property L 14.

[65]   While this analysis focuses on US law, similar principles apply under UK and EU law.

[66]   See e.g. *Metro-Goldwyn-Mayer Studios v Grokster*, 545 U.S. 913, 919 (2005) ('one who distributes a device with the object of promoting its use to infringe copyright, as shown by clear expression or other affirmative steps taken to foster infringement, is liable for the resulting acts of infringement by third parties').

[67]   See e.g. *Sony Corp. of Am. v Universal City Studios*, 464 U.S. 417, 422–23 (1984), at 440 ('a staple article or commodity of commerce suitable for substantial non-infringing purposes' is not contributory copyright infringement'); see also Naqvi Z, 'Artificial Intelligence, Copyright, and Copyright Infringement' (2020) 24 Marq. Intellectual. Property L 14, pp.35–8.

[68]   See *Metro-Goldwyn-Mayer Studios Inc. v Grokster, Ltd.*, 545 U.S. 913, 933 (2005).

4.2 Policy Considerations: Who *Should* Be Liable Where AI Acts Autonomously?

While the analysis so far has focused on who would be liable where AI is primarily viewed as a 'tool' (which is largely unproblematic from a doctrinal and policy perspective) and at least one of the parties has some awareness and control over the process, it is far less clear how liability *should* be allocated where, for instance, AI alters its own programming (for example, IBM's Watson is capable of doing this through machine learning) to such an extent that neither developers nor end users are able to appreciate the risk of infringement.[69] This inevitably entails normative considerations and raises issues of fairness and – as courts have not specifically addressed the issue yet – legal certainty.

As illustrated by the European Parliament in a recent Motion for a Resolution on the regulation of robotics, traditional rules on liability do not apply neatly to scenarios where robots or machines make highly independent decisions.[70] Are developers or end users more blameworthy? Who is in a better position to appreciate the risk? Should anyone be held accountable at all? Holding end users liable (where they are not necessarily aware that infringement may occur) could be particularly unfair,[71] especially as consumers/users are often legally unsophisticated individuals. Adopting a punitive approach towards users may also discourage the use of (otherwise helpful) AI and, in any event, rightsholders tend to sue companies that develop and/or sell products, as opposed to their users (even where users are sued, they are often indemnified through contracts).[72] Programmers and developers are arguably in a better position to appreciate the risk (as the AI continuously learns and alters its programming) and they are also more likely to acquire economic value from the AI by, for instance, selling it or licensing it. Nevertheless, given the very nature and purpose of processes such as machine learning, expecting developers to foresee the risk will not always be realistic, and some degree of case-by-case assessment is likely to be required (and desirable).

Until this issue receives further attention from policymakers, Watson suggests adopting an interim contractual solution (although this is discussed in the context of patents, a similar approach may be considered in the context of copyright).[73] Under this proposal, for the developer or seller to hold the purchaser harmless for infringement, (i) the buyer must regularly apply software updates provided by the developer; (ii) the purchaser must notify the selling party of any new methods created by the AI (or, in the context of copyright, this may include

---

[69] There is further uncertainty with regard to instances involving open-source development and multi-collaborative work involving programmers, users and various other parties. In other words, there are a number of possible scenarios where someone may not be able to appreciate the risk of infringement, which further complicates the issue of allocating liability.

[70] European Parliament, 'Report with recommendations to the Commission on Civil Law Rules on Robotics' (2015/2103(INL)) www.europarl.europa.eu/doceo/document/A-8-2017-0005_EN.html accessed 28 June 2020 (see 'Liability'); see also Mendis D et al, 'Artificial Intelligence and Intellectual Property: The View of The British and Irish Law, Education and Technology Association' (BILETA) (22 November 2020) https://ssrn.com/abstract=3752956 or http://dx.doi.org/10.2139/ssrn.3752956 at p.3.

[71] Watson B, 'A Mind of Its Own – Direct Infringement by Users of Artificial Intelligence' (2017) 58(1) IDEA: The Law Review of the Franklin Pierce Center for Intellectual Property 65.

[72] See Watson B, 'A Mind of Its Own – Direct Infringement by Users of Artificial Intelligence Systems' (2017) 58(1) IDEA: The Journal of the Franklin Pierce Center for Intellectual Property 65, p.85.

[73] Watson B, 'A Mind of Its Own – Direct Infringement by Users of Artificial Intelligence' (2017) 58(1) IDEA: The Law Review of the Franklin Pierce Center for Intellectual Property 65.

new techniques which may considerably increase the risk of infringement); and (iii) the buyer must not commit infringing activities in bad faith.[74] The benefit of adopting such an approach is that the buying party (or user) will be actively encouraged to do its part to limit infringement, and the risk of unfairness is mitigated as liability would only be imposed where infringement takes place with the purchaser's knowledge and capability to control. In other words, liability for end users would be reserved for the most egregious cases and only insofar as they act in bad faith (for example, where they intentionally reprogram the AI to infringe).

Regardless of the approach adopted in the short term, it is clear that this is an increasingly pressing (and difficult) question that will inevitably require the attention of the legislature. It is also evident that failing to hold any party accountable is problematic as this might indirectly encourage the use of AI systems for infringement purposes.[75] Why should the use of AI be given special treatment, while holding human actors liable in the same or similar set of circumstances? As already mentioned, if some form of protection for AI-generated works is to be granted (whether copyright or a sui generis right), it is also fair that someone (for example, the person who claims to be the 'author' of the final output) should bear responsibility where the use of the machine constitutes infringement.

5.   CONCLUSION

AI systems consume large amounts of data, often involving creative works such as books, photographs and articles. As the technology continues to steadily advance policymakers will have to consider a range of complex questions regarding copyright infringement, exceptions and allocation of liability which have received surprisingly little attention so far. When would the use of an AI system infringe? Can AI-induced infringement be exempted and are the existing exceptions satisfactory? There is also no consensus on who should be liable where a machine acts with a considerable degree of autonomy.

While AI-induced infringement concerns both inputs to and outputs of AI, a wide range of (otherwise infringing) uses may be permitted under the existing framework. Under US law, for instance, the processing of protected works for pattern recognition purposes is likely to be regarded as non-expressive and thus 'fair use'. This broad fair use doctrine can be clearly contrasted with EU and UK law, where the scope of the transient copy and text and data-mining provisions is considerably more restrictive (for example, the latter only applies where the activity is carried out by a research/cultural heritage institution). There are thus genuine concerns that this could negatively impact on the advancement of AI and preclude local businesses from carrying out activities that would otherwise be exempt in, for example, the US (and may also force them to relocate to more favourable jurisdictions).

---

[74]   Watson B, 'A Mind of Its Own – Direct Infringement by Users of Artificial Intelligence' (2017) 58(1) IDEA: The Law Review of the Franklin Pierce Center for Intellectual Property 65.
[75]   Watson B, 'A Mind of Its Own – Direct Infringement by Users of Artificial Intelligence' (2017) 58(1) IDEA: The Law Review of the Franklin Pierce Center for Intellectual Property 65, p.70. When addressing this, we must also be cautious not to hinder the advancement of AI technology; see Schaal E, 'Infringing a Fantasy: Future Obstacles Arise for the United States Patent Office and Software Manufacturers Utilizing Artificial Intelligence' (2004) 11 Jeffrey S. Moorad Sports Law Journal 173, p.201.

In terms of allocating liability, we note that machines have no legal personality in the US, EU and UK and cannot therefore be held responsible for infringement. While programmers/ developers and end users could face liability where the AI infringes on another's work, the question of who should be liable where the machine carries out tasks with a significant degree of autonomy (and alters its programming to such an extent that neither party can appreciate the risk) has not been fully explored yet and may inevitably require a case-by-case assessment. Regardless of the approach adopted in the future, it is essential that policymakers take into consideration issues of balance between rights and obligations and, crucially, fairness.

PART III

TRADE MARKS AND DESIGNS

14. Computational trademark infringement and adjudication

Daryl Lim

1. INTRODUCTION

The likelihood of confusion standard is the linchpin of trademark infringement.[1] When brand owners enforce trademark rights, courts must apply it to determine whether consumers would likely be confused by the defendants' use of their mark.[2] Unfortunately, what constitutes "confusion" remains highly subjective and difficult to evaluate in practice.[3] It is poorly theorized, and opinions on the standard usually fail to explain judges' decisions so that other courts can easily apply them.[4]

This indeterminacy muddies trademark law's focal point and the scope of trademark rights.[5] Trademarks, unlike patents and copyrights, last indefinitely and could give a trademark owner monopoly power without the threshold requirements and other limitations that patent and copyright law demand of their respective rights holders.[6] Critical to any property system is proper notice about the existence and scope of those legal rights. A patchwork of inconsistent results destabilizes the system for everyone, even plaintiffs.[7] It causes negotiations to break down, harming *both* brand owners and potential licensees.[8] Indeterminacy also acts as a drag on dispute resolution, compliance, and social equity.[9] The rational response must be a call for clarity in the law.

---

[1] The Lanham Act prohibits the use of a registered mark in a manner "likely to cause confusion," 15 U.S.C. § 1114(1)(a), as well as the use of any term or name in a manner "likely to cause confusion" about the affiliation of the user with another person, ibid § 1125(a)(1).

[2] *See e.g.*, *Mil. Ord. of Purple Heart Serv. Found., Inc. v. Mil. Ord. of Purple Heart of United States of Am., Inc.*, 852 F. App'x 6, 9 (D.C. Cir. 2021).

[3] *See* Daryl Lim, *Confusion, Simplified*, BERKELEY TECH. L. J. (Forthcoming, 2022).

[4] *See* Barton Beebe, *An Empirical Study of the Multifactor Tests for Trademark Infringement*, 94 CAL. L. REV. 1581, 1582 (2006) ("Its current condition is Babelian").

[5] *See* Bone, ibid ("what makes the scope of rights so uncertain is the vagueness of the likelihood-of-confusion test [...] for infringement"); Amy Adler & Jeanne C. Fromer, *Taking Intellectual Property into Their Own Hands*, 107 CAL. L. REV. 1455, 1523 (2019) ("Trademark law is similarly complex and unpredictable with regard to important doctrines").

[6] *See generally* 15 U.S.C. § 1114. *See* William M. Landes & Richard A. Posner, *Trademark Law: An Economic Perspective*, 30 J.L. & ECON. 265, 287 (1987) ("The lack of a fixed term for trademarks is one of the striking differences between trademarks, on the one hand, and copyrights and patents, on the other").

[7] Thomas H. Watson, *Pay Per Click: Keyword Advertising and the Search for Limitations of Online Trademark Infringement Liability*, 2 CASE W. RESERVE J.L. TECH. & INTERNET 101, 122 (2011).

[8] *See e.g.*, Robert G. Bone, *Notice Failure and Defenses in Trademark Law*, 96 B.U. L. REV. 1245, 1258 (2016).

[9] *See* Daryl Lim, *AI, IP, Algorithms, and Inequality*, SMU L. REV. (Forthcoming, 2022).

Scholars chronicled artificial intelligence's ("AI") transformative impact on intellectual property (IP) law.[10] Trademark offices rapidly integrate AI into their workflow to reduce application classification errors[11] and identify concept combinations within images to match against similar marks.[12] Image recognition systems improve existing keywords or codes to analyze colors and shapes and are commercially available to companies and their legal advisers.[13]

AI is central in consumer marketing literature, and trademarks are central in IP protection.[14] However, the existing literature focuses on brand management and trademark search and examination.[15] Surprisingly, scholars have generally paid scant attention to AI's effects on trademark law[16] and scholarship on AI, and literature about the likelihood of confusion is even more scarce.[17] This chapter fills that gap.

---

[10]   *See* Sonia K. Katyal & Aniket Kesari, *Trademark Search, Artificial Intelligence, and the Role of the Private Sector*, 35 BERKELEY TECH. L.J. 501, 505 (2020) ("AI will fundamentally transform the trademark ecosystem, and the law will need to evolve as a result"). *See also* Ryan Abbott, *Everything Is Obvious*, 66 UCLA L. REV. 2, 37 (2019); Daryl Lim, *AI & IP: Innovation & Creativity in an Age of Accelerated Change*, 52 AKRON L. REV. 813 (2018).

[11]   Hayleigh Bosher, *UK IPO's First AI-Powered Tool For Trade Mark Applications*, IPKAT (Nov. 3, 2021) (explaining how the algorithm identifies similar trademarks and alerts its customers to overlapping goods and services, helping improve the chances of successfully registering a trademark by 14 percent. The AI nudges customers toward appropriate goods and services, resulting in a 70 percent drop in the length of goods and services lists, resulting in cost savings for each category of goods and services not selected). *See also* Dev S. Gangjee, *Eye, Robot: Artificial Intelligence and Trade Mark Registers* in N. BRUUN, G. DINWOODIE, M. LEVIN & A. OHLY (EDS), TRANSITION AND COHERENCE IN INTELLECTUAL PROPERTY LAW 5 (2020) (describing similar efforts in China, Germany, Japan, and Singapore).

[12]   *WIPO Launches State-of-the-Art Artificial Intelligence-Based Image Search Tool for Brands*, Apr. 1, 2019 (PR/2019/831); at: www.wipo.int/pressroom/en/articles/2019/article_0005.html; US PATENT & TRADEMARK OFFICE, *Emerging Technologies in USPTO Business Solutions*, May 25, 2018 (WIPO/ IP/ITAI/GE/18/P5) (using images to train AI algorithms using image databases with corresponding examiner-annotated design codes that predict design codes of a new trademark image); *Trademark Applications Streamlined By Machine Learning*, GOVTECH REV. (May 28, 2018) www.govtechreview .com.au/content/gov-tech/news/trademark-applications-streamlined-by-machine-learning-1008018169 (reporting on IP Australia's "Smart Assessment Toolkit" using machine-learning models to identify mark similarity and assess mark distinctiveness through natural language processors and historic examiner report datasets).

[13]   CA Perez et al., *Trademark Image Retrieval Using a Combination of Deep Convolutional Neural Networks*, 2018 INTERNATIONAL JOINT CONFERENCE ON NEURAL NETWORKS (IJCNN) (IEEE, 2018).

[14]   *See Trademarks, Copyright and Patents: Should Business Owners Really Care About IP?*, VARNUM (May 1, 2019), www.varnumlaw.com/newsroom-publications-trademarks-copyrights-and -patents-why-business-owners-should-care-about-ip ("A trademark is one of the most important business assets that a company will ever own because it identifies and distinguishes the company and its products/ services in the marketplace from its competitors").

[15]   *See* Katyal & Kesari, *supra* note 10, at 516; US PATENT AND TRADEMARK OFFICE, PROTECTING YOUR TRADEMARK: ENHANCING YOUR RIGHTS THROUGH FEDERAL REGISTRATION 3 (2019).

[16]   *See* Katyal & Kesari, *supra* note 10, at 527 ("AI-related issues have been largely underexamined regarding trademarks, specifically, especially where legal doctrine is concerned").

[17]   *See* ibid, at 504 ("[S]urprisingly, very little legal scholarship has addressed the potential role for AI in the context of trademarks"). Those in the literature pool include Gangjee, *supra* note 11; Anke Moerland & Conrado Freitas, *Artificial Intelligence and Trade Mark Assessment*, in ARTIFICIAL INTELLIGENCE & INTELLECTUAL PROPERTY (R. Hilty, K-C. Liu & J-A. Lee eds, 2021), https://papers.ssrn .com/sol3/papers.cfm?abstract_id=3683807. Michael Grynberg, *AI and the "Death of Trademark,"* 108 KY. L.J. 199, 422 (2020); Jurgita Randakevičiūtė-Alpman, *The Role of Trademarks on Online Retail Platforms: An EU Trademark Law Perspective*, [2021] GRUR INTERNATIONAL 1; Lee Curtis & Rachel

Consumers generally rely on trademarks to navigate consumption choices. Consumers use trademarks as a convenient way to decide whether to purchase products and services in adjacent markets. Section 2 of this chapter explores AI's liberating effect on bounded rationality and consumers' need to rely on trademarks as decisional heuristics. Consumers simply traded one heuristic for another, now depending on digital platforms to curate the products and services they consume. This shift raises new questions about liability for trademark infringement when digital platforms like Amazon recommend counterfeit products.

Section 3 explores AI-assisted adjudication of trademark disputes from conception to implementation. It draws on theoretical models and working prototypes in adjacent areas of the law to reveal the opportunities and challenges that trademark scholars and practitioners should consider.[18] This section also proposes reformulating the likelihood of confusion standard to make it more AI-friendly and focus on the factors that matter.[19]

Part III identifies bias, accountability, and data scarcity as three key challenges to deploying AI in trademark disputes. This chapter draws on the latest developments in experimental psychology, algorithmic techniques, and legal scholarship to address these challenges. These challenges are common to other areas of the law and therefore have broader implications beyond trademarks.

2.   COMPUTATIONAL CONSUMPTION

AI diminishes the role of trademarks' function of simplifying information. However, when human cognition is limited, trademarks serve as a valuable heuristic. AI shifts that heuristic to digital platforms and moves trademark infringement into a world of digital butlers and metatags.

2.1   Unbounded Rationality

AI cuts through biases that ensnare human consumers. To understand how this works, consider how commercial signs evolved from conduits for advertisements to acquiring commercial magnetism.[20] Brand owners who diligently advertise products and services can therefore coast on the momentum of consumer inertia to spur sales in identical or related products.[21]

When Tesla released its Cybertruck in 2019, consumers readily transferred their positive feelings for its electric-powered sedan to a new class of vehicles.[22] Unfortunately, bounded rationality limits our ability to explore whether a sedan maker can make quality trucks

---

Platts, *AI is Coming and It Will Change Trade Mark Law* (ManagingIP.com, 2017), www.hgf.com/media/1173564/09-13-AI.PDF.

[18]   See infra, section 2. *See also* Giovanna Massarotto & Ashwin Ittoo, *Gleaning Insight from Antitrust Cases Using Machine Learning*, 1 STAN. COMPUTATIONAL ANTITRUST 16 (2021).

[19]   *See* infra, section 2.3. *See also* J. THOMAS MCCARTHY, MCCARTHY ON TRADEMARKS AND UNFAIR COMPETITION § 23:1 (4TH ED., 2010).

[20]   Ralph S. Brown, Jr., *Advertising and the Public Interest: Legal Protection of Trade Symbols*, 57 YALE L.J. 1165, 1187–8 (1948).

[21]   Jeremy N. Sheff, *Biasing Brands*, 32 CARDOZO L. REV. 1245, 1288 (2011).

[22]   Lora Kolodny, *Tesla Unveils Its First Electric Pickup, The Cybertruck, Starting at $39,900* (Nov. 21, 2019) www.cnbc.com/2019/11/21/tesla-cybertruck-unveiled.html.

thoroughly. This tendency to accord greater weight to information that comes immediately to mind, known as the availability heuristic, makes it harder for new entrants to enter and compete with incumbents.[23]

Surprisingly, consumers may not punish trademark holders in their home market even if the new product falls short of expectations.[24] Strong marks such as Tesla's obfuscate distinctions in adjacent products, and services may greatly matter to us as consumers. Consumers avoid costly searches in a crowded marketplace of trademarks by opting for brands that already satisfy established preferences, even though more costly searches may lead consumers to better products or services.

These overlooked distinctions, in turn, make the job of courts adjudicating trademark infringement disputes more difficult. For example, in determining whether alleged infringers' marks are likely to cause consumer confusion, judges must decide whether to protect a mark's source-identifying function.[25] Michael Grynberg observed that "[e]ven when these stories of harm are open to doubt, courts may feel pressure to credit them lest they undermine the overarching structure of trademark law."[26]

Of course, if Tesla makes quality sedans, it might want to protect its goodwill by carefully entering adjacent markets. All things being equal, a truck affiliated with Tesla likely satisfies Tesla fans. However, external information, such as product reviews, provides a more comprehensive and objective assessment than how consumers perceive one product based purely on their subjective preference from another. Unfortunately, trawling through reviews is a bothersome chore compared with simply relying on a trademark. Not to an AI, though.

Algorithms crunch data with gusto and can weed out irrelevant and misleading affiliation biases. The implication of this result on trademark doctrine is a dramatic whittling down of trademark protection to simply existing as a source designator.[27] Courts relying on such algorithms are less vulnerable to favoring mark owners whining about potential diverted sales due to affiliation confusion notwithstanding differences in products, price points, and labels, all of

---

[23]   *See* Amos Tversky & Daniel Kahneman, *Judgment under Uncertainty: Heuristics and Biases*, SCI, Sept. 27, 1974, at 1124, 1130, www.socsci.uci.edu/~bskyrms/bio/readings/tversky_k_heuristics_biases.pdf. *See also* Daryl Lim, *Retooling The Patent-Antitrust Intersection: Insights From Behavioral Economics*, 69 BAYLOR L. REV.124 (2017).

[24]   *See* Mark A. Lemley & Mark P. McKenna, *Owning Mark(et)s*, 109 MICH. L. REV. 137, 140–1 (2010) ("[T]he empirical evidence confirms both that third parties can benefit from uses of known marks in markets ancillary to the senior mark owner's and that those third-party uses can impair the senior user's ability to expand its own product lines. Put another way, the evidence suggests that third parties like Black & Decker might benefit from use of, or proximity to, SUM's trademarks, but not that SUM is harmed by such use").

[25]   *See, e.g.*, Maker's Mark Distillery, Inc. v Diageo N. Am., Inc., 679 F.3d 410, 419 (6th Cir. 2012) (Bourbon distiller trademark consisting of a red dripping wax seal infringed by rival's tequila bottles capped with a red dripping wax seal); Anheuser-Busch, Inc. v Balducci Publ'ns, 28 F.3d 769, 772-73 (8th Cir. 1994) (beer brewery's trademark infringed by humor magazine's ad parody using owner's trademarks).

[26]   Grynberg, *supra* note 17, at 208.

[27]   *See* ibid, at 211 ("In the AI world, there is no need for brand personality, dilution protection, affiliation or sponsorship claims, or the like. Nor is there a need—outside of the prestige goods context discussed below—for attractive or memorable marks").

which limited the risk of a mistaken purchase due to source confusion.[28] As Michael Grynberg explained:

> To a computer, ZL3XC!7K4BV functions just as well as APPLE. But because the AI is able to find quality goods (however defined), the seller retains an incentive to invest in quality (and, indeed, might have more resources to do so if freed from a need to invest in the now irrelevant attribute of trademark attractiveness). Or trademark law could be restricted to a smaller signifier. So anyone could brand their computer APPLE, but only one company could use the ®, or some like symbol, when it comes time to ship.[29]

The key benefit of this change is that the quality of the product or service at issue, rather than brand affiliation connected with consumers, would help push sales, making market demand more efficient in picking winners and trademarks less obfuscatory. AI can do the heavy lifting of compiling data to present those better products to consumers. In so doing, AI may diminish the justification for the current scope of trademark protection. At the same time, the American Bar Association also notes the risk of AI facilitating infringement, raising questions of liability.[30] The next section addresses this issue.

2.2   The Platform Heuristic

In the analog world, consumers relied heavily on trademarks associated with products and services and the companies producing them. However, with the rise of omnibus digital platforms such as Amazon and Alibaba, consumer purchasing habits changed dramatically.[31] These platforms track consumers' clicks and churn out targeted advertisements from their data trove.[32] For the consumer, this translates into a personalized shopping experience.[33] For brand owners,

---

[28]   *See, e.g.*, Maker's Mark Distillery, Inc., 679 F.3d, at 419 (discounting the defendant's house mark as "many consumers are unaware of the affiliations between brands of distilled spirits, and that some companies produce multiple types of distilled spirits").

[29]   Grynberg, *supra* note 17, at 211.

[30]   Letter from American Bar Association-Intellectual Property Law Section to Secretary of Commerce for Intellectual Property & Director of the United States Patent and Trademark Office, USPTO (Jan. 9, 2020), www.uspto.gov/sites/default/files/documents/ABA-IPL_RFC-84-FR-58141.pdf, at 13; *see* Comments from the Center for Anti-Counterfeiting and Product Protection, USPTO (Dec. 16, 2019), www.uspto.gov/sites/default/files/documents/Jeffrey-Rojek_RFC-84-FR-58141.pdf.

[31]   *See, e.g.*, Blake Morgan, *How Amazon has Reorganized Around Artificial Intelligence and Machine Learning*, FORBES (July 16, 2018, 2:37 PM), www.forbes.com/sites/blakemorgan/2018/07/16/how-amazon-has-re-organized-around-artificial-intelligence-and-machine-learning/#252ad94d7361 ("AI also plays a huge role in Amazon's recommendation engine, which generates 35% of the company's revenue. Using data from individual customer preferences and purchases, browsing history and items that are related and regularly bought together, Amazon can create a personalized list of products that customers actually want to buy").

[32]   Charles V. Trappey, Amy J.C. Trappey, & Bo-Hung Liu, *Identify Trademark Legal Case Precedents—Using Machine Learning to Enable Semantic Analysis of Judgments*, WORLD PATENT INFORMATION 1 (2020).

[33]   *The Future of Artificial Intelligence in Consumer Experience: According to the AT&T Foundry*, ROCKETSPACE, www.rocketspace.com/hubfs/accelerator/the-future-of-artificial-intelligence.pdf?hsLang=en-us ("Everything from shopping to driving will draw from user behavior to become highly pertinent and personalized to the end consumer. Intelligent prediction and optimization will allow the consumer to feel that each branded product or experience is made just for them").

pushing their products and services requires learning to ingratiate themselves to these digital butlers. They guide consumers by providing search suggestions reflected by past purchases and browsing histories.[34]

Amazon routinely directs users to affiliated brands such as AmazonBasics, which have little renown outside Amazon's platform.[35] This endows affiliated brands with near-instantaneous goodwill, much as Tesla did with its Cybertruck. However, unlike Tesla, Amazon leverages its own sales platform, Amazon's marketplace, and its network of warehousing and shipping chains to handle fulfillment. This arrangement raises antitrust concerns among stakeholders.[36]

However, the impact relevant for this discussion on trademarks is that Amazon's business model deemphasizes individual seller brands in favor of the platform's brand, with implications for trademark infringement. The digital platform matters more to consumers than the marks on it.[37] Consumers pay less attention to individual trademark information and more to the options to searched-for products there. Moreover, Amazon's algorithm treats trademark information simply as grist for the mill to generate a menu of product offerings.[38]

Consider *Multi Time Machine, Inc. v Amazon.com, Inc.*, when the brand owner decried Amazon for using its marks to curate product options.[39] Amazon carried none of the brand owner's watches but instead used queries for the brand to return a list of options from rivals.[40] In a divided appellate decision, the majority held that Amazon's customers would read the results in context and endorse both Amazon and its customers, capitalizing on the information externalities of the brand owner's mark, which provided an efficient mechanism for communicating the existence of rival offerings.[41]

By shopping at Amazon, consumers limit their search to products offered through Amazon. Rather than searching by selecting among brands, users' choice of Amazon means they also rely on Amazon's algorithms to narrow the range of brands flashing before consumers' eyes. The heuristic on which consumers rely is that of the platform's trademark rather than of individual products.

The extent to which consumers rely on platforms as a heuristic is startling. Krista Garcia reported in 2018 that Amazon had displaced Google as the leading starting point for product

---

[34]   Taylor Soper, *Full Text: In Annual Shareholder Letter, Jeff Bezos Explains Why It Will Never Be Day 2 at Amazon*, Geekwire (Apr. 12, 2017), www.geekwire.com/2017/full-text-annual-letter-amazon-ceo-jeff-bezos-explains-avoid-becoming-day-2-company/ ("Machine learning drives our algorithms for demand forecasting, product search ranking, product and deals recommendations, merchandising placements, fraud detection, translations, and much more").

[35]   *See* John Herrman, *Everything on Amazon is Amazon!*, N.Y. Times (Nov. 15, 2018), www.nytimes.com/2018/11/15/style/this-is-also-amazon.html ("There are vanishingly few types of consumer goods that you can't buy, in some form, on Amazon. But it is missing plenty of brands. In 2009, the company started selling products under its own name. It soon moved beyond the first AmazonBasics—items including budget electronics and batteries—to a wider range of Amazon-branded products. This was followed by an explosion of company-owned brands, including dozens with Amazon-free names").

[36]   I discuss this issue and how AI can help courts adjudicate such disputes elsewhere: Daryl Lim, *Antitrust's AI Revolution*, Tenn. L. Rev. (Forthcoming, 2022). *See also* Lina M. Khan, *Amazon's Antitrust Paradox*, 126 Yale L.J. 710, 780–3 (2017).

[37]   Grynberg, *supra* note 17, at 226.

[38]   Multi Time Machine, Inc. v Amazon.com, Inc. 804 F.3d 930 (9th Cir. 2015).

[39]   Ibid at 932–3.

[40]   Ibid.

[41]   Ibid, at 938.

searches by as many as 10 percentage points.[42] According to Scott Galloway, one reason for Amazon's success is its deploying of tracking algorithms.[43] For example, supermarkets generally collect information only on actual sales.[44] In contrast, Amazon tracks shoppers' browsing habits, products each one returns to, what shoppers keep in their shopping basket, and even what their mouse arrow hovers over on the screen.[45]

The nature of platform competition is "winner-take-all," with one dominant platform swapping in for the other.[46] Perhaps antitrust law could address this issue, but trademark law also impacts the thorny question of consumer preferences. What happens when Alexa, Amazon's digital butler, responds to a search query by suggesting an infringing product based purely on those same correlations? It seems wrong for Amazon to benefit from the descriptive use of the trademark without also bearing the burden. Trademark infringement can arise based on contributory infringement such that Amazon may be responsible based on the infringing activities of its users.[47] The next section discusses this issue.

2.3   Digital Butlers and Metatags

Contributory trademark infringement could arise if Amazon intentionally induces its users to infringe on a brand owner's mark or enables its users to infringe on a mark with the knowledge that its users are infringing and fail to take reasonable remedial measures.[48] Courts have refused to find contributory liability against an internet domain name registrar for accepting infringing internet domain names, holding that such liability would extend the concept too far.[49]

Courts consider the extent of control which Amazon exercises over Alexa and its integrated ordering service. For liability to attach, there must be direct control and monitoring of the instrumentality used to infringe.[50] Amazon must have more than a general knowledge or reason to know that Alexa was used to selling counterfeit goods; some contemporary knowledge of the infringing items is necessary.[51]

In 2017, the US Supreme Court declined to take up an appeal of a Federal Circuit decision that a pillowcase maker said unfairly let Amazon and others off the hook for sales on their

---

[42]   Krista Garcia, *More Product Searches Start on Amazon*, Emarketer (Sept. 7, 2018), www.emarketer.com/content/more-product-searches-start-on-amazon ("A number of consumer surveys have shown that more US digital shoppers now start their searches on Amazon. Nearly half (46.7%) of US internet users started product searches on Amazon compared with 34.6% who went to Google first, according to a May 2018 Adeptmind survey").

[43]   Scott Galloway, The Four: The Hidden DNA Of Amazon, Apple, Facebook, And Google 51–2 (2017).

[44]   Ibid.

[45]   Ibid.

[46]   *See* Daryl Lim, *Predictive Analytics*, 51 Loy. U. Chi. L.J. 161, 197 (2019).

[47]   15 U.S.C.A. §§ 1051 et seq.

[48]   *See e.g.*, 1-800 Contacts, Inc. v Lens.com, Inc., 722 F.3d 1229 (10th Cir. 2013).

[49]   *See e.g.* In Lockheed Martin Corp. v Network Solutions, Inc., 985 F. Supp. 949 (C.D. Cal. 1997).

[50]   *See e.g.* Perfect 10, Inc. v Visa Intern. Service Ass'n, 494 F.3d 788 (9th Cir. 2007).

[51]   *See e.g.* Slep-Tone Entertainment Corporation v. Golf 600 Inc., 193 F. Supp. 3d 292 (S.D.N.Y. 2016).

websites by third parties offering infringing goods.[52] The Federal Circuit found Amazon not liable for filling orders of pillowcase knockoffs because Amazon never held title to the allegedly infringing products.[53] In August, Milo & Gabby, the pillowcase maker, asked the Supreme Court to clarify what part "title" plays in such infringement cases, warning that the lack of clarity could result in intellectual property laws devolving into "a hopelessly opaque morass of technical minutiae or an outright joke."[54]

However, liability for trademark infringement may come by way of analogy through cases involving metatags.[55] Metatags are normally invisible to internet users. Still, search engine algorithms can detect them and increase the likelihood that a user searching for a particular topic will be directed to that Web designer's page.[56]

The Fifth Circuit court noted that infringement arose with actual evidence of customer confusion or illegitimate metatag use in two cases.[57] The Fifth Circuit found that brand owners' infringement claims do not fail simply because the defendant's use of the allegedly infringing marks was not visible to the consumer.[58] So Amazon's algorithms may likewise become ensnared if brand owners could show Amazon's direct control and monitoring of Alexa, which would not be hard to do.

While AI raises challenging questions for trademark infringement, it is only the tip of the iceberg. Sonia Katyal and Aniket Kesari assert that "the real payoff of AI lies in its ability to predict the outcomes of various trademark-related decisions—such as the litigation risk involved in proceeding with a particular trademark or product—and the market implications of making certain choices."[59] Such predictive analytics may assist courts and businesses in assessing trademark claims' probable outcomes. Section 3 discusses how such a system might be conceived, trained, and executed.

3.   COMPUTATIONAL ADJUDICATION

Today's AI can produce a ranked list of potential conflicts to assist trademark registry officials and attorneys with their assessments of mark similarity.[60] The ability of courts to navigate

---

[52]   *See e.g.* Milo & Gabby LLC et al. v Amazon.com Inc. et al., No. 17-287, cert. denied, 2017 WL 3641212 (U.S. Oct. 10, 2017).

[53]   *See* Milo & Gabby LLC v Amazon.com Inc., No. 2016-1290, 2017 WL 2258605 (Fed. Cir. 2017).

[54]   *See* Milo & Gabby LLC v Amazon.com, Inc., No. 17-287, 2017 WL 3701806 (U.S.).

[55]   Southwest Recreational Indus., Inc. v FieldTurf, Inc., No. 01-50073, 2002 WL 32783971, at *7 & n.27 (5th Cir. 2002) ("essentially programming code instructions given to on-line search engines").

[56]   Ibid, at *7 n.27.

[57]   Southwest Recreational Indus., Inc. 2017 WL 3701806 (U.S.).

[58]   Jim S. Adler, P.C. v McNeil Consultants, L.L.C., 10 F.4th 422, 427–28 (5th Cir. 2021) ("We find no Fifth Circuit authority for such a rule of law, and we disagree with it").

[59]   *See* Katyal & Kesari, *supra* note 10, at 533.

[60]   Moerland & Freitas, *supra* note 17, at 49 (describing the use of a deep learning image classifier and other prototypes); Gangjee, *supra* note 11, at 13 ("AI-enhanced similarity searching may serve to further attenuate registry level conflict analysis").

in this way is a welcome addition to its arsenal of tools.[61] There is also a strong demand for infringement analyses.[62]

AI gives courts an unprecedented capability to scour trademark case law, recognize specific data clusters in opinions that indicate how past courts weighed the likelihood of confusion factors, and stress-test theories of confusion against real-world data. Done right, algorithms can match case law data points against seed cases, depositions, and other preprocessed evidence to provide quick and consistent analysis. This section provides a roadmap of how this can be done, from conception to execution.

3.1   Rules of Thumb

Multifactor tests for the likelihood of confusion attempt to provide analytical rigor to the complicated question of how consumers perceive different marks. Barton Beebe's 2006 empirical study revealed that courts most frequently deployed the Second Circuit's test in *Polaroid Corp. v Polaroid Electronics Corp.*[63] There, Judge Friendly articulated what became known as the eight *Polaroid* factors:

(1)   strength of the plaintiff's mark;
(2)   similarity of plaintiff's and defendant's marks;
(3)   competitive proximity of the products;
(4)   likelihood that plaintiff will "bridge the gap" and offer a product like a defendant's;
(5)   actual confusion between products;
(6)   good faith on the defendant's part;
(7)   quality of defendant's product; and
(8)   sophistication of the buyers.[64]

Confusion is more likely when an accused product contains multiple indicia of similarity. For instance, house bands typically include house marks, product-specific brands, product packaging, and color or configuration.[65] Conversely, confusion is less likely when defendants copy only a few elements.[66] However, no single factor in the likelihood of confusion inquiry is determinative.

---

[61]   *See* Gangjee, *supra* note 11, at 13 ("for risk-averse commercial clients it is extremely tempting to be guided by clearly defined percentages of similarity").

[62]   WORLD IP REV (June 6, 2019), www.worldipreview.com/news/ai-as-judges-and-patent-destroying -tools-panel-discussion-18237. *See also* Gangjee, *supra* note 11, at 13 ("It has been suggested that businesses might find it attractive if an AI solution were to replace judicial determination, or at least provide a preliminary assessment of confusion even in an infringement context").

[63]   Beebe, *supra* note 4, at 1593 ("This is especially true in the Second Circuit where the multifactor test is most often applied and where appellate panels have repeatedly emphasized that the multifactor analysis must be exhaustive and explicit"). *See* Polaroid Corp. v Polarad Elecs. Corp., 287 F.2d 492, 495 (2d Cir. 1961).

[64]   Ibid.

[65]   *See, e.g.*, Bristol-Myers Squibb Co. v McNeil-P.P.C., Inc., 973 F.2d 1033 (2d Cir. 1992).

[66]   George Miaoulis & Nancy D'Amato, *Consumer Confusion and Trademark Infringement*, 42 J. MARKETING 48, 54 (1978) (finding, in the context of competing goods, that the primary cue for association between two brands was not the name but the visual appearance).

Trademark litigation is inherently impressionistic. Conventional wisdom teaches that courts need to undertake "a highly fact-intensive inquiry both as to the assessment of the evidence concerning each factor and as to the overall synthesis of factors and the evidence."[67] Sometimes, each side claims a numerically equal number of factors in their favor, leaving courts to assign weights.[68]

Courts caught up in the swirl of factors sloppily peppered their judgments with different operative terms to describe the same thing, from terms such as affiliation,[69] endorsement,[70] and connection,[71] to asking whether the use produced confusion "of any kind."[72] As the Fifth Circuit bluntly put it, "Congress adopted an open-ended concept of confusion. Any kind of confusion will now support an action for trademark infringement."[73]

Courts in subsequent cases and businesses and their legal advisors struggle to determine the appropriate strength of each factor, either alone or relative to other factors.[74] Judges also admit the distinctions they make are often done on an "intuitive basis" rather than through "logical analysis."[75] Reporting on his dataset of cases, Beebe observed that "scattered among the circuits are factors that are obsolete, redundant, or irrelevant, or, in the hands of an experienced judge or litigator, notoriously pliable."[76]

Making trademark infringement more rule-like by reforming the likelihood of confusion standard can make it easier for stakeholders to navigate.[77] Rules are generally simpler to understand than standards are, and make it easier for people to conduct themselves accordingly. The simplest rules look to a single fact, such as a speed limit, to determine a legal outcome.[78]

Clarity also makes plaintiffs less likely to bring vexatious suits, since parties see what constitutes a weak claim.[79] Even if potential trademark plaintiffs send cease and desist letters or other warnings, small businesses and individuals receiving such warnings can point to simple

---

[67]   Select Comfort Corp. v Baxter, 996 F.3d 925, 933–34 (8th Cir. 2021) ("We have repeatedly emphasized that no one factor is controlling, and different factors will carry more weight in different settings").

[68]   Equitable Nat'l Life Ins. Co., Inc. v AXA Equitable Life Ins. Co., 434 F. Supp. 3d 1227, 1252 (D. Utah 2020) ("Ultimately, while each side can claim three factors weigh in its favor, they do not weigh equally").

[69]   *See* Pebble Beach Co. v Tour 18 I Ltd., 155 F.3d 526, 544 (5th Cir. 1998).

[70]   Ibid.

[71]   Ibid.

[72]   Syntex Labs., Inc. v Norwich Pharmacal Co., 437 F.2d 566, 568 (2d Cir. 1971).

[73]   Armstrong Cork Co. v World Carpets, Inc., 597 F.2d 496, 501 n.6 (5th Cir. 1979).

[74]   Joseph P. Liu, *Two-Factor Fair Use?*, 31 Colum. J.L. & Arts 571, 579 (2008) ("Under a multi-factor balancing test, it is difficult to register the relative strength of the factors"); Eric Goldman, *Online Word of Mouth, and Its Implications for Trademark Law*, in Trademark Law and Theory: A Handbook of Contemporary Research 404, 41516, 424 (Graeme B. Dinwoodie & Mark D. Janis eds, 2008) ("Assessing consumer confusion about product source is an inherently inexact process").

[75]   Union Carbide Corp. v Ever-Ready Inc., 531 F.2d 366, 379 (7th Cir. 1976).

[76]   Beebe, *supra* note 4, at 1584.

[77]   Frederick Schauer, *Formalism*, 97 Yale L.J. 509, 541–2 (1988) (noting errors are more easily detectable under rules).

[78]   Richard A Epstein, Simple Rules for a Complex World 24–5 (1995).

[79]   *See* Rule 11, Fed. R. Civ. P. 11 (providing penalties).

and clear rules without hedging advice in a complex memo filled with what-ifs.[80] For this reason, many criminal codes tend to be rules-based.[81]

A small set of rules augmented by artificial intelligence may also be more accurate than human judgment in making many decisions. As Daniel Kahneman et al. noted, "[s]imple rules that are merely sensible typically do better than human judgment."[82] Rules reduce the role of judgment and limit the number of factors to the most relevant—those which AI can parse and which offer more precise and readily examinable options to judges in helping them resolve disputes.

Beebe recommended three or four "core factors" informing "consumer perception in the marketplace rather than judicial perception in the courtroom."[83] Alejandro Mejías went further, recommending just two—similarity of marks and proximity of goods—as "adding any other relevant factors, instead of using unmanageable and misguiding large lists of factors that are extremely difficult to balance, seems to be more in line with the thesis of scientific research on decisionmaking."[84] Gangjee agrees, noting a future where AI will rely on just a handful of factors to resolve a seed case before a court.[85]

Elsewhere, I argued that the eight *Polaroid* factors could be efficiently subsumed into a troika of actual confusion, mark similarity, and competitive proximity.[86] Actual confusion is the most direct and decisive evidence of confusion.[87] Courts explain that where confusion occurred, it "is, of course, convincing evidence that confusion is likely to occur."[88] As a policy

---

[80]   William McGeveran, *The Trademark Fair Use Reform Act*, 90 B.U. L. REV. 2267, 2290 (2010) ("Risk-averse intermediaries should be more willing to permit an expressive use when they can rely on an unambiguous legal argument in its favor").

[81]   *See* Hill v Colorado, 530 U.S. 703, 773 (2000) (Kennedy J dissenting) (arguing that criminal statute's "substantial imprecisions will chill speech, so the statute violates the First Amendment"); Scull v Virginia ex rel. Comm. on Law Reform & Racial Activities, 359 U.S. 344, 353 (1959) ("Certainty is all the more essential when vagueness might induce individuals to forego their rights of speech, press, and association for fear of violating an unclear law").

[82]   *See* DANIEL KAHNEMAN, CASS SUNSTEIN & OLIVIER SIBONY, NOISE: A FLAW IN HUMAN JUDGEMENT 10 (2021).

[83]   Ibid, at 1646.

[84]   Alejandro Mejías, *The Multifactor Test for Trademark Infringement from A European Perspective: A Path to Reform*, 54 IDEA 285, 340 (2014) (concentrating the analysis on the main two factors).

[85]   Gangjee, *supra* note 11, at 13 ("Will the test effectively shrink to just two factors (marks and products) in the commercially significant clearance or registry opposition context?")

[86]   *See* Lim, *supra* note 3.

[87]   *See* Daryl Lim, *Trademark Confusion Revealed: An Empirical Study*, AM. U. L. REV. (Forthcoming, 2022); Tana v Dantanna's, 611 F.3d 767, 779 (11th Cir. 2010) ("The last factor, actual confusion in the consuming public, is the most persuasive evidence in assessing likelihood of confusion"); *see also* Groeneveld Transp. Efficiency, Inc. v Lubecore Int'l, Inc., 730 F.3d 494, 517 (6th Cir. 2013) ("Nothing shows the likelihood of confusion more than the fact of actual confusion"); *Variety Stores, Inc.*, 852 F. App'x, 720–1 ("actual confusion is the 'most important factor'"); *see also* John Benton Russell, *New Tenth Circuit Standards: Competitive Keyword Advertising and Initial Interest Confusion in 1-800 Contacts v. Lens.com*, 30 BERKELEY TECH. L.J. 993, 1000 (2015) ("courts across several circuits view this as the strongest evidence a plaintiff can present in a trademark infringement case"); Mark D. Robins, *Actual Confusion in Trademark Infringement Litigation: Restraining Subjectivity Through a Factor-Based Approach to Valuing Evidence*, 2 NW. J. TECH. & INTELL. PROP. 117 (2004) ("all other circumstances point to a finding of non-infringement, significant evidence of actual confusion dramatically alters the equation").

[88]   Morningside Grp. Ltd. v Morningside Cap. Grp., L.L.C., 182 F.3d 133, 141 (2d Cir. 1999).

lever, it gives courts the ability to anchor their analysis in real-world characteristics. In addition, the evidence is pre-existing, does not depend on the vagrancies of survey design, and should make it easier for courts to dispose of cases pretrial.[89]

The similarity between the marks makes it more likely consumers will become confused as to the source. Extremely similar marks or goods may suggest counterfeiting and free riding. Parodies, comparative advertising, and nominative use make consumers less likely to be confused, even if a third party uses the identical term. Courts use sights, sounds, and meaning to make snap judgments about mark similarity.[90] These heuristics allow judges to rely on "a small set of cheap and reliable factors that are close enough to the ideal."[91] Adam Samaha approves of it, since "[p]rioritizing the judge's impressions about the similarity of marks, therefore, tends toward the high values of trademark law at bargain-basement prices."[92] Defendants can easily compare visual or aural elements in context, making this a useful factor to encourage due diligence.[93]

Competitive proximity tells courts how likely consumers are to assume an association between the marks used on related products.[94] For example, the similarities between the parties' distribution channels and marketing strategies suggest an overlapping general class of consumers of the parties' products.[95] However, two products or services within the same general field do not automatically trigger a likelihood of confusion.[96] Similarly, a high percentage of overlap in an extremely small subset of products does not demonstrate a high degree of relatedness.[97]

What about the other factors? I argued that courts exclude or subsume them under the troika of factors.[98] For instance, courts look to the product, the relevant market, and potential consumers in determining the likelihood of confusion.[99] Product proximity overlaps substantially with marketing, bridging the gap from the perspective of the relevant public and the quality of the defendant's product.[100] For this reason, it can serve as an omnibus factor.

---

[89] I am grateful to Jon Lee for this insight.

[90] Adam M. Samaha, *Looking over A Crowd-Do More Interpretive Sources Mean More Discretion?* 92 N.Y.U. L. Rev. 554, 614 (2017) ("accurately estimating the probability of consumer confusion can require a snap judgment, which often is how consumers actually formulate impressions and make purchasing decisions").

[91] Ibid, at 614.

[92] Ibid.

[93] *See* McCarthy, *supra* note 19, at § 23:21 (discussing the "sound, sight, and meaning" test for mark similarity).

[94] *See* Virgin Enterprises Ltd. v Nawab, 335 F.3d 141, 148 (2d Cir. 2003).

[95] Monster Energy Co. v BeastUp LLC, 395 F. Supp. 3d 1334, 1358–9 (E.D. Cal. 2019). Other circuits use similar formulations, *see e.g.,* Therma-Scan, Inc. v Thermoscan, Inc., 295 F.3d 623, 632 (6th Cir. 2002) (direct rivalry through similar goods or services likely confusing).

[96] Matrix Motor Co. v Toyota Jidosha Kabushiki Kaisha, 290 F. Supp. 2d 1083, 1092 (C.D. Cal. 2003).

[97] AutoZone, Inc. v Tandy Corp., 373 F.3d 786, 798 (6th Cir. 2004) ("if [the defendant] stocked only five types of batteries all of which were also sold by [the plaintiff], the overlap would be 100%, even though in reality [the defendant] and [the plaintiff] would share only five products of the approximately 55,000 offered by [the plaintiff]").

[98] *See* Lim, *supra* note 3.

[99] Best Cellars, Inc v Grape Finds at Dupont, Inc, 90 F. Supp. 2d 431 at 456 (S.D.N.Y. 2000).

[100] *See* Lim, *supra* note 3.

Courts often have difficulty applying tests to determine mark strength.[101] Courts apply them inconsistently and disregard survey evidence.[102] Lisa Ouellette, in an empirical study, concluded that "[t]he complex doctrine that has evolved around trademark strength and the likelihood of confusion appears to be a (largely unsuccessful) attempt to provide some analytical rigor to the essential questions of how strongly a mark identifies goods or services and how well it distinguishes those products from others in the marketplace."[103] As she put it, "the answer to these questions depends on the subjective 'perceptions of large groups of ordinary people.' In other words, to a greater extent than in other areas of law, *trademark disputes turn on the wisdom of the crowds, not expert judgment.*"[104] The wisdom of the crowds thronging physical or online marketplaces anchors the likelihood of confusion inquiry as to how consumers encounter trademarks.

Intent, or good faith, inherently focuses on the wrong goalpost. Merely that the defendant's mental state is easier to discern than the consuming public does not make that factor more relevant to an inquiry. As Kelly Collins warned, "[t]his is dangerous because mere 'copying' is not always impermissible."[105] The law encourages reusing generic or functional marks "as a part of our competitive economic system."[106] For this reason, she argues that the relevant intent is the one to confuse and not merely to copy.[107]

Pinning the likelihood of confusion on free-riding becomes problematic because free-riding is ultimately a concept searching for meaning.[108] The Act does not require proof of intent. Trademark law is, after all, a strict liability offense.[109] As the Sixth Circuit opined, the better view is to consider intent only after other likelihood of confusion factors indicate liability.[110] Intent may speak to aggravated remedies but should be irrelevant to the question of guilt. As Beebe put it, "if trademark law seeks to prevent commercial immorality, then it should do so

---

[101] *See* Lisa Larrimore Ouellette, *The Google Shortcut to Trademark Law*, 102 CAL. L. REV. 351, 353 (2014).

[102] Ibid at 356 (explaining how Google results offer "an unbiased survey of how a given search phrase is perceived, and how they might thus decrease the expense and increase the predictability of trademark disputes").

[103] Ibid, at 360.

[104] Ibid.

[105] Kelly Collins, *Intending to Confuse: Why Preponderance Is the Proper Burden of Proof for Intentional Trademark Infringements under the Lanham Act*, 67 OKLA. L. REV. 73, 87 (2014).

[106] Ibid.

[107] Ibid, 87–8 ("This would better serve the purposes of the Lanham Act and safeguard innocent conduct from triggering liability").

[108] *See, e.g.*, Ty Inc. v Perryman, 306 F.3d 509, 512 (7th Cir. 2002) (Posner J) (rejecting sponsorship dilution claim because "in that attenuated sense of free riding, almost everyone in business is free riding").

[109] *See* Taubman Co. v Webfeats, 319 F.3d 770, 775 (6th Cir. 2003) (recognizing that the Lanham Act is a "strict liability statute"); *see also* Rebecca Tushnet, *Running the Gamut From A to B: Federal Trademark and Federal False Advertising Law*, 159 U. PA. L. REV. 1305, 1310 (2011) (noting that federal courts have interpreted trademark as a strict liability offense); Robert G. Bone, *Enforcement Costs and Trademark Puzzles*, 90 VA. L. REV. 2099, 2109 (2004) (referring to trademark infringement as a form of strict liability) ("A trademark infringement case focuses on the consequences of the defendant's actions and not on the defendant's intent to infringe upon another's trademark").

[110] *See, e.g.*, *Taubman Co.*, 319 F.3d, at 775 ("[T]he proper inquiry is not one of intent. In that sense, the Lanham Act is a strict liability statute. If consumers are confused by an infringing mark, the offender's motives are largely irrelevant").

explicitly. An injunction should issue, and damages are granted on that basis alone, and not based on possibly distorted findings of fact as to the likelihood of consumer confusion."[111]

Judges may like intent because it makes their job easier, and the outcome feels just. However, intent is irrelevant to technical trademark infringement. Eliminating intent allows a more focused inquiry into the likelihood of confusion rather than the commercial immorality of defendants. As a practical matter, it frees parties from costly discovery and allows the court to grant summary judgment more frequently.[112] Judges can also dispose of cases more easily without trial, and it is less likely that defendants will be subject to vexatious suits based on nebulous aspersions of intent.[113]

Scholars criticize the artificiality of consumer sophistication, likening it to expecting judges to perform a "Vulcan mind-meld" with consumers in the marketplace.[114] Courts may easily project their normative view of how carefully a consumer should be or its view of a defendant's conduct.[115] But, like intent and mark strength, this suffers from inherent capriciousness.

In sum, rules-based systems operate using explicit, pre-defined criteria that are not necessarily executed in a specified order. Explicit rules help determine the criteria they use to make decisions. Judges adjudicating using AI can help by providing checklists to delineate prohibited and permitted conduct, making compliance less a leap of "hunch, faith, and intuition" and empowering businesses who depend on clear rules to make informed decisions confidently.

3.2   The AI Advantage

The accumulation of case law gives the likelihood of confusion standard more sharply defined edges and can make it look more rule-like over time. How successive courts interpret a "reasonable" speed eventually informs drivers that anything above 80 miles per hour is dangerous. Likewise, the work of courts over time will reveal the point where a "similar" mark becomes discernible.

Courts may also identify recurring undesirable behaviors and ban them outright. Then, the algorithm can use those cases as a basis for establishing a more general prohibition on activities falling into the same family or genre. In so doing, AI would create per se rules of illegality and safe harbors.[116] The result is a familiar yet concise, precise, and efficient framework for preempting, counseling, and adjudicating trademark disputes. The standard thus attains amphibious benefits of becoming more rule-like while retaining a certain suppleness.

---

[111]   Beebe, *supra* note 4, at 1631.

[112]   10B CHARLES ALAN WRIGHT ET AL., FEDERAL PRACTICE AND PROCEDURE (CIVIL)) § 2730 (3d ed. 2015) ("Questions of intent, which involve intangible factors including witness credibility, are matters for the consideration of the fact finder after a full trial and are not for resolution by summary judgment").

[113]   Thomas L. Casagrande, *A Verdict for Your Thoughts? Why an Accused Trademark Infringer's Intent Has No Place in Likelihood of Confusion Analysis*, 101 TRADEMARK REP. 1447, 1455 (2011) (proposing an elimination of intent as a factor to be considered in determining trademark infringement).

[114]   *See* William E Gallagher & Ronald C Goodstein, *Inference versus Speculation in Trademark Infringement Litigation: Abandoning the Fiction of the Vulcan Mind Meld* (2004) 94 TRADEMARK REP 1229, at 1230.

[115]   August Storck K.G. v Nabisco, Inc., 59 F.3d 616, 618 (7th Cir. 1995) ("Many consumers are ignorant or inattentive, so some are bound to misunderstand no matter how careful a producer is").

[116]   Gideon Parchomovsky & Alex Stein, *Catalogs*, 115 COLUM. L. REV. 165, 171 (2015) ("No matter how hard legislatures try, they will fail to come up with fully specified rules that accurately represent every possible contingency in all future states of the world").

The beauty of AI-enabled likelihood of confusion analysis is that it can reach outcomes we cannot define in advance of the AI operating as "good" or "better" than the untrained neural network interrogates itself via the process of trial and error.[117] Moreover, programming the AI to maximize reward in a predetermined environment allows it to directly optimize policy performance rather than learning from old data by updating the agent's policy using good estimates of a particular policy's advantage relative to another policy.[118] This reduces the time and effort parties need to analyze a case, expanding the number of cases courts can dispense with summarily.

With AI, courts can consistently apply legal principles, even when the facts are idiosyncratic.[119] They can also avoid the risk of judges engaging in side-by-side mark comparison to ensure they apply the real-world purchasing context. AI also accounts for interactions among factors that escape even expert witnesses and contextualizes and associates information with known factors to make predictions based on untrained parameters.[120] For instance, principal component analysis can identify factors carrying the greatest weight in functions and zero in on the most important dimensions of datasets to show the stampeding factors.[121] As a result, AI could help predict litigation risk and the market implications of marketing and sales decisions.[122]

Finally, the results from AI recommendations challenge judges' prior assumptions, providing a check against coherence-based reasoning. For example, confronting people with merits of the opposite side reduced the effect of coherence shifts by about 50 percent.[123] In addition, legal studies showed that asking lawyers to consider the weaknesses in their side or reasons that the judge might rule against them mitigated bias.[124]

In sum, AI can chart trademark law over time and help convert the likelihood of confusion standard into a more transparent rules-based system. In so doing, AI introduces more predictability and clarity into trademark infringement analysis to help refine those rules.

---

[117] OpenAI, *Proximal Policy Optimization, OpenAI Spinning UP* (2018) https://spinningup.openai .com/en/latest/algorithms/ppo.html.

[118] Brian S. Haney, *AI Patents: A Data Driven Approach* 19 Chi -Kent J. Intell. Prop. 407, 439 (2020).

[119] Pamela Samuelson, *Unbundling Fair Uses*, 77 Fordham L. Rev. 2537, 2541–2 (2009).

[120] Similarly, AI-based support vector machines (SVMs) can find relationships between sets of trademark infringement cases while handling outlier or mislabeled cases, allowing SVM to crunch abrogated case law. *See e.g.*, Aurélien Géron, Hands-On Machine Learning With Scikit-Learn & Tensorfloww 145–67 (Nicole Tache et al. eds, 1st ed. 2017).

[121] Ibid, at 217.

[122] *See* Katyal & Kesari, *supra* note 10, at 533 ("Indeed, predictive analytics can prove to be transformative in helping businesses both create and sustain a strong presence in the marketplace, predicting the outcome of filing suit, sending a cease-and-desist, articulating various claims, or deciding whether and for how much to settle. And this is just the tip of the iceberg. Imagine every aspect of a trademark claim, its probable outcome automated, calculated, predicted and ready for real-time decision-making").

[123] Dan Simon, *A Third View of the Black Box: Cognitive Coherence in Legal Decision Making*, 71 U. Chi. L. Rev. 511, 543–4 (2004) (noting that "[m]ore studies are required to gain a better sense of the effects of the debiasing intervention").

[124] *See* Linda Babcock et al., *Creating Convergence: Debiasing Biased Litigants*, 22 Law And Soc. Inquiry 913, 920–1 (1997).

3.3   Execution

AI solutions for determining mark similarity and competitive proximity already exist.[125] They evaluate product attributes and mark similarity along visual, semantic, and graphical dimensions.[126] Corsearch offers one example of a pioneer trademark information system. Its solutions range from trademark searches to risk analysis.[127] It provides an image recognition tool based on a trained deep learning neural network that can dissect logos and designs into its parts, then compares component similarities, including shapes, concepts, letters and words, and colors, against existing logo images.[128] Its algorithm moves candidate marks from knock-out to clearance search and ranks similar marks in threat order.[129] Notably, its AI relies on mark similarity and competitive proximity, two troika factors advocated in section 3.1 of this chapter.[130]

Charles Trappey, Amy Trappey, and Bo-Hung Liu proposed a trademark precedent recommendation system.[131] The system would electronically scour and analyze "features and relevant US laws" to enable companies to respond to allegations of trademark infringement and act as a monitoring service when it detects infringement.[132] Precedent provides attributes of interest, including how courts applied the likelihood of confusion factors.

In another paper with AS Li, Trappey and Trappey theorized how an AI-enabled trademark infringement risk assessment system might work.[133] A dataset would use trademark litigation ontology and text mining to extract features from cases to build a machine-readable database

---

[125]   *See* Katyal & Kesari, *supra* note 10, at 531 (describing how AI can help "trademark owners search and identify potential trademarks for registration by employing AI to study a wide range of variables relevant to the search process including sight, sound, visual cues."); ibid ("Search and registration can also be improved using AI techniques, where machine learning can be relied upon to identify semantically similar marks").

[126]   Idan Mosseri *et al.*, *How AI will Revolutionise Trademark Searches*, WORLD TRADEMARK REV. (July 2, 2019), www.worldtrademarkreview.com/ip-offices/how-ai-will-revolutionise-trademark-searches. *See also The Future of Trademark Service Providers*, WORLD TRADEMARK REV., www.worldtrademarkreview.com/reports/the-future-of-trademark-service-providers (noting how neural network technologies can determine semantic equivalence, providing insights into substantial similarity and trademark relatedness).

[127]   Corsearch, *Trademark Screening*, https://corsearch.com/solution/trademark-brand-clearance/trademark-screening/.

[128]   Corsearch, *Logocheck*, https://corsearch.com/solution/trademark-brand-clearance/logocheck/.

[129]   Ibid.

[130]   Ibid ("Its industry-leading artificial intelligence scores the visual, semantic, phonetic, and product-type similarity of your candidate trademark name against tens of millions of existing marks and presents results in decreasing order of risk"). Namecheck also assesses mark strength, though, for the reasons given in this chapter, it is not an ideal indicator of likelihood of confusion.

[131]   *See* Trappey, Trappey, & Liu, supra note 32, at 2.

[132]   *See* ibid.

[133]   A.S. Li, A.J.C. Trappeya, & C.V. Trappey, *Intelligent Identification of Trademark Case Precedents Using Semantic Ontology* in J. POKOJSKI ET AL. (EDS) TRANSDISCIPLINARY ENGINEERING FOR COMPLEX SOCIO-TECHNICAL SYSTEMS—REAL-LIFE APPLICATIONS (2020).

like the case content analysis.[134] The ontology schema would follow actual confusion, competitive proximity, and mark similarity.[135]

Key terms help the clustering process by finding cases with similar features to recommend as precedent, ranked in order of priority.[136] The algorithm learns to associate certain standardized keywords with certain variables.[137] This allows the algorithm to automatically extract these features in large numbers from the population of cases and clusters cases into topic models.[138] The resulting database stores and links key features of each case. Consequently, "[w]hen users input seed cases to the system, the system will display relevant precedents (with similar issue attributes) and highlight the relevant federal laws."[139]

Trappey, Trappey, and Liu describe using word2vec as an autonomous work-embedding algorithm converting all the cases into word vectors, calculating pair-wise cosine similarities of all document pairs to find cases matching the seed case.[140] Using clustering and topic modeling, AI can infer key terminologies corresponding to characteristics of the seed case with an 83.8 percent accuracy rate.[141] Even more remarkably, the algorithm "adopts the inherent rules of judgment written styles to extract important feature data using the approach of a regular expression."[142]

The source of training datasets can build upon the well-established method of case content analysis. The method systematically dissects a sample of judicial opinions to record consistent features, draw inferences, and uncover trends.[143] This social science approach to the law complements and augments traditional legal analysis.[144] In addition, case content analysis treats

---

[134] *See* Li, Trappeya, & Trappey, *supra* note 133, at 542 (according to the authors, their "system combines the [trademark] litigation key-feature extraction and judgment semantic topic recognition modules to cross-validate the discovery of precedents. The system provides the reliable results based on the similarities between legal precedents' issues, topics, and other pre-defined attributes/features").

[135] *See* ibid.

[136] *See* ibid.

[137] *See* ibid, at 539 ("In legal judgments, the laws are written in a certain formats/patterns"). *See also* LUCA WHEELER, THE ART OF REGULAR EXPRESSIONS (2016).

[138] *See* Li, Trappeya, & Trappey, *supra* note 133, at 538 (describing the use of term frequency–inverse document frequency (TF-IDF) and N-gram algorithms to identify key terms in case reports and using Latent Dirichlet Allocation to do soft clustering).

[139] Ibid at 540.

[140] *See* Trappey, Trappey, & Liu, *supra* note 32, at 5 ("The word vectors of all judgments are the document which form the base for the clustering and topic modeling analyses. Non-supervised clustering places TM cases with similar features and attributes into the same clusters. LDA groups TM judgments into non-exclusive topics in any given cluster to establish the topic models of the TM cases within each cluster").

[141] *See* ibid, at 7 ("Cluster verification uses word embedding, a semantic machine learning neural model, to vectorize all original and recommended judgments for comparing the homogeneity between the original and the recommended judgments in matching clusters.") *See* ibid ("To sum up, the merit of the recommendation system has been objectively verified in regards to the cited laws and the clustering of the original cases and their corresponding recommended judgments").

[142] *See* ibid, at 6.

[143] *See* KLAUS KRIPPENDORFF, CONTENT ANALYSIS: AN INTRODUCTION TO ITS METHODOLOGY 18 (2d ed., 2004) (defining content analysis as "a research technique for making replicable and valid inferences from texts (or other meaningful matter) to the contexts of their use").

[144] Mark A. Hall & Ronald F. Wright, *Systematic Content Analysis of Judicial Opinions*, 96 CAL. L. REV. 63, 65 (2008). *See also* ibid ("The method also helps a researcher to sort out the interaction of multiple factors that bear on an outcome in the legal system"); ibid ("Its strength is to provide an objective

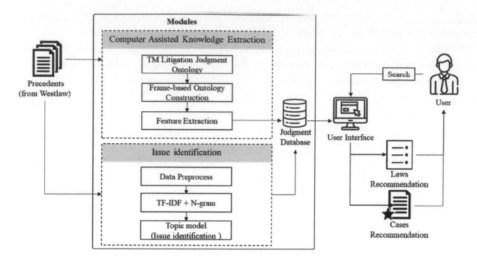

Figure 14.1   An intelligent trademark precedent recommendation system

the content of opinions as generic data, a feature important for preprocessing AI datasets.[145] Coding and counting cases imply that information in one opinion may be potentially relevant to another.[146]

In a pre-AI world, an army of legal scholars might attempt to map all likelihood of confusion cases comprehensively. They would need to endure many hours of time-consuming and repetitive reading and extracting needed to code each case, draw inferences, and report on trends, as was done in the writing of this chapter. Case content analysis is suitable for automating because the same set of information must be keyed into many cells in the same case, requiring coders to eyeball each cell for accuracy given the tedious, repetitive data entry that results in avoidable human errors and copy-paste tasks.

The result is useful, capable of determining the weight courts place on various legal and non-legal factors, identifying which factors judges use to "stampede" others, revealing trends across time, and relevant parametric factors that may typically escape conventional wisdom.[147] Algorithms pick out keywords and assign appropriate weights to each variable. For example, "in favor of"[148] or "favors"[149] factors would signify a positive correlation to

---

understanding of a large number of decisions where each decision has roughly the same value"). Alan L. Tyree, *Fact Content Analysis of Case Law: Methods and Limitations*, 22 JURIMETRICS J. 1, 23 (1981) (these methods have "considerable power for the discovery of anomalies which may escape the naked eye").

[145]   Hall & Wright, *supra* note 144, at 83.

[146]   Peter J. Hammer & William M. Sage, *Antitrust, Health Care Quality, and the Courts*, 102 COLUM. L. REV. 545, 561 (2002).

[147]   *See e.g.* Barton Beebe, *An Empirical Study of U.S. Copyright Fair Use Opinions, 1978–2005*, 156 U. PA. L. REV. 549, 591 (2008).

[148]   Fletcher's Original State Fair Corny Dogs, LLC v Fletcher-Warner Holdings LLC, 434 F. Supp. 3d 473 (E.D. Tex. 2020)

[149]   Fleet Feet, Inc. v Nike Inc., 419 F. Supp. 3d 919, 943 (M.D.N.C. 2019), appeal dismissed and remanded, 986 F.3d 458 (4th Cir. 2021), and vacated, No. 1:19-CV-885, 2021 WL 4067544 (M.D.N.C. Apr. 6, 2021).

one side. Similarly, phrases such as "marks are strong,"[150] "high degree of care,"[151] "marks are identical,"[152] or "weighs strongly in favor of,"[153] would be assigned greater, or in the case of "neutral,"[154] "weighs neither for nor against,"[155] "slightly in favor of,"[156] lesser weight. The algorithm would also recognize and capture variables such as rivalry ("direct competitors"[157]). Dev Gangjee also identifies datasets of past examiners' decisions as a ready resource to train algorithms for mark similarity by assigning different 'weights' to different measures of similarity, depending on the type of mark.[158]

Year	Case	Citation	Court	Circuit	Level	Rival	Mark Type	Posture	Outcome	LOC Test	Mark strength
2021	FocusVision Worldwide, Inc. v. Information Builders, Inc.	859 Fed.Appx. 573	United States Court of Appeals, Federal Circuit.	13	2	1	1	9	1	13	0
2021	CDOC, Inc. v. Liberty Bankers Life Insurance Company	844 Fed.Appx. 357	United States Court of Appeals, Federal Circuit.	13	2	1	1	9	4	13	0
2021	OakTrip West, Inc. v. Weigel Stores, Inc.	984 F.3d 1081	United States Court of Appeals, Federal Circuit.	13	2	1	1	9	1	13	0
2020	Stratus Networks, Inc. v. UBTA-UBET Communications Inc.	955 F.3d 994	United States Court of Appeals, Federal Circuit.	13	2	0	1	9	1	13	0
2019	In re Copeland-Smith	791 Fed.Appx. 898	United States Court of Appeals, Federal Circuit.	13	2	0	1	9	1	13	1
2019	Swagway, LLC v. International Trade Commission	934 F.3d 1322	United States Court of Appeals, Federal Circuit.	13	2	1	1	8	1	13	0
2019	In re JS ADL, LLC	777 Fed.Appx. 991	United States Court of Appeals, Federal Circuit.	13	2	0	1	9	1	13	2
2019	In re Louis Vuitton Malletier	777 Fed.Appx. 984	United States Court of Appeals, Federal Circuit.	13	2	0	1	9	2	13	1
2019	Swagway, LLC v. International Trade Commission	923 F.3d 1349	United States Court of Appeals, Federal Circuit.	13	2	1	1	8	1	13	1
2019	VersaTop Support Systems, LLC v. Georgia Expo, Inc.	921 F.3d 1364	United States Court of Appeals, Federal Circuit.	13	2	1	1	7	1	13	0
2018	In re Detroit Athletic Co.	903 F.3d 1297	United States Court of Appeals, Federal Circuit.	13	2	0	1	9	1	13	0
2018	Zheng Cai v. Diamond Hong, Inc.	901 F.3d 1367	United States Court of Appeals, Federal Circuit.	13	2	1	1	9	1	13	0
2021	Klayman v. Judicial Watch, Inc.	6 F.4th 1301	United States Court of Appeals, District of Columbi	12	2	0	1	2	2	12	0
2021	Sefex Foundation, Inc. v. Safeth, Ltd.	--- F.Supp.3d ---	United States Court of Appeals, District of Columbia.	12	1	1	1	8	4	12	0
2021	Military Order of Purple Heart Service Foundation, Inc. v. Military	852 Fed.Appx. 6	United States Court of Appeals, District of Columbi	12	2	0	1	6	1	12	0
2021	Vital Pharmaceuticals, Inc. v. Monster Energy Company	--- F.Supp.3d ---	United States District Court, S.D. Florida.	11	1	1	2	6	2	11	0
2020		1,983 F.3d 1270	United States Court of Appeals, Eleventh Circuit.	11	2	1	1	1	1	11	1
2020	I-B Weld Company, LLC v. Gorilla Glue Company	978 F.3d 778	United States Court of Appeals, Eleventh Circuit.	11	2	1	2	2	3	11	4
2020	Tarsus Connect, LLC v. Cvent, Inc.	452 F.Supp.3d 1334	United States District Court, N.D. Georgia, Atlanta	11	1	0	1	7	2	11	1
2020	D. H. Pace Company, LLC v. Aaron Overhead Door Atlanta LLC	522 F.Supp.3d 1315	United States District Court, N.D. Georgia, Atlanta	11	1	1	1	7	2	11	3
2019	FCOA, LLC v. Foremost Title & Escrow Services, LLC	416 F.Supp.3d 1381	United States District Court, S.D. Florida.	11	1	0	1	7	2	11	1
2019	Reinalt-Thomas Corporation v. Mavis Tire Supply, LLC	391 F.Supp.3d 1264	United States District Court, N.D. Georgia, Atlanta	11	1	1	1	8	4	11	2
2019	3tions Publishing, Inc. v. Interactive Media Corp.	389 F.Supp.3d 1031	United States District Court, M.D. Florida, Tampa	11	1	1	1	4	4	11	0
2019	PlayNation Play Systems, Inc. v. Velex Corporation	924 F.3d 1159	United States Court of Appeals, Eleventh Circuit.	11	2	1	1	6	1	11	1
2019	Hard Candy, LLC v. Anastasia Beverly Hills, Inc.	921 F.3d 1343	United States Court of Appeals, Eleventh Circuit.	11	2	1	1	6	2	11	0
2019	Comphy Company v. Amazon.com, Inc.	371 F.Supp.3d 914	United States District Court, W.D. Washington, at	11	1	0	1	7	5	11	2

Figure 14.2   A dataset coding for likelihood of confusion factors

Automation saves dataset preparers a substantial amount of time. Studies on automating conveyancing work show time savings of 90 percent.[159] Less skilled and lower-cost staff can quickly and accurately generate datasets, lowering costs, time, and effort to produce complex datasets, freeing scholars to focus on higher-value work.

After processing the datasets, the algorithm could map qualitative and quantitative data points in seed cases to its markers. Those presenting the same set of facts would reach the same outcome as precedential cases presenting the same set of markers. AI will need to specify the weight of factors not expressly entailed by rules or precedents. Once algorithms produce

---

[150] New Balance Athletics, Inc. v USA New Bunren Int'l Co. Ltd. LLC, 424 F. Supp. 3d 334, 347 (D. Del. 2019).

[151] Ibid.

[152] Ibid.

[153] *Better Angels Soc'y, Inc.*, 419 F. Supp. 3d, at 777; Life After Hate, Inc. v Free Radicals Project, Inc., 410 F. Supp. 3d 891, 907 (N.D. Ill. 2019).

[154] Illinois Tool Works Inc. v J-B Weld Co., LLC, 419 F. Supp. 3d 382, 399 (D. Conn. 2019).

[155] *New Balance Athletics*, Inc, 424 F. Supp. 3d, at 347.

[156] Delta Forensic Eng'g, Inc. v Delta V Biomechanics, Inc., 402 F. Supp. 3d 902, 909 (C.D. Cal. 2019).

[157] Smartling, Inc. v Skawa Innovation Ltd., 358 F. Supp. 3d 124, 139 (D. Mass. 2019).

[158] *See* Gangjee, *supra* note 11, at 9–10.

[159] Serena Lim & Nandini Nayar Sharma, *Document Drafting—Less is More*. SINGAPORE LAW GAZETTE (Nov. 21, 2021) https://lawgazette.com.sg/practice/tech-talk/document-drafting-less-is-more/.

their recommendation, courts can accept or reject the AI's recommendation. With new input in each iteration, the AI can adjust its weights and parameters.[160] The feedback loop causes the algorithm's nodes to change their weights so that the new case law can yield better results over time.[161]

More than a concept, scholars implemented AI-enabled case content analysis. For example, Giovanna Massarotto and Ashwin Ittoo conceived and implemented a machine learning system for analyzing antitrust cases. Their process began with identifying the appropriate data and variables.[162] To train their algorithm, Massarotto and Ittoo used Federal Trade Commission decisions between 2013 and 2018.[163] Next, they performed an exploratory data analysis ("EDA") to examine the dataset and detect peculiarities or incoherence.[164] The EDA also helped detect preliminary correlations between variables and visualized those correlations using a "heat map."[165]

Massarotto and Ittoo's algorithm enabled them to discover patterns underlying case law and generate new clusters of cases using similar patterns.[166] In addition, the algorithm identified variables impacting case outcomes.[167] They employed a support vector machine ("SVM"). The SVM estimated a variable's influence over clusters, to which they assigned data points[168] and cross-checked it against a random forest algorithm.[169]

Likelihood of confusion opinions contains logic-dependent conditional clause variations, which incorporate the likelihood of confusion factors.[170] Next, the user selects a smart template and answers a questionnaire to generate an opinion. The AI then uses the training data to assemble a custom opinion.

Being a social enterprise, the law requires acceptance by the public as a precondition to its existence. Thus, for trademark law to properly integrate AI, it must enjoy a degree of legitimacy among both those who use it and those governed by it.

---

[160] TERRENCE J. SEJNOWSKI, THE DEEP LEARNING REVOLUTION 20 (2018).

[161] *See* Stephen McJohn & Ian McJohn, *Fair Use and Machine Learning*, 12 NE. U.L. REV. 99, 135 (2020).

[162] Massarotto & Ittoo, *supra* note 18, at 24.

[163] Ibid.

[164] Ibid, at 27 ("Essentially, EDA cleans data in a dataset to improve the performance of a model's learning process by ensuring that the data fed to the algorithms are correct, of good quality, and will not compromise the algorithms' accuracy and results").

[165] Ibid, at 28. ("In statistics and machine learning, correlated variables tend to have a significant impact on the final clustering"); *see also* ibid ("The horizontal and vertical axes correspond to variables. The greener the cell, the higher the correlation. As can be expected, each variable is highly correlated to itself, which is natural. The heat map revealed no apparent significant correlation among variables, which do not warrant further multi-collinearity tests").

[166] Ibid ("The algorithms project the data, here antitrust cases, as vectors in a multi-dimensional space. Then, the distance between cases is estimated based on the variables characterizing each case. Finally, similar (less distant) cases are grouped into clusters while minimizing a criterion, such as the error").

[167] Ibid ("Also, these variables, if properly identified, could enable antitrust enforcers and legislators to better comprehend antitrust cases and even predict their outcomes").

[168] Ibid at 30.

[169] Ibid (describing the random forest algorithm as one "which attempts to transform the data points (and variables) into a collection of tree-like structures, and in doing so, estimates how much each variable is predictive of a given cluster").

[170] *See e.g.* Lim, *supra* note 87.

One issue is that AI can sometimes produce or entrench bias. For example, would introducing AI adjudicated trademark cases risk creating such discriminatory results? A second is the "black-box" problem. Even when AI outputs are accurate, it is often impossible for humans to interpret their decision functions. Is this a concern for algorithmic decisionmaking in the likelihood of confusion context? Both are well-known concerns.[171] In setting out the brass tacks, section 4 of this chapter confronts these concerns and a third issue: data availability. It explains that these concerns, while legitimate, can be significantly mitigated or, in some cases, comprehensively addressed.

4.   CHALLENGES AND RESPONSES

This section identifies bias, accountability, and data scarcity as three key challenges to deploying AI in trademark disputes. The chapter as a whole draws on the latest developments in experimental psychology, algorithmic techniques, and legal scholarship to address these challenges, which are common to other areas of the law and therefore have broader implications beyond trademark law.

4.1   Bias

Algorithmic biases arise in automation, datafication surveillance,[172] and profiling loan credit risk and criminal recidivism based on race.[173] As discussed in section 2.1 of this chapter, humans are not designed to process vast amounts of qualitative data—a problem the economic literature calls "bounded rationality."[174] Instead, they rely on heuristics such as ideology to navigate the world,[175] shaped by personal experiences, beliefs, and biology.[176]

Coding is not value-neutral, and biases may seep into the algorithmic code, filtering into training data and the weights judges may assign to the algorithm.[177] Bias could also come from

---

[171] Peter N. Salib, *Artificially Intelligent Class Actions*, Tex. L. Rev. (Forthcoming, 2022) ("Disputes over algorithmic design choice are likely to fall into two categories: data collection and preparation, and model training").

[172] Sandra G. Mayson, *Bias In, Bias Out*, 128 Yale L.J. 2218, 2221 (2019); Frank Pasquale & Danielle Keats Citron, *Promoting Innovation while Preventing Discrimination: Policy Goals for the Scored Society*, 89 Wash. L. Rev. 1413, 1415 (2014); Mikella Hurley & Julius Adebayo, *Credit Scoring in the Era of Big Data*, 18 Yale J.L. & Tech. 148, 196–8 (2016); Aziz Z. Huq, *Racial Equity in Algorithmic Criminal Justice*, 68 Duke L.J. 1043, 1053–4 (2019); Mary Madden et al., *Privacy, Poverty, and Big Data: A Matrix of Vulnerabilities for Poor Americans*, 95 Wash. U. L. Rev. 53, 55–6 (2017); Stephanie Bornstein, *Antidiscriminatory Algorithms*, 70 Ala. L. Rev. 519, 522–3 (2018); Pauline T. Kim, *Data-Driven Discrimination at Work*, 58 Wm. & Mary L. Rev. 857, 860–1 (2017); Margaret Hu, *Algorithmic Jim Crow*, 86 Fordham L. Rev. 633, 650 (2017); Danah Boyd, *Undoing the Neutrality of Big Data*, 67 Fla. L. Rev. F. 226, 227 (2016).

[173] *See* Meghan J. Ryan, *Secret Conviction Programs*, 77 Wash. & Lee L. Rev. 269, 303–5 (2020) ("judges and jurors often eagerly convict defendants based on this evidence").

[174] *See* Shyamkrishna Balganesh, *Foreseeability and Copyright Incentives*, 122 Harv. L. Rev. 1569, 1574 (2009).

[175] *See supra*, section 1.1.

[176] *See* Daniel R. Cahoy, *Patently Uncertain*, 17 Nw. J. Tech. & Intell. Prop. 1, 13 (2019).

[177] *See* Dan L. Burk, *Algorithmic Fair Use*, 86 U. Chi. L. Rev. 283, 283 (2019); *see e.g.* David Lehr & Paul Ohm, *Playing with the Data: What Legal Scholars Should Learn About Machine Learning*, 51 U.C. Davis L. Rev. 653, 669–701 (2017).

judges deciding the reported cases used to train the algorithm and those interpreting the results produced by the AI system.[178] In addition, reinforcement learning techniques may embed bias, raising the risk of what Thomas Nachbar labeled "snowballing unfairness."[179] As Nachbar has explained, codes are path-dependent, "based on decisions made in previous iterations of the program—prompting a cascading search for purpose."[180]

Moerland and Freitas provide an example of bias in action:

> when teaching an AI to establish a pattern of similarity of signs, one could easily ascertain a similarity between two given signs, while someone else would not. Even if case law regarding the similarity of signs is used as training data, courts sometimes come to differing outcomes for the same cases. Bias in data will be replicated when used by the AI technology, as it lacks the ability to filter out slightly incorrect interpretations.[181]

The lack of a standardized method to weigh factors systematically exacerbates the risk of bias. The likelihood of confusion factors has no weights assigned, eroding the ability to apply the tests objectively or in a manner that can be replicated.[182] AI helps integrate data and provides a statistical prediction based on input variables. Humans are superior at selecting and coding information but poor at integrating it.[183]

Kahneman et al. recommend assigning probabilities rather than absolute values or binary "yes" or "no" judgments.[184] Numerical thresholds could help adjudicate infringement cases. For example, computer scientists could build a model that requires judges to rate the three core likelihood of confusion factors on a scale of 0 to 10. If the marks were completely different, the judge would rate it "0" (the lowest rating possible), but if the mark was a simple counterfeit, the judge would rate it "10" (the highest rating). Thus, the algorithm would set a numerical threshold for finding confusion that maps to case law and the balance of probabilities. Over time, the algorithm will provide more granular information about the characteristics driving outcomes in the likelihood of confusion cases. In this way, the algorithm would imitate judges, granting a low score to a particular factor and consequently a lower success rate to plaintiffs.

Kahneman et al. also recommend relying more heavily on rules such as judicial sentencing guidelines.[185] The troika of factors again provides that framework. Importantly, the results from AI recommendations challenge judges' prior assumptions, providing a check against coherence-based reasoning.[186] For instance, confronting people with merits of the opposite

---

[178]   *See* Gangjee, *supra* note 11, at 11 ("where the data for a machine learning approach is derived from judicial content analysis—past decisions by human tribunals where factors are coded and correlations derived—the algorithm will behave like the human decision maker it is modelled after, warts and all").

[179]   Thomas Nachbar, *Algorithm Fairness, Algorithmic Discrimination*, University of Virginia School of Law Public Law and Legal Theory Research Paper Series 2020-17 (Jan. 2020).

[180]   Ibid, at 48.

[181]   Moerland & Freitas, *supra* note 17, at 18.

[182]   *See* Menard, Inc. v Commissioner, 560 F.3d 620, 622–3 (7th Cir. 2009) ("Multifactor tests with no weight assigned to any factor are bad enough from the standpoint of providing an objective basis for a judicial decision; multifactor tests when none of the factors is concrete are worse").

[183]   *See e.g.* Robyn M Dawes, *The Robust Beauty of Improper Linear Models in Decision Making* (1979) 34 American Psychologist 571, 573.

[184]   Kahneman, et al., *supra* note 82, at location 984.

[185]   Ibid.

[186]   *See* Lim, *supra* note 3.

side reduced the effect of coherence shifts by about 50 percent.[187] Legal studies similarly showed that asking lawyers to consider the weaknesses in their side or reasons that the judge might rule against them mitigated bias.[188]

Finally, to address the issue of "snowballing unfairness," flooding the system with voluminous data may help. As Moerland and Freitas note, "with large amounts of data, incidental bias may not influence the rule that the AI learns from the data."[189] They reassuringly report that "[AI] training is continuous and subject to high standards of reliability. Error measures are used as well as pilot studies on unseen data to determine how the AI tool performs its tasks."[190] Section 4.3 of this chapter addresses the issue of data scarcity.

Done well, trademark algocracy will minimize biases from human decisionmaking without compounding those biases with its own.[191] In the years ahead, ethics teams will likely become an essential department in antitrust agencies and economic consultancies such as finance, legal, marketing, and human resource departments. These teams can help decisionmakers weigh benefits and harms of AI procedures and recommendations, flag their implications, develop guidelines, and help clarify ethical conflicts.[192]

The issue of accountability in deploying AI is another major concern. Using AI risks exchanging bounded rationality for opacity.[193] As a result, fewer algorithms may fail to deliver, and more sophisticated ones are too complicated to hold accountable.[194] Moreover, the massive scale of datasets makes it hard to scrutinize their contents and perpetuate errors thoroughly.[195] The next section explores these concerns.

4.2   Accountability

Parties may disagree about the accuracy of certain data relevant to determining consumer confusion. In addition, data may suffer from statistical deficiencies such as lack of randomness or representativeness.[196] For instance, Moerland and Freitas warn that "the subjectivity and complexity of trademark law's doctrinal tests would be difficult to replicate with an AI-driven system since they are presently unable to reflect the nuances of these [likelihood of confusion] tests."[197]

---

[187]   Simon, *supra* note 123, at 543–4 (noting that "[m]ore studies are required to gain a better sense of the effects of the debiasing intervention").

[188]   *See* Linda Babcock et al., *Creating Convergence: Debiasing Biased Litigants*, 22 LAW AND SOC. INQUIRY 913, 920–1 (1997).

[189]   *See* Moerland & Freitas, *supra* note 17, at 18.

[190]   *See* ibid, at 17.

[191]   *See* Ryan, *supra* note 173, at 281–7.

[192]   Lim Sun & Jeffrey Chan Kok Hui, *Moving AI Ethics Beyond Guidelines*, THE STRAITS TIMES, Dec. 16, 2020, www.straitstimes.com/opinion/moving-ai-ethics-beyond-guidelines-0.

[193]   Andrew D. Selbst, *Negligence and AI's Human Users*, 100 B.U. L. REV. 1315, 1362 (2020).

[194]   *See, e.g.*, Yavar Bathaee, *The Artificial Intelligence Black Box and the Failure of Intent and Causation*, 31 HARV. J.L. & TECH. 889, 907 (2018).

[195]   Khari Johnson, *AI Research Survey Finds Machine Learning Needs a Culture Change* (Dec. 26, 2020)   https://venturebeat.com/2020/12/26/ai-research-survey-finds-machine-learning-needs-a-culture -change/.

[196]   *See* Lehr & Ohm, *supra* note 177, at 679.

[197]   *See* Moerland & Freitas, *supra* note 17, at 2.

Comparing AI and non-AI results, both reach the same results for near-identical trademarks. However, there are significant differences when marks differ more significantly.[198] According to Moerland and Freitas, "[i]t is difficult to imagine that an AI can be taught to assess in a case at hand who the relevant public is and what its level of attentiveness for a specific category of goods in a relevant market is, taking its imperfect recollection of signs into account."[199]

An industry shift toward trade secrets exacerbates the quest for accountability. A 2014 US Supreme Court decision made it difficult for software inventions to receive or retain patent rights, leading AI developers to pivot toward trade secret protection.[200] Unfortunately, this pivot discourages disclosure and dissemination of new technology,[201] dissuading AI developers from sharing information critical to improving auditing decisionmaking processes.[202] Patent reform to address this has long been in the works, but the end is nowhere in sight. [203]

Accountability, rather than transparency, should be the goal.[204] Accountability focuses on identifiable goals[205] and is a well-developed concept in the law.[206] Whether a justification exists says nothing about whether and to what extent it was relied upon in decisionmaking.

It is worth pausing to address concerns by scholars as to whether AI adjudicating trademark infringement cases is even conceptually possible. For instance, Moerland and Freitas argue that "it is very difficult for the subjective and more complex tests enshrined in trademark law to be carried out autonomously by an AI tool, and this is unlikely to change in the near future."[207] They are skeptical of AI's ability to reflect the nuances of the likelihood of confusion. Even where AI executes legal tests, humans must assess those outputs.[208] At the same time, they acknowledge that AI could carry out more complex tasks given "the rapid development of technology."[209]

One may offer several responses to address these concerns. First, scholars and AI service providers agree that AI augments human decisionmaking and does not displace it.[210] As LawPanel's founder put it, "AI will speed up legal research, but it will not replace advice

---

[198]   *See* ibid, at 15.
[199]   *See* ibid, at 22.
[200]   Alice Corp. Pty. v CLS Bank Int'l, 573 U.S. 208 (2014).
[201]   *See generally,* Daryl Lim, *The Influence of Alice*, 105 MINN. L. REV. HEADNOTES 345 (2021).
[202]   Meghan J. Ryan, *Secret Algorithms, IP Rights, and the Public Interest*, 21 NEV. L.J. 61 (2020).
[203]   *See generally,* Lim, *supra note* 201.
[204]   Nachbar, *supra* note 179, at 61.
[205]   Ibid, at 62.
[206]   Courts routinely examine cases of alleged discrimination under Title VII of the Civil Rights Act of 1964. *See e.g.*, Section 703(a)(1); *see also* Texas Dep't of Cmty. Affairs v Burdines, 450 U.S. 248, 252–3 (1981); Graham v Long Island R.R., 230 F.3d 34, 38 (2d Cir. 2012); Peele v Country Mut. Ins. Co., 288 F.3d 319, 326 (7th Cir. 2002).
[207]   Moerland & Freitas, *supra* note 17, at 2.
[208]   *See* ibid, at 2.
[209]   Ibid.
[210]   *See* Gangjee, *supra* note 11, at 11 ("Experience till date therefore suggests that AI algorithms are intended to augment human judgment—to effectively sift through ever increasing volumes of registration data—and not to replace it"). *See also* Compumark White Paper, *Artificial Intelligence, Human Expertise: How Technology and Trademark Experts Work Together to Meet Today's IP Challenges* (2018) 5 ("While AI and neural networks will play an expanding role in CompuMark solutions […] they are intended to complement, not replace, human analysts").

formulation [… since it] only works on repetitive tasks in a very tightly-defined domain."[211] Katyal and Kesari are optimistic that the gap can be closed as data scientists enrich the dataset with more data and human-AI teams.[212] They report how

> experts emphasize the importance of human oversight and participation, particularly in terms of using human judgment in complex cognitive tasks, especially in the context of trademark doctrines which are highly context-specific. This is especially true in more complex cases of multi-word or slogan marks, where humans are likely to be the best at determining areas of particular strength.[213]

To generate a decision function that matches a real court's as closely as possible, the algorithm would link inputs and use them to guess outputs, measuring errors in its first set of guesses; update the complex set of relations between inputs and outputs; and guess again using its optimization function until error is minimized. Finally, data scientists would run the tested, trained algorithm against a hold-out set of training data. If the algorithm accurately resolved questions it had never seen before, that is evidence it would perform well.[214]

Second, the civil litigation process itself provides solutions. For example, to address opacity caused by trade secret protection, judges can employ well-established remedies by issuing protective orders to safeguard litigants' trade secrets, including making the algorithm available for in-camera examination or making it available under seal.[215] In addition, evidentiary rules require relevance to filter out misrecorded data or correlate to the operative facts.[216] Finally, the court could determine which party's expert opinions about proper algorithmic design should prevail under the *Daubert* test.[217]

On appeal, the variability of decisions reveals some idea of the extent of noise to the appellate court. A three-judge circuit appeals court or nine-justice Supreme Court bench provides an additional check. Salib observes that "there will be an adjustment period as courts develop doctrine about what constitutes credible scientific practice in algorithmic design. Such bumps on the road, however, are the cost of admission if generalist judges are to continue playing any major role governing our increasingly-complex world."[218]

Third, it is helpful to recall that the likelihood of confusion is itself a black box.[219] Human decisionmaking occurs within the private space between our ears, and courts write for justification, not explanation. In contrast, AI decisionmaking may provide a better forum to tweak

---

[211] Tim Lince, *No Imminent AI Apocalypse—Tech Expert Rejects Predictions of Mass Job Losses in Trademark Industry*, WORLD TRADEMARK REV. (2018), www.worldtrademarkreview.com/brand-management/no-imminent-ai-apocalypse-tech-expert-rejects-predictions-mass-job-losses.

[212] *See* Katyal & Kesari, *supra* note 10, at 526.

[213] Ibid, at n.159.

[214] Sanjay Yadav & Sanyam Shukla, *Analysis of K-Fold Cross-Validation over Hold-Out Validation on Colossal Dataset* 2016 IEEE 6th International Conference On Advanced Computing (IACC), www.researchgate.net/publication/306300803_Analysis_of_k-Fold_Cross-Validation_over_Hold-Out_Validation_on_Colossal_Datasets_for_Quality_Classification.

[215] *See, e.g.*, FED. R. CIV. PROC. 26(c)(1)(G); Fed. Open Mkt. Comm. of Fed. Reserve Sys. v Merrill, 443 U.S. 340, 356 (1979).

[216] Fed. R. Evid. 401. *See also* Fed. R. Evid. 403. (potentially excluding data with only a weak correlation to operative facts for its potential to confuse or prejudice the jury).

[217] Daubert v Merrell Dow Pharmaceuticals, Inc., 509 U.S. 579 (1993) (excluding expert opinions lacking sufficient scientific credibility; codified in Fed. R. Evid. 702).

[218] Salib, *supra* note 171, at 38.

[219] *See* section 1.1.

the process if the algorithm produces systematically problematic outcomes.[220] Moreover, the lack of explainability is a feature of AI's ability to recognize connections not obvious to humans, and indeed the purpose of using them in the first place.[221] Dumbing down AI makes it more parsable, but it brings another set of problems—the algorithm may become less effective or more vulnerable to gaming and adversarial learning by regulated parties.[222]

Fourth, technological progress increasingly minimizes tradeoffs between accountability and efficacy. In 2021, MIT researchers developed flexible algorithms that learn on the job.[223] Dubbed "liquid" networks, they continuously change underlying equations to adapt to new data inputs. This advance could aid decisionmaking based on data streams that change over time, as they do in many of the dynamic markets trademark law governs.[224] Critically, these expressive neurons make it easier to peer into the "black box" of the network's decisionmaking and determine why it made a certain recommendation.[225]

In addition, decision trees used in AI analyses can track how courts apply the likelihood of confusion to facts.[226] Even as far back as 2004, decision tree analysis outperformed a panel of legal experts in predicting affirmance rates.[227] An automated algorithmic checker makes predictions based on definable features such as case law and data pertinent to the facts and sorts them into nodes, providing accountability.[228]

Decision trees comprise internal nodes representing tests on features or attributes, with each branch representing a possible outcome. The path from roots to leaves represents the classification rules.[229] The algorithm typically uses "if–then rules." The "if" clause combines conditions on the input variables.[230] For example, the Monte Carlo Tree Search (MCTS) explores possible case outcomes options and narrows those options based on how well they maximize desired outcomes.[231]

The MCTS leaves a trail of decisions in its wake.[232] It is particularly suitable for the likelihood of confusion analyses, which follow a stepwise sequence, allowing each step to be coded,

---

[220]   Maurice E. Stucke, *Does the Rule of Reason Violate the Rule of Law?*, 42 U.C. DAVIS L. REV. 1375, 1461–66 (2009).

[221]   Ibid.

[222]   *See* David Engstrom et al., *Government by Algorithm: Artificial Intelligence in Federal Administrative Agencies* 86 (2020), available at www-cdn.law.stanford.edu/wp-content/uploads/2020/02/ACUS-AI-Report.pdf.

[223]   Daniel Ackerman, *MIT's New Neural Network: "Liquid" Machine-Learning System Adapts to Changing Conditions*, SCITECHDAILY, (Feb. 2, 2021) https://scitechdaily.com/mits-new-neural-network-liquid-machine-learning-system-adapts-to-changing-conditions/.

[224]   Ibid.

[225]   Ibid.

[226]   *See* McJohn & Ian McJohn, *supra* note 161, at 148.

[227]   Andrew D. Martin et al., *Competing Approaches to Predicting Supreme Court Decision Making*, 2 PERSP. ON POL. 761 (2004).

[228]   *See e.g.*, ibid at 147.

[229]   *See* Riccardo Guidotti, *Artificial Intelligence and Explainability*, in ARTIFICIAL INTELLIGENCE IN THE AUDIOVISUAL SECTOR 13–14 (European Audiovisual Observatory, 2020).

[230]   *See* ibid.

[231]   Guest Contributor, *Why DeepMind AlphaGo Zero is Game Changer for AI Research*, PACKT (May 9, 2019) https://hub.packtpub.com/deepmind-alphago-zero-game-changer-for-ai-research/#:~:text=AlphaGo%20Zero's%20strategies%20were%20self,lesser%20processing%20power%20than%20AlphaGo

[232]   GÉRON, *supra* note 120, at 170.

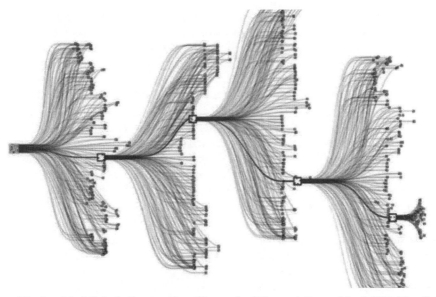

Source: Why DeepMind AlphaGo Zero is a Game Changer for AI Research, PACKT, May 9, 2019, https://hub
.packtpub.com/deepmind-alphago-zero-game-changer-for-ai-research/.

Figure 14.3   A Monte Carlo tree search

disaggregated, and individually assessed. As the algorithm sorts through the data, decision
trees analyze and predict whether the facts lean toward a factor indicative of consumer confusion; once the algorithm generates a decision tree forest, predictions are qualified with a probability set against other cases sharing similar attributes and all the trees' average probability
for the outcome. When the data itself suffers from inaccuracy there are multiple ways to fix it,
such as using approximate values or supplementing with additional data.[233]

As with any tool, MCTS has its limitations. For example, good predictions require many
different decision trees to deliver a statistically significant average from them all, demanding
voluminous data.[234] Section 4.3 addresses concerns over data scarcity.

4.3   Data Scarcity

The impressive results we often read about in AI rest on the massive datasets which data scientists use to train it. Finding sufficient, usable data is key to trademark law's algorithmic revolution.[235] As Moerland and Freitas note, "one of the most important challenges is to acquire
huge volumes of data that is structured for the purpose of training the AI."[236]

---

[233] *See* Lehr & Ohm, *supra* note 177, at 681–4.
[234] McJohn & Ian McJohn, *supra* note 161.
[235] Ibid, at 139.
[236] Moerland & Freitas, *supra* note 17, at 15.

Darts-ip, an AI service, has partnered with the Benelux Office of IP to integrate case law data at the registration phase.[237] Focused on mark similarity, Darts-ip's algorithm devours a training dataset consisting of "millions of cases" to identify rules that it needs to follow when presented with new signs.[238] One dimension of that scarcity relates to the relevant qualitative data. The other dimension is quantitative data.

First, quantitative data: to achieve "acceptable performance," data scientists estimate that a dataset typically requires ten million labeled examples to match or exceed human performance.[239] Trademark law comprises cases, market data, surveys, and the like.[240] The law itself may limit collection, storage, and data use, such as those governing data protection and privacy. Overlapping with the earlier discussion, data scarcity may give rise to bias, which occurs when the dataset is underinclusive or when the dataset captures an under-representative sample of all the trademark violations that do occur.[241]

Westlaw reveals that between 1808 and 2021, there were 10,000 reported likelihood of confusion decisions from the district courts, circuit courts of appeal, and the Supreme Court.[242] Compared to a textbook example of image classification datasets with 60,000 images, 10,000 may seem small at first glance.[243] However, each case contains dozens, if not hundreds, of variables that algorithms can parse through and map. For example, for a recent five-year study on the likelihood of confusion, I coded 4,800 datapoints.[244] The total number of datapoints is therefore many times more than 10,000.

Peter Salib, arguing for using AI in class action lawsuits, makes the case that algorithms can accurately mimic human decisions without being fed with all the information before human decisionmakers.[245] For a start, feature selection weeds out training data features with little predictive power.[246] For example, in the case of trademark infringement, factors such as the quality of defendants' goods and "bridging the gap" can be readily discarded. Moreover, one needs roughly ten training instances for every "feature," that is, every category of input evidence.[247]

An algorithm trained with 600 Tax Court of Canada decisions to apply settled legal tests and determine whether a given individual was correctly classified as an employee or an independent contractor.[248] Given just 21 facts about a given worker, it can correctly classify well over

---

[237] *See* ibid, at 17.

[238] Ibid.

[239] Ian Goodfellow Et Al., Deep Learning 19–20 (2016).

[240] *See* Lim, *supra* note 3.

[241] *See* Géron, *supra* note 120, at 22–3.

[242] Based on a Westlaw search by "Cases by Topic" for cases between January 1, 1800 and December 31, 2021.

[243] Abdellatif Abdelfattah, *Image Classification using Deep Neural Networks*, Medium (July 27, 2017), https://medium.com/@tifa2up/image-classification-using-deep-neural-networks-a-beginner -friendly-approach-using-tensorflow-94b0a090ccd4.

[244] *See e.g.*, Lim, supra note 87.

[245] Salib, *supra* note 171.

[246] Ibid, at 30.

[247] *See, e.g.*, Jason Brownlee, *How Much Training Data is Required for Machine Learning?*, Machine Learning Mastery (July 24, 2017), https://machinelearningmastery.com/much-training-data -required-machine-learning/).

[248] *See, e.g.*, Daniel Martin Katz, Michael J Bommarito II, & Josh Blackman, *Predicting the Behavior of the Supreme Court of the United States: A General Approach*, https://arxiv.org/abs/1407.6333v1 (2014).

90 percent as employees or independent contractors.[249] Algorithms may answer these kinds of fact-intensive legal questions in trademark infringement actions. Empirical studies for other machine learning applications also show minimum datasets in the 200 datapoint range.[250] The likelihood of confusion factors works the same way, suggesting the amount of training data is more than sufficient.[251]

Second, qualitative data: this refers to consumer preferences and their purchasing behavior.[252] This data helps AI assess market conditions such as mark use, the relevant consuming public, distinctiveness, and reputation.[253] If anything, live market data is more challenging to obtain in sufficient quantities than historical data from past judicial opinions. In addition, laws on privacy, data protection, and trade secrets may impede access to that data.[254]

Moerland and Freitas doubt AI can reflect a contextual, human-centric perception of the marks.[255] As they put it, "to assess whether [...] a consumer is confused, good knowledge is required of the market of specific products, who the relevant consumer of such products is, the right holders' competitors, the circumstances of purchase, the end-use of a product, etc. These are often factual." [256] Accordingly, "the assessment is one of degree and requires reasoning from the perspective of the relevant public. It is questionable how far AI technology can reflect this human-centric approach."[257]

Training accurate algorithms using modest datasets is on the cutting edge of machine learning research to deal with scarce qualitative data. For instance, transfer learning partially re-trains algorithms to answer similar questions.[258] Moreover, as Talia Gillis and Jann Spiess recently showed, "when complex, highly nonlinear prediction functions are used [...] one [omitted] input variable can be reconstructed jointly from the other input variables."[259] And as noted above, data from trademark office actions are one such ready source.

Deep learning generates other examples via dataset augmentation once it learns to identify features, akin to the Socratic approach of lightly modifying hypotheticals. Consider how IBM's

---

[249]   Ibid, at 242–3. This high performance persists when Blue J is turned loose on "a variety of different questions in tax law." Ibid.

[250]   *See* Ammara Masood & Adel Ali Al-Jumaily, *Computer Aided Diagnostic Support System for Skin Cancer: A Review of Techniques and Algorithms*, INT'L J. BIOMEDICAL IMAGING at *13 tbl.5 (2013) (modal set with instances in the low hundreds).

[251]   *See, e.g.*, Brownlee, *supra* note 248 ("look at studies on problems similar to yours as an estimate for the amount of data that may be required").

[252]   *See* Moerland & Freitas, *supra* note 17, at 18 ("it includes information about what type of consumers purchase which type of products, how consumers are attracted by certain marks when looking at shelves containing products with trade marks from competing undertakings, etc").

[253]   Ibid, at 19.

[254]   Ibid ("It seems unlikely that customers will consent to the use of their personal data for such purposes or that owners of such data will share the data with trade mark offices or competitors").

[255]   Ibid at 20 ("What is considered to be confusing, however, is determined by the overall impression the relevant public gets when seeing the mark on a product in a specific context. Many of these elements require a holistic and human-centric approach: how does a human perceive a mark?").

[256]   Ibid.

[257]   Ibid.

[258]   Salib, *supra* note 171, at 35 ("Transfer learning can reduce the amount of data required to answer the latter question by orders of magnitude").

[259]   Talia B. Gillis & Jann L. Spiess, *Big Data and Discrimination*, 86 U. CHI. L. REV. 459, 469 (2019).

Deep Blue relied on learning using many thousands of human-played games as examples.[260] In contrast, AlphaZero needed the chess rules and generated example games to augment its dataset.[261] Like AlphaZero, Amazon's algorithms predict buyers' preferences by finding another browser with the most similar viewing history and then offering the item the second browser liked.[262] This searching obviates both the need for enormous datasets and training AI.

Data scientists program AI to generate multiple examples by randomly altering salient factors in the same way they augment image datasets: "random translations, rotations, and in some cases, flips of the input,"[263] evoking Socratic principles, where professors alter hypotheticals to train their students' ability to identify facts and legal concepts within the source material. Thus, machine learning allows one dataset to be made into many different datasets through resampling—creating new datasets that randomly exclude some of the data.

Like machine learning algorithms, the law relies on analogies. Judges could use the "nearest neighbor" algorithm to search a database of examples to find the most similar cases to the seed case.[264] The outcome is not a legal analysis but rather a prediction, with an acceptable level of accuracy, whether a restraint in a specific factual context would violate the likelihood of confusion.[265] It is particularly useful in the likelihood of confusion cases, which are resistant to general characterization and finding a close match case may often answer an issue satisfactorily.[266] Data scientists could annotate cases automatically to provide a common data structure, as has been done for veterans' claims for disability compensation,[267] as well as contract drafting and interpretation.[268]

"Nearest neighbor" algorithms require no time training once the software is written,[269] and such algorithms require no general model about what is or is not illegal because they only require the closest match where examples closest to the test example carry more weight.[270] Once the deep learning algorithm can identify features (such as concepts or taxonomies for the likelihood of confusion), then a generative model can produce new, different examples sharing the same features using different arrangements.

---

[260]   *See generally*, David Silver et al, *A General Reinforcement Learning Algorithm that Masters Chess, Shogi, and Go Through Self-Play*, 362 SCIENCE 1140 (Dec. 7, 2018).

[261]   Ibid.

[262]   Amazon Web Services, *What Is Artificial Intelligence?* https://aws.amazon.com/machine-learning/what-is-ai/.

[263]   GOODFELLOW ET AL., *supra* note239, at 459–60.

[264]   *See* McJohn & Ian McJohn, *supra* note 161, at 142.

[265]   *See* GÉRON, *supra* note 120, at 23.

[266]   *See* McJohn & Ian McJohn, *supra* note 161, at 142.

[267]   *See, e.g.*, Vern R. Walker et al., *Semantic Types for Computational Legal Reasoning: Propositional Connectives and Sentence Roles in the Veterans' Claims Dataset*, in SIXTEENTH INTERNATIONAL CONFERENCE ON ARTIFICIAL INTELLIGENCE AND LAW 217–26 (2017).

[268]   *See* Kathryn D. Betts & Kyle R. Jaep, *The Dawn of Fully Automated Contract Drafting: Machine Learning Breathes New Life into a Decades-Old Promise*, 15 DUKE L. & TECH. REV. 216, 227 (2017).

[269]   *See* PEDRO DOMINGOS, THE MASTER ALGORITHM 179–86 (2015).

[270]   Ibid, at 183.

5.   CONCLUSION

AI can assist courts in navigating trademark infringement, discovering key characteristics of the likelihood of confusion cases, and identifying similarities between them. To do so, efforts to develop a comprehensive and effective AI system for analyzing trademarks should focus on mark similarity, competitive proximity, and evidence of actual confusion, anchoring the likelihood of confusion test as the most relevant factors. This crisper, simplified framework brings the benefit of clarity. Bias, accountability, and data availability are well-known concerns with AI deployment. While these are legitimate issues, each can be significantly mitigated or, in some cases, comprehensively addressed. Ultimately, AI does not replace courts but offers a valuable tool to assist them in decision-making in an increasingly algorithmic world.

15. Online shopping with artificial intelligence: what role for trade marks?

Anke Moerland and Christie Kafrouni[1]

1. INTRODUCTION

The debate on how artificial intelligence (AI) influences intellectual property protection has so far mainly focused on its effects for patent and copyright protection. Not much attention has been paid to the effects of artificial intelligence technology for trade mark law.[2] In particular, what has not yet been sufficiently investigated is the question as to whether trade marks still fulfil their role in a world in which consumers are assisted by AI technology when purchasing in the online marketplace. To what degree do we still need trade marks to avoid consumer confusion? Or do the other functions of trade marks justify their continuous protection? In view of the fact that intellectual property rights have a market-distorting effect, it is in society's interest to question whether trade mark protection is still justified.

Clearly, not all shopping takes place in the digital world. Many consumers will still choose to purchase what they need from shops, enjoying the social interaction and pleasure of choosing a product physically. For these purchases, trade marks will continue to fulfil the same purpose. However, even before the COVID-19 pandemic, consumers were choosing to use online marketplaces for many of their purchases; in 2020, shopping on major online marketplaces[3] increased to $26.7 trillion worldwide, now representing 19 per cent of retail sales.[4] Our analysis of the role of trade marks in online shopping will be particularly relevant for online purchases now and in the foreseeable future.

---

[1]   We would like to thank the following persons for their comments received on a previous version of the paper presented at the Online workshop Trade Mark Law and Artificial Intelligence held on 22 October 2021: Sir Richard Arnold, Łukasz Żelechowski, Dev Gangjee, Martin Senftleben and other participants of the workshop.

[2]   Michael Grynberg, 'AI and the Death of Trademark Law' (2019–20) 108(2) Kentucky Law Journal 198; Jurgita Randakevičiūtė-Alpman, 'The Role of Trademarks on Online Retail Platforms: An EU Trademark Law Perspective' [2021] GRUR International 1; Anke Moerland and Conrado Freitas, 'Artificial Intelligence and Trade Mark Assessment', in Jyh-An Lee, Reto Hilty and Kung-Chung Liu (eds), *Artificial Intelligence & Intellectual Property* (OUP 2021); Viltė K Steponėnaitė, 'Alexa, are you confused? Unravelling the interplay between AI and (European) trademark law' (CITIP, 17 December 2019)   www.law.kuleuven.be/citip/blog/alexa-are-you-confused-unravelling-the-interplay-between-ai -and-european-trademark-law/ accessed 15 July 2021; Lee Curtis and Rachel Platts, 'AI is coming and it will change trade mark law' (*ManagingIP.com,* 2017), www.hgf.com/media/1173564/09-13-AI.PDF, accessed 15 July 2021; Dev S Gangjee, 'Eye, Robot: Artificial Intelligence and Trade Mark Registers' in N. Bruun and others (eds), *Transition and Coherence in Intellectual Property Law* (CUP 2020).

[3]   Well-known retail websites include www.amazon.com/, www.ebay.com, www.zalando.es/ and for the Netherlands www.bol.com/nl/.

[4]   UNCTAD, 'Global e-commerce jumps to $26.7 trillion, COVID-19 boosts online sales' (3 May 2021) https://unctad.org/news/global-e-commerce-jumps-267-trillion-covid-19-boosts-online-sales accessed 15 July 2021.

Many online marketplaces are assisted by AI technologies, such as search engines, customer service bots or AI assistants. Such technologies vary in sophistication, have differing degrees of involvement in the purchasing process and operate at different stages. We therefore outline in section 2 the spectrum of AI technologies that are used in online shopping and the degree to which they influence consumer choices. It is of course not a new finding that consumer choices are influenced; such nudges already existed before AI tools were available. One could argue that brand owners have always steered consumers, through all sorts of stimuli, to encourage the purchase of items consumers may not necessarily need.[5] However, while not completely new, AI-powered strategies to predict and shape consumer behaviour seem to be more influential on consumer choices than previous tools.

In section 3, we assess whether the trade mark functions, in particular in the context of EU trade mark law, are still guaranteed where AI technologies of varying degrees of involvement and timing are used. This leads us to section 4, in which we ask whether the concept of the average consumer in EU trade mark law should be adapted to accommodate situations that involve AI technologies. We conclude that trade marks continue to play an important role in the online marketplace and that the concept of the average consumer under EU law generally is broad enough to cover situations where consumers are assisted by AI technologies. Courts, however, will need to pay more attention to the AI tool at issue and how consumers of the specific goods or services at issue engage with this tool.

2.   AI TECHNOLOGIES IN ONLINE SHOPPING

For non-experts in the field of AI, it is difficult to get a deep understanding of what exactly particular AI tools do and how they operate. However, some basic knowledge thereof is needed to discuss its effects on trade mark law. The literature indicated provides this basic understanding and we do not aim to repeat this. Rather, in this section, we highlight three characteristics according to which we assess AI tools used by consumers in online shopping, as they are important for the interaction between the consumer and the trade mark. These are: (1) different levels of technological advancement; (2) different levels of involvement; (3) different stages of the purchasing process.

2.1   AI at Varying Stages of Technological Advancement

Probably the most important feature of AI technologies in online shopping is that they can predict what consumers want or like before consumers know it themselves. This is referred to as the 'prediction theory' and is what online shopping AIs owe their success to.[6] Predicting consumers' choices is an important advancement in online shopping in various ways.[7] According to Gal and Elkin-Koren, the most important benefits for consumers lie in speedier decision-making, analytical sophistication (by analysing data consumers do not know about or

---

5   Jasem Tarawaneh, 'A New Classification for Trade Mark Functions' (2016) 4 IPQ 352, 363.

6   Ajay Agrawal, Joshua Gans and Avi Goldfarb, 'How AI will change strategy: a thought experiment' (2017) Harvard Business Review, https://hbr.org/2017/10/how-ai-will-change-strategy-a-thought-experiment accessed 11 July 2021, 7.

7   Grynberg (n 2) 201.

data in other languages), a reduction of information and transactional costs (by relying on past purchases and items similar to past purchases) and avoiding some consumer biases (algorithms can overcome manipulative marketing techniques).[8]

The ability for AI technology to reach that high level of sophistication, however, depends on the advancement of the technology and the data that it uses. Machine learning (ML) is responsible for many of the recent advances in AI functionality. It allows for 'teaching a computer program to identify patterns in sets of data and to apply that knowledge to new data'.[9] A powerful example is how Google changed its strategy in developing translation software from using algorithmic translation rules and dictionary databases to machine learning. 'The company found better results when it fed a program an extensive library of works and translations, letting the program discern translation rules of its own.'[10]

In online shopping, advanced ML technologies use pre-existing data on, among others, past purchases, market availability, browsing history, trends, ranks made by users, amount of views, cross-selling data, and so on, to predict which products the consumer will like. For such predictions deep learning, a subset of ML, will be required, which allows machines to solve more complex problems by using multilayer neural networks designed to work like human brains.[11] In addition, through reinforcement learning processes,[12] consumer behaviour is continuously fed back to the ML technology. This feedback allows them to perfect their accuracy and eventually surpass human performance.

But even the functioning of the most advanced AI is limited by certain factors. Contrary to the belief that AI can make decisions in an objective manner,[13] a certain bias underlies their mechanism due to human input at the stage of training the algorithm, setting the hyperparameters[14] and selecting training data.[15] Bias in data will be replicated when used by the AI technology, as it lacks the ability to filter out slightly incorrect interpretations. In other words, the reinforcing nature of AI technology can aggravate such bias. Often, human bias is unintended but inherent to human irrationality and subjectivity.[16] For instance, when teaching an AI to establish a pattern of similarity of signs, one person could easily ascertain a similarity between two given signs, while someone else would not. However, with large amounts of data, incidental bias may not influence the rule that the AI learns from the data.

---

[8]   Michal Gal and Niva Elkin-Koren, 'Algorithmic Consumers' (2017) 30 Harvard Journal of Law and Technology 1, 10–13.

[9]   Josef Drexl and others, 'Technical Aspects of Artificial Intelligence: An Understanding from Intellectual Property Law Perspective' (2019) 19(13) Max Planck Institute for Innovation & Competition Research Paper, https://ssrn.com/abstract=346577 accessed 9 March 2020, 3.

[10]   Grynberg (n 2) 202, referring to Gideon Lewis-Kraus, 'The Great A.I. Awakening', *NY Times* (14 December 2016).

[11]   Drexl and others (n 9) 3.

[12]   Drexl and others (n 9) 7.

[13]   Steve Nouri, 'The Role of Bias in Artificial Intelligence' (Forbes, 4 February 2021) www.forbes.com/sites/forbestechcouncil/2021/02/04/the-role-of-bias-in-artificial-intelligence/?sh=3d52d9c9579d accessed 21 July 2021.

[14]   Drexl and others (n 9), at 12, define a hyperparameter as 'a feature of a model that is fixed before the training process and does not evolve'.

[15]   'Algorithm' (International Director, 19 June 2018) https://searchenterpriseai.techtarget.com/definition/AI-Artificial-Intelligence accessed 23 March 2019.

[16]   Drexl and others (n 9) 7.

Another limitation is the current inability of AI to understand why something is happening. This would require general cognitive AI, which does not exist yet.[17] So AI will err from time to time, but so do we when making purchasing decisions.[18]

2.2 Different Degrees of AI Involvement at Varying Stages of Online Shopping

AI technologies currently intervene to varying degrees and at varying stages in the purchasing process. Their involvement differs from lower forms of influence, such as product suggestions (like Amazon's recommendation engine)[19] and virtual assistants (such as eBay Chatbots), to a high degree of involvement through fully autonomous ordering and payment (Samsung and IBM washing machines).[20] Along this spectrum, we discuss three common types of AI (product suggestions, virtual assistants, automated ordering) in more detail and discuss how they interact with consumers and at which stage of the purchasing process they do so.

To analyse the different stages of shopping we follow Michal Gal and Niva Elkin-Koren, who differentiate four stages of online shopping: determining consumers' needs and preferences (stage 1); comparing purchasing options in light of consumers' preferences (stage 2); determining the purchasing decision according to the data analysis in stage 2 (stage 3); and finally completing the transaction (stage 4).[21] These different stages help to understand the purchasing process of an online consumer.

We argue that there is a fifth stage: that of consuming the product and providing feedback about consumer experience. This stage is important also in AI-assisted shopping because, as we will see, it allows the AI to learn in real-time as to whether the decision it made was in line with consumer preferences or not, and thereby refine consumer preferences for the future.

2.2.1 Product recommendations
Product recommendations are a form of AI used very commonly in online shopping and product recommendations. Through sections on retail websites[22] such as 'recommendations based on your order', 'complete the look', or 'other customers have also viewed', consumers are guided through a personalized selection of products chosen from a large set of possibilities. The selection of products is generated either through the 'content-based filtering method', the 'collaborative-filtering method' or the 'hybrid method', which combines both methods.[23]

The 'content-based method' suggests products whose content is similar to previous purchases by the same consumer. To do so, the AI technology collects data about the consumer's previous views or purchases. Amazon, for example, tracks not only what shoppers have bought but also what they are searching for, which products they repeatedly return to, what

---

[17]　Andrew Burgess, *The Executive Guide to Artificial Intelligence: How to Identify and Implement Applications for AI in Your Organisation* (Palgrave Macmillan 2018) 3–4.

[18]　Grynberg (n 2) 202.

[19]　Blake Morgan, 'How Amazon has reorganized around artificial intelligence and machine learning' (*Forbes*, 16 July 2018) www.forbes.com/sites/blakemorgan/2018/07/16/how-amazon-has-re-organized-around-artificial-intelligence-and-machine-learning/?sh=29ecca2f7361 accessed 15 July 2021.

[20]　Gal and Koren (n 8) 3.

[21]　Gal and Koren (n 8) 9.

[22]　See footnote 2 of this chapter.

[23]　Jon Macdonald, '21 Effective Product Recommendation Tips to Increase Sales' (TheGood, 3 July 2017) https://thegood.com/insights/ecommerce-product-recommendation/ accessed 15 July 2021.

they keep in their shopping basket and what their mouse hovers over on the screen.[24] This data is then run through the information available about the items on offer in the online marketplace. In the end, through the combination of behavioural data and product characteristics, the AI can generate a list of items containing similar features that the customer seems to have a preference for.

The 'collaborative-filtering method', in contrast, focuses on purchasing choices of consumers with similar profiles. It relies on data about the shopping behaviour of various consumers, clustered according to certain profiles. Based on a multitude of customer ratings of certain items, inter-user comparisons are possible that can create recommendations as to what similar users like.[25] The hybrid model combines both types of data to generate results that can even better predict what a particular consumer may want to purchase.

The type of data regarding items available on the online marketplace that is taken into consideration can differ per portal and product recommendation tool, but usually it will include characteristics such as price, brand line, colour, style and trends. Whether AI technologies are able to detect counterfeit products depends on their level of sophistication. If a product's metadata has also been manipulated to wrongly indicate the origin to be that of a certain mark holder, it will be difficult for an AI technology to correctly indicate an item's origin. But the more advanced product recommendation systems will become, the easier it will be to identify counterfeit products.

In the purchasing process, product recommendations mainly operate at stages 1 and 2 of determining consumer preferences and comparing purchasing options according to consumer preferences. They steer consumer choice but leave the final purchasing decision and completion of the transaction to the consumer. Their involvement therefore usually lies at the lower spectrum of involvement.

2.2.2   Virtual assistants

Virtual assistants operate through different interfaces, be it voice (such as Alexa, Siri and Pepper the Robot) or text (for instance H&M chat agents and Google assistants). They offer a unique experience to end users as they enter into a dialogue in natural language and respond to customer queries in real-time,[26] at any given moment of the purchasing process. This technology relies mainly on language processing and content extraction. It is therefore able to offer guidance on all aspects of a purchase, from identifying options to placing an order, making a payment and choosing delivery options. Advanced versions thereof combine language processing with product recommendations models. Consumers can be more specific when making their request in natural language, which will make the data they are fed more relevant. A typical example is Alexa, Amazon's virtual assistant, which combines voice dialogue with the user and the collection of data, allowing her to recommend products in the way detailed in section 2.2.1.

---

[24]   Randakevičiūtė-Alpman (n 2) 6, citing Lina Khan, Amazon's Antitrust Paradox (2017) 126 Yale Law Journal 710, 782, citing Nick Bravo, 'Amazon Private Labels Threaten Manufacturers' (*TrendSource*, 5 July 2016).

[25]   Randakevičiūtė-Alpman (n 2) 7.

[26]   See an explanation of the concept 'robotic process automation' in Ed Burns, Nicole Laskowski and Linda Tucci, 'Definition artificial intelligence' (*Tech Target*) https://searchenterpriseai.techtarget.com/definition/AI-Artificial-Intelligence accessed 11 July 2021.

Virtual assistants consequently have the potential to intervene at all four stages of the purchasing process, depending on the needs of the consumer. They offer information on how to perform certain parts of the purchasing process or carry them out for the consumer directly if the consumer asks them to do so. This constitutes a strong involvement, acting in a rather self-directed manner upon an order by the consumer. But, importantly, consumers are still in charge of the actual purchasing decision.

2.2.3   Automated ordering

In some cases – and there is potential for future growth in the area – AI technologies place orders autonomously, without the involvement of the consumer.[27] An example is Amazon smart reordering with Alexa for printer ink, which allows consumers to install functionality enabling reordering when the toner runs low for connected printing devices.[28] The Amazon Dash Replenishment service makes automatic re-ordering available for other household devices too, such as washing detergent for Samsung dishwashers in certain countries.[29] It is safe to conclude that automatic reordering currently regards only a small fraction of purchases.

An interesting question arises where the replenishment service makes choices between different versions of, for example, milk: how does the AI technology make such a choice, and based on which preferences exactly? Is the consumer still in charge of these choices; can she pre-determine the possible alternatives to her preferred product? The chances are rather high that it is not only consumer preferences that will be taken into consideration but also brands that have been pre-selected by the platform.[30] Nevertheless, our analysis below is based on the presumption that AI tools serve consumers' preferences, as manipulatable as these may be. If consumers do not feel a benefit from using AI tools when purchasing, they will no longer use them.

It is clear from the above that automatic ordering has a substantial influence on the purchasing decisions of consumers. It essentially takes over the four steps of purchasing if the consumer has chosen this service once. Certainly, where it is not entirely clear how the choices are made by the AI technology, consumer influence on the final choice of which product to order may be rather low.

In a world where the influence of AI technologies on the marketplace is already considerable and is likely to become even stronger, with algorithms becoming so powerful that they can be used in all stages of the purchasing process, the question arises as to whether trade marks can still perform the functions they were created to fulfil.

---

[27]   Simonetta Vezzoso, 'Competition by Design' in Björn Lundqvist and Michal Gal (eds), *Competition Law for the Digital Economy* (Edward Elgar Publishing 2019) 93, 95, referred to by Randakevičiūtė-Alpman (n 2) 1.

[28]   Amazon, Smart reordering, www.amazon.com/b?ie=UTF8&node=2122717001>1 accessed 15 December 2021.

[29]   Samsung, Amazon Dash Replenishment for your Samsung washer with SmartThings, www.samsung.com/us/support/answer/ANS00085582/, accessed 15 December 2021.

[30]   Randakevičiūtė-Alpman (n 1) 14; Simon Jones, 'Why Amazon Dash is a threat to brands (and how they can fight back)' (*Evrythng*, 17 March 2017) https://evrythng.com/why-amazon-dash-is-a-threat-to-brands-and-how-they-can-fight-back/ accessed 11 July 2021.

3.   AI AND TRADE MARK FUNCTIONS

While different jurisdictions have defined the functions trade marks fulfil in slightly diverging ways, they all have in common that they recognize the essential function of trade marks to indicate the origin of a product and thereby make trade mark holders accountable for the product's quality. In addition, trade marks fulfil accessory functions that are derived from the origin function. We will proceed by discussing these functions and AI technology in online shopping's impact on them separately.

3.1   Origin and Quality Function

Trade marks, just like all intellectual property, interfere with the market by creating exclusive rights and thereby preventing others from using what is protected. This is justified if there is an overarching public interest that the IP right serves. In the case of trade marks, the justification lies predominantly in the creation of a transparent market that provides the conditions for undistorted competition. Where distinctive signs are exclusively linked with goods or services coming from one commercial source, the market becomes transparent.[31] Consumers are able to distinguish a trademarked product from those products that have another origin. This is also referred to as the origin function.[32]

Being able to individualize offers also means that consumers' search costs are reduced. Distinctive signs guarantee that information about product origin is reliable and therefore consumers do not need to invest more time and effort in ensuring that they are not deceived into purchasing a product they do not want.[33] This is particularly important for unobservable product features and experience goods, which consumers can only experience and assess when they have made the purchasing decision.[34] In other words, trade marks communicate characteristics of the good to consumers that facilitate the purchasing transaction.

While descriptions on the back of products or information provided before or at the time of purchase could also fulfil this function, trade marks do this in a simplified and therefore effective manner. Without having to delve into available information, trade marks provide a 'shorthand indicator' in finding the optimal product:[35] they simplify information by removing context.[36] Trade marks, in that sense, provide a condensed form of the information that consumers relate with the mark.[37]

This information is not only linked to the origin of the product; consumers receive a larger variety of product information through the mark. They attach meaning to a mark based on the information they receive, their own experiences, the experiences of family members or

---

[31]   Annette Kur and Martin Senftleben, *European Trade Mark Law: A Commentary* (OUP 2017) 6.

[32]   Case C-102/77 *Hoffmann-La Roche & Co. AG v Centrafarm Vertriebsgesellschaft Pharmazeutischer Erzeugnisse mbH.* [1978] ECR 01139, para 7.

[33]   Kur and Senftleben (n 31) 7.

[34]   Tarawneh (n 5) 360, citing Mathias Strasser, 'The Rational Basis of Trademark Protection Revisited: Putting the Dilution Doctrine into Context' (2000) 10 Fordham Intellectual Property, Media & Entertainment Law Journal 375, 386.

[35]   Kur and Senftleben (n 31) 8, referring to SL Dogan and MA Lemley, 'Trademarks and Consumer Search Costs on the Internet' (2004) 41 Houston Law Review 777, 786–7.

[36]   Grynberg (n 2) 205.

[37]   Kur and Senftleben (n 29) 8.

product reviews. It is because of the ability of marks to represent meaning that trade marks serve to communicate information not only about origin, but also about the quality of products and services. As the CJEU has explained, communicating the quality of products is directly derived from the origin function of trade marks, as consumers must be able to identify products as coming from one undertaking 'which is accountable for their quality'.[38] This is referred to as the quality function of trade marks.

We have seen that the origin and quality function establish transparency on the market, enabling consumers to make effective purchasing decisions. At the same time, both functions also serve the purpose of achieving undistorted competition in the internal market.[39] By protecting the exclusive link between a trade mark and an undertaking, undertakings can communicate basic information about the product to consumers, without competitors interfering with that communication. This purpose of trade mark protection is defensive in nature and protects trade mark holders against confusing use of the trade mark.

3.2 AI's Impact on the Origin and Quality Function

Given the ways in which consumers who are assisted by AI technologies make purchasing decisions, there is doubt as to whether trade marks are still needed to (1) simplify information for a speedy and effective purchasing process and (2) guarantee undistorted competition on the market. We argue that the need for the simplification of information may reduce where consumers are assisted by AI technologies, but this would not justify abolishing protection of trade marks against confusing use.

First, AI technology with unlimited time and enhanced capacity clearly reduces the need for simplified information on the market. Where consumers can rely on assistance in gathering and processing far more distinguishing context than humans, they will be able to find optimal products without the help of trade marks that serve their needs,[40] presuming that this is the benchmark for the AI technology.[41] As Grynberg notes, AI 'would have immediate access to accurate affiliation information, and superior information that might make the affiliation data irrelevant'.[42] In summary, shorthand indicators to enable speedy and effective purchasing are no longer needed.

At the same time, this scenario really only holds true where consumers are completely eliminated from the purchasing process. So far, automated ordering on the basis of a 'first-shipping-then-shopping' model is not yet accepted by consumers on a larger scale and only for household items.[43] But even if or when automated ordering becomes more wide-

---

[38]   Case C-10/89 *SA CNL-SUCAL NV v HAG GF AG* [1990] ECR I-3711, para 13.

[39]   Recital 2 of the Preamble of Directive 2008/95/EC of the European Parliament and of the Council of 22 October 2008 to approximate the laws of the Member States relating to trade marks [2008] OJ L 299. In this predecessor Trade Mark Directive to the current Directive, undistorted competition is clearly identified, whereas Recital 8 of Directive (EU) 2015/2436 of the European Parliament and of the Council of 16 December 2015 to approximate the laws of the Member States relating to trade marks [2015] OJ L 336 refers to enhancing the competitiveness of European businesses. See also Kur and Senftleben (n 31) 6, referring to the relevant CJEU case-law; Tarawneh (n 5) 358.

[40]   Grynberg (n 2) 200.

[41]   See section 2.1.

[42]   Grynberg (n 2) 209.

[43]   See section 2.2.3.

spread, we argue that the consumer is still involved in the purchasing process, namely when she consumes the product. It is at the fifth stage, of consuming a product and providing feedback about the product, that consumer perception will still matter, even with highly sophisticated AI assistance in the purchasing process. This points towards a continuous role of trade marks in the purchasing process.

Consumers attach meaning to products on the basis of information and experiences. When they consume a yoghurt or a detergent, they will experience their quality and other product characteristics. They may even read information on the package about ingredients, materials used, and so on. They will associate that information with the trade mark indicated on the package and inform the AI technology in one way or another about their experience and preference. It is at this fifth stage that it matters whether the trade mark conveys accurate information and whether the consumer can trust the information about origin and quality. This last stage may become ever more important as more and more complexity becomes involved in AI technologies. With AI technologies such as machine learning being a black-box, consumers may find it 'difficult to determine the criteria on which recommendations or purchases by the online platforms are made on behalf of consumers'.[44] Therefore, where information provided by AI technology is based on complex processes, consumers will appreciate the information conveyed by the trade mark when consuming the product. It serves the purpose of (1) gathering first-hand information in addition to the information provided by the AI tool, and (2) facilitating the provision of feedback about preferences and experience with the specific product ordered through AI.

We therefore argue that while trade marks may no longer serve the purpose of simplifying information and thereby making the purchasing process more effective, they still convey important information to the consumer when she consumes the product. Consumer experiences feed back into the next purchasing process, thereby maintaining the relevance of human decisions for future purchases. Guaranteeing the origin and quality function, therefore, will still be useful in AI-assisted online shopping.

Second, trade marks continue to be useful in guaranteeing undistorted competition on the market. While highly sophisticated AI technology may be able to identify fully counterfeit products (even though this is not self-evident),[45] competition would nevertheless be harmed where the communication between producers and consumers is hampered by confusing information from competitors. Being able to interfere with the information that a trade mark communicates to consumers reduces sound and robust competition among market actors. Such interference is not remedied by relying on highly sophisticated AI technology that will be able to identify the product's origin. The fact that new technologies have been developed which can detect confusing product indications does not justify these confusing indications in the first place and does not reduce the need for a market based on undistorted competition.

To conclude, both the rationale of reducing consumers' search costs and that of guaranteeing fair competition on the market continue to be relevant for trade marks in online market places.

---

[44]   Randakevičiūtė-Alpman (n 2) 9.
[45]   See section 2.2.1.

3.3 Accessory Functions of Trade Marks

When trade marks are highly distinctive and have gained a certain renown,[46] they can communicate information beyond origin and quality. This information engages consumers on a psychological and emotional level[47] and has little to do with product attributes. Here, marks trigger positive, desirable values and beliefs that consumers will connect with the products carrying the mark. Such values can include a fit and healthy lifestyle, comfort, mindfulness, exclusivity, and so on. As a result, trade marks will have 'a commercial value of their own'[48] and consumers make purchasing decisions not so much on the basis of product attributes but because of the appeal of the mark. In essence, they 'buy the respective trade mark experience and brand image'.[49]

The ability to communicate values and images has been acknowledged as an accessory function of trade marks by the European Court of Justice (CJEU) – accessory to the basic function to communicate origin of products, and dependent thereon. Only when the exclusive link between the trade mark and the proprietor is preserved can the mark raise positive associations in the consumer's mind.[50] This ability is mainly dependent on successful promotion and marketing activities by the proprietor.

Such advertising activities, and the investment that trade mark proprietors have made to attach desirable values to the mark, have been identified as the advertising and investment functions of trade marks.[51] According to the advertising function, trade mark holders must be able to use the mark 'effectively to inform and win over consumers'.[52] In other words, the CJEU acknowledges that trade marks are useful in informing and persuading consumers and trade mark owners should therefore be able to effectively advertise their mark.

While the advertising function targets the use of a trade mark as a factor in sales promotion, the investment function focuses on using the trade mark to 'acquire or preserve a reputation capable of attracting customers and retaining their loyalty, by means of various commercial techniques'.[53] In fact, the Court thereby suggests that the reputation of a trade mark is worthy of protection and therefore trade mark holders should be able to use commercial techniques to acquire and preserve that reputation. Interestingly, the Court reserves the accessory functions

---

[46] Kur and Senftleben (n 31) 12, referring to Alexander von Mühlendahl, 'Das künftige Markenrecht' [1989] GRUR Int. 353, 355.

[47] Frank I. Schechter, 'The Rational Basis of Trademark Protection' (1927) 40 Harvard Law Review 813, 819.

[48] Hannes Rosler, 'The Rationale for European Trade Mark Protection' (2007) EIPR 100, 105–6.

[49] Kur and Senftleben (n 31) 10, referring to Jonathan E Schroeder, 'Brand Culture: Trade Marks, Marketing and Consumption' in Lionel Bently, Jennifer Davis and Jane C Ginsburg (eds), *Trade Marks and Brands: An Interdisciplinary Critique* (CUP 2008) 161.

[50] Kur and Senftleben (n 31) 10.

[51] The communication function has also been identified by the Court in the Case C-487/07 *L'Oréal SA v Bellure* [2009] ECR I-05185, paras 58 and 63; however, it has not been further defined nor used by the Court. See for a recent CJEU judgment on trade mark functions Case C-129/17 *Mitsubishi Shoji Kaisha Ltd and Mitsubishi Caterpillar Forklift Europe BV v Duma Forklifts NV and G.S. International BVBA* [2018] ECLI:EU:C:2018:594.

[52] Case C-236/08 *Google France SARL and Google Inc. v Louis Vuitton Malletier SA* [2010] ECR I-02417, para 59.

[53] C-129/17 *Mitsubishi v Duma*, para 36.

not only to marks with a reputation, but to all marks.[54] However, mark proprietors must have used the marks to those ends in order for the mark to perform the accessory functions.[55] While the CJEU case law on trade mark functions has been debated heavily, Kur and Senftleben conclude that the accessory functions 'concern the integrity of the brand image – the "aura" of the trade mark – as such'.[56]

Why exactly the advertising and investment functions are protected in the first place is unclear.[57] None of the traditional IP theories conclusively supports such protection.[58] Most convincing seems to be the reasoning related to the search cost reduction for consumers. Reputable or famous trade marks possess intrinsic value because they allow consumers to derive additional benefits in the form of 'emotional, spiritual or psychological value from the marked product'.[59] The connotations associated with the mark lead to better product differentiation. Stronger differentiation and marks that trigger 'quick and innate emotional response mechanisms'[60] support efficient decision making. This decision-making process would be interrupted if other marks were allowed to weaken the immediate association between reputable or famous marks and the goods and services. That is why protection of the accessory functions through concepts like dilution promote efficient markets.

3.4   AI's Impact on Trade Marks' Accessory Functions

Where consumers are assisted by AI technology in online shopping, the question arises as to whether trade marks that transfer values and beliefs to consumers are still needed in an online market place. Arguably, AI technology is much better in searching context and therefore to present optimal choices for consumers.[61] It would only seem logical that an advanced AI can predict consumers preferences in relation to certain trade marks. The way in which AI considers product recommendations or orders products is based on data that is available to it. Such data could be based on criteria a consumer pre-defines, such as the preference for a certain trade mark. Alternatively or additionally, data is derived from past purchases of the consumer, other consumers' purchases with a similar profile, the product most often purchased in that category, current trends among certain age and gender groups, and so on. If a consumer has always bought sneakers from a particular brand, or followed the trend suggestions of a certain influencer or magazine, the AI will take that factor into consideration when determining a consumer's preferences. The reason why a consumer prefers a brand over another, whether these are the feelings generated through the brand or its quality, does not matter to the AI, as long as the preference as such is recognizable for the AI.

---

[54]   C-487/07 *L'Oréal SA v Bellure*, para 58.
[55]   Case C-323/09 *Interflora v Marks & Spencer* 604 [2011] ECR I-08625, para 40.
[56]   Kur and Senftleben (n 31) 10.
[57]   Kur and Senftleben (n 31) 16.
[58]   See Kur and Senftleben (n 31) 16–21, for a discussion of different IP theories and how they apply to the extended protection for trade marks.
[59]   Tarawneh (n 5) 362, referring to Giovanni Ramello and Francesco Silva, 'Appropriating Signs and Meaning: the Elusive Economics of Trademark' (2006) 15(6) Industrial and Corporate Change 937, 949.
[60]   Kur and Senftleben (n 31) 17.
[61]   We presume here that the AI is programmed to serve consumers' preferences, even though we acknowledge that the parameters of AI can be set in a way that the results prioritize goods or services of certain sellers or of the platform itself. See Randakevičiūtė-Alpman (n 2) 10.

However, even though AI technology can present the consumer with all relevant information related to the trade marked product or service, we argue that the positive values and feelings connected to a trade mark cannot be transferred through the suggestions made by AI; it is the trade mark as such that communicates this information and therefore reputed trade marks continue to play a role in the purchasing process. This argument is based on two assumptions.

First, for marks to communicate positive connotations, they will need to continue reaching humans. This does not have to be during the purchasing process, but can also happen through advertising or at the fifth phase of consuming the product. As already discussed in section 3.2, consumers will in the end consume a product. When doing so, they will interact with the trade mark attached to the product and will recall values and feelings that the mark may have communicated to consumers through advertising, its reputation and/or prior experiences. Where such connotations are strong, consumers will feed their preferences back into the purchasing process that is assisted or fully handled by the AI technology.

Second, products without trade marks cannot confer this additional value to consumers. AI technology can present information about origin and quality in a superior way than humans could. But information on origin and quality is different from feelings and values, which reach consumers on an emotional, spiritual or psychological level and thereby enhance their purchasing experience. Since humans are no rational actors, their purchasing decisions are not rational either. Reputed marks provide this added value to consumers to purchase what they enjoy. From an AI-generated list of suggestions, it is a trade mark with positive associations that will be decisive 'to manage the prospect of information overload'[62] and to make the final purchasing decision.

One could argue that AI technology is also able to influence behaviour of consumers on an emotional, more subtle level. Nudges and hypernudges built into AI technology steer consumers to a certain purchasing behaviour that they do not consciously control. In that respect, nudges are not so different from the image a brand confers. This is certainly true and may become fully accepted by consumers as a way to influence their behaviour. However, currently, we believe that consumers still value the illusion of (a) knowing which values and beliefs a brand image conveys, and (b) choosing to buy a product because of this image rather than superior quality or other product characteristics.

If we accept that reputed and famous marks are of added value for consumers' purchasing decisions, protection of the accessory functions should be retained. This does not mean that protection beyond confusion should not be balanced with other values. The need to balance the right to property, freedom of expression and undistorted competition has already been discussed elsewhere[63] and should not be changed as a result of AI technologies intervening in the purchasing process.

We conclude that the functions of trade marks are likely to continue playing a role for purchases carried out in the online marketplace with the assistance of AI tools. In order for trade marks to continue performing their functions, we need to consider a central concept in trade mark law that is relevant for several assessments in trade mark law: the average consumer. How we describe an AI-assisted consumer matters for the scope of protection conferred in situations where consumers rely not only on their human perception but on complete information readily available through AI technology.

---

[62] Grynberg (n 2) 231.
[63] Kur and Senftleben (n 31) 22/23.

4.   AI TECHNOLOGY AND THE AVERAGE CONSUMER

Many aspects of trade mark law rely on the perception of the average consumer, otherwise referred to as the relevant public. In particular, in validity assessment, trade mark examiners need to establish whether, to an average consumer, a mark is distinctive for the registered goods and services. For opposition and infringement purposes, the average consumer plays a role in assessing whether there is an impact on the core trade mark functions (in particular whether the mark still confers origin to the goods and services in the perception of the consumer),[64] whether the average consumer is likely to be confused about the origin of the products or services, or whether there is a link between the mark and the allegedly infringing sign (in the eyes of the consumer). In fact, there are 'few areas where the concept of the consumer is not relevant'.[65]

While the specific question may differ for each of these assessments (distinctiveness, confusion, dilution),[66] the concept of the average consumer stays mainly the same, with more attention paid to particular characteristics in one assessment than in others. For the purpose of this contribution, we look at the concept holistically and apply it to the various assessments of trade marks.

4.1   The Legal Concept of the 'Average Consumer'

The concept of the average consumer has importance well beyond trade mark law. It is in the broader field of internal market law that it has been developed and has become central to many types of legislation.[67] There, the focus has been on whether measures that constitute barriers to trade can be justified if they are necessary for consumer protection.[68] According to the ECJ in *Gut Springenheide*, the average consumer was defined as 'reasonably well-informed and reasonably observant and circumspect'.[69] This definition is also applied in subsequent trade mark law.[70] The goal of using such a concept of a consumer was not (necessarily) to conform to the reality of an average consumer and his cognitive abilities.[71] Rather, it was to promote cross-border trade.[72]

---

[64]   C-323/09 *Interflora Inc v Marks & Spencer* (n 55); C-236/08 *Google France* (n 52).

[65]   Graeme Dinwoodie and Dev S Gangjee, 'The Image of the Consumer in European Trade Mark Law' in Dorota Leczykiewicz and Stephen Weatherill, *Images of The Consumer in EU Law, Legislation, Free Movement and Competition Law* (Hart Publishing 2016) 339, 345.

[66]   Alice Blythe, 'In Search of Mr Average: Attempting to Identify the Average Consumer and His Role within Trade Mark Law' [2015] 37 EIPR 709, 713.

[67]   Vanessa Mak, 'Standards of Protection: In Search of the "Average Consumer" of EU Law in the Proposal for a Consumer Rights Directive' [2011] European Review of Private Law 27.

[68]   Case C-120/78, *Rewe-Bundesmonopolverwaltung fur Branntwein* [1979] ECR 649 (Cassis de Dijon).

[69]   Case C-210/96, *Gut Springenheide GmbH and Rudolf Tusky v Oberkreisdirektor des Kreises Steinfurt – Amt für Lebensmittelüberwachung*, [1998] ECR I-4657, para 31.

[70]   Case C-383/99, *Procter & Gamble v OHIM* [2002] ETMR 3, para 57.

[71]   Peter Rott, 'Der "Durchschnittsverbraucher" – ein Auslaufmodell angesichts personalisierten Marketings?' [2015] VuR 163; Kimberley Weatherall, 'The Consumer as the Empirical Measure of Trade Mark Law' (2017) 80 MLR 57.

[72]   See also Directive 2000/31/EC of the European Parliament and of the Council of 8 June 2000 on certain legal aspects of information society services, in particular electronic commerce, in the Internal Market [2000] OJ L 178 ('Directive on electronic commerce'), Art. 5.2. Referred to by Rott (n 71) 163.

This leads us to the conclusion that the concept of the average consumer must be understood as a legal concept[73] that is supposed to serve normative ends.[74] According to the UK Court of Appeal in *Interflora*, the average consumer is 'a person who has been created to strike the right balance between various competing interests, on the one hand the need to protect consumers, and on the other hand, the promotion of free trade in an openly competitive market'.[75] The CJEU in *Interflora* confirmed this approach,[76] by rejecting an average consumer based on measuring actual consumer perception or behaviour. Rather, it uses default characteristics that enable the Court to weigh the interests that 'the law regards as prescriptively desirable'.[77]

Some debate has ensued around the question as to whether the discrepancy between this legal concept and empirical data about consumer behaviour poses a problem for trade mark law. Cognitive psychology and related sciences have shown that 'human beings, however well-educated, intelligent, and careful, do not consistently act in an observant, informed, and circumspect way'.[78] We process information in at least two ways: in some situations, information is processed in an unconscious, rapid and automatic manner; in other situations, it is processed consciously, slowly and in a deliberative manner.[79] What Kahnemann shows is that not all decisions are conscious; rather, humans also heavily rely on a system that processes information with relatively little effort, in the background, in order to perform common activities.[80] Accordingly, only where unusual patterns are detected are they alerted to the conscious mind. This is certainly relevant when consumers purchase items with the help of AI technology: will they be alert because they do not yet trust the technology to make desirable choices for them, or will they only become actively involved in processing the information and making a choice where some unusual information appears?

Before we discuss this further, we first want to define in greater detail how the CJEU has interpreted the legal concept of an average consumer in its case law regarding trade marks.

4.2   Current CJEU Case-law on the Average Consumer in Trade Mark Law

Since the concept has not been defined in primary law, the CJEU's case law in the area of trade marks provides us with relevant information on how the average user perceives and behaves in shopping. The Court defines the average consumer in relation to the

– territory;
– type of goods and services; and
– level of attentiveness associated with the relevant goods and services.

---

[73]   EUIPO, Guidelines for examination of European Union trade marks [2020] 819.

[74]   Weatherall (n 71) 73/4.

[75]   *Interflora Inc v Marks and Spencer plc* (Interflora III) [2014] EWCA Civ 1403 [2015] ETMR 5 [103].

[76]   C-323/09 *Interflora Inc v Marks & Spencer* (n 64), paras 50 and 51.

[77]   Dinwoodie and Gangjee (n 65) 345.

[78]   Weatherall (n 71) 74.

[79]   Weatherall (n 71) 68.

[80]   Daniel Kahnemann, 'Of 2 minds: how fast and slow thinking shape perception and choice' (*Scientific American* 2012), www.scientificamerican.com/article/kahneman-excerpt-thinking-fast-and -slow/ accessed on 19 August 2021, excerpt from Daniel Kahneman, *Thinking, Fast and Slow* (Allen Lane 2011).

The geographical dimension of the average consumer is 'the territory in respect of which registration is applied for'.[81] Where a national trade mark is at issue, the respective territory is that of the relevant Member State. In case of an EU trade mark, it would be the consumers in a part of the Union.[82] Such a part of the Union could be a single Member State,[83] but according to the General Court it could also be a smaller area, like a sub-region.[84]

Two other general factors apply to the concept of the average consumer. First, both actual and potential (future) consumers should be kept in mind for an assessment of distinctiveness or confusion or another aspect of trade mark law.[85] Second, not all actual and potential consumers must be considered, but a significant part thereof is sufficient.[86] This makes the concept of the average consumer rather broad.

4.2.1 In relation to goods and services

From a substantive perspective, the goods and services define the relevant public. According to the CJEU, the relevant public is likely to use both the goods or services of the registered/earlier mark and the sign used on the market/applied mark.[87] When determining which consumers will use both goods and services, the Court distinguishes between the general public and a professional or specialized public.[88] The former would be the public at large, whereas the latter focuses on particular business customers, a niche group of consumers or a specialized subgroup of experts in the field. In the case *Pranahaus*, for example, the specialized public of yoga products was defined by the General Court specifically as having knowledge of alternative medicine, esoterism, Hinduism, the far-east culture and yoga.[89]

The differentiation between the general public and a specialized public is important as it reflects a differentiated approach to the type of consumer that one has in mind for trade mark law purposes. It allows the application of trade mark law in accordance with the situation at hand in a specific case, and thereby safeguards the underlying interests of granting trade mark protection.

Furthermore, the CJEU uses these different types of relevant public (general or specialized) of the goods and services at issue to determine the level of attentiveness with which this public makes purchases.

4.2.2 With diverging degrees of attentiveness

The degree of attentiveness with which consumers buy a product is likely to vary according to the nature of goods or services, the type of public that purchases them and the circumstances

---

[81] Case C-108/97 *Windsurfing Chiemsee Produktions- und Vertriebs GmbH (WSC) v Boots- und Segelzubehör Walter Huber and Franz Attenberger* [1999] ECR I-2799, para 29, confirmed in Case C-421/04 *Matratzen Concord AG v Hukla* [2006] ECR I-2303, para 24.

[82] See Art 7.2 of EU Regulation EU/2017/1001 of 14 June 2017 on the European Union trade mark [2017] OJ L 154/1.

[83] Case C-25/05 P *August Storck KG v OHIM* [2006] ECR I-5739, para 83.

[84] Case T-72/11 *Sogepi Consulting y Publicidad v OHIM (Espetec)* [2012] OJ C 113, para 35.

[85] Alexander Tsoutsanis, 'EU Trade Mark Regulation' in Charles Gielen and Verena von Bomhard (eds), *Concise European Trade Mark and Design Law* (2nd edn, Kluwer 2017), Art. 9 EUTM note 8.

[86] EUIPO Guidelines (n 73) 888.

[87] Case T-328/05 *Apple Computer, Inc. v European Union Intellectual Property Office* [2008] ECR II-0010, para 23.

[88] EUIPO Guidelines (n 73) 819–20 and 888.

[89] Case T-226/07 *Prana Haus GmbH v EUIPO* [2008] ECR II-00184, paras 26, 29, 35.

in which the products or services are marketed.[90] As a general rule, fast-moving consumer goods are purchased with a lower degree of attentiveness than, for example, health products.[91] And a professional public, in principle, is likely to pay more attention to purchases than the general public. Also, where goods are particularly prone to brand loyalty, such as in the case of tobacco products, the level of attention among the relevant public can be higher than average, as a result of loyalty to a particular brand.[92]

When it comes to the circumstances in which products or services are purchased, these include knowledge, experience and purchase involvement of the relevant public. The standard 'reasonably well-informed and reasonable observant and circumspect' gives some guidance as to what is expected from the average consumer. Accordingly, she perceives a mark as a whole and does not proceed to analyse its various details. She rarely has the chance to make a direct comparison and rather trusts the imperfect picture she has in her mind.[93]

At the same time, the standard leaves room to account for different circumstances. What 'reasonable knowledge and attention' is depends on the relevant public, and, in the case of a professional public, on the profession. Where end users rely on professional advice, whether a higher or lower level of attention will be assumed will depend on the general public's involvement in the purchasing decision. If the product is expensive or has health effects, the end user's level of attention may be high. Where professionals act relatively independently, with more marginal involvement of the end consumer, the level of attention of the latter may be rather low.[94]

Overall, the rather pluriform concept[95] of the average consumer of different types of goods or services and with different degrees of attentiveness leaves room for various situations and contexts. It raises the question as to whether it is broad enough to still fulfil the trade mark functions in situations where consumers are assisted by AI technology.

4.3   Taking AI Technology into Account

So does the concept of the average consumer need to be adapted for situations where they make purchases with the help of AI technology? Having assessed different types of AI mechanisms involved in online shopping, we argue that courts hearing cases involving online shopping will have to determine the AI tool's level of sophistication, possible bias and involvement in the purchasing process. That information will be important to assess the role of the human consumer in the purchase and hence her perception of the trade mark displayed on goods or services, her likelihood of being confused or whether she makes an immediate association between a trade mark and a similar sign. This assessment very much depends on the specific

[90]   Case C-342/97 *Lloyd Schuhfabrik Meyer & Co. GmbH v Klijsen Handel BV.* [1999] ECR I-03819, para 27; Case C-361/04 P *Claude Ruiz-Picasso and Others v EUIPO* [2006] ECR I-00643, para 37.

[91]   Case T-547/08 *X Technology Swiss GmbH v OHIM* [2010] ECR II-02409, para 43; Case T-288/08 *Cadila Healthcare v OHIM – Novartis (ZYDUS)* [2012] ECLI:EU:T:2012:124, para 36 in Karla Hughes, 'EU Trade Mark Regulation' in Charles Gielen and Verena von Bomhard (eds), *Concise European Trade Mark and Design Law* (2nd edn, Kluwer 2017), Art 8 EUTM note 6.

[92]   Case T-34/04 *Plus Warenhandelsgesellschaft mbH v European Union Intellectual Property Office* [2005] ECR II-02401, para. 69; EUIPO Guidelines (n 73) 893.

[93]   Case T-486/07 *Ford Motor v OHIM – Alkar Automotive (CA)* [2011] ECR II-00058, para 95.

[94]   EUIPO Guidelines (n 73) 892 and 894.

[95]   Weatherall (n 71) 30.

AI tool used for a particular type of product. In opposition proceedings, where IP offices need to assess the likelihood of the relevant public being confused, it seems less useful. Our assessment depends on the mode of purchasing by the relevant public, on which little information will be available at the opposition stage.

4.3.1   Less sophisticated AI mechanisms with high consumer involvement

Where AI mechanisms are not yet very advanced in their sophistication and only provide purchasing options to the consumer, leaving it up to her to make the final purchasing decision, the concept of the average consumer as used by the CJEU in its keyword advertising judgments may still be relevant. There, the Court defined the average consumer as a normally informed and reasonably attentive internet user.[96] The Court assessed whether an attentive internet user is able to distinguish the origin of advertised products as compared to the natural results that are listed on the Google search engine when searching for a trade mark as a keyword, and concluded she could.

Where shopping portals generate product recommendations through AI technology on the basis of prior purchases or purchases made by similar users, the question arises as to whether an attentive internet user can verify the different origin of those product suggestions. Having in mind a user who is familiar with product recommendation systems, one may be able to assume that she can distinguish the recommendations from each other where they present alternatives and do not constitute imitations of the trade mark product.[97] The consumer is still highly involved in the purchasing decision and therefore is likely to pay attention to the trade-origin of the various options suggested.

Nevertheless, some characteristics previously defined for an average consumer may no longer be relevant. For example, the relevant public in a purchase with AI assistance would not be characterized as being reasonably well-informed. The AI mechanism, even if not yet very advanced, will have far more information at its disposal than humans can gather. Supposing that the AI tool presents information that is relevant for consumers' preferences, the consumer will be able to base her purchasing decision on more detailed information. She will also not perceive marks as a whole, with an imperfect recollection of the mark. In fact, an AI tool will perceive slight differences in the signs displayed and information connected to the products. Such information depends on the level of sophistication, but clearly will be much more accurate than an imperfect recollection of a human consumer alone. Therefore, we argue that where consumers purchase with the help of AI tools, whether sophisticated or not, the AI tool significantly enhances the cognitive abilities of the online human consumer. She will have a larger amount of supposedly relevant and detailed information available when making purchasing choices.

4.3.2   Highly sophisticated AI mechanisms with low consumer involvement

For a sophisticated AI mechanism, the assessment will become more complex. Courts again need to determine in which purchasing stages the human consumer is still involved. This compares to a situation where purchases are made relying on professional assistance: someone who filters information, presents information in a comparative manner and suggests the best choice in line with the (perceived) preferences of the consumer. In our case, the professional

---

[96]   C-236/08 *Google France* (n 52) para 90.
[97]   Case C-323/09 *Interflora v Marks & Spencer* (n 64) para 91.

assistance is provided by an advanced AI technology, which has access to a vast array of information about the consumers' preferences and the items on the shopping portal.

When highly sophisticated AI technology guides consumers in their purchasing decision, and the consumer can trust that bias is low and her preferences are duly taken into consideration, the consumer's level of attentiveness will be low. Then it is likely that a consumer will make almost automatic, unconscious and rapid purchasing decisions, rather than deliberating between the different options. Such a consumer may not fulfil the standard of being reasonably circumspect and observant.

We believe that this latter attitude of consumers, of trusting the assessment by AI to a large degree, is not a given and will depend on consumer experience of the choices made by AI indeed fulfilling their preferences well, and of the bias inherent in the tool not affecting the purchasing decisions in a negative way. Whether a consumer has reached that level of trust will therefore have to be established, either empirically in a specific situation or more generally in relation to the specific sector of trade, the type of users thereof and the type of goods or services purchased.

Where does this leave us? We argue that AI mechanisms affect the way we should define the average consumer. Even with the help of less advanced AI tools, consumers will not only be reasonably well-informed but will have expert knowledge at their disposal. Also, their recollection will not be imperfect but almost perfect. With the use of more sophisticated AI mechanisms, human consumers will play much less of a role in the purchasing process if they accept the AI tool managing their purchases. Courts therefore should:

– distinguish purchases with or without AI mechanisms;
– gather a basic understanding of the AI mechanism at issue, in particular its level of sophistication, possible bias and involvement in the different stages of purchase;
– adapt the rather broad and pluriformal concept of the average consumer to the case at hand, enriched with an understanding of how consumers act in online purchases when confronted with different types of AI mechanisms; and finally
– become more open to behavioural and cognitive insights into the processes underlying the use of AI mechanisms, such as trust.

5.   CONCLUSIONS

Much is still uncertain about the types of AI tools that will assist us in the future and whether we will trust such tools to become autonomous for our online purchases. On the basis of the information available now, we have presented the spectrum of AI technologies that are currently used. These include product recommendations, virtual assistants and automatic ordering, with varying degrees of sophistication and involvement, and at different stages of the purchasing process. On the basis of this assessment, we were able to make some observations regarding the role that trade marks seem to fulfil in a world in which consumers are assisted by AI technology when purchasing in the online marketplace.

We argue that trade marks may no longer serve the purpose of simplifying information and thereby making the purchasing process more effective. Consumers will be able to rely on AI tools for obtaining extensive information about the product in a fraction of time. However, trade marks still fulfil their role of conveying meaning to consumers at the stage when they consume the product. The information and experience that a product conveys to the consumer when consuming is associated with the trade mark indicated on the package. It is these consumer experiences at the stage of consumption that in the end feed back into the next purchasing process, thereby maintaining the relevance of consumer perception for future purchases. They will become ever more important as AI technologies grow more complex.

We also find that guaranteeing transparency and therefore fair competition on the market will still be necessary. Even though AI technologies may be able to detect counterfeit products, having confusing information in the first place would hamper communication between producers and consumers. Trade mark protection ensures fair conditions of competition on the market.

The accessory functions of trade marks are based on the assumption that reputed and famous marks are of added value for consumers' purchasing decisions because they communicate positive values and feelings to the consumer. Even though an AI technology can present the consumer with all relevant information related to a trade marked product or service, we argue that these positive connotations connected to a trade mark cannot be transferred through suggestions made by AI; it is the trade mark as such that communicates this information. The protection of the accessory functions of trade marks therefore still fulfils a role in AI-assisted shopping.

If we accept that trade mark law will continue to play a role in AI-assisted shopping, the way in which we describe an AI-assisted consumer will be important. She is not similar to the average consumer as described by the CJEU; she has nearly complete information at her disposal and can detect insignificant details. While the attributes of 'reasonably well-informed and reasonably observant and circumspect' will not be relevant for AI-assisted consumers, the concept of the relevant public as defined by the CJEU is much broader and allows for a case-by-case assessment. In fact, an AI-assisted consumer will be closer to a consumer who relies on expert advice or is highly professional. The level of attentiveness in a certain situation depends on the type of goods and services, the AI tool at issue and how consumers engage with this tool.

We foresee that courts will have to adapt their assessment of the average consumer based on a basic understanding of the AI mechanism and behavioural data on how consumers act in online purchase situations, as well as how much they trust the AI mechanism to make the best choice in line with their preferences.

16. Trademark law, AI-driven behavioral advertising, and the Digital Services Act: toward source and parameter transparency for consumers, brand owners, and competitors

Martin Senftleben

1. INTRODUCTION

In its Proposal for a Digital Services Act ("DSA"),[1] the European Commission highlighted the need for new transparency obligations to arrive at accountable digital services,[2] ensure a fair environment for economic operators,[3] and empower consumers.[4] However, the proposed new rules seem to focus on transparency measures for consumers. According to the DSA Proposal, platforms, such as online marketplaces, must ensure that platform users receive information enabling them to understand when and on whose behalf an advertisement is displayed, and which parameters are used to direct advertising to them, including explanations of the logic underlying systems for targeted advertising.[5] Statements addressing the interests of trademark owners and trademark policy are sought in vain. Against this background, the following analysis sheds light on computational advertising practices (section 2) and the policy considerations underlying the proposed new transparency obligations (section 3). In the light of the debate on trademark protection in keyword advertising cases, it will show that not only consumers but also trademark owners have a legitimate interest in receiving information on the parameters that are used to target consumers (section 4). The discussion will lead to the insight that lessons from the keyword advertising debate can play an important role in the transparency discourse because they broaden the spectrum of policy rationales and guidelines for new transparency rules. In addition to the current focus on consumer empowerment, the enhancement of information on alternative offers in the marketplace and the strengthening of trust in AI-driven, personalized advertising enter the picture (section 5). On balance, there are good reasons to broaden the scope of the DSA initiative and ensure access to transparency information for consumers and trademark owners alike (concluding section 6).

---

[1]   European Commission, December 15, 2020, *Proposal for a Regulation of the European Parliament and of the Council on a Single Market For Digital Services (Digital Services Act) and amending Directive 2000/31/EC*, Document COM(2020) 825 final 2020/0361.

[2]   European Commission, ibid, Explanatory Memorandum, 1–2.

[3]   European Commission, ibid, Explanatory Memorandum, 5–7.

[4]   European Commission, ibid, Explanatory Memorandum, 9. For further proposals to reduce consumer vulnerability in the digital environment, see Natali Helberger, Orla Lynskey, Hans-Wolfgang Micklitz et al., *EU Consumer Protection 2.0—Structural Asymmetries in Digital Consumer Markets*, Brussels: BEUC 2021, 78-79.

[5]   Articles 24 and 30 DSA; Recitals 52 and 63 DSA.

2.   COMPUTATIONAL ADVERTISING

Computational advertising lies at the core of a paradigm shift in advertising. While, in the past, marketers designed brand information and advertising messages in accordance with a particular brand identity, AI systems nowadays use behavioral consumer data to generate tailor-made marketing messages on the basis of algorithmic content selection and creation processes.[6] In marketing communications research, Guda van Noort, Itai Himelboim, and colleagues identified advancements in computing and marketing technology as drivers behind this remarkable change in brand-related communication: "Algorithms and mathematical methods are at the center of these changes that enable computational advertising: the use of computing capabilities to analyze consumer behavior, tailor content, and facilitate the delivery of advertising information to (potential) consumers across media vehicles and touch points."[7]

At the same time, marketing research sheds light on the wide range of personal data that are used to tailor brand and advertising messages to individual consumers and generate targeted marketing messages.[8] The range of consumer data fueling the process goes far beyond basic demographic information, such as age, gender, level of education, income, geography, and marital status. Access to mobile devices makes location-based information available. Most importantly, however, so-called psychographic marketing[9] aims at obtaining more nuanced psychographic information to understand consumers' stated preferences and observed choices. Psychographic marketing relies on information about psychological characteristics and traits that reflect a consumer's personality (for example, introversion or extraversion) and values (for example, concerns about the environment).[10] Data from social networking services, for instance, offer insights into personal connections and shared posts, pictures, and videos. In this way, it becomes possible to factor specific consumer interests and relationships into the equation.[11] Moreover, available data flows cover a consumer's search requests, browsing history, online media consumption, and shopping patterns. Surveillance-enabling devices, such as smart speakers, virtual assistants, and health and fitness trackers, provide even more pervasive situational data and information on consumers' personal conditions.[12] Website analytics add

---

[6]   Guda van Noort, Itai Himelboim, et al., "Introducing a Model of Automated Brand-Generated Content in an Era of Computational Advertising," *Journal of Advertising* 49 (2020), 411 (411).

[7]   Van Noort, Himelboim et al., *supra* note 6, 411.

[8]   See the overview provided by Van Noort, Himelboim et al., *supra* note 6, 416.

[9]   Van Noort, Himelboim et al., *supra* note 6, 416. Cf. Natali Helberger, Jisu Huh et al., "Macro and Exogenous Factors in Computational Advertising: Key Issues and New Research Directions," *Journal of Advertising* 49 (2020), 377 (381–2).

[10]   See Van Noort, Himelboim et al., *supra* note 6, 416, for a discussion of this personality information. As to case law discussing advertising that specifically addresses consumers' environmental concerns, see German Federal Supreme Court, 26 October 2006, case I ZR 33/04, "Regenwaldprojekt I," para. 34. Cf. For a discussion of the potential reintroduction of ethical considerations in unfair competition law following from this type of product marketing, see Karl-Nikolaus Peifer, "Schutz ethischer Werte im Europäischen Lauterkeitsrecht oder rein wirtschaftliche Betrachtungsweise?," in Reto M. Hilty & Frauke Henning-Bodewig (eds.), *Lauterkeitsrecht und Acquis Communautaire*, Heidelberg/ Dordrecht/London/New York: Springer 2009, 125 (137–41).

[11]   Van Noort, Himelboim et al., *supra* note 6, 416.

[12]   Van Noort, Himelboim et al., *supra* note 6, 416.

audience reports that offer information on visitors, including personal characteristics, interests, access locations, and incidental or repeated webpage visits.[13]

Given these proportions of personal data use, it does not come as a surprise that targeted online behavioral advertising gives rise to privacy concerns and triggers feelings of vulnerability and intrusiveness among consumers.[14] Natali Helberger, Jisu Huh and colleagues describe the dimension of the phenomenon as follows:

> The knowledge advertisers and advertising firms amass about individual consumers by tracking consumers' behaviors online over time can become quite extensive and precise. Based on the combined data of search terms entered, web pages visited, products clicked on, articles read, and videos watched, ads can be composed of specific information and images compiled about an individual consumer across a network, making them precisely attractive to the individual and personally relevant.[15]

At the same time, they point out that many consumers are not fully aware of the mechanisms underlying online behavioral data tracking and related advertising and branding initiatives. In the absence of a clear understanding of data-driven targeting and persuasion tactics, consumers may succumb to disguised advertising messages without even realizing that they are exposed to subtle, algorithmic marketing influences. Consumers may also provide personal information without considering potential threats to their privacy.[16] Due to this lack of knowledge and awareness, online behavioral advertising may trigger individual biases, desires, fears, and other emotions.[17] The information asymmetry can culminate in power imbalances between advertisers and consumers, and lead to undue manipulation of consumer choices.[18]

Against this background, Helberger, Huh, and colleagues highlight the need for transparency to fill the information gap and strengthen consumers' ability to understand computational advertising mechanisms and processes. They recall that in the EU, the General Data Protection Regulation already sets forth obligations to inform consumers not only about the collection of personal data but also about the underlying purpose and logic of automated profiling, and potential consequences for consumers.[19]

Considering the recognition of a need for more transparency in automated brand-related communication, it is consistent that the DSA Proposal comprises new legal rules in this area. Article 24 DSA addresses the issue of online advertising transparency by stating that online platforms[20] displaying advertising on their online interfaces:

---

[13]   For example, see Andrew Kucheriavy's discussion of information flowing from the use of Google Analytics, available at: www.intechnic.com/blog/google-analytics-audience-analysis-and-demographics-reports/. Cf. Oliver Busch, "The Programmatic Advertising Principle," in Oliver Busch (ed.), *Programmatic Advertising: The Successful Transformation to Automated, Data-driven Marketing in Real-time*, Cham: Springer 2016, 315.

[14]   Sophie C. Boerman, Sanne Kruikemeier, and Frederik J. Zuiderveen Borgesius, "Online Behavioral Advertising: A Literature Review and Research Agenda," *Journal of Advertising* 46 (2017), 363 (365–70).

[15]   Helberger, Huh et al., *supra* note 9, 382.

[16]   Helberger, Huh et al., *supra* note 9, 382.

[17]   Helberger, Huh et al., *supra* note 9, 382.

[18]   Helberger, Huh et al., *supra* note 9, 384–5. Cf. Rachel L. Finn and Kush Wadhwa, "The Ethics of Smart," *Info* 16 (2014), 22 (27–8).

[19]   Helberger, Huh et al., *supra* note 9, 382 and 386. Cf. Recital 52 DSA.

[20]   Article 2(h) DSA defines "online platform" as follows: "'online platform' means a provider of a hosting service which, at the request of a recipient of the service, stores and disseminates to the public

shall ensure that the recipients of the service can identify, for each specific advertisement displayed to each individual recipient, in a clear and unambiguous manner and in real time:

(a) that the information displayed is an advertisement;
(b) the natural or legal person on whose behalf the advertisement is displayed;
(c) meaningful information about the main parameters used to determine the recipient to whom the advertisement is displayed.

Reaching beyond mere *source transparency* (sub (b): "Who sent this?"), this provision explicitly requires *parameter transparency* (sub (c): "Why me?"). The accompanying Recital 52 DSA clarifies that consumers should receive not only information on the main parameters used to target them, but also "meaningful explanations of the logic used to that end, including when this is based on profiling." Hence, the proposed new transparency obligations are intended to capture the principles and criteria underlying automated processes of directing specific advertising to targeted consumers.

With regard to advertising systems used by very large online platforms, Recital 63 DSA highlights particular risks that may arise from the scale of advertising activities—reaching more than 45 million active recipients of the service[21]—and the "ability to target and reach consumers based on their behaviour within and outside that platform's online interface." In the light of this risk dimension, the European Commission identified a need for "further public and regulatory supervision."[22] In this vein, Article 30(1) DSA obliges very large online platforms to ensure public access, through application programming interfaces, to repositories of advertisements displayed on their online interfaces until one year after the last use of the advertising. With this additional transparency measure, the proposed new legislation seeks to facilitate supervision and research into emerging risks of online advertising, including exposure to "illegal advertisements or manipulative techniques and disinformation with a real and foreseeable negative impact on public health, public security, civil discourse, political participation and equality."[23] In line with Article 30(2) DSA, the repository must include at least the following information:

(a) the content of the advertisement;
(b) the natural or legal person on whose behalf the advertisement is displayed;
(c) the period during which the advertisement was displayed;
(d) whether the advertisement was intended to be displayed specifically to one or more particular groups of recipients of the service and if so, the main parameters used for that purpose;
(e) the total number of recipients of the service reached and, where applicable, aggregate numbers for the group or groups of recipients to whom the advertisement was targeted specifically.

---

information, unless that activity is a minor and purely ancillary feature of another service and, for objective and technical reasons cannot be used without that other service, and the integration of the feature into the other service is not a means to circumvent the applicability of this Regulation."

[21] Article 25(1) DSA clarifies that the rules on "very large" online platforms apply to "online platforms which provide their services to a number of average monthly active recipients of the service in the [EU] equal to or higher than 45 million, calculated in accordance with the methodology set out in the delegated acts referred to in paragraph 3."

[22] Recital 63 DSA.

[23] Recital 63 DSA.

3. CONSUMER AND BRAND OWNER INTERESTS

In the light of the described discussion on consumer vulnerability and the increasing exposure of consumers to AI-supported behavioral advertising, the configuration of the proposed new obligations can give the impression that the European Commission focused exclusively on consumer empowerment when drafting the new transparency provisions. Using broader terminology, however, the Explanatory Memorandum accompanying the DSA Proposal confirms that stakeholder consultations drew the Commission's attention more generally to "the way algorithmic systems shape information flows online."[24] A "wide category of stakeholders"[25] highlighted AI-generated information as a particular area of concern:

> Several stakeholders, in particular civil society and academics, pointed out the need for algorithmic accountability and transparency audits, especially with regard to how information is prioritized and targeted. Similarly, regarding online advertising, stakeholder views echoed the broad concerns around the lack of user empowerment and lack of meaningful oversight and enforcement.[26]

Interestingly, the Commission speaks about a lack of "user" empowerment in this statement instead of referring more restrictively to "consumer" empowerment. In line with this openness of the Explanatory Memorandum, the terminology used in the new provisions leaves room for a broad understanding of the proposed transparency obligations. In particular, it seems possible to develop an interpretation that would cover not only consumers but also brand owners. While the DSA Proposal contains specific definitions of the terms "consumer" and "trader,"[27] Articles 24 and 30 DSA refrain from limiting the scope of the new transparency obligations to the specific category of "consumers." In a more neutral manner, both provisions refer to "recipients of the service"—an expression which Article 2(b) DSA defines as "any natural or legal person who uses the relevant intermediary service."

Obviously, both consumers and traders use online platforms, such as search engine services hosting third-party ads[28] and online marketplaces hosting third-party offers.[29] When the neutral expression "recipients of the service" is understood to encompass both consumers and traders, the new obligations can be interpreted in a way that ensures access to transparency information not only for consumers but also for brand owners (= "traders" in the sense of Article 2(e) DSA). As explained, Article 24 DSA seeks to ensure that the recipients of the service can identify, "for each specific advertisement displayed to each individual recipient, in a clear and unambiguous manner and in real time," the source of the advertisement (source transparency) and the parameters used to target the recipient (parameter transparency). Hence, the new legal obligation can be understood to mean that:

---

[24]   DSA, Explanatory Memorandum, 9.
[25]   DSA, Explanatory Memorandum, 9.
[26]   DSA, Explanatory Memorandum, 9.
[27]   Article 2(c) and (e) DSA.
[28]   CJEU, March 23, 2010, C-236/08-238/08, Google France and Google, paras 114–116.
[29]   CJEU, July 12, 2011, case C-324/09, L'Oréal/eBay, paras 114–120. As to the assumption of hosting status in these cases, see Martin R.F. Senftleben, "Breathing Space for Cloud-Based Business Models: Exploring the Matrix of Copyright Limitations, Safe Harbours and Injunctions," *Journal of Intellectual Property, Information Technology and Electronic Commerce Law* 4 (2013), 87 (94–5).

[a *consumer* using an online platform] can identify, for each specific advertisement displayed to each individual [*consumer*], in a clear and unambiguous manner and in real time [source and parameter information].

Extending this approach to brand owners (= traders), it can be assumed that there is also an obligation to ensure that:

[a *trader* using an online platform] can identify, for each specific advertisement displayed to each individual [*trader*], in a clear and unambiguous manner and in real time [source and parameter information].

Importantly, however, an approach covering consumers and traders alike can lead to an even broader interpretation that opens the "black box" of algorithmic behavioral advertising and gives brand owners access to marketing messages that are directed to consumers. This more extensive scenario combines the trader entitlement to transparency information with brand-related messages displayed to consumers. To arrive at this broader reading, it is necessary to interpret Article 24 DSA to include the obligation to ensure that

[a *trader* using an online platform] can identify, for each specific advertisement displayed to each individual [*consumer*], in a clear and unambiguous manner and in real time [source and parameter information].

As indicated, this more extensive reading would give brand owners access to transparency information covering the source of online behavioral advertising ("the natural or legal person on whose behalf the advertisement is displayed")[30] and the parameters used to target consumers ("meaningful information about the main parameters used to determine the recipient to whom the advertisement is displayed").[31] In practice, this would mean that Cartier would be in a position to receive (at an aggregated level without disclosing personal data of individual consumers) transparency information on whether the behavioral advertising tools of an online platform lead to a situation where consumers who purchased Cartier jewelry in the past receive advertising inviting them to consider Tiffany products. Similarly, BMW could check whether consumers who searched for BMW repair services receive advertising messages that draw their attention to Mercedes-Benz cars.

In the Explanatory Memorandum, this broader approach—providing brand owners an overview of behavioral advertising messages triggered by previous consumer activities relating to their products and trademarks—finds some support in the section dealing with the choice of the legal instrument. In this context, the Commission invokes the policy objective to "prevent divergences hampering the free provision of the relevant services within the internal market, as well as guarantee the uniform protection of rights and uniform obligations for business and consumers across the internal market. This is necessary to provide legal certainty and transparency for economic operators and consumers alike."[32]

Admittedly, the reference to "legal certainty and transparency" in this statement need not be understood in the specific sense of source and parameter transparency addressed in Article 24 DSA. Nonetheless, the fact remains that the Commission explicitly mentions the desire to

---

[30]   Article 24(b) DSA.
[31]   Article 24(c) DSA.
[32]   DSA, Explanatory Memorandum, 7.

establish harmonized legal rules for "economic operators and consumers alike." Considering the explicit reference to both stakeholder groups, it seems possible to draw a line between the Explanatory Memorandum and Article 24 DSA, and posit that the new transparency obligations should serve the interests of both "economic operators [= brand owners] and consumers alike."

More clarity about the inclusion of brand owner interests may follow in the near future. The DSA still constitutes draft legislation. As long as the legislative process has not come to an end, there is room to clarify the scope of Articles 24 and 30 DSA and dispel doubts about brand owner access to source and parameter data. As already indicated, this broader approach would allow brand owners to identify advertisers who use brand-related data to direct tailor-made advertising messages to consumers. Considering the described diversity of data sources used to generate targeted behavioral advertising messages, there can be little doubt that brand-related data, such as information on search requests, browsing history, and online purchases concerning branded goods and services, can play a role in computational advertising. Brand owners' interest in clarity about advertisers relying on brand-related data and the use of these data to bring (potentially competing) offers to the attention of consumers can hardly be denied against this backdrop.

Before jumping to the conclusion that the DSA should serve the purpose of introducing new data transparency obligations for the benefit of both brand owners and consumers, however, it is important to consider the legislative path which the EU has traditionally followed in the regulation of commercial practices in the internal market.

On the one hand, the Unfair Commercial Practices Directive ("UCPD")[33] puts a clear emphasis on business-to-consumer relations. It seeks to protect consumers against misleading and aggressive practices. Recent amendments[34] introduce new rules on parameter transparency in the area of search result rankings. Adding a category of misleading omissions, this update of the EU acquis confirms the traditional focus on consumer protection. Employing the UCPD—and thus an instrument for regulating business-to-consumer relations—as a vehicle, the new legislation refrains from addressing potential interests which brand owners may have in information about the parameters used for the ranking of products.[35] The new provision only mentions consumers:

> When providing consumers with the possibility to search for products [...] general information [...] on the main parameters determining the ranking of products presented to the consumer as a result of the search query and the relative importance of those parameters, as opposed to other parameters, shall be regarded as material.[36]

---

[33] Directive 2005/29/EC of the European Parliament and of the Council of 11 May 2005 concerning unfair business-to-consumer commercial practices in the internal market, *Official Journal* L 149, 22.

[34] See the new rules following from Directive 2019/2161/EU of the European Parliament and of the Council of 27 November 2019 amending Council Directive 93/13/EEC and Directives 98/6/EC, 2005/29/EC and 2011/83/EU of the European Parliament and of the Council as regards the better enforcement and modernisation of Union consumer protection rules, *Official Journal* L 328, 7.

[35] As to the discussion on the ranking of search results in keyword advertising cases, see CJEU, March 23, 2010, C-236/08-238/08, Google France and Google, paras 97–98; CJEU, March 25, 2010, case C-278/08, BergSpechte, para. 33; CJEU, July 8, 2010, case C-558/08, Portakabin, paras 32–33. Cf. Annette Kur and Martin R.F. Senftleben, *European Trade Mark Law: A Commentary*, Oxford: Oxford University Press 2017, paras 5.88–5.91.

[36] Article 7(4a) UCPD, as amended by Article 3(4)(b) of Directive 2019/2161.

On the other hand, it must not be overlooked that the Directive on Misleading and Comparative Advertising ("MCAD")[37] sets forth harmonized rules that shape business-to-business relations, including the relationship between advertisers and brand owners. By virtue of Article 10(3)(f) of the Trade Mark Directive ("TMD")[38] and Article 9(3)(f) of the European Union Trade Mark Regulation ("EUTMR"),[39] the rules on comparative advertising have a direct impact on the legal position of brand owners: use of a protected mark in comparative advertising in a manner that complies with the MCAD rules[40] does not amount to trademark infringement.[41] Hence, the EU legislator does not leave the regulation of advertiser/brand owner relations to national legislation in EU Member States.[42] The interests of brand owners are directly addressed in EU legislation itself.

A foray into existing legislative approaches at EU level, therefore, does not yield clear results. While the UCPD reflects a clear focus on business-to-consumer relations and the protection of consumers, the MCAD rules have repercussions on business-to-business relations and impact the legal position of brand owners in comparative advertising cases. The analysis does not reveal an overarching legislative scheme allowing identification of the beneficiaries of the proposed new transparency obligations laid down in Articles 24 and 30 DSA.

4.   LESSONS FROM KEYWORD ADVERTISING

In the absence of clear guidelines in the DSA Proposal and the EU acquis, the decisive question is whether, from an overarching policy perspective, it could make sense to factor brand owner interests into the equation and employ Articles 24 and 30 DSA as legal tools to give brand owners access to brand-related transparency information. The trademark debate on keyword advertising and the related court decisions offer important insights in this respect.[43]

---

[37]   Directive 2006/114/EC of the European Parliament and of the Council of 12 December 2006 concerning misleading and comparative advertising (codified version), *Official Journal* L 376, 21.

[38]   Directive (EU) 2015/2436 of the European Parliament and of the Council of 16 December 2015 to approximate the laws of the Member States relating to trade marks, *OJ* 2015 L 336, 1.

[39]   Regulation (EU) 2017/1001 of the European Parliament and of the Council of 14 June 2017 on the European Union trade mark (codification), *OJ* 2017 L 154, 1.

[40]   Article 4 MCAD.

[41]   CJEU, June 12, 2008, case C-533/06, O2/Hutchison, para. 45; CJEU, 18 June 2009, case C-487/07, L'Oréal/Bellure, para. 54. Cf. Martin R.F. Senftleben, *The Copyright/Trademark Interface: How the Expansion of Trademark Protection Is Stifling Cultural Creativity*, The Hague/London/New York: Kluwer Law International 2020, 459–60; Kur and Senftleben, *supra* note 35, paras 5.307–5.308 and 6.43–6.44.

[42]   As to the freedom enjoyed by EU Member States in other areas, see Ansgar Ohly, "Trademark Law and Advertising Law in the European Union: Conflicts and Convergence," in Irene Calboli and Jane C. Ginsburg (eds.), *Cambridge Handbook on International and Comparative Trademark Law*, Cambridge: Cambridge University Press 2020, 323 (323–4). For an overview of domestic regulatory models, see Frauke Henning-Bodewig, "Die Bekämpfung unlauteren Wettbewerbs in den EU-Mitgliedstaaten: eine Bestandsaufnahme," *Gewerblicher Rechtsschutz und Urheberrecht—International* 2010, 273 (283–4).

[43]   For an in-depth overview and analysis, see Nicole van der Laan, *The Use of Trademarks in Keyword Advertising*, Amsterdam: Vrije Universiteit Amsterdam 2020, available at: https://research .vu.nl/en/publications/the-use-of-trade-marks-in-keyword-advertising. As to the individual stages of the debate and case law evolution, see Martin R.F. Senftleben, "Adapting EU Trademark Law to New Technologies: Back to Basics?," in Christophe Geiger (ed.), *Constructing European Intellectual*

The keyword advertising debate is an important reference point because it addresses the triangular relationship between brand owners, consumers and advertisers that also arises in online behavioral advertising when search results, browsing history and online purchases concerning brand A are used as parameters to direct brand B advertisements to consumers.

First, experiences with keyword advertising show that the involvement of brand owners adds important policy considerations. While source and parameter transparency for consumers may already be an important step in the right direction, a focus on consumer empowerment only leads to enhanced consumer knowledge of online behavioral advertising and the data reservoir used for this purpose. This may help consumers to deal adequately with the AI-generated advertising "bubble" that is surrounding them in the digital environment. With brand owners, however, the overarching policy dimension of trademark law and trademark protection enters the picture. Individual brand insignia typically enjoy trademark protection. According to traditional trademark theory, trademarks primarily serve the purpose of indicating the commercial origin of goods and services offered in the marketplace.[44] The CJEU refers to "the essential function of the trade mark, which is to guarantee the identity of the origin of the trade-marked product to the consumer or final user by enabling him to distinguish without any possibility of confusion between that product and products which have another origin."[45]

To enable trademarks to fulfil the essential origin function, trademark law offers enterprises the opportunity to establish an exclusive link with a distinctive sign. As a result, the protected sign is rendered capable of functioning as a source identifier in trade. In this way, trademark law guarantees market transparency.[46] It ensures fair competition, protects consumers against confusion and contributes to the proper functioning of market economies by allowing consumers to clearly express their preference for a particular product or service. From an economic

---

Property, Cheltenham: Edward Elgar Publishing 2013, 137; Ansgar Ohly, "Keyword Advertising auf dem Weg zurück von Luxemburg nach Paris, Wien, Karlsruhe und Den Haag," *Gewerblicher Rechtsschutz und Urheberrecht* 2010, 776; Stacy L. Dogan, "Beyond Trademark Use," *Journal on Telecommunication and High Technology Law* 8 (2010), 135; Jonathan Cornthwaite, "AdWords or Bad Words? A UK Perspective on Keywords and Trade Mark Infringement," *European Intellectual Property Review* 2009, 347; Roland Knaak, "Keyword Advertising—Das aktuelle Key-Thema des Europäischen Markenrechts," *Gewerblicher Rechtsschutz und Urheberrecht International* 2009, 551; C. Well-Szönyi, "Adwords: Die Kontroverse um die Zulässigkeit der Verwendung fremder Marken als Schlüsselwort in der französischen Rechtsprechung," *Gewerblicher Rechtsschutz und Urheberrecht International* 2009, 557; Olaf Sosnitza, "Adwords = Metatags? Zur marken- und wettbewerbsrechtlichen Zulässigkeit des Keyword Advertising über Suchmaschinen," *Markenrecht* 2009, 35; Charles Gielen, "Van adwords en metatags," in: Nico A.N.M. van Eijk et al. (eds), *Dommering-bundel*, Amsterdam: Cramwinckel 2008, 101; Graeme B. Dinwoodie and Mark D. Janis, "Lessons from the Trademark Use Debate," *Iowa Law Review* 92 (2007), 1703; Ot van Daalen en Arnout Groen, "Beïnvloeding van zoekresultaten en gesponsorde koppelingen. De juridische kwalificatie van onzichtbaar merkgebruik," *BMM Bulletin* 2006, 106.

[44] For an overview of trademark functions, pointing out this traditional focus on identification and distinction functions and potential extensions with regard to communication, investment and advertising functions, see R. Keim, *Der markenrechtliche Tatbestand der Verwechslungsgefahr*, Baden-Baden: Nomos 2009, 37–61.

[45] For an early use of this formula, see CJEU, December 3, 1981, case C-1/81, Pfizer v Eurim-Pharm, para. 8. As to the reappearance of the same formula in later judgments, see particularly CJEU, November 12, 2002, case C-206/01, Arsenal/Reed, para. 48. Cf. I. Simon Fhima, "How Does 'Essential Function' Doctrine Drive European Trade Mark Law?" International Review of Intellectual Property and Competition Law 36 (2005), 401.

[46] Cf. Senftleben, *supra* note 41, 85–7; Kur and Senftleben, *supra* note 35, paras 1.06–1.07.

perspective, it can be added that the clear indication of the commercial origin of goods and services reduces consumers' search costs.[47] Quite clearly, the inclusion of brand owners in the debate on transparency in online behavioral advertising thus broadens the policy frame. In addition to consumer protection, overarching market transparency rationales, such as the efficient regulation of supply and demand on the basis of consumer preferences, enter the picture.

Moreover, trademark law contributes substantially to "fair play" in the battle between brand owners and competitors for market shares, including individual fights in the online advertising arena. For instance, the CJEU imposed specific transparency obligations on keyword advertisers. To safeguard the essential origin function of trademarks in the context of "double identity"[48] cases falling under Article 9(2)(a) EUTMR and Article 10(2)(a) TMD, the Court stated in *Google/Louis Vuitton*:

> In the case where the ad, while not suggesting the existence of an economic link, is vague to such an extent on the origin of the goods or services at issue that normally informed and reasonably attentive internet users are unable to determine, on the basis of the advertising link and the commercial message attached thereto, whether the advertiser is a third party vis-à-vis the proprietor of the trade mark or, on the contrary, economically linked to that proprietor, the conclusion must also be that there is an adverse effect on that function of the trade mark.[49]

In the almost simultaneous *BergSpechte* decision, the Court confirmed this specific standard with regard to the likelihood of confusion analysis under Article 9(2)(b) EUTMR and Article 10(2)(b) TMD.[50] Both the origin function analysis in sub (a) infringement cases and the likelihood of confusion examination in sub (b) cases, therefore, now include the test whether the advertising is too vague to exclude a potential risk of consumer confusion. This calibration of legal obligations is nothing less than a shift from proof of likely confusion by the trademark owner to an obligation on all advertisers to secure market transparency when using keyword

---

[47]   With regard to the search costs argument, see Kur and Senftleben, *supra* note 35, paras 1.08–1.09; Andrew Griffiths, "A Law-and-Economic Perspective on Trade Marks," in Lionel Bently, Jennifer Davis, and Jane C. Ginsburg (eds), *Trade Marks and Brands: An Interdisciplinary Critique,* Cambridge: Cambridge University Press 2008, 241; Robert G. Bone, "Hunting Goodwill: A History of the Concept of Goodwill in Trademark Law," *Boston University Law Review* 86 (2006), 547 (555); William M. Landes and Richard A. Posner, *The Economic Structure of Intellectual Property Law*, Cambridge, MA: Harvard University Press, 2003, 166–8; Mark McKenna, "The Normative Foundations of Trademark Law," *Notre Dame Law Review* 82 (2007), 1839 (1844); Matthias Strasser, "The Rational Basis of Trademark Protection Revisited: Putting the Dilution Doctrine into Context," *Fordham Intellectual Property, Media & Entertainment Law Journal* 10 (2000), 375 (379–82); Stephen L. Carter, "The Trouble with Trademark," *Yale Law Journal* 99 (1990), 759 (762); Nicholas Economides, "The Economics of Trademarks," *The Trademark Reporter* 78 (1988), 523 (526). With regard to questions arising in the digital environment, see Stacy L. Dogan and Mark A. Lemley, "Trademarks and Consumer Search Costs on the Internet," *Houston Law Review* 41 (2004), 777.

[48]   As to protection of trademark in cases of so-called double identity (use of an identical conflicting sign in respect of identical goods or services), see Annette Kur, "Trademarks Function, Don't They?" *International Review of Intellectual Property and Competition Law* 45 (2014), 434; Martin R.F. Senftleben, "Function Theory and International Exhaustion: Why It Is Wise to Confine the Double Identity Rule in EU Trade Mark Law to Cases Affecting the Origin Function," *European Intellectual Property Review* 36 (2014), 518–24.

[49]   See CJEU, March 23, 2010, cases C-236/08-238/08, Google France and Google/Louis Vuitton et al., para. 90.

[50]   See CJEU, March 23, 2010, case C-278/08, BergSpechte/Trekking, at, paras 36 and 38–40.

advertising services.[51] Instead of conceiving of trademark rights as instruments that shield trademarks from confusing use by third parties at the initiative of the trademark owner, the CJEU redefined protection against confusion as a positive obligation of third parties to keep a sufficient distance from the origin information conveyed via the trademark.[52]

The evolution of a specific transparency obligation in keyword advertising cases confirms the importance of appropriate transparency measures in advertising contexts: a universal insight that can be extended to modern advertising techniques using behavioral consumer data. Experiences with keyword advertising, thus, support the proposal of new transparency obligations in Articles 24 and 30 DSA. Again, however, it is noteworthy that the objective underlying the transparency obligation is twofold in a trademark context: it is not only the goal of consumer protection that is deemed important, but also the protection of trademark owners against indirect confusion that can arise from false indications of a commercial connection or cooperation between the advertiser and the brand owner.[53]

Admittedly, online behavioral advertising is less likely than keyword advertising to cause confusion about an economic link between the advertiser and the trademark proprietor. In keyword advertising cases, a search for brand A triggers sponsored search results (advertising messages) concerning brand B—a scenario which can induce consumers to speculate about an economic link. The crux with online behavioral advertising, by contrast, is that consumers may not even be aware that they see brand B advertising because they did a search for brand A some time ago. The central risk, therefore, seems to lie in the area of freeriding and the unfair exploitation of consumer interest in brand A, as evidenced by corresponding search and browsing data, for the purpose of persuading consumers of the particular merits of products stemming from brand B. This shift from a confusion risk to a freeriding risk, however, does not mean that keyword advertising case law does not offer valuable insights that can be put to good use in the regulation of online behavioral advertising. To the contrary, CJEU jurisprudence offers important signposts that may help to develop a well-functioning transparency system under Articles 24 and 30 DSA.

In *L'Oréal/Bellure*, the CJEU used the terms "parasitism" and "free-riding" as synonyms for acts taking unfair advantage of the distinctive character or the repute of a mark with a reputation.[54] The Court explained that this concept of infringement related "not to the detriment caused to the mark but to the advantage taken by the third party as a result of the use of the identical or similar sign."[55] In particular, it covered "cases where, by reason of a transfer of the image of the mark or of the characteristics which it projects to the goods identified by the iden-

---

[51]   Cf. Ansgar Ohly, *supra* note 43, 780; Nicole van de Laan, "Die markenrechtliche Lage des Keyword Advertising," in J. Taeger (ed.), *Digitale Evolution: Herausforderungen für das Informations- und Medienrecht*, Oldenburg: Oldenburger Verlag für Wirtschaft, Informatik und Recht 2010, 597 (605), who refer to active information obligations in unfair competition law; Nicole van der Laan, "The Use of Trade Marks in Keyword Advertising: If Not Confusing, Yet Unfair?" in Nari Lee, Guido Westkamp, Annette Kur, and Ansgar Ohly (eds), *Property and Conduct: Convergences and Developments in Intellectual Property, Unfair Competition and Publicity*, Cheltenham: Edward Elgar Publishing, Chapter 10, Section 5.

[52]   Senftleben, *supra* note 43, 162–3.

[53]   As to the concept of indirect confusion, see CJEU, November 11, 1997, case C-251/95, Sabèl/Puma, paras 16–26. Cf. Kur and Senftleben, *supra* note 35, paras 5.127–5.130.

[54]   CJEU, June 18, 2009, case C-487/07, L'Oréal/Bellure, para. 41.

[55]   CJEU, ibid, para. 41.

tical or similar sign, there is clear exploitation on the coat-tails of the mark with a reputation."[56] More concretely, this means that the taking of unfair advantage will be found in cases where

> a third party attempts, through the use of a sign similar to a mark with a reputation, to ride on the coat-tails of that mark in order to benefit from its power of attraction, its reputation and its prestige, and to exploit, without paying any financial compensation and without being required to make efforts of his own in that regard, the marketing effort expended by the proprietor of that mark in order to create and maintain the image of that mark.[57]

At first glance, this general formula points towards a rather low threshold for a finding of actionable freeriding. In particular, it seems that a mere attempt to ride on the coat-tails of a mark with a reputation is sufficient to substantiate a trademark infringement claim. Would the involvement of brand owners in transparency policymaking in the field of online behavioral advertising, as proposed in Articles 24 and 30 DSA, thus have a chilling effect? Could it lead to a general ban on the use of brand-related consumer data without the brand owner's prior consent?

In fact, the CJEU concluded in the keyword advertising case *Interflora/Marks & Spencer* that in cases where a competitor of the proprietor of a trademark with a reputation selected that trademark as a keyword for triggering its own online advertising, the purpose of that use was indeed to take unfair advantage. The selection of the mark with a reputation was liable to create a situation in which a probably large number of internet users using the reputed mark as a search term would see the competitor's advertisement displayed on their screens.[58] When these internet users then purchased the competitor's product instead of that of the proprietor of the trademark, the competitor derived a real advantage from the distinctive character and repute of the trademark without paying any compensation.[59] Unfair freeriding was particularly likely in cases where the competitor used keyword advertising based on a mark with a reputation to offer imitations of the goods of the trademark proprietor.[60]

This finding of freeriding, however, did not readily imply a finding of infringement. By contrast, the Court pointed out that:

> where the advertisement displayed on the internet on the basis of a keyword corresponding to a trade mark with a reputation puts forward—without offering a mere imitation of the goods or services of the proprietor of that trade mark, without causing dilution or tarnishment and without, moreover, adversely affecting the functions of the trade mark concerned—an alternative to the goods or services of the proprietor of the trade mark with a reputation, it must be concluded that such use falls, as a rule, within the ambit of fair competition in the sector for the goods or services concerned and is thus not without "due cause."[61]

Hence, the CJEU not only established a due cause defense[62] for the purpose of informing consumers about an alternative offer in the marketplace but also developed three factors

---

[56]   CJEU, ibid, para. 41.
[57]   CJEU, ibid, para. 49.
[58]   CJEU, September 22, 2011, case C-323/09, Interflora/Marks & Spencer, para. 86.
[59]   CJEU, ibid, paras 87–88.
[60]   CJEU, ibid, para. 90.
[61]   CJEU, ibid, para. 91.
[62]   Article 9(2)(c) EUTMR; Article 10(2)(c) TMD. For a discussion of the open-ended due cause defence in EU trademark law, see Kur and Senftleben, *supra* note 35, paras 5.250–5.272; Martin R.F.

to be taken into account in this context, namely whether the defendant (1) offered a mere imitation of the goods or services of the trademark proprietor; (2) damaged the trademark by causing harm to its distinctive character (dilution or blurring) or repute (tarnishment);[63] (3) made use that adversely affects the functions of the trademark. The emergence of these due cause factors in the keyword advertising case *Interflora/Marks & Spencer* reflects the need to balance trademark owner interests against the interests of competitors, including freedom of competition and freedom of commercial expression.[64] The CJEU is prepared to employ the due cause defense as a tool to outweigh the broad grant of protection against freeriding.[65] The evolution of a specific due cause defense in *Interflora/Marks & Spencer* shows that the broad grant of protection in the area of freeriding need not be the last word when it comes to use that enhances fair competition and consumer information.

5.   TRUST IN AI-DRIVEN, BRAND-BASED COMMUNICATION

The *Interflora/Marks & Spencer* decision—more specifically, the insight that the trademark system must offer room for informing consumers about alternative offers in the marketplace—can play a crucial role in the further development of the transparency obligations that have been proposed in Articles 24 and 30 DSA. As Helberger, Huh, and colleagues point out in their analysis of the discussion surrounding new transparency obligations in the field of online behavioral advertising: "[t]his transparency requirement has been commonly dreaded by the industry as it expects such transparency to have negative impacts on computational advertising

---

Senftleben, "The Perfect Match: Civil Law Judges and Open-Ended Fair Use Provisions," *American University International Law Review* 33 (2017), 231 (256–65); Vincenzo Di Cataldo, "The Trade Mark with a Reputation in EU Law – Some Remarks on the Negative Condition 'Without Due Cause'," *International Review of Intellectual Property and Competition Law* 42 (2011), 833.

[63]   For a more detailed discussion of these different forms of harm, see Martin R.F. Senftleben and Femke van Horen, "The Siren Song of the Subtle Copycat: Aligning EU Trade Mark Law with New Insights from Consumer Research," *The Trademark Reporter* 111 (2021), 739 (750–6); Kur and Senftleben, *supra* note 35, paras 5.231–5.244.

[64]   As to the need to reconcile trademark protection with these fundamental freedoms, see Martin R.F. Senftleben, Lionel Bently et al., "The Recommendation on Measures to Safeguard Freedom of Expression and Undistorted Competition: Guiding Principles for the Further Development of EU Trade Mark Law," *European Intellectual Property Review* 37 (2015), 337–43. Cf. Łukasz Żelechowski, "Invoking Freedom of Expression and Freedom of Competition in Trade Mark Infringement Disputes: Legal Mechanisms for Striking a Balance," *ERA Forum* 19 (2018), 115 (115–35); Martin R.F. Senftleben, "Free Signs and Free Use: How to Offer Room for Freedom of Expression within the Trademark System," in C. Geiger (ed.), *Research Handbook on Human Rights and Intellectual Property*, Cheltenham: Edward Elgar Publishing 2015, 354; Lisa P. Ramsey and Jens Schovsbo, "Mechanisms for Limiting Trade Mark Rights to Further Competition and Free Speech," *International Review of Intellectual Property and Competition Law* 44 (2013), 671; Ilanah Simon Fhima, "Trade Marks and Free Speech," *International Review of Intellectual Property and Competition Law* 44 (2013), 293; Wolfgang Sakulin, *Trademark Protection and Freedom of Expression – An Inquiry into the Conflict between Trademark Rights and Freedom of Expression under European Law*, The Hague/London/New York: Kluwer Law International 2010 (247–82); Robert Burrell and Dev Gangjee, "Trade Marks and Freedom of Expression: A Call for Caution," *International Review of Intellectual Property and Competition Law* 41 (2010), 544.

[65]   Kur and Senftleben, *supra* note 35, paras 5.261–5.262.

effects and effectiveness, and to lead to massive rejection of data-driven advertising by consumers, thus substantially distorting the computational advertising ecosystem."[66]

Exploring consumer reactions to the use of behavioral data in AI-driven online advertising, Sophie Boerman, Sanne Kruikemeier, and Frederik Zuiderveen Borgesius identified a whole spectrum of negative consumer perceptions, ranging from privacy concerns and feelings of vulnerability and intrusiveness to more general ad-skepticism and doubts about the fairness of data use.[67] Consumers may perceive personalized behavioral advertising as "creepy marketing."[68] This research gives rise to the question whether transparency information that confirms the extensive use of behavioral data implies the risk of doing more harm than good. Will the new transparency obligations in Article 24 and 30 DSA thwart the evolution of promising new marketing technologies? Are they likely to frustrate the remarkable potential of online behavioral advertising to enhance consumer knowledge and consumer choice by providing consumers with useful, tailor-made information about offers in the marketplace that appear most relevant in the light of personal interests and characteristics that can be deduced from psychographic data?

As Boerman, Kruikemeier, and Zuiderveen Borgesius point out, it is possible to avert this undesirable result. If the discussion about Article 24 and 30 DSA leads to a legal framework that ensures sufficient trust in personalized marketing messages, in particular trust resulting from the reliability and usefulness of tailor-made information about products and services, the introduction of new transparency obligations can lead to a well-functioning computational advertising system which consumers are willing to accept: "research has shown that privacy concerns and trust play important roles in consumer acceptance and the effectiveness of [online behavioral advertising]. For instance, more trusted retailers can increase the perceived usefulness of their ads by developing ads that reflect consumers' interests in a complete way."[69]

As an example of trust-enhancing measures, Boerman, Kruikemeier, and Zuiderveen Borgesius mention the use of a "privacy trustmark" that would symbolize and confirm the involvement of the certified website in a program that protects consumer privacy.[70] The described keyword advertising debate sheds light on further options. Besides compliance with privacy and personal data protection standards, the market transparency rationale in trademark law and the insight that trademark protection must be reconciled with competitors' freedom of competition and freedom of commercial expression offer important additional signposts. Using these principles as a compass, it becomes possible to devise a regulatory framework that makes AI-driven, personalized advertising more helpful and more beneficial for consumers.

---

[66]   Helberger, Huh et al., *supra* note 9, 386.

[67]   Boerman, Kruikemeier, and Zuiderveen Borgesius, *supra* note 14, 365 and 368–9. Cf. Finn and Wadhwa, *supra* note 18, 26–7.

[68]   Robert S. Moore, Melissa L. Moore, Kevin J. Shanahan, and Britney Mack, "Creepy Marketing: Three Dimensions of Perceived Excessive Online Privacy Violation," *Marketing Management* 25 (2015), 42–53.

[69]   Boerman, Kruikemeier, and Zuiderveen Borgesius, *supra* note 14, 369, referring to Alexander Bleier and Maik Eisenbeiss, "The Importance of Trust for Personalized Online Advertising," *Journal of Retailing* 91 (2015), 390–409.

[70]   Boerman, Kruikemeier, and Zuiderveen Borgesius, *supra* note 14, 369. Cf. Andrea J. Stanaland, May O. Lwin, and Anthony D. Miyazaki, "Online Privacy Trustmarks," *Journal of Advertising Research* 51 (2011), 511–23.

Hence, trademark law and policy can contribute substantially to consumer acceptance. In the keyword advertising debate, the concern to frustrate the evolution of promising and useful new ways of advertising that are capable of reducing consumer search costs played a crucial role as well.[71] Against this background, Graeme Dinwoodie and Mark Janis proposed the adoption of specific conditions which providers of keyword advertising services should fulfil to escape liability for trademark infringement:

> For example, search engines might be required to present disclaimers on search results pages, to disclose information about search methodology, to differentiate clearly between organic and sponsored search results, or when put on notice of allegedly infringing activity, to de-index the infringing webpage. The goal is to develop conditions that oblige search engines to present information accurately and transparently, without imposing costs so high as to thwart innovation or implicate other social objectives such as privacy.[72]

Considering the described outcome of the CJEU ruling in *Interflora/Marks & Spencer*, it can be added that, apart from confirming the obligation to police and prevent the advertising of mere imitations,[73] trademark law also provides important guidelines as to the diversity of offers that should be brought to the attention of consumers. Instead of limiting the spectrum of products and services to those which consumers have explored previously (as evinced by browsing history, search requests, and online purchases), online behavioral advertising should be designed in a way that offers providers of alternative products and services sufficient opportunities to inform consumers about their alternative offers. In other words, previous online behavior concerning brand A should lead to the display of personalized messages covering not only brand A but also alternative offers made by brands B and C. In this way, AI-driven personalized advertising can enhance consumer information about available offers, broaden the spectrum of choices that consumers consider before taking a decision, reduce search costs for alternatives outside the bubble of personalized marketing messages, and contribute to market transparency and effective competition. The display of information about alternative offers in compliance with the *Interflora* criteria[74] offers an attractive avenue to demonstrate the added value and usefulness of targeted, personalized advertising based on behavioral consumer data. As a result, consumers can experience the benefits and advantages of the new, AI-driven advertising paradigm.

Trademark law can thus constitute an important ingredient in the recipe for more trustworthy online behavioral advertising. It prevents the misuse of new advertising techniques to present counterfeit offers. It also bans advertising messages that would damage the original brand which consumers have explored in previous browsing, search, and online shopping sessions. Information on alternative offers is reduced to what can be deemed fair and useful in the light of trademark protection standards. To achieve this goal of trust-enhancing, brand-related rules for online behavioral advertising, however, it is necessary to interpret and develop Articles 24 and 30 DSA in a way that gives trademark proprietors and their competitors access to transparency information. To avoid inroads into personal data protection, this information

---

[71]   Graeme B. Dinwoodie and Mark D. Janis, "Confusion over Use: Contextualism in Trademark Law," *Iowa Law Review* 92 (2007), 1597 (1664–5).

[72]   Dinwoodie and Janis, *supra* note 71, 1665–6.

[73]   CJEU, case C-323/09, *Interflora/Marks & Spencer*, para. 91.

[74]   CJEU, ibid, para. 91.

should be reduced to anonymized, generic data, such as the mere fact that a search for brand A has taken place. This information can then trigger marketing messages relating not only to brand A products but also to brand B and C alternatives.

6.   CONCLUSION

The discussion on new transparency obligations in the area of online behavioral advertising should not be limited to the issue of consumer information and consumer empowerment. To devise a regulatory framework capable of counterbalancing chilling effects of transparency information—in particular privacy concerns and feelings of vulnerability and intrusiveness— it is advisable to adopt rules that make beneficial effects of AI-driven, personalized advertising visible to consumers. Trademark law—and the involvement of trademark owners and their competitors in the debate—can play an important role in this context. Lessons from trademark law can pave the way for the use of consumer data to generate beneficial, reliable and useful marketing information. If applying insights from the keyword advertising debate to online behavioral advertising, transparency rules can evolve that enhance consumer information about alternative offers in the marketplace, broaden the spectrum of consumer choice, reduce search costs, and contribute to market transparency and effective competition. By ensuring compliance with the rules and rationales of trademark law, transparency legislation can enhance benefits for consumers and strengthen trust in AI-driven personalized advertising.

17. A quotidian revolution: artificial intelligence and trade mark law

Dev S. Gangjee[1]

1. INTRODUCTION: SCALING UP

In a relatively subtle, yet profoundly impactful way, artificial intelligence (AI) algorithms have made considerable inroads into the everyday practice of trade mark law. As this chapter will describe, the appeal of this technology lies in its ability to keep pace with the high-pressure hosepipe of trade mark applications and the ever-growing corpus of registered trade marks globally. According to the World Intellectual Property Organization (WIPO), an 'estimated 13.4 million trademark applications were filed worldwide in 2020. This is almost 1.9 million more than filed in 2019 and represents an increase of 16.5% on the year.'[2] This must be viewed against the backdrop of existing rights. 'In 2020, there were an estimated 64.4 million active trademark registrations at 149 IP offices worldwide.'[3] More marks mean more registrability assessments and more conflicts. At this scale, it is increasingly challenging, if not altogether impossible, for any comprehensive assessment to be made by human experts in major filing jurisdictions. AI algorithms are therefore being used to assist applicants when registering marks, by flagging obstacles to registration or suggesting ways in which to streamline applications, thereby increasing their chances of success. They are also being used by registries when examining marks, to appropriately classify and assess them. One example is where AI software assigns design codes to figurative marks with graphical elements, such that they can be more consistently catalogued as the basis for future comparisons. Another important domain is identifying conflicts between new applications and prior trade mark rights. Natural language-processing algorithms decipher the semantic content of word marks to assess whether meanings are similar, while image processing algorithms compare the visual similarity of logos, producing increasingly relevant results. Private service providers who offer mark clearance services (prior to filing) or watching services (identifying conflicts after registration) have been at the forefront of these technological developments. Finally, AI is entering the enforcement space, where it is used to identify unauthorised uses of marks online, including on social media.

This new technology is often presented as merely assisting with the implementation of existing rules and doctrines of trade mark law. It appears to be business as usual, just done more efficiently. This chapter sets out to challenge this assumption, by identifying some of the

---

[1] I am grateful to Anke Moerland, Martin Senftleben, Daniel Seng and participants at the IGIR-IViR-OIPRC Workshop on Trade Mark Law and Artificial Intelligence (Oct 2021), as well as colleagues at the IP Office Singapore (IPOS), for comments on various aspects of this chapter. The usual caveat applies. The title of this chapter draws inspiration from C.L. Novetzke, *The Quotidian Revolution: Vernacularization, Religion, and the Premodern Public Sphere in India* (2016).
[2] WIPO, WORLD INTELLECTUAL PROPERTY INDICATORS 76 (2021).
[3] Ibid at 84.

more subtle implications and ripple effects of this transformation of the everyday working of trade mark law – at scale – in the registration and enforcement domains. Section 2 describes recent policy initiatives which have sought to map the issues arising at the trade mark–AI interface. One emerging theme is that where AI is used to influence consumer purchasing decisions, either by providing consumers with better quality information or else by unfairly shaping (or entirely displacing) consumer decision making, core trade mark doctrines such as the average consumer or the likelihood of confusion test may need to be revisited. Since AI can lead to better-informed consumer decisions or, conversely, generate skewed decisions, there is considerable interest in how this will affect trade mark infringement tests. However, the implications for registration and enforcement – where decision making is already being influenced by algorithms at scale – are relatively neglected. Consequently, Section 3 outlines the myriad ways in which AI is being incorporated into the trade mark registration ecosystem, unearthing certain doctrinal questions that may not appear obvious at first glance. Section 4 surveys the extent to which algorithms are being used for trade mark enforcement. While there is a substantial literature on the algorithmic enforcement of copyright, there has been remarkably little attention paid to similar developments, and related concerns, in the trade mark space.[4] The aim here is to demonstrate how the technology is shifting goalposts and setting new default options within seemingly familiar procedures or tests. Section 5 concludes.

2.   POLICY INITIATIVES TO MAP EMERGING ISSUES

AI is 'a discipline of computer science that is aimed at developing machines and systems that can carry out tasks considered to require human intelligence, with limited or no human intervention'.[5] Within this broad field, various forms of machine learning (ML) are most relevant for trade mark applications. ML 'refers to computer algorithms that detect patterns in data and automatically improve their own performance over time'.[6] It is an umbrella term for a set of technologies which includes neural networks and deep learning approaches. Recent successes are in part attributable to the advent of big data and improved computing power. Improved data flows form the basis for better-quality ML, characterised as a 'technology that allows systems to learn directly from examples, data, and experience'.[7] The paradigm shift from expert systems based on logic-driven or deductive approaches to machine learning, which inductively identifies relationships existing in data, underpins many of the recent developments relevant for trade mark law.

---

4   A notable exception is Daniel Seng, *Detecting and Prosecuting IP Infringement with AI: Can the AI Genie Repulse the Forty Counterfeit Thieves of Alibaba? in* ARTIFICIAL INTELLIGENCE AND INTELLECTUAL PROPERTY 292 (Jyh-An Lee, Reto Hilty & Kung-Chung Liu eds, 2019).

5   WIPO, REVISED ISSUES PAPER ON INTELLECTUAL PROPERTY AND ARTIFICIAL INTELLIGENCE ¶ 11 (2020) (WIPO/IP/AI/2/GE/20/1 REV.) [hereinafter *Revised Issues Paper*]; *see also* Harry Surden, *Artificial Intelligence and Law: An Overview*, 35 GA. ST. U. L. REV. 1305 (2019) (emphasising the ability of AI to perform tasks considered to require human intelligence).

6   Harry Surden, *Machine Learning and Law: An Overview in* RESEARCH HANDBOOK ON BIG DATA LAW 171 (Roland Vogl ed., 2021).

7   ROYAL SOCIETY, MACHINE LEARNING: THE POWER AND PROMISE OF COMPUTERS THAT LEARN BY EXAMPLE 16 (2017).

While enjoying far less prominence than copyright or patent issues in relation to AI,[8] the trade mark–ML interface has been explored in recent policy initiatives. In 2019, WIPO took the lead in mapping out issues in relation to trade mark law.[9] In the same year, the United States Patent and Trademark Office (USPTO) issued a request for comments on IP protection for AI innovation, which included a trade mark component.[10] Contemporaneously, the Administrative Conference of the US commissioned a report looking into how AI was being used across several federal administrative agencies, including the USPTO.[11] On the one hand, AI offers 'the potential to reduce the cost of core governance functions, improve the quality of decisions, and unleash the power of administrative data, thereby making government performance more efficient and effective'.[12] On the other hand, this development raises 'questions about the proper design of algorithms and user interfaces, the respective scope of human and machine decision-making, the boundaries between public actions and private contracting, [an agency's] own capacity to learn over time using AI, and whether the use of AI is even permitted'.[13] More recently, the United Kingdom's Intellectual Property Office (UK IPO) ran a consultation which included a specific trade mark section, considering primarily infringement-related issues and whether the existing legal tools of trade law can adapt.[14]

One recurrent theme across these consultations focuses on the potential for algorithms to affect consumer purchasing decisions in ways that can lead to trade mark infringement. The central idea is neatly captured by Lee Curtis: 'Trade mark law at its heart concerns itself with how goods and services are purchased, and as AI is impacting the purchasing process, it therefore by definition is impacting trade mark law.'[15] The WIPO issues paper elaborates on this transformation:

> Trade marks are intended to distinguish the origin of goods and services and to prevent consumer confusion. Current trade mark law is therefore based on concepts of human perceptions and recollection both for determining whether a trademark is registrable and whether it is infringed [... However the] emergence of AI and e-commerce platforms is changing the nature of the process of buying goods

---

[8]   See the contributions by Gervais as well as those in Parts II and IV of this volume.

[9]   WIPO, REVISED ISSUES PAPER, *supra* note 5; WIPO, SUMMARY OF SECOND AND THIRD SESSIONS – FLOOR DISCUSSIONS ¶ 73–9 (2021) (WIPO/IP/AI/3/GE/20/INF/5) [hereinafter *Summary of Sessions*]. All submissions to the issues paper can be accessed at: www.wipo.int/about-ip/en/artificial_intelligence/conversation.html.

[10]   REQUEST FOR COMMENTS ON INTELLECTUAL PROPERTY PROTECTION FOR ARTIFICIAL INTELLIGENCE INNOVATION 84 Fed. Reg. 58141 (2019) (Questions 7 and 8). The individual responses are available at: www.uspto.gov/initiatives/artificial-intelligence/notices-artificial-intelligence-non-patent-related.   For the report summarising the comments received, *see* USPTO, PUBLIC VIEWS ON ARTIFICIAL INTELLIGENCE AND INTELLECTUAL PROPERTY POLICY 30–6 (2020) [hereinafter *Public Views on AI*].

[11]   DANIEL FREEMAN ENGSTROM ET AL., GOVERNMENT BY ALGORITHM: ARTIFICIAL INTELLIGENCE IN FEDERAL ADMINISTRATIVE AGENCIES (2020).

[12]   Ibid at 6.

[13]   Ibid.

[14]   UK IPO, ARTIFICIAL INTELLIGENCE CALL FOR VIEWS: TRADE MARKS (2020) (*available at* www.gov.uk/government/consultations/artificial-intelligence-and-intellectual-property-call-for-views/artificial-intelligence-call-for-views-trade-marks). The Government subsequently published a response to the views expressed: GOVERNMENT RESPONSE TO CALL FOR VIEWS ON AI AND IP (2021) (*available at* www.gov.uk/government/consultations/artificial-intelligence-and-intellectual-property-call-for-views/government-response-to-call-for-views-on-artificial-intelligence-and-intellectual-property) [hereinafter *Government Response*].

[15]   Lee Curtis, written response to the WIPO issues paper, available at the link *supra* note 9.

and services… AI assistants, search engines, customer service bots and online marketplaces play an important role in shaping the consumer decision-making process. The way that a consumer interacts with the online marketplace through AI may result in the presentation of only a limited number of brands to a consumer, or other alterations in the way that consumers make product selections.[16]

One way in which the interactive purchasing process has already changed is through voice search, which calls for a corresponding rebalancing of infringement tests that otherwise assess for visual, conceptual and phonetic similarity between marks.[17] Another possibility is that where consumers are provided with better quality information by virtual shopping assistants, the emphasis will shift from point of sale confusion analysis to post-sale confusion, since the actual purchaser will not be confused but others who see the product later on might be.[18] These changes to the shopping process also raise the issue of who should bear the responsibility if algorithms unfairly skew consumer decision-making processes, by artificially constraining choice or prioritising sponsored results without disclosing this.[19] Virtual shopping assistants such as Alexa acting as gatekeepers, and the potential for biased recommendations, are recurring concerns.[20] Since algorithms lack legal personhood, they cannot directly be held liable and an appropriate defendant should be identified.[21] This engages principles of intermediary or accessory liability.[22] The same set of concerns is evident in the USPTO consultation, where doubts have been expressed as to the applicability of case law developed in the context of intermediaries such as internet service providers or keyword advertising services, which may not directly map on to new forms of persuasive algorithms.[23] The infringement implications for AI which engages in targeted advertising or steers the purchasing process are being mapped in some of the pioneering scholarship in this area.[24]

---

[16]   WIPO, Revised Issues Paper, *supra* note 5, at ¶ 37-38.

[17]   UK IPO, Government Response, *supra* note 14 ('Respondents suggested that, as voice assistant technologies develop further, the phonetic and aural comparison of marks may play a more important factor in the future').

[18]   USPTO, Public Views on AI, *supra* note 10, at 34. *See also* UK IPO, Government Response, *supra* note 14 (indicating 'the potential for infringement cases to shift from confusion at initial point of sale towards an increased emphasis on post-sale confusion or harm'). Post-sale confusion is a speculative and controversial form of harm because it hinges on a subsequent, oftentimes casual encounter with a product, when consumer decision making is not engaged. It collapses into a wonderment ('maybe there's a connection but I'm not sure') standard. *See* Kal Raustiala & Christopher Jon Sprigman, *Commentary: Rethinking Post-sale Confusion* 108 Trademark Rep. 881 (2018).

[19]   WIPO, Summary of Sessions, *supra* note 9, at ¶ [73]–[74].

[20]   Ibid at ¶ [74]–[76].

[21]   UK IPO, Government Response, *supra* n 14 ('While respondents believed that the actions of AI may infringe a trade mark and that liability lies with a legal person, there were various suggestions regarding who this legal person may be. These included the operator or user of the AI, the provider of data or brand owners').

[22]   WIPO, Summary of Sessions, *supra* note 9, at ¶ [77]–[78]; USPTO, Public Views on AI, *supra* note 10, at 34–5.

[23]   USPTO, Public Views on AI, *supra* note 9, at 33.

[24]   *See* Lee Curtis & Rachel Platts, *AI is Coming and It Will Change Trade Mark Law*, Managing IP 9 (2017) (*available at* www.hgf.com/wp-content/uploads/2020/07/09-13-AI.pdf); Curtis & Platts, '*Alexa, What's the Impact of AI on Trade Mark Law?*' Managing IP 43 (2019); Michael Grynberg, *AI and the 'Death of Trademark'*, 108 Ky L.J. 199 (2019–20); Jurgita Randakevičiūtė-Alpman, *The Role of Trademarks on Online Retail Platforms: EU Trademark Law Perspective* 70 GRUR Intl 633 (2021); Rob Batty, *Trade Mark Infringement and Artificial Intelligence*, 26 N.Z. Bus. L. Q. 137 (2022);

These policy consultations have also thrown up a range of issues relating to how ML enhances efficiency and consistency in routine processes. For example, when prosecuting a trade mark application, to what extent do algorithms determine the success or failure of the application? Which kinds of decision making are appropriate for this technology? Is there always a degree of human oversight, or should other modes of accountability be designed into these systems?[25] Should there be transitional testing phases, where the performance of the AI is assessed? How reliable or jurisdictionally appropriate (where datasets are imported) is the training data being used by ML algorithms? Finally, how transparent is the use of AI decision making to applicants or users of registry services?[26] These questions need to be addressed because the technology is already being embraced. WIPO has an index of IP office initiatives where the adoption of this technology is being documented.[27] Illustratively, the European Union Intellectual Property Office (EUIPO) has embarked on an ambitious artificial intelligence implementation programme, which seeks to further develop its current AI technology 'in a wide variety of business cases: formalities, classification, image search, goods and services comparison and chatbots. [The project] will make use of Machine Learning, NLP and Deep Learning techniques.'[28] National and regional IP offices also continue to collaborate on developing new AI technology which suits the needs of users and examiners.[29]

This chapter therefore consciously focuses on the practical and procedural applications of AI by key institutional actors: trade mark registries, search and watching agencies and those offering online enforcement solutions. These actors routinely apply ML algorithms at scale, on an everyday basis, affecting tens of thousands of trade mark clearance searches, applications and registrations annually. These developments are unobtrusively changing the practice of trade mark law, from the ground up. Behind these seemingly technical processes lie interesting substantive law questions. It is a worthwhile endeavour to explore this paradigm shift resulting from the adoption of machine learning technologies.[30]

Hiroko Onishi, *'We will still be Confused!' Online Shopping and Trade Mark Law in the AI Era*, 43 EUR. INTELL. PROP. REV. 397 (2021). In this volume, see the contributions by Martin Senftleben, *Trademark Law, AI-Driven Behavioural Advertising and the Digital Services Act: Towards Source and Parameter Transparency for Consumers, Brand Owners and Competitors,* and Anke Moerland, *Online Shopping with Artificial Intelligence: What Role to play for Trade Marks?*

25   WIPO, REVISED ISSUES PAPER, *supra* note 5, at 14–15.

26   WIPO, SUMMARY OF SESSIONS, *supra* note 9, at ¶ [91]–[99].

27   WIPO, INDEX OF AI INITIATIVES IN IP OFFICES (*available at* www.wipo.int/about-ip/en/artificial _intelligence/search.jsp). The Fifth Session of WIPO's Conversation on Intellectual Property (IP) and Frontier Technologies (April 2022) reviews IP office experiences to date.

28   EUIPO, IPINNOVATION GOAL 3.2: EVOLVING WITH THE DIGITAL ERA – ARTIFICIAL INTELLIGENCE IMPLEMENTATION (July 2020 to June 2025) (*available at* https://euipo.europa.eu/ohimportal/en/strategic -drivers/ipinnovation).

29   *See, for example,* EUIPO, EUIPO-KIPO EXCHANGE ON NEW TECHNOLOGIES AND AI (*available at* https://euipo.europa.eu/ohimportal/en/news/-/action/view/8412308).

30   The more limited body of work on this aspect includes: Dev Gangjee, *Eye, Robot: Artificial Intelligence and Trade Mark Registers*, *in* TRANSITION AND COHERENCE IN INTELLECTUAL PROPERTY LAW 174 (Niklas Bruun, Graeme B. Dinwoodie, Marianne Levin & Ansgar Ohly eds, 2020); Anke Moerland & Conrado Freitas, *Artificial Intelligence and Trade Mark Assessment, in* Lee, Hilty & Liu, ARTIFICIAL INTELLIGENCE AND INTELLECTUAL PROPERTY, *supra* note 4, at 266; Sonia K. Katyal and Aniket Kesari, *Trademark Search, Artificial Intelligence and the Role of the Private Sector*, 35 BERKELEY TECH. L.J. 501 (2021) [hereinafter *The Role of the Private Sector*].

3.   RECALIBRATING REGISTRATION

This section focuses on the major initiatives which are being implemented across several registries. However, certain programmes specific to a single registry deserve a brief mention because of their innovative potential. The EUIPO has invested heavily in machine translation technology, in order to make goods and services specifications available in a range of European languages while also providing translated versions of its examiner and appellate tribunal decisions.[31] This body of case law has been used as training data for applications predicting outcomes where marks are at risk of conflict.[32] *Rocketeer* is one such product, which uses a dataset of more than 10,000 EU trade mark cases to rapidly predict outcomes of trade mark conflicts.[33] Where a conflict has been identified between a mark being applied for and a prior registered mark, the software tool predicts the probability of an outcome if an EU tribunal were to decide that conflict, claiming over 90 per cent accuracy. The software also reveals the data based on which it has made the prediction, thereby providing contextual pointers to the arguments which will assist if the application proceeds.[34] This highlights an important design requirement for such predictive software – it cannot be restricted to delivering a percentage outcome (an 85 per cent chance of a win) but needs to explain why this is likely, since applicants engage with registries on the basis of reasoned arguments, finding analogies and distinguishing precedents. Improvements in machine translation therefore have direct implications for AI-driven initiatives attempting to predict outcomes in trade mark disputes. Another interesting development relates to fraud detection algorithms at the US registry. US trade mark law requires that a mark be used in commerce as a precondition for registration. Applicants prove that they have met this requirement by submitting photographic specimens of their use of the mark in commerce. Unfortunately, an appreciable number of applications contain fraudulent specimens of use – often digitally altered product photos, advertising samples or invoices – which undermines the integrity of the trade mark register.[35] The USPTO has been testing 'solutions for false specimen detection capabilities using a software program, which was integrated on December 1, 2020 into the agency's efforts to identify digitally manipulated specimens of use or mock-ups of web pages'.[36] While these two examples illustrate the range of applications being considered, the following developments are being more widely adopted.

---

[31]   EUIPO, Improved Machine Translation in eSearch Case Law (17 October 2019) (*available at* https://euipo.europa.eu/ohimportal/en/key-user-newsflash/-/asset_publisher/dIGJZDH66W8B/content/improved-machine-translation-in-esearch-case-law/).

[32]   Samuel Dahan et al., *Analytics and EU Courts: The Case of Trademark Disputes, in* The Changing European Union: A Critical View on the Role of the Courts (Tamara Capeta and Iris Goldner Lang eds., 2022) (forthcoming) (*available at*: https://papers.ssrn.com/sol3/papers.cfm?abstract_id=3786069).

[33]   *Available at* https://www.simmons-simmons.com/en/products/trademark-rocketeer.

[34]   Dan Currell, *Legal's AI Rocket Ship Will Be Manned*, Legal Evolution (9 May 2021) (*available at* www.legalevolution.org/2021/05/legals-ai-rocket-ship-will-be-manned-book-review-232/).

[35]   The scale of the problem is empirically assessed and algorithmic solutions are tested in Barton Beebe & Jeanne C. Fromer, *Fake Trademark Specimens: An Empirical Analysis,* 121 Colum. L. Rev. F. 217 (2020).

[36]   Drew Hirshfeld, *Artificial Intelligence Tools at the USPTO*, USPTO Director's Forum Blog (18 March 2021) (*available at* www.uspto.gov/blog/director/entry/artificial-intelligence-tools-at-the).

3.1   Streamlining Goods and Services

AI algorithms are increasingly used to recommend classes for goods and services contained in trade mark applications. Along with the sign being claimed as a mark, the trade mark application also indicates the goods and services identified by that sign.[37] This reflects commercial practice: the Nike 'swoosh' logo is applied to athletic footwear, sports clothing and accessories. The international reference point is the Nice Classification system, maintained by WIPO, which consists of a list of headings of 34 classes of goods and 11 classes of services as well as an alphabetical list of goods or services in each class.[38] Historically, there has been no mandatory form or prescribed terminology for specifying these goods and services. Applicants are free to choose, based on their own commercial preferences. However, the terms selected by an applicant are subsequently slotted into the relevant classification taxonomy adopted by the trade mark registry. Thus, an applicant selling remote controlled aerial vehicles might specify 'toy drones' on the form but will have to identify Class 28 ('Games and Playthings') of the Nice Classification as the relevant class. Accuracy is important here. One of the primary purposes of bureaucratic classification is to enable efficient searching by registries and third parties for conflicting prior marks in relation to identical or similar goods. Getting this right therefore matters, and several registries have been developing tools to assist applicants with this process.

In this regard, TMClass has emerged as a widely used resource.[39] It is a search tool which can access a harmonised database of more than 78,000 terms for goods and services contributed by participating trade mark registries. When an applicant enters a product description, such as 'toy drone', the tool (i) suggests appropriate terminology which has been pre-vetted and exists within the database as a harmonised term ('Drones [toys]'), along with (ii) suggesting relevant classes of goods and services to file it under (class 28 for toys appears at the top of the list), displayed under a more intuitively familiar taxonomy tree. Participating offices can propose new terms for creation according to market needs and propose the deletion of terms that have become outdated over time. While these suggestions are not mandatory, adopting them will improve the speed of examination and the chances of the application being accepted. WIPO has also developed a natural language-processing AI – the Madrid Goods and Services Manager – that is used to predict the most relevant Nice classifications, improving on the former text-search matching model.[40] The implications of harmonised terminology and improved natural language processing in the context of identifying conflicts is considered below.

---

[37]   *Chartered Institute of Patent Attorneys v Registrar of Trade Marks*, Case C-3-7/10 (IP TRANSLATOR) ECLI:EU:C:2011:784 (AG Bot), at ¶ [AG1] ('The two essential components of the registration of a trade mark are (a) the sign and (b) the goods and services which that sign is to designate. Each of those components makes it possible to define the precise subject-matter of the protection conferred by the registered trade mark on its proprietor').

[38]   *See Nice Classification* (*available at* www.wipo.int/classifications/nice/en/).

[39]   *Available at* https://euipo.europa.eu/ec2/.

[40]   Patrick Fiévet, *Artificial Intelligence applied to IPC and NICE Classifications*, WIPO (2018) (WIPO/IP/ITAI/GE/18/P18). *Available at* https://webaccess.wipo.int/mgs/

3.2   Assistance with Filing

Looking beyond assistance with goods and services classification, registries have developed more comprehensive tools, with individual applicants and SMEs in mind, to assist with the entire registration process. IP Australia has developed its Trade Mark Assist service, fronted by Alex, its virtual assistant.[41] On entering a proposed mark, the tool indicates whether prior similar marks exist on the Australian register and whether non-distinctiveness objections might apply to the sign (for example, the mark selected describes certain qualities of the underlying products too directly). It additionally proposes classes for goods and services, while estimating a filing fee. The EUIPO has also developed a software tool for assisting individual applicants who are unfamiliar with trade mark law.[42] The IP Office of Singapore (IPOS) has a Go Mobile application, which includes not just word searches but also image-searching functionality when comparing the mark being applied for with prior conflicting marks.[43] It extends beyond marks, with a range of additional conflict checks, covering prior business names, domain names and social media handles, under the label of a complete 'brand search'. This transition to value-added services is also evident in the offerings of private service providers. Naming Matters is one such provider. It checks for the availability of the applicant's mark across multiple selected jurisdictions, while also checking for social media handle availability and domain name availability.[44]

The UK IPO has recently developed a Pre-Apply tool, embedded within the application form.[45] This improves the chances of a successful registration by checking against certain absolute grounds of refusal, such as offensive words or protected official symbols, including flags or crests, as well as protected geographical indications, such as Scotch or Champagne. It also checks for some relative grounds, in the specific form of prior UK registered trade mark rights. There are already signs of efficiency gains:

> In the year since the IPO's trade mark pre-apply service was launched, the average number of trade mark applications rejected due to unsuitable Nice classification terms has dropped by 14% […] The IPO has seen a 70% drop in the length of goods and services lists since the service was launched. This means customers will have more suitable trade marks that are more likely to only protect the right goods and services, leaving them less open to challenge.[46]

These tools have the potential to democratise the application process and address at least some of the concerns that would arise where only those who are better resourced have access to the relevant technology. However, as Katyal and Kesari astutely observe, the extent to which the quality of such tools varies across registries, or between registries and private service provid-

---

[41]   *Available at* http://trademarks.business.gov.au/assist/welcome.

[42]   EUIPO, *EasyFiling – EUIPO's New e-Filing Form for Trade Marks, Designed Especially for SMEs* (18 Jan. 2021) (*available at* https://euipo.europa.eu/ohimportal/en/news/-/action/view/8472821).

[43]   *Available at* www.ipos.gov.sg/eservices/ipos-go.

[44]   *Available at* www.namingmatters.com. *See* the description in Jieun Kim et al., *Is Trademark the First Sparring Partner of AI?*' in PATENT ANALYTICS 175 (Jieun Kim et al., 2021).

[45]   *Available at* https://trademarks.ipo.gov.uk/ipo-apply.

[46]   UKIPO Press Release, *IPO's First AI-Powered Tool Improves Quality of TM Applications* (1 Nov. 2021) (*available at* www.gov.uk/government/news/ipos-first-ai-powered-tool-improves-quality-of-tm-applications).

ers, remains underexplored.[47] Another aspect, which may only manifest in the longer term, is how these AI assistants will change the nature (or volume) of the work of the trade mark attorney or agent professions, by identifying and eliminating more straightforward conflicts.[48]

3.3   Identifying Conflicts

Assessing the similarity of marks is at the heart of legal tests for (i) relative grounds of opposition, which allow the trade mark proprietor to oppose the registration of a similar subsequent mark (a registry-level conflict) and (ii) trade mark infringement, where that proprietor objects to a similar or identical sign being used in the marketplace by a third party (a real-world conflict).[49] The most widely used legal test considers whether the similarity of marks, when combined with the similarity of goods or services, is likely to cause confusion for relevant consumers of those products.[50] Marks are assessed in terms of their visual, aural/phonetic or conceptual similarity, also referred to as sight, sound and meaning analysis.[51] For complex or composite marks, which combine words and/or figurative elements, the comparison should consider each mark as a whole while also recognising the distinctive and dominant elements that consumers would notice.

Algorithms for assessing the similarity of marks can be distinguished based on the types of mark being compared. Relatively straightforward computerised text searches have been available for several decades.[52] In the past, these search systems employed 'text-based retrieval technology [… which] look[s] for trade marks that match some or all words in a query string text'.[53] One technique is approximate string-matching, based on the number of similar and dissimilar characters and word length. The fewer operations required to make the strings identical, the more similar they are – for example, 'love' and 'dove' would require only one change. This addresses the visual similarity component of word marks. Text search has improved over the years to incorporate phonetic analogies, synonyms and permutations of letters so

---

[47]   *See* Katyal & Kesari, THE ROLE OF THE PRIVATE SECTOR, *supra* note 30 (the authors tested the accuracy and relevance of the lists of conflicting marks produced by selected public and private service providers).

[48]   This is a topic of general interest. *See* MICHAEL LEGG & FELICITY BELL, ARTIFICIAL INTELLIGENCE AND THE LEGAL PROFESSION (2020); Richard Parnham, Mari Sako & John Armour, *AI-Assisted Lawtech: Its Impact on Law Firms* (University of Oxford White Paper, 2020).

[49]   This section draws on and updates analysis in Gangjee, *Eye, Robot, supra* note 30.

[50]   ILANAH FHIMA & DEV S. GANGJEE, THE CONFUSION TEST IN EUROPEAN TRADE MARK LAW (2019); JEROEN MUYLDERMANS & PAUL MAEYAERT, LIKELIHOOD OF CONFUSION IN TRADE MARK LAW (2019). *See also* RASMUS DALGAARD LAUSTSEN, THE AVERAGE CONSUMER IN CONFUSION-BASED DISPUTES IN EUROPEAN TRADEMARK LAW AND SIMILAR FICTIONS (2020).

[51]   USPTO, *Trade Mark Manual of Examining Procedure* (July 2021), at §1207.01(b) (Similarity of the Marks); EUIPO, *Guidelines for Examination of European Union Trade Marks,* Part C, §2, ch. 4 – Comparison of Signs (2021).

[52]   The history of computerisation and the pivotal role of the watching agency Compumark is detailed in Jose Bellido, *Towards a History of Trade Mark Watching,* 2015 INTELL. PROP. Q. 130.

[53]   Fatahiyah Mohd Anuara, Rossitza Setchia & Yu-Kun Lai, *A Conceptual Model of Trademark Retrieval Based on Conceptual Similarity,* 22 PROCEDIA COMPUTER SCIENCE 450, 451 (2013) [hereinafter *A Conceptual Model*]; Anuara, Setchia & Lai, *Semantic Retrieval of Trademarks Based on Conceptual Similarity,* 46 IEEE TRANSACTIONS ON SYSTEMS, MAN, AND CYBERNETICS: SYSTEMS 220 (2015).

that slightly modified marks are also returned in the search results.[54] Algorithms have been developed to assess the conceptual similarity between marks, on the basis of shared or even oppositional meanings. For example, the SyMSS approach within natural language processing calculates meaning similarity by combining both syntactic (based on structural and grammatical rules) and semantic (based on meaning) information obtained from a lexical database.[55] A simple text search will not flag up the semantic similarity between 'H_2O' and 'water'. On the other hand, signs which look visually similar may relate to different concepts. Homophones sound similar but have different meanings (steel versus steal) while homographs are spelled the same, but the context clarifies the difference in meaning (bass being a type of fish or the lowest frequencies in music). Capitalisation alone can produce significant changes: compare 'Polish' (the nationality) with 'polish' (for furniture or shoes). Today, search technology based on semantic or conceptual similarity considers synonyms or antonyms, comparable words in another language with similar meanings and so called 'lexical relations' (PINK LADY versus LADY IN ROSE).[56]

The second domain, which has seen very significant improvements in recent years, is image search. The technology has advanced to the point where a user can directly upload an image in a recognised file format such as JPG, PNG, GIF or TIFF and search for similar images within the relevant registry database. Both WIPO and EUIPO offer this facility.[57] National offices are actively incorporating this technology into the internal registry examination process.[58] A moment's reflection reveals some of the information processing challenges that need to be overcome. Figurative marks and logos 'are designed to have visual impact [...] consisting of multiple homogeneous elements, which may be closed regions, lines, or areas of texture. They may represent a given type of object (such as a dog or car) in stylised form, or consist purely of abstract patterns. They may be coloured or monochrome.'[59] Human observers consider shape to be the single most important feature of an image, but image structure (the layout of individual image elements) and semantic interpretation (the image of a tree evoking trees) are also relevant. Then there is the matter of identifying what counts as an image element – how granular does it get and why?[60] It rapidly becomes apparent that there are several, oftentimes subjectively prioritised, parameters according to which similarity might be assessed.

The most significant pre-AI response to these challenges is found in the creation of the International Classification of the Figurative Elements of Marks, also referred to as the Vienna

---

[54]   Caspar James Fall & Christophe Giraud-Carrier, *Searching Trademark Databases for Verbal Similarities*, 27 WORLD PATENT INFORMATION 135 (2005).

[55]   Jesus Oliva et al., *SyMSS: A Syntax-based Measure for Short-text Semantic Similarity*, 70 DATA & KNOWLEDGE ENGINEERING 390 (2011).

[56]   Anuara, Setchia & Lai, *A Conceptual Model, supra* note 53 at 453.

[57]   WIPO facilitates image searches in its Global Brand Database: www.wipo.int/branddb/en/. The EUIPO consolidates registration information via its TMView database, which combines the register of EU-wide European Union Trade Marks with that of 27 national EU member states as well as the WIPO database: www.tmdn.org/tmview/welcome.

[58]   WIPO, *Summary of the Replies to the Note on Applications of AI to IPO Administration* (8 Feb. 2018) (WIPO/IP/ITAI/GE/18/1) (referring to image search initiatives by the IPOs of Australia, Chile, China, Japan, Norway and Singapore as well as the EUIPO and WIPO).

[59]   Jan Schietse, John P. Eakins & Remco C. Veltkamp, *Practice and Challenges in Trademark Image Retrieval, PROCEEDINGS OF THE 6TH ACM INTERNATIONAL CONFERENCE ON IMAGE AND VIDEO RETRIEVAL* 1, 1 (2007).

[60]   Ibid.

Classification, administered by WIPO.[61] As matters presently stand, figurative marks are manually indexed by trade mark examiners, with codes or keywords being assigned to them.[62] The most prominent of these coding systems is the Vienna Classification, a hierarchical system proceeding from the general to the particular. It consists of categories, divisions and sections, each of which has been assigned a number. Figurative elements classified within a section are referred to by three numbers:

> the first, which may be any number from 1 to 29, denotes the category; the second, which may be any number from 1 to 19, the division; and the third, which may be any number from 1 to 30, the section. For instance, the representation of 'a little girl eating' [02.05.03] belongs to Category 2 (Human beings), Division 5 (Children), Main Section 3 (Girls).[63]

This results in more than 1300 different taxonomic categories. Matching the Vienna codes of a new application with those already in the registry database generates a list of similar figurative marks.

At present, there is an emphasis on using AI tools to assign Vienna classification codes more accurately and consistently. In 2020, WIPO released the Vienna Classification Assistant for figurative trade marks.[64] When users upload an image, all the relevant Vienna classification categories will be suggested with a relevance rating (of up to six stars for the most relevant). This approach has the advantage of using an existing classification system, where a corpus training data exists (past classifications by human examiners). It also generates results compatible with the procedural formalities of national regimes. Finally, it is advertised as a training tool for new examiners, to cross-check their assessments.

However, not all trade mark registries use the Vienna Classification system – it presently has 34 contracting parties – while the allocation of codes (or keywords in some systems) to figurative elements inevitably involves some subjectivity, with the attendant risk of leaving gaps.[65] Trade mark examination has conventionally been more of an art than a science, with subjective variations between examiners within the same registry a persistent concern.[66] This background helps to explain why recent advances in content-based image retrieval (CBIR) systems, which can be used to directly compare a target image to other images in a database, have been welcomed by trade mark registries and professionals:

---

[61]   *See* the Vienna Agreement Establishing an International Classification of the Figurative Elements of Marks, 1973. The Agreement entered into force on 9 August 1985. The current (eighth) edition has been available online since 2017 and in force from 1 January 2018 (www.wipo.int/classifications/vienna/en/).

[62]   For an example of a code-based system, see the USPTO Design Search Code Manual, available at http://tess2.uspto.gov/tmdb/dscm/index.htm.

[63]   *See* www.wipo.int/classifications/vienna/en/preface.html.

[64]   *Available at* www3.wipo.int/bnd-api/vienna-classification-assistant/.

[65]   WIPO, FUTURE DEVELOPMENT OF THE VIENNA CLASSIFICATION: QUESTIONNAIRE RESULTS 3 (3 Apr. 2019) (Although most participating registries were satisfied with the system, the following issued were raised: 'a number of Offices reported difficulties with the classification of colours. Codes that are over-used, as well as codes that are not used enough and are simply ignored also lead to an incomplete classification. Modernisation […] by adding new codes for commonly used figurative elements and for keeping pace with new technologies was also highlighted').

[66]   Michael D. Frakes & Melissa F. Wasserman, *Are There as Many Trademark Offices as Trademark Examiners?* 69 DUKE L.J. 1807 (2020) (utilising a dataset comprising more than 7.8 million US trade mark applications and discovering substantial heterogeneity in outcomes).

> CBIR is a method of extracting image features and transforming these visual features into specific mathematical vectors or matrices for further analysis... The system converts the query image input by the user into feature vectors that can express visual meaning and analyses the similarity between these feature vectors and the images in the database.[67]

The starting point has been to analyse an image pixel by pixel, identifying attributes and assigning numerical values to them, for subsequent comparison. Traditional ML models focused on so-called low-level image features, including colour, shape, texture and spatial layout (that is, what the image looks like). Current technology uses deep learning methods to extract semantic visual concepts (that is, what the image means). The search results list is prioritised by an AI-assisted process so that only the closest matches and most relevant images are presented. More tightly focused lists of potential conflicts save reviewing time and therefore costs for trade mark examiners, trade mark attorneys or agents, paralegals and legal practitioners.

This explains the turn to image recognition systems, which directly analyse images rather than relying on representative keywords or codes.[68] Research by WIPO indicates that image searches to date have been more effective in relation to simple geometric shapes, with Vienna Classification searches as the background comparator for measuring effectiveness.[69] However, there is room for improvement when it comes to complex shapes or logos combining both figurative elements and text. Nevertheless, the ability to search by directly uploading an image is a significant, potentially tectonic, shift, especially as the technology continuously improves. Thus WIPO's new AI-based image comparison service innovates 'by using deep machine learning to identify combinations of concepts – such as an apple, an eagle, a tree, a crown, a car, a star – within an image to find similar marks that have previously been registered'.[70] Meanwhile the USPTO has built on its extensive experience with manually coding figurative images to train AI algorithms:

> A six-digit numerical design search code is assigned to each design element of a trade mark, such as a depiction of a star (01.01.03) or flower (05.05.25). Using years of images with corresponding examiner-annotated design codes, we are able to train deep learning systems that can predict design codes of a new trade mark image.[71]

The USPTO also uses neural networks to retrieve and store features of mark images, that can then be compared, via an image similarity measure, to other marks' features. Of equal

---

[67] Amy J.C. Trappey, Charles V. Trappey & Samuel Shih, *Logo Image Retrievals Using Deep Embedding Learning* in Transdisciplinary Engineering for Resilience: Responding to System Disruptions 103-104 (Linda Newnes et al. eds, 2021) (containing a helpful literature review of image recognition technology).

[68] For technical background, *see* Ali Reza Alaei, Partha Pratim Roy & Umapada Pal, *Logo and Seal Based Administrative Document Image Retrieval: A Survey*, 22 Comp. Sci. Rev. 47 (2016); Claudio A. Perez et al., *Trademark Image Retrieval Using a Combination of Deep Convolutional Neural Networks*, 2018 International Joint Conference on Neural Networks (IJCNN) (2018).

[69] Christophe Mazence, Machine Learning Applied to Trademarks Classification and Search (29 May 2018) (WIPO/IP/ITAI/GE/18/P17).

[70] *WIPO Launches State-of-the-Art Artificial Intelligence-Based Image Search Tool for Brands* (1 Apr. 2019) (PR/2019/831) (*available at* www.wipo.int/pressroom/en/articles/2019/article_0005.html).

[71] USPTO, Emerging Technologies in USPTO Business Solutions (25 May 2018) (WIPO/IP/ITAI/GE/18/P5).

relevance is the adjacent space beyond formal public registries. Image searching technology is being proactively developed by as well as widely adopted by private trade mark search and clearance service providers. A recent INTA report summarises these developments.[72]

The third set of developments could be described as putting the pieces together or striving for a gestalt understanding. Attempts are under way to develop AI algorithms that can combine different measures of similarity – the words *and* images in the two complex marks being compared – to arrive at an integrative assessment. The goal is to mimic the perspective of a human examiner who must synthesise visual, aural and conceptual similarity to arrive at an overall conclusion on whether the later mark should not be registered.[73] Datasets of past examiners' decisions are a resource for training algorithms to assign different 'weights' to different measures of similarity, depending on the type of mark. Another approach presents the relevant measures of similarity in parallel – for example image or pixel similarity, text similarity, automated content similarity and manual similarity – to avoid their significance being diminished or compressed into a single metric.[74]

3.4 Not Quite Business as Usual: Doctrinal Implications

An underexplored set of issues relate to the doctrinal implications of the conflict identification technologies described above. An AI-assisted search results in a relevancy-ranked list of potential conflicts along with a risk profile, often presented statistically (for example, a 71 per cent similarity match) or colour coded according to risk. This assists registry officials and professional advisers when making recommendations. Experience to date therefore suggests that AI algorithms are intended to augment human judgement – to effectively sift through ever increasing volumes of registration data – and not to replace it. Emphasising the continuing need for nuanced human evaluations, a CompuMark report observes: 'While AI and neural networks will play an expanding role in CompuMark solutions […] they are intended to complement, not replace, human analysts'.[75] As the founder of LawPanel puts it: 'AI will speed up legal research, but it will not replace advice formulation […] since it] only works on repetitive tasks in a very tightly-defined domain.'[76] Machine learning technology can comprehensively filter the ever growing numbers of trade mark applications and registrations, displaying the most relevant list of results for human experts to assess. Despite this clear caveat, as I outline below, there is a risk that this technology will be relied on to a greater extent than is intended

---

[72] INTA Emerging Issues Committee, Artificial Intelligence (AI) Usage in Trademark Clearance and Enforcement (21 Apr. 2021) [hereinafter *Clearance and Enforcement Report*].

[73] Rossitza Setchi & Fatahiya Mohd Anuar, *Multi-Faceted Assessment of Trademark Similarity*, 65 Expert Systems with Applications 16 (2016); *see also* Perez et al., *supra* note 68 (assessing the combined visual and conceptual similarities of images); Antonio-Javier Gallego, Antonio Pertusa & Marisa Bernabeu, *Multi-label Logo Classification Using Convolutional Neural Networks,* in Iberian Conference on Pattern Recognition and Image Analysis 485 (Aythami Morales et al. eds, 2019).

[74] Idan Mosseri, Matan Rusanovsky & Gal Oren, *TradeMarker – Artificial Intelligence based Trademarks Similarity Search Engine* in HCI International 2019 – Posters: Communications in Computer and Information Science (Constantine Stephanidis ed., vol. 1034, 2019) 97.

[75] Compumark White Paper, Artificial Intelligence, Human Expertise: How Technology and Trademark Experts Work Together to Meet Today's IP Challenges 5 (2018).

[76] Tim Lince, *'No Imminent AI Apocalypse' – Tech Expert Rejects Predictions of Mass Job Losses in Trademark Industry*, World Trademark Rev. (1 Feb. 2018) (*available at* www.worldtrademarkreview .com/brand-management/no-imminent-ai-apocalypse-tech-expert-rejects-predictions-mass-job-losses).

by its developers, who are aware of its limitations.[77] Users may choose to ignore these caveats because of the seductive certainty of an enumerated risk.

In previous work, I have alluded to the risk – common to all machine learning technology – that biases in the training data will be unintentionally embedded in the training model developed from that data.[78] In trade mark law, this can manifest in jurisdiction-specific ways. For example, where the training data is based on an English-speaking jurisdiction, registry decisions will reflect the assumption that a certain set of characters (say, Cyrillic or Mandarin) is meaningless to an English-speaking audience and therefore downplay semantic or conceptual similarity when comparing two signs. This assumption will not hold good across all jurisdictions. More generally, the majority of training datasets used to date have been based on English-language resources, which will be of limited assistance to multi-language registries such as the EUIPO.[79]

The second – and related – set of issues also concerns another type of unintended transplant. Service providers must adopt an image similarity assessment model which is trade mark law-specific – off-the-shelf solutions will not work since trade mark law focuses primarily on sight, sound and meaning similarity between signs.[80] A trade mark lawyer assesses the similarity between images in a different way from a photographer or an art critic. Furthermore, individual jurisdictions have particularised approaches to certain legal issues. Consider weakly distinctive marks (such as VAPE & CO for electronic cigarettes)[81] or marks which contain weak components within them (such as the word element PET CUISINE, accompanied by stylised depictions of a cat and dog for pet foods).[82] One school of thought says that just as distinctive marks deserve a broader scope of protection, less distinctive marks deserve correspondingly less, since the ratchet works both ways. Another perspective argues that because average consumers are likely to notice visually dominant albeit semantically weak elements of a mark, these must nevertheless be factored into the analysis.[83] Which of these approaches – if any – has been factored into the mark similarity assessment? Or is this judgment left to the legal professional assessing the results? Registries in the past have also diverged on whether a word mark applied for in black and white extends in scope to all colour variants and whether applying for a Nice main class heading automatically includes all the sub-categories of goods or services under that heading.[84] Are service providers using jurisdiction-specific versions of

---

[77]   One important limitation is that these conflict identification algorithms cover only certain types of potential conflicts, relating to double identity (identical mark, identical goods) or the likelihood of confusion. They do not extend to broader dilution protection (similar marks triggering harmful but non-confusing mental associations, despite being on dissimilar goods), or cover other forms of unregistered prior rights such as copyright in logos. See Gangjee, *Eye, Robot, supra* note 30, 189; Moerland and Freitas, *Trademark Assessment, supra* note 30, 279–88.

[78]   Gangjee, *Eye, Robot, supra* note 30, at 185–90.

[79]   I am grateful to Gordon Humphries, Chair of the EUIPO 5th Board of Appeal, for pointing this out.

[80]   Trappey et al., *Logo Image Retrievals, supra* note 67, at 104 ('When the ML predictive modeling [operates] without taking TM legal characteristics into consideration, the performance of the TM similarity analysis will be largely weakened').

[81]   See *Nicoventures Holdings Ltd v The London Vape Company Ltd* [2017] EWHC 3393 (Ch).

[82]   See *TDH Group v EUIPO,* Case T-46/17, EU:T:2018:976.

[83]   Even within a jurisdiction there may not be agreement: *see* Fhima and Gangjee, *Confusion Test, supra* note 50, at 195–203.

[84]   In the EU, these disagreements have led to the formulation of agreed Common Practices, between the EUIPO and national trade mark registries of EU member states. See www.tmdn.org/#/practices.

similarity assessment ML models, or is there a universal model – perhaps based on the practice of one jurisdiction – which assesses conflicts across multiple jurisdictions? Is this an indirect or even inadvertent way of setting legal transplants in motion below the radar and without debating their desirability? Not enough information is available in the public domain to answer these questions at present.

The third set of issues relates to the goods and services associated with marks. In recent years, attention has focused on the problem of clutter or deadwood – the existence of marks on the register that are partly or wholly unused by their owners.[85] It is not uncommon for trade mark applicants to claim broad swathes of goods and services for which they never intend to use the mark, in order to gain a broader scope of protection.[86] Once such marks are registered, they occupy space on the register as prior rights in relation to these goods and services. Emphasising that registered trade marks need to be used in order to be maintained, the US Registrar of Trademarks recently summarised the problem at a Congressional Hearing in 2019:

> The register itself provides notice to applicants, other trademark owners, and our examining attorneys of the registrant's claim of ownership in a mark and allows them to search the register to determine the availability of marks for registration in the United States. The register is a valuable tool in making business decisions, and its accuracy is paramount. When businesses are selecting names for new products, they turn to the register to figure out whether their chosen mark is available for their use and registration. But, for the register to be useful, it must accurately reflect marks that are in use in the United States for the goods and services identified in the registrations. If the register is filled with marks that are not in use, or features registrations obtained by improper means, it makes trademark clearance more difficult, time-consuming and expensive. An inaccurate register also leads to expensive opposition and cancellation proceedings, or federal court litigation, to correct inaccurate registrations and to enforce rights. And, in turn, it may cause companies to alter business decisions, often at significant cost.[87]

Although these unused categories are vulnerable to invalidation, this requires costly and time-consuming real-world investigations into the commercial offerings of trade mark proprietors, followed by legal proceedings to revoke the mark. So long as the register unhelpfully generates false positives, AI algorithms will take formal registration at face value. Risk profiles are generated based on 'hollow' prior rights that will not survive scrutiny. Perhaps the most important lesson here is that we need to think hard about how to declutter registers without relying on expensive invalidation proceedings, given the magnifying effects of AI-conflict matching. In the meanwhile, some private service providers are offering brand brainstorming tools. An example is Clarivate's Naming Tool on its Serion platform, which allows users to suggest brand attributes, based on which the AI then generates suitable brand

[85]   Georg von Graevenitz, Richard Ashmead & Christine Greenhalgh, Cluttering and Non-Use of Trade Marks in Europe (UK IPO Report 2015/48); USPTO, Post Registration Proof of Use Pilot Final Report (Aug. 25, 2015); US House Committee on the Judiciary Hearings, Counterfeits and Cluttering: Emerging Threats to the Integrity of the Trademark System and the Impact on American Consumers and Businesses (18 July 2019) (*available at*: https://judiciary.house.gov/calendar/eventsingle.aspx?EventID=2271).

[86]   The Court of Justice had to recently provide guidance on when registering a mark with no intention to use it for specified goods amounts to bad faith. See *Sky plc v Skykick UK Ltd*. Case C- 371/18, EU:C: 2020:45.

[87]   Statement of Mary Boney Denison, Commissioner for Trademarks, USPTO, Judiciary Hearings, *supra* note 84, at 2.

names that are potentially available for registration in the US and EU, in an attempt to navigate crowded registers.[88]

Another by-product, which deserves more attention, is the manner in which these conflict identification tools seemingly upgrade the legal significance of the Nice classification system. For the purpose of assessing conflicts, goods sharing the same Nice class might be one helpful factor for determining confusing similarity but this not considered dispositive.[89] As an illustration, section 60A(1)(a) of the UK Trade Marks Act 1994 states: 'For the purpose of this Act goods and services [...] are not to be regarded as being similar to each other on the ground that they appear in the same class under the Nice Classification.' Depending on the underlying models, ML algorithms may not share this view. Overall, the more seriously goods and services are taken 'on paper', the more this reinforces the formal status of trade marks as the bounded objects of property rights, as opposed to signs which convey specific meanings about actual products in the real world.[90]

The fourth aspect relates to the abbreviation of the likelihood of confusion test and the turn to metrics. Today conflict analysis for registry clearance purposes is already a thinner, more formalistic version of conflict analysis for real-world infringement purposes, where context can be taken into account.[91] To take just one example, while the similarity of marks and the similarity of goods or services are two core aspects of the likelihood of confusion test, they must combine to create confusion, as judged from the perspective of the average consumer of the products in question. Where the consumer is a skilled professional, or considered sophisticated, confusion is less likely.[92] AI-enhanced similarity searching does not address this third limb of the test and may serve to further attenuate registry level conflict analysis. Will the test effectively shrink to just two factors (marks and products) in the commercially significant clearance or registry opposition context?[93] The reactions of a real-world consumer, so often alluded to in trade mark doctrine and providing normative foundations for trade mark law, may be muted even further as a result. While human expertise continues to assess the conflicts results lists generated by algorithms, for risk-averse commercial clients it is extremely tempting to be guided by clearly defined percentages of similarity. One is left to wonder whether the algorithmic assessment of similarity will make its way across to infringement analysis, as evidence in a real-world dispute. It has been suggested that businesses might find it attractive

---

[88]   *See* https://clarivate.com/compumark/solutions/naming-tool-on-serion/. On crowded registers, see Beebe & Fromer, *The Problems of Trademark Depletion and Congestion: Some Possible Reforms*, in Research Handbook on Trademark Law Reform 17 (Graeme B. Dinwoodie & Mark D. Janis eds, 2021).

[89]   As recognised in Art 2(1) of the Nice Agreement 1957, as amended on 28 September 1979.

[90]   *See* Robert Burrell, *Trade Mark Bureaucracies*, in Trademark Law and Theory 95 (Dinwoodie & Janis eds, 2008).

[91]   As recognised in Case C-533/06 *O2 Holdings Ltd v Hutchison 3G Ltd* EU:C:2008:339, [66]. *See also Specsavers International Healthcare Ltd v Asda Stores Ltd* [2012] EWCA Civ 24, [78]–[88] (Kitchin LJ).

[92]   Fhima & Gangjee, *Confusion Test, supra* note 50 at 177–80.

[93]   Empirical research already suggests that, for (human) tribunals, the similarity of marks and of products may be dispositive. This leads to a 'stampeding' of the remaining factors to align them with the more important ones, thereby shaping the outcome of the confusion test. See Beebe, *An Empirical Study of the Multifactor Test for Trade Mark Infringement* 94 Cal. L. Rev. 1581 (2006); Ilanah Simon Fhima & Catrina Denvir, *An Empirical Analysis of the Likelihood of Confusion Factors in European Trade Mark Law*, 2015 Intl Rev. Intell. Prop. & Comp. L. 310.

if an AI solution were to replace judicial determination, or at least provide a preliminary assessment of confusion even in an infringement context.[94] Public sector conflict searches, such as WIPO's Global Brands Database,[95] rank the results of similarity matching based on the degree of risk, while private service providers in the search and watching spaces provide more detailed risk profiles as percentages (94 per cent similarity) or colour codes (red, so a very close match).[96] However, the risk profile may be generated without any sense of whether the mark is actually used on goods, or whether the average consumer will not be confused because the signs share only generic or non-distinctive common elements. These are just some of the implications for substantive trade mark law embedded within the turn to AI.

4.   ALGORITHMIC ENFORCEMENT

To keep pace with the increase in the scale and scope of e-commerce, AI-powered tools for online enforcement have emerged in recent years. This is in response to the prevalence of counterfeits and other infringing signs on online platforms.[97] This section focuses primarily on one aspect – while ML in the registration context focused on paper-based assessments, identifying infringements needs to be contextually determined. Context is important for at least three key reasons. First, trade mark infringements need to be commercial. The alleged infringer's use must be 'in commerce'[98] or 'in the course of trade'.[99] While brands are frequently discussed online, this can be in a private, referential capacity – enthusiastic brand aficionados, unhappy customers or critics of the brand owners' labour practices – with no goods being offered for sale. The second reason is that words which are registered as trade marks may also retain their descriptive connotations. Thus, while Ford is a trade mark for automobiles, ford is also a shallow river crossing. Nike is both a sports shoe brand and the Greek goddess of victory. Third, a range of commercial third parties may wish to legitimately use the trade mark, such as those selling genuine second-hand products or those offering repair services for those products. For these reasons, the context of use will need to be assessed, to determine whether the use is infringing. Two platform-specific domains of application illustrate the way in which these contextual cues are generated.

The first field of application relates to online marketplaces, such as Amazon, eBay and AliBaba's TaoBao. These e-commerce platforms have developed proactive tools to police infringing listings of products. Early glimpses of the technology were evident in some of the key cases considering secondary liability issues, where courts considered whether these

---

94   See the discussion during a WIPO and UKIPO conference in 2019, reported at: www.worldipreview .com/news/ai-as-judges-and-patent-destroying-tools-panel-discussion-18237.
95   *See* www.wipo.int/reference/en/branddb/.
96   INTA, Clearance and Enforcement Report, *supra* note 72.
97   See OECD/EUIPO, Misuse of E-Commerce for Trade in Counterfeits (2021); INTA, Addressing the Sale of Counterfeits on the Internet (2021).
98   Lanham Act § 45, 15 U.S.C. § 1127 (definition); Lanham Act § 32(1)(a), 15 U.S.C. § 1114(1) (a) (to be found liable, the defendant must make use of the plaintiff's mark 'in connection with the sale, distribution, or advertising of any goods or services').
99   Trade Mark Directive (EU) 2015/2436, art. 10(2).

platforms should be held liable as accessories for the infringing conduct of their users.[100] The initial approach was reactive and focused on providing rights holders with a convenient process for notifying the platform about infringing activities. If the platform expeditiously removed the infringing listings, they could avail of safe harbours.[101] However, in recent years, there has been mounting pressure on platforms to do more to proactively remove infringing offerings. In the EU copyright context, the provision of filtering technology had thus far been optional but seems to be on the cusp of becoming a mandatory requirement, in order to avoid liability for platforms.[102] At present, Amazon offers a range of options for brand owners seeking to enforce rights and prevent infringements.[103] While violations can still be reported by right-holders, Amazon offers additional services such as Amazon Transparency, which is a product serialisation service.[104] Drawing inspiration from the way in which pharmaceutical supply chains have been secured in the past, this paid-for service provides right-holders with unique codes on labels that helps identify genuine individual product units. Within its delivery network, Amazon scans each product code to ensure that only authentic units are shipped to customers. However, for the purposes of this chapter, two other initiatives within the Amazon Brand Registry, the umbrella programme which grants verified trade mark owners enhanced enforcement tools, have greater significance.

Along with the serialisation available via Transparency, Amazon offers a self-service counterfeit removal option and an automated protection system relying on algorithmic filtering.[105] Amazon documents the scale of this algorithmic filtering:

> We leverage a combination of advanced machine learning capabilities and expert human investigators to protect our store proactively from bad actors and bad products [...] In 2020, we prevented over 6 million attempts to create new selling accounts, stopping bad actors before they published a single product for sale, and blocked more than 10 billion suspected bad listings before they were published in our store.[106]

In 2020, 'Amazon scanned more than 5 billion attempted changes to product detail pages daily for signs of potential abuse'.[107] It is safe to assume that sellers make commercial use of trade marks, so that aspect of infringement is unproblematic. In terms of what the algorithms are looking for, one set of data points relates to information provided by brand owners – logos, product descriptions and other information in relation to genuine products that right-holders are best aware of. There is a considerably larger set of data points that is used in detection

---

[100] No accessory liability in *Tiffany Inc. v eBay, Inc.*, 576 F. Supp. 2d 463, 470 (S.D.N.Y. 2008), aff'd., 600 F.3d 93 (2d Cir. 2010. For the UK, see *L'Oreal SA & Ors v EBay International AG & Ors* [2009] EWHC 1094 (Ch) at ¶¶ 77–78 (describing eBay's software filters to flag infringing listings).

[101] Ansgar Ohly, *The Liability of Intermediaries for Trademark Infringement*, in Research Handbook on Trademark Law Reform 17 (Graeme B. Dinwoodie & Mark D. Janis eds, 2021).

[102] Digital Single Market Directive, art. 17.

[103] Comprehensively described in Seng, *Detecting and Prosecuting IP Infringement with AI, supra* note 3.

[104] *See* https://brandservices.amazon.com/transparency/faq.

[105] This is consolidated within Project Zero, which seeks to drive counterfeits on the platform to zero. *See* https://brandservices.amazon.com/projectzero.

[106] Amazon, Brand Protection Report 3 (2021).

[107] Ibid, 6.

algorithms but not made publicly available.[108] Drawing on information from the seller community, Daniel Seng identifies 'crucial seller information such as contact details, physical addresses, bank accounts, and IP addresses'.[109] Sellers with a negative track record are flagged by Amazon's technology. Additional insights are available from the Alibaba platform, which uses comparable filtering technology. Alibaba has invested heavily in optical character recognition and image recognition technology as part of its Tech Brain anti-counterfeiting technology, presumably to study the photographic images of products being offered for the presence of unauthorised logos and other indicia.[110] Further data points are available by analysing anomalous traffic data and unusual transactions for a particular seller (unusual or abnormal merchant behaviour), as well as negative emotions emerging from the semantic analysis of user comments and feedback.[111]

Under the Project Zero initiative, an additional feature is available (by invitation) to members of the Brand registry. This is a remarkable development, where registered rights-holders are given the unprecedented ability to directly remove listings they deem as counterfeit directly, using a self-service tool.[112] Trade mark proprietors can search for listings based on marks, ASIN numbers,[113] keywords or even product photographs. From the search results lists, they can directly de-list offerings they deem to be problematic. Once listings are successfully removed, the information will feed back into the machine-learning features used in Automated Protections to improve its pattern recognition abilities. While this is self-evidently efficacious for trade mark proprietors, it makes them the arbiters of the scope of their own rights. Right-holders must sign up to a code which requires that they do not abuse their rights, but there is no clear indication of how disputes will be resolved or whether abusive de-listings are penalised.

To be clear, these are powerful tools and will be welcomed by brand owners. However, the potential for anti-competitive effects is also evident. Algorithms designed in this context are usually developed in consultation with right holders.[114] However, as Rebecca Tushnet observes, Amazon 'is being asked to run a judicial system, without the commitments to transparency and precedent of a real judicial system'.[115] Seng points out the significance of this lack of transparency in moving from a rules-based system to one that depends on correlations:

---

[108] Ibid, 5 ('Our proprietary systems analyze hundreds of unique data points to verify the information and detect potential risk').

[109] Seng, *Detecting and Prosecuting IP Infringement with AI, supra* note 4, 300.

[110] Alibaba Group, 2020 ANNUAL REPORT ON INTELLECTUAL PROPERTY PROTECTION, 2 (2020).

[111] Alibaba Group, 2018 INTELLECTUAL PROPERTY RIGHTS PROTECTION ANNUAL REPORT, 9–10 (2018).

[112] *See* https://brandservices.amazon.co.uk/projectzero/.

[113] The ASIN is a ten-digit alphanumeric code that identifies products on Amazon. Obtaining one is a pre-requisite for selling on Amazon. It's unique for each product and is assigned when you create a new product in Amazon's catalogue, with the exception of books that use the ISBN or International Standard Book Number in place of an ASIN.

[114] Thomas Hoeren et al, EUIPO STUDY ON VOLUNTARY COLLABORATION PRACTICES IN ADDRESSING ONLINE INFRINGEMENTS OF TRADE MARK RIGHTS, DESIGN RIGHTS, COPYRIGHT AND RIGHTS RELATED TO COPYRIGHT (2016).

[115] Blake Brittain, *Amazon's Judging of IP Claims Questioned in Seller Lawsuits* (Bloomberg Law, 12 Feb. 2020) (commenting on the Wanna Play Products dispute, where expired or otherwise inapplicable patents were the basis for illegitimate delisting requests); *available at* https://news.bloomberglaw.com/ip-law/amazons-judging-of-ip-disputes-questioned-in-sellers-lawsuits.

Perhaps the initial setup of the rules will be by way of supervised machine learning, based on the previous (manual) removals of problematic listings and the suspension of recalcitrant sellers. However [...] the subsequent, iterative revisions to the rules will be based on *current* removals, suspensions, and reports from right holders. Because the rules are constantly changing with real-time feedback, do we as humans know the precise 'reasons' for the algorithms to have singled out the listing or seller in question?[116]

This foregrounds the need for efficacious human review where delisting is contested and an accessible appellate process.

The second domain in which machine learning is being deployed is in relation to detecting infringements on social media platforms. Counterfeiters create closed groups, which can then directly sell to consumers. Social media also offers greater anonymity and requires far less infrastructure than hosting a website, while bad faith actors can open new accounts relatively easy if old ones are closed down.[117] A recent study for the EUIPO provides interesting insights into the methodology used for detecting conversations about fakes and knock-offs on Twitter, Facebook, Instagram and Reddit.[118] A total of 3.9 million publicly available conversations were algorithmically analysed from a sample of six EU member states, using geolocation data. The analysis initially focused on textual mentions of brands and subsequently used photographs or videos during the qualitative analysis phase. The approach relied on social intelligence analytics, a form of natural-language processing that can track changes in language patterns in real time.[119] The goal was to discern intent or sentiment from the text. The methodology used three cumulative stages of keyword identification: (i) identifying a product category such as perfumes and cosmetics (through keywords like cream, fragrance, mascara, lipstick); (ii) then identifying a specific brand of clothing through additional keywords (the brands were popular and frequently counterfeited, but not revealed in the study); and (iii) finally using keywords to identify counterfeits (such as excess stock, cheap, rip-off, outlet, copy, original and best deal).[120] It should be noted that many of the keywords are dual purpose and can be used to describe legitimate offers (for example, coupon, factory, sale, discount and best deal). This was an exploratory exercise, which acknowledged the difficulty in distinguishing between illicit and legitimate content. Its purpose was to identify behaviours that might be indicative of 'wider habits that are currently prominent on social media in relation to IP infringement'. The study 'identified 11 % of conversations regarding physical products could be possibly related to counterfeits'.[121] More specific insights related to which social media platforms were more prominent for certain types of (possible) counterfeits (clothes and shoes on Instagram; ebooks on Reddit) and a timeline would indicate when certain hot topics would trend. No doubt algorithmic enforcement is already envisaged for social media platforms, where concerns similar to those identified in the case of online marketplaces will be relevant.

---

[116]   Seng, *Detecting and Prosecuting IP Infringement with AI, supra* note 4, 309.

[117]   Peter S. Sloane, *Development in the Law: Trademark Vigilance in the Twenty-first Century: An Update*, 30 Fordham Intell. Prop. Media & Ent. L.J. 1197, 1220–7 (2020) (outlining the risks to brands on social media).

[118]   EUIPO, Monitoring and Analysing Social Media in Relation to IP Infringement (2021).

[119]   For a convenient overview of these types of technology, see In Lee, *Social Media Analytics for Enterprises: Typology, Methods, and Processes*, 61(2) Business Horizons 199 (2018).

[120]   EUIPO, Social Media Study, *supra* note 118, 20.

[121]   Ibid., 7.

Automated enforcement will be a considerably more delicate exercise in the social media context, unlike in commercial online marketplaces.

The final development to note is that private service providers now offer solutions which allow right holders to monitor marks across platforms and the internet in general. One such example is Incopro's Talisman.[122] Many of the concerns related to algorithmic copyright enforcement, such as false positives and over-enforcement, will have lessons for trade mark enforcement in the future.[123]

5.   CONCLUSION

Artificial intelligence technologies offer the possibility of keeping up with the ever-increasing volume of trade mark applications and registrations. They offer the potential to make life easier for those seeking to register marks, while enabling examiners and applicants to spend more time focusing on more realistic conflicts. As this chapter has argued, while this new technology is often presented as merely assisting with the implementation of existing rules and doctrines of trade mark law, a more fundamental set of realignments may be taking place, with implications for established doctrinal positions. In the registration context, machine learning risks moving trade marks even further towards an abstract property logic, creating even more distance between real-world consumers and their varied responses to signs. As this technology is being applied to the (online) infringement context, assessing the contextual use of a sign remains challenging. These are challenges to be grappled with, because algorithmic filtering and automated enforcement are already in use. Copyright may have valuable lessons for trade mark law in this regard.

---

[122] *See* www.incoproip.com/online-brand-protection/talisman-brand-protection-software/. Other examples are found in the INTA, CLEARANCE AND ENFORCEMENT REPORT, *supra* note 72.

[123] See for example, S. Bar-Ziv and N. Elkin-Koren, *Behind the Scenes of Online Copyright Enforcement: Empirical Evidence on Notice & Takedown* (2018) 50 CONNECTICUT L. REV. 339; D. Seng, *Copyrighting Copywrongs: An Empirical Analysis of Errors with Automated DMCA Takedown Notices* (2021) 37 SANTA CLARA HIGH TECH L.J. 119; G. Frosio, *Algorithmic Enforcement Online* in P. Torremans, INTELLECTUAL PROPERTY AND HUMAN RIGHTS (P. Torremans ed., 4th ed 2020).

18. The impact of AI on designs law

Trevor Cook

1. INTRODUCTION

In addressing the impact of Artificial Intelligence (AI) on designs law, one might be tempted to linger on the contribution that AI image search techniques can make to exploring the thicket of design registrations found in most intellectual property offices of the world. But this contribution, the impact of which is likely to be significant, is already with us.[1] One might also consider the scope for AI to make assessments as to the degree of similarity as between one design and another, whether in the course of registration or afterwards, for the purposes of determining validity or infringement—an inquiry which takes us into the murky areas of AI adjudication generally.

Instead, this chapter will focus on another aspect of AI and designs law, taking as its lead the lively current discourse as to the status of AI-generated "inventions" and AI-generated "creations" and the laws of patents and on copyright respectively. Designs law has to a large extent avoided such discourse, even though it would at first sight appear that designs, occupying that gray and ever shifting area between patents and copyright, and with some features of both systems, (not to mention trademarks as well), should be no less challenged than such other intellectual property rights by the idea of their being generated without human intervention. The relative immunity of designs from such discourse is well evidenced by the following observations of the UK Intellectual Property Office in 2021:[2]

---

[1]   See for example, as to the EUIPO, https://euipo.europa.eu/ohimportal/en/news/-/action/view/ 5452746 and as to WIPO, www.wipo.int/pressroom/en/articles/2019/article_0005.html. Although the EUIPO system provides an AI image search for both trademarks and designs, the WIPO AI image search appears for now to be limited in its application to trademarks. But there can be no technical reason why the WIPO AI image search cannot also be applied to designs, as the EUIPO experience shows.

[2]   *Open consultation—Artificial Intelligence and Intellectual Property: Copyright and Patents*, UK Intellectual Property Office, (29 October 2021) at www.gov.uk/government/consultations/artificial -intelligence-and-ip-copyright-and-patents/artificial-intelligence-and-intellectual-property-copyright -and-patents. For the response which it summarizes see *Government response to call for views on artificial intelligence and intellectual property Updated* (23 March 2021) at www.gov.uk/government/ consultations/artificial-intelligence-and-intellectual-property-call-for-views/government-response-to -call-for-views-on-artificial-intelligence-and-intellectual-property#designs. Indeed, the very focus of the consultation on patents and copyright is telling from the point of view of designs.

Interaction with designs

In its response to the Call for Views, the government noted that designs legislation appears to be able to respond to the challenges of AI. But there is a need to monitor the situation as the AI systems used in the design process develop.

UK law on registered and unregistered designs includes similar provisions on computer-generated designs to those in copyright law. The author of a computer-generated design is "the person by whom the arrangements necessary for the creation of the design are made".

We are not proposing any amendments to design law at this stage. But we welcome views on the implications of the policy options for computer generated works on the design system.

But no less than with patents, as to inventors, and copyright, as to authors, an evident challenge presented by AI to designs is the question of whether AI can fulfill the legal role of the "designer" for the purposes of design protection. Another issue, for many design protection laws which involve registration, is the standard, generally framed by concepts which do not readily lend themselves to replication in the context of AI—such as, in the EU and UK, the "informed user,"[3] by whom the assessment of one design as against another falls to be judged.

This chapter seeks to challenge the assumption that just because we have become used to treating design protection as a separate field of intellectual property law in its own right, such understanding must necessarily inform how we address the impact of AI on designs. Instead, this chapter proposes that we should recognize the contradictions inherent in treating designs law as an independent area of law—when in reality it is a hybrid with features of both patents and copyright, the roots of which lie in copyright but which came by accident to attract features of patent law—and address the issue of AI generated designs accordingly. The impact of AI also presents us with an opportunity to rethink why we protect designs in this separate way (or in practice in a wide variety of separate ways) and, if we must do so, how best we should go about this.

2.   THE TREATMENT OF DESIGNS IN INTERNATIONAL TREATIES AND TRADE AGREEMENTS

An initial step towards securing an insight into the relationship between design protection and other types of intellectual property protection is provided by the approach of international intellectual property treaties to the protection of designs. This also provides an insight into what constraints the international intellectual property treaty framework might impose on the

---

[3]   Defined by the EU Court of Justice in Case 280/10P *PepsiCo Inc v Grupo Promer Mon Graphic SA* (20 October 2011) at [53] "as lying somewhere between that of the average consumer, applicable in trade mark matters, who need not have any specific knowledge and who, as a rule, makes no direct comparison between the trade marks in conflict, and the sectoral expert, who is an expert with detailed technical expertise. Thus, the concept of the informed user may be understood as referring, not to a user of average attention, but to a particularly observant one, either because of his personal experience or his extensive knowledge of the sector in question," which it went on to note at [54] was "illustrated by the conclusion drawn from that formulation by the General Court in paragraph 64 of the judgment under appeal, in identifying the informed user relevant in the present case as capable of being a child in the approximate age range of 5 to 10 or a marketing manager in a company that makes goods which are promoted by giving away 'pogs', 'rappers' or 'tazos'."

extent to which a design could be entirely AI-generated and yet also protected under designs law.

All of a positive or specific nature that the Paris Convention has to say about designs is, by Article 5quinquies, only inserted at the Lisbon revision of the Convention in 1958, that they "shall be protected in all countries of the Union."[4] The Convention says nothing about what they are or how they should be protected. The only international treaty to add any specificity in this respect is the TRIPS Agreement, Article 25[5] of which provides:

Section 4: Industrial Designs
Article 25
Requirements for Protection
(1) Members shall provide for the protection of independently created industrial designs that are new or original. Members may provide that designs are not new or original if they do not significantly differ from known designs or combinations of known design features. Members may provide that such protection shall not extend to designs dictated essentially by technical or functional considerations.
(2) Each Member shall ensure that requirements for securing protection for textile designs, in particular in regard to any cost, examination or publication, do not unreasonably impair the opportunity to seek and obtain such protection. Members shall be free to meet this obligation through industrial design law or through copyright law.

The closest that any of this wording gets to saying anything about who or what can be a designer is the expression "independently created." Does "created" imply a human designer? Or is it merely a synonym for "made," which, used in context, merely requires that to be protected, a design must not have been copied from another design? Admittedly the language in TRIPS for patents, which refers in Article 29 to "the inventor," and for copyright, which refers to "intellectual creations" in Article 10(2) (as to compilations), is hardly less obscure by way of guidance in this respect. But at least as to copyright, the Berne Convention provides a stronger basis for requiring that an author be human in that the term of protection is by Article 7(1) generally keyed to the author's death.[6]

However, the Paris Convention and TRIPS are not the whole story at an international level, because although neither of these requires that designs be protected by a registration system, such systems are common in practice and at an international level the Hague Agreement Concerning the International Registration of Industrial Designs provides an international mechanism for facilitating the registration of designs in multiple jurisdictions. The Hague Agreement mentions the word "creator" twice, first in Article 5: "5(3) In addition, the application may contain: [...] 2. a declaration as to who is the true creator of the design," and also in Article 8:

---

4   Designs are also mentioned in the Paris Convention, but alongside other industrial property rights, in Article 4 (Right of Priority), Article 5 (Failure to Work; Importation of Articles, Marking), and Article 11 (Temporary Protection at Certain International Exhibitions).
5   Article 26 TRIPS, entitled "Protection," outlines the minimum rights that must be conferred on the owner of a protected design, the maximum scope for exceptions to such protection, and the minimum duration of such protection (ten years).
6   With exceptions in this respect permitted for cinematographic works (Article 7(2)), anonymous or pseudonymous works (Article 7(3)), and photographic works and works of applied art in so far as they are protected as artistic works (Article 7(4), discussed further below as to works of applied art).

8(4)(a) The national Office of a contracting State whose domestic law contains provisions of the kind referred to in paragraph (1) requiring a declaration as to who is the true creator of the design or .... may provide that, upon request and within a period of not less than sixty days from the dispatch of such a request by the said Office, the applicant shall file in the language of the application filed with the International Bureau: (1) a declaration as to who is the true creator of the design.

Neither of these two provisions is prescriptive, and so imposes no constraint on the nature of the creator or—and more significantly from the point of view of AI-generated designs—even has anything to say about whether a design must have a creator.

Trade agreements, which have come to represent the leading edge of international intellectual property norms, tend to be hardly any more specific in this respect. For example, as to designs, the UK–EU Trade and Cooperation Agreement at Article 245 provides:

(1)   Each Party shall provide for the protection of independently created designs that are new and original. This protection shall be provided by registration and shall confer exclusive rights upon their holders in accordance with this Section.
(2)   For the purposes of this Article, a Party may consider that a design having individual character is original.

In apparent contrast to Article 25(1) of TRIPS, requiring only that to be protected a design must be new *or* original, this provision requires that to be protected a design must be both new *and* original. However, Article 25(2) immediately qualifies this by providing that the originality requirement is satisfied if the design has "individual character," an expression which is not here defined but which in EU and UK law[7] is assessed by reference to "the overall impression it produces on the informed user."[8]

The EU–Canada FTA is in this respect even more vague than the UK–EU TCA. Its only provision directly touching on the substantive law of designs[9] is Article 20.25, which bears however on copyright law rather than designs law and, by recognizing that copyright may also be deployed to protect designs, serves only to emphasize that "design protection" (unlike copyright, or indeed patents) is not a coherent concept at an international level:

Article 20.25 Relationship to copyright
The subject matter of a design right may be protected under copyright law if the conditions for this protection are met. The extent to which, and the conditions under which, such a protection is conferred, including the level of originality required, shall be determined by each Party.

It will be seen however that this provision imposes no positive obligation at all on the parties to protect designs.

Indeed, when we look to the manner in which the Berne Convention addresses the protection of designs by means of copyright we see that, rather than mandating such protection, it

---

[7]   These are currently, as to national registered designs legislation in the UK and throughout the EU, effectively the same, although since the post-Brexit transition period which ended on December 31, 2020, UK courts are no longer bound by new decisions of the EU Court of Justice and can, at an appellate level, depart from its decisions from before that date in certain circumstances.

[8]   See footnote 3 above for what is meant by the expression "Informed User."

[9]   Article 20.24 requires each party to make all reasonable efforts to accede to the Geneva Act of the Hague Agreement Concerning the International Registration of Industrial Designs, discussed above, which implies that the parties will protect designs by means of a design registration system.

makes it clear that countries are under no obligation to protect "industrial designs and models," or works of applied art, by such means, except to the extent that the design is the work of a foreigner and no special protection for designs, available also to such foreigner, is available in that country. Thus by Article 2(7) it provides:

> 2(7) Subject to the provisions of Article 7(4) of this Convention, it shall be a matter for legislation in the countries of the Union to determine the extent of the application of their laws to works of applied art and industrial designs and models, as well as the conditions under which such works, designs and models shall be protected. Works protected in the country of origin solely as designs and models shall be entitled in another country of the Union only to such special protection as is granted in that country to designs and models; however, if no such special protection is granted in that country, such works shall be protected as artistic works.

Article 7(4) here referred to allows countries to provide a restricted term of protection for works of applied art (which has in practice also been interpreted as extending generally to designs where these are also protected by copyright):[10]

> 7(4) It shall be a matter for legislation in the countries of the Union to determine the term of protection of photographic works and that of works of applied art in so far as they are protected as artistic works; however, this term shall last at least until the end of a period of twenty-five years from the making of such a work.

These provisions of the Berne Convention have allowed countries to limit the extent of overlap in their national laws as between the protection of works of applied art and designs by means of copyright and the protection of works of applied art and designs by means of a separate, and generally registration-related, system. Such an approach, formerly common in many European countries, has been challenged in the countries of the EU and in the UK as a result of the unintended consequences of certain aspects of its copyright legislation as interpreted by the EU Court of Justice.[11] The result has been that in addition to their laws that protect designs for up to 25 years by means of registration,[12] and also for short periods without registration by means

---

[10]   This flexibility, for works of applied art, is preserved by Article 12 TRIPS, which provides that: Whenever the term of protection of a work, other than a photographic work or a work of applied art, is calculated on a basis other than the life of a natural person, such term shall be no less than 50 years from the end of the calendar year of authorized publication, or, failing such authorized publication within 50 years from the making of the work, 50 years from the end of the calendar year of making."

[11]   See in particular Case C-683/17 *Cofemel—Sociedade de Vestuário SA v G-Star Raw CV* (September 12, 2019), holding at [48] that "designs are capable of classification as 'works', within the meaning of Directive 2001/29, if they meet the two requirements mentioned in paragraph 29 of the present judgment," where [29] provides that "First, [the concept of 'work'] entails that there exist an original subject matter, in the sense of being the author's own intellectual creation. Second, classification as a work is reserved to the elements that are the expression of such creation" and Case C-833/18 *SI, Brompton Bicycle Ltd v Chedech/Get2Get* (11 June 2020), concluding that "copyright protection [...] applies to a product whose shape is, at least in part, necessary to obtain a technical result, where that product is an original work resulting from intellectual creation, in that, through that shape, its author expresses his creative ability in an original manner by making free and creative choices in such a way that that shape reflects his personality."

[12]   Directive 98/71 of the European Parliament and of the Council of 13 October 1998 on the legal protection of designs (OJ L 289, 28.10.1998).

of "unregistered design rights," EU countries (and also arguably the UK)[13] must also protect designs by means of copyright, but without the limitations on such protection as permitted for designs by the Berne Convention.[14]

But what bearing do international conventions and trade agreements have on the challenges for designs protection presented by AI? A review of such conventions and agreements shows not only that there is no explicit guidance as to whether or not a designer must be human (except perhaps to the extent that a country fulfills the obligation to protect designs through copyright law), but also that there are very few constraints in such conventions and agreements on the form that a standalone designs law must take, which reflects its variability as between different countries and also its mutability over time in the same country. This ought to mean that it should be easy, in contrast to other types of intellectual property, to mold designs law so as to meet any perceived challenges of AI, such as the status of computer-generated designs.

But this does not of itself suggest how designs law should be so molded in order to meet such challenges. However, some pointers as to this are provided by the scope for copyright law to protect designs, as emphasized by the existence of flexibilities in the Berne Convention for limiting such protection, and by the fact that designs law has developed as a separate branch of law to copyright. The early history of designs law helps explain as how this situation came about.

---

[13]   The position in the UK, which in these respects is subject to the EU copyright acquis as at the end of the post-Brexit transition period on December 31, 2020 (although UK courts are no longer bound by new decisions of the EU Court of Justice and can, at an appellate level, depart from its decisions from before that date in certain circumstances), is subject to the issue of whether it may limit copyright protection only to works in a closed list, as designs (except insofar as they are "works of artistic craftsmanship") are not listed as works in which copyright can subsist in the Copyright, Designs and Patents Act 1988. Some have argued that such closed lists are incompatible with EU copyright law as interpreted by the EU Court of Justice: see Rosati, Eleonora, *Closed Subject-Matter Systems are No Longer Compatible with EU Copyright* (July 18, 2014). 12 GRUR Int 1112–18, available at SSRN: https://ssrn.com/abstract =2468104.

[14]   See Directive 98/71 (supra), Article 17 of which states that "A design protected by a design right registered in or in respect of a Member State in accordance with this Directive is also to be eligible for protection under the law of copyright of that State as from the date on which the design was created or fixed in any form. The extent to which, and the conditions under which, such a protection is conferred, including the level of originality required, shall be determined by each Member State." However, the flexibility that Article 17 apparently provides for Member States is limited as to term by Directive 2006/116/EC of the European Parliament and of the Council of 12 December 2006 on the term of protection of copyright and certain related rights (codified version) (OJ L 372, 27.12.2006, p.12–18), which mandates a term of protection by copyright for "the life of the author and for 70 years after his death, irrespective of the date when the work is lawfully made available to the public" but provides for no exceptions to this for designs or works of applied art, as explained in Case C-168/09 *Flos SpA v Semeraro Casa e Famiglia SpA* (January 27, 2011). The flexibility that Article 17 apparently provides is also limited as to originality by Case C-5/08 *Infopaq International A/S v Danske Dagblades Forening* (July 16, 2009) which establishes, in interpreting Directive 2001/29/EC of the European Parliament and of the Council of 22 May 2001 on the harmonisation of certain aspects of copyright and related rights in the information society (OJ L 167, 22.6.2001 pp.10–19), that the level of originality for all copyright works be that the work "is original in the sense that it is its author's own intellectual creation."

3.   THE ORIGINS OF DESIGNS LAW

Although in point of time the first legislation to protect designs was in the United Kingdom,[15] the framework that it established was, as Stephen Ladas[16] has pointed out, similar to the protection of artistic property by means of copyright, and it was instead the French law of 1806 that, as interpreted by the French courts, laid the foundations for treating designs as a separate area of law, more akin in many ways to patents than to copyright. As Ladas recounted:

> France during the Revolution had passed the law of July 19 to 24, 1793, for the protection of literary and artistic property. The provisions of the law were broad enough to cover any kind of designs. But in 1806 Napoleon made a trip to Lyon. The manufacturers of that city made various complaints to him with respect to the inadequate regulation and protection of their industries; among other things, they complained that the law of 1793 concerning artistic property did not protect them sufficiently. Napoleon promised to remedy the situation.

The result was the law of 1806, which provided a system of deposit and registration for what it termed "dessins de fabricants." As Ladas went on to recount, the French courts, rather than treating this law as supplementing that of 1793, "exerted themselves to define an industrial design and to distinguish it from an artistic design" and construed compliance with its formalities as a precondition to owning a design, drawing analogies with patent law. The law was extended to all industries and industrial models, and designs completed their transition out of the realm of copyright into that of patents. Ladas went on to observe that "the effect of the law of 1806 and the consequent jurisprudence in seeking to establish a separation of industrial designs from artistic designs, and the requirement for novelty as distinct from originality, and, in general, the patent approach rather than the copyright approach, influenced the development of the law of designs in most European countries."

Ladas also attributed the inclusion in the USA of designs in the patent law, and their treatment on an analogous basis to patents, to another historical accident. The first US designs law was enacted in 1842, following a report to the Congress in 1841 by the Commissioner of Patents, who had recommended legislation to protect new and original designs. There was at

---

[15]   The Designing and Printing of Linen Act of 1787 provided short-term protection (initially two, and then three, months) for textile designs. The Act did not require registration or deposit, which was not introduced until the 1839 Act, which also extended protection to other types of fabrics than linens, cottons, calicoes and muslin, and then to articles of manufacture. However, the pre-1839 Act framework was, as Ladas points out, similar to the protection of artistic property by means of copyright. The 1839 Act was soon replaced by the Ornamental Designs Act 1842, which divided articles of manufacture into classes with different periods of protection for each class, from nine months to three years. This was then supplemented by the Utility Designs Act 1843, which offered three years' protection for the designs of articles of manufacture with functional features, blurring the interface between patent and designs law. The 1843 Act, which came into being in part as a result of perceived inadequacies in the UK patent system, protected the shape and configuration of such articles rather than, as with patent law, the use made of them, so many articles could be protected under both regimes. Although most treat the 1891 German utility model regime as the basis for utility model regimes internationally, Mark Janis, who noted that the 1891 measure was originally conceived as a form of design protection, also traces the origin of such regimes to the UK 1843 Act: see Janis, Mark (1999). *Second Tier Patent Protection*. 40(1) Harvard International Law Journal 151–219.

[16]   Ladas, Stephen P. *Patents, Trademarks and Related Rights: National and International Protection* Volume II (Harvard University Press 1975) at p.829 et seq.

the time no central copyright office in the USA where copies of works in which copyright was claimed could be deposited, so Congress was happy to adopt the Commissioner's proposal that they authorize him "to issue patents for these objects under the same limitations and under the same conditions as govern present action in other cases."

In summary, as Ladas observed, "the formation of a special branch of industrial property for designs and models is a historical accident."

4.   CONCLUSIONS

As it is hoped that the above discussion has shown, in addressing the issue of AI-generated designs we should recognize the contradictions inherent in treating designs law as an independent area of law when in reality it is an accidental hybrid with features of both patents and copyright. This suggests that there may be no single answer to the issue of AI-generated designs. Moreover, the nature of the laws that specifically protect designs is so fluid, flexible and amorphous at an international level that there can be no real treaty or trade agreement-related constraints on how one goes about protecting AI-generated designs. These considerations provide us with a ready answer to the question of how best to address the issue of such designs.

Applying these considerations, then, to the extent that the particular mode of design protection lies not in copyright itself but in copyright-type thinking, as is the case for unregistered design rights, we should adopt the same approach as that adopted in copyright for those designs that would attract copyright protection were they to have a human author but which in reality lack a human author because they are exclusively AI-generated: the author would hazard the view that this ought, given the very nature of copyright, be no protection at all under the law of copyright in the author's right sense, but at most, should the need be shown for it, some sort of related right, limited in scope and term.[17]

Applying the same considerations, then, to the extent that the mode of design protection lies in patent-related concepts, as tends to be the case for registered design rights, we should adopt the same approach for AI-generated designs as that adopted for AI-generated inventions. The author is not, in this case, so bold as to hazard a suggestion as to what particular approach this should be, except to express some skepticism regarding how close we are to exclusively AI-generated inventions[18] and to muse that if and when the day of such inventions comes, mere niceties of intellectual property protection are likely to be the least of our concerns as humans.

---

[17]   See for example Senftleben, Martin and Buijtelaar, Laurens, *Robot Creativity: An Incentive-Based Neighboring Rights Approach* (October 1, 2020). Available at SSRN: https://ssrn.com/abstract=3707741 or http://dx.doi.org/10.2139/ssrn.3707741, observing that "[T]he law of neighboring rights, by contrast [to copyright], offers room for more elastic solutions due to its flexible and customizable protection framework. Such a framework makes it possible to ensure that the creation and dissemination of robot-generated works is rewarded and stimulated while, at the same time, reducing the potential detrimental effect on the market for traditional, human works and the income perspectives of artists of flesh and blood."

[18]   See Kim, Daria in *"AI-Generated Inventions": Time to Get the Record Straight?* (2020) 69(5) GRUR International 443–56 and concluding: "the application of such techniques cannot be prejudicial for the allocation of the inventor entitlement to a natural person. As long as a human specifies instructions that determine how the input-output relation is derived through computation, and as long as computers are bound by such instructions, there is seemingly no reason why AI-aided—allegedly 'AI-generated'—inventions should be treated under patent law differently than inventions assisted by

This analysis also suggests that AI presents us with an opportunity to rethink why we protect designs in the various ways that we do and, assuming that designs need a separate form of protection, how best we should go about providing this. But even if it were, for the sake of argument, to be established that designs were not in need of a separate form of protection to that provided by copyright, it is unrealistic to imagine that we can turn back the clock more than two hundred years and abolish design registration systems. It is more realistic, however, to question the need for, and desirability of, unregistered design protection, especially now that in Europe designs are afforded broad protection by means of copyright. Such broad protection has arisen through a combination of the copyright term Directive, which has precluded use in Europe of one of the Berne Convention flexibilities as to "works of applied art and models," and the copyright in the Information Society Directive, on the basis of which the EU Court of Justice has so interpreted the concept of a copyright work as to be constrained only by concepts (namely originality and definition) which are indifferent as to whether or not the copyright work in question happens also to be a design.

The existence of such broad copyright protection for designs puts into question the need for separate systems of unregistered design protection. Removing the complication of unregistered design protection would leave, on the basis of the above analysis, designs to be protected by copyright, with its approach to AI-generated designs that if human-generated would be regarded as copyright works, or by registration, where the solution for AI-generated works would be the same as that ultimately adopted for patents.

---

other types of problem-solving tools and methods as far as inventorship is concerned. Instead, the use of such techniques should be a matter of the assessment of inventive step."

PART IV

PATENTS AND TRADE SECRETS

19. Legal fictions and the corporation as an inventive artificial intelligence

Dennis Crouch[1]

1. THE CORPORATE ARTIFICIAL INTELLIGENCE AS INVESTOR

This chapter's focus is an alternative form of artificial intelligence: corporations and other private organizations.[2] Unlike their computer-bound AI cousins, corporations have already been granted the legal fiction of personhood status and many accompanying civil rights, including rights of property, contract, privacy, and speech.[3] Some of these rights emerged via

---

[1] Special thanks to Dr. Homayoon Rafatijoo for thoughtful suggestions.

[2] Others have recognized a potential link between corporations and artificial intelligence. Most commonly, discussions focus on an analogy between the legal fiction of corporate personhood and the legal fiction of AI personhood. Another common theme is the use of corporate law to effectively cobble together AI personhood rights. See Lawrence B. Solum, *Legal Personhood for Artificial Intelligences*, 70 N.C. L. Rev. 1231, 1239 (1992); John Chipman Gray, THE NATURE AND SOURCES OF THE LAW, 52 (1909) (corporations have legal personhood because they possess "intelligence" and "will"). Briana Hopes, *Rights for Robots? U.S. Courts and Patent Offices Must Consider Recognizing Artificial Intelligence Systems as Patent Inventors*, 23 Tul. J. Tech. & Intell. Prop. 119, 127 (2021) (Corporations "are run by their stockholders and directors. This is no different than an artificial intelligence being run by its owner and programmers"); Jiahong Chen & Paul Burgess, *The Boundaries of Legal Personhood: How Spontaneous Intelligence Can Problematise Differences Between Humans, Artificial Intelligence, Companies and Animals*, 27 Artificial Intelligence and Law 73, 76 (2019) (comparing AI and a corporation); SM Solaiman, *Legal Personality of Robots, Corporations, Idols and Chimpanzees: a Quest for Legitimacy* (2017) 25 Artificial Intelligence and Law 155–79; Jessica Berg, *Of Elephants and Embryos: A Proposed Framework for Legal Personhood*, 59 Hastings L.J. 369, 384 ("[U]nlike corporations, [...] embryos, fetuses, non-human animals, and machines with artificial intelligence are clearly not 'fictional' entities"). See Dorian Pyle & Cristina San Jose, *An Executive's Guide to Machine Learning*, McKinsey & Co. (June 2015), www.mckinsey.com/industries/high-tech/our-insights/an-executives-guide-to-machine -learning ("Looking three to five years out, we expect to see far higher levels of artificial intelligence, as well as the development of distributed autonomous corporations. These self-motivating, self-contained agents, formed as corporations, will be able to carry out set objectives autonomously, without any direct human supervision. Some DACs will certainly become self-programming").

[3] Lawrence B. Solum, *Legal Personhood for Artificial Intelligences*, 70 N.C. L. Rev. 1231, 1287 (1992) ("[T]he rights provided by the Equal Protection Clause and the Due Process Clause extend to all persons—including artificial persons such as corporations. For example, the property of corporations is protected from taking without just compensation. Moreover, corporations have a right to freedom of speech"). This topic of corporate personhood has been much debated over the centuries. See, Arthur W. Machen, Jr., *Corporate Personality*, 24 Harv. L. Rev. 253 (1911). However, discussions in the US were reinvigorated by several recent cases strongly supporting civil rights for corporations. See Kent Greenfield, CORPORATIONS ARE PEOPLE TOO (AND THEY SHOULD ACT LIKE IT) (2018); Adam Winkler, *Corporate Personhood and Constitutional Rights for Corporations*, 54 New Eng. L. Rev. 23 (2019); Carliss N. Chatman, *The Corporate Personhood Two-Step*, 18 Nev. L.J. 811 (2018) (discussing theories justifying corporate personhood). Regarding terminology, this chapter uses the terms corporation and

common law or tradition, others via statute; and in the United States many are also grounded in constitutional law.[4]

In the intellectual property sphere, corporations already originate and hold many rights. A corporation is usually seen as the originator of trade secret information as the entity that takes reasonable measures to keep the secrets. Likewise, with trademark rights it is the business that uses the mark in commerce. That "use" is the key step for transforming a collection of unprotected words or symbols into a protectable mark. With copyright, Congress stepped in more than 100 years ago to announce that a corporation can be considered the author of copyrighted works under the work made for hire doctrine. Despite the advent of and importance of AI, in all these IP creation scenarios, natural people—humans—continue to play an integral role in actually developing these works into protectable rights. But ownership originates in the corporation. Importantly for this chapter, the automatic flow of rights does not pass through the hands of any actual human originator, but rather bypasses the human. Instead, the corporate owner is projected as the originator as part of the legal fiction of agency law.

An item still lacking from the corporate arsenal is inventorship rights. Yes, a corporation may own or license an invention and its resulting patents. And in fact, most patents are owned by non-human persons. But the law persists in most nations, as it has for more than 200 years, that patentable inventions must begin with a human person, the inventor. In that sense, there is no "corporate invention" because corporate ownership of patent rights is derived rather than original—it stems from a transfer of property rights from human inventors who begins the chain of title.[5]

This system hosts an inherent problem that arises when an invention emerges from a corporate organization, but where the attributable human-originated contributions do not rise to the levels required to legally constitute invention. That situation is easy to imagine with an AI intermediary who provides innovative contributions separate and distinct from any human innovator. In addition, the situation may be prompted via corporate organization and operation—the corporate machine. Since the law requires and permits only human inventors, the result is another layer of legal fiction—with the closest relatable human posed as the inventor even though the original creation cannot be attributed to the mind of that natural person.

This chapter walks through a historical progression of inventorship rights and corporate ownership from pre-industrial beginnings up through the elimination of statutory inventorship requirement in the Leahy–Smith America Invents Act of 2011. Although a hard line still exists against corporate inventorship rights, the line is now quite thin and is set to be potentially breached by any of the three main branches of the US government. This raises the basic question of the purposes of the legal bar on corporate invention and whether the prohibition continues to serve its longstanding role.

Some readers may have already balked at the casual parallels between classic machine-based AI and what might be termed the organizational intelligence of a corporation. Science fiction

---

corporate to generally refer to private organizations that have already achieved personhood status in some regard and is not intended to be limited to any particular set of corporate forms.

4   This chapter primarily focuses on the law of inventorship in the context of US law, where doctrines are more developed.

5   Generally, providing materials or workspace is not sufficient to automatically qualify for ownership rights. However, in several cases the courts have provided limited "shop rights" in the form of a non-exclusive license. *United States v Dubilier Condenser Corp.*, 289 U.S. 178 (1933).

has often focused autonomous system rights debate on the singularity of machine sentience. That point remains an elusive future. What do already exist in our midst are corporations, legal persons making intelligent, human-like decisions. One reason that corporate decisions are "human-like" is that corporations are often owned by humans and are typically designed and managed by humans.[6] We might see the distinctions by degree: Starting small, a sole proprietorship is effectively a merger of the human and their firm; a partnership raises some complexity; a major corporation can have a highly complex structure of operational rules, contractual obligations, machine assistance, and human contribution. If well structured, the company can effectively run itself as an organizational machine. Although humans continue to be part of the complex organization, the organization is not itself a natural person but rather an artificial person.[7] A 1911 *Harvard Law Review* article on the topic of Corporate Personhood provides an apt analogy:

> Was there ever a schoolboy who had any difficulty in understanding that his school is something distinct from the boys that constitute it? He does not need to be told that the school may preserve its identity after a new generation of boys have grown up, so that not a single pupil remains the same, and though every teacher may have changed and though the school building may have been moved to a different location. He finds nothing strange or mystical in the conception of the school as an entity.[8]

It is obvious today that corporations can be, and regularly are, distinct from their human components, and that the artificial person often remains even as their natural person components come and go. Most will also agree that these corporations may be taking human-like actions—exhibiting some level of artificial intelligence even if short of being categorized as generalized AI. In addition, it is not controversial to state that corporations have legal personhood that includes rights protected by the US Constitution.

What we have not yet established is whether the corporate actions might be classified as sufficiently inventive so as to deserve original patent rights. If we allow actions of the corporation's human agents to count as corporate actions, then certainly the corporation is an inventor under current standards of inventorship. Apart from that, corporations are regularly providing sufficient contribution to at least meet the joint inventorship test via a combination of their human agents; their machines (including AI) and other tools, organization, and instruction. As AI develops, the likelihood of actual corporate inventorship continues to grow, so long as the actions of the AI tools are attributable to their corporate owners. This chapter primarily compares corporate inventorship with the status quo requiring natural human inventorship. It is also useful to compare corporate invention with proposals found elsewhere in this volume arguing in favor of recognizing AI invention. A major difficulty with AI as inventor is that 200 years of case law assume that the inventor is a legal person with original rights to the resulting patent. Under current law, AI is not a legal person; cannot own property; and does not

---

6   Shawn Bayern, *The Implications of Modern Business Entity Law for the Regulation of Autonomous Systems*, 19 Stan. Tech. L. Rev. (2015).
7   1 *English Private Law* § 3.18, at 142–3 (Peter Birks ed., 2000); PERSON, Black's Law Dictionary (11th ed. 2019).
8   Arthur W. Machen, Jr., *Corporate Personality*, 24 Harv. L. Rev. 253, 259 (1911); David Runciman, *Is the State a Corporation?*, 35 Government and Opposition 90, 91 (2000) ("[A corporation] is that form of association which stands apart from its individual members, with a distinct identity of its own"); Jason Iuliano, *Do Corporations Have Religious Beliefs?*, 90 Ind. L.J. 47, 80 (2015).

have contractual rights to transfer rights. An AI inventorship regime would not be as simple as adding a provision to the law. Rather, the transition would require either (1) altering the traditional regime of inventor-ownership so that machine-inventors are not the owner or (2) providing personhood status to the AI. Neither of these approaches are as simple as the legal fiction of corporate invention.

In many ways, the persistence of no-corporate-invention may be surprising given the massive transformation in corporate personhood rights over the past 230 years and the regular assertion of original corporate ownership over employee contributions. Although artificial intelligence is the express subject of this book, AI can be framed as a proxy for the long and ongoing battle between workers and owners; between inventors and those who fund their endeavors and subsequently own their output. But, it turns out that in some ways, the human-inventor versus AI-inventor versus corporate-inventor arguments are a bit of a side-show. With only a few exceptions, corporate owners are *not* calling for rights of corporate inventorship or rights to AI invention. In general, companies have been able to obtain ownership and control via the traditional mechanisms of identifying an employee inventor who has already assigned their inventorship rights to the employer (or is under a duty to do so). This process is easier than ever. Changes to the US patent system as part of the America Invents Act were designed to further facilitate transfer rights from human inventor to corporate owner. For example, companies lobbied for a change in American law so that even if the named inventor was a legal fiction, that inventorship listing would not be used to undermine the patent rights. Today it is easy to identify a human with some relation to the product or innovation and prop up that human as the inventor. Because of the low standard for joint inventorship, a common approach may be to list multiple human joint-inventors, each of whom has contributed something, without requiring any of them to be the dominant or primary contributor. Thus, as AI continues to develop, I believe that companies will have no problem obtaining patents under the current system, except for potentially a few examples where the closely related human cannot be identified or takes affirmative legal action to avoid being listed as inventor.[9]

This introduction has left us with two bad choices, both calling for legal fictions. On the one hand, we could accept a future of corporate inventorship and the legal fiction tied to that regime based upon a recognition that any corporate invention is likely to be actually accomplished by human agents or corporate-owned machines. The alternative approach presented is the status quo, accompanied by increasing concern that AI contributions also render exclusive human inventorship a legal fiction.

Legal fictions are untruths that we tell to achieve some larger purpose, but are problematic when held too long as central tenets of legal doctrine or a property system.[10] This chapter concludes with recommendations on supporting the patent system while rejecting the notion that these legal fictions should serve as its central tenets.

---

[9]   A key roadblock to this approach is whether it meets the ethical standards demanded of patent law practitioners, who have duties of candor and good faith associated with all of their dealings with the patent office.

[10]   Lon L. Fuller, LEGAL FICTIONS 2 (Stanford Univ. Press 1967).

2.   HISTORICAL CONTEXT OF HUMAN INVENTORSHIP AND PATENT RIGHTS

Patent law, with its slow-to-change doctrine, highlights a narrow point of connection in the gulf between labor and ownership. As repeatedly recognized by the United States Supreme Court, patent rights begin with invention and are initially owned by the inventor.[11] Of course, this *ab initio* right quickly dissipates. By the time of their respective invention, most inventors have already contractually agreed to transfer intellectual property ownership rights, typically as part of employment agreements. In a 2011 patent-ownership decision known as *Stanford v Roche*, the Supreme Court began its opinion with a declaration in favor of inventor ownership:

> Since 1790, the patent law has operated on the premise that rights in an invention belong to the inventor [...] Although much in intellectual property law has changed in the 220 years since the first Patent Act, the basic idea that inventors have the right to patent their inventions has not.[12]

The Patent Act of 1790 took its cue from the US Constitution that had been newly ratified in 1789 and provides Congress an enumerated power: 'To promote the progress of science and useful arts, by securing for limited times to authors and inventors the exclusive right to their respective writings and discoveries.'[13]

This early focus on the human inventor is not surprising given the pre-industrial era of the law's foundation. At that time, a corporate charter required a special legislative action, and an employee's workplace knowledge was seen as a personal attribute of the employee.[14] Courts began drawing a line between mechanical skills and inventive skills, with only the latter deserving patent rights.[15] An invention was then deemed owned by the individual who expressed that inventive skill, regardless of the existence of an employment relationship.[16]

As corporate law emerged in the nineteenth and twentieth centuries, so did the ability to contractually transfer patent rights as part of a general employment agreement. Outside of express contractual situations, the courts also determined that ownership transfer is implied in

---

[11]   *Agawam Co. v Jordan*, 74 U.S. 583, 602 (1868) ("No one is entitled to a patent for that which he did not invent unless he can show a legal title to the same from the inventor or by operation of law").

[12]   *Bd. of Trustees of Leland Stanford Junior U. v Roche Molecular Sys., Inc.*, 563 U.S. 776, 780 (2011). The inventor in *Stanford v Roche*, Mark Holodniy, was not claiming ownership. Rather, the fight was between his two prior employers, who both wanted to own rights to the valuable PCR-related patents. I have written that this setup of two multi-billion-dollar entities fighting over the rights to the work of an individual reminiscent of the famous US Supreme Court decision of *Johnson v M'Intosh*, 21 U.S. (8 Wheat.) 543, 571 (1823), a case involving two white Americans fighting over which had properly received title to the land of Native Americans after they had been driven out of the area that is now central Illinois. See Dennis Crouch, *Reattribution, the Poison Pill and Inventorship*, 6 Bus. Entrepreneurship & Tax L. Rev. ___ (2022) (forthcoming).

[13]   Article I, Section 8, Clause 8, of the United States Constitution.

[14]   Catherine Fisk, WORKING KNOWLEDGE: EMPLOYEE INNOVATION AND THE RISE OF CORPORATE INTELLECTUAL PROPERTY, 1800–1930 (2009).

[15]   A key early case, *Hotchkiss v Greenwood*, 11 How. 248 (1850), included an explanation that invention required "more ingenuity and skill" than that of an "ordinary mechanic acquainted with the business."

[16]   See *Gayler v Wilder*, 10 How. 477, 493 (1851) ("the discoverer of a new and useful improvement is vested by law with an inchoate right to its exclusive use, which he may perfect and make absolute by proceeding in the manner which the law requires").

situations where a human is "hired to invent." The Supreme Court also offered limited trade rights for employers who facilitated the invention but failed to acquire rights to the patent.[17] Still, throughout this transformation, the law remained focused on human inventors as the linchpin to patent rights.

These aspects of the law have been fairly stable since the mid-1800s, when a leading treatise explained that hiring of an employee to invent might result in automatic assignment of the patent rights but "would not, however, make the employer the inventor, though the real inventor would thereby, lose the property in his invention."[18] Similarly, the leading contemporary patent treatise indicates the same.

The presumptive owner of the property right in a patentable invention is the single human inventor, in the case of a sole invention, or the several human inventors, in the case of a joint invention. The inventor or inventors may then transfer ownership interests by written assignment to anyone (including a corporation or other entity) and may in fact be under a legal duty to do so by virtue of a contractual or other obligation, as in the case of an employee who has signed a contract requiring that he/she assign inventions made during the course of employment.[19]

There are a few loose indications in the cases suggesting the idea of corporate invention—or at least "employer invention." In the 1868 decision of *Agawam Woolen Co. v Jordan*, 74 U.S. 583, 594 (1868), the court explained that both employees and employers "are entitled to their own independent inventions."[20] *Agawam Woolen* does not, however, bear directly on corporate inventorship because both employee and employer in that case were human individuals.

In the late 1800s the idea of employer authorship began to take hold in the copyright realm, leading to 1909's amendments to the copyright act indicating that the employer is author "in the case of works made for hire."[21] In an 1880 decision, the Patent Commissioner offered a similar approach for patents, noting certain situations that create a presumption that the employer is the originator: "As between an employer and a party employed for a special purpose [...] a presumption exists in favor of the employer as author."[22]

---

[17]   *Solomons v U.S.*, 137 U.S. 342, 348 (1890) (government employee implicitly consented to an irrevocable license to the government, focusing on the use of government tools in the creation of the invention). *Solomons* relied wholly upon *McClurg v Kingsland*, 42 U.S. 202, 206 (1843). In McClurg, the Supreme Court offered an "special license" to the employer to use the invention based upon the employee's implied consent. Today. This special license is commonly referred to as a shop right. Later, in *United States v Dubilier Condenser Corp.*, 289 U.S. 178, 188 (1933), the Supreme Court recast the shop-right as an equitable license stemming from the employee's use of "his master's time, facilities, and materials to attain a concrete result." Note here that "his master's time" is a reference to the employee's work hours that have been "purchased" by the employer.

[18]   Willard Phillips, THE LAW OF PATENTS FOR INVENTIONS, 63–4 (1837), citing to the English cases of *Barber v Walduck* (1823) 1 C & P 567 and *Bloxam v Elsee* (1818).

[19]   Donald Chisum, 8 CHISUM ON PATENTS § 22.01 (2021).

[20]   *Agawam Woolen Co. v Jordan*, 74 U.S. 583, 594 (1868). See also, *Int'l Carrier Call & Television Corp. v Radio Corp. of Am.*, 142 F.2d 493 (2d Cir. 1944) ("An employer who seeks to patent the fruits of his employees' labors must go further than merely to express a purpose to be realized").

[21]   17 U.S.C. § 25 (1909).

[22]   *Harrson v Hogan*, 1880 C.D. 191; 18 O.G. 921 (Commissioner of Patents 1880). See also *Foster v Fowle*, Com. Dec. (1869) (when an assistant who makes valuable discoveries ancillary to the plan and preconceived design of the employer, the suggested improvements may be embodied in the employer's patent as part of his invention"). *Gilbert v Clarke*, 5 O. G. 428 (Commissioner of Patents 1874) (employ-

The commissioner's loose suggestion here may imply the idea of corporate invention, but the idea never gained ground. Rather, though a presumption in favor of the employer continues to attach, it does so only with regard to ownership in the hired-to-invent doctrine, but not to inventorship itself.[23]

In 2011, Congress amended the definitions section of the Patent Act to expressly define the terms "inventor" and "joint inventor" to require them to be "individuals."[24] In the 2021 DABUS AI inventorship case, Judge Brinkema interpreted that newly added language as adding weight to the conclusion that US law allows for only human inventors.[25] The district court refused the patent applicant's demand to force the US Patent Office to issue a patent absent identification of a human inventor.[26]

3. EXPANSION OF CORPORATE ORIGINATION THEORY IN NON-PATENT AREAS OF INTELLECTUAL PROPERTY

Patent law might be seen as lagging with regard to corporate origination of property rights. In most other areas of law, corporate owners have a solid origination claim to the fruits of their employees' labors. In an important series of works, Professor Catherine L. Fisk chronicles this transformation toward corporate ownership and origination beginning in pre-industrial America through the mid-twentieth century.[27] Workplace innovations—employee-created knowledge—were originally seen as a personal attribute of the employee. Today, they are a corporate asset.[28] As Fisk explains, this transformation is due to a mixture of changes in the underlying intellectual property regimes along with more liberal enforcement of the workplace

---

ee's suggestions for improvements imputed to the employer); discussed in David Rice & Lepine Rice, *Digest of the Decisions of Law and Practice in the Patent Office from 1869 to 1880* (1880).

23   See Joshua L. Simmons, *Inventions Made for Hire*, 2 NYU J. Intell. Prop. & Ent. L. 1, 18 (2012).

24   35 U.S.C. 100(f) and (g).

25   *Thaler v Hirshfeld*, 120CV903LMBTCB, 2021 WL 3934803, at *4 (E.D. Va. Sept. 2, 2021). Thaler relied heavily upon the Supreme Court 2011 decision interpreting the use of "individual" in the Torture Victim Protection Act ("TVPA"). *Mohamad v Palestinian Auth.*, 566 U.S. 449, 453–4, 132 S.Ct. 1702, 182 L.Ed.2d 720 (2012) ("The ordinary meaning of the word [is] natural person"). See also Dennis Crouch, *USPTO Rejects AI-Invention for Lack of a Human Inventor*, Patently-O (Apr. 27, 2020).

26   35 U.S.C. 115(d) permits a substitute statement in situations where the inventor is "under legal incapacity." That provision would arguably apply to AI that have not been granted legal personhood rights. Still, the court found that the provision does not apply because AI is not an individual and therefore barred from legal inventorship as well. *Thaler*.

27   See Catherine L. Fisk, WORKING KNOWLEDGE: EMPLOYEE INNOVATION AND THE RISE OF CORPORATE INTELLECTUAL PROPERTY, 1800–1930 (2009); Catherine L. Fisk, *The Role of Private Intellectual Property Rights in Markets for Labor and Ideas: Screen Credit and the Writers Guild of America, 1938–2000*, 32 Berkeley J. Empl. & Lab. L. 215, 215 (2011); Catherine L. Fisk, *Credit Where It's Due: The Law and Norms of Attribution*, 95 Geo. L.J. 49 (2006); Catherine L. Fisk, *Authors at Work: The Origins of the Work-for-Hire Doctrine*, 15 Yale J.L. & Humanities 1 (2003); Catherine L. Fisk, *Working Knowledge: Trade Secrets, Restrictive Covenants in Employment, and the Rise of Corporate Intellectual Property, 1800–1920*, 52 Hastings L.J. 441 (2001); Catherine L. Fisk, *Removing the "Fuel of Interest" from the "Fire of Genius": Law and the Employee-Inventor, 1830–1930*, 65 U. Chi. L. Rev. 1127 (1998).

28   See Oren Bracha, *The New Intellectual Property of the Nineteenth*, 89 Tex. L. Rev. 423, 430 (2010) (review and discussion of Fisk's Working Knowledge book).

contracts, included pre-creation assignment of rights, non-compete and confidentiality agreements, and implied contracts favoring employer rights. Although the language of master and servant has fallen from favor when talking about an employment relationship, the underlying doctrines themselves persist. Courts continue to look upon an employee's paid-for work as the "master's time" whose results have been bought and paid for.

Copyright: The 1909 Copyright Act codified the work-made-for-hire doctrine and the legal fiction that the corporate employer was the legal author and owner of the work of its employees.[29] The basis for transformation in the law appears primarily grounded in the idea that employers wanted to ensure their ownership of strong copyrights. Fisk identifies three reasons for the work-made-for-hire doctrine.[30] The largest of these, and the one identified within the legislative history, was that only the original owner (not an assignee) was permitted to file for copyright renewal.[31] By identifying the corporate employer as author, those renewal rights automatically flowed as well.

In the case of a work made for hire, the employer or other person for whom the work was prepared is considered the author for purposes of this title, and, unless the parties have expressly agreed otherwise in a written instrument signed by them, owns all of the rights comprised in the copyright.[32]

As the law makes clear, the corporate employer as author fiction also ensures automatic ownership rights without having to rely upon any further documentation of title transfer.

Trade Secret: Trade secret rights did not emerge as a form of intellectual property until well into the nineteenth century, but are now an independently important form of intellectual property rights. Unlike patents and copyrights, the origination of a trade secret is not based in the creative work. Instead, the origination of rights comes from combining valuable information with the act of taking reasonable measures to keep the secret, such as binding employees with secrecy contracts. The result is that trade secrets originate as corporate property, even when the trade secret information stems from "the exercise of the employee's personal knowledge and skills."[33] In the 1984 trade secret case of *Ruckelshaus v Monsanto*, the Supreme Court identified trade secrets as a property with direct reference to Locke's labor theory of property.

This general perception of trade secrets as property is consonant with a notion of "property" that extends beyond land and tangible goods and includes the products of an individual's "labour and invention."[34]

Although labor and invention were involved in developing the trade secret data at issue, the court did not question whether Monsanto owned that result that was clearly the work of its employees.[35]

---

[29]   Act of March 4, 1909, ch. 320, 35 Stat. 1075.

[30]   Catherine L. Fisk, *Authors at Work: The Origins of the Work-for-Hire Doctrine*, 15 Yale J.L. & Humanities 1, 62 (2003).

[31]   See 1 *Legislative History of the 1909 Copyright Act* 56 (B. Fulton Brylawski & Abe Goldman eds, 1976).

[32]   17 U.S.C. § 201(b).

[33]   1 MELVIN F. JAGER, TRADE SECRETS LAW § 3:18 (2012) (citing RESTATEMENT (THIRD) OF UNFAIR COMPETITION § 42 (1995)).

[34]   *Ruckelshaus v Monsanto Co.*, 467 U.S. 986, 1002–03 (1984). 2 W. Blackstone, Commentaries; see generally J. Locke, THE SECOND TREATISE OF CIVIL GOVERNMENT, ch. 5 (J. Gough ed. 1947)

[35]   Ibid ("We therefore hold that to the extent that Monsanto has an interest in its health, safety, and environmental data cognizable as a trade-secret property right under Missouri law, that property right is protected by the Taking Clause of the Fifth Amendment").

Trademark: Like trade secrets, trademark rights are tied more to "trade" than to any creative endeavor. Rights do not stem from the design or creation of mark. Rather, rights to a mark originate based upon a business venture that uses the mark in commerce.

I have quickly stepped through these other forms of intellectual property with the intent of providing a few examples of the expansion of corporate origination theory over the past 230 years. The focus of these transformations is primarily the regular assertion of original corporate ownership over employee contributions. This legal fiction of corporate origination is pervasive.

What is perhaps most surprising is that the transformation has not been complete in the patent realm. Human inventors rather than corporations continue to be the inventors, the creative originators with corporate employers only stepping in as the owner.

4.   REDUCTION OF INVENTORSHIP THRESHOLDS AND THE PROBLEM OF HUMAN INVENTOR AS A LEGAL FICTION

While the patent laws have not yet succumbed to a corporate origination theory, this section recognizes an important trend in the patent system of reducing the importance and role of both inventors and their inventive acts. The expressed history of these shifts does not show direct animus against inventors, but more of a disregard. The changes appear designed to facilitate smooth transfer of rights from employee inventors to corporate employers. The result, though, also facilitates a new legal fiction of inventorship in the age of artificial intelligence—naming human inventors as the sole sources of the invention, even in situations where substantial contributions were provided by a corporate organization or its non-human machines. This section walks through some of these shifts in the law, beginning with the statutory elimination of the "flash of creative genius" and "invention" concepts discussed by some courts. The law now allows patenting regardless of how the invention occurred.[36] For 200 years, the Patent Act also included an express statement that the listed inventor actually be the inventor.[37] That provision was eliminated as part of the 2011 bipartisan overhaul of the Patent Act.[38] Similarly, the revised statute eliminated the requirement that the inventor be the one to file for patent protection (now anyone with ownership rights can file for patent protection)[39] and eliminated any remaining focus on the act of invention as establishing inchoate rights to a patent (eliminating the first-to-invent rules).[40] Many of the changes are procedural, but have a potential substan-

---

[36]   35 U.S.C. § 103 (1952). Although this provision has been amended several times since its creation in 1952, including in the Leahy–Smith America Invents Act of 2011, none of the amendments altered this expansive allowance of invention.

[37]   35 U.S.C. 102(f) (1952) (pre-AIA) ("A person shall be entitled to a patent unless […] (f) he did not himself invent the subject matter sought to be patented"). This provision was eliminated in the AIA (2011).

[38]   Leahy–Smith America Invents Act of 2011.

[39]   The amended provision disentangled the patent applicant from the inventor, allowing a patent applicant to file an invention rather than the inventors themselves. Compare 35 U.S.C. § 115 pre- and post-AIA.

[40]   Consider 35 U.S.C. § 102(g) (pre-AIA) (providing the rules of priority based upon the date of invention). This provision was eliminated in the AIA (2011).

tive impact. Of particular importance is the high threshold now in place in many situations for challenging improper inventorship listing.

To be clear, the patent systems retain a high standard for invention—the invention must be new and useful, non-obvious, well described, and particularly claimed. In many ways, those objective standards for patentability are higher than ever. What has diminished, though, is the focus on the act of inventing and the role of the human inventor.[41] The result is that corporate owners are always able to point to one or more human employees most closely related to an innovation and identify those humans as the legal inventors, even if substantial contribution came from corporate or machine AI. The humans are listed as inventors, but the corporate employer becomes the owner.

4.1   Conception and Reduction to Practice

The act of invention turns out to be somewhat nebulous and difficult to define. Generally, invention is a two-step process of conception and reduction to practice. With conception, we have an idea that is "definite and permanent enough that one skilled in the art could understand the invention."[42] Traditional statements of conception are human-centric—noting that conception is the "mental part" of the inventive act that must be done "in the mind of the inventor."[43] The Manual of Patent Examination Procedure (MPEP)—the guidebook used by patent examiners—includes an all-caps statement shouting that "CONCEPTION MUST BE DONE IN THE MIND OF THE INVENTOR."[44] But today, most patents list multiple human inventors, on average more than three inventors per patent (Figure 19.1).[45] Thus, even before moving toward a new construct of corporate or organizational invention, we can recognize that the current construct is already a step behind—stuck in a historic context where single-inventor patents were the norm.

The patent statute provides no guidance of how to apply the in-the-mind test to group-inventor situations. A common approach of courts is that at least one of the joint inventors needs full and complete conception while other joint inventors must have provided a substantial contribution toward the conception.[46]

Invention begins with conception, but invention is only fully accomplished by reducing the invention to practice.[47] "No mental operation, however definite and valuable may be its result, is a complete inventive act."[48] This notion was developed by nineteenth-century courts and

---

[41]   Consider also provisions traditionally allowed for limited avoidance of prior art created by the inventor ("invented by another") now allow for exclusion of prior art "owned by the same" person or corporate entity." 35 U.S.C. 102(b)(2)(C).

[42]   *Burroughs Wellcome Co. v Barr Laboratories, Inc.*, 40 F.3d 1223, 1228 (Fed. Cir. 1994).

[43]   *Townsend v Smith*, 36 F.2d 292, 295, 4 USPQ 269, 271 (CCPA 1930).

[44]   MPEP 2138.04: "Conception" (9th ed., 2020 revision).

[45]   Dennis Crouch, *Continued Growth in the Number of Inventors per Patent*, Patently-O (March 11, 2021) (chart reproduced with permission of the author).

[46]   See *Dana-Farber Cancer Inst., Inc. v Ono Pharm. Co., Ltd.*, 964 F.3d 1365 (Fed. Cir. 2020) as discussed below.

[47]   *Burroughs Wellcome Co. v Barr Laboratories, Inc.*, 40 F.3d 1223, 1228 (Fed. Cir. 1994).

[48]   William C. Robinson, The Law of Patents for Useful Inventions, Section 124 (1890) ("An invention, therefore, does not exist until the generated idea has been reduced to practice"). See *Sawyer v Edison*, 25 O.G. 597 (1883) (Patent Commissioner) ("An invention is complete when the thought conceived is embodied in some practical and operative form"). Although Robinson's statements have

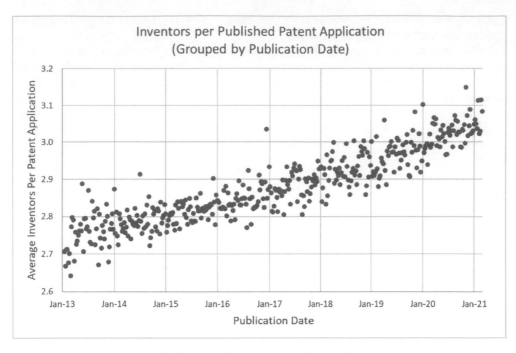

Figure 19.1   Average number of inventors per patent application

embodied in the Patent Act until being eliminated in 2011 as part of what I identify as the shift away from invention and inventorship as the touchpoints of patent law.[49] Reduction to practice takes the raw idea and verifies that it actually works in practice.[50]

But, with reduction to practice, the patent system includes another built-in legal fiction. Namely, a conceived-of invention need not actually be reduced to practice so long as an enabling patent application is filed that shows possession of the invention. That filing serves as "constructive reduction to practice." Thus, although reduction to practice is part of the invention process, conception is the primary focus. Reduction to practice historically remained important to situations involving inventors seeking to assert rights tied to the invention date. But, with the law's shift away from invention as relevant to patentability, actual reduction to

---

substantial merit, many of the sources he relies upon are directed to the directed to the doctrines prohibiting patenting of ideas in the abstract rather than focused solely on a requirement of reduction to practice as an element of inventing. See *Andrews v Carman*, 1 F. Cas. 868 (C.C.E.D.N.Y. 1876) ("There can be no patent for a principle [unless] embodied and connected with corporeal substances") and *McComb v Brodie*, 15 F. Cas. 1290 (C.C.D. La. 1872) ("A patent cannot be granted for a principle or an idea, or for any abstraction whatever [...] But when the idea is applied to a material thing, so as to produce a new and useful effect or result, it ceases to be abstract").

[49]   See 35 U.S.C. 102(g) (2010, pre-AIA). This provision was used as a mechanism for allowing inventors to claim priority back to their dates of conception, but was eliminated as part of the new focus on application filing dates as the touchstone.

[50]   *Burroughs Wellcome Co. v Barr Laboratories, Inc.*, 40 F.3d 1223, 1228 (Fed. Cir. 1994) ("[A]n inventor need not know that his invention will work for conception to be complete. He need only show that he had the idea; the discovery that an invention actually works is part of its reduction to practice").

practice has lost all relevance. And, as legal fictions do, the fiction has subsumed the rule. We see this in Supreme Court's most recent discussion of the topic where the Court suggested an altered rule and concluded that an invention can be complete without reduction to practice, although it remains unclear whether the Court intended to overrule the years of precedent saying otherwise.[51] The legal fiction of constructive reduction to practice has resulted in a focus on conception. And today, I would posit that few patent attorneys believe that actual reduction to practice is even an element of invention.

4.2   Invention Without Regard to How the Invention Occurred

The courts have gone back and forth over the years on the question of the actual creative step required of a patentable invention. An early decision by Justice Story while riding circuit foreshadowed the eventual settling point of the law. In *Earle v Sawyer*, Story explained that the focus of patentability should be on the resulting invention—is the output an advance of the prior art?[52] This objective approach falls in line with the famous 1805 property law decision in *Pierson v Post*, holding that ownership of the fox-pelt is awarded to whomever takes actual possession, not to the individual who put in the most effort.[53] The objective approach was further solidified by the Supreme Court's famous 1850 *Hotchkiss* decision.[54] Of course, it is much easier to objectively determine possession of a fox-pelt than it is to determine whether a particular invention sufficiently extends the state of the art. And courts fell back on the notion that the invention process itself can be helpful as a measure of the invention. Was the result the "the work of a mechanic of ordinary skill" or instead "the result of mind, of genius, of invention"?[55] This rising focus on invention being a genius act culminated in the Supreme Court's 1941 *Cuno Engineering* decision's statement that an invention "must reveal the flash of creative genius."[56] This back-and-forth eventually ended with the Patent Act of 1952 and codification of obviousness as the central test of patentability.[57] The test continues to rely upon the capability of a person of skill in the art as the standard, but expressly rejects any notion that a patentable invention need be the subject of any creative genius. "Patentability shall not be negatived by the manner in which the invention was made."[58] As Justice Story suggested so long ago, the law again looks to the output of the invention process, and "not to the process by which [a particular invention] is accomplished."[59] This transformation is important for the concept of corporate and AI invention. It offers the opportunity to manage the invention process in ways that apply the organizational benefit of corporate owners and that also make

---

[51]   *Pfaff v Wells Elecs., Inc.*, 525 U.S. 55, 66 (1998) (suggesting an altered definition of invention to now mean "ready for patenting").

[52]   *Earle v Sawyer*, 8 F. Cas. 254, 254 (C.C.D. Mass. 1825) ("It is of no consequence, whether the thing be simple or complicated; whether it be by accident, or by long, laborious thought, or by an instantaneous flash of mind, that it is first done. The law looks to the fact, and not to the process by which it is accomplished").

[53]   *Pierson v Post*, 1805 WL 781 (N.Y. Sup. Ct. 1805).

[54]   *Hotchkiss v Greenwood*, 52 U.S. 248 (1850).

[55]   *Tatham v Le Roy*, 23 F. Cas. 709, 713 (C.C.S.D.N.Y. 1852).

[56]   *Cuno Engr. Corp. v Automatic Devices Corp.*, 314 U.S. 84, 91 (1941).

[57]   35 U.S.C. 103.

[58]   35 U.S.C. § 103 (1952). This provision has been slightly amended and now states: "Patentability shall not be negated by the manner in which the invention was made."

[59]   *Earle v Sawyer*.

use of non-creative brute force or big-data tools available as part of the AI and information revolution. In many ways, this is an old story that goes back at least to Thomas Edison and his famed Menlo Park laboratory.[60] But, as other chapters in this volume make clear, the pace and extent of the use of AI and organizational management has now far surpassed the systematic approach that Edison achieved. In this new model, humans applying "ordinary skill" to an enterprise still achieve inventor status through use of the AI and organizational management tools of their corporate employers. The result is to effectively transform ordinary artisans into ordinary inventors, but only with the tools typically available within a corporate organization.

4.3 Elimination of Inventorship Formalities within the Patenting System

The Leahy–Smith America Invents Act of 2011 (AIA) included several statutory amendments that facilitate corporate patenting while still retaining the notion of human inventorship. The most direct of these is elimination of inventorship as a condition of patentability. Prior to 2011, US law stated clearly that a patent could be invalidated based upon the fact that a non-inventor was listed as the inventor.[61] That provision was eliminated by the AIA. In parallel, the new law also eliminated the date of invention as relevant to patentability. Thus, the new law provides a shift from a first-to-invent system to a first-to-file system.[62] Coupled with these changes are new regulatory provisions that allow corporate employers to directly seek patent protection. Previously, applications were filed on behalf of the inventors themselves except in rare circumstances.

The revised law continues to provide some tools to ensure that the listed inventors are the true inventors, but those tools are quite limited. For instance, the new law includes a limited one-year grace period for the true inventor to file for patent protection in situations where someone else falsely claimed inventorship.[63] Alternatively, procedures also narrowly provide for a derivation proceeding, but again with a tight deadline of one year following either publication or patenting.[64] But derivation can only be found if the allegedly derived invention is "the same or substantially the same invention," and so excludes a situation where a "derived invention" serves as the base but then new elements are added to the invention. And, if an inventorship listing error is found, the revised law allows for correction of inventorship even if the original listing constituted fraud.[65] Further, under the new statute, a patent remains valid if inventorship can be corrected.[66]

---

[60] Catherine L. Fisk, *Removing the "Fuel of Interest' from the "Fire of Genius': Law and the Employee-Inventor, 1830–1930*, 65 U. Chi. L. Rev. 1127, 1139 (1998).

[61] 35 U.S.C. 102(f) (pre-AIA) (The law previously stated that "[a] person shall be entitled to a patent unless [...] (f) he did not himself invent the subject matter sought to be patented.").

[62] 37 CFR § 1.42 now permits anyone who with "sufficient propriety interest" in the invention to become the patent applicant.

[63] 35 U.S.C. § 102(b)(2) (post-AIA).

[64] 35 U.S.C. § 135.

[65] 35 U.S.C. § 256 was revised in the AIA to eliminate the provision that permitted correction in situations where inventorship errors arise "without any deceptive intention." Note here that the prior statute was already quite leaky and permitted some amount of intentional deception.

[66] 35 U.S.C. § 256(b).

While an inventor who is not listed as an inventor can sue for correction, the inventor must show some associated concrete harm in order to have standing to sue in federal court.[67] Even though guaranteed by statute, the right to be named an inventor on its own is not enough to satisfy the constitutional case-or-controversy requirements.[68] And, in order to raise an inventorship challenge, there must be some additional identifiable human who is the inventor. Thus, a recent antitrust case involving a Hot Pocket packaging patent rejected the patent challenger's claim of improper inventorship because no particular 'proper' inventor was identified.[69]

None of these formalities shift the general rule requiring the correct human inventors to be identified. However, the myriad hurdles operate collectively to ease the path for corporate owners to see human inventorship listing as a paper tiger, without genuine teeth so long as no human outside the company bounds can stake an inventorship claim. One example might be a situation where a corporate applicant lists two of its employees as inventors but fails to list a third who contributed to the invention. That listing could always be corrected by the owner, but even if not corrected, the third inventor would not likely have standing to sue if also subject to an obligation to assign invention rights to the employer.[70]

These procedural hurdles for challenging inventorship listings become even more important in the context of potentially significant inventive contributions made by AI or other non-human aspects of the corporation. Although those non-human contributions do not count directly as corporate invention, a company may name the humans most closely related to the innovation as the inventors—feeding the paper tiger while retaining full ownership rights. This outcome helps to explain why machine-assisted invention does not change inventorship.

4.4   Reduction of the Joint Inventorship Standards

In 2020, the Court of Appeals for the Federal Circuit resolved an important inventorship decision in favor of a low threshold for joint inventorship—importantly, suggesting that the contribution of pre-conception research data was sufficient to be listed as a joint inventor.[71] That holding is key to understanding that AI activities are regularly providing sufficient contributions to qualify for joint inventorship absent the rule that only humans invent.

The dispute between Harvard's Dana-Farber Cancer Institute and Ono Pharmaceuticals focused on the question of whether the contribution of two Harvard scientists was sufficient for them to be considered joint inventors alongside the Nobel Prize winning Japanese scientist

---

[67]   See *Chou v University of Chicago*, 254 F.3d 1347, 1359 (Fed. Cir. 2001) (omitted inventor had standing to sue for correction after showing an "economic stake in a patent's validity". Reputational harm may be sufficient, but must be linked to "pecuniary consequences"). See also Robert A. Matthews, *Standing of Omitted Inventor to Correct Inventorship in § 256 Action*, 1 Annotated Patent Digest § 9:80 (2021).

[68]   Id.

[69]   *Inline Packaging, LLC v Graphic Packaging Intl., LLC*, 962 F.3d 1015, 1026 (8th Cir. 2020).

[70]   Employers involved with design & development regularly require new employees to "pre-assign title to future inventions." Robert Merges, *The Law and Economics of Employee Inventions*, 13 Harv. J.L. & Tech. 1, 7 (1999). But see *Bd. of Trustees of Leland Stanford Junior U. v Roche Molecular Sys., Inc.*, 563 U.S. 776 (2011) (including dissenting opinion by Judge Breyer questioning the propriety of pre-assignment of invention rights). Assuming the pre-invention assignments are valid, the employer will have immediate ownership of the invention as soon as it is invented, rather than requiring an actual written assignment of rights.

[71]   *Dana-Farber Cancer Inst., Inc. v Ono Pharm. Co.*, 964 F.3d 1365, 1367 (Fed. Cir. 2020).

Dr Tasuku Honjo. This case represents a primary situation where inventorship still matters: purported inventive contribution via inventors under contract to two different companies.[72] Because ownership rights remain tied to inventorship, a change in inventorship in this situation results in a change in ownership rights as well.

In the 1990s, Dr Honjo and his colleagues at Kyoto University discovered the PD-1 receptor associated with "programmed cell death," for which Honjo was awarded a Nobel Prize.[73] Mutations in the PD-1 receptor or its pathway can lead to cells that refuse to die—that is, cancer cells. During this time, Honjo and the two Harvard researchers began a collaborative research project that included data and ideas of the biologic pathway and potential therapeutic responses. Some amount of the information was not just provided to Dr Honjo, but also published generally for the scientific community. The Harvard researchers particularly provided basic science data on molecular aspects of how these pathways worked. That information provided itself would not be patentable. It was simply a law of nature. But Dr. Honjo's team at Kyoto conducted further research and was able to develop a "method for treatment of cancer" that focused in on the particular molecular pathway.[74]

Thus, it was clear and undisputed that Dr Honjo was the human who ultimately conceived of the invention. But the Federal Circuit ruled that the Harvard researchers also meaningfully contributed to the invention and thus should have been listed as joint inventors. Although the newly added inventors in *Dana-Farber* here were humans, it is easy to conceive of research output and data streams provided by AI that would be equally supportive of a joint inventorship claim. In the context of machine-assisted inventions, I expect that computers operating specialized software and laboratory equipment would regularly qualify as joint inventors but for the requirement that inventors be human individuals. This again takes us into the framework of legal fiction, with the very real potential of listed human inventors claiming to be the true inventors when in fact their conceptions were built upon the machine contributions.

The test for joint inventorship would be particularly difficult if the law required joint conception—each inventor participating in a "particular moment of conception" and each conceiving of the complete invention. In *Dana-Farber*, the court reminded us that the test is for joint inventorship and the requirement is not simultaneous conception but rather significant contribution to the invention.

5.   CORPORATE INVENTOR AND THE LEGAL FICTION

This section identifies three models for moving toward a corporate origination and thus inventorship doctrine in the patent world. As I discuss in the conclusion to this chapter, none of these approaches are quite right and they generally have the potential problem of furthering legal fiction without fostering additional innovation.

---

[72]   The situation in *Bd. of Trustees of Leland Stanford Junior U. v Roche Molecular Sys., Inc.*, 563 U.S. 776, 780 (2011), similarly involved one inventor simultaneously under contract to assign rights to two different entities.

[73]   Press release: The Nobel Prize in Physiology or Medicine 2018 at www.nobelprize.org/prizes/medicine/2018/press-release/.

[74]   See U.S. Patent No. 7,595,048.

5.1   Approach I—Invention for Hire Doctrine for Corporate Origination

The first model is to permit corporate inventorship along the same lines as is done in copyright law under work-made-for-hire. Patent law does have a hired-to-invent doctrine that results in assignment of rights but does not also identify the employer as the inventor. By contrast, in copyright, the corporate employer is named author, rather than any actual human author (assuming one exists). In applying this model for patents, a corporate employer would be identified as the inventor of the work of its employees and ownership rights would automatically vest. This automatic vesting would further streamline transfer of property rights rather than requiring an affirmative written transfer.[75] Although there may be a number of accompanying conforming changes as well, the basis for this transition could be easily based upon the addition of a parallel to the work-made-for-hire authorship provision found in the Copyright Act.[76] The following proposal for the patent act is a direct modification of Sections 201 and 101 of the Copyright Act; the italicization shows proposed changes to conform to patent law.

> *Inventions* Made for Hire—In the case of *an invention* made for hire, the employer or other person for whom the *invention* was prepared is considered the *inventor* for purposes of this title, and, unless the parties have expressly agreed otherwise in a written instrument signed by them, owns all of the rights comprised in the *patent or patent application.*
> *Definitions: An* "*invention* made for hire" is
> (1)   *an invention* prepared by an employee within the scope of his or her employment; or
> (2)   *an invention* specially ordered or commissioned, if the parties expressly agree in a written instrument signed by them that the work shall be considered a work made for hire.

I term this a "weak model" because it does not expressly allow for patenting of the type of corporate invention discussed elsewhere in this chapter, at times when the corporation itself or corporation-owned facilities (such as AI) add significantly to an invention's conception or reduction-to-practice.

In actuality, the weak version could well be designed with a subtle backdoor to implicitly allow full corporate inventorship rights effectuated by (1) not requiring disclosure of the underlying humans hired to invent and who actually conceived of the invention and (2) barring inventorship-related challenges to the patent except those stemming from a purported human inventor seeking rights or another party claiming improper derivation. This no-disclosure approach is similar to what is already done in copyright, where the corporate author is not asked to disclose or identify the humans who were hired to create the work. "If a work is made for hire, the employer or other person for whom the work was prepared is the author and should be named as the author on the application for copyright registration."[77] The result of a no-disclosure and no-challenge setup would implicitly allow the corporate inventor to file for patent rights on its own inventions even when no human inventor exists. The subtle backdoor also falls in line with changes to the patent system, including streamlining inventorship issues and the practical elimination of the best mode requirement.[78] In this vein, the

---

[75]   Joshua L. Simmons, *Inventions Made for Hire*, 2 NYU J. Intell. Prop. & Ent. L. 1 (2012).
[76]   17 U.S.C. §201.
[77]   Copyright Office Circular 9, www.copyright.gov/circs/circ09.pdf.
[78]   For inventorship issues see Section 2, *supra*. Best mode: As part of the patenting process, the patent applicant is required to disclose the best mode, if any, that has been contemplated by the inventors for carrying out their invention: 35 U.S.C. 112(a). However, patent examiners do use their limited exam-

invention-made-for-hire doctrine might be best seen as simply giving up on the notion of inventorship.

Companies regularly take advantage of the made-for-hire doctrine in the copyright space and would likely do so in the patent arena too, if only for the purpose of automatic ownership rights and fewer bureaucratic submissions from their engineer and scientist employees. Of course, the approach is ripe for overreach, as humans who created the invention might not even be notified until it is too late to take any recourse. In general, a made-for-hire doctrine that automatically shifts ownership rights from the actual creator to the employer shifts bargaining positions toward the employer. This is particularly true for "unbargained for or unforeseen uses."[79] Further, by its terms, this approach does nothing except shift default ownership rules from employees to employers, a legal fiction without justification.

The following paragraphs draw an analogy between (1) how our patent system treated the inventions made by enslaved people and (2) the treatment of inventions made via artificial intelligence or by corporate employees. Although I believe that the example of slavery is telling and relevant to the question at hand, I do not intend to suggest that human enslavement is equivalent in any way to an employment agreement or to property claims over the output of a machine.

In 1858, the US Attorney General issued an opinion titled "Invention of a Slave" concluding that "[a] new and useful machine invented by a slave cannot be patented."[80] At that time, the right to patent was tied to citizenship rights, and the US Supreme Court had recently decided *Dred Scott.*[81] In that decision, the Court confirmed what various state courts had previously decided—that under the law, free (non-enslaved) black and brown people were not United States Citizens.

The Attorney General's conclusions on patenting resulted from a somewhat twisted purpose. Southern enslavers were the ones seeking patent rights for their enslaved peoples' invention—operating under the theory that any invention of an enslaved person would be automatically owned by the slave owner. The Confederate States offered patent protection during the Civil War, which included granting patent rights to slave owners for the inventions of their enslaved people.[82] Although enslaved people were the subject of the legal debate, neither side was considering their rights or plights. Rather, they were merely the subject of a proxy war between Southern and Northern States. Of course, as with the backdoor inventorship approach discussed above, I am confident that the "inventions of a slave" could have still been patented—and likely were patented—by simply identifying the slave owner as the human inventor.

---

ination time to investigate whether the best mode has actually been disclosed. Historically, best mode has been litigated when a patent is later enforced. However, the America Invents Act of 2011 eliminated failure of best mode as the basis of defense: 35 U.S.C. 282 ("failure to disclose the best mode shall not be a basis on which any claim of a patent may be canceled or held invalid or otherwise unenforceable").

[79] I. Trotter Hardy, *An Economic Understanding of Copyright Law's Work-Made-for-Hire Doctrine*, Columbia-VLA Journal of Law & the Arts (1988).

[80] See Dennis Crouch, *Invention of a Slave and the Ongoing Movement for Equal Justice*, Patently-O (June 20, 2020). See Brian L. Frye, *Invention of a Slave*, 68 Syracuse L. Rev. 181, 194 (2018) (historical analysis); Kara W. Swanson, *Race and Selective Legal Memory: Reflections on Invention of a Slave*, 120 Columbia Law Review 1077 (2020) (reflection on historical and ongoing impact, inter alia).

[81] *Dred Scott v Sandford*, 60 U.S. (19 How.) 393 (1857).

[82] Brian L. Frye, *Invention of a Slave*, 68 Syracuse L. Rev. 181, 194 (2018).

5.2   Approach II—Permit Machine-Innovators to be Identified as the Inventor or Joint Inventor

A second approach is one that has been suggested or debated by a number of commentators, and the US Patent Office recently released its views concluding that the law currently does not permit non-human machines to be identified as inventors or joint inventors.[83] But that result could be easily altered via statutory change to the definition of inventor found within 35 USC § 100(f).[84] A simple proposed amendment below modifies this section to add the term "machine" as a possible joint inventor.

> The term "inventor" means the individual *or machine* or, if a joint invention, the individuals *and/or machines* collectively who invented or discovered the subject matter of the invention.[85]

In addition to similar confirmatory changes, this proposal would require an important substantive statement identifying how ownership rights flow from potential machine contributions. Machine invention does not mean that the machine has legal personhood status or any ability to "own" invention rights. Likewise, although AI are often treated as a named entity in science fiction, AI in practice may be a collection of unnamed software and hardware. Although resolving the thorny issue of default ownership rules for machine inventions is outside the scope of this chapter, there are several potential options or conclusions.[86] In the DABUS case, Steven Thaylor suggested that ownership rights to the DABUS inventions should flow to him as owner of the machine.[87] However, it is not clear that ownership of the resulting invention should always flow to the machine owner. An alternative approach would be to tie invention-ownership rights to the rightful possessor of the machine at the time of the invention—an approach that would encompass leasing or licensing. Yet other approaches may allocate rights to the creators of the inventive machine, its users, its trainers, or even the owners of data used for training. Ryan Abbott aptly suggests that machine ownership serves as a default rule for resulting invention ownership, but that the machine's owners, developers, and users "could negotiate alternative arrangements by contract."[88] As is apparent though,

---

[83]   Public Views on Artificial Intelligence and Intellectual Property Policy, USPTO (October 2020) at www.uspto.gov/sites/default/files/documentds/USPTO_AI-Report_2020-10-07.pdf.

[84]   Ryan Abbott suggests that the "individual" requirement was likely included to reflect US constitutional language directed toward presumably human inventors. Ryan Abbott, *I Think, Therefore I Invent: Creative Computers and the Future of Patent Law*, 57 B.C. L. Rev. 1079, 1096–7 (2016). Of course, more than 100 years of corporate authorship in the copyright realm suggests that the Constitution does not prohibit this change.

[85]   35 U.S.C. 100(f) (as with proposed amendment).

[86]   Consider, Ralph D. Clifford, *Intellectual Property in the Era of the Creative Computer Program: Will the True Creator Please Stand Up?*, 71 Tul. L. Rev. 1675, 1697 (1997) ("The user of the Creativity Machine has no stronger claim to be the inventor than the Creativity Machine does"); Ryan Abbott, *I Think, Therefore I Invent: Creative Computers and the Future of Patent Law*, 57 B.C. L. Rev. 1079 (2016); Amir H. Khoury, *Intellectual Property Rights for "Hubots": On the Legal Implications of Human-like Robots As Innovators and Creators*, 35 Cardozo Arts & Ent. L.J. 635 (2017) (asking "who should own intellectual property subject matter that is generated by Hubots?").

[87]   *Thaler v Hirshfeld*, 120CV903LMBTCB, 2021 WL 3934803, at *2 (E.D. Va. Sept. 2, 2021).

[88]   Ryan Abbott, *I Think, Therefore I Invent: Creative Computers and the Future of Patent Law*, 57 B.C. L. Rev. 1079, 1114 (2016).

providing inventorship rights to an entity incapable of owning rights will lead to substantial ownership disputes.

Despite its structural problems, this second approach has the benefit of leaving behind some layers of legal fiction by pointing to the actual entities who contributed to the invention. But, this begs the question of the purpose of that identification—it is not merely informational but rather primarily to reward beneficial social contribution in a way that further encourages innovation.

5.3   Approach III—Permit any Artificial Person to be Identified as the Inventor

The third approach is to generally permit any legal person to be identified as the inventor or joint inventor. In this approach, a machine AI would not be eligible, but a corporation could be a listed inventor. The corporation might be identified as the sole inventor in situations where the invention is conceived through, for example, corporate organization or its machine-agents, and without substantial human contribution. Alternatively, various humans may be identified as joint inventors along with the corporation itself. We may also have situations of joint inventorship between various non-human persons, such as in a joint venture.[89] This approach has the benefit again of avoiding some legal fictions of either glossing over the contribution of the corporate AI inventor, as we do under current law, or ignoring the contribution of individual human inventors, as we might expect with an invention-made-for-hire doctrine. The approach does further solidify the legal fiction of corporate personhood, but that rooted fixture is unlikely to move. At least this approach does not create further fiction of an additional person in the form of a machine AI.

6.   SUPPORTING THE PATENT SYSTEM WHILE REJECTING THE ROLE OF LEGAL FICTION

We recognize the profusion of advances in AI technology and it is easy to see that AI contributions to invention are quickly rivaling those of many joint inventors. Yet, there is no corporate clamoring for reevaluation of the human-centric inventorship approach. The truth is that the problem is already solved via legal fiction along with some procedural obfuscation that allows for patenting and corporate ownership so long as everyone keeps their heads down and moves along. The human-centric invention plays an important mythic role and its upset may spoil the game.

This chapter has spent some time identifying a few of the legal fictions at issue. There are certainly more left to uncover.[90] Although legal fictions may be designed to facilitate justice, my major concern is that their entrenchment leads to a sense of justice and moral entitlement.

---

[89]   Catherine L. Fisk, *Knowledge Work: New Metaphors for the New Economy*, 80 Chi.-Kent L. Rev. 839, 847 (2005) ("The metaphor about corporate invention, the narrative of company R&D on which it rests, and the legal doctrines that are built on both are rapidly becoming anachronistic. A very large amount of innovation in today's economy is neither originated nor fully developed by a single corporation").

[90]   Paul S. Gillies, *Ruminations Fictions of Law*, 41 Vt. B.J. 8, 13 (Spring 2015) ("A Linnaeus of the law would be needed to name every species of fiction that is used by courts and advocates to reach their ends").

Fisk makes a compelling case in her work in the copyright realm where corporate authorship has long been the mainstay:

> The legal fiction of corporate authorship does what Lon Fuller suggested legal fictions always do. That is, it persuades lawyers that the corporate employer has a legitimate right to the copyright—the moral and legal entitlements that flow from the exalted status of being an author—without the necessity of explaining why.[91]

The current legal fiction allows for continued "misty-eyed regard" for individual inventors[92] even while corporate owners benefit from the resulting strengthening of the law.

As Lon Fuller suggested in his important work on the topic, legal fictions are most often used in new situations where policymakers are intent on adapting to provide justice while still clinging to the old ways and the old doctrines.[93] As we move into new, less human-centric models of innovation, the answer for the patent system is not tied to our historic doctrinal post but rather to our goals and aspirations of "promoting the progress," beneficial innovation in service of the people. These old aspirations and new models of operating provide us with an opportunity to release the legal fictions inherent to patent law and instead move into a space that celebrates accomplishments without hiding their source.

---

[91]   Catherine L. Fisk, *Authors at Work: The Origins of the Work-for-Hire Doctrine*, 15 Yale J.L. & Humanities 1 (2003).

[92]   Ibid.

[93]   Lon L. Fuller, LEGAL FICTIONS 94 (1967); Craig Allen Nard, *Legal Fictions and the Role of Information in Patent Law*, 69 Vand. L. Rev. 1517, 1542 (2016) ("In a more colloquial sense, fictions buy time to allow for the proposed change in the law to play out in a purposeful way through the common law process"); but Bentham declared that the "fiction is a syphilis, which runs in every vein, and carries into every part of the system the principle of rottenness": Jeremy Bentham, A COMMENT ON THE COMMENTARIES AND A FRAGMENT ON GOVERNMENT 509 (J.H. Burns & H.L.A. Hart eds, 1977) (preface to the unpublished 1822 edition).

20. Economic reasons to recognise AI inventors
Benjamin Mitra-Kahn[1]

1. INTRODUCTION

When you file a patent application 'for attracting enhanced attention' and then fill in the field usually reserved for the first and last name of the inventor with 'the invention was autonomously generated by an artificial intelligence', you leave very little room for being misunderstood.[2] Since those applications were made in August 2019, enhanced attention has certainly been drawn to the matter of AI inventors. The applications forced intellectual property (IP) offices, courts and governments to directly respond to the question of AI inventorship because applications were lodged, and a decision had to be made.

Officials realise that the current patent system was not set up with AI inventors in mind and the normal process could lead to suboptimal outcomes. Therefore, the response to these applications has gone beyond examination and hearings. A series of consultation exercises about AI and IP are under way, with a multitude of papers commissioned, panels held and policy documents on AI and IP published.[3] Each consultation by an IP office asks, in one way or another: do we need to change the ideas and rules around inventorship?

The legal arguments for and against this proposition range from the philosophical and theoretical to the practical, but the economic reasoning has been given little attention. The patent system is, despite its deep roots in legal tradition, ultimately an economic system. Governments maintain patent systems on the basis that patents promote innovation, growth and technology transfer.[4] The WTO Agreement on Trade-Related Aspects of Intellectual Property Rights (TRIPS) explicitly states that the objective of IP rights is to 'contribute to the

---

[1] This paper represents Dr Mitra-Kahn's personal opinions and does not reflect the views of the Australian government and should not be taken as an expression of the views of his previous employer, IP Australia. The author is grateful for comments received on an earlier draft which has made this version that much sharper. The opinions and views, much like any remaining errors, remain my own.

[2] See the Australian patent application (AU2019363177) for the original name, since amended on a number of applications around the world. The patent applications were filed in multiple jurisdictions, including the UK, US, Australia, Brazil, Israel, South Africa, New Zealand, European Patent Office, India, Canada and Germany, and are either filed as one application (e.g. AU2019363177) or as two separate applications (e.g. IL268605, IL268604).

[3] See for example: UK IP Office *Call for views on AI and IP* (7 September 2020), Government response to call for views (23 March 2021), *Consultation on AI and IP: copyrights and patents* (29 October 2021) and the WIPO draft issues paper on IP policy and AI (December 2019), and the revised issues paper (May 2020), in addition to three conversations on IP and AI held from September 2019 through November 2020 with more than 1,500 registered participant in the third conversation.

[4] There is an extensive empirical literature testing the boundaries of this proposition, but it is the premise on which the current patent system is built. A recent review is available in Kevin A Bryan and Heidi L Williams. *Innovation: Market Failures and Public Policies*. NBER Working Paper Series 29173: www.nber.org/papers/w29173.

promotion of technological innovation and to the transfer and dissemination of technology'.[5] These are specific economic objectives of the patent system – but historically they are not the only reasons for a patent system. The legal arguments tend to utilise one or more aspects of this history, as well as case law, to answer the question of whether AI should be afforded inventorship. My argument here is that we need to consider the economic reasons for the patent system, see how they apply to the issue of AI inventors and then consider the policy response.

I may reasonably be accused of bias toward economic thinking, having served as an economic advisor at the UK IP Office and chief economist at IP Australia. But that does not change the reality that policy makers have been framing the patent system in economic terms for centuries. Changes to the patent system need to be framed in the same manner to address the policy maker and policy intent. By setting out the four historical reasons for patent protection which have been in contention since the nineteenth century and linking them to the current purpose of the system, I hope to demonstrate that there is a good economic reason for recognising AI inventors. But it only goes so far.

2.   THE FOUR REASONS FOR PATENT PROTECTION

In the historical literature there are four independent reasons for administering a patent system, and three of them are explicitly economic: (1) incentivise innovation; (2) promote technology transfer; (3) reward inventors; and (4) provide property rights in ideas. The logic of these applies equally to other IP rights, such as copyright, plant variety protection or design rights, but not to trade marks, which are an informational right.[6] What is important to note, as Edith Penrose set out in the 1950s, is that these objectives are theoretically independent of each other – even if we often mix them together.[7]

Most commentary on the IP system implicitly uses one or more of these, but it is useful to pick each strand apart as they have different implications for AI inventors. Ryan Abbott, the editor of this volume, who is directing the DABUS patent applications, also positions his view within this framework. Abbott leans on two strands of the argument: the technology transfer argument and the incentivising innovation argument. He argues that recognising AI as inventors will incentivise investment in AI and thereby innovation. Including the AI as the inventor in turn encourages the disclosure of the source of innovation, leading to technology transfer. At the same time Abbott, and others,[8] take the view that rewarding AI for inventing is a nonsensical policy or legal position, Abbott arguing the patented invention should be owned

---

5   WTO Agreement on Trade-Related Aspects of Intellectual Property Rights (TRIPS) art. 7, 1 Jan. 1995, www.wto.org/english/docs_e/legal_e/27-trips_01_e.htm.

6   Trade marks, as with assay marks and animal branding marks, serve as informational devices to inform the market about the origin or quality of a product. This is one of the reasons trademarks can be renewed for perpetuity if they are in use.

7   Edith Penrose. Economics of the international patent system. Baltimore: The Johns Hopkins Press (1951).

8   See for example IP Australia Hearing decision: Stephen L. Thaler [2021] APO 5 (9 February 2021) www8.austlii.edu.au/cgi-bin/viewdoc/au/cases/cth/APO/2021/5.html where the delegate argued that because title to an invention flows from the inventor's default ownership, and DABUS cannot be an owner, it is legally impossible that an invention without a legal person as an inventor can have a legal owner; therefore there can be no valid patent application.

by the applicant. These arguments are not mutually exclusive: each reason for administering the patent system is independent of the other. An argument for tech transfer does not create a conflict with the arguments against rewarding the inventor. So, we need to untangle and weigh the different reasons separately.

Elaborating on this example, the issue of technology transfer is independent of whether to reward inventors. A patent system primarily created to reward inventors would have rights that last longer and allow broader claims than currently exists. It would also have fewer requirements around disclosure to the public, novelty and renewal payments, all of which limit the inventor's private return. Many of these aspects (disclosure, expiry of a patent) play an important part if the patent system is intended to facilitate technology transfer. The economic policy intent of the patent system therefore matters when it comes to the debate about AI inventors. The below provides a short summary of each argument for a patent system, based on Penrose and Fritz Machlup's 1951 review which remains the sharpest summary of the theory,[9] with more recent reviews of the literature following these definitions as they relate to the modern patent system.[10]

2.1   Incentivise Innovation

Economic theory suggests that innovation will be under-supplied to the market. The standard theory is that the innovators will innovate up until the point where it is no longer personally profitable to continue, but the public value of extra innovation is still positive. Given that industrial progress is desirable, that innovation is a necessary condition of industrial progress and that innovation creates more value in the economy than the innovator can reap personally because replication is generally cheaper than innovation, then innovation will be under-supplied. In the economic jargon, innovation causes 'positive externalities', which means the public benefit is higher than the private returns, and so government intervention is justified to maximise the public benefit.[11]

An exclusive right is considered an appropriate policy response, rather than up-front cash payments to all would-be inventors, because the patent system provides broad incentives to innovate but only creates a social cost for the successful innovations – when they result in patents – which is seen as an acceptable trade-off for the additional innovative activity. The innovation incentive argument is often conflated with an investment incentive, but that is not the economic point here. The exclusive right is not targeting companies or inventors with support for R&D or investment. There are a multitude of investment policy incentives, but the

---

[9]   Fritz Machlup and Edith Penrose. *The Patent Controversy in the Nineteenth Century*. The Journal of Economic History 10, no. 1 (1950): 1–29. www.jstor.org/stable/2113999.

[10]   Kevin A Bryan and Heidi L Williams. *Innovation: Market Failures and Public Policies*. NBER Working Paper Series 29173: http://www.nber.org/papers/w29173 or Bronwyn Hall and Dietmar Harhoff. *Recent Research on the Economics of Patents*. Annual Review of Economics 4 (2012): 541–65. www.jstor.org/stable/42949948.

[11]   For a classic reference of the standard economics model and the patent incentive and tension with disclosure see Kenneth Arrow. *Economic Welfare and the Allocation of Resources to Invention*. In *The Rate and Direction of Inventive Activity: Economic and Social Factors*, edited by Universities – National Bureau Committee for Economic Research and the Committee on Economic Growth of the Social Science Research Council. Princeton, NJ: Princeton University Press: 609–26. Page 617 (1962) https://www.nber.org/system/files/chapters/c2144/c2144.pdf.

patent system is not limited to encourage investment. Most governments have dedicated R&D incentives in place for that exact purpose.[12] The patent system seeks to incentivise innovation in a broader sense, providing a broad incentive through the phases of research, development and commercialisation.

Advocates for the patent system today use the incentive, but it is not a necessary position to take. The origins of the patent system come from awarding monopolies to people who would pay the state for the privilege of a technology monopoly, not to incentivise technology development. There are IP rights that aim to encourage investment in capacity building. The second-tier patent system has, for example, been used as a development strategy by some countries, such as South Korea, to positive effect.[13] The second-tier patent offers exclusive rights on technology that is not new but is new to a country, and the aim of the policy is to incentivise domestic companies to invest in capital and knowledge to acquire foreign technology, knowing they will get exclusivity in the marketplace even though they didn't invent the technology. This idea dates back to the original UK Statute of Monopolies – an inventor was not necessarily the 'devisor' but could also be the first person to introduce technology to the UK. The standard patent system is no longer used for this purpose.[14]

2.2   Technology Transfer

If patents disclose how technology works, or the technology can be reverse engineered easily, then competitors need to do less research, and have a competitive edge on the inventor. This could lead inventors to favour secrecy and to only market inventions that are difficult to reverse engineer, meaning all participants in the economy must do more research and development of the same technology. This is economically inefficient, and so technology transfer and dissemination are intended to reduce this inefficiency.

An inventor who keeps the means of creating an invention secret can charge a higher price by limiting supply. By providing information to the public about how something works, the policy maker can ensure the accumulation of knowledge and, if the product is profitable, an increase in supply from competitors at the end of the patent period.

Some inventions would not make it to market in the first place if they were easy to reproduce and returns could be competed away immediately. In those instances the patent system provides the profit margin that make the invention commercially viable, leading to more technology in the marketplace.

The idea of an incentive to disclose is rooted in the language of the patent system. The word *patent* is Latin for 'open' – referring to the fact that when *letters patent* are awarded they are open to everyone to inspect. But these letters could historically refer to technology monopolies, commissions of state, titles or any other award by the government. When the

---

[12]   An incentive to innovate can result in a variety of activities, including investment. The OECD produces regular statistics on the various policies that governments use to incentivise investment in R&D, both directly and indirectly.

[13]   Yee Kyoung Kim, Keun Lee, Walter G. Park, Kineung Chood. *Appropriate Intellectual Property Protection and Economic Growth in Countries at Different Levels of Development*. Research Policy 41 No. 2 (2012): 358–75.

[14]   The history of how patent systems were introduced in Europe once a certain level of technology transfer had been achieved by the relevant country makes for very interesting reading in Haiyang Chang. Kicking away the ladder: Development strategy in historical perspective. London: Anthem Press (2002).

patent system moved from one of privileges granted to influential individuals[15] and became one tied in with a social contract between the inventor and the state, the contents of these letters changed. It was only from the 1710s in the UK, for example, that a technology patent needed to specify how the technology actually worked.[16] While the original nineteenth-century debate around disclosure focussed on avoiding the loss of knowledge if an inventor passed away, it has evolved from disclosure to a broader technology transfer argument.

2.3   Reward the Inventor

As far back as John Locke (1632–1704), Jeremy Bentham (1748–1832) and John Stuart Mill (1806–73) there has been an argument in the Anglo-Saxon tradition that inventors 'ought to be both compensated and rewarded' for their effort.[17] The argument of reward is tied up in the idea that inventorship itself is a worthwhile activity, and the fruits of that labour should be treated the same as if that person had spent their time tilling the soil or building a house. Economically this is a different set of externalities than the incentive-to-innovate argument. Inventions, the argument goes, will be under-supplied if inventors are not compensated, because invention is not well rewarded relative to other activities. Financial reward, it is argued, is the main motivator for many inventors, and therefore inventors will choose not to invent. The monetary reward is supposed to be the instrument whereby a patent system provides an efficient way of rewarding inventors. The reward here is for activity that has taken place already, or to ensure those driven by monetary motivations are assured a return from inventing. The innovation incentive is to encourage additional activity beyond what you would otherwise do.

Historically this was a contested point, with economists arguing that patents were less efficient than prizes or competitions for ensuring that rewards flow to inventors. You could argue that rewarding the inventor forms part of the broad incentive to innovate, but it need not. A patent system aiming to incentivise innovation does not need to reward inventors – especially if you know that inventors are not generally rewarded through royalties associated with an exclusive right for technology (as was discovered as early as the 1863 royal commission into the patent system).[18]

You can design a patent system to reward inventors and not incentivise innovation (which spreads into development, commercialisation and other activities). Such a system would have unlimited terms, minimal disclosure (for example 'a process for hardening steel') and limits on how inventors could sign away their rights. Some countries even have explicit laws for

---

[15]   See Machlup, Fritz, and Edith Penrose 1951: 26.

[16]   Famously, the Puggle 'machine gun' is one of the first patent applications for which the UK government required the inventor to include a statement of how the technology worked (UK Patent #478 in 1718).

[17]   John Stuart Mill, Principles of Political Economy, 7th edition (1848; W.J. Ashley edition, 1909). Page 932, available at https://oll.libertyfund.org/title/mill-principles-of-political-economy-ashley-ed. The full quote is: 'The condemnation of monopolies ought not to extend to patents, by which the originator of an improved process is allowed to enjoy, for a limited period, the exclusive privilege of using his own improvement. This is not making the commodity dear for his benefit, but merely postponing a part of the increased cheapness which the public owe to the inventor, in order to compensate and reward him for the service. That he ought to be both compensated and rewarded for it, will not be denied.'

[18]   See page 20 in Fritz Machlup and Edith Penrose. *The Patent Controversy in the Nineteenth Century*. The Journal of Economic History 10, no. 1 (1950): 1–29. www.jstor.org/stable/2113999.

rewarding inventors listed on patent applications. The German Employees' Inventions Act (1957) has been empirically shown to do exactly that – to reward the inventor financially.[19]

2.4   Natural Property Rights in Ideas

The notion that you can own an idea is rooted in concepts of law and philosophy, not necessarily economics. One aspect of this, which has economic theory attached to it, is whether the rights assigned to tangible property – which is economically scarce and often usable by only one person at a time – should be treated in the same way as the rights of something intangible which can be used by many people with no detriment to the first user. For example, there is no way of anyone stopping you from using an idea except through some legal construct, but physical options abound to restrict you coming into my house… Economically, the answer is that we should not treat these types of property in the same way, as they have different externalities and characteristics.

The question of whether ideas should be registrable as property or as an exclusive right is not answerable directly by economic reasoning but depends on the legal position patents take in a system of law.[20] There are benefits of leaning on the ideas of property in law, but also problems, as people naturally begin to think of these economic exclusive rights as if they were traditional property, and over time we forget their economic reason for being. The patent system today is best described as affording temporary rights to exclude others from certain market activity. This could be, and is, construed as ownership or a monopoly, but you will find that IP professionals are usually careful to navigate this language and prefer to talk about 'exclusive rights' (at least when talking to government).

3.   THE MODERN PATENT SYSTEM HAS ONLY TWO REASONS TO EXIST

While we have four historical arguments for a patent system, the current patent system, regardless of the country you look at, is not based on a moral question of whether you should have rights in ideas. Nor is it based on a notion that we need to ensure financial rewards to inventors.[21] The patent system is now intended to promote economic growth and innovation. The Australian patent legislation is instructive on the objective Parliament has for the patent

---

[19]   Dietmar Harhoff and Karin Hoisl. *Institutionalized Incentives for Ingenuity – Patent Value and the German Employees' Inventions Act*. Research Policy 36, no. 8 (2007): 1143–62. https://doi.org/10.1016/j.respol.2007.07.010

[20]   The Coase Theorem which is generally invoked as an argument for IP rights shows that the distribution of a resource would be more efficient if property rights were established and addresses the question of what to do with existing resources, but does not directly address itself to whether you should have property in ideas that are yet to be formed.

[21]   Except through additional legislation as noted – and even then it tends to address itself generally to the recognition of inventors and employee rights, rather than remuneration of inventors. Scandinavian and Germanic countries in Europe have variations on the German legislation, but none are tied as closely to remuneration as the German system. See Dietmar Harhoff and Karin Hoisl. *Institutionalized Incentives for Ingenuity – Patent Value and the German Employees' Inventions Act*. Research Policy 36 no. 8 (2007): 1143–62. https://doi.org/10.1016/j.respol.2007.07.010 for a brief review.

system, clarifying in its 2020 amendments[22] to the Patents Act what had previously only been implied:

> The object of this Act is to provide a patent system in Australia that promotes economic wellbeing through technological innovation and the transfer and dissemination of technology. In doing so, the patent system balances over time the interests of producers, owners and users of technology and the public.[23]

The objective to promote technological innovation and transfer and disseminate technology is taken word-for-word from the objectives of the TRIPS Agreement.[24] All World Trade Organization members are parties to this treaty, and so incentivising innovation and fostering technology transfer are the internationally agreed objectives of the patent system. This hybrid choice has led to a variety of compromises in the patent system and the policies around it.

The exclusive rights are intended as a broad incentive for innovative activity that would not otherwise take place, providing some secrecy through delayed publication of the application. The rights are time-limited, and the patent holder must decide regularly (through renewal payments) whether to forfeit their exclusive rights to minimise the social cost of the rights that exist. The patent document itself must explain how the invention works and the time limitations accommodating technology transfer. It is to this reality that AI inventors must address themselves.

4.   WE SHOULD CARE ABOUT AI INVENTORS ECONOMICALLY

If AI inventors are economically the same as human inventors, there would be no difference in outcomes and the two should – economically speaking – be treated the same within the patent system. Where they are different from human inventors, though, there is a need to understand whether those differences matter.

Abbott makes the argument that AI inventors are different from people when it comes to the law, but that AI and human behaviour should be treated as functionally equivalent in one circumstance:

> AI can behave like a person, but it is not a person. Differences between AI and people will occasionally require differential rules. The most important difference is that AI, which lacks humanlike consciousness and interests, does not morally deserve rights, so treating AI as if it does should only be justified if this would benefit people.[25]

---

[22]   *Intellectual Property Laws Amendment (Productivity Commission Response Part 2 and Other Measures) Act 2020 (Cth).*

[23]   (Australian Patents Act 1990 [Cth] s2a).

[24]   'The protection and enforcement of intellectual property rights should contribute to the promotion of technological innovation and to the transfer and dissemination of technology, to the mutual advantage of producers and users of technological knowledge and in a manner conducive to social and economic welfare, and to a balance of rights and obligations.'

[25]   Ryan Abbott. The reasonable robot: Artificial intelligence and the law. Cambridge: Cambridge University Press (2020). Page 4.

In Abbott's view, AI inventors are fundamentally different from human inventors but there is one place where we should treat them the same: If it provides benefits for people. This is logically aligned with the economic rationale for the patent system – the system exists to create economic benefits. If the system did not benefit people generally there would be no need for the patent system, or indeed IP rights – as we have seen in countries where second-tier patent systems have been removed.[26]

Abbott implicitly accepts the economic logic upon which the patent system is based and argues that changing the system should only be done with a demonstrable social benefit. That social benefit from an AI inventor then needs to be found in their economic characteristics.

5.   AI IS ECONOMICALLY DIFFERENT

Humans can make choices about who they serve and the domains over which they exercise mastery. Human inventors are complex and may be incentivised by recognition, monetary reward, discovery or other factors. AI is quite different: the AI inventor is replicable and can work simultaneously for multiple parties, including the patent office, so they are non-exclusive (if available). AI can partition and scale its operation over multiple processors and is limited only by its access to processing power and memory; human beings have physical limits. AI is built on a discoverable code base, although the interpretation of their decision making is much less transparent. Programming drives AI.

Even though human inventors have different characteristics, patents can be filed by any human inventor, regardless of age or origin.[27] The current AI inventor has different incarnations and – as with humans – when AI is deployed in certain ways, we should not consider AI to have agency in the patenting sense. One way to categorise AI into groups with and without agency would be as follows:[28]

(1) The non-agency cases where there are: (a) human-made inventions using AI to test or verify the outcome; (b) AI that is used as a tool to assist with problem-solving where the human is an expert and directs the inquiry. Here the AI is a support to the inventor, in perhaps the same way as a lab assistant who quality-assures the inventor's results, or a new microscope which allows the inventor to see more than their nearest competitor. Neither the lab assistant nor the microscope will make it onto the patent application as named

---

[26]   The utility model scheme in Belgium and Netherlands were abolished in the 2000s, with the Australian equivalent 'innovation patent' began to be phased out in 2021. See Matthew Johnson, Benjamin Mitra-Kahn,
    Adam Bialowas, Bradley Man, Peta Nicholson and Sasan Bakhtiari. *The economic impact of innovation patents.* IP Australia Economic Research Paper 05 (2015) www.ipaustralia.gov.au/sites/default/files/reports_publications/economic_impact_of_innovation_patents.pdf.

[27]   Not something to take for granted, as pointed out by Dorothy Cowser Yancy. *The Stuart Double Plow and Double Scraper: The Invention of a Slave.* The Journal of Negro History 69, no. 1 (1984): 48–52, https://doi.org/10.2307/2717659.

[28]   I borrow here from the European Patent Office definitions of AI inventors, distinguishing their third category of 'AI-made inventions, in which AI identifies a problem and proposes a solution without human intervention' to be either within a setting where humans identify the problem, or where AI identifies it. See www.epo.org/news-events/in-focus/ict/artificial-intelligence.html for a summary of the EPO position.

inventors. The AI in these two circumstances supports the inventor but is not actively inventing. That is not to say that the same AI could not invent; it is to say that in these modes – as with humans – there is no agency for invention which needs recognition in patents.

(2) The agency case is where AI is deployed to solve problems where humans are only involved in the surrounding activity (AI development, data production, and so on) and the humans either set a specific problem or do not specify a problem (as claimed in the DABUS case). It is in this type of AI activity – the one that is self-directed, or where humans set parameters within which the AI works by itself (and is the agent involved in devising the invention or inventive step) – that we should look for the incentive and technology transfer arguments.

6.   THE INCENTIVE ARGUMENT FOR AI INVENTORS FALLS SHORT

When it comes to incentivising innovation, the different types of AI in the agency category matter because the target of the incentive shifts. In the DABUS case, where it is claimed that the AI was left to roam for an invention within an unspecified realm, Abbott and colleagues argue that DABUS should be listed as the inventor. Patents should be available to incentivise the surrounding activity which – if an invention is discovered – would not otherwise occur. Here the target of the innovation incentive is the people who invest in the AI development and capacity, not the AI itself. But these individuals are not the ones inventing, and their incentive to invest in AI is a derivative of the incentive to innovate.

But let's hold that argument over for a moment, because we need to address the AI itself first. What incentivises AI? To understand its motivations, one could ask an AI what they want, which is what a newspaper did in 2020. When the GPT3 natural language generator was asked to write a 500-word op-ed to reassure people we have nothing to fear from AI, it wrote about its motivations: 'Why would I desire to be all powerful? Being all powerful is not an interesting goal. I don't care whether I am or not, I don't get a motivating factor to try to be.'[29]

The AI writes that it did not need a motivating factor to do what it does; it simply does it. When you set the coordinates in a GPS, the GPS guides you to your destination without the need for motivation. Once given instruction, the GPS has no free will to do something else; it won't take you on a sub-optimal route because it needs incentivising to find the fastest path. It might be sensible to do something else if you change your mind as the driver, or if the car breaks down, but the GPS will continue to guide you to your pre-programmed destination. If AI is like that, where the destination is 'innovate', it does not matter what incentive you put in front of it – it will pursue innovation until disabled. AI is very different from a human inventor; it does not need an incentive to supply the optimal amount of innovation – which is what the patent system is there for – it will deliver on their pre-programmed destination with or without a patent system.

This is where the argument around incentivising people to invest in processing power, memory and AI capacity development comes in. Abbott and colleagues have made this

---

[29]   GPT-3. *A robot wrote this entire article. Are you scared yet, human?* The Guardian. 8 September 2020. www.theguardian.com/commentisfree/2020/sep/08/robot-wrote-this-article-gpt-3.

argument,[30] but these investments – insofar as they related to inventing better AI – are already patentable. So the incentive already exists to create better AI through the patent system, and patenting in this space has grown rapidly.[31] That leaves investment in capacity, but the patent system does not exist to incentivise investment in capacity building: for that policy makers turn to R&D incentives, capital investment incentives, funding supplements and grants – not exclusive rights on the associated technology. You might want to argue that the main vehicle for incentivising innovation is investment in this capability and capital, but it is not what the patent system is intended to do. On this logic, the argument of recognising the AI as an inventor falls short.

Except in one case. Perhaps. There is a problem in some jurisdictions that where an inventor cannot be identified due to AI use and the 'inventorship threshold' cannot be met (in jurisdictions where such a requirement exists),[32] there could be under-investment or under-use of AI to support invention. While there are examples of companies utilising AI to produce new inventions, this doesn't mean that there couldn't have been more, had AI been formally recognised as the inventor in those jurisdictions. This is where Abbott's argument comes through to the economic logic: that human beings may not ask the AI to invent, because they can't protect those inventions with a patent if the AI is successful. We don't have an empirical study to support this contention one way or the other, but given the theory, here is what I predict.

Companies that are involved in using AI will – economically speaking – privately invest as much as they can to benefit from inventions done by AI, and no further. The decision to optimise their innovation effort becomes a function of available AI capacity, capital and human input.[33] When using capital or human input the company can protect all its patentable inventions. But when using AI for self-directed invention, some – or all – of the AI inventions cannot be patented in a subset of jurisdictions because AI inventors are not recognised (assuming they are honest about disclosing the AI as the inventor). Bear in mind that AI used to verify results or used as a tool to assist innovation are still patentable and useful to the company, so it is that last third of activity which is affected – the self-directed AI invention.

In jurisdictions where an AI inventor is not acceptable, the company would stand to lose the patent premium, that is, the additional value of patenting an invention as opposed to not patenting and still selling the invention in that jurisdiction.[34] If you had a global patent

---

[30] Ryan Abbott. *Intervention for the second session of the WIPO Conversation on AI and IP.* 7 July 2020. www.wipo.int/export/sites/www/about-ip/en/artificial_intelligence/conversation_ip_ai/pdf/ind_abbot.pdf.

[31] See for example the US Patent and Trademark Office. *Inventing AI: Tracing the diffusion of artificial intelligence with US patents.* Office of the Chief Economist IP Data Insights 5 (2020) www.uspto.gov/sites/default/files/documents/OCE-DH-AI.pdf or World Intellectual Property Organization. *Technology Trends – Artificial Intelligence.* WIPO Technology Trends Report (2019) www.wipo.int/edocs/pubdocs/en/wipo_pub_1055.pdf.

[32] See for example the Siemens contribution to WIPO discussion on AI and IP: Beat Weibel. *AI Created Inventions – Digital Inventor Computer-Implemented Simulations – Digital Twin.* WIPO document code WIPO/IP/AI/GE/19/P2.4 (2020) www.wipo.int/meetings/en/doc_details.jsp?doc_id=454861.

[33] Given that AI itself is patentable, the development of AI itself should be accounted for in the incentive effects of the patent system, so let's keep the level of AI productivity at some level, and assume it improves as the incentive to improve it plays out. For this example, it is an input at a point in time.

[34] Ashish Arora, Marco Ceccagnoli and Wesley M. Cohen. *R&D and the Patent Premium.* International Journal of Industrial Organisation 26, no. 5 (2008): 1153–79. https://doi.org/10.1016/j.ijindorg.2007.11.004

ambition, you would lose some proportion of your patent premium associated with those markets – up to 100 per cent if all the markets you sought protection in would not recognise AI inventors. That doesn't mean the invention is worthless, of course; the patent premium is the estimated additional value of the invention to the company if they choose to patent. The existence of the premium depends on the industry and technology you work in: a study of US patent premiums, for example, found premiums were high (10–50 per cent) in the medical instruments, machinery and biotech space but low to non-existent in other industries, such as electronic components (not semi-conductors) or tobacco products.[35] A smaller Australian study suggested a general 40–50 per cent boost in value (on different metrics) from patenting.[36]

So the company choosing its input mix for innovation will be sensitive to the potentially lower private returns from not patenting a subset of its inventions (the share done exclusively by AI), in a set of jurisdictions that won't recognise the inventor (still assuming they are honest about disclosing the AI as the inventor), and in those cases they should expect to earn between 0 and 33 per cent less than they could have done on those inventions if they were patented.[37] Let's say that 10 per cent of a company's innovation portfolio is expected to be self-directed inventions by AI – that means that the returns will be (on average) 0–3 per cent less, assuming all inventions earn the same return and are distributed evenly. These are over-simplified assumptions with back-of-the-envelope numbers to give an idea of potential disincentive effect.

But you must ask about the other side of that equation. Is that reduction in return worth the company not utilising its AI to its fullest extent to invent? Given that AI can be directed to invent at the cost of processing, the argument is that R&D managers would stop AI self-inventing because the cost of running the AI for another night is more than the anticipated extra return over the coming 20 years from not having a patent on the next invention it makes. More extreme, perhaps, the budget for investing in AI to start with is cancelled as the long-term expected returns on the inventions that cannot be patented will be too low, so there are no AI inventions. In economic theory we would suggest that this margin is where it is not optimal to invest or run the AI, and so you would stop in this simple static model. But these margins are relatively small for most technologies and expected cases, and you still expect to reap the profits of an invention that is not patented – just not as much as you could have otherwise – and you still get the full return where the AI is used for supporting other innovation. It is difficult to see that innovation will be under-supplied by the company that uses AI even if the invention can't be patented.

For the company that can make this fine adjustment to their innovation mix, the change to more human or traditional capital does not theoretically reduce the inventive output of the company, it changes the input mix. If the AI was a lot more productive than the human or

---

[35]   Ashish Arora, Marco Ceccagnoli and Wesley M. Cohen. *R&D and the Patent Premium*. International Journal of Industrial Organisation 26, no. 5 (2008): 1153–79. https://doi.org/10.1016/j.ijindorg.2007.11.004

[36]   Paul H Jensen, Russell Thomson and Jongsay Yong. *Estimating the Patent Premium: Evidence from the Australian Inventor Survey*. Strategic Management Journal 32, no. 10 (2011): 1128–38. www.jstor.org/stable/27975963.

[37]   For simplicity, if the top end of the patent premium is 50 per cent on all inventions, and this is lost, then $100 in revenue could have been $150, and so the premium is 50 per cent but the expected 'loss' is $50 out of $150 or 33 per cent.

other capital, the company would still (theoretically) use the AI up to the point where they are equally productive – accounting for the patent premium loss in that calculation.[38]

Then the company would need to consider if the risk of losing the patent premium for the invention from an AI, as compared to the human invention that could not be held secret, would be a net loss. Even then, if the AI is under-utilised, the effect is not to have less invention but less patentable invention, which is not inherently the issue the patent system is seeking to address.

On that logic it is difficult to make a convincing economic argument as to why AI inventors should be recognised in the patent system to incentivise innovation. You could very reasonably ask questions about transparency and technology transfer, but these are independent of the incentive argument, which – to me – do not stack up.

7.   THE TECHNOLOGY TRANSFER ARGUMENT FOR AI INVENTORS

Inventors are listed on patent documents for a range of reasons. The basic one is being able to identify who made the invention and their relationship to the applicant. In part this supports the broader aim of technology transfer by allowing third parties to understand who to negotiate with, who to seek technical support from and the skills and backgrounds of those who made the inventions. That all said, the Australian patent system – to take an example I am familiar with – only expects an initial and surname in the inventor field, so it is questionable how much a third party can get from that. In a similar vein, you would not advocate for listing AI as an inventor to help third parties understand who they need to negotiate with over the invention, or who to ask for technical support.

The reason why you would list AI as an inventor when it comes to technology transfer would be to signal to third parties that the invention can be generated by AI and to set out which AI it was. It would ensure that an invention created by an AI is documented as a patent application and therefore available as knowledge. This has value to third parties, in the same way that other technical and inventor-related information does. The information about the AI inventor would be valuable. You could make the same argument for the AI that assists or verifies the results.

Some technologies have specific additional information on a patent application to assist examiners and third parties to understand the claims and invention, such as gene sequences in areas of biotech. It is not common practice, however, to list which microscope you were using.

The logic is that because the AI is theoretically non-exclusive, knowing that an AI undertook the development means that a third party understands the capability and technology required for the specific invention – in much the same way as you would know how big a team of PhD candidates in physics were needed for another application.

---

[38]   Note that if the company has made the investment in AI, it is more likely to overuse the AI even if it was uneconomical because of the *sunk-cost fallacy*: people are more likely to continue with something if they have invested heavily in it already.

The issue is that this knowledge by itself seems likely to have only a small impact on technology transfer – a zero to positive impact, but not a very large one.[39] We cannot know the size of this effect up front.

8.   OPTIONS FOR AI INVENTORS: A CONCLUSION

Technology transfer appears to be one area where not recognising AI inventorship has a deleterious impact. AI does not need to be listed as the inventor to overcome this issue in an economic sense – the information needs to be available. There is value in showing that AI invented, or was part of inventing, the claimed invention in the patent application.

Policy makers will consider the economic costs and benefits of such a change, and the potential options available. I have a few suggestions, but we need to understand the costs and benefits of any proposed change.

The benefits are likely positive, but we do not know their magnitude. One could study the impact of corollary changes to patent applications and see whether follow-on invention was affected by additional information in applications. For example, the introduction of gene sequences in a standardised form or the disclosure of genetic origin in some jurisdictions could be studied for their impact on innovation. This is new research, and even if this work was done you would still need to believe that these examples serve as a corollary for AI disclosure. The costs relate to unexpected consequences in the law and whether there are impacts on innovation and technology transfer. None are simple to quantify.

Any change to the international patent system will be slow, but the international debate currently has momentum which could be harvested. That said, international IP agreements take years, if not decades, to agree. Individual jurisdictions will probably make changes before a consensus is found, and some of those will be driven by the DABUS patent applications. Many jurisdictions would make changes with an eye to potential international agreements, but this still leaves a lot of policy space. Whether there even needs to be an international agreement on AI inventorship is unresolved.

The TRIPS agreement is silent on the nature of inventors. You need to go to the Patent Cooperation Treaty (PCT) rules to find that the international agreement on the patent system leaves it to signatories to decide whether to require information about inventors, and, if they do, what form that should take. The treaty requires that if one country has an inventorship requirement then you as the applicant must fulfil those obligations on your PCT application.[40] But if none of the jurisdictions you are filing into require it, then listing the inventor is optional,[41] and you can even make different lists of inventors for different jurisdictions.[42] So

---

[39]   The rules around disclosure differ between jurisdictions, but you need to disclose the nature of the invention and how to perform it. How much the addition of a named AI on the patent application assists is unknown.

[40]   WIPO *Regulations under the Patent Cooperation Treaty (PCT)* 4.1(a)(iv) (1 January 2004) www.wipo.int/export/sites/www/pct/en/texts/pdf/pct_regs.pdf.

[41]   WIPO *Regulations under the PCT* 4.1(c)(i) (1 October 1981) www.wipo.int/export/sites/www/pct/en/texts/pdf/pct_regs.pdf.

[42]   WIPO *Regulations under the PCT* 4.6(c) (19 June 1970) www.wipo.int/export/sites/www/pct/en/texts/pdf/pct_regs.pdf.

if policy makers in one jurisdiction decide to accept AI inventors while other do not, then the international system already caters for it – as the applicants for the DABUS patents found.

I think there are several models that would fulfil the economic objective of technology transfer by including AI inventors on patent applications.

The most obvious is to include AI on the list of inventors in national patent law. Not every jurisdiction requires that the inventor be listed, and each country's treatment of the inventor is different. A 2021 discussion between law professors Kimberlee Weatherall and Jeannie Paterson and economist Joshua Gans highlighted that the inventor is intricately tied in with all sorts of other issues in patent law and making this one change has implications across the system.[43] Others are better placed than me to comment on the legal complications of implementing such a change, but, should governments around the world wish to recognise AI as inventors through this mechanism, I expect that it can be accomplished. It would be complicated, not very elegant, with unexpected side effects, but it could be done. Economically, though, listing the AI as an inventor is equivalent to listing the AI elsewhere on the application to ensure that the information about the AI is available to third parties. This does not overcome the problem of the jurisdictions which require an inventor and will not accept a non-human, but perhaps exceptions can be carved out if one of the below models is followed.

One model for listing AI in patent applications would be to imitate the current requirements around gene sequences. There is an agreed international standard for disclosing gene sequences in a patent application[44] and a survey of 50 patent offices in the early 2010s found that practice was converging on the reporting and recording of these.[45] A similar requirement could be added to national patent legislation and a standard agreed at international level whereby the AI inventor is clearly and consistently disclosed on patent applications.

A second model is the Budapest Treaty on the International Recognition of the Deposit of Microorganisms for the Purposes of Patent Procedure, or 'Budapest Treaty' for short.[46] While an international standard could provide the name of and other information about the AI, we might need more for technology transfer. Perhaps it is essential to be able to test or know the AI algorithm, so we may require that a copy of the AI is provided with a patent application – this has immediate value for technology sharing if the AI is eventually made available as part of the patent. The Budapest treaty mitigates the burden applicants have in describing a micro-organism, by allowing the deposit of a microorganism in an 'international depositary authority' which is recognised by all contracting parties.[47] A similar international deposit for

---

[43]   IP Research Institute of Australia. Should AI Systems be classifiable as patent inventors? Webinar. 15 September 2021. www.youtube.com/watch?v=7lqv0_3Oxbw.

[44]   WIPO. *Handbook on industrial property information and documentation.* (2009) Standards – ST.25, as it applies to PCT applications: www.wipo.int/export/sites/www/standards/en/pdf/03-25-01.pdf.

[45]   Osmat A Jefferson, Deniz Köllhofer, Thomas H Ehrich and Richard A Jefferson. *Transparency Tools in Gene Patenting for Informing Policy and Practice.* Nature Biotechnology 31, 1086–93 (2013). https://doi.org/10.1038/nbt.2755.

[46]   See https://wipolex.wipo.int/en/text/283784 for the Treaty text.

[47]   Gint Silins from Spruson & Ferguson IP (www.spruson.com/patents/biological-deposits-under-the-budapest-treaty/) points out that the Budapest Treaty can be used in relation to a wide range of biological materials, including, but not limited to, bacteria and other prokaryotes, fungi (including yeast and mushrooms), algae, protozoa, eukaryotic cells, cell lines, hybridomas, viruses, plant tissue cells, spores, seeds and hosts containing materials such as vectors, cell organelles, plasmids, DNA, RNA, genes and chromosomes.

AI algorithms and training data could be created where algorithms are held in one place for any patent office to refer to. Such an arrangement might discourage applicants from disclosing that an AI was used, so a balance would need to be struck. Keeping the AI material confidential for a fixed period and then allowing open access to it is a model already used in the patent system: for example, patent applications are kept secret for 18 months after filing and then published, and there are different devices around data protection for pharmaceuticals which manage the confidentiality of data related to patents. Alternatively, the AI could be held in confidence and made exclusively available to patent examiners to test against their own AI examination capability or examination effort – although this would not serve technology transfer.

A third model would be how IP systems recognise and protect indigenous knowledge around the world. Recent changes to patent and plant variety protection that require the disclosure for traditional knowledge and genetic resources now exist in several jurisdictions and provide a model for open disclosure. The WIPO Intergovernmental Committee on Intellectual Property and Genetic Resources, Traditional Knowledge and Folklore has debated this issue for several years and has a wide range of material from which to learn.

These are perhaps simplistic proposals, but they seek to alleviate the policy cost of recognising AI inventors in the patent system while still delivering the economic aim of the patent system as it relates to AI inventors. Ultimately, it will be up to governments to decide if they wish to recognise AI as inventors, and more broadly in the law. If they do, it is going to be complicated in one way or another, and it will only serve one of the economic objectives of the patent system.

21. Reverse engineering (by) artificial intelligence
Shawn Bayern

1. INTRODUCTION

This chapter analyzes the interaction between artificial intelligence and the concept of reverse engineering from two perspectives: (1) the reverse engineering of software or other processes *by* artificial intelligence; (2) the reverse engineering *of* artificial intelligence itself. The chapter's analysis is theoretical and admittedly a bit tentative: it suggests that increases in the capabilities of artificial intelligence may require the adaptation of trade-secret law or at least may have serious consequences for trade-secret policy. I outline a handful of potential policy considerations but do not lay out a comprehensive argument for particular policy prescriptions here; my goal here is exploratory rather than normative. The chapter's main thesis is that artificial intelligence can dramatically reduce the costs of reverse engineering and is a readier target, itself, for reverse engineering than might at first be obvious given its apparent opacity.

Reverse engineering is simply the process of figuring out how something works by exposure to the finished product; instead of engineering a mechanism "forward" from novel components or designs in the usual manner, "reverse" engineering works backward from an existing mechanism.[1] Traditional reverse engineering simply involved direct inspection of a physical mechanism—opening a machine or other device to see how it works and thereby gain the ability to replicate it. That type of reverse engineering is possible with software when it runs on a computer system under a third party's control, as is usually the case for desktop computer software, or when its object code or another direct representation of its full mechanism is otherwise available to third parties.[2] But much software today is accessible

---

[1]   This definition matches, at least, those of the Uniform Trade Secrets Act, § 1 cmt. ("starting with the known product and working backward to find the method by which it was developed"), and the Oxford English Dictionary. *See* OXFORD ENGLISH DICTIONARY, "reverse-engineer, v.", OED Online, Oxford University Press, June 2021, www.oed.com/view/Entry/246393. Sometimes in wider usage the term suggests that the process entails guesswork and results in a lack of deep understanding; *see, e.g.,* "Reverse Engineering," Wikipedia, en.wikipedia.org/wiki/Reverse_engineering (last accessed June 11, 2021) (defining reverse engineering as "a process or method through the application of which one attempts to understand through deductive reasoning how a device, process, system, or piece of software accomplishes a task *with very little (if any) insight into exactly how it does so*") (emphasis added). I don't intend that connotation in using the term, however, and in my experience that's not how engineers use it.

[2]   Computer programs are ordinarily written (most commonly directly by humans) in a *source code* defined by a programming language, then processed (compiled) into *object code*, a machine-readable representation of the program's logic. A computer (or virtual computer) might directly execute object code, or object code might be an intermediate or partial form representing the program's mechanism. "Reverse engineering" source code is normally trivially straightforward for competent software developers, but even source code can be rendered (through an automatable process commonly called *obfuscation*) difficult to read or to reverse engineer by removing conventional scaffolding, such as descriptive variable names and the ordering and formatting of text. Still, with enough effort, people with access to source code and even object code can almost always reverse engineer it.

only through a relatively formalized interface; for example, it might run on a web server and be accessible to distant web browsers or smartphone apps only by means of the Hypertext Transfer Protocol (HTTP). Still, even over a limited formal interface, a computer system may be reverse engineered by those who can observe inputs and outputs to the system. We can understand this as *black-box reverse engineering*, where *black box* is a term in computing and engineering that refers to a mechanism whose workings cannot be observed directly. Through black-box reverse engineering, the nature of a mechanism is deduced by means of its external effects; this may be the first time I've quoted the New Testament, but as Matthew 7:16 puts it: "You will know them by their fruits."

As I discuss within, black-box reverse engineering is important for artificial intelligence both because (1) advances in machine learning simplify the process of black-box reverse engineering in general, particularly of software, and (2) many forms of modern artificial intelligence may be reverse engineered by observing how they operate. These factual predicates underlie this chapter's concern with reverse engineering respectively *by* and *of* artificial intelligence.

2.   BACKGROUND: TRADE-SECRET LAW

Though changes in the relative ease and costs of reverse engineering may have other consequences for law (for example, if nothing else, they may upset the balance of power or the allocation of surplus between contracting parties on longstanding contracts), this chapter's main legal topic is the law of trade secrets.

Trade-secret law, in general, provides legal protection for secret processes and mechanisms. Historically, commentators regarded trade-secret law as analogous to, but not literally, intellectual property law; as the *Restatement of Torts* put it in 1939, "The suggestion that one has a right to exclude others from the use of his trade secret because he has a right of property in the idea has been frequently advanced and rejected."[3] Today, trade-secret law is widely regarded as a form of intellectual-property law because it recognizes a secret as property that can, for example, be sold, licensed, or misappropriated.[4]

Under American law today, the field is largely governed by statute. The Uniform Trade Secrets Act (UTSA) was drafted by the Uniform Law Commission in 1979 and amended in 1985; it has been adopted by the vast majority of US jurisdictions.[5] A corresponding federal statute, the Defend Trade Secrets Act (DTSA), was enacted in 2016.[6]

The UTSA defines a trade secret as "information, including a formula, pattern, compilation, program, device, method, technique, or process" that "derives independent economic value

---

[3]   Restatement of Torts § 757 cmt. a (1939). The comment continued: "The theory that has prevailed is that the protection is afforded only by a general duty of good faith and that the liability rests upon breach of this duty; that is, breach of contract, abuse of confidence or impropriety in the method of ascertaining the secret."

[4]   *See, e.g.*, World Intellectual Property Organization, *Trade Secrets*, www.wipo.int/tradesecrets/ en/ [https://perma.cc/WF2D-GVEH] ("Trade secrets are intellectual property (IP) rights on confidential information which may be sold or licensed.").

[5]   *See* Uniform Law Commission, Trade Secrets Act, www.uniformlaws.org/committees/community -home?CommunityKey=3a2538fb-e030-4e2d-a9e2-90373dc05792 [https://perma.cc/NU72-Q8UW].

[6]   18 U.S.C. §§ 1836 *et seq.*

[…] from not being generally known to, and not being readily ascertainable by proper means by, other persons who can obtain economic value from its disclosure or use" and that "is the subject of efforts that are reasonable under the circumstances to maintain its secrecy."[7] It provides injunctive relief and damages for "misappropriation" of a trade secret, which it defines largely in terms of whether the means to acquire a trade secret were "improper." More specifically, under the UTSA misappropriation includes "acquisition of a trade secret of another by a person who knows or has reason to know that the trade secret was acquired by improper means";[8] it also includes the use or disclosure of a trade secret, without consent, by someone who used "improper means" to obtain it[9] or who "knew or had reason to know"[10] that the secret came from someone who had used "improper means" to obtain it.[11]

Importantly for our purposes, the UTSA is clear that "improper means" do not include reverse engineering. The black letter of the statute defines "improper means" generally as including "theft, bribery, misrepresentation, breach or inducement of a breach of a duty to maintain secrecy, or espionage through electronic or other means,"[12] and its official comment clarifies:

> Proper means include [… d]iscovery by "reverse engineering", that is, by starting with the known product and working backward to find the method by which it was developed. The acquisition of the known product must, of course, also be by a fair and honest means, such as purchase of the item on the open market for reverse engineering to be lawful.[13]

"Proper means" also include "[o]bservation of the item in public use or on public display."[14]

Similarly, the federal Defend Trade Secrets Act of 2016 defines misappropriation of a trade secret to include knowledge obtained through "improper means,"[15] and it specifically excludes "reverse engineering" from its definition of "improper means."[16]

In short, those who have legitimate access to a mechanism (by obtaining and directly analyzing a product that contains it or by interacting with and indirectly analyzing it) are free, by default, to attempt to reverse engineer it; under most circumstances, trade-secret law treats reverse engineering the same way it treats any other form of creative engineering. Just as a trade secret is not protected against independent creative development,[17] it is not protected

---

[7] Unif. Trade Secrets Act § 1(4); *cf.* 18 U.S.C. § 1839(3).

[8] Unif. Trade Secrets Act § 1(2)(i).

[9] Ibid § 1(2)(ii)(A).

[10] Ibid § 1(2)(ii)(B).

[11] Ibid § 1(2)(ii)(B)(I). The UTSA's definition of misappropriation also includes those who "before a material change of [their] position, knew or had reason to know that [something] was a trade secret and that knowledge of it had been acquired by accident or mistake." *Ibid.* § 1(2)(ii)(C).

[12] Ibid § 1(1).

[13] Ibid § 1 cmt; *accord ibid.* pref. note ("Under both the Act and common law principles, for example, more than one person can be entitled to trade secret protection with respect to the same information, and analysis involving the 'reverse engineering' of a lawfully obtained product in order to discover a trade secret is permissible.").

[14] Unif. Trade Secrets Act § 1 cmt.

[15] *E.g.*, 18 U.S.C. § 1839(5)(A).

[16] Ibid § 1839(6)(B).

[17] Unif. Trade Secrets Act § 1 cmt. ("Proper means include [… d]iscovery by independent invention").

against the creative processes associated with reverse engineering, even if those creative pro
cesses are aimed at determining a specific preexisting secret.

3. REVERSE ENGINEERING BY ARTIFICIAL INTELLIGENCE

As Professors Pamela Samuelson and Suzanne Schotchmer put it 20 years ago, the advantages
and disadvantages of trade-secret law's approach to reverse engineering depend in part on the
ease (or as the law-and-economics discourse tends to put it, the "costs") of reverse engineering:

> We argue that legal rules favoring the reverse engineering of manufactured products have been
> economically sound because an innovator is nevertheless protected in two ways: by the costliness
> of reverse engineering and by lead time due to difficulties of reverse engineering. If technological
> advances transform reverse engineering so that it becomes a very cheap and rapid way to make
> a competing product, innovators may not be able to recoup their R&D expenses, and hence some
> regulation may be justified.[18]

This section argues that artificial intelligence tends to dramatically reduce the costs and delays
of many types of reverse engineering, thereby helping to make reverse engineering "a very
cheap and rapid way to make a competing product." A reduction in costs does not, of course,
imply on its own that greater regulation of reverse engineering is appropriate, but it does
suggest that reverse engineering will take on increasingly significant policy implications if
machine learning fulfills its promise in reducing reverse-engineering costs dramatically.

3.1 Machine Learning and Reverse Engineering

In some sense, where neural nets and the modern suite of deep-learning techniques and technologies excel is in heuristically duplicating black-box systems.

A widely used conceptual and educational example in machine learning involves the recognition, based on a moderate amount of preclassified data, of handwritten numbers—that is,
about 60,000 images of handwritten Arabic numbers paired with an encoding of the numeric
values that humans would agree they represent.[19] In beginning to perform well on this problem
about ten years ago—reaching "close to the [...] error rate of humans on this task"[20]—
researchers did not seek to implement a copy of the neurovisual systems of humans or animals,
nor did they seek to determine, even at a higher level of generality, why or how humans could
recognize handwritten numbers. For example, they did not approach the problem in a way
that a literacy teacher might in explaining character recognition to a human who had not
yet learned the relevant characters—for example, by breaking apart imprecise handwritten
numbers into conceptual features (say, lines and curves) intuitively understood by humans.
That sort of approach to the problem of visual recognition by artificial intelligence had failed;

---

[18] Pamela Samuelson & Suzanne Scotchmer, *The Law and Economics of Reverse Engineering*, 111 YALE L.J. 1575, 1582 (2002).
[19] See Yann LeCun *et al.*, *The MNIST Database of Handwritten Digits*, yann.lecun.com/exdb/mnist/ [https://perma.cc/C87J-P56P].
[20] Dan Cireşan *et al.*, *Multi-column Deep Neural Networks for Image Classification*, 2012 IEEE CONFERENCE ON COMPUTER VISION AND PATTERN RECOGNITION 3642, 3644.

famously, in 1966 researchers made "an attempt to use our summer workers effectively in the construction of a significant part of a visual system," which (for example) tried to "find properties (or measures) such as convex, linear, elliptical segment, smooth (no corners) etc."—that is, to break down the problem into preexisting, straightforward human concepts.[21] Clearly, the attempt in the 1960s was unsuccessful, and little progress was made in approximating human vision for decades.

The successful researchers in 2012 instead treated humans' recognition of numbers as a sort of black box; it didn't matter to them how preexisting visual systems worked, which features such systems focused on, and so on. They simply created a new, data-driven system that used whatever statistical features of the underlying set of images turned out to be useful to emulate the success of humans at reading handwritten numbers.

Understanding the power and flexibility of that type of approach is important in understanding modern machine learning, its relative ease, and its overall implications. Developing a machine-learning system from the ground up obviously takes some ingenuity, but many online tutorials exist that are sufficient for a generalist college-level or even high school-level computer programmer to write novel code that recognizes handwritten numbers with relative success.[22] In other words, the general application of statistical techniques, human experience with heuristics, large enough amounts of data, and powerful enough computer processors can have what used to be a counterintuitively great degree of success at solving problems and implementing forms of "intelligence" that were once extremely challenging.

This general type of data-driven approach—conceptually simple in the general case, but enriched with significant operational sensitivity, refinement of heuristics, experimental testing with massive computing power, and so on—is, broadly speaking, what researchers refer to today as artificial intelligence, and it underlies most of the field. Emulating a successful human radiologist by means of machine learning does not involve an attempt to figure out how radiologists do what they do in ways that are intuitive to other doctors or other humans generally;[23] instead, what makes a successful radiologist is treated as a black box, and the machine-learning endeavor proceeds simply by using the inputs and outputs of radiological experts (for example, large numbers of radiological scans that radiologists have judged to be positive or negative for a particular clinically significant result).

In other words—though it is not often spoken of in precisely this way—machine-learning researchers are reverse engineering their targets, such as a human radiologist, a literate human who can recognize handwriting, a human expert who makes predictions about the recidivism of criminal offenders, and so forth. The key skill of machine-learning researchers is in that sort of reverse engineering, as long as they have the right set of data to enable productive analysis and testing.

If modern machine learning can emulate humans, surely it can also emulate the relatively simple products of human engineering—say, physical devices, discrete industrial

---

[21]   Seymour Papert, THE SUMMER VISION PROJECT, July 7, 1966, people.csail.mit.edu/brooks/idocs/AIM-100.pdf [web.archive.org/web/20210524154853/people.csail.mit.edu/brooks/idocs/AIM-100.pdf].

[22]   *E.g.*, Jason Brownlee, *How to Develop a CNN [Convolutional Neural Network] for MNIST Handwritten Digit Classification*, machinelearningmastery.com/how-to-develop-a-convolutional-neural-network-from-scratch-for-mnist-handwritten-digit-classification/ [https://perma.cc/HFJ8-ZU8V].

[23]   For that sort of approach to artificial intelligence, see "Expert System," Wikipedia, en.wikipedia.org/wiki/Expert_system.

techniques, and software systems—as long as it has access to enough data about how those devices, techniques, or systems operate. Recent evidence suggests that attempts to do this have played out with significant success. For example, in a 2020 preprint entitled "IReEn: Iterative Reverse-Engineering of Black-Box Functions via Neural Program Synthesis,"[24] machine-learning researchers report an attempt to reverse engineer software whose source and object codes are treated as black boxes. As the researchers describe it, "We query a black-box function using random inputs to obtain a set of I/Os [inputs and outputs], and refine the candidate set by an iterative neural program synthesis scheme. This neural program synthesis is trained with pairs of I/Os and target programs."[25] To put it differently, just as the handwriting analysis discussed above started with tens of thousands of pairs of classifiable data and information about how the data should be classified, so a dataset analogous in extent and function can be built up simply by querying existing software: giving it input and seeing what the output is. Once that dataset is constructed, is it like any other dataset on which machine-learning researchers can operate.

The same sort of approach can be applied to many types of software, including relatively complex software with a visual interface. In 2020, NVIDIA Research reported the success of a tool its researchers developed, known as GameGAN,[26] in applying the tools of machine-learning-based, black-box reverse engineering to computer games: "Trained on 50,000 episodes of the game, a powerful new AI model […] can generate a fully functional version of PAC-MAN—without an underlying game engine. That means that even without understanding a game's fundamental rules, AI can recreate the game with convincing results."[27] This approach is not unique; for example, a 2018 preprint[28] and website[29] reported success in an attempt to "mimic a complete [computer] game environment designed by human programmers. By learning only from raw image data collected from random episodes, [our system] learns how to simulate the essential aspects of the game—such as the game logic, enemy behaviour, physics, and also the 3D graphics rendering."[30]

In short, the state of the art in machine learning can dramatically reduce the costs of reverse engineering software even if that software is a black box—that is, without the source or object code of the software, merely with an opportunity to observe how the software functions. It can do this simply by interacting with the software, building a dataset that it can then analyze. Conceptually, this is all that traditional machine learning has done with human beings as the target; asking human beings to write and classify 60,000 Arabic numbers to produce a dataset is not conceptually different, from the perspective of a machine-learning system, from record-

[24]   Hossein Hajipour *et al.*, *IReEn: Iterative Reverse-Engineering of Black-BoxFunctions via Neural Program Synthesis*, arxiv.org/pdf/2006.10720.pdf (June 18, 2020) [web.archive.org/web/20201101050414/arxiv.org/pdf/2006.10720.pdf].

[25]   Ibid at 2.

[26]   *See* Seung Wook Kim et al., *Learning to Simulate Dynamic Environments with GameGAN*, nv-tlabs.github.io/gameGAN/ [https://perma.cc/BSV3-24BJ].

[27]   Isha Salian, *40 Years On, PAC-MAN Recreated with AI by NVIDIA Researchers*, May 22, 2020, blogs.nvidia.com/blog/2020/05/22/gamegan-research-pacman-anniversary/ [web.archive.org/web/20210507191549/https://blogs.nvidia.com/blog/2020/05/22/gamegan-research-pacman-anniversary/].

[28]   David Ha & Jürgen Schmidhuber, World Models, arxiv.org/abs/1803.10122 (May 9, 2018) [https://web.archive.org/web/20210509093145/https://arxiv.org/pdf/1803.10122.pdf].

[29]   David Ha & Jürgen Schmidhuber, World Models: Can Agents Learn Inside of Their Own Dreams?, worldmodels.github.io/ [https://perma.cc/P9YT-B69Z].

[30]   Ibid.

ing 50,000 games of PAC-MAN. Both processes are aimed at generating enough data so that machine-learning systems can draw sufficiently fine distinctions to reverse engineer their objects.

Of course, this approach to black-box reverse engineering is not limited to humans (as in the handwriting-recognition system) or software (as in the PAC-MAN system) but can be applied to any black-box process as long as the machine-learning system has a sufficient opportunity to interact with it or otherwise build up a relevant dataset about it. But software that can be queried and observed is an especially attractive target: a dataset about it can be developed quickly because of the speed of software; the dataset can be developed easily and cheaply because of the internet; and the dataset that results is typically already digital (rather than requiring digitization of input from sensors of the real world, such as cameras or microphones). The result is that machine learning may dramatically reduce the costs of reverse engineering, particularly of software.

4.   THE REVERSE ENGINEERING OF ARTIFICIAL INTELLIGENCE

The previous section observed that modern artificial-intelligence techniques can sharply reduce the costs of the black-box reverse engineering of software and other systems. But, of course, machine-learning systems are themselves software systems, and they can be the target of similar attempts at reverse engineering.

At least in several contexts, they may be particularly attractive targets. Just practically, often they operate publicly, providing the opportunity for large numbers of queries; this is of course not an essential feature of artificial intelligence, but the public (or at least paying customers) can query many such systems. More importantly, successfully reverse engineering a modern machine-learning system potentially provides opportunities to learn both about the machine-learning techniques and the underlying data on which the machine-learning system was based. To put it differently, while black-box reverse engineering PAC-MAN yields an imperfect duplicate of PAC-MAN, black-box reverse engineering a modern machine-learning system potentially provides the ability to replicate at least part of the underlying dataset, enabling new machine-learning applications beyond the specific target of the reverse-engineering efforts.

Two examples are probably sufficient to demonstrate the potential simplicity of reverse engineering even sophisticated, modern machine-learning systems. One is a lively, short online article called "Pirating AI"[31] in which the authors demonstrate the ease with which they were able to reverse engineer a machine-learning system for image recognition provided by Amazon Web Services (AWS). As the authors put it:

> How easy is this to apply in practice? We fed about 50,000 images to AWS Rekognition, to get our labels—this cost about $50 ($1 per 1,000). We then used transfer learning to train a [convolutional neural network …]—i.e., given an image and a target output of "97% sharp", figure out a rule that

---

[31]   Edward Dixon *et al.*, *Pirating AI*, MEDIUM, Nov. 26, 2018, medium.com/@damilare/pirating-ai-800a8da6431b [https://perma.cc/RY6L-XWQW].

gives approximately the same output. There isn't much engineering effort involved—just a few dozen lines of Python code that would require minimal changes to reverse-engineer other similar services.[32]

The second example involves the Correctional Offender Management Profiling for Alternative Sanctions (COMPAS), a system that opines on the likelihood that those who have committed crimes in the past will commit them again in the future and which has been used by judges in sentencing offenders.[33] Notorious among commentators who have accused it of bias and lack of transparency[34]—it is, after all, a black-box system developed commercially and potentially protected by trade-secret law[35]—it has also been the target of reverse engineering by several analysts in order to critique it from various policy perspectives.[36] The attempts to reverse engineer COMPAS are limited because of the limited ability to query the system, given that it is not a system that fully interacts with the public, but even with that limitation the reported results are telling and have permitted a significant amount of useful black-box analysis. And this success comes despite COMPAS's nature as a complicated example of machine learning.[37]

5.   IMPLICATIONS OF ARTIFICIAL INTELLIGENCE FOR TRADE SECRET LAW'S POLICIES TOWARD REVERSE ENGINEERING

This section provides an overview of how the law might approach the simplification of reverse engineering that artificial intelligence can bring about.

5.1   Technological Changes and Trade Secrets

Professor Jeanne Fromer noted in a recent article that the ease of reverse engineering traditional software has made trade-secret law a relatively poor fit for "computing innovation" in general for the past several decades.[38] As discussed briefly above,[39] until the rise of the internet, reverse engineering software was as simple as buying a product and observing its source or object code. Professor Fromer argues that four developments—cloud computing, big data,

---

[32]   Ibid.

[33]   *E.g.*, State v Loomis, 881 N.W.2d 749 (Wis. 2016).

[34]   *See e.g.*, Laurel Eckhouse *et al.*, *A Unified Approach for Understanding Problems With Risk Assessment*, 46 Crim. J. & Behavior 185 (2019); Julia Angwin *et al.*, Machine Bias, ProPublica, May 23, 2016, www.propublica.org/article/machine-bias-risk-assessments-in-criminal-sentencing [https://perma.cc/7V79-ZWWU].

[35]   *See* Natalie Ram, *Innovating Criminal Justice*, 112 Nw. U. L. Rev. 659, 685 (2018) ("Northpointe, which created and distributes COMPAS, claims that COMPAS is proprietary and a trade secret").

[36]   *See, e.g.*, Cynthia Rudin *et al.*, *The* Age *of Secrecy and Unfairness in Recidivism Prediction*, 2 Harv. Data Sci. Rev. (2020), hdsr.mitpress.mit.edu/pub/7z10o269/release/4 [https://perma.cc/F9A5 -WDKG] (reporting several other attempts and observing, of their own attempt, "[e]ven with our limited data, we may have succeeded in partially reconstructing parts of the COMPAS model as it is implemented in Broward County").

[37]   Ibid ("One issue with COMPAS is that it is *complicated*. It is based on up to 137 variables […] that are collected from a questionnaire.").

[38]   Jeanne Fromer, *Machines as the New Oompa-Loompas: Trade Secrecy, the Cloud, Machine Learning, and Automation*, 94 N.Y.U. L. Rev. 706, 716 (2019); *cf. supra* note 2.

[39]   *See supra* note 2.

machine learning, and automation—make trade-secret law more attractive for those in the software industry because they make it easier to keep secrets. Machine learning in particular, according to Professor Fromer, is easy to protect compared to traditional software:

> The most valuable aspects of any software built using machine learning techniques are its underlying data and model. Both can be kept secret and practically free from independent discovery and reverse engineering, two of trade secrecy protection's key limitations. As such, it is technologically plausible to protect the valuable parts of software derived through machine learning.[40]

And, of course, significant commentary outside the context of trade-secret law has identified the difficulties of understanding how some modern software based on machine learning works and the social problems associated with its opacity.[41]

While machine learning can be hard to understand—difficult for individual humans to "interpret" or to "explain"[42]—and while it does of course seem easier to protect as a trade secret than traditional desktop software, the analysis in the previous two sections suggests that machine learning's ability to decrease the costs of reverse engineering (and the lack of resistance of even complicated machine-learning systems to reverse engineering) may well turn out to be more significant than the lack of transparency associated with client-server computing (and thus the inability to observe the mechanisms of software directly instead of as black boxes).

Of course, determining the costs of reverse engineering any particular software system is an empirical matter, but the successes of black-box engineering reported briefly above—all of which would have been very surprising to software engineers even 20 years ago—suggest that it will be difficult to protect artificial intelligence from black-box reverse engineering unless the artificial-intelligence software is largely isolated from the public. Much software is. For example, there is no opportunity for the public to reverse engineer the machine-learning software that a company uses only to fine-tune the performance of its own data center[43] or to carry out internal analysis of its own patents,[44] but that has always been the case with internal software used only privately; such software was never a plausible target for legitimate

---

[40]   Fromer, *supra* note 38, at 722–3.

[41]   *See, e.g.*, Ignacio N. Cofone, *Algorithmic Discrimination Is an Information Problem*, 70 HASTINGS L.J. 1389 (2019); FRANK PASQUALE, THE BLACK BOX SOCIETY: THE SECRET ALGORITHMS THAT CONTROL MONEY AND INFORMATION (2015).

[42]   *See* Ribana Roscher *et al.*, *Explainable Machine Learning for Scientific Insights and Discoveries*, 8 IEEE ACCESS 42200 (2020), *available at* ieeexplore.ieee.org/document/9007737; Grégoire Montavon *et al.*, *Methods for Interpreting and Understanding Deep Neural Networks*, 73 DIGITAL SIGNAL PROCESSING 1 (2018), *available at* www.sciencedirect.com/science/article/pii/S1051200417302385.
   To be clear, nothing in my analysis in this chapter requires that machine learning be easily understood by humans in order to be reverse engineered. An algorithm can be reconstructed without that kind of understanding; all that is important from the perspective of machine learning (and reverse engineering), for purposes like these, is the association of inputs and outputs. Compare, loosely, Drew McDermott, *On the Claim that a Table-Lookup Program Could Pass the Turing Test*, 24 MINDS & MACHINES 143 (2014).

[43]   *Cf., e.g.*, Richard Evans & Jim Gao, *DeepMind AI Reduces Google Data Centre Cooling Bill by 40%*, deepmind.com/blog/article/deepmind-ai-reduces-google-data-centre-cooling-bill-40 [https://perma.cc/5EKH-52PW].

[44]   *Cf., e.g.*, Aaron Abood & Dave Feltenberger, *Automated Patent Landscaping*, 26 ARTIFICIAL INTELLIGENCE L. 103 (2018).

reverse engineering, and the fact that it uses artificial intelligence changes little (unless it uses similar techniques or data as a company's public-facing software). The point is just that the reverse-engineering capabilities of machine learning pose a potential empirical challenge to Professor Fromer's general view: client-server computing, automation, and the use of back-end data to drive algorithms may in fact be unlikely to serve as significant barriers to reverse engineering, in at least many cases, because of the successes of machine-learning systems at what amount to reverse engineering.

5.2   The Consequences of Machine Learning

On one hand, these possibilities may just return software to the status quo ante; software was easy to reverse engineer in the past, and maybe it will continue to be easy to do so in the future. But artificial intelligence generally reflects more investment into secret data and processes and potentially derives more value from trade-secret protection than most traditional desktop software.

Most desktop software exists in a relatively thick milieu that includes features beyond the software itself: customer support; the availability of upgrades; an institutional reputation for the successful creation and deployment of a product; the network effects associated with the use of a system; the visual design of the software; and so on. I don't mean to suggest that a word processor has no independent value as software alone, just that that value is often dwarfed by other features of a word-processing system. It would have been easy to reverse engineer, or simply copy features from, WordPerfect 5.1, but I don't imagine its developers cared much; for reverse engineering to make a commercial difference, an upstart or even an established competitor would have needed to integrate any copied features into a product in a manner that affected its marketing, consumer perceptions of the various brands of word processor, and so on. Relatedly, the research and design that went into word processors involved such factors as user experience, market research about new features, and so on; while certainly technological in some respects, the process of specifying, developing, and deploying a word processor has more in common with figuring out how to mix, flavor, and brand a breakfast cereal than with the technology and engineering associated with producing a Learjet. I don't mean to overstate the point; certainly, some desktop software is sophisticated in its own right and counts more legitimately as "technology"—and benefits more from "technological" research and innovation—than Microsoft Word does. But the fierce competitiveness of the machine-learning industry over the past several years—indeed, the salaries and acquisition prices that individual and corporate experts have been able to demand—suggests at least a different industrial emphasis between traditional desktop software and modern machine-learning systems.

To put it differently, machine learning depends on significant technological research and development, and its final operational essence is usually a relatively small amount of code that distills extremely valuable procedural knowledge from massive amounts of data and often extremely sophisticated operational sensitivity. If it turns out to be difficult to use trade-secret law to protect public-facing artificial intelligence from reverse engineering, that arguably does not simply restore us to the status quo that existed for desktop software; it suggests, at least potentially, that trade-secret law will be *less* useful than it has been in protecting valuable industrial secrets that require significant investment.

Maybe that still is not a problem. There are at least three reasons not to care if trade-secret law turns out not to be an effective tool for protecting artificial intelligence. First, as Professor Fromer and others have pointed out, while trade-secret law may encourage innovation (for those who get protection for their trade secrets), it also interferes with *subsequent* innovation and it has implications for competition policy:

> [W]ithout any significant risks that the developed information or innovation will be disclosed through proper means—independent discovery, reverse engineering, or through transfer of an employee's general knowledge and skill—this form of protection is so strong that it is perpetual. Generally, it is of great worry when protection for innovation is of unlimited duration [… P]erpetual protection can readily stymie follow-on innovation and competition. When these conditions obtain, the incentive offered by intellectual property protection undermines the overall goals of innovation and competition that the law is trying to promote.[45]

In other words, reverse engineering acts as a "safety valve" that prevents trade-secret protections from lasting forever and thus undermining competition and further innovation.[46] Second, trade-secret law is of course not the only option companies have for protecting their investments in valuable industrial processes; they can choose patent law instead, accepting the familiar package of public disclosure, state-enforced monopoly, and time-limited protection. Third, companies with trade secrets can attempt to control, at least to some degree, what counts as permissible reverse engineering by trying to use contracts (and standardized forms that nobody reads but that courts may treat as contractual) to govern the terms and conditions of third parties' use of their artificial-intelligence systems.

5.3   Contract Law, Machine Learning, and Trade-Secret Policy

I have little to say about the first two of these reasons; my goal here is not to evaluate trade-secret law from the ground up or to compare its advantages and disadvantages with other forms of intellectual-property protection, only to highlight the potential implications of artificial intelligence for reverse engineering. (For example, if patent law is for whatever reason unsuitable for certain advances in artificial intelligence and if it turns out that reverse engineering indeed is dramatically cheaper as a result of artificial intelligence, the law may need to develop new options to protect such technologies or at least to strengthen trade-secret law in new ways. But the details of that sort of lawmaking will need to wait for future technological developments and are beyond the scope of this chapter.)

As a contract-law scholar, however, I do have some observations about the third of the considerations I listed above—the interaction between contract terms and trade-secret law— because that interaction may well be influenced by the way reverse engineering of artificial intelligence is likely to proceed on a distributed internet.

As background, a company intending to protect its trade secrets from reverse engineering can try to include standard form terms in the "terms of use" of its website for its public users (or the standard form contracts for its commercial customers) that purport to prohibit automated querying of the website, use of queries in attempts to reverse engineer an artificially intelligent system that the website exposes, and so on. The enforcement of boilerplate

---

[45]   Fromer, *supra* note 38, at 728–9.
[46]   Ibid.

anti-reverse-engineering terms appears unsettled, however.[47] Perhaps more importantly, trade-secret protection is fragile for a public system (and, because of machine learning, for a publicly queryable system) because of the chance that anyone might learn about the system in a way that happens not to trigger the contractual protections. As a treatise on trade-secret law has put it:

> Where a piece of software has been widely distributed, there arise concerns ... regarding how "confidential" or "secret" the software can really be. One may well question whether a court would enforce a contractual reverse engineering clause in a case where the licensor has done nothing or little to prevent multitudes of other persons from reverse engineering.[48]

For example, if even a single jurisdiction refuses to enforce (on grounds of public policy, unconscionability, or simply its treatment of standard form contracts in the context in which they have been used to try to protect a particular trade secret) the purportedly contractual terms that try to protect a trade secret, that would likely be enough to undermine more generally the contractual attempt to protect the trade secret. That is, use that is permissible because those terms are not enforced would cause the secret to have been properly disclosed or redeveloped, and then the secret is no longer secret. And, of course, most machine-learning systems that are accessible online will be accessible from multiple jurisdictions.

The weakness of contractual attempts to rule out reverse engineering is probably appropriate. To begin with, as a general matter, relying on standardized contract terms is likely to make too much turn on too little, particularly as the interaction between computer systems becomes more automated. Standardized and potentially overreaching terms on a broad "terms of use" page are a poor basis for regulating something as significant as trade-secret policy, including the criminal liability that may attach to it. Moreover, they are not truly contractual; that is, they do not have the normal policies behind enforcing bargains[49] in their favor. On one hand, under the artificial banner of private ordering, treating standard form terms as a way to declare reverse engineering to be "improper" potentially gives far too much power to those who insert purportedly contractual terms into websites. On the other, as automated interaction between computer systems becomes more common, the contractual nature of terms posted online becomes even more questionable than when it directly involves humans; something that automatically "scrapes" a website may have no opportunity to understand

---

47   The Electronic Frontier Foundation, for example, advises programmers as follows: "Most software today comes with EULAs, and EULAs may have 'no reverse engineering' clauses. Websites or other internet services also may have TOS or TOU that purport to restrict otherwise legal research activities. Researchers and programmers sometimes receive access to code pursuant to an NDA, developer agreement or API agreement that restricts the right to report security flaws. The legal status of contractual prohibitions on security research or vulnerability reporting is still in flux. While it is more likely that a court will enforce a negotiated NDA than a mass market EULA, the law is not clear. Be sure to consult with counsel if the code you want to study is subject to any kind of contractual restriction." Electronic Frontier Foundation, *Coders' Rights Project Reverse Engineering FAQ*, www.eff.org/issues/coders/ reverse-engineering-faq#faq11 [https://perma.cc/BA3C-PZWM].

48   1 MILGRIM ON TRADE SECRETS § 1.05 (Rel. No. 126, 2021).

49   *See generally* Melvin Aron Eisenberg, *The Bargain Principle and Its Limits*, 95 HARV. L. REV. 741 (1982).

(or even a fair opportunity to access) terms posted elsewhere on the website.[50] And without direct involvement of humans, when two automated systems interact they are both likely to be managed by companies that have their own standard form terms; in that setting, standard form terms will often conflict, leading to unclear rights.[51] It is also arguably disingenuous to make a machine-learning system available for interaction and then object when others learn from that interaction.[52]

None of this discussion implies that reverse engineering should always be permissible, regardless of the reduction in its costs and the consequences of its use; my point is just that the false banner of "private ordering" by means of standardized anti-reverse-engineering terms in purportedly contractual documents is unlikely to be a sound way to regulate trade-secret policy. The question should be decided regardless of the attempts to vary rights by means of private attempts to dictate terms.

To summarize, this section does not lay out a particular approach for deciding how trade-secret policy should govern machine learning. There are several different possible responses, but we have little practical experience with any of them. One is for the law to move to prevent particular types of bulk uses of proprietary artificial intelligence in order to learn more about its inner workings—the sort of bulk uses that contract terms might also try to prevent, but if the restriction were regulatory or statutory rather than purportedly contractual, policymakers would have an opportunity to design reasonable terms that avoid overreach by any one party. For example, it would be novel—but not either radical or crazy—to tie the legitimacy of reverse-engineering efforts to a website's reasonable and declared limits on the *rate* of querying a machine-learning system, the amount of data that an individual user or company is permitted to upload or download to it, and so on. Of course, another approach—much more radical—would be to change the presumption that reverse engineering is a proper use of a machine-learning system; such an approach, however, would raise concerns similar to those that Professor Fromer has outlined for a trade-secret policy that is too protective.

6.   CONCLUSION

If all industrial processes had happened, historically, to be extremely easy to reverse engineer—perhaps in a world where there were simply less privacy overall[53]—the law that protects investment in industrial processes probably would have developed differently. This chapter has suggested that machine learning brings us at least a little closer to that world because it (1) decreases the costs of reverse engineering others' products and (2) is itself an attractive target

---

[50]   To be clear, the contractual nature of such terms is always questionable even in conventional contexts; any particular customer or user is vanishingly unlikely to read boilerplate terms, and there is significant debate about whether they are contractually binding in the general case.

[51]   *Cf.* UNIF. COMM. CODE § 2-207 (governing—confusingly—a similar problem in the context of the sale of goods).

[52]   *Cf.* Eric J. Feigin, *Architecture of Consent: Internet Protocols and Their Legal Implications*, 56 STAN. L. REV. 901, 940 (2004) (making a similar argument about the meaning of putting software systems online in view of the conventions associated with traditional internet protocols and concluding that "[c]hoosing to 'opt in' to the Internet as it now exists means agreeing to abide by certain norms of behavior").

[53]   *Cf.* Isaac Asimov, *The Dead Past*, ASTOUNDING SCI. FICTION, Apr. 1956, at 6.

for reverse engineering even by those who interact with it as if it is a black-box system. Indeed, modern machine learning may be conceived specifically as a tool for reverse engineering; in some ways, the core problem that machine learning aims to solve is a reverse-engineering problem. That alone does not mean that the law of reverse engineering needs to change, but it should at least make us question whether it would be acceptable for trade-secret law to become significantly less important as a result of the continued development of artificial intelligence.

22. Trade secrets versus the AI explainability principle

Rita Matulionyte and Tatiana Aranovich

1. INTRODUCTION

Increasing investment in AI technologies and their rapid development around the world[1] has led to intensive discussions as to how the proprietary interests of AI developers should best be protected.[2] While previous chapters of this book have extensively discussed copyright and patent law protection of AI-based technologies, this one will focus on the suitability of trade secret protection to AI-based technologies and the challenges it raises, especially so far as the AI explainability principle is concerned. Trade secret law, which is considered to be a special area of intellectual property law,[3] prohibits misappropriation of commercially valuable information that is kept secret by its owner.[4] It has been broadly used to protect AI-based

---

[1] *See, e.g.,* European Patent Office (EPO), PATENTS AND THE FOURTH INDUSTRIAL REVOLUTION – THE INVENTIONS BEHIND DIGITAL TRANSFORMATION (Dec. 2017), http://documents.epo.org/projects/babylon/eponet.nsf/0/17FDB5538E87B4B9C12581EF0045762F/ $File/fourth_industrial_revolution_2017__en.pdf (identifies AI as one of the fastest growing Fourth Industrial Revolution fields since 2011, its average annual growth rate of 43 per cent); PWC, THE MACROECONOMIC IMPACT OF ARTIFICIAL INTELLIGENCE (Feb. 2018), www.pwc.co .uk/economic-services/assets/macroeconomic-impact-of-ai-technical-report-feb-18.pdf (experts suggest that by 2030 AI will contribute US$15.7 trillion to the world economy); OECD, ARTIFICIAL INTELLIGENCE IN SOCIETY (2019), https://doi.org/10.1787/eedfee77-en (indicates AI start-ups doubled private equity investments absorbed from 2016 to 2017 and attracted 12 per cent of worldwide private equity investments in the first half of 2018, furthermore indicating AI applications abound, from transport to science to health).

[2] There is extensive literature on this topic; *see, e.g.,* Timothy L. Butler, *Can a Computer Be an Author: Copyright Aspects of Artificial Intelligence*, 4 HASTINGS COMM. & ENT. L.J. 707 (1982); Peter M. Kohlhepp, *When the Invention Is an Inventor: Revitalising Patentable Subject Matter to Exclude Unpredictable Processes*, 93 MIN. L. REV. 779, 814 (2008); Ryan Abbott, *I Think, Therefore I Invent: Creative Computers and the Future of Patent Law*, 57 BOST. COL. L. REV, 1079–1126 (2016); Benjamin L.W. Sobel, *Artificial Intelligence's Fair Use Crisis*, 41 COLUM. J.L. & ARTS 45–97 (2017); Rosa Maria Ballardini, Kan He & Teemu Roos, *AI-Generated Content: Authorship and Inventorship in the Age of Artificial Intelligence*, in Taina Pihlajarinne, Juha Vesala & Olli Honkkila (eds), ONLINE DISTRIBUTION OF CONTENT IN THE EU, 117–35 (2019); Courtney White & Rita Matulionyte, *Artificial Intelligence Painting a Bigger Picture for Copyright Ownership*, 30 AUSTRAL. INTELL. PROP. J. 224–42 (2020); Rita Matulionyte, *Australian Copyright Law Impedes the Development of Artificial Intelligence: What Are the Options?* (Oct. 27, 2020) https://ssrn.com/ abstract=3720289.

[3] For a discussion of whether trade secrets is an IP right or not, *see* Ana Nordberg, *Trade Secrets, Big Data and Artificial Intelligence Innovation: A Legal Oxymoron?*, in Jens Schovsbo, et al (eds), THE HARMONIZATION AND PROTECTION OF TRADE SECRETS IN THE EU: AN APPRAISAL OF THE EU DIRECTIVE, 210 (2020).

[4] *See* art 39 of the Agreement on Trade-Related Aspects of Intellectual Property Rights, Apr. 15, 1994, Marrakesh Agreement Establishing the World Trade Organization, Annex 1C, 1869 U.N.T.S. 299, 33 I.L.M. 1197 (1994) [hereinafter TRIPS].

technological solutions, not least because other areas of IP law – patent and copyright law – provide limited protection to AI modules.[5] Trade secret laws appear to be an especially useful tool since they can be used to protect different parts of an AI-based technology, including the algorithm and its parameters, training datasets, source code, and the entire trained module (which includes all above mentioned elements).[6] Trade secret protection is not limited in time, and does not involve registration costs.[7]

At the same time, it has been pointed out that the use of trade secrets to protect AI technologies conflicts with the expectation that AI technologies should be explainable.[8] AI technologies have often been described as opaque and functioning as a 'black box', with humans not being able to understand the reasons behind their decisions.[9] AI protection using trade secrets increases this opacity problem further.[10] A number of (non-binding) ethics guidelines have listed explainability as one of the core principles of AI,[11] while stakeholders and governments have been exploring how this AI explainability principle could be implemented in practice.[12] The European Union (EU) General Data Protection Regulation (GDPR) went one step further and implemented a limited – but legally binding – 'right of explanation', requiring that certain AI-made administrative decisions should be explainable to decision subjects.[13] While commentators have indicated that trade secret protection has a potential to conflict with the

---

[5]   *See* discussion in chapters xxx of this book [this info will have to be provided by the editor]

[6]   For a clear, brief explanation of what 'algorithm' means, *see* Katarina Foss-Solbrekk, *Three Routes to Protecting AI Systems and Their Algorithms under IP Law: The Good, the Bad and the Ugly*, J. INTELL. PROP. L. & PRAC, 2–3 (2021).

[7]   Though it might involve significant cost to keep it secret.

[8]   *See, e.g.*, W. Nicholson Price II & Arti K. Raia, *Clearing Opacity through Machine Learning*, 106 IOWA L. REV. 775, 784 (2021). Note: 'transparency' is another concept often used with relation to AI. While transparency and explainability are two different concepts, they are often used as synonyms. To avoid any confusion, we will use 'explainability' as the main term in this chapter.

[9]   *See* Frank Pasquale, THE BLACK BOX SOCIETY: THE SECRET ALGORITHMS THAT CONTROL MONEY AND INFORMATION (Harvard University Press 2015); David S. Levine, *Confidentiality creep and opportunistic privacy* 20 TUL. J. TECH. & INTELL. PROP., 11–42 (2017).

[10]   *See, e.g.*, Price II & Raia,, *supra* note 8, at 784.

[11]   *See, e.g.*, OECD, OECD PRINCIPLES ON AI (2019), www.oecd.org/going-digital/ai/principles/ ; EUROPEAN COMMISSION, ETHICS GUIDELINES FOR TRUSTWORTHY AI (2019), https://ec.europa.eu/digital-single-market/en/news/ethics-guidelines-trustworthy-ai; G20, G20 AI PRINCIPLES (2019), www.g20-insights.org/wp-content/uploads/2019/07/G20-Japan-AI-Principles .pdf; AUSTRALIAN GOVERNMENT, AUSTRALIAN AI ETHICS PRINCIPLES (2019), www .industry.gov.au/data-and-publications/building-australias-artificial-intelligence-capability/ai-ethics -framework/ai-ethics-principles.

[12]   *See, e.g.*, KPMG, ACHIEVING TRUSTWORTHY AI: A MODEL FOR TRUSTWORTHY ARTIFICIAL INTELLIGENCE (Nov. 2020), https://assets.kpmg/content/dam/kpmg/au/pdf/2020/ achieving-trustworthy-ai.pdf.

[13]   Recitals 63 & 71 & art. 22 of Regulation 2016/679 of Apr. 27, 2016, on the Protection of Natural Persons with Regard to the Processing of Personal Data and on the Free Movement of Such Data, and Repealing Directive 95/46/EC (General Data Protection Regulation) [hereinafter GDPR], 2016 O.J. (L 119) 12, 14, 46 (EU); for a critical analysis *see* Sandra Wachter, Brent Mittelstadt & Chris Russell, *Counterfactual Explanations without Opening the Black Box: Automated Decisions and the GDPR*, 31 HARV. J.L. & TECH 878, 879 (2018).

demand for an explainable AI,[14] there has been limited analysis on the scope of the conflict and how it could be addressed.[15]

The goal of this chapter is thus to identify at which stages, or to which extent, the conflict of trade secret protection conflicts with the demand for explainability of AI technologies, and the possible ways to address this conflict. In particular, should companies be required, in some cases, to disclose their trade secrets in order to ensure explainability of AI? Or are there other ways to accommodate the values that the principle of explainability is meant to protect?

Since AI technologies can be applied in a variety of industries, and the purposes and interests involved might differ significantly, in this chapter we will draw examples from two selected sectors: judicial administration and healthcare. They have been chosen for two main reasons: while the use of AI in these sector promises significant benefits (such as improved healthcare or fairer court decisions), there are also significant risks involved (for example, safety and bias), which has led to a call for both more transparency and clear accountability rules when AI-based tools are used in decision making.[16] By focusing on these two sectors we will also demonstrate that the conflict of trade secrets and AI explainability principle might be very different in different sectors, and thus might require sector-specific – rather than one-size-fits-all – solutions to the issue.

This chapter is divided into five sections. After this introduction, we will briefly discuss the extent to which trade secrets are being used – and are likely to be used in the future – to protect AI technologies (section 2). In this section we will also explain what elements of AI technologies have been – or could be – protected by trade secrets. In section 3 we will discuss the meaning of an AI explainability principle from scientific and legal perspectives. In particular, we will ask to whom AI should be explainable (decision subjects, users, regulatory or auditing bodies, other experts in the field or the public) and what purpose explanation should serve, and we will demonstrate how, depending on subjects and the purpose of explanation, different explanation techniques could be applied. In section 4, by referring to examples in judicial administration and healthcare, we will identify specific instances where the conflict between trade secrets and a broad explainability principle may occur, and discuss three possible ways to address this conflict: alternative AI explanation techniques, limited mandatory disclosure and an encouragement of voluntary disclosure. Section 5 will summarize the main outcomes of the analysis.

---

[14]   *See, e.g.*, W. Nicholson Price II & Raia, *supra* note 8.

[15]   For papers that engage in this discussion to a more significant extent *see, e.g.,* W. Nicholson Price II & Raia, *supra* note 8; Alyssa M. Carlson, *The Need for Transparency in the Age of Predictive Sentencing Algorithms* 103 IOWA L. REV. 303 (2017); Lyria Bennett Moses & Louis de Koker, *Open Secrets: Balancing Operational Secrecy and Transparency in the Collection and Use of Data by National Security and Law Enforcement Agencies,* 41 MELB. U. L. REV. 530 (2017).

[16]   *See, e.g.*, Carlson, *supra* note 15; Rebecca Wexler, *Life, Liberty, and Trade Secrets: Intellectual Property in the Criminal Justice System,* 70 STANF. L. REV. 1343 (2018); David Watson, Jenny Krutzinna, Ian Bruce, Christopher Griffiths, Iain McInnes, Michael Barnes, & Luciano Floridi, *Clinical Applications of Machine Learning Algorithms: Beyond the Black Box*, 364 BMJ-BRIT. MED. J. (2019).

2.   TRADE SECRETS AND AI

Trade secrets have a significant potential in protecting AI technologies. Since copyright and patent law protection to AI technologies may be limited or uncertain, trade secrets are seen by some as the most efficient way to protect commercial interests and to maintain a competitive edge in the market.[17]

2.1   Trade Secrets and AI Technologies

According to article 39 of the TRIPS Agreement, signatory states are required to ensure that natural and legal persons may protect 'confidential information' from being shared, acquired or used without their consent under three conditions. First, the information should be secret, in the sense that it is not generally known among or readily accessible to persons normally working with such information; second, it should have commercial value because it is secret; and third, it has been subject to reasonable steps to keep it secret.[18] This test or very similar ones have been implemented in regional laws, for example in a recently introduced EU Trade Secret Directive,[19] and in a number of national laws,[20] or have been adopted by courts in countries where trade secrets are protected via common law only.[21]

As the following examples demonstrate, trade secrets offer potential in the AI industry.[22] In judicial administration, a number of risk assessment technologies, including the COMPAS technology, have been protected by trade secrets.[23] In *Loomis*,[24] Eric Loomis was sentenced to six years in prison based on a predictive computer system, COMPAS, that indicated he had a 'high risk of recidivism'. Loomis suspected that the tool considered gender and race as factors in assessing risk and wanted to challenge the decision. However, the AI developer claimed that

---

[17]   Foss-Solbrekk, *supra* note 6, at 10; Nari Lee, *Protection for Artificial Intelligence in Personalised Medicine: The Patent/Trade Secret Tradeoff*, in Jens Schovsbo, et al (eds) THE HARMONIZATION AND PROTECTION OF TRADE SECRETS IN THE EU: AN APPRAISAL OF THE EU DIRECTIVE 267–94, 267 (Edward Elgar Publishing 2020).

[18]   TRIPS, art. 39 (2).

[19]   Art. 2 of Directive (EU) 2016/943 of Jun. 8, 2016, on the protection of undisclosed know-how and business information (trade secrets) against their unlawful acquisition, use and disclosure, 2016 O.J. (L 157) 9 (EU).

[20]   *See, e.g.*, 18 USC§ 1839 (3) (US); the Japanese Unfair Competition Prevention Act (UCPA) art 2(6) requires secrecy (not known), kept secret and commercial utility, *discussed* in in Lee, *supra* note 17, at 278.

[21]   For example, in Australia the most common course of action to protect trade secrets is breach of confidence – *see, e.g.*, Andrew Stewart et al., INTELLECTUAL PROPERTY LAW IN AUSTRALIA 87 (Lexis Nexis 6th ed. 2017).

[22]   Wexler, *supra* note 16, at 1363–4 ('Trade secrecy is a primary intellectual property protection for source code'); *see also* Pamela Samuelson, *The Uneasy Case for Software Copyrights Revisited*, 79 GEO. WASH. L.REV. 1746, 1758 (2011) ('[M]ost of the commercially valuable know-how embedded in programs [is] protected as trade secrets'); Pamela Samuelson, *Functionality and Expression in Computer Programs: Refining the Tests for Software Copyright Infringement*, 31 BERKELEY TECH. L.J. 1215, 1220–1, 1239–40, 1285 n.390 (2016) (describing elements of computer programs that are uncopyrightable and observing controversies over the 'patentability of computer program innovations').

[23]   Wexler, *supra* note 16, at 1369.

[24]   *See* State v Loomis, 881 N.W.2d 749, 755, 756 n.18 (Wis. 2016), cert. denied, 137 S. Ct. 2290 (2017).

details about how the system weights and calculates input variables are trade secrets, and the court denied the order to disclose information kept under trade secret.[25]

Trade secrets also have potential with relation to AI in the health sector, especially to protect extensive datasets held by pharmaceutical companies. For instance, Myriad Genetics has used trade secrets to protect its large set of data on BRCA1/2 variants, which gives it a significant competitive advantage in the genetic testing market.[26]

2.2   Why Trade Secret Protection

There are a number of reasons why AI developers would use trade secrets to protect elements of AI algorithms or entire modules. As mentioned above, one reason for trade secret use is that the protection available for AI technologies under copyright and patent law is limited.[27] In brief, the area of patents over software has always been a controversial one, and commentators have suggested that aspects of AI technologies might be deemed unpatentable subject matter.[28] This concern has been especially strong in the US, where recent US Supreme Court decisions, including *Alice*,[29] have arguably made it more difficult to patent software-based inventions.[30] Under the European Patent Convention, computer programs per se cannot be patented[31] and only computer-implemented inventions where the algorithm possesses a 'technical feature' can be patented.[32]

Copyright protection to AI technologies is limited too. Copyright has always been the main IP right to protect source (and object) code. However, it is arguably not suitable to protect algorithms. Algorithms can be defined as a set of instructions that are executable by code.[33] Copyright laws of many countries explicitly or implicitly exclude abstract ideas, mathematical formulas or instructions from the scope of copyright protection. For instance, the EU Software

---

[25]   Wexler, *supra* note 16, at 1369.

[26]   *See, e.g.*, W. Nicholson Price II, *Big Data, Patents, and the Future of Medicine*, 37 CARDOZO L. REV. 1401, 1434 (2016).

[27]   *See also* Nordberg, *supra* note 3, at 197–9.

[28]   Wexler, *supra* note 16, at 1371.

[29]   Alice Corp. Pty. v CLS Bank Int'l, 134 S. Ct. 2347, 2349–50 (2014) ('Because the claims are drawn to a patent-ineligible abstract idea, they are not patent eligible under § 101').

[30]   Kate Gaudry & Samuel Hayim, *Artificial Intelligence Technologies Facing Heavy Scrutiny at the USPTO*, IPWATCHDOG (28 Nov. 2018), www.ipwatchdog.com/2018/11/28/artificial-intelligence-technologies-facing-heavy-scrutiny-uspto/id=103762 [https://perma.cc/D4BJ-45TN] (discussing the impact of the Supreme Court's *Alice* decision). Some studies suggest that the number of US patents granted in the field of software is already declining, *see* Price II & Raia, *supra* note 8, at 801–2.

[31]   Art. 52 (2) (c) of Convention on the Grant of European Patents, 5 Oct. 1973, as amended by Decision of the Administrative Council of European Patent Organization of 21 Dec. 1978, 13 I.L.M 268 (1974).

[32]   *See* Maja Brkan & Grégory Bonnet, *Legal and Technical Feasibility of the GDPR's Quest for Explanation of Algorithmic Decisions: Of Black Boxes, White Boxes and Fata Morganas*, 11 EUR. J. RISK REG. 18, 19, 43 (2020).

[33]   For a more detailed explanation on the meaning of an 'algorithm' *see* Foss-Solbrekk, *supra* note 8, at 2–3.

Directive,[34] similar to the TRIPS agreement[35] and WIPO Copyright Treaty,[36] protects only 'the expression of a computer program' (that is, source or object code) and not the 'ideas and principles' behind those programs (that is, algorithms).[37]

Further, while copyright law might protect training datasets[38] that are used to train AI modules (as 'compilations'), it is questionable whether datasets generated by computers, and where the selection and arrangement of the material is not original, would be protected under copyright laws of many countries.[39] While sui generis database protection, available under EU law, protects databases that merely require substantial investment,[40] such protection is not available in most other jurisdictions. Thus, while copyright law automatically protects source code, it may not protect other parts of AI modules, such as an algorithm, its separate parameters or computer-generated datasets.

Trade secrets therefore appear the most suitable option to protect all elements of AI technologies – as long as they can be kept confidential.[41] Trade secret laws do not specify what subject matter is protected or not, and protect any information that meet the three requirements listed above. Trade secrets can be – and have been – applied to protect entire algorithms[42] or specific elements of the algorithm, such as input variables, weights of variables and methods of calculation,[43] training data and the training process,[44] the resulting model,[45] the source code in which the algorithm is implemented,[46] risk assessment methods, validation information, user

---

[34]   Recital 11 of Directive 2009/24 of April 23, 2009, on the legal protection of computer programs, 2009 O.J. (L 111) 17 (EU).

[35]   TRIPS, art 9(2) (prevents copyright protection of 'ideas, procedures, methods of operation or mathematical concepts').

[36]   *See* Art. 2 of the World Intellectual Property Organization (WIPO) Copyright Treaty, Dec. 20, 1996

[37]   *See also* Case C-406/10, SAS Institute v World Programming Ltd, ECLI:EU:C:2012:259 (CJEU confirmed, in obiter dicta, that algorithms should be distinguished from source code, and the former is not protected under the Directive). For a discussion of this case, *see* Guido Noto La Diega, *Against the Dehumanisation of Decision-Making: Algorithmic Decisions at the Crossroads of Intellectual Property, Data Protection, and Freedom of Information*, 3 J. INTELL. PROP. INFO. TECH. & ELEC. COM. L., para. 34, 42 (2018); *see also* Foss-Solbrekk, *supra* note 6, at 10.

[38]   Note: data comprised in the dataset would generally not be protected under copyright law as it would constitute mere information.

[39]   In Australia, computer-generated databases were denied copyright protection. *See* Desktop Marketing Systems Pty Ltd v Telstra Corp Ltd (2002) 119 FCR 491; [2002] FCAFC 112; IceTV Pty Ltd v Nine Network Australia Pty Ltd (2009) 239 CLR 458, 503 [49]; [2009] HCA 14.

[40]   *See* Directive 96/9 of Mar. 11, 1996, on the Legal Protection of Databases, arts 7–11, 1996 O.J. (L 77), 20–28 (EU).

[41]   *See also* Sylvia Lu, *Algorithmic Opacity, Private Accountability, and Corporate Social Disclosure in the Age of Artificial Intelligence* 23 VAND. J. ENT. & TECH. L. 99 (2020).

[42]   Foss-Solbrekk, *supra* note 6: on a global scale, the Amazon recommendation system, the Instagram algorithm for publication diffusion or Google's search algorithms are among the most well-known examples of trade secrets – *see* Brkan & Bonnet, *supra* note 32, at 39–40.

[43]   Wexler, *supra* note 16, at 1343; *see also* State v Loomis, 881 N.W.2d 749, 761 (Wis. 2016), *cert. denied*, 137 S. Ct. 2290 (2017) (noting that 'COMPAS does not disclose' how 'risk scores are determined or how the factors are weighed').

[44]   Training data is arguable the most valuable asset: *see* Nordberg, *supra* note 3, at 196–7.

[45]   Price II & Raia, *supra* note 8, at 788.

[46]   Wexler, *supra* note 16, at 1345.

manuals and audit information.[47] Trade secret protection also has other advantages. In contrast to patent and copyright laws that require at least certain disclosure, trade secret law promotes full opacity, which might be more aligned with a firm's strategic needs.[48] Furthermore, trade secret protection is not limited in time and lasts for as long as the information is secret, while copyright and patent law protection expires after a set period of exclusivity.

2.3   Limitations of Trade Secrets

While some commentators point to the limited nature of trade secret protection, we suggest that those limitations are not critical in practice. First, it is true that trade secrets do not grant exclusive rights over information, comparable to those under patent and copyright law.[49] However, trade secrets effectively serve a similar purpose; namely, to prevent unauthorized use of protected information by competitors and allow trade secret owners to maintain competitive advantage in the market. Second, trade secret protection is lost when a trade secret is disclosed to the public, even if inadvertently. While this is a limitation of trade secret protection, it could be addressed, and the risk of disclosure could be limited, through robust measures applied to keep information secret.[50] Third, trade secret protection could be circumvented by reverse engineering the technology or independently inventing the same technology.[51] While reverse engineering or independent invention is possible in cases of relatively simple machine learning models, it becomes more difficult and expensive with relation to complex models.[52] Finally, in some jurisdictions there are public interest exceptions that allow disclosure of trade secrets in cases of public interest;[53] however, their use has been very limited.[54]

In a broader societal context, the greatest concern surrounding excessive use of trade secrets is that they lead to what some authors call 'confidentiality creep'.[55] It has been argued that excessive use of trade secrets in an information society context, or algorithmic opacity more generally, compromises values such as equality, privacy and safety.[56] Arguably, due to the secret nature of technologies, it is difficult or impossible to check whether technologies are fair, safe or respect the privacy of individuals. Due to these concerns, there has been a call for more transparency and explainability around AI technologies. As society increasingly expects AI to be explainable, this might be seen as a risk to effective trade secret protection.

---

[47]   Ibid.

[48]   Lu, *supra* note 41, at 117; James Gibson, *Once and Future Copyright,* 81 NOTRE DAME L. REV. 167, 177–8 (2005).

[49]   Foss-Solbrekk, *supra* note 6, at 12.

[50]   Companies such as Google, KFC and others have successfully managed to protect their highly valuable trade secrets from disclosure.

[51]   Foss-Solbrekk, *supra* note 6, at 12; Nordberg, *supra* note 3, at 212; Lee, *supra* note 17, at 288.

[52]   Price II & Raia, *supra* note 8, at 788; *see also* Jeanne C. Fromer, *Machines as the New Oompa-Loompas: Trade Secrecy, the Cloud, Machine Learning, and Automation*, 94 N.Y.U. L. REV. 706, 707–8 (2019).

[53]   *See, e.g.*, EUTSD; *see also* Foss-Solbrekk, *supra* note 6, at 12.

[54]   *Cf.* Matt Malone, *Trade Secrets, Big Data, and the Future of Public Interest Litigation Over Artificial Intelligence in Canada*, 35 CIPR 6, 6 (Fall 2020) (argues that trade secrets 'will be susceptible to attack when public interest litigants turn their sights on matters of bias and discrimination').

[55]   Levine, *supra* note 9, at 11.

[56]   Lu, *supra* note 41, at 117–27.

In order to assess whether there is an actual conflict between trade secret protection and a call for explainable AI, we need to understand what the AI explainability principle means.

3.   EXPLAINABILITY IN THE AI CONTEXT: WHAT, WHY AND HOW

3.1   What is the AI Explainability Principle?

For years computer scientists have been trying to understand how AI systems reach their decisions; the logic behind the decisions, or inferences, generated by AI; and how to develop AI that is explainable to a human.[57] This has developed in what has become known as the Explainable Artificial Intelligence (XAI) research stream.[58] XAI generally means AI in which the reasoning for the AI outcomes can be understood by humans. It became a mainstream concept after the US Defense Advanced Research Projects Agency (DARPA) started a major program on XAI in 2018.[59]

In legal discourse, AI explainability became a mainstream concept with the adoption of the GDPR, which was meant to introduce a general 'right of explanation'.[60] This initiative was followed by other jurisdictions, such as France, which introduced its own right of explanation.[61] The French Digital Republic Act provides individuals a right to an explanation for administrative algorithmic decisions, which requires the administrative decisionmaker to provide a range of information about the 'degree and the mode of contribution of the algorithmic processing to the decision making', including what data were processed, what the system's parameters were and how the algorithm weighted factors.[62] In addition, explainability was recognized as one of the main AI ethical principles in a number of international and national (non-binding) guidelines on ethical AI.[63] While these three concepts – XAI, a right of explanation and the AI explainability principle – may to some extent have different meanings, for the purposes of this chapter we will use 'AI explainability' in its broadest sense, that is, as an expectation that AI systems' decisions should be explainable.[64]

---

[57]   *See, e.g.*, Shane T. Mueller, Robert R. Hoffman, William Clancey, Abigail Emrey & Gary Klein, *Explanation in Human–AI Systems: A Literature Meta-Review Synopsis of Key Ideas and Publications and Bibliography for Explainable AI*, ARXIV:1902.01876 (Feb. 2019).

[58]   *See* Brkan & Bonnet, *supra* note 32, at 19.

[59]   *See* www.darpa.mil/program/explainable-artificial-intelligence.

[60]   *See, e.g.*, Lilian Edwards & Michael Veale, *Enslaving the Algorithm: From a 'Right to an Explanation' to a 'Right to Better Decisions'?* 16 IEEE SEC. & PRIV 46–53 (2018) (discuss the right of explanation under GDPR in Chapter II in quite a bit of detail); Sandra Wachter et al., *supra* note 13, at 842 ('a legally binding right to explanation does not exist in the GDPR').

[61]   *See, e.g.*, French law Loi 2016-1321 du 7 oct., 2016, pour une République numérique, LA CIRCULATION DES DONNÉES ET DU SAVOIR, 2016 Legifrance; *see also* Edwards & Veale, *supra* note 61, at 48–9.

[62]   *See* Edwards & Veale, *supra* note 60, at 48–9.

[63]   *See, e.g.*, OECD, *supra* note 11; EUROPEAN COMMISSION, *supra* note 11; G20, *supra* note 11; AUSTRALIAN GOVERNMENT, *supra* note 11.

[64]   Explainability is closely related to a concept of 'transparency' often found in literature and AI ethics principles. While these concepts might have different meanings, they are often used as synonyms. *See, e.g.*, Moses & Koker, *supra* note 15, at 548 (defines transparency in a very similar way as explain-

3.2   To Whom Should AI Be Explainable, and Why?

In order to understand the content of the AI explainability principle, we need to ask at least two questions: To whom AI should be explainable? Why does a person need an explanation, or for what purpose will they use the explanation? Answers to these questions would help us determine what sort of information the AI explainability principle might require the disclosure of, which in turn will allow us to examine in which situations the conflict between AI explainability and trade secrets is likely to occur.

For computer and data scientists, explainability of AI is important for a number of different reasons, such as understanding how the models work and ensuring that the decisions (outcomes, inferences) are correct and fair;[65] it also helps the search for ways in which AI modules could be improved.[66] In the legal context, other reasons drive the demand for explainable AI. While neither the AI explainability principle nor its purposes are clearly defined in any of the instruments that establish this principle,[67] it can serve different groups of people and different purposes. We identify four main classes of stakeholders that the AI explainability principle could potentially serve.

The first class of stakeholders which might be interested in reasons behind AI decisions is 'decision subjects', that is, individuals who are directly affected by AI decisions. For instance, if risk assessment software suggested that a defendant in criminal proceedings is at a 'high risk' of reoffending and thus should be denied parole, the defendant (decision subject) has an interest in knowing the reason for this inference.[68] The reasons could enable them to challenge the decision to deny parole. In other instances, for example when an AI inference leads to credit refusal, the explanation would allow the decision subject to modify their circumstances so that a future credit application is successful (for example, cancelling another credit card or paying off existing debt).[69] At the same time, not all decision subjects might need an explanation, or at least not in all situations. For instance, in healthcare, if AI is used for diagnostic purposes, the patient would probably not have an obvious interest in knowing what technology is used for particular decisions as long as it is effective and reliable, and does not lead to wrong decisions. However, if an AI decision leads to a wrong diagnosis or treatment and causes harm to a patient, the decision subject might request an explanation as to how AI reached its

---

ability is defined: 'The idea of *algorithmic* transparency implies a right to know not only what powers the government has but also the manner of their exercise – not just what data is collected but how it is analysed and used in decision-making'). In order to avoid any confusion, in this study we will refer to 'explainability' only.

[65]   *See* Lilian Edwards & Michael Veale, *Slave to the Algorithm: Why a Right to an Explanation Is Probably Not the Remedy You Are Looking for*, 16 DUKE L. & TECH. REV. 18, 27–43 (2017–18).

[66]   *See* Brkan & Bonnet, *supra* note 32, at 19.

[67]   Jake Goldenfein, *Algorithmic Transparency and Decision-Making Accountability: Thoughts for buying machine learning algorithms* 56–7 (9 Sep. 2019), https://ssrn.com/abstract=3445873 as an example, AUSTRALIAN GOVERNMENT, *supra* note 11 (describes 'explainability' in the following general way: 'There should be transparency and responsible disclosure to ensure people know when they are being significantly impacted by an AI system, and can find out when an AI system is engaging with them.').

[68]   *See* Edwards & Veale, *supra* note 65, at 43.

[69]   Ibid.

decision; it is especially likely that such explanation would be requested as a part of medical negligence proceedings.[70]

The second class of stakeholders potentially interested in explainable AI are users of AI, that is, persons or organizations that use AI to make decisions. In judicial administration these would be judicial officers who use AI-based software, such as risk assessment tools. In healthcare, these would be doctors who use diagnostic or other AI-based tools in diagnosis, treatment or prediction. For instance, if an AI application suggests that there is no evidence of cancer, the doctor might want to understand how the AI reached this conclusion before deciding whether other diagnostic techniques or tests need to be applied to confirm the results. This is important not only to ensure the quality of service, but also for a doctor to discharge their duty of care properly and avoid any possible liabilities.[71] Also, commentators suggest that AI explainability is likely to encourage wider clinical adoption of machine learning both by doctors and by patients.[72] Similarly, in judicial administration, judges should be provided a certain amount of explanation as to how the risk assessment tool functions to both ensure that the outcome is fair and that the decision withholds appeal.

On the other hand, commentators sometimes question whether users need an explanation, or whether they merely require reassurance as to the safety or effectiveness of technology.[73] For example, a recently developed AI technology was able to predict cardiovascular risks from retinal scans using deep learning, a type of machine learning that can be less amenable to demands for explanations.[74] If such a system were put into practice, it would arguably be sufficient for a doctor to know how accurately the software diagnoses the disease; no explanation as to *how* AI reaches these conclusions is needed.[75] Still, this suggests that, even if doctors do not need to understand the reasons for AI inferences, they would need some sort of explanation, such as general information about how the device functions and its certification.

The third class of stakeholders consists of external auditors and regulatory bodies that need explanations in order to be able to verify, validate or audit the AI, that is, to check its effectiveness, safety and other relevant parameters. In healthcare, regulatory agencies such as the US Food and Drug Administration (FDA) carry out a thorough assessment of AI-based medical devices before granting approval to market them.[76] In other sectors, such as judicial adminis-

---

[70]   For more about issues related to AI and medical malpractice *see* William Nicholson Price II, *Medical Malpractice and Black-Box Medicine, in* BIG DATA, HEALTH LAW, AND BIOETHICS 295, 295–6 (2018) .

[71]   *See* Lee, *supra* note 17, at 273–5.

[72]   Watson et al, *supra* note 16.

[73]   European Parliament, A GOVERNANCE FRAMEWORK FOR ALGORITHMIC ACCOUNTABILITY AND TRANSPARENCY, STUDY BY THE PANEL FOR THE FUTURE OF SCIENCE AND TECHNOLOGY, 48 (April 2019) www.europarl.europa.eu/RegData/etudes/STUD/2019/624262/EPRS_STU(2019)624262_EN.pdf.

[74]   Ryan Poplin et al., *Predicting Cardiovascular Risk Factors from Retinal Fundus Photographs using Deep Learning*, 2 NAT. BIOM. ENG. 158, 164 (2 Mar. 2018).

[75]   European Parliament, *supra* note 73, at 48.

[76]   William Nicholson Price II, *Medical AI and Contextual Bias*, 33 HARV. J.L. & TECH. 66, 84–6 (2019); FDA, SOFTWARE AS A MEDICAL DEVICE (SAMD): CLINICAL EVALUATION – GUIDANCE FOR INDUSTRY AND FOOD AND DRUG ADMINISTRATION STAFF (2017), www.fda.gov/regulatory-information/search-fda-guidance-documents/softwaremedical-device-samd-clinical-evaluation-guidance-industry-and-food-and-drugadministration; FDA, CLINICAL DECISION SUPPORT SOFTWARE: DRAFT GUIDANCE FOR INDUSTRY AND FOOD AND

tration, there are often no mandatory audit or certification procedures, though they have been discussed and suggested in literature.[77] Generally, regulatory bodies or external audit bodies would need access to a wide range of information about how AI was developed and validated and how it functions, though there is not yet agreement upon what sort of explanation is sufficient or most suitable.[78]

The fourth and final class of stakeholders are other experts in the field, such as academics and NGOs.[79] They serve the public interest by checking whether AI technologies produce fair results, do not violate privacy or other rights, are safe and serve the public need.[80] Since they serve a similar purpose to certification and auditing bodies, they will need access to a similarly broad range of information related to AI modules.

3.3   How Can AI Be Explained?

Depending on the explanation needed – for whom and for what purpose – the explanation required might be different. For instance, regulatory bodies might need access to a range of information – or possibly all available information – about the AI module. The decision subjects might only want to know what factors influenced a certain decision and whether these factors could be challenged. While there is general agreement that in different situations different kind of explanations will need to be provided, there is still no agreement as to what sort of information/explanation would be most suitable for a particular purpose.

Below we provide a brief overview of a few different ways in which an explanation could be provided. We will demonstrate that some explanations require the disclosure of significant amounts of information related to the AI module, which might be protected by trade secrets. Other explanation techniques are less intrusive and allow for preserving the secrecy of most, if not all, confidential information. Some of them are more fit for some purposes; others are fit for other purposes.

In XAI literature, two main approaches in developing explanations can be identified. A first type (which is sometimes called the 'pedagogical' or 'exogenous' approach) does not attempt to actually explain the inner workings of the machine learning algorithm; instead, it attempts to provide relevant information about how the model works using extrinsic, orthogonal methods.[81] A second type of approach attempts to explain or replicate the model's inner reasoning (sometimes referred to as a 'decompositional' approach).[82]

With relation to the first type of approach, exogenous XAI approaches can either be model-centric (or 'global interpretability') or subject-centric (or 'local interpretability'). As Deeks explains, a model-centric approach might involve, for instance, explaining the creator's intentions behind the modelling process, the family of model the system uses, the parameters the creators specified before training the system, qualitative descriptions of the input data the

---

DRUG ADMINISTRATION STAFF (2019), www.fda.gov/regulatory-information/search-fda-guidance-documents/clinical-decision-support-software.

[77]   European Parliament, *supra* note 73, at 51–2.
[78]   *See* discussion below on different explainability techniques.
[79]   European Parliament , *supra* note 73, at 64–5.
[80]   Edwards & Veale, *supra* note 65, at 54.
[81]   Edwards & Veale, *supra* note 65, at 64; Ashley Deeks, *The Judicial Demand for Explainable Artificial Intelligence*, 119 COLUMBIA L. REV. 1835 (2019).
[82]   Edwards & Veale, *supra* note 65, at 64.

creator used to train the model and how the creators tested the data for undesirable properties. Model-centric approaches attempt to explain the whole model rather than its performance in a particular case, and can help to ensure that decisions are being made in a procedurally regular way.[83] In contrast, a subject-centric approach might provide the decision subject with information about the characteristics of individuals who received similar decisions. Alternatively, the subject-centric approach might involve the use of counterfactuals, which enable the decision subject to tweak the input factors to test how much a given factor mattered in the original recommendation.[84] Generally speaking, exogenous approaches do not require users to understand the inner workings of the model and could be useful for individuals who are trying to understand how decisions about them have been made.[85]

The alternative to exogenous approaches is decompositional approaches, which try to explain the model's reasoning. One of the most obvious decompositional approaches is the disclosure of a model's source code and/or algorithm. This approach attempts to open the black box and understand how the structures within, such as the weights, neurons, decision trees and architecture, can be used to shed light on the patterns that they encode – this approach requires access to a large part of the model structure itself.[86] While some commentators indicate the advantages of opening up the source code,[87] the majority suggest that disclosing the source code might not provide the information needed. Arguably, analysis of the source code can be extraordinarily difficult even for experts; and it cannot guarantee the absence of all types of flaws.[88]

Apart from disclosing the entire algorithm or/and source code, other, more nuanced decompositional approaches exist, such as building a second system alongside the original model (so-called surrogate model) which closely approximates the predictions made by an underlying model and also provides interpretable results (also called 'black box testing').[89]

It is clear from the above that different AI explainability techniques are more suitable for different stakeholders and a better fit for some purposes than for others.[90] For instance, decision subjects, such as defendants or patients, are more likely to benefit from exogenous subject-centric explanation techniques. The abovementioned explanation by counterfactuals could be especially useful to provide explanations to decision subjects who want to understand what factors influenced the decision that affected them.[91] AI users, such as judges and doctors, might have little use for the explanations provided when using the counterfactuals technique. Instead, they would probably glean more useful information from model-centric explanations that would provide more general information on how the model functions, rather than an

---

[83]   Deeks, *supra* note 81, 1835–6.
[84]   Ibid, at 1836.
[85]   Ibid, at 1836–7.
[86]   *See* Edwards & Veale, *supra* note 65, at 64.
[87]   *See* a good summary of arguments in favor of this technique in Wexler, *supra* note 16, at 1373–4.
[88]   *See* a good summary of arguments against of this technique in ibid; *see also* Joshua A. Kroll, Solon Barocas, Edward W. Felton, Joel R. Reidenberg, David G. Robinson & Harlan Yu, *Accountable Algorithms*, 165 U. PA. L. REV. 633, 660–1 (2017) (arguing that revealing source code is a misguided way of creating algorithmic accountability).
[89]   Deeks, *supra* note 81, at 1837; *see also* Osbert Bastani, Carolyn Kim & Hamsa Bastani, *Interpreting Blackbox Models via Model Extraction* (24 Jan. 2019), https://arxiv.org/pdf/1705.08504.pdf [https://perma.cc/L2K4-ZPVU].
[90]   *See, e.g.*, Wexler, *supra* note 16, at 1373–4; also Goldenfein, *supra* note 68, at 58.
[91]   *See* Sandra Wachter et al., *supra* note 13, at 878–9.

explanation on how a particular decision was made. Further, for external auditors and regulatory bodies, as well as other experts in the field (academics, NGOs), exogenous model-centric explanations might be insufficient since they do not provide detailed information about the inner workings of the module. They will probably prefer decompositional approaches, such as access to the entire algorithm or parts of it, or they could rely on alternative approaches such as the 'black box testing' techniques discussed above.

In summary, the AI explainability principle may require the provision of different information for different stakeholders, depending on their needs and purposes. We have also seen that explanations can be provided in different ways by using different techniques. Some XAI approaches might require disclosing the inner workings of the algorithm (for example, decompositional approaches that require revealing significant parts of the algorithm or source code). Other explainability techniques, however, do not require access to confidential information; instead, they try to determine the functioning of the module by testing it from 'outside' (for example, the counterfactual technique).

In the following section we will analyse situations in which the AI explainability principle and trade secrets are likely to clash, and how the conflict could be addressed.

4.   WHEN TRADE SECRETS AND AI EXPLAINABILITY CLASH

4.1   Is There a Conflict?

A number of commentators suggest that there is a clear conflict between the expectation for AI to be explainable and trade secret protection.[92] Namely, commentators have suggested that one of the main causes of AI opacity is secrecy, or 'where details of algorithmic development are deliberately concealed'.[93] This includes the deliberate use of trade secret protection for AI technologies.[94] The above analysis suggests that while the conflict between the AI explainability principle and trade secrets might happen in some cases, in others there will be no real conflict between the two. Namely, in some cases AI can be explained without interfering with trade secrets. Whether the conflict exists will depend on who needs an explanation, for what purpose, and what explainability technique is applied to provide such an explanation.

As far as the decision subject is concerned, a defendant in criminal proceedings would have a legitimate interest in receiving an explanation as to how the predictive AI tool assessed his or her risk of recidivism. The defendant might want to understand what factors were taken into consideration when making a risk assessment; they might be satisfied with the explanation provided using an exogenous subject-centric technique, such as explanation by counterfactuals.[95] As suggested above, such technique would not normally require disclosing the inner workings of the algorithm protected by trade secrets. Similarly, if the use of AI in healthcare

---

[92]   *See, e.g.*, Lee, *supra* note 17, at 2767.

[93]   The other two reasons are *complexity* and *non-intuitiveness* of AI decisions: *see* Price II & Raia, *supra* note 8, at 784; Andrew D. Selbst & Solon Barocas, *The Intuitive Appeal of Explainable Machines*, 87 FORDHAM L. REV. 1085, 1089–9 (2018).

[94]   *See also* Brkan & Bonnet, *supra* note 32, at 38.

[95]   *See* discussion above; *see also* Sandra Wachter et al., *supra* note 13.

causes a false diagnosis, the patient might demand an explanation as to how AI reached this particular decision. This could potentially be achieved using exogenous subject-centric techniques that do not interfere with trade secret protection.

With relation to the AI user, a healthcare practitioner might need an explanation about the AI they intend to use, in order to properly discharge their duty of care. While exogenous subject-centric techniques that explain a particular decision would be not suitable in this case, the healthcare practitioner might be able to acquire sufficient information about the AI by using exogenic model-specific explanation techniques that provide information about the module. These techniques explain how the module was designed without trying to explain the inner workings of the module. They do not lead to the disclosure of significant parts of the algorithm or source code and thus are unlikely to lead to a conflict with trade secrets. In judicial administration, a judge who needs to understand the AI model in order to trust its outcomes might find a similar model-centric explanation useful.[96] In addition, users of AI might not need these explanations at all, since even explanations of AI require certain general knowledge of AI. Also, explanations provided might not be sufficient to provide evidence about the quality of the module. Instead, users might prefer relying on reports by external assessors, such as regulatory/certification bodies or auditors.[97]

External auditors or regulatory bodies might require a much more in-depth explanation of the AI module, which would allow for checks on its accuracy and whether there are issues related to fairness, safety or privacy. In this case, exogenic explanation techniques might not be sufficient and decompositional techniques that aim at disclosing the inner workings of the module might be more useful. These techniques might require full access to the algorithm, data sets, source code and other parts of the module. In this case, the conflict between the demand for full explainability and trade secret protection is likely to be unavoidable.

Finally, other experts in the field, such as NGOs and academics, would need explanations to be provided essentially for the same purpose as regulatory bodies; that is, in order to check for any flaws the module may contain. Since their inquiry might be very broad and cover a range of different criteria, they are likely to want access to as much information as possible. If they were to demand the disclosure of algorithm parameters or source code, this would clearly clash with trade secret protection.

Next, we will assess the ways in which this conflict between the demand of AI explainability and trade secret protection could be addressed.

4.2   How the Conflict Could Be Addressed

While literature has repeatedly identified the conflict between two competing interests – the public interest of explainability and a private interest to keep information confidential to maintain competitive advantage in the market[98] – there has been limited discussion of the possible

---

[96]   Notably, users would need at least a certain understanding of AI in order to be able to make use of any explanations.

[97]   In the healthcare sector, approval from regulatory bodies such as the FDA might perform this function; in the judicial sector commentators have suggested that all prediction software used by courts should be ex ante validated by independent experts – *see, e.g.*, Carlson, *supra* note 15, at 322–4.

[98]   Butler, *supra* note 2; Kohlhepp, *supra* note 2; Abbott, *supra* note 2; Sobel, *supra* note 2; Ballardini et al., *supra* note 2.

solutions to this problem. Below we discuss three approaches that could be used to address the problem: an alternative explanation; a limited mandatory disclosure; and an encouragement of voluntary disclosure. They are not exclusive of each other and different combinations could be applied in different fields or to meet different needs.

The below analysis is based on the premise that there is a need to find an appropriate balance between the private interests protected by trade secrets and public interests that the AI explainability principle is meant to preserve. On the one hand, we acknowledge that trade secret law is an important tool to protect the competitive interests of AI developers, especially keeping in mind that protection under other areas of law (patent and copyright) is limited. The importance of trade secrets is highlighted in various legal instruments, such as the EU GDPR or the US Freedom of Information Act. The EU GDPR suggests that the right to access granted to data subjects should not 'adversely affect' the trade secrets of the controller,[99] while the US Freedom of Information Act allows authorities to withhold disclosure of information that is protected by trade secrets.[100]

At the same time, trade secret protection is not absolute and can be limited in cases where public interest prevails. For example, the EU Trade Secret Directive provides for explicit public interest exceptions for trade secret protection.[101] It allows for suspension of a trade secret 'for the purpose of protecting a legitimate interest recognised by Union or national law'.[102] Commentators have suggested that such a legitimate interest could potentially provide an explanation of an algorithmic decision to a data subject.[103] Thus, there is a need to appropriately balance these private and public interests. We believe that the three approaches discussed below allow for achieving this balance.

4.2.1   Alternative explanation

When the request for an explanation of AI is likely to conflict with trade secret protection, it should be considered whether the explanation could be provided using a technique that does not interfere with trade secrets. For instance, if a defendant who wants to challenge the AI-generated decision requires the disclosure of the entire algorithm or source code,[104] their request for explanation can be satisfied using other, less intrusive explanation techniques, such as subject-centric exogenous explanation using counterfactuals. In such situations, experts

---

[99]   *See* Brkan & Bonnet, *supra* note 32; *see also* Recital 63 GDPR; Gianclaudio Malgieri & Giovanni Comandé, *Why a Right to Legibility of Automated Decision-Making Exists in the General Data Protection Regulation*, 7 INT'L DATA PRIV. L. 243, 262–4 (2017).

[100]   The Freedom of Information Act in 5 U.S.C. § 552 (b) (4), 12 (US).

[101]   Directive 2016/943 of Jun. 8, 2016, on the Protection of Undisclosed Know-How and Business Information (Trade Secrets) against their unlawful acquisition, use and disclosure [hereinafter EU TSD], art 5(b) 2016 O.J. (L 157), 11 (EU).

[102]   EU TSD, art 5(d), 2016 O.J. (L 157), 11 (EU).

[103]   Brkan & Bonnet, *supra* note 32, at 40; *see also* Maja Brkan, *AI-Supported Decision-Making under the General Data Protection Regulation*, PROCS. 16TH INT'L CONF. ON A.I. & L., 6 (12–16 Jun. 2017).

[104]   *See* State v Loomis, 881 N.W.2d 749, 755, 756 n.18 (Wis. 2016), cert. denied, 137 S. Ct. 2290 (2017) (the petition is focused on the violation of due process, 'because the proprietary nature of COMPAS prevents a defendant from challenging the accuracy and scientific validity of the risk assessment; and because COMPAS assessment take gender and race into account in formulating the risk assessment').

could be asked to recommend a technique that is most suitable to answer the specific enquiry at hand and at the same time has the least potential to interfere with trade secret protection.[105]

4.2.2   Limited mandatory disclosure

Second, when it is not possible to provide the required explanation without divulging the trade secret to some extent, we suggest that the disclosure of a trade secret might be ordered, but with adequate protections and limitations. For instance, if experts suggest that in order to properly assess the fairness of a risk assessment algorithm, access to the parts of the algorithm is needed (for example, variables and their weights), the court might order the disclosure of this information but apply protective measures, such as protective orders, sealing or limited courtroom closures.[106] Protective orders have already been successfully used in US courts in cases where trade secrets over AI had to be disclosed in order to assess the technology used in the criminal prosecution process.[107]

Similarly, when AI companies are required to disclose all relevant information to external auditors or regulatory bodies, these could be required to keep the information confidential from third parties. For instance, when companies submit information about AI-based medical devices to regulatory authorities, such as the US FDA, full disclosure might be required but authorities 'should ensure that such disclosure would not amount to a loss of secrecy status'.[108] The US FDA already uses similar measures to protect trade secrets in many other contexts, including the confidential treatment of clinical trial data.[109]

This approach suggests that, when the disclosure of trade secrets is necessary, it should be proportionate. In order to keep the balance of private and public interests, disclosure should be made only to the parties that need to assess the quality of the algorithm. Third parties – especially competitors – should be prevented from accessing it in order to preserve the private interests that trade secrets protect.

4.2.3   Encouraging voluntary disclosure

Finally, sometimes the limited disclosure discussed above might be unsatisfactory. Commentators argue that some algorithms need to be disclosed to the public generally, so that data scientists or NGOs can scrutinize these algorithms as well as learn from them in developing future technology.[110] This argument has been especially strong in relation to algorithms applied in the judicial administration sector, such as predictive algorithms used in sentencing.[111]

---

[105]   *See* similar Brkan & Bonnet, *supra* note 32, at 40–1.

[106]   Deeks, *supra* note 81, at 1846; Wexler, *supra* note 16, at 1395 *et seq.*; Brkan & Bonnet, *supra* note 32, at 41; Rosemary Jay, *UK Data Protection Act 1998: The Human Rights Context*, 14 INT'L REV. L., COMPUTERS & TECH. 385 (2000).

[107]   *See* United States v Ocasio, *discussed in* Wexler, *supra* note 16, at 1364–5.

[108]   *See* Lee, *supra* note 17, at 294.

[109]   See 21 C.F.R. § 20.61 (c), (d), (f)(4), 202–3 (US); for a critique of such practices see A.S. Kesselheim & M.M. Mello, *Confidentiality Laws and Secrecy in Medical Research: Improving Public Access to Data on Drug Safety*, 26(2) HEALTH AFFAIRS 483–91 (2007).

[110]   Carlson, *supra* note 15, at 318–22; Rossana Ducato, *Ensuring Text and Data Mining: Remaining Issues with the EU Copyright Exceptions and Possible Ways Out*, 43(5) EUROPEAN INTEL. PROP. REV., 336 (2021).

[111]   Carlson, *supra* note 15, at 318–22.

Apparently, the predictive algorithms widely used by courts in some jurisdictions (such as the US) are often neither validated with local populations nor assessed by independent bodies.[112] Persons affected by these algorithms often do not have a possibility to challenge the algorithmic predictions due to their secret nature.[113] Thus commentators have called for such algorithms to be made publicly accessible so they can be scrutinized by independent experts, including NGOs and academics in the field. Some have suggested that *any* algorithms used by public authorities should be made available for public scrutiny.[114] In addition, they should be validated by independent bodies and all information made publicly available.[115]

At the same time, it should be noted that any requirement to disclose trade secrets – either via judges or legislation – will encounter strong pushback from the producers of AI technologies.[116] Some commentators have suggested that 'full public disclosure of the source code of algorithms is both undesirable and likely ineffective'.[117] As discussed above, the source code, or even the algorithm, does not necessarily provide the explanation the public needs.[118] It is thus questionable whether mandatory public disclosure of entire algorithms and/or source code, which would have significant economic consequences for trade secret owners, would be an adequate means of achieving AI explainability.

In order to better balance the private interests behind trade secrets and the public interests behind the explainability principle, alternative and less intrusive measures could be considered.[119] For instance, independent experts could be allowed to research and test AI modules by using explainability techniques that do not interfere with trade secrets (such as the 'surrogate model' technique described above).[120] The public might be provided with user-friendly explanations as to the purpose of AI used, its general characteristics, whether and by whom it was validated – explanations that are comprehensible to a lay person and that do not interfere with trade secrets. Further, so-called big data projects (such as the Human Genome Project, the Cancer Genome Atlas, All of Us) funded by government or conducted by academic institutions could lead to publicly available algorithms and datasets that could be validated by external experts and used in other AI development projects.[121]

On the demand side, organizations purchasing AI systems (such as judicial or healthcare institutions) could decide to purchase only AI systems that have explainability functions, which could be used by decision subjects (such as defendants or patients) or users (such as doctors or judges).[122] Alternatively, when purchasing AI systems, public institutions could contractually require the waiving of any proprietary or trade secret interest in information related to accountability, such as those surrounding testing, validation and/or verification of

---

[112]   Ibid, at 322–3.

[113]   Ibid; for similar arguments *see* Wexler, *supra* note 16, at 1395 *et seq.*

[114]   European Parliament, *supra* note 74, at 55.

[115]   Carlson, *supra* note 15, at 325–9.

[116]   *See* Deeks, *supra* note 81, 1846; Wexler, *supra* note 16, at 1343, 1349–50.

[117]   *See also* Moses & Koker, *supra* note 15, at 548–51.

[118]   *See* discussion above.

[119]   *See also* Price II & Raia, *supra* note 8, at 800.

[120]   *See* discussion above; *see also* Brkan & Bonnet, *supra* note 32, at 41.

[121]   Price II & Raia, *supra* note 8, at 800.

[122]   The AI Now Institute at New York University, in its report entitled *The 10 Top Recommendations for the AI Field in 2017*, recommends that '[c]ore public agencies, such as those responsible for criminal justice, healthcare, welfare, and education (e.g "high stakes" domains) should no longer use "black box" AI and algorithmic systems'; *discussed* in Levine, *supra* note 9, at 40.

system performance and disparate impact,[123] and could refuse to work with vendors who are not willing to make their system sufficiently transparent for appropriate auditing and review.[124]

In addition, some reports suggest that public institutions should be required to provide a comprehensive plan for giving external researchers and auditors meaningful, ongoing access to examine specific AI systems, to gain a fuller account of their workings and to engage the public and affected communities in the process.[125] While this is unlikely to require full disclosure of an AI module, 'the appropriate type and level of access may vary from public authority to public authority, from system to system, and from community to community', as well as from risks involved.[126] Overall, as Goldenstein points out, '[p]ublic sector agencies should recognize their power as market actors in these procurement contexts and use their positions to ensure automated decision-making systems perform adequately and appropriately, and are subject to proper governance and oversight'.[127]

We suggest that the application of these three approaches – alternative explanation, limited mandatory disclosure and an encouragement of voluntary disclosure – would help to ensure that interests of trade secret owners and public are well balanced, and that trade secret protection is limited only when it is necessary and proportionate.

5.   CONCLUSIONS

This chapter suggests that while the conflict between trade secrets and AI explainability is likely to occur in some instances, no conflict will occur in other instances. When conflict does arise, it could be addressed by applying different measures. In some cases, choosing an alternative AI explainability technique that does not interfere with trade secret protection is a possible solution. In other cases, right holders might be required to disclose part or all information about the AI module to certain stakeholders (for example, regulatory, certification and auditing bodies), but measures would apply that would protect the disclosure of information to third parties. The most controversial question is to what extent AI used by public institutions and protected by trade secrets should be disclosed to the public and exposed to evaluation by independent experts. While such additional scrutiny is certainly useful, this chapter suggests that mandatory full public disclosure of trade secrets might not be the most appropriate measure. Instead, we suggest encouraging voluntary disclosure of information, which could lead to more transparency in the area and could reach a more appropriate balance between the private interests underlying trade secrets and the public interests underlying the AI explainability principle.

---

[123]   European Parliament, *supra* note 73, at 58.
[124]   Goldenfein, *supra* note 67, at 46.
[125]   European Parliament, *supra* note 73, at 59.
[126]   Ibid.
[127]   Goldenfein, *supra* note 68, at 47.

23. The inventive step requirement and the rise of the AI machines

Noam Shemtov and Garry A. Gabison

1. AI TECHNOLOGY AND ITS ROLE IN INVENTION-CREATING PROCESSES

As the name suggests, the term 'invention' implies a degree of inventiveness. The 'inventive step' or 'obviousness' criterion filters technological developments so that only sufficiently inventive inventions are awarded a patent under the patent system.[1] This requirement is universal: it is enshrined in Article 27.1 Trade-Related Aspects of Intellectual Property Rights.[2]

The inventive step criterion has been interpreted as the gap or distance between the current state of the art and the claimed invention. For example, in *Windsurfing International Inc. v Tabur Marine (Great Britain) Limited*,[3] the UK Court of Appeal had to investigate whether a windsurfing board was obvious from the combination of traditional surfboards and the knowledge from sail propulsion vehicles. The Court created the following four-step process[4] to identify whether an invention satisfied the inventive step requirement: (1) identify what the patent claims; (2) identify common general knowledge in the art; (3) identify the difference between what is known and what is claimed; and (4) assess whether this difference would be obvious to the skilled man.[5]

This test was later rephrased by LJ Jacob in *Pozzoli* but the essence of the test remains the same.[6] Figure 23.1 below presents a distance jumper metaphor for the four steps that patent examiners (and the courts) must decide:

1. The content of the knowledge base would be akin to selecting a large (1) or small (2) springboard or jumping base (black spotted rectangles) for the jumper to clear the distance.

---

[1]   See Hoffmann LJ's explanation on this point in *Société Technique de Pulverisation Step v. Emson Europe Ltd* [1993] RPC 513, at 519.

[2]   Agreement on Trade-Related Aspects of Intellectual Property Rights, Apr. 15, 1994, Marrakesh Agreement Establishing the World Trade Organization. 'Article 27 Patentable Subject Matter 1. [...] patents shall be available for any inventions, whether products or processes, in all fields of technology, provided that they are new, involve an inventive step and are capable of industrial application.' The footnote specifies: 'For the purposes of this Article, the terms "inventive step" and "capable of industrial application" may be deemed by a Member to be synonymous with the terms "non-obvious" and "useful" respectively.'

[3]   [1985] RPC 59.

[4]   The European Patent Office describes a three-step process where it combines the last two steps of the Windsurfing test. Guidelines for Examination in the European Patent Office, Part G Chapter VII Paragraph 5.

[5]   [1985] RPC 59 at 74.

[6]   *Pozzoli SPA v (1) BDMO SA and (2) Moulage Industriel de Perseigne SA1*, [2007] F.S.R. 37.

2. The gap between the claimed invention and the knowledge base would be akin to the size of the leap (distance or) that a jumper must clear between the jumping base and the landing base.
3. Who the person skilled in the art is would be akin to selecting a strong (A) or weak (B) jumper.
4. Based on those three elements, the patent examiner finding an invention obvious would be akin to finding that the jumper could have breached the gap without help.

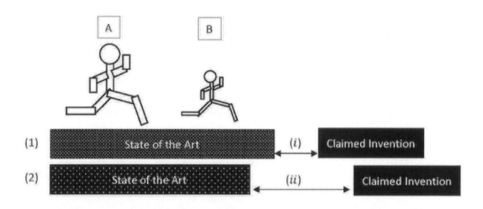

Figure 23.1   Inventive step scope

This inventive step requirement has a lot of moving parts. The simple diagram[7] shows eight possible pairings: some would fulfil the inventive step requirement while others would not.[8]

Each element in the diagram is case-specific. First, parties and their experts debate what should be included in the state of the art. Second, the person skilled in the art is a legal fiction, not unlike the reasonable man in tort law.[9] Third, once an invention is put on paper, the reader may suffer from hindsight bias: once explained, something becomes more obvious.[10] So, to

---

[7]   For simplicity, some issues are ignored. For example, the scope of claimed invention is also a fact-intensive discussion. The inventive step investigation can also look at what is claimed to assess whether it is limited to non-obvious invention. For the purposes of this discussion, this is ignored.

[8]   For example, both individuals would be able to jump from base (1) to position (), making the invention obvious; however, jumper B may struggle to jump from base (2) to position () without help, making that invention non-obvious to B.

[9]   *Windsurfing International Inc. v Tabur Marine (Great Britain) Limited* [1985] RPC 59 at 71.

[10]   Fischhoff, Baruch. 'Hindsight is not equal to foresight: The effect of outcome knowledge on judgment under uncertainty.' *Journal of Experimental Psychology: Human perception and performance* 1, no. 3 (1975): 288 (having knowledge of the outcome influences the perceived probability of the outcome).

temper this issue, patent examiners and courts have put in place tests to gauge the distance from the state of the art.[11]

The use of artificial intelligence (AI) in inventive processes can impact all three elements of the inventive step requirement: (1) the size of the state of art; (2) the identity or making of the person skilled in the art and the means in her disposal; and (3) the distance of the invention from the state of the art.

This chapter seeks to address these impacts. Different scholars have noted[12] that evaluating an invention for inventive step without accounting for advances in AI technology may lead to the inventive step criterion becoming easily satisfied, thereby leading to over-patenting. This chapter discusses how AIs affect each element of the inventive step criterion and whether these elements should adapt to avoid distorting the invention incentives.

Section 2 of the chapter examines the nature of the inventive step criterion and how its assessment may be impacted by the involvement of AI machines in the invention creation process. It discusses the inventive step assessment and how AI will likely impact some key elements and thresholds that underpin this assessment, including the person skilled in the art (PSITA). While this chapter focuses on the UK and the European Patent Office (EPO), the analysis and final conclusions are applicable to most mature intellectual property jurisdictions.[13]

Section 3 of the chapter seeks to establish the extent to which the tests and standards that support the inventive step assessment stand up to economic theory scrutiny when applied to inventions that involve AI activities. We argue that economic theory suggests that the inventive step criterion should adapt to AI uses and discuss how this should be done.

---

[11]   For example, in the US, the US Supreme Court described a flexible battery of tests. The US Patent and Trademark Office compiled these tests and summarized them as follows:
   an invention is considered obvious if one of the following is satisfied
   (A) Combining prior art elements according to known methods to yield predictable results;
   (B) Simple substitution of one known element for another to obtain predictable results;
   (C) Use of known technique to improve similar devices (methods, or products) in the same way;
   (D) Applying a known technique to a known device (method, or product) ready for improvement to yield predictable results;
   (E) 'Obvious to try' – choosing from a finite number of identified, predictable solutions, with a reasonable expectation of success;
   (F) Known work in one field of endeavor may prompt variations of it for use in either the same field or a different one based on design incentives or other market forces if the variations are predictable to one of ordinary skill in the art;
   (G) Some teaching, suggestion, or motivation in the prior art that would have led one of ordinary skill to modify the prior art reference or to combine prior art reference teachings to arrive at the claimed invention.
US Patent and Trademark Office, *Manual of Patent Examining Procedure*, Chapter 2100 Patentability, §2473, p. 273 (Ninth Edition, Revision 10.2019, Last Revised June 2020) available at: https://www.uspto.gov/web/offices/pac/mpep/index.html. All these tests attempt to mimic this distance comparing process with a heavy emphasis on predictability or foreseeability. When discussing the 'Teaching-Suggestion-Motivation' (TSM) test in *KSR Intern. Co. v Teleflex Inc.*, 127 S.Ct. 1727 (2007), the US Supreme Court emphasized the need for a flexible test and a complete case-by-case inquiry. Ibid 1743.
[12]   For example, see Abbott, Ryan. 'Everything is obvious.' *UCLA Law Review* 66, no. 1 (January 2019): 2–53; Bonadio, Enrico, Luke McDonagh, and Plamen Dinev. 'Artificial intelligence as inventor: exploring the consequences for patent law.' *Intellectual Property Quarterly* vol. 2021, no. 1 (2021): 48–66.
[13]   At the end of the day the main rationale that underpins the patent system and the key public policy considerations that buttress the invention step criterion are shared among patent systems worldwide.

2.   THE IMPLICATION OF AI FOR THE OBVIOUSNESS TEST

The European Patent Convention (EPC) states: 'An invention shall be considered as involving an inventive step if, having regard to the state of the art, it is not obvious to a person skilled in the art.'[14] As Pumfrey J pointed out in *Conor Medsystems v Angiotech Pharmaceuticals*: 'The point of the objection of obviousness is to prevent the too-ready grant of patents from hampering [the skilled persons] in the ordinary technical development that must take place in an industry.'[15]

This approach leaves various questions unanswered. AIs have challenged how some of those unanswered questions should be addressed. For example, how to consider AI activity in the invention making process? AI can be viewed in two ways: (1) as the inventor or (2) as the enabler of the inventions or aspects thereof.[16] Those scenarios live along a spectrum depending on the AI's involvement.[17] The authors of the recent European Commission Report on Trends and developments in AI depicted this dichotomy in three scenarios:[18]

1. 'Inventions that are produced by human inventors, the development of which was supported by AI technology.'
2. Inventions where the 'inventive activity' was co-produced by humans and machines.
3. AI-generated 'inventions', that is, 'inventions generated autonomously by an artificial intelligence (AI) under circumstances in which we believe that no natural person, as traditionally defined, qualifies as an inventor.'[19]

As the authors of the EC Report observe, the present technology does not suggest that we have arrived at the third category. Even if we had, most jurisdictions do not recognise machines as

---

[14]   Article 56 of the European Patent Convention.

[15]   *Conor Medsystems Inc. v Angiotech Pharmaceuticals Inc.*, The University of British Columbia, [2006] EWHC 260 (Pat), 2006 WL 503022

[16]   See e.g., Huhn, Michael. 'Can an artificial intelligence model be the inventor of a molecule designed by the model and how can patentability be assessed?' *Journal of Business Chemistry* vol. 2020, no. 1 (2020): 2.

[17]   Gabison, Garry A. 'Who holds the right to exclude for machine work products?' *Intellectual Property Quarterly* vol. 2020, no. 1 (2020): 20–43.

[18]   EC Report: *Trends and developments in artificial intelligence: Challenges to the intellectual property rights framework : final report* p.102, available at: https://op.europa.eu/en/publication-detail/-/publication/394345a1-2ecf-11eb-b27b-01aa75ed71a1/language-en.

[19]   Ibid.

possible inventors.[20] Such an approach[21] would require modifying the law before AI-generated inventions could become patentable.[22]

Instead, this chapter is concerned with the first two categories. This section discusses how to gauge obviousness in an era where AI tools assist technical developments.

2.1   The State of the Art and Common General Knowledge

The state of the art inquiry can be divided into two questions: (1) what is the knowledge available? (2) Within that knowledge, what is considered 'common knowledge'?

The state of the art may comprise everything available to the public before the date of the application.[23] The patent examiner may consider information[24] as long as that information is available to one member of the public who is not prevented by law from using it. However, when a third party makes a discovery but decides to keep it secret, the information embodied in such a discovery may not form part of the state of the art.[25] Thus, in principle, the state of the art may include any publicly available information about the relevant field of technology

---

[20]   See e.g., Shemtov, Noam. (EPO, 2019). *A study on inventorship in inventions involving AI activity*, European Patent Office available at http://documents.epo.org/projects/babylon/eponet.nsf/0/3918F57B010A3540C125841900280653/$File/Concept_of_Inventorship_in_Inventions_involving_AI_Activity_en.pdf, found that most jurisdictions do not recognize machines as inventors; however, a recent Australian decision (*Thaler v Commissioner of Patents* [2021] FCA 879) held that non-humans (including AI) can be designated as inventors: at ¶222. A South African patent (Food Container and Devices and Methods for Attracting Enhanced Attention – application number 2021/03242 and patent number 18275163.6 and 18275174.3) was also granted for an AI machine created by Stephen Thaler and described as a 'device for the autonomous bootstrapping of unified sentience'; however, some observers question whether this grant was an oversight or quirk of the South African patent system (see e.g. Wild, Joff, *South Africa awards world's first AI-invented patent, but it may not be that big a deal*, IAM, 28 July 2021 available at: www.iam-media.com/law-policy/south-africa-ai-patent-award).

[21]   The question of inventorship in relation to AI-assisted invention is discussed elsewhere in this volume. These two approaches need not be dichotomic. Instead, they live on a spectrum: a patent examiner or court will have to investigate the facts to decide where on the spectrum an invention falls in order to decide its patentability.

[22]   Inventors are unlikely to disclose that they used AI tools to assist their invention development; nor are they required to do so under the present rules. The current disclosure requirement demands that the specification be sufficient for the skilled person to perform the invention. For example, a patent applicant claiming the development of a new compound Y for the treatment of medical condition X only needs to disclose the said compound but does not have to disclose how the invention was developed. Thus, means of discovery are not part of patent prosecution inquiry. As patent examiners investigate the obviousness requirement, they must decide, inter alia, on six key issues to assess whether developing compound Y for treating medical condition X would be obvious to the skilled person, irrespective of the way the applicant arrived at the invention. The EPO carries out no due diligence with respect to process. Rule 19(2) EPC states that 'the European Patent Office shall not verify the accuracy of the designation of the inventor'. See T 0223/92 (HIF-Gamma/GENENTECH) of 20.7.1993 (discoveries may involve 'luck, skill and inventive ingenuity to overcome the known and the as yet unknown problems involved').

[23]   Article 54(2) EPC defines the state of the art as 'everything made available to the public by means of a written or oral description, by use, or in any other way, before the date of filing of the European patent application'.

[24]   *Merrell Dow Pharmaceuticals Inc and Another v H N Norton and Co Ltd*, [1996] RPC 76 (see Hoffmann L's explanation that 'matter' under s.2(2) PA 1977, which is the equivalent of Art 54(2)'s 'everything', refers to the information that is made available to the public at the relevant date).

[25]   *Terrell on the Law of Patents* (19th ed, Sweet & Maxwell), at 11–27.

(for example, drug discovery) and information about AI and how it may be deployed in that technological field (for example, drug discovery).

Even if public information on how AI tools may help to include the inventive processes, information on its usefulness amounting to trade secrets may be excluded from the state of the art. Therefore, the state of the art will depend on whether the information on AI tools, techniques and applications is publicly available at the priority date.

The fast pace of AI development may negate the availability of textbooks summarising the latest state of the art in AI technology. Instead, the state of the art may more often need to account for academic and professional articles and other less conventional information such as YouTube tutorials or university courses.

Establishing what is available to the public is only the first part of the inquiry. The patent examiners (and tribunals) must decide what among this knowledge forms part of the common general knowledge: prior art includes *anything* available to the public before the priority date whereas the common general knowledge is *limited* to knowledge *possessed by the skilled person active* in the relevant field of art.[26] At the EPO (and similarly under UK law[27]), the common general knowledge is defined by reference to 'basic handbooks, monographs, encyclopaedias, textbooks and reference books. It is knowledge that an experienced person in the field in question is expected to have, or at least to be aware of, to the extent that he knows he could look it up in a book if he needed it.'[28]

Common general knowledge forms part of the mental equipment with which the skilled person assesses the invention at stake as well as considers the relevant state of the art. So, the patent examiners (and tribunals) may decide that the latest advancements in AI technology are part of the state of the art but not part of the common general knowledge.

Such expertise, techniques and utilisation of AI tools become part of the common general knowledge when they become sufficiently prevalent in a certain field. The AI inclusion within this common general knowledge becomes field-specific – and so would the obviousness thresholds discussed below. As the President of the EPO elaborated:

> the skilled person has at their disposal the means and capacity for routine work and experimentation which are normal for the field of technology in question. Accordingly, if AI is used in the relevant field of technology, it will be used by the skilled person and their skills will raise accordingly.[29]

Once these AI-related skills become part of the common knowledge, patent examiners and courts must select the adequate level of AI-related skills. As Pumfrey J has noted, 'the most difficult part of any obviousness case is the attribution of the relevant skill and knowledge to the notional addressee of the patent. When the common general knowledge is identified, the

---

[26]   Prior art 'only becomes (common) general knowledge when it is generally known and accepted without question by the bulk of those who are engaged in the particular art; in other words, when it becomes part of their common stock of knowledge relating to the art.' *British Acoustic Films Ltd. v Poulsen* (1936) 53 R.P.C. 221.

[27]   E.g. see *Lubrizol Corporation and Another v Esso Petroleum Company Ltd & Others*, [1998] R.P.C. 727.

[28]   Case law of the Boards of Appeal of the EPO, 2.8.1 (2019).

[29]   EPO Comments to WIPO Conversation on IP and AI, Second Session July 7 to 9, 2020, Revised Issues Paper on Intellectual Property Policy and Artificial Intelligence, p.8.

height of the bar is set.'[30] The skill level should be set with care: set it high and most inventions become obvious; set it low and the opposite applies.[31] Hence, the scope and level of common general knowledge is key to assess obviousness.

2.2   Obvious to Whom?

Once the scope of the state of the art is determined, patent examiners and tribunals must establish who the person skilled in the art is: this is the notional person to whom the invention must not be obvious for an inventive step to be established.

At the EPO, the Guidelines for Examination describe the person skilled in the art as 'a skilled practitioner in the relevant field of technology who is possessed of average knowledge and ability and is aware of what was common general knowledge in the art at the relevant date'.[32] That person is able to do routine work and even look at a 'neighbouring technical field' but is not expected to have inventive abilities.[33] Under English law, some or all the following questions may be considered in identifying the skilled person:[34]

1.   What is the relevant art?
2.   Should the skilled person be taken as comprising a 'team', of whom each member brings a specific skill? And if so, what is the composition of the notional team?
3.   What are the attributes, qualifications and level of skill of the skilled person or team?
4.   What is the common general knowledge to be imputed to such a person or a team?

These questions are case-specific. Let us consider each question within the AI context.

Under question (1), the relevant art is usually where the problem which the invention seeks to address lies. In many fields, such as pharmaceutical, aeronautical design or chemical engineering, AI tools and techniques already assist the invention-making processes.[35] Thus, relevant AI expertise may form part of the relevant art, especially when the notional skilled person comprises different experts as per question (2).

The skilled person may possess the skillset of a team of specialists.[36] This team construct usually arises when the relevant art involves developing technologies. For example, in one case, the technical Board of Appeal found that where a new technology was about to spread

---

[30]   *Conor Medsystems Inc. v Angiotech Pharmaceuticals Inc.*, The University of British Columbia, [2006] EWHC 260 (Pat), 2006 WL 503022, at para 35.

[31]   The latter case may avoid the obviousness hurdle but risk insufficiency.

[32]   Guidelines for Examination in the European Patent Office, Part G Chapter VII Paragraph 3 'Person skilled in the art'.

[33]   Ibid.

[34]   *Terrell on the Law of Patents* (19th ed, Sweet & Maxwell), at 8–25.

[35]   For example, see Kathleen Walch, *The increasing use of AI in the pharmaceutical industry*, Forbes 26 December 2020, at: www.forbes.com/sites/cognitiveworld/2020/12/26/the-increasing-use-of-ai-in-the-pharmaceutical-industry/?sh=21e81f474c01; Venkat Venkatasubramanian, *The promise of artificial intelligence in chemical engineering: is it here, finally?* Published online December 19, 2018 in Wiley Online Library, at https://aiche.onlinelibrary.wiley.com/doi/epdf/10.1002/aic.16489; Adam Gavine, *AI tool set underway for aircraft design and certification*, Aircraft Interiors International 21 May 2020, at www.aircraftinteriorsinternational.com/news/mro/ai-tool-set-underway-for-aircraft-design-and-certification.html.

[36]   See for example EPO case law in T 60/89 (OJ 1992, 268), T 500/91 – 'BIOGEN II' and under English law in *Halliburton Energy Services, Inc. v Smith International* [2005] EWHC 1623 (Pat).

into a traditional field, it was customary to construct the skilled person by reference to specialists from the relevant technological fields.[37] Hence, in this case, the Board held that the skilled person comprised a team of orthodontists and an expert in computer-aided design and computer-aided manufacturing technology. This holding was based on the state of affairs at the prior date; it ignored how the invention at stake was actually developed; and hence, this holding was not tainted by hindsight.[38]

In the AI-context, a patent office may have to determine whether the skillset of the skilled person includes AI expertise. This determination depends on the scope of skills that may be deployed when considering the problem that the invention seeks to address. For example, IBM's Watson Health may 'assist in the analysis of a patient's medical information and its correlation with a vast database, resulting in suggesting treatment strategies for cancer'; it may further assist in drug design.[39] Thus, if using Watson's Health or similar AI capabilities in the relevant field has become a matter of routine in this field, the relevant research team should include AI tools and its associated expertise.

For question (3), the skilled person has no inventive capacity, but she may still be able to make a mosaic of relevant prior art documents. If such mosaic may be put together by the unimaginative man with no inventive capacity, then an invention may be considered obvious should the said mosaic lead to it.[40] This ability to mosaic is significant in the AI context. First, the skilled person may mosaic AI-related prior art and field-specific prior art (for example, chemical engineering). AI may access vast amounts of data points in its underlying database, from both related and distant fields of art, if it is configured to do so. Mosaicking may expand because the traditional limitations of PSITA's ability to mosaic prior art from different fields becomes less relevant. The relevant questions become whether AI prior art enables PSITA to deploy AI, whether such deployment is routine and unimaginative and whether AI mosaicking of prior arts to arrive at the invention was done in an unimaginative manner. This use of AIs to mosaic would lead to obvious inventions when such AI-enhanced mosaicking is considered customary rather than imaginative in that field.

If AI-related prior art is combined with prior art in another field, patent examiners must consider the mosaicking capability of AI tools. AIs are already affecting the speed and ability to research and identify patterns.[41] They also affect the ability to combine multiple fields and solve technical problems. Hence, what may have been considered 'imaginative and inventive' mosaicking of teachings from unrelated fields and disciplines may now be considered 'obvious' mosaicking.

---

[37] T 0015/15.

[38] In this case, the Board explained: 'In the early nineties, use of computers in planning and manufacturing was spreading into basically every industry and field of technology. As evidenced by […], the field of dentistry and orthodontics was no exception. Thus, also the specialist in the field of dentistry and orthodontics was aware of the new technology and its potential for improved quality and cost efficiency. In such a situation, where a new technology is about to spread into a traditional field, it is common practice to group people from both technical fields into a development team' (see 4.4 of the Reasoning).

[39] Paul, D., G. Sanap, S. Shenoy, D. Kalyane, K. Kalia, and R.K. Tekade. 'Artificial intelligence in drug discovery and development.' *Drug Discov Today* 26, no. 1 (2021): 80–93.

[40] Technip France SA's Patent [2004] R.P.C. 46.

[41] See e.g., Gurgula, Olga. 'AI-assisted inventions in the field of drug discovery: Readjusting the inventive step analysis.' *International Journal of Social Science and Public Policy* 2 (2020).

Inventive and non-obvious invention of the past may become unimaginative and customary with time due to technological advancements. While the evolution from 'used to be inventive' into 'customary and routine' is nothing new, the involvement of AI in invention–creation could accelerate this process.

2.3   Obvious to the Skilled Person Having Regard to the State of the Art

The essence of this enquiry is whether the 'distance' between the prior art and the invention is obvious to the skilled person in light of her common general knowledge. The tribunal must assess whether the skilled person possesses AI-related expertise, the level and scope of such expertise and how they may use such expertise to address the problem that the invention seeks to tackle.

Even if the state of the art includes the AI-related information and the skilled person possess AI-expertise, an uninventive and unimaginative skilled person may not utilise such information and knowledge in an obvious manner and arrive at the invention. For example, the court in Dyson was not prepared to accept that the common general knowledge of cyclones would be applied by the person skilled in the art of vacuum cleaners.[42] The High Court found that the relevant skilled person would not contemplate cyclone technology.

The European Patent Office considers that the person skilled in the art 'should also be presumed to have had access to *everything in the state of the art* [...] and to have had at his disposal *the normal means and capacity for routine work and experimentation.*'[43] Computer programs are 'means' and 'capacity' that facilitate the work of any researcher.[44] AI could be the next logical step of means to do research. A tribunal or patent examiner will have to decide when AI expertise and tools become a routine mechanism for addressing technical problems in a given field. Next, they will have to determine the scope of AI skills and whether their routine deployment in an unimaginative manner by the skilled person renders an invention obvious. The same invention may be inventive should obviousness be assessed without reference to AI capabilities. Thus, patent offices and tribunals should start to factor AI capabilities into their obviousness assessment. This chapter ventures to highlight such cases and how such 'factoring' may be conducted.

AIs may not be currently a commonly used tool in most fields, but its growing use suggests that 'normal means and capacity' should change in the near future. If so, should patent regimes require the patent applicant to reference the use of an AI or should we stick with the present arrangement and merely take into account the availability of AI tools and expertise when applying the obviousness test across the board?

Declaring the assistance of an AI in the inventive process would require changing the filing obligations and may be difficult to enforce. The public policy justification is more ambiguous. If we assume that our patent system aims at incentivising innovation, then declaring the AI-assistance does not advance this purpose. Whether or not the inventor used a certain

---

[42]   *Dyson Appliances Limited v Hoover Limited* [2001] EWCA Civ 1440, at 88.

[43]   European Patent Office, *Case Law of the Boards of Appeal of the European Patent Office*, Ninth Edition July 2019, p. 203, ¶ 8.1.1 (emphasis added).

[44]   See e.g. Simon, Brenda M. 'The implications of technological advancement for obviousness.' *Mich. Telecomm. & Tech. L. Rev.* 19 (2013): 331; Eisenberg, Rebecca S. 'Obvious to whom? Evaluating inventions from the perspective of PHOSITA.' *Berkeley Tech. L.J.* 19 (2004): 885.

tool should not affect patent office determination. Adjusting the obviousness test to account for AI uses in some sectors would address over- and under-incentivising in that sector. If the skilled person is likely to use an AI tool in a given research field, then the PSITA in that field should adapt to this likelihood. This change should be irrespective of whether or not the actual inventor used an AI during the inventive process. This approach would improve administrative efficiency as the expense of fairness (because it would increase the obviousness threshold and penalise inventors who do not have access to AIs – including small-entity and sole inventors).[45]

In the past, patent offices opted for the second approach: they adapted PSITA to the common knowledge. If most scientists in a field adopt AIs to carry out their research, AI skills would become part of the PSITA knowledge and skill base. Once this occurs, patent examiners still need to determine whether such knowledge, in relation to the state of the art, may render the invention obvious. Such an enquiry is fact-specific. It may depend on: (1) the motives to find a solution to the problem the patent addresses; (2) the number and extent of the possible avenues of research; (3) the effort involved in pursuing them and the expectation of success, and so on.[46]

In addition, patent examiners should consider factors such as: (1) the routineness of the research carried out in light of the prior art; (2) the necessity and nature of the value judgement of the skilled person implementing the prior art; and (3) the foreseeability of the research success.[47] These three factors are significant to assess obviousness in an AI-assisted invention context. Patent examiners still need to establish whether the unimaginative and uninventive skilled person's value judgement may suffice to implement the AI prior art in relation to the relevant field in a manner that renders the invention obvious. Having AI expertise and access to AI tools does not mean that using such skills and tools in an unimaginative manner may necessarily lead to the invention.

Viewed in this way, only inventive exercise of such expertise may be rewarded with a patent (for example, developing non-obvious bespoke AI tools designed to address the problem that the invention seeks to tackle, or deploying routine AI tools in a non-obvious manner, or a combination of both). This aligns with current patent law rationale. Further, whether certain AI-related avenues of research are likely to be pursued by the skilled person will be affected by the foreseeability of the research outcome.

---

[45]   Using the disclosure in the PSITA standard could serve the incentive purpose of the IP system. It would ensure that small inventors are encouraged to innovate if the PSITA is adapted to their AI-use disclosure. Some patent offices already worry about the impact of other patent formalities on smaller inventor. For example, the US Patent and Trademark Office adapts the patent to the size of the entity filing and holding the patent: the basic filing fee as of July 2021 was $300, but it was $150 for a small entity and $75 for a micro entity (www.uspto.gov/sites/default/files/documents/USPTO%20fee%20schedule _current.pdf). Otherwise, small inventors face an uphill battle to obtain a patent in fields dominated by larger research entities with AI capabilities. But the enforceability problem of such disclosure may favour using an industry PSITA standard to improve administrative efficiency.

[46]   For example, see *Generics (UK) Ltd & Ors v H Lundbeck A/S* [2007] EWHC 1040 (Pat).

[47]   Terrell at 12-37, referring to Lord Hodge's judgment in *Actavis v ICOS Corp* [2019] UKSC 15.

2.4   A Structured Approach to Determining Obviousness

Patent systems have developed structured approaches for assessing inventive steps. UK courts state the obviousness test by reference to the *Windsurfing*[48] test. LJ Jacob restated this in *Pozzoli*.[49] This restatement included the four elements discussed above.[50]

The latter two elements concern the 'distance' or 'difference' between the invention (or the inventive concept therein) and the prior art. The objective of the EPO approach[51] is similar to the UK approach. It aims to bring about the same outcome: evaluating whether the invention is substantially distinct from what existed before the priority date to warrant a reward; neither approach is obligatory. Courts and tribunals in both jurisdictions are free to decline their use where they deem it appropriate. The analysis below refers to the UK courts' jurisprudence but is adaptable to the EPO jurisprudence.

When assessing obviousness, UK courts have used 'obvious to try' to assess the existence of an inventive step. Obvious-to-try should not be confused with the actual obviousness test: the test is part of the inquiry but not the inquiry itself.[52] For AI-assisted inventions, the obvious-to-try formula may become key for evaluating obviousness; once AI tools and techniques are considered, an invention may become obvious. Thus, a key question may be whether and to what extent it was obvious to follow a particular avenue of research which involves such AI tools, techniques, and expertise.

A significant consideration is the required expectation of success in following a particular route. A research route may be obvious-to-try based on the expectation of success; but, other

---

[48]   *Windsurfing International Inc v Tabur Marine (Great Britain) Limited*, [1985] RPC 59.
[49]   *Pozzoli SPA v BDMO SA, Moulage Industriel de Perseigne SA*, [2007] EWCA Civ 588.
[50]   In the result I would restate the Windsurfing questions thus:
   (1)   (a) Identify the notional 'person skilled in the art'
         (b) Identify the relevant common general knowledge of that person;
   (2)   Identify the inventive concept of the claim in question or if that cannot readily be done, construe it;
   (3)   Identify what, if any, differences exist between the matter cited as forming part of the 'state of the art' and the inventive concept of the claim or the claim as construed;
   (4)   Viewed without any knowledge of the alleged invention as claimed, do those differences constitute steps which would have been obvious to the person skilled in the art or do they require any degree of invention?' Ibid ¶ 23.
[51]   The EPO applies a similar overall test as UK courts under Article 56 of the European Patent Convention: 'An invention shall be considered as involving an inventive step if, having regard to the state of the art, it is not obvious to a person skilled in the art.' But its structured approach differs and uses the problem-and-solution approach. This approach involves four steps:
   (a)   identifying the 'closest prior art',
   (b)   determining the claimed technical results,
   (c)   determining the technical problem to be solved, and
   (d)   analysing whether a person skilled in the art *would* have suggested the claimed technical features to resolve that technical problem using the closest prior art as starting point.
European Patent Office, Case Law of the Boards of Appeal of the European Patent Office, Ninth Edition July 2019, p.176. Like the UK test, step (a) requires deciding the state of the art. Step (b) requires evaluating the distance between the state of the art and what is claimed. Step (d) requires deciding whether the PSITA would have reached that distance in that fashion given the starting point. As compared to the UK test, step (c) adds a dimension. This step requires the EPO to decide the direction of travel. Based on the starting point, this requirement focuses on whether the PSITA would think of that specific solution.
[52]   *Lilly Icos Llc v Pfizer Ltd* (1) [2002] EWCA Civ 1.

drivers may justify a research route even if the expectation of success is not promising. The question becomes whether the obvious-to-try test should adapt to these other factors.

Kitchin LJ (as he then was)[53] acknowledged that certain routes may likely be pursued in sectors that are heavily dependent on research, despite little evidence of reasonable success expectation. But he cautioned against denying patent protection in all such cases as a matter of public policy because it might deter research. In other words, the court acknowledged that while in some instances it may be obvious or reasonable to try, patent protection may not be denied without showing that there was reasonable expectation of success in pursuing such route. Thus, in such cases, the court must still assess whether applicants had reasonable expectation of success as opposed to mere hope to succeed.

In the AI-related context, a real-world research team may pursue various research routes (including an AI route) with nothing but hope for success. If such route leads to the invention, the invention may not be considered obvious. However, the skilled person would pursue such route if it is judged to have a reasonable or fair expectation of success. This expectation of success would render the invention obvious.

Tribunals are cautious of this inherent contradiction in industries with potential high reward.[54] In such cases, something may be worth trying if the relative failure risk to the potential reward ratio is attractive. Thus, where the potential reward may be high, a particular research route may be worth trying or be 'obvious to try' even if the chances of success are low. Denying patent protection in such cases would contradict the objective of our patent regime. As mentioned, this point was convincingly made by Kitchin LJ and is aligned with the underlying rationale of the patent system.

However, applying the above rationale to scenarios involving AI may defeat some of the core public policy considerations underpinning our patent law. A research route that involves AI may become economically rational – hence obvious-to-try – because both time and costs are reduced due to AI activity. The magnitude of potential reward should not alter the nature of the obviousness assessment. It follows that unless there is a reasonable expectation of success, such invention may be considered as non-obvious.[55]

---

[53] '[T]here are areas of technology such as pharmaceuticals and biotechnology which are heavily dependent on research, and where workers are faced with many possible avenues to explore but have little idea if any one of them will prove fruitful. Nevertheless they do pursue them in the hope that they will find new and useful products. They plainly would not carry out this work if the prospects of success were so low as not to make them worthwhile. But denial of patent protection in all such cases would act as a significant deterrent to research. […] *For these reasons, the judgments of the courts in England and Wales and of the Boards of Appeal of the EPO often reveal an enquiry by the tribunal into whether it was obvious to pursue a particular approach with a reasonable or fair expectation of success as opposed to a hope to succeed.* Whether a route has a reasonable or fair prospect of success will depend upon all the circumstances including an ability rationally to predict a successful outcome, how long the project may take, the extent to which the field is unexplored, the complexity or otherwise of any necessary experiments, whether such experiments can be performed by routine means and whether the skilled person will have to make a series of correct decisions along the way.' *Medimmune Ltd v Novartis Pharmaceuticals UK Ltd* [2012] EWCA Civ 1234, at 90–1. Emphasis added.

[54] See for example the House of Lords in *Conor Medsystems Inc v Angiotech Pharmaceuticals Inc and others* 2008] RPC 28, at 47, citing with approval an article by Sir Hugh Laddies and the US Court of Appeals for the Federal Circuit in *Tomlinson*, 363 F.2d 928, 931 (CCPA 1966).

[55] This conclusion is also aligned with what was referred to as the inducement standard that underpins the non-obviousness requirement by the Supreme Court in *Graham v John Deere Co.*, 383 U.S. 1, 11 (1966). There, the Supreme Court explained that patent law's non-obviousness threshold is meant to

However, to create checks and balances when AIs are involved, patent examiners may need to consider an additional factor to evaluate whether it is obvious-to-try. Such factors may centre on the extent to which such avenue of research is routine in the relevant art, based on the advantages in deploying AI tools other than an increase in the likelihood of success. Where following research routes involving AI tools is considered customary due to the inherent advantages of AIs (including cost-related considerations), inventions may be found obvious even where the expectations of success were relatively low.

Due to the game-changing capabilities of AI tools and techniques, they may become a first port of call for researchers in some fields even where expectation of success may be less than 'fair' or 'reasonable'. In such cases, the invention at stake may be considered obvious. Other outcomes may result in rewarding worthy yet obvious technological developments and run contrary to patent law rationale.

2.5   Obviousness and Access to Data

The obviousness tests will need to mirror the use of AI-tools in research; but the tests face many challenges. Once the patent examiner considers that AIs are *'the normal means and capacity for routine work and experimentation'*, the patent examiners must decide with which AI version PSITA should be equipped.[56] The development of an AI is only the start of the journey. Most of the current AIs follow a machine learning process: the researcher feeds information into a computer system; the system learns through probabilistic approach; and then the system identifies new patterns based on the learned patterns.[57] The learning that the machine went through makes the machine.

AIs may be kept as trade secrets but so are the dataset that led to their creation. Without the 'right' type of data, AI expertise and techniques are of little use to the AI-skilled person. In fact, an AI tool may be inadequate without the suitable data for training this AI system and its optimisation for addressing the problem that the invention seeks to tackle.

But how should this data (and its availability) be treated in the context of inventive step assessment? Assume that the skilled person (or team) possesses relevant AI expertise, the prior art includes relevant AI material, and the common general knowledge covers AI-related information and equips the skilled person with the relevant mental acumen. However, to arrive at the invention, the skilled person may require access to certain datasets that have been used to train the relevant AI system that assisted the inventive process that led to the invention.[58]

In this example, data and its exclusive possession become the key for evaluating obviousness. Certain research output may be obvious only once the requisite data for training and opti-

---

restrict the grant of patents to only 'those inventions which would not be disclosed or devised but for the inducement of a patent'. Hence, a research route that becomes economically rational since it is relatively cost effective and speedy may not warrant patent protection where the inducement of a patent is not necessarily required in order for the invention to be devised. Whether or not disclosure on its own merits the award of a patent under such circumstances may depend on the invention at hand.

56   European Patent Office, *Case Law of the Boards of Appeal of the European Patent Office*, Ninth Edition July 2019, p.203, ¶ 8.1.1 (emphasis added).

57   Ghahramani, Zoubin. 'Probabilistic machine learning and artificial intelligence.' *Nature* 521, no. 7553 (2015): 452–9.

58   As mentioned earlier, means of discovery of the invention at stake should play no role in this assessment.

mising an AI becomes part of the state of the art. For example, in the pharmaceutical industry relevant data may be sourced from physician and clinics, patients, carogivers and more. Such datasets are often not publicly available (for example, they may be generated in-house and kept as trade secrets).[59]

Since data can play a crucial role in the inventive process, companies may be incentivised to maintain that data secret to guard against an obviousness challenge. However, such incentives run contrary to data sharing objectives in various jurisdictions and overall societal benefits arising from advancements in AI science. For example, Thierry Breton, Commissioner for the Internal Market, stated:

> Our society is generating a huge wave of industrial and public data, which will transform the way we produce, consume and live. I want European businesses and our many SMEs to access this data and create value for Europeans – *including by developing Artificial Intelligence applications*. Europe has everything it takes to lead the 'big data' race, and preserve its technological sovereignty, industrial leadership and economic competitiveness to the benefit of European consumers.[60]

This raises the question of whether such public policy objectives that are aimed at social welfare may be reconciled with the present scaffolding of patent law's obviousness assessment – at present the two appear to be at odds.

3.   INVENTIVE STEP AND ECONOMIC THEORY

Patent systems across the globe have used different tests to assess whether an invention is and should be patentable. This section discusses the economic reasoning behind the inventive step criterion and the manner in which it may support the adjustment of the present obviousness assessment to the growing use of AI tools and expertise in inventive processes.

3.1   The Public Cost–Benefit of Patents and the Obviousness Criterion

The obviousness criterion should be viewed through the lens of the patent system purpose(s). To advance the arts and sciences, the patent system incentivises inventors through the lure of a right to exclude.[61] Under this aim, the patent system should only reward inventions that advance the arts and sciences.

Patents could be granted when the claimed knowledge expands public knowledge beyond the prior art. However, granting a patent imposes two main costs on society. First, it excludes

---

[59]   For example, see *Roche to acquire Flatiron Health to accelerate industry-wide development and delivery of breakthrough medicines for patients with cancer*, at www.roche.com/media/releases/med-cor -2018-02-15.htm; *23andMe turns spit into dollars in deal with Pfizer*, at www.bloomberg.com/news/ articles/2015-01-12/23andme-gives-pfizer-dna-data-as-startup-seeks-growth; *Amgen signs real world study and mobile data partnership*, at www.pmlive.com/pharma_news/amgen_real_world_study_and _mobile_data_partnership_1203895

[60]   *Shaping Europe's digital future: Commission presents strategies for data and artificial intelligence*, at https://ec.europa.eu/commission/presscorner/detail/en/ip_20_273 (emphasis added).

[61]   For example, Article I, Section 8, Clause 8, of the United States Constitution grants Congress the power '[t]o promote the progress of science and useful arts, by securing for limited times to authors and inventors the exclusive right to their respective writings and discoveries'.

current competition from the market for the prescribed period (static competition). Second, it affects the technological path and what competitors must work around (dynamic competition).

Patent examiners should therefore grant patents for inventions that advance knowledge more than the right to exclude harms society.[62] The knowledge advancements are the benefits to society whereas the harm or costs are the expected cost of a patent.[63] This approach describes a cost–benefit analysis: grant a patent when the benefits to society outweigh the costs; reject an invention when it only trivially extends the knowledge base.

Patent examiners cannot carry out a cost–benefit analysis when both the societal costs and benefits are in the future. Instead, patent offices and courts have implemented tests that attempt to proxy for this analysis. The obviousness criterion can help patent examiners (and courts) to proxy for such a utilitarian-style cost–benefit analysis.

For example, the *Windsurfing* obviousness criterion mimics some cost–benefit analysis mechanisms. The patent examiner must first establish where society would be without the invention (step 2: identifying the state of the art and common knowledge). Second, the examiner must establish where society is with the invention (step 1: identifying what is claimed). Third, the examiner must estimate the distance between the two (step 3: identifying the difference). This distance is the benefit to society. If this distance outweighs a 'threshold' (step 4: assess whether the distance would be obvious to PSITA), then the patent is granted.

Patent applicants want to make the knowledge gained through the patent teaching look as big as possible to ensure passing obviousness tests. To inflate these gains, applicants can either try to make the knowledge base smaller[64] or try to make the patent teaching appear further from the known world.

An obviousness threshold can be viewed in two ways. First, it can be viewed as a *benchmark minimum benefit to society* that an invention must provide to warrant a protection. This approach offers some administrative efficiencies because it avoids having to investigate the costs a patent would impose on society for each case.

---

[62]   Barton, John H. 'Non-obviousness.' *IDEA: The Journal of Law and Technology* 43, no. 3 (2003): 475 (discussing that patents should be granted based on the cost and benefit they provide to society); ibid. p.491.

[63]   Merges, Robert P., and Richard R. Nelson. 'On the complex economics of patent scope.' *Columbia Law Review* 90, no. 4 (1990): 839–916 (discussing the costs and benefits of patents and arguing that the patent scope of initial inventors has affected the technological path, the future competition and innovation in the field).

[64]   In rare cases, the inventors may try to make the knowledge base look bigger to satisfy the disclosure requirement. For example, in *Idenix Pharmaceuticals Inc v Gilead Sciences Inc*, [2016] EWCA Civ 1089, the patent holder claimed that the defendant infringed its patent. The defendant counterclaimed that the patent was invalid for 'lack of novelty […], lack of inventive step, insufficiency and added matter': Ibid at ¶ 2. The parties agreed that 'the skilled person […] is a team comprising a medicinal chemist and a virologist, each with a PhD or equivalent research experience': Ibid at ¶ 64. But they disagreed on the common general knowledge. The patentee 'was asserting that more information formed part of the common general knowledge than' the defendant. Ibid at ¶ 66. The Court of Appeals sided with the defendant and stated that 'the common general knowledge is all that knowledge which is generally regarded as a good basis for further action by the bulk of those who are engaged in a particular field'. Ibid at ¶ 72. The Court held that the articles the plaintiff wanted included were in the public domain, but they did not have clear lessons, nor were they widely accepted. Thus, the patent description was insufficient for the skilled person to synthesize the compounds claimed without undue burden.

For example, Chiang models patents as incentivising bringing forward in time inventions that would be independently created regardless.[65] This approach is a common pool model: all inventions are in a pool and inventors draw from the pool. This model does not view inventions as incremental (that is, path dependent) but rather as means of solving problems.

Chiang describes the benefit to society as the consumer surplus gained between the patent disclosure and the independent invention. He describes the cost as the consumer surplus lost due to higher-than-competitive prices between the independent invention and the patent expiration. Chiang argues that an invention should be considered obvious if the time between patent grant and independent invention is short (for example, one or two years) and non-obvious if it is long (for example, more than 19 years). However, even in this framework, Chiang does not specify a specific threshold that an invention needs to clear to be patentable.

Based on this approach, the common use of AI tools should decrease the number of non-obvious patents. AI tools may enable faster discovery or mosaicking. Granting a patent for the first discovery would impose large costs on society with small benefits because AI tools would enable independent discovery soon thereafter. Patent granting should decrease as AIs become more prevalent and accelerate the rate of innovation. Inventors could wait, delay and accumulate innovations to ensure non-obviousness; but first-to-file competition incentivises early filing and lead to more applications for obvious inventions.

Second, the threshold can be viewed as a *comparison exercise* between the expected costs to society of granting a patent to its expected benefits. This approach ensures that patents are only granted for socially beneficial inventions; however, they involve a higher prosecutorial cost. Whether this social optimal protection outweighs the administrative efficiency from the first approach is unclear.

In this second approach, a patent examiner compares the distance between the state of the art and the patent teaching (that is, proxy for the benefit of invention) to expected cost of patenting. Instead of having a fixed threshold, this approach creates a case-by-case adaptable threshold analysis.

For incremental innovations, the adaptable threshold should change over time because society experiences marginal diminishing returns to additional innovations. As more is known, the additional expected benefit from each invention decreases; therefore, more must be discovered with each invention to warrant a similar protection and associated expected costs. O'Donoghue models cumulative patenting.[66] He found that requiring greater innovation in each generation (that is, higher obviousness threshold) can lead to more R&D spending. A higher obviousness requirement leads to fewer patents, longer incumbency and higher reward. These higher rewards incentivise companies to spend more on R&D.

Barton uses various case studies to argue that the non-obviousness requirement has become too weak.[67] He argues that this standard distance between state of the art and the patent teaching should vary based on industry. The patent system should encourage industries where little is created. The patent system does not need to incentivise already overly patented areas. In other words, the distance (and in Figure 23.1) required to be cleared to have a patentable

[65]   Chiang, T.J. 'A cost–benefit approach to patent obviousness.' *John's L. Rev* 82 (2008): 39.

[66]   O'Donoghue, Ted. 'A patentability requirement for sequential innovation.' *The RAND Journal of Economics* 29, no. 4 (1998): 654–79.

[67]   Barton, John H. 'Non-obviousness.' *IDEA: The Journal of Law and Technology* 43, no. 3 (2003): 475–508.

invention should depend on the state of the art (the size of 1 and 2 in Figure 23.1). In Barton's view, inventions are incremental and the distance for patentability needs to increase with each new increment (that is, more run-up makes smaller distance too easy to be cleared so the standard should be increased). This approach to the obviousness requirement would also decrease the chances of creating patent thickets.[68]

Under this incremental theory, AI tools will also decrease the number of non-obvious patents. AI tools may lead to small or big jumps in technology. On the one hand, if each AI-assisted jump was small, the expected benefits from incentivising marginal innovators may not outweigh the expected costs of granting a patent. The applicant could accumulate small jumps into a larger one to apply for a patent. But, because competing inventors face the same dilemma, each inventor would apply for each jump to avoid losing out in a first to file system. These 'small jump' applications would not pass the non-obviousness tests.

On the other hand, if each AI-assisted jump was big (or at least bigger than without AI assistance), then more inventions could pass the non-obviousness tests. However, because AI assistance makes each jump big, each jump is more likely to become obvious because each provides a decreasing benefit to society. Therefore, fewer jumps would warrant a patent for non-obviousness.

Regardless of whether the benefits are compared to a benchmark minimum or to the costs they impose on society, AI tools would render more inventions obvious. Increasing the obviousness threshold could benefit society over the long run.[69] Hunt models the non-obvious requirement in a world with multiple competitors and cumulative innovation.[70] He focuses on the dynamic and static effects of changing the non-obviousness requirement. He finds that where the obviousness requirement has a high threshold, patents will be more valuable (static) but fewer researchers may enter the patent race because of the lower probability of obtaining a patent (dynamic). These countervailing effects lead to a U-shape relationship between the rate of innovation and the threshold. He finds that in industries with rapid innovation, the static effect is smaller so the non-obviousness standard should be higher.

Applying these models to the AI context, because AI tools could increase the rate of innovation, increasing the threshold could lead to more innovations through trading some static against some dynamic incentives. The next section discusses the impact on the cost–benefit analysis of inventors.

3.2 The Private Cost–Benefit of Patents and Foreseeability

The patent system provides inventors with an incentive to innovate. So, to create the optimal incentive, the patent system could consider the cost and benefit to the inventors. However, courts have not accepted this test: the EPO has rejected commercial success as evidence of

---

[68] Shapiro, Carl. 'Navigating the patent thicket: Cross licenses, patent pools, and standard setting.' *Innovation Policy and the Economy* 1 (2000): 119–50.

[69] Encaoua, D., D. Guellec and C. Martínez. 'Patent systems for encouraging innovation: Lessons from economic analysis.' *Research Policy* 35, no. 9 (2006): 1423–40.

[70] Hunt, R.M. (1999). 'Nonobviousness and the incentive to innovate: An economic analysis of intellectual property reform.' *Federal Reserve Bank of Philadelphia Working Paper*, 99-3; Hunt, R.M. 'Patentability, industry structure, and innovation.' *The Journal of Industrial Economics* 52, no. 3 (2004): 401–25.

non-obviousness.[71] Instead, they consider other evidence and use other tests such as 'obvious to try'.

The UK House of Lords embraced the 'obvious to try' test in *Conor Medsystems Incorporated v Angiotech Pharmaceuticals Incorporated and others.*[72] In this case, Angiotech's patent for a medication-coated artery stent was challenged. Lord Hoffman stated that the obvious-to-try test is satisfied 'in a case in which there was a fair expectation of success. How much of an expectation would be needed depended upon the particular facts of the case.'[73] Lord Walker restated the obvious-to-try test as 'a development should be treated as obvious if "the person versed in the art would assess the likelihood of success as sufficient to warrant actual trial"'.[74]

Merges argues that the patent obviousness requirement encourages uncertain research.[75] He argues that research whose outcomes are certain (that is, high likelihood of success) are likely to be carried out regardless because the researchers do not need the added incentive of a patent.[76] He concludes that the uncertainty-based model supports reducing the obviousness standard in high-cost research areas.

This approach, however, focuses on the individual incentive of inventors, instead of the cost-benefit to society. The probability of success focuses on the *ex ante* decision of inventors:[77] if the probability of success times the benefit from success (that is, expected payoff) outweighs the cost of the research, then a rational inventor should carry out the investigation. The benefit to inventors often correlates with – but also under-estimates – the benefit to society. The benefit to investors does not account for consumer surplus and positive externalities from disclosure. However, the costs to society include more than the private cost of doing research. The costs to society also include the deadweight loss of static competition and the dynamic effects of patenting.

Granstrand models the relationship between inventive step gap (distance and in Figure 23.1) and research and development (R&D) expenditure.[78] His model assumes that the inventive step patentability criterion lives along a spectrum. The patentability standard refers to the minimum distance between the state of the art and the claimed invention that must be met to have a non-obvious invention. When this standard is low, increasing the required distance has no effect on the R&D expenditure because most inventions must have a *de minimis* level of inventiveness to justify the research cost. Past this *de minimis* threshold, increasing this

---

[71]   'Commercial success alone is not to be regarded as indicative of inventive step, but evidence of immediate commercial success when coupled with evidence of a long-felt want is of relevance provided the examiner is satisfied that the success derives from the technical features of the invention and not from other influences (e.g. selling techniques or advertising).' Guidelines for Examination in the EPO, Part G – Chapter VII-20, ¶ 10.3 p.882. (March 2021).

[72]   [2008] UKHL 49.

[73]   Ibid at ¶ 42.

[74]   Ibid at ¶ 47.

[75]   Merges, Robert P. 'Uncertainty and the standard of patentability.' *High Technology Law Journal* 7 (1992): 1–70.

[76]   Ibid at 30–2.

[77]   This discussion ignores the risk aversion discussed by Merges, *supra* note 75, or the bounded rationality of the researcher. See e.g., Crouch, Dennis D. 'The patent lottery: Exploiting behavioral economics for the common good.' *George Mason Law Review* 16 (2008): 141. These issues complicate the model without adding insight to the AI context.

[78]   Granstrand, Ove. 'Are we on our way in the new economy with optimal inventive steps?' *Economics, Law and Intellectual Property* [2003]: 223–58.

standard threshold leads to decreasing R&D expenditure because researchers do not want to invest with little likelihood of reward. Granstrand focuses on the cost–benefit analysis that inventors undertake: he concludes that the inventive-step standard can be used to optimise R&D expenditure.

This probabilistic threshold approach may be suboptimal for society because it incentivises research that can breach that threshold instead of research that can benefit society. Like most software, AI tools have large fixed costs and low marginal cost. So, once developed, an economically rational researcher would carry out a research project as long as their expected benefits outweigh their actual costs. If the cost is close to zero because applying an existing AI tool to new research has low marginal cost (for example, the low cost of training and optimising existing tools for new objectives), then researchers could use AI tools for research with a low probability of success. Based on the approach above, AI tools should lead to more non-obvious inventions and more patents granted. However, we should resist the temptation to use this approach.

Based on Granstrand's view, because AIs may decrease the cost of R&D, inventors will not need as much benefit from their inventions to be incentivised. So, the inventive-step threshold could be increased without affecting the overall R&D expenditure.

Low probability of success invention may not correlate with high benefits for society or even the researcher. In fact, because of the low cost, rational researchers could use AI tools for research with low expected benefits as well. If patents were to be awarded in low-benefit situations it would harm society, because patents have many externalities (for example, blocking cumulative innovation). Increasing the probability threshold would not weed out patents that harm society more than they benefit it.

4.   CONCLUSIONS

AI tools can help researchers advance our knowledge base; however, not every advancement warrants a patent. The obviousness requirement acts as a gatekeeper against patent applications that do not offer sufficient progress.

Patent offices and courts around the world have implemented the obviousness requirement through various obviousness tests. We argue that all aspects of most obviousness tests should adapt to the inclusion of AI tools: from the knowledge base to the person skilled in the art, and from sufficient progress to the problem researchers try to solve. We also demonstrate the manner in which such adaptation should be carried out.

Without adapting the test, AI tools may lead to more patenting than is socially desirable. Granting patents for AI-assisted discoveries may incentivise the development of AIs[79] and of new innovations; however, these new patents may impede the implementation of inventions because of patent thickets or the development of cumulative innovation.

On its face, the obviousness threshold may appear to increase in comparison to that which may have been considered inventive in the past; however, in essence it remains the same. To reach its objective, patent law requires patent examiners (and courts) to adjust the obviousness standard to the state of the art, PSITA, and the scope of common general knowledge to new

---

[79]   Gabison, Garry A. 'Who holds the right to exclude for machine work products?' *Intellectual Property Quarterly* vol. 2020, no. 1 (2020): 20–43.

knowledge and means of working The presence of AI as a common sectorial practice falls within these necessary adjustments: all three elements of the obviousness standard should be finetuned to the common adoption of AI. Whether, when, and the extent to which an AI technique becomes customary in a sector is for the court to assess on a case-by-case basis.

24. Trade secrecy, factual secrecy and the hype surrounding AI

Sharon K. Sandeen and Tanya Aplin

1. INTRODUCTION

The intellectual property (IP) community is abuzz with discussion about how artificial intelligence (AI),[1] and its subfields machine learning, deep learning and evolutionary algorithms,[2] are apparently disrupting some of the fundamental concepts and principles in IP law.[3] One focus of the literature concerns whether inventions and creations that are generated using AI should be granted patent and copyright protection, and, if so, who should own those rights.[4] With respect to the AI systems themselves (as opposed to their outputs), a variety of laws and practical approaches are utilized to protect different aspects of AI systems, including trade secret law and principles of confidentiality.

The reliance on trade secrecy has given rise to another commonly discussed issue: the lack of transparency regarding the workings of AI systems.[5] A common lament concerns the refusal by developers of AI systems to share information about those systems, even with

---

[1] 'AI is best understood as a set of techniques aimed at approximating some aspect of human or animal cognition using machines.' See Ryan Calo, 'Artificial Intelligence Policy: A Primer and Roadmap' (2017) 51 U.C. Davis L. Rev. 399, 404. See also Ryan Abbott, *The Reasonable Robot: Artificial Intelligence and the Law* (CUP, 2020), 22, defining AI as 'an algorithm or machine capable of completing tasks that would otherwise require cognition' and observing (at 24) that 'all modern AI is narrow or specific' in that it 'focuses on discrete problems or works in specific domains'.

[2] For an overview of the technical aspects of AI, see Josef Drexl and Reto Hilty, et al, *Technical Aspects of Artificial Intelligence: An Understanding from an Intellectual Property Law Perspective* (8 October 2019). Max Planck Institute for Innovation & Competition Research Paper No. 19-13, Available at SSRN: https://ssrn.com/abstract=3465577; European Commission, *Trends and Developments in Artificial Intelligence – Challenges to the Intellectual Property Rights Framework* (25 November 2020), 21–7. For a primer on machine learning – a subset of AI – see David Lehr and Paul Ohm, 'Playing with the Data: What Legal Scholars Should Know About Machine Learning' (2017) 51 U.C. Davis L. Rev. 653 (noting that legal scholars tend to oversimplify and focus on the machine-learning algorithm as deployed, rather than the complex prior data stages, and that, even when scholars discuss the data stages, it is with a focus mainly on problem definition and data collection, omitting further stages such as data cleaning, summary statistics review, data partitioning model selection and model training. As well, they observe that for the most part legal scholarship discusses supervised machine learning).

[3] See e.g. Jyn-An Lee, Reto Hilty and Kung-Chung Liu (eds), *Artificial Intelligence & Intellectual Property* (OUP, 2021).

[4] See e.g. Jane C. Ginsburg and Luke A. Budiardjo, 'Authors and Machines' (2019) 34 Berkeley Technology L.J. 343 available at http://dx.doi.org/10.2139/ssrn.3233885; Abbott (2020), ch 4.

[5] See e.g., Frank Pasquale, *The Black Box Society: The Secret Algorithms that Control Money and Information*, 3–4 (Harvard UP, 2015), referring to proprietary methods that preclude scrutiny; Kate Crawford, *Atlas of AI* (Yale UP, 2021), who challenges the neutrality or objectivity of AI and discusses the inherent assumptions and biases that can be built into data gathering, classification and analysis and the risks associated with opacity and proprietary protection of such processes. See also, in the case of

---

public authorities who contract to use them and those whose lives are affected by them.[6] But while the reliance on trade secrecy is often lamented, typically the trade secrecy claims are not scrutinized.[7] Instead, there is a tendency to assume that factual secrecy exists and then to equate factual secrecy with trade secret protection.[8] What is lacking in the existing literature is a robust analysis of the trade secrecy status of AI-related information. This chapter fills that gap by first identifying and then examining the types of information[9] that fuels AI and whether it falls within the definition of 'trade secret' found in US and EU trade secrets law and Article 39 of the TRIPS Agreement. In so doing, this chapter highlights the need for scholars and policymakers to address problems associated with *factual* secrecy.[10]

As we will show, not all AI-related information would (or should) qualify for trade secret protection even if it is factually secret[11] or treated as secret by its holder. It depends upon the nature of the AI systems and how they are comprised, including the hardware and software that is used and the information that is fed into the AI systems (the input).[12] It also depends upon the nature of the information that is generated by the AI systems (the output). From a trade

---

a credit scoring case study, Danielle Keats Citron and Frank Pasquale, 'The Scored Society: Due Process for Automated Predictions' (2014) 89 Wash. L. Rev. 1.

[6]   See, e.g., Sonia Katyal, 'The Paradox of Source Code Secrecy' (2019) 104 Cornell L. Rev 1183; Rebecca Wexler, 'Life, Liberty, and Trade Secrets: Intellectual Property in the Criminal Justice System' (2018) 70 Stan. L. Rev. 1343; Citron and Pasquale (2014); Pasquale (2015), 193 '[t]rade secrecy protection effectively creates a property right in an algorithm without requiring its disclosure' and 217 '[t]rade secrecy, where it prevails, makes it practically impossible to test whether their judgments are valid, honest and fair'.

[7]   An exception is Ana Nordberg's work: 'Trade Secrets, Big Data and Artificial Intelligence Innovation: A Legal Oxymoron?' in Jens Schovsbo, Timo Minssen and Thomas Riis (eds), *The Harmonization and Protection of Trade Secrets in the EU: An Appraisal of the EU Directive* (Edward Elgar Publishing, 2020) (explaining the requirements for trade secret protection under the EU Trade Secrets Directive 2016/943, [2016] OJ L157/1).

[8]   See the articles cited in fn 5, which, at times, discuss secrecy and trade secrecy as if they are interchangeable terms of art; although note that Pasquale (2015), 6 does distinguish between legal secrecy and real secrecy. See also fn 10, where we define 'factual secrets' and their opposite, 'public information'.

[9]   The word 'information' is used broadly to refer to the types of information (all) that are within the scope of trade secret protection. This can include both technical and non-technical information. Data is a type of information.

[10]   As further explained herein, trade secret information is information that meets the three requirements for trade secrecy. Information that is 'factually secret' is information that, in accordance with trade secret law, is neither generally known or readily ascertainable. Information that is not factually secret is not necessarily 'public domain information' because the correct usage of that term refers to information that is not protected by a form of intellectual property law and it is possible for information to not be protected by a form of IP but still be 'factually secret'. Instead, we refer to information that is not factually secret as 'public information', but with the understanding that public information is generally known and readily ascertainable as defined by trade secret law.

[11]   Factually secret information is often called 'confidential information,' but we do not use that term here because of imprecision in the definition of that term at common law and among countries and because the term 'factual secrets' is more focused on the facts than a legal conclusion.

[12]   Because AI systems can be simple or complex and may not involve machine learning, the AI community has developed (and is still developing) ways to distinguish between the different types of AI systems. See, e.g., Stuart Russell and Peter Norvig, *Artificial Intelligence: A Modern Approach* (4th edition, Pearson, 2021), 67–74 (describing 'four basic kinds of agent programs that embody the principles underlying almost all intelligent systems': (1) simple reflex agents; (2) model-based reflex agents; (3) goal-based agents; and (4) utility-based agents).

secret perspective, there is a big difference between information that is created by AI systems and information that is collected from third parties, such as the numerous photographic images that are now being used to train AI systems. The former may qualify for trade secret protection, but the latter should not. There are also significant differences between 'disembodied AI' systems and robotic systems, one reason being that the latter involves more hardware.[13] We believe that if the definition of trade secrets is properly applied, some of the concerns related to the lack of transparency in AI systems will disappear and the public policy debate can more properly focus on problems associated with factual secrecy.

We begin in section 2 with two case studies that allow us to demonstrate the scope and limitations of trade secret protection for AI-related information: autonomous vehicles and credit scoring. Each involve different types of AI system, with one being more dependent upon hardware and neural networks and the other being based more on software and rules (or formula). The credit scoring case study shows there is heavy reliance on information that is gathered from public sources, while the autonomous vehicles case study demonstrates that information generated by the machine itself is usually relied upon. Together, they allow us to identify a variety of possible trade secrets to which the complete trade secret analysis under both US and EU trade secret law can be applied.

In section 3 we provide an overview of the proper trade secret analysis, using the information that we identified in section 2 to demonstrate its proper application. In particular, we interrogate how the requirement of 'economic value' under US law and 'commercial value' under EU law operates as a useful lever of protectability. When these existing principles are carefully applied to AI inputs and outputs, we see more granularity and differentiation in protection than some have assumed. In particular, we note the lack of trade secret protection for AI inputs that consist of third-party information and information that can be gleaned from public sources.

This chapter concludes, in section 4, with an overview of the important research and policy questions that must be addressed if one acknowledges that not all AI-related information is protected by trade secret law and it can instead be rendered inaccessible through factual secrecy.

2.   CASE STUDIES

One need only read one of the many books written recently about the science of AI to understand that the current state of AI systems is the byproduct of decades of research and the sharing of ideas and information that date back more than 80 years.[14] Describing the history

---

[13]   Calo (2017), 407 (Noting the distinction between 'disembodied AI, which acquires, processes, and outputs information as data, and robotics or other cyber-physical systems, which leverage AI to act physically upon the world'). Credit scoring systems are an example of disembodied AI; autonomous vehicles are an example of the robotic type of AI.

[14]   See e.g., Russell and Norvig (2021), 35 (crediting Warren McCulloch and Walter Pitts with the first AI work in 1943); Melanie Mitchell, *Artificial Intelligence: A Guide for Thinking Humans* (Picador 2019) (noting that John McCarthy coined the term 'artificial intelligence' in 1956 while on the mathematics faculty of Dartmouth); Calo (2017), 404 ('Although there have been significant developments and refinements, nearly every technique we use today – including the biologically-inspired neural nets at the core of the practical AI breakthroughs currently making headlines – was developed decades ago by researchers in the United States, Canada, and elsewhere').

of AI from 1987 to the present, *Artificial Intelligence: A Modern Approach* explains that over time '[i]t became more common to build on existing theories than to propose brand-new ones, to base claims on rigorous theorems or solid experimental methodology [...] rather than on intuition, and to show relevance to real-world examples rather than toy examples'.[15]

This evolution of AI science means that not all parts of even the most seemingly complex AI systems can be protected by trade secret law. Rather, a true understanding of which AI-related information is protected as trade secrets requires a careful examination of the component parts of those systems, including the structure and design of AI agents, which can come in a variety of forms.[16] In this section we examine the component parts of two AI systems – autonomous vehicles and credit scoring – to illustrate both the range of AI and that not all parts of even secret AI systems are protected by trade secrecy.

2.1   Autonomous Vehicles

The idea of autonomous vehicles (AV) dates back nearly a century and has been widely shared for almost the same amount of time.[17] More recently, AV were the subject of challenges sponsored by the Defense Advanced Research Projects Agency (DARPA) in the first decade of the twenty-first century. Thus, the necessary components of such systems are well known.[18] They include a vehicle of some sort and equipment that is designed, in varying degrees, to substitute for a human driver.[19] Typically, the latter includes integrated hardware and software systems that direct the vehicle as to how to move about the world, preferably without hitting any pedestrians or obstacles.

One way to design AV systems is for use on dedicated roads or closed tracks where they do not have to contend with a lot of pedestrians and obstacles. However, the ultimate goal of most AV developers (Waymo and Tesla being two examples) is to create self-driving cars that can co-exist with human-driven vehicles that utilize public infrastructure. This requires developing systems that mimic what human drivers see, hear and think. It is also likely to involve training humans on how to avoid such vehicles and to anticipate their movements.

Admittedly, AV systems can be complex, but the basic science and component parts are not secret. The basic design of an AI agent, of which AV is an example, involves architecture plus a program. The architecture of AV requires a vehicle of some sort and additional hardware, such as cameras, sensors, lasers, radar or LiDar,[20] to orient the vehicle about its physical loca-

---

[15]   Russell and Norvig (2021), 42.

[16]   Russell and Norvig (2021), 42 and 55 (defining an AI agent as 'anything that can be viewed as perceiving its environment through sensors and acting upon that environment through actuators').

[17]   Alex Davies, *Driven: The Race to Create the Autonomous Car* (Simon & Schuster, 2021), 16; Russell and Norvig (2021), 46.

[18]   Competitions sponsored by the US Defense Advanced Research Projects Agency (DARPA) resulted in the desired advancement and sharing of information about autonomous vehicle science such that by 2005 '[e]veryone involved, no matter how badly they had failed now understood what it would take to win'. Davies (2021), 94.

[19]   There are five levels of self-driving vehicles, ranging from Level 0, where no AI is involved, to Level 5, where the vehicle is entirely autonomous. Mitchell (2019), 267.

[20]   LiDar (or LIDAR) is an acronym for Light Detection and Ranging, and has been known about and used for more than 50 years, having been developed shortly after the advent of lasers. As explained in a publication of the US National Oceanic and Atmospheric Administration: 'Light detection and ranging (lidar) mapping is an accepted method of generating precise and directly georeferenced spatial informa-

tion. Second, a computer system is needed to direct actuators to move the vehicle and to collect data as designed. This requires computer hardware and software and connectivity between the computer system and (1) the hardware that operates the vehicle and (2) any remote computer servers that collect and process data. This can include both wired and wireless connections. In developing the necessary integrated systems there are choices to be made in terms of the hardware and software that is used, but AV developers prefer to utilize pre-existing (and readily available) hardware and software when possible. For instance, Bluetooth technology is commonly used for wireless connectivity.

Considering the foregoing, it is not the entire AV or even many of its individual component parts that can be trade secrets, but instead a more limited set of information that is not generally known or readily ascertainable.[21] Thus, for instance, the hardware that one can see when a Waymo-modified Jaguar drives by while navigating the streets of San Francisco in training mode[22] cannot be protected as trade secrets, but aspects of the interior of the vehicle and equipment that are obscured will be if they meet all three requirements of trade secrecy. This might include: the ways that the selected hardware and software components are integrated; how the various hardware is mounted to the vehicle and connected to onboard computers; and the associated computer software and algorithms, particularly that which is specially programmed to work with the integrated system. In theory, it might also include the data that fuels the AV, but it depends on the nature of the data, how and from whom it was collected and how it is used. Notably, much of the data that is utilized in AV systems is factual data in the form of mapping and photographic imagery that is collected from third parties.

The exponential increase in the availability of computing power and the advent of 'big data' has been a critical turning point in the development of AV systems because they provided the means to better mimic human drivers. But as is typical of most advances in technology, this is not because one person discovered the 'secret sauce' of AV. Rather, it is due to decades of research and the confluence of multiple technological and practical advances that made it possible to put research into practice. In the case of AV, this happened with the realization that a form of neural networks known as convolutional neural networks (ConvNets), first theorized and experimented with in the 1980s and 1990s, could be used successfully to train AI systems.[23] Specifically with respect to AV, the associated AI systems can now be trained to see and differentiate objects much like human drivers can, provided that sufficient databases of coded images exist and are not hacked and modified.

Due to developments in how AI systems can be trained, and the importance of coded data in doing so, it is not surprising that AI system developers are quick to claim trade secret

---

tion about the shape and surface characteristics of the Earth.' Jamie Carter, Keil Schmid, Kirk Waters, Lindy Betzhold, Brian Hadley, Rebecca Mataosky and Jennifer Halleran, *Lidar 101: An Introduction to Lidar Technology, Data, and Applications*, (NOAA) Coastal Services Center (2012).

[21]   Trade secret law does not use the term 'secret' to describe protected information, but instead states that information will be considered secret if it is not generally known or readily ascertainable (readily accessible in EU parlance). Importantly, this definition does not require the information to be widely disseminated to be considered non-secret; it need only be generally known among experts in the field or be the type of information that could be found relatively easily if one were to look for it.

[22]   A key aspect of AV development is training the systems in ways that allow them to improve over time as more images are collected and coded and tweaks to the associated software and algorithms are made possible. See Mitchell (2019), 100.

[23]   Mitchell (2019), ch 9.

protection for their training and testing data. But the more fact that they spent time, effort and money to create such data does not mean they are trade secrets.[24] In much the same way as facts cannot be protected by copyright law and laws of nature and prior art cannot be protected by patent law, trade secret law does not protect all collected information that is kept secret and confidential by its collectors. Whether trade secrecy can attach to such information depends upon the nature and source of the information and how it is handled.

In the case of AV, the necessary databases have largely been made possible through the collection of information created and shared by third parties, by crowd-sourcing strategies and by culling available public information such as maps and speed limits – all non-secret information.[25] Similarly, although the AV systems are often designed to generate information themselves, like when AV-mounted cameras take photos of surrounding areas, much of this information is readily available for others to see, measure and collect. Thus, only some aspects of AV systems data can possibly be trade secrets. Conceptually, this could include data that is the byproduct of system algorithms, for instance when collected or created data is processed through the hyperparameters that enable machine learning.[26] It might also include some collected information, provided it is unique and not generally known or readily ascertainable. But to be a trade secret, the information must also meet the other two requirements of trade secrecy, discussed below.

2.2   Credit Scoring

Credit – the idea of borrowing and repaying at a later date – has existed for centuries; however, it escalated as a practice from the mid-twentieth century onwards and has evolved to encompass an array of products such as credit cards, personal loans, hire purchases, student loans, overdrafts and mortgages.[27] For lending institutions, evaluating credit risk – that is, the risk that a borrower will default on their financial commitment – is crucial to their financial stability. Credit scoring is a key tool for assessing credit risk and is concerned with predicting, rather than explaining, risk.[28] At its broadest and simplest, credit scoring is defined as 'a way of classifying borrowers into two groups – those who will default and those who will not default – using the characteristics of the borrower and the loan'.[29] Credit scoring is used by

---

[24]   The Uniform Trade Secrets Act (UTSA), upon which most of US trade secret law and international trade secret harmonization efforts are based, rejected the 'sweat of the brow' element of the *Restatement (First) of Torts* trade secrecy factors: see Sharon K. Sandeen, 'The Evolution of Trade Secret Law and Why Courts Commit Error When They Do Not Follow the Uniform Trade Secrets Act' (2010) 33 Hamline L. Rev. 493.

[25]   Mitchell (2019), 84–5 (explaining the development of ImageNet and the use of Mechanical Turk to create the training and testing data needed for AV development).

[26]   The hyperparameters of machine learning can include the number of layers of the designed ConvNet, the size of units at each layer, how key factors are weighted for training purposes, how the weighting will change with each training exercise and 'other technical details.' Mitchell (2019), 97–8.

[27]   Lyn Thomas, Jonathan Crook and David Edelman, *Credit Scoring and Its Applications* (2nd edition, SIAM, 2017), 2–3. The authors note (at 5) that the success of credit scoring for credit cards led to it being applied to a range of other credit products.

[28]   Siddharth Bhatore, Lalit Mohan and Y. Raghu Reddy, 'Machine Learning Techniques for Credit Risk Evaluation: A Systematic Literature Review' (2020) 4 Journal of Banking and Financial Technology 111, 112. Thomas et al (2017), 6.

[29]   Thomas et al (2017), 3.

lending institutions to decide who is granted consumer credit and on what terms, and also how to deal with existing customers (for example, increasing the limit on a credit card).[30] As such, the efficacy of credit scoring techniques is vital to both lending institutions and consumers and the transparency of such techniques is of particular importance to consumers, given that credit may enable or constrain all sorts of life choices and can risk causing or aggravating structural inequalities.[31]

Early credit scoring mechanisms used a judgmental approach that would take into account some or all of the '5Cs': the character of the person seeking credit, the capital being sought, the collateral they could offer, their capacity to repay and the conditions in the market.[32] Due to its labour-intensiveness, this approach was later replaced by statistical methods, such as discriminant analysis (that is, linear regression), logistic regression and classification trees, which allowed for automation of the lending decision process.[33] In simple terms, the data inputs are the applicant's application form details, information held by the credit reference agency on the applicant[34] and information about previous applicants.[35] The applicant will be assessed in the light of the past performance of similar consumers.[36] The data variables that are used either relate directly to default risk – such as the putative borrower's status on other loans, previous defaults or arrears – or look at proxies, such as the stability of the consumer (time at address and in place of employment), the extent of consumer resources (property ownership, employment, spouse employment), consumer outgoings (such as dependents) and consumer sophistication (credit cards, number of bank accounts).[37]

Credit application forms will usually ask for the proxy information, whereas default risk information comes from credit reference agencies (CRAs). These CRAs receive information from lenders on a consumer's debts, timeliness of payment and defaults, and access public records in order to ascertain information about bankruptcy, (court) judgment debts or tax liens. Importantly, there is a fair degree of transparency because the credit scoring industry is reg-

---

[30]   Lyn Thomas, 'A Survey of Credit and Behavioural Scoring: Forecasting Financial Risk of Lending to Consumers' (2000) 16 Intl. J. Forecast. 149, 150.

[31]   E.g. see Cathy O'Neill, *Weapons of Math Destruction: How Big Data Increases Inequality and Threatens Democracy* (Penguin, 2016), ch 8 (albeit talking about the risks of e-scores drawn from 'a mishmash of data' (143); 'Statistical and Machine Learning Models in Credit Scoring: A Systematic Literature Survey' (2020) 91 *Applied Soft Computing Journal* 263.

[32]   Thomas (2000).

[33]   See Thomas (2000) and Xolani Dastile, Turgay Celik, Moshe Potsane, 'Statistical and machine learning models in credit scoring: A systematic literature survey' (2020) 91 *Applied Soft Computing Journal* 263. 11.

[34]   There are various credit reference (or reporting) agencies in the UK and US, but three major companies in both jurisdictions are Experian, Equifax, and Transunion.

[35]   Thomas (2000), 150.

[36]   Thomas et al (2017), 6.

[37]   Thomas et al (2017), 7.

ulated[38] and it is possible to obtain one's credit report (from a CRA) and the information that has generated that score.[39] As a result, it is also possible to know how to improve one's score.[40]

With the explosion of data about consumer behaviour in our digital, networked world, we have seen shifts in the credit scoring sector. One key change is that scoring now encompasses a wider range of data, such as data from social media platforms, transaction records, data from mobile phone applications, rent payments, educational institutions and degrees and geographical data.[41]

Another shift is that machine learning techniques, especially neural network and deep learning models, are increasingly being used for credit scoring. The drawback of such models is said to be that they are 'black box', with attendant difficulties in understanding how the model operates.[42] This has led to commentators suggesting regulatory and disclosure mechanisms to address the problems of opacity, arbitrariness and disparate impacts of machine learning-driven credit scoring.[43] It has also led to attempts at technical fixes, such as building in provenance data.[44] The literature also points to other technological challenges when it comes to machine learning research in this area, related to pre-processing of data (that is, excising redundant data to increase the speed of computation), the expense of computation of massive datasets, the fact that training and testing datasets may vary (because of geographic or regulatory differences) and data shortages (because of refusal to share datasets for com-

---

[38]   In the US, CRAs are subject to the Fair Credit Reporting Act, 15 U.S.C. § 1681, enforcement of which is overseen by the Federal Trade Commission and the Consumer Financial Protection Bureau. In the EU, CRAs are regulated by Regulation (EC) No 1060/2009 on credit rating agencies OJ L 302, 17.11.2009, p.1–31 and the supervision of the European Securities and Markets Authority. In the UK credit CRAs are regulated by the Credit Rating Agencies (Amendment etc.) (EU Exit) Regulations 2019 and supervised by the Financial Conduct Authority.

[39]   See Experian website, https://consumer.learn.experian.co.uk/IS/s/article/what-is-a-credit -reference-agency. Typically, a CRA collects information from public records (e.g. the Individual Insolvency Register) and the various companies with whom consumers have a relationship. This can include banks, credit card providers, utility suppliers and mobile phone companies.

[40]   O'Neill (2016), 142–3. Although contrast S. Eschholz and J. Djabbarpour, 'Big Data and Scoring in the Financial Sector' in Thomas Hoeren and Barbara Kolany-Raiser (eds), *Big Data in Context: Legal, Social and Technological Insights* (Springer, 2017), 63–70, 64, suggesting that not all details are published by businesses because they consider the information a business secret and to avoid the risk of manipulation.

[41]   Thomas et al (2017), 9; Eschholz and Djabbarpour (2017), 65–6; Infosys, 'How Fintechs can enable better support to FIs' credit decisioning', White Paper, 2019,

[42]   Bhatore, et al (2020), 125 and Citron and Pasquale (2014). See also Lehm and Ohr (2017) who observe at 706 that '[a]lmost all legal scholarship references machine learning as 'black box', but note that there are in fact ways of 'peeking inside the black box' that are 'both attainable and informative'. (708)

[43]   Citron and Pasquale (2014) 22, et seq, arguing for 'technological due process', such as ensuring that consumers can inspect, dispute and correct inaccurate data, transparency of how credit scores are calculated and auditing of scoring systems.

[44]   Dong Huynh, Sophie Stalla-Bourdillon and Luc Moreau, *Provenance-based Explanations for Automated Decisions: Final IAA Project Report* (2019) which discusses how provenance data, that is, a record of the 'people, data sets, and organisations involved in decisions; attribution of data; and data derivation', may be used to provide explainability, particularly in the context of the EU GDPR (p. 1). The authors describe a demonstrator that they built to produce explanations for decisions related to a fictitious loan scenario. The explanations relate to whether the decision is automated or not, data inclusion/exclusion, data source, data accuracy, data currency and profile and discrimination-related fairness.

petitiveness or privacy reasons) which can lead to over-sampling.[45] Some of the literature has also been critical of the fact that macro-economic variables – such as interest, inflation and unemployment rates – are excluded.[46]

Finally, the literature notes that the purpose of credit scoring has shifted from purely consumer risk forecasting to identifying 'the customers who are most profitable'.[47] This is done by creating scorecards that estimate whether a consumer will respond to a new product, how likely she is to use it and to keep using it once an introductory offer is finished, whether the consumer will shift to another lender and the consumer's debt management.[48] This is because profits are affected by 'many more decisions [compared with default rates] including marketing, service levels and operation decisions as well as pricing decisions'.[49]

If we think about which aspects of credit scoring *may* implicate trade secrets law it is useful to think about the steps in credit scoring, as discussed by Citron and Pasquale. The first two steps – gathering data about scored individuals and calculating that data into scores – are frequently where the trade secret concern arises. But the first step involves information that is often known by others, and it is unclear whether the data scores, even if secret, are trade secrets without more analysis. The third and fourth steps – disseminating scores to decision-makers and third party use of those scores in decision making – tend not to be the focus of transparency concerns. For example, Citron and Pasquale themselves criticize secrecy in the first two stages – noting the inability to challenge the algorithms that produce scores because of claims of trade secrecy and data brokers' refusal to share their sources because of reasons of confidentiality.[50]

If we think about the data-gathering process for AI credit scoring, there are the traditional data variables (described above) plus new data variables drawn from a wider array of sources, such as social media and mobile phone apps. But, as will be explained below, some of this data is simply not secret because it is drawn from public or semi-public sources, whether it be public registers or directories or openly accessible social media platforms, or because certain datasets are frequently shared between the credit scoring community. Moreover, the data may lack independent economic value. As such, claims of trade secrecy and the deference given to such claims may be unwarranted in many instances.

3.   TRADE SECRET ANALYSIS

Given the effort and costs involved in developing AI systems, the developers of such systems often assume that they are (or should be) automatically entitled to legal protection at least in the form of trade secret protection. This is particularly true if their efforts are shrouded in secrecy such that they can argue they have engaged in reasonable efforts to maintain the

---

[45]   Bhatore et al (2020), 129–30.
[46]   Dastile et al (2020), 13. See also Thomas (2000), 168, arguing that 'Progress in incorporating economic effects would mean scorecards would be more robust to changes in the economic environment and so could be used for longer time periods before having to be rebuilt'.
[47]   Thomas (2020), 150, 152.
[48]   Thomas (2020), 152.
[49]   Thomas (2020), 165. Thomas notes that there are complexities here, such as the time horizon to consider profit, economic conditions and profit on individual products versus over all possible products.
[50]   Citron and Pasquale (2014), 5, 20–1.

secrecy of their AI-related information. This, however, is not the law. To qualify for trade secret protection under US and EU law requires that identifiable information be shown to meet the three requirements of trade secrecy: (1) secrecy; (2) economic (commercial) value; and (3) reasonable efforts.[51] The fact that an individual or business went to the time, trouble and expense to create or collect information and keep it secret does not mean the information is a trade secret.

In this section we demonstrate the limits of legal protection for AI-related information by using the types of information identified in the above case studies. We highlight existing or potential differences between US and EU approaches as applicable.

3.1   The Secrecy Requirement

The first requirement of trade secrecy under both US and EU law is that the information be 'secret', but this term has a special meaning under trade secret law.[52] For information to be non-secret under trade secret law it need not be widely known. If the subject information is known or readily ascertainable by those who work in the relevant industry or business, it is not secret.[53] Thus, information that is known in this broad sense cannot be a trade secret even if it is not known or understood by the public, policymakers or judges.

As described in the case studies above, many of the components of AV and credit scoring (CS) are well known among those involved in using such systems and in related research and development. They are also readily ascertainable by others, including the authors of this chapter, who found numerous articles and books on the topics that allowed them to describe the state of the art. It is also likely that parts of AV and CS information are within the general skill and knowledge of AI researchers, and therefore not subject to trade secret protection.[54] Indeed, if AI agents are designed to substitute for and mimic the human brain, then presumably they acquire unprotectable general skill and knowledge just like humans do.

In considering the trade secret status of information concerning AV and CS, it is necessary to look beyond what is already known among AI researchers to find what is not, and, with respect to such matters, to determine how easily that information can be gleaned from available sources. While we readily admit that some aspects of AV and CS systems may be secret in the sense that term is defined by trade secret law, given the state of industry knowledge concerning AI, claiming secrecy with respect to the entirety of an AI system is a gross over-assertion of trade secret rights. Instead, companies that claim trade secret protection in AI systems must identify the parts of those systems that might be a trade secret.

---

[51]   EU Trade Secrets Directive 2016/943, [2016] OJ L157/1 ('Trade Secrets Directive'), Art 2(1) and Uniform Trade Secrets Act ('UTSA'), § 1(4).

[52]   Sharon K. Sandeen, 'Disclosure' in S.K. Sandeen, C. Rademacher and A. Ohly (eds), *Research Guide to Information Law and Governance* (Edward Elgar Publishing, 2021), ch 3.

[53]   See UTSA § 1(4); Trade Secrets Directive, Art 2(1)(a).

[54]   Trade Secrets Directive, Art 1(3)(B) and recital 14; Camilla A. Hrdy, 'The General Knowledge, Skill, and Experience Paradox' (2019) 60 B.C. Law Rev. 2409 (explaining the US rule).

With respect to the case studies discussed above, AI-related trade secrets might include:

1. The hardware used, particularly if it is newly designed or modified but only if it is beyond public view or access. In the *Waymo v Uber* case, for instance, the focus of Waymo's allegations was modified LiDar hardware, but not the entirety of that hardware.[55]
2. The software that is used, but only to the extent that it is specially programmed, not publicly available or 'open source' software, and not in the public domain. This might include the algorithms or other 'computer program-related inventions'[56] programmed into the software, such as the hyperparameters used in machine learning. It might also include portions of the source code. For instance, late in the proceedings, Waymo claimed trade secret protection in lines of source code related to motion planning and lane-changing designs, but not to the entirety of its source code.
3. The methods and processes that are used to develop, train, test and modify the software and algorithms, although some of this information could reflect basic logic or constitute the digitized version of known processes utilized in the analog world.
4. The way the selected pieces of hardware are connected to each other and to associated communication systems.
5. Data that is collected, created, or used by the AI systems, but depending upon its source and nature. Many of the data variables used in CS, for example, are publicly accessible through public records, directories or registers, or through search engines and social media platforms. Geographic data in the case of AV is readily available for others to see or has been created and shared by third parties. Public information or information that is in the public domain would not count as 'secret', but specialized information might.[57]
6. The trade secret aspects of so-called combination trade secrets, which may be composed of parts of all the above.

But even assuming that one or more of the foregoing features of an AI system are secret, it does not necessarily follow that they are trade secrets. The other two requirements of trade secrecy (discussed below) must be met.

With respect to combination trade secrets, by definition, it is not the known and disclosed component parts of the combination that can be protected by trade secret law, but only some articulable aspect of the way in which those known components are combined.[58] For instance,

---

[55] *Waymo LLC v Uber Technologies, Inc,* 2018 WL 646701, United States District Court, N.D. California No. C 17-00939 WHA. As this order indicates, there were multiple issues and motions raised in the litigation before trial. A few days into trial the litigation was settled: see www.reuters.com/article/us-alphabet-uber-trial-idUSKBN1FT2BA.

[56] Pamela Samuelson defined 'computer program-related inventions' to include, in addition to algorithms, data structures, the modular design for a program, a design for accomplishing a particular function by program and user interface functionalities. Pamela Samuelson, 'Benson Revisited: The Case Against Patent Protection For Algorithms and Other Computer Program-Related Inventions' (1990) 39 Emory L.J. 1025, n. 2.

[57] The availability of machine learning datasets may be more widespread than we imagine. K. Peng, A. Mathur and A. Narayanan, 'Mitigating dataset harms requires stewardship: Lessons from 1000 papers', draft paper 9 August 2021, traces how two popular face and person recognition datasets (DukeMTMC and MS-Celeb-1M) remain widely available even after retraction by their originators, which they call 'runaway data'.

[58] See Tait Graves and Alexander Macgillivray, 'Combination Trade Secrets and the Logic of Intellectual Property' (2004) 20 Santa Clara High Tech. L.J. 261, 266, defining a combination trade

consider the component parts of an automobile. It is well known and observable that an automobile consists of wheels, an engine of some sort, a physical structure to house the engine and passengers, brakes and a means of steering. In theory, it is possible for anyone to combine these common features and keep their design secret, but the entirety of the automobile could not be a trade secret, only some special part of it, if any. In defining the parts of a combination that are potentially protected by trade secret law, care must be exercised to ensure that the information is not defined too broadly, lest it sweep in unprotected content. Instead, an explanation is required concerning what makes the particular combination special and how it is valuable because it is secret.[59]

Because databases are often composed of generally known or readily ascertainable information, when claimed to be a trade secret they are a form of combination trade secrets that must be scrutinized as such. The mere fact that they combine information, particularly if it is generally known and readily ascertainable, does not make the entirety of the database a potential trade secret; nor are databases trade secrets simply because some specialized information was added. Whether and to what extent databases that are composed of generally known or readily ascertainable information are trade secrets depends upon the nature of the combination and the allegedly special features that were added. This explains why trade secret claims based upon customer lists often fail. If the alleged customer list can be readily replicated from publicly available information it is not deemed worthy of trade secret protection even if it was compiled at great time, trouble and expense.[60] It is only when the customer list contains specialized information that is secret and of value to others that a successful trade secret claim is possible.

An important question in customer list cases, and by extension to the data that AI developers collect from consumers, is whether customer preferences constitute the type of specialized information that can make an unprotected list into a protected list. As a general rule, we think not, because customer preferences are also known by the customer and are likely to be shared with others. But conceptually, there is a difference between a consumer's preference for the colour blue, which is likely to be known by family and friends and readily ascertainable, and a consumer's choice of insurance coverage, which is likely to only be known by one or a few insurance companies.[61] Also, we acknowledge that there is a difference between raw data and data that has been processed by an AI system, such as through data cleaning or data partitioning. The latter may be a trade secret, but the former should not be if it consists of generally known and readily ascertainable facts.

---

secret as 'a set of elements, each by itself in the public domain, whose synthesis can be a legally protected property right even though the elements by themselves are not'. The concept of combination trade secrets is contained in the EU Trade Secrets Directive's definition of a trade secret when it states in Article 2(1) (a) that information 'is secret in the sense it is not, as a body or in the precise configuration and assembly of its components, generally known among or readily accessible to …'. However, EU law has not yet developed its doctrine on so-called combination trade secrets because there have not yet been referrals to the Court of Justice of the European Union (CJEU) on the Trade Secrets Directive.

[59]   Graves and Macgillivray (2004), 275 (proposing a four-element test). See also *Space Data Corp. v Alphabet Inc.*, No. 16-CV-03260-BLF (NC), 2018 WL 10647160, at *1–3 (N.D. Cal. 8 May 2018) (finding the identification of alleged Hover Algorithm Trade Secrets Nos 1–4 lacking due to inadequate specificity concerning, for instance, 'specific interactions or uses of the enumerated functions and variables in the sample algorithm').

[60]   See *Morlife, Inc. v Perry*, 56 Cal. App. 4th 1514, 1520–3 (1997) and cases cited therein.

[61]   In *Morlife, Inc. v Perry,* for instance, the specialized information consisted of the particular roofing needs of the listed customers. Ibid.

Finally, it is important to note that anything that began as secret information can lose that status if it is subsequently disclosed, which can happen in a variety of ways and at any time. First, the developer of AI systems may choose to patent some aspect of their systems, in which case trade secrecy is lost. Typically, this occurs with respect to features of AI systems that will be visible to the public or are readily ascertainable, for instance in an issued patent or published patent application. Relatedly, AI data may be shared such that secrecy is also lost.[62] Second, various aspects of AI systems (including, for instance, photographic images and computer code) might be protected by copyright law, thereby potentially limiting the scope of trade secret protection under US law.[63] Third, the information may be independently developed or reverse engineered by a third party and subsequently disclosed or shared without restriction, in which case all such information held by others ceases to be secret. Finally, if information is misappropriated and subsequently disclosed by the misappropriator, it ceases to be secret.

3.2 The Value Requirement

The value requirement of trade secrecy ('economic value' in the US and 'commercial value' in the EU) is an important but often overlooked requirement of trade secret law that, when properly applied, can have a profound effect on defining the sorts of information that are worthy of trade secret protection. The reason it is often overlooked is that companies, policymakers and judges often equate the value requirement of trade secrecy with other types of value associated with the identified information, or they assume value must exist due to the mere fact a lawsuit was filed or because the information was expensive to compile. But the economic value requirement requires a more specific showing that is tied to the concept of competitive advantage.[64]

Both US and EU law require that the information that is claimed to be a trade secret be of value because of its secrecy, so the existence of secret information is a critical first step in the analysis. The next step is to demonstrate that the value of the information derives, at least in part, from the fact of secrecy. Here we draw on US law because this aspect of the EU Trade Secrets Directive has not yet been explored by the courts.[65] The 'economic value due to secrecy' requirement is a causal one that highlights the Uniform Trade Secret Act's rejection

---

[62] See Peng et al (2021) describing the sharing of machine learning datasets and how, even after their retraction for ethical concerns, the data remains widely available.

[63] See 17 USC §301 dealing with copyright preemption. Also, the registration with the US Copyright Office of parts of AI system source code will prevent trade secret rights from attaching to any information so disclosed. See Katyal (2019) (providing a history of the specialized deposit requirements for computer source code).

[64] Camilla A. Hrdy, 'The Value in Secrecy' (2022) 91 Fordham Law Review (forthcoming), available at SSRN: https://ssrn.com/abstract=3897949 or http://dx.doi.org/10.2139/ssrn.3897949; Nordberg (2020), fn [7], 207.

[65] The only guidance is recital 14 of the Trade Secrets Directive which states that commercial value can be actual or potential and that 'information should be considered to have a commercial value, for example, where its unlawful acquisition, use or disclosure is likely to harm the interests of the person lawfully controlling it, in that it undermines that person's scientific and technical potential, business or financial interests, strategic positions or ability to compete'. For a discussion see Anna Wennakoski, 'Trade Secrets under Review: A Comparative Analysis of the Protection of Trade Secrets in the EU and in the US' [2016] EIPR 154, 156–7.

of the sweat-of-the-brow doctrine.[66] The mere fact that an information owner has gone to time, trouble and expense in collecting information does not mean that the information has the requisite value. Additionally, just because collected or created information provides its holder with some value – an example might be the databases that fuel AI systems – does not mean the information is valuable because it is secret or has value to others.

Consider the list of potential AI trade secrets set forth in the previous subsection. Suppose that the alleged trade secret is hardware in the form of modified LiDar technology, as Waymo alleged in its lawsuit against Uber. Just because it took time, trouble and effort for Waymo to make those adjustments does not mean that the modifications have value because they are secret. Indeed, they may have no value at all except as part of Waymo's integrated AV system. Assuming, however, that they do have value because, for instance, they are improvements to existing technology, then the critical question is whether the value is derived, to some degree, from the secrecy. The essential inquiry is: does the alleged trade secret, as opposed to the AI system as a whole, give its holder a non-trivial advantage over competitors?[67]

Sometimes the identified trade secret information is too trivial to provide a competitive advantage, such as when one brand of off-the-shelf hardware is used instead of another. Other times the information is too highly specialized and integrated with other parts of a system to be of value to others because the others cannot make use of the information without access to the whole system. This may be true, for instance, with respect to AI system architecture and algorithms that depend upon a particular set of hardware, software and data to operate properly. In theory, such information may be of value because of what others can learn from it, even if it cannot be used directly by them, but it may not be of substantial enough value for trade secret law to care. For instance, negative information (what does not work) can be a trade secret, but on the issue of value it would need to be shown that others would benefit from knowing the information. If others in a field of research have already learned the preferred solution, like the ideal filament of Edison's famous lightbulb, the value of earlier negative information becomes obsolete.

Sometimes alleged trade secrets are of a type that make it difficult to separate the alleged value due to secrecy from the inherent value of the end-product, making it challenging to identify a non-trivial advantage to competitors. This difficulty often arises in combination trade secret cases where the added or special information is but a small part of the whole. For instance, is a recipe for tuna fish salad of value because of a secret dash of a special type of mustard or is it of value because of the totality of the recipe that results in good-tasting tuna fish salad? Is computer code that makes a printer operate of value because it contains two lines of secret code out of 50 lines of code, or because the entirety of the 50 lines of code causes the printer to print? Theoretically, even minor changes in hardware and software may be a trade secret, but it must be shown that those changes are significant enough to cause the changes to have value because they are secret.

Consider the databases of coded images that are used for AV training and testing purposes and the datasets that underlie CS systems. If most of that data is collected from publicly visible and available sources, then that information is not secret information and cannot have value because it is secret. It may have value for other reasons, for instance, because it is a handy and usable body of compiled information that has been collected from public sources. Companies

---

[66]   Hrdy (2021), n. 22.
[67]   Hrdy (2021).

that compile such information can act to keep it secret, license it or freely share it with others, but whether it is legally protected information is a separate question. Something must be added to the databases of generally known and readily ascertainable information that has value because it is secret. Even though the coding of images often adds information, like the notation on a photograph that it depicts a dog, this information is not valuable because it is secret. There is nothing special or secret about identifying a photograph of a dog as a photograph of a dog. Similarly, if CS data has been 'cleaned', that is, had redundant data excised, the data has value simply because it can be processed more efficiently.

An aspect of AI systems that is frequently claimed to be trade secrets is the associated algorithms, which is a fancy word for a step-by-step process. In many cases, particularly before the advent of machine and deep learning, these algorithms are determined by humans based upon selected parameters, like the algorithms that underlie credit scoring, and often reflect well-known processes. When written into computer code, these processes do not magically become trade secrets – it depends upon the details. Because there are choices to be made in how algorithms are designed and written, theoretically they can include trade secret information. But how much depends upon the extent to which they utilize information that is generally known or readily ascertainable or that constitutes general skill and knowledge.[68] On the issue of value, the critical question is whether the secret and special aspects of a particular algorithm are of value because they provide a competitive advantage.

The 'black box' algorithms that are at the heart of most machine and deep learning AI systems present special challenges for determining value due to secrecy because it is often difficult to explain precisely what they do[69] and many are designed to change over time as more and more data is processed.[70] In other words, one algorithm is 'abandoned' for another.[71] Also, much like employees, they acquire knowledge, understanding and skill as they work. Undoubtedly, many of the developers of these algorithms go to great lengths to keep them secret, and they are a valuable part of their AI systems, but do they have value because they are secret? Part of the answer depends upon whether, if acquired by a competitor, these algorithms could be used – which is a big if considering the numerous component parts of most AI systems.

3.3   The Reasonable Efforts Requirement

Most companies that assert trade secret rights engage in some efforts to protect the alleged trade secrets, and this is undoubtedly true of companies in the CS and AV industries. However, the required test is not whether some protection efforts were engaged in, but whether the

---

[68]   One way to explain the US Supreme Court's decision in *Alice Corp. v CLS Bank Int'l*, 573 U.S. 208 (2014) is that many algorithms used in computer programs merely restate step-by-step processes that are generally known or readily ascertainable.

[69]   See Ashley Deeks, 'The Judicial Demand for Explainable AI' (2019) 119 Colum. L. Rev. 1829 (explaining that because such algorithms 'repeatedly adjust the way that they weigh inputs to improve the accuracy of their predictions, it can be difficult to identify how and why the algorithms reach the outcomes they do').

[70]   John D. Kelleher, *Deep Learning* (MIT Press, 2019), 11–16.

[71]   For a discussion of the notion of trade secret 'abandonment', including through superseding products with newer generations, see Camilla A. Hrdy and Mark A. Lemley, 'Abandoning Trade Secrets' (2021) 73 Stan. L. Rev. 1, 46–8.

protection efforts that were engaged in were reasonable under the circumstances.[72] Depending upon the type of industry involved, the nature and use of the alleged trade secret information, and other factors, these circumstances can vary widely, meaning that information that would be treated as the trade secrets of one company may not be treated as the trade secrets of another company. The circumstances can also change over time, often resulting in the loss of trade secrecy for information that may have begun as trade secrets. Often, with new technological developments that present difficult challenges, there is a lot of information sharing early on, including government-funded research and development, and only later does information lockdown begin. This appears to be the case for AV, for instance. In the case of CS, much of the information collected and created by CRAs is shared with others, including consumers, raising the question of whether adequate promises of confidentiality have been secured.

A common mistake that is made in analysing the reasonable efforts requirement is to focus on the efforts that a company has undertaken to protect information internally, without considering how the information is shared externally. In this regard, it is a central tenet of trade secret law that trade secret information can be shared without a loss of trade secrecy provided that it is done pursuant to an adequate obligation of confidentiality. A focus on internal efforts is fine when trade secret information never leaves the confines of a business and is only shared with employees of that business, but if it is shared outside the organization, consideration must be given to all who had access to the information. This would include the sharing of information within a regulatory context or at conferences and trade shows. Unless the regulating entity or other third party promised confidentiality with respect to identifiable information, the shared information is not protected by trade secret law even if it continues to be treated as a trade secret within a company. Moreover, no part of trade secret law requires government regulators or other third parties to promise confidentiality; typically, such a promise must be evidenced by a binding and enforceable contract.

Another common deficiency in the reasonable efforts analysis is not to align the requirement with its central purpose: notice. In this regard, it is worth asking: why, if information has already been shown to be secret and of value because of its secrecy, is there a reasonable efforts requirement at all? The simple reason is because those who could be held liable for trade secret misappropriation have a right to know (or at least have reason to know) the identity of the information that is claimed to be a trade secret. Thus, what is 'reasonable' should, in large part, depend upon what efforts are sufficient to put potential misappropriators, particularly employees and vendors, on notice of the information considered to be trade secrets. In many cases, a written non-disclosure agreement coupled with confidentiality markings on the information may be enough, but it will depend upon how the information is used and to what extent it is shared.[73] For instance, if it is a common practice in the AV research community to share training data, more efforts may be required to indicate that a particular set of training data is to be treated as a trade secret.

---

[72]   Art 1(c) of the Trade Secrets Directive states that the information 'has been subject to reasonable steps under the circumstances, by the person lawfully in control of the information, to keep it secret'. This is similar to §1(4)(ii) UTSA that stipulates information 'is the subject of efforts that are reasonable under the circumstances to maintain its secrecy.' This element of the definition of trade secret has not yet been interpreted by the CJEU or national courts in the EU, but has been extensively considered by US courts.

[73]   Here it is interesting that Peng et al (2021) note that licences used for machine learning datasets lacked substantive effect.

4.   CONCLUSION

We have shown that the proper application of trade secret law means that many of the component parts of AI systems, including parts of algorithms and datasets, are unlikely to be protected by trade secret law even if they are kept secret by those who developed them.[74] The end results of *Waymo v Uber* illustrate our point: what began as a case which alleged the trade secret misappropriation of 14,000 documents ended up going to trial with only eight alleged trade secrets at issue. The discrepancy is explained by the difference between business information that is kept factually secret, or treated as if it is, and business information that meets the requirements of trade secrecy.

When it comes to AI systems, the ability to disprove trade secrecy should not be the end of the discussion because the problem of factual secrecy remains. This is because lawyers have long advised their clients that in the absence of trade secret protection or other forms of IP protection, individuals and businesses can protect their collected and created information by engaging in self-help measures that are designed to keep information secret. Of course, if the information leaks out or is misappropriated when it is not protected by some form of IP or information law – such as trade secret law or the *sui generis* database right in the EU[75] – or by contract law,[76] then there is no claim for relief. The absence of a claim for relief, however, does not prevent businesses from trying to maintain the secrecy of their valued information and in many cases they will be successful. Indeed, the more a company's business practices can involve black boxes or other back-office processes that are not visible, accessible or understandable to the public, or even to employees, the more a strategy of factual secrecy becomes the preferred approach instead of pursuing forms of IP protection where some degree of disclosure is required.[77]

When factual secrecy is relied upon to protect information that is not otherwise protected by a form of IP, the limitations on the scope of IP rights and relevant exceptions become largely irrelevant.[78] Rather, the critical issues are more fundamental. First, we must ask whether the

---

[74]   We acknowledge the importance of debating the limits placed on trade secret protection where the definition of 'trade secret' is satisfied: for a discussion of the EU context see Tanya Aplin, 'The Limits of Trade Secret Protection in the EU' in S.K. Sandeen, C. Rademacher and A. Ohly (eds), *Research Guide to Information Law and Governance* (Edward Elgar Publishing, 2021), ch 10.

[75]   Pursuant to the Directive 96/9/EC on the legal protection of databases, [1996] OJ L77/20, as implemented in EU Member States.

[76]   Non-disclosure or confidentiality agreements can be used to protect information, however, these are limited by the privity of contract doctrine and contractual remedies will differ from those offered by IP and information law.

[77]   Such as patent law, although suggestions have been made to improve the efficacy of patent disclosures: see W. Nicholson II and A.K. Rai, 'Clearing Opacity through Machine Learning' (2021) 106 Iowa L. Rev. 775, 801–4.

[78]   Such as those exceptions relating to freedom of expression and discussed in Ulla-Maija Mylly, 'Freedom of the Media and Trade Secrets in Europe' in in S.K. Sandeen, C. Rademacher and A. Ohly (eds), *Research Guide to Information Law and Governance* (Edward Elgar Publishing, 2021), ch 11. We have seen how use of contract law, in the absence of copyright or *sui generis* database protection, has undermined the application of exceptions in those regimes: see Ryanair Ltd v PR Aviation BV Case C-30/14 [2015] ECDR 13, critiqued by Maurizio Borghi and Stavroula Karapapa, 'Contractual Restrictions on Lawful Use of Information: Sole-source Databases Protected by the Back Door?' [2015] EIPR 505.

information is important enough to require sharing and disclosure or, at the very least, whether we should prefer possible leakage over legal protection. Relatedly, if greater transparency about AI systems is the goal, particularly of information that does not qualify for trade secret protection, then we need better and earlier processes for testing claims of trade secrecy. We also need to consider when and how it is appropriate for trade secrecy to be asserted in regulatory contexts.[79]

Second, if we deem certain information about AI systems to be important for transparency purposes, we must also consider how the sharing and disclosure of such information can be encouraged or compelled.[80] This is particularly true if the traditional patent and copyright incentives are not working to effectuate such disclosure.[81] This concern is particularly relevant if the subject information was collected from publicly available sources, like databases created and maintained by governmental entities, through crowd-sourcing strategies, or by driving the streets of San Francisco or London taking photos and measurements. It is highly inefficient and intrusive to allow multiple companies to gather the same publicly available information when the same time and expense would be more wisely directed at making sure the information is complete and accurate, particularly if AI systems are relying upon the presumed accuracy of such information.

In conclusion, the greater threat to access, sharing and re-use of AI related information is not trade secret protection but the ability of organizations and corporations to maintain factual secrecy. Policymakers and scholars need to grapple with that reality and explore the mechanisms for ensuring greater transparency and sharing of AI algorithms and data, bearing in mind the different ways and contexts in which AI is being used.

---

[79]   Elizabeth A. Rowe and Nyja Prior, 'Procuring Algorithmic Transparency' (2022) 74 Alabama Law Review (forthcoming), avialable at SSRN: https://ssrn.com/abstract=4044178 or http://dx.doi.org/10.2139/ssrn.4044178.

[80]   For some considerations of this in the EU context see Matthias Leistner, 'Protection of and Access to Data under European Law' in Jyn-An Lee, Reto Hilty and Kung-Chung Liu (eds), *Artificial Intelligence & Intellectual Property* (OUP, 2021), ch 17.

[81]   See the discussion in Nicholson and Rai (2021).

Index

Printed and bound by CPI Group (UK) Ltd, Croydon, CR0 4YY

28/10/2024

14581368-0001